A History of
Musical Thought

A HISTORY OF MUSICAL THOUGHT

By Donald N. Ferguson

EMERITUS PROFESSOR OF MUSIC
UNIVERSITY OF MINNESOTA

THIRD EDITION

APPLETON—CENTURY—CROFTS, INC.

New York

Preface to the First Edition

THIS BOOK is designed to offer, primarily to college students, but also to the general reader who is interested in penetrating beneath the surface, an approach to the endless riches of musical literature. It is first of all a textbook in the history of music; but it gives also an expanded view of the field more narrowly covered by the many current books on musical appreciation.

To those who are beginning the serious study of the subject, such a combination of historical and appreciative treatment is necessary; for the technical history of music is intelligible only to those whose background of appreciation is already largely established. Adequate appreciation of music, on the other hand, is impossible without a considerable awareness of the historical evolution of the art.

The current literature of appreciation presents the forms and processes of musical structure as self-existent, arbitrary facts, originated by creative genius, and authenticated by the theoretical analyst. But the history of music reveals that these forms are not arbitrary at all, and that both the forms and the expressive values of music are to a great extent a result of the endeavor to represent, through these forms, a wide region of thought and feeling which is originally quite unrelated to music. Like language or any of the other arts, music is a *conventional* utterance, assuming, in different periods, the form to which it is constrained by its relation to other existing conventions of life. It has its own intrinsic laws, to be sure, dictated by the nature of the musical substance. But it grows, not by virtue of these laws but in spite of them. That is, the forms of music are to be understood as a product of the fertilization of music through the world of human experience. Genius is the agent, not the source, of such creations.

The sonata, for example, viewed as a purely musical fact, is only an ingenious musical pattern, presenting contrasts and intensifications agreeable to the analytical mind, but of no other than purely artistic interest. Even the expressive value of its themes and their treatment is minimized in such a view; for consideration of the form aspect of the work overrides attention to the emotional values represented. Observed as a product of more

v

than musical evolution, however, the sonata, while losing none of its true artistic value, takes on a vastly augmented interest. It is impossible for the hearer to value the *Eroica* Symphony at its full worth ("appreciation" is valuation) merely by observing its themes as such, and pursuing their rhetorical evolution throughout the piece. There are countless implications and characteristics in this music which can be apprehended only by one whose awareness of the symphonic form includes an awareness of the long process of its growth. To this broader appreciation there can be no other than the historical approach.

This approach is hardly provided by purely historical study, however. The immediate purpose of scientific history is to exhibit the politics or the economic life or the musical art of a past age *as it once was*. The larger purpose of the historian, always implied but seldom persistently expressed, is to present this account of the past as an explanation of the way in which things of the present *came to be as they are*. But the average student, confronted with the mass of detailed fact which delineates a past epoch, and confronted, too, with an ultimate examination which will test his knowledge of fact, misses this implication. In the field of music especially he fails to grasp, beneath the surface of fact, the actual working of the historic forces which brought about the changes he observes in musical practice. For anything he can see, men merely tired of the old and evolved the new out of that same desperation of boredom which he feels as he peruses the so-called history of his art.

Our persistent aim, accordingly, has been to give, not a mere account of music as it once was, but an explanation of the way in which it came to be as it is. In pursuit of this aim, very considerable alterations in the usual plan of the historical narrative have been found desirable.

The actual relation of present to earlier efforts is not perceptible unless some fundamental impulse can be shown to be common to the two efforts. This it is entirely possible to show. In even the most primitive music there exist two types of impulse or effort which are still fundamental for the music of today. These are impulses of tone organization and rhythm organization. Our narrative accordingly begins with an examination of these impulses as they appear in simple examples of contemporary music, and then proceeds to show how these same impulses generated the almost wholly dissimilar music of the Greeks.

As we have already said, however, the whole purpose of music is not achieved by satisfying the instinct for form (which is another name for completed efforts toward tone and rhythm organization). Music expresses feeling, and is thus related to other media of expression from which it may borrow, and by which it may to a large extent be conditioned. The music of the Greeks, to an extent hardly imaginable today, was conditioned by its intimate association with poetry. The emancipation of the fundamental musical impulse from the original tyranny of words, and its gradual adaptation to the expression of the inner sense of the words, is really the main objective of musical effort until the advent of independent instrumental literature. Many such forces, religious, humanistic, or whatever, constantly deflect the course of purely musical thought. These forces also have to be exhibited in their relation to the musical impulse, and the resultant lines of force must be determined.

Once determined, these lines have been followed—even to lengths which sometimes override the usual period divisions of history. The tone-organizing effort of the Greeks, for example, has been pursued uninterruptedly up to the moment of the adoption by the Christian Church of what in the older system was valid for its needs. Similarly, the ancient rhythmic scheme, conditioned by the system of quantitative verse, is discussed without a break until, in the fourth century A.D., the substitution of accent for quantity gave a new release to the rhythmic impulse of music. The student must derive from these separate discussions of the elements and their adjuncts his total picture of the music of the Greeks. But this is much easier than it would be to gain, from such a static picture of the Greek period as is usually given, an awareness of the actual lines of continuity between the earlier and the following period.

To a large extent, the same plan of longitudinal rather than cross-sectional treatment of the subject matter has been pursued throughout the book. The opera has been discussed separately from other musical forms. The evolution of instruments, from the ancient prototypes to the modern examples, has been dealt with in a single chapter. Instrumental forms have been very carefully traced from their obscurest origins to their completed state. Technical discussions—inevitable in any intelligible account of actual musical developments—have been given in such detail as to make them comprehensible to students of relatively slight advancement in such matters. Comment has been generously offered on the nature and value of the contributory forces affecting musical developments. Great care has been expended on making continuous the transitions of musical progress from one stage to another. Continuity in the narrative, indeed, has been the first concern of the author.

An extensive Bibliography appears in an appendix. It is so classified that references pertinent to the matter under consideration may readily be found. It naturally lists the literature about music rather than the music itself that is discussed in the text. Although the great collections of music such as the German and Austrian *Denkmäler* and the complete editions of the works of the older masters are now readily obtainable on microfilm, the student will probably find that the Harvard and Gleason anthologies, mentioned in the text, will sufficiently amplify the necessarily brief examples that appear in the book. These, however, have been chosen with great care for their illustrative value, and the teacher will find that many of them—for example, the simpler forms of organum, the *Agincourt Song*, and *Sumer is icumen in*—can easily be performed either by the whole class or by selected members.

It is a pleasure not untinged with a sense of humility to indicate the many obligations I am under for advice, correction, and constructive suggestions of all sorts. Professor Paul J. Weaver of Cornell University, the editor, gave endless time to the careful scrutiny of the whole manuscript. Among my colleagues in this university, Professor Krey gave many valuable corrections of the book's historical perspective; Professor Pepinsky supplied voluminous matter regarding the history of instruments; Professors Searles and Kroesch, both passionate amateurs of music, gave invaluable help in clarifying many of my statements; Professor Upjohn supplied me with much matter concerning the history of art—more matter, unfortunately, than I have been able to use; and Mr. Stump, a rare example of the musician really conversant with Greek, translated the texts of the examples of Greek music, and reassured me on many points regarding the relation of Greek music to poetry.

PREFACE TO THE SECOND EDITION

The present revision of this book has been designed to rectify certain disproportions and deficiencies which, while perceptible from the beginning, have been made more apparent by the almost phenomenal growth of musicological interest in America since 1935. What then seemed an over-emphasis on the subject of Greek music will now seem normal. What then seemed (at least to the average class) a sufficient discussion of the Middle Ages and the Renaissance is now not only meager in detail but often considerably false in perspective. That whole portion of the book dealing with these two periods has accordingly been completely rewritten.

It was imperative, however, if practical classroom requirements were to be met, that this greatly expanded field should nevertheless be covered in only slightly expanded space. Considerable areas of interest, such as that of Byzantine music, or the remoter contributions of Syrian, Coptic, and even Jewish music, are therefore either wholly ignored, or are given an occasional glance, more indicative of courtesy than of real recognition. The main stream of musical thought, however, has been carefully mapped; and even though its channel will prove on closer acquaintance to be more tortuous than it here appears, the author believes that the student who undertakes to explore the backwaters will not, after such orientation as is here offered, be likely wholly to lose his bearings.

The twentieth century has also been dealt with at greater length; but there has naturally been no attempt to render final judgment on contemporary problems. Neither has any effort been made to capture the curiosity of the reader by bringing the chronicle of contemporary events up to the last three weeks before the date of publication. Such reporting is the business of periodicals, not of histories.

The book is chiefly addressed, as formerly, to the student who is making his first contact with the serious aspect of the subject. But the general reader, whose interest is often as deep as that of the formally enrolled student, and who seems to have found considerable satisfaction with the book as it was, has also been kept in mind. Great care has been expended on the maintenance of continuity in the narrative, and on the clarification of the many technical details incidental thereto.

The Bibliography will reveal the sources to which the author has appealed for assistance. It will be apparent that one work in particular—Gustave Reese's *Music in the Middle Ages*—has been a constant guide, whether on matters of opinion or for remoter bibliographical direction. Personal inquiry, which was most cordially responded to, seemed needful in but one instance; but that fact only indicates the more sharply the author's sense of obligation to the epoch-making book and to its writer. My thanks are also gratefully tendered to Professor Roy Dickinson Welch of Princeton University, for his careful editorial supervision.

The kindly interest awakened by the book on its first appearance brought to the author almost an embarrassment of gratification. He ventures to hope that the revision will not diminish that interest.

PREFACE TO THE THIRD EDITION

The third edition of this book will show (throughout its earlier portions, many corrections of error—whether of statement or omission—that appeared in the second edition. These, in order to keep the dimensions of the book within reasonable bounds, have been introduced within the existing space.

The principal alterations will be found in the last two chapters, which deal with the twentieth century. These replace, expand, and rectify the one chapter on that period appearing in the second edition. They attempt to describe and (of course, tentatively) to evaluate those great changes in the musical idiom which—at first appearing as no more than extravagant adventures in tonal structure—have in the last thirty years become established as normal, not only in the writings of the learned but even in the musical language of the cinema and the dance hall.

The battles of the theorists—a kind of civil war—which began in the 'teens of the century after the first strident trumpet-calls of the *avant-garde,* and which raged so violently among their followers and opponents during the 'twenties, have now all but ceased. Many of the dead, on both sides, have been decently buried. The ideal of liberty and equality among notes (as unattainable as among humans) has not, indeed, brought about untroubled fraternity among composers. But the victory is unquestionably with the moderns.

History records, but does not celebrate, victories. It attempts to evaluate them. In this effort it must take into account not merely the embattled forces and their maneuvers but the vast number of noncombatants whose interests, ignored in the heat of battle, prove in the long run the truest measure of the victory.

As after our civil war, a process of reconstruction has begun. In that process, changes at first assessed as gains turn out to be losses, severe enough so that they must somehow be retrieved. (Such losses, as this book records, have several times been retrieved, and always in the interest of the seeker for more than purely musical meaning in music.) England and America—perhaps because they are more skilled than other nations in the difficult practice of democracy—appear to this writer as regions where losses of this kind have been more justly assessed and where practical retrieval is more unhampered than elsewhere. For this reason these two have been dealt with in a separate chapter.

I am grateful to my colleagues, Ian Morton, Vincent Carpenter, and Thomas Nee (for next season, assistant conductor of the Minneapolis Symphony Orchestra), and especially to Robert Laudon, one of the most percipient students of contemporary music among my acquaintance, for their careful scrutiny of my manuscript. These young men have offered many rectifications of my somewhat presbyopic perspective.

D.N.F.

Minneapolis, Minn.

Contents

&ℰ *CHAPTER I* ℰ&

The Problems

MUSIC is a mode of thought—a way of thinking in tones. Many possible aspects of tone-thinking will appear in the course of our study. But what do we mean by *thinking in tones?* The substance of tone seems hardly to form either the substance or the vehicle of thought in the ordinary meaning of that word. Except in the physical sense, indeed, tones are almost incapable of definition. A single tone, no matter how sensuously attractive, has (apart from that attractiveness) no real meaning in itself. But melodies or harmonies, which are but successions or combinations of tones, have a value not discoverable in isolated tones—a value which we apprehend, however, with such slight effort that the understanding of simple music seems hardly to constitute an act of thinking. But even the hearing of such simple music stimulates in our minds several different types of awareness; and to examine, no more than superficially, these types is to perceive that in hearing music we are following the course of what can truthfully be described as *thought*.

First of all, we are aware that music makes sense—sense, that is, in the tones themselves without reference to anything else. And this making of sense is fundamental to the other pleasures and interests which music offers, which we roughly describe as coming from the beauty of the music and from its expression of various emotions. These qualities of beauty and expression have puzzled the minds of philosophers and aestheticians and psychologists ever since their branches of knowledge came into being; and it sometimes seems as if they had made no progress toward a solution of their problems. But it is certain that in order to be either beautiful or expressive, music must first make sense. If, then, the musical mode of thought is a complex vehicle for the suggestion of ideas of beauty and emotion, our first task must be to discover the principle according to which musical sounds are organized so as to make sense.

The analogy with language is here very helpful; for language is also a mode of thought—a way of thinking in words. Words are symbols—symbols for things and acts, for their qualities, and for the relations between them. From the beginning of consciousness, almost, we learn to associate these symbols with objects and facts of experience. Presently we combine words into sentences—word groups whose structure conforms in a general way to the relations or the behavior of those facts or objects as we know them. The rules of syntax lay down the principles of sentence structure; but it is presupposed that sentences will be made out of words which symbolize objects behaving in a way compatible with ordinary human experience. The succession of words *Henry and biology to perfectly those black involves* makes no sense whatever, although the meaning of the individual words is known, partly because there is no semblance of syntax in the word order, and partly because the objects symbolized have no relation to each other in human experience. On the other hand, *And black biology perfectly involves those to Henry*, although it conveys no real idea, has a faint and irritating resemblance to sense because it conforms to syntactical principles and because there is just enough of relativity between the suggested symbols to make us search for a hint of possible human experience. Verbal syntax—the fundamental convention of speech—has its roots in human experience. Is this possibly true of musical syntax also?

It is as easy to make nonsense with notes as with words. The following sequence of notes is probably as unintelligible as our senseless group of words, although the notes themselves are familiar:

A beginning of sense can be made out of the same note sequence by giving it a definite rhythm pattern:

The motion of the notes has now become suggestive of some kind of human reality—whether of the possible movement of our feet in the dance, or of some other motion, is no matter. For motion is definitely characteristic of almost all human behavior; and many types of feeling find an almost instinctive "expression" in appropriate types of bodily movement. Musical rhythm, at least, is founded in human experience.

Is it also possible that the tone relations of music have a similar foundation? This is a question more difficult to answer. Certainly the pure tone-patterns of great sonatas and fugues have no immediate counterpart in human activity. But it is true that the inflection of the voice in impassioned speech is in a way imitated and much intensified in melody. And it is true, as we shall see, that the first effective steps toward the definite organization of our scale were made directly out of a certain type of experience—the experience of concord and discord. Concord and discord in their elemental form are apprehended alike by almost everybody. It is certainly safe to say that even tone organization—which at first seems like the most purely imaginative and unrelated to earth of all human achievements—is to some degree developed out of human experience, part of which is of a nonmusical sort.

We are concerned at the moment, however, not with these abstractions but with a single element of the whole problem: that of the basis of musical syntax. We have made nonsense and partial sense out of notes. Let us now take a simple tune which makes complete sense, and by examination and comparison try to find the principle of syntax which binds these notes together. The example is simple and familiar, which makes easier our search for the secret of its sense:

Here, without any thought of the words, is something which clearly resembles an English sentence. It is, however, punctuated at the same points, and comes to the same complete stop, as the familiar words to which the music is set. How, without noun tones or verb tones (for music has neither), is this punctuation effected? And why do the notes in the musical phrase cohere as do the words in the verbal phrase?

The rhythm pattern, obviously, helps to define the sense. Yet the rhythm has nothing directly to do with the tone sense, which would be equally clear with quite another rhythm pattern. How can one phrase end with a sense of *going on*, and another end with a sense of *stop?* If we recognize certain notes as saying "go on," it must be that we already recognize some other note as capable of saying "stop." But if no single note in itself has the invariable meaning *stop*, it must also be that from the notes which go on we recognize the note which stops. This is only a tedious way of saying what everybody knows, that in all our music there is this one note toward which all melody ultimately tends—a note which we call the *keynote* or *tonic*.

But if we go a step farther, and ask why or how this sense of tonic comes to be so universally felt, we cannot answer. About all we can say is that, as the music begins, we assume a certain note to be the tonic; and, as it goes on, prove the truth of our assumption by observation. Sometimes, indeed, we cannot be sure. The following, for example, can make two different kinds of sense, accordingly as we take C or A to be the tonic:

just as we can see this little boxlike figure as having two different positions or shapes, accordingly as we see the point A or the point B as representing the corner of the box which is nearest us. It is plain, however, that we must read sense into the music, just as we read sense into the figure. In the case of the figure, this sense comes from a previous knowledge of the shapes of boxes. But what previous knowledge can we have about tones?

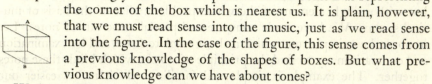

We have already said that an awareness of concord seems to exist almost universally. Can it be that there is in this awareness, which is a kind of "previous knowledge," an explanation of the mystery of the tonic? Some confirmation of this idea is offered by the physicist. Examining and measuring the phenomena of sound, he first shows us that tones are produced by sound waves having a uniform rate of vibration; and that they are thus distinguished from noises, in which many waves of very different rates of vibration are combined. (Noises, it will be seen, are from the physicist's point of view a very extreme type of discord.) Then, considering tones in combination, he shows us that the higher of two tones which are exactly an octave apart (as C and c) vibrates exactly twice as fast as the lower tone. Expressing this ratio as 2 : 1, he goes on to find the ratio of the fifth (C to G) to be 3 : 2; that of the fourth, 4 : 3. These are physically the smoothest consonances; but to our ears (trained in the elaborate conventions of harmony) the major third (5 : 4) and the minor third (6 : 5) are far more attractive.

Thus the *physical* distinction between the perfect concords (unisons, fourths, fifths, and octaves) and the imperfect concords (major and minor thirds and sixths) seems falsely descriptive of the *musical* values of these intervals. It will be noted that the perfect concords are expressed in simpler ratios (that is, ratios in smaller numbers) than are the imperfect. Discords have still higher ratios, such as 9 : 8 for the major second (whole step), and 16 : 15 for the minor second (half step). Physicist and musician agree in describing all seconds and sevenths, and all augmented and diminished intervals, as discords.

With this very meager summary of the physicist's contribution, let us return to our problem: How far can the sense of tonic be explained on the basis of the perception of consonance and disonance?

The identity of octaves (the almost complete similarity of two notes an octave apart) may to some extent explain why, when we ascend or descend the scale, we stop at the octave of the note on which we started. But this does not explain why C, for example, in the scale of C, is keynote; for if we go from D to d (always with the white keys of the piano only) we still feel that C is keynote. It is obviously the arrangement of the whole and half steps in the series rather than the identity of octaves which points out the keynote to our minds.

Let us then observe for a moment that arrangement. Our major scale consists of two tone groups (in the C scale, C–D–E–F and G–A–B–c) which are identical in interval pattern. In spite of this similarity, the homologous tones in the two groups function very differently to the musical ear. B, especially, tends much more actively toward C than E tends toward F. Is this because in hearing the whole series we are aware that B, sharply discordant with c, gains its tendency from the fact of discordance? If so, why should not E, equally discordant with F, point out F as tonic? The obvious answer is that our sense of the activity of B is intensified by another and still stronger discord impression—that conveyed by the interval F–B. This relation is not paralleled for E by the homologous interval B′–E.

But there is a further question involved. Physicist and musician agree that discord implies motion toward concord. To the physicist it would appear that for the dissonant interval F–B, the *perfect* concord F–c should offer a more satisfactory resolution than the *imperfect* concord E–c. But this supposition the musical ear denies. Even when we approach from F–B the concord F–c, but still more with the *inversion* of these intervals (B′–F to C–F), we feel that F is actually not concordant with C at all. Even if we strike the combination C–F without approach, the impression is the same. Exactly as if it were a dissonant note, F *wants to move*. It wants to go to E—or at least we want it to; and all the physics in the world will not convince us that the perfect concord is a more satisfying tone combination than the imperfect. The musician's way of looking at discord and concord differs, apparently arbitrarily, from the physicist's way. Thus, although it appears true that the physical fact of discord relationship establishes for us the sense of tonic in our scale, it must be admitted that the implications of physical science are also denied in the structure of our scale; and that physics does not fully account for the sense of tonic.

Nor do physiology and psychology offer any complete explanation. The physiologist offers us only the mechanism of the ear—a mechanism which has no choice but to transmit to the brain every sound impulse which strikes upon it. The ear does somehow transmute sound waves into nerve impulses. This is a very remarkable and a much disputed transmutation; but no one contends that the aural mechanism itself can be responsible for the change in meaning of an interval. The psychologist is confronted with a bewildering complexity of processes in the reception of even the simplest of musical stimuli. In answer to our question, about all he can tell us is that if the sense of key is not a necessary result of the physical stimulus itself, then some other activities in the brain must combine with the hearing process to produce the result which we all agree is produced. He will show us that such judgments as this (of the tonic as the gravitational center of the scale, or of the perfect fourth as almost a discord) are really habits of thought—habits which are the result of the mind's primordial necessity to make sense out of the stimuli which come to it through the sense organs.

Is our sense of key, then, largely a mental habit? The psychologist knows that this is entirely possible. We are continually combining and readjusting raw sense impressions into ideas; and to a large extent these adjustments are habits. It is so with sight. We must test our sight perceptions—our judgments of the size and position of objects—by means of parallel observations with other senses (that of touch, chiefly), and must learn to correct the somewhat erratic and insufficient suggestions which our eyes alone convey. No matter how good our eyes are, we must *learn* to see; and the product of this learning is a habit of sight. Our whole attitude toward music, too, is a habit of thought which is the result of our observing and relating tones. Rhythm, which greatly aids any succession of tones in assuming recognizable shape, and harmony, which is a great aid in tone organization, are both factors in our complex habit of musical thought. But the principal clue to all understanding of tone relations is the sense of tonic or key.[1]

Our habits of musical thought, then, are really *conventions*—habits which have a history. We say that the elements of music are melody, rhythm, and harmony; but these are not exactly the elements of musical thought. Of the three, rhythm is probably the only true and irreducible element. For behind all melody lies an essential principle of tone organization which, however various the actual tone series among different peoples, seems invariably to rest upon the conventional elevation of one tone in the series to a position of supremacy; while harmony is not only a

---

[1] This statement apparently takes no account of the current ultramodern attitude toward tonality. There are many modern composers who assume that tonic centrality has been overthrown. But there are many more who view modernistic practice as a loosening rather than as a complete overthrow of the influence of the tonic. And in view of the recent subsidence of militant atonalism, both in theory and practice, it seems best to let the statement stand. It should by no means be inferred, however, that what might be called a mid-Victorian attitude in the matter is advocated.

product of our own diatonic scale alone, but is relatively a late invention and is thus by no means elemental. Our own art, however, does derive from these elemental impulses of rhythm and tone organization; and full understanding of the forms and characteristics which our present-day music assumes is impossible without some realization of the history of its development from these actual elements.

In this study we shall be concerned only with those facts which show the evolution of our present way of thinking music. We shall watch the development of our scale almost from its birth; and shall see how the groping search for a keynote is retarded by other conventions. We shall study the sources from which rhythm comes, and the hindrances to purely rhythmic thought which kept music for many centuries in bondage to verse. We shall see how, out of the solution of these problems of rhythm and tonic sense, other problems arose—the problems of harmony and of an adequate notation for the ever increasing complexities of music; the problems of musical syntax and rhetoric whose solution must precede the larger problems of form; and the problems of sweeping readjustment of form to meet the needs of a time in which new ideas of the relations of men to each other or to God have generated new emotions which it must be the business of music to express. We shall see, that is, how out of a condition of almost complete dependence either on speech or on the dance, music throws off this subservience to other modes of thought and becomes self-existent. Only through its history shall we have any adequate idea of the wonderful art which in our own day appeals to more people, perhaps, than any other.

The First Scales and the Beginnings
of Keynote Feeling

THE MUSIC OF ANCIENT GREECE

ORIGINS AND ANTECEDENTS

THE problem of the actual beginning of music can be solved only by speculation. Was music developed, as Darwin thought, from the love calls of our antehuman ancestors? Was it suggested by the song of birds? Did it arise before speech? Or was it, as Herbert Spencer held, a natural product of excitement arising out of, or wedding itself to, the already existing expression of speech? No one knows, or can know. The nearest approach to the actual origins of music which can now be made is of course through the study of the music of primitive peoples—American Indians, Murray Islanders, Salomon Islanders, Patagonians, and others. Even here, however, a very great variety of accomplishment is manifest, so that no more than very general conclusions can be drawn.

All primitive peoples make up chants of religion, of war, of the chase, of love, or of death. That is, they associate musical tone with the chief experiences of life. Such as it is, this music is always directly associated with words or with bodily movements which assume the rhythmic form of the dance. With most primitive tribes, the words (which are rhythmic) or the dance steps, rather than the tone patterns, seem to be the chief element. The tone patterns are of the simplest kind, often repeated almost endlessly, and exactness of intonation seems of little importance. The tone element of music, that is, is subordinate to the rhythm element. There is no self-sufficient tonal idea. Tones are valued rather for their character suggestion, in association with words or steps, than for their pitch or form relations. Extended melody, coherently knitting together a variety of phrases, hardly exists in primitive music. Consequently, primitive scales (the orderly succession of the notes which are used for melody) differ widely from our own, and often appear to us irrational or even unintelligible.

Nevertheless, these melodies and scales make sense to their habitual users; and even to our ears, attentive listening reveals at last a kind of reasonableness. Certain intervals, in many types of primitive scale, are essentially the same as intervals in our own series. Along with these familiar intervals, however, occur others which we do not use—intervals smaller than a half step, for instance, which our conventional expectancy of harmonic sense makes it almost impossible for us to accept as musical. It appears possible, out of all this confusion, to classify scales into two general types, each of which involves the consonant intervals of the octave, the fifth, or the fourth, and is probably based on some fundamental recognition of consonance. The fifth, when taken as the basic interval, gives a rising pentatonic (five-note) scale. The fourth gives a descending heptatonic (seven-note) scale. Pentatonic scales are characteristic of the Far East (China, Japan, the Pacific Islands) and are found also in the primitive music of Western Europe, notably in that of the Celtic peoples of Ireland and Scotland. Heptatonic scales develop (of course, with many variations) in Western Asia (Persia, Arabia, and India) and ancient Egypt and appear at last in Greece, from which source, as we shall see, our own type of heptatonic scale has been derived.

The music of the great civilizations of antiquity is almost as difficult to reconstruct as the primitive art out of which it grew. Verbal records, mural decorations, even the remains of musical instruments in large variety, indicate that music played a large part both in the religious and royal ceremonial and in the social life of such peoples as the Egyptians, the Babylonians, and the Persians. The strange wailing of Asiatic music as we now hear it bears, doubtless, some traces of the ancient musical language of these peoples; but the actuality of that music, or the influence of one ancient system upon another, will probably remain a matter of conjecture. A flute with seven holes, apparently more than 3000 years old, has been found in Egypt. This may be taken as sufficient proof of the currency at that time of a heptatonic scale; but without knowledge of the music which was played on that flute we can have no exact idea of the way these seven tones were understood. We are even ignorant of the degree to which later Egyptian music influenced that of Greece. When one remembers the many dynasties which succeeded each other in Egypt, and considers the racial interminglings which these dynasties represent, one sees the impossibility of drawing any sure inferences from the few facts in our possession.

If it had been a direct ancestor of our own system, the music of China, reflecting the most unbroken continuity of culture which has been recorded, would have contributed invaluably to our understanding of the evolution of our own art. It is our scale and our music, however, which has influenced that of China. The fundamental Chinese scale, as we have said, is the anhemitonic pentatonic (the five-note scale without the half step), f g a c d' f'. Theoretically, indeed, this scale was altered to a scheme of six whole-tone steps, f g a b c sharp' d sharp'; and this series of six "masculine" tones was supplemented, as early as 2700 B.C., by another group of six "feminine" tones, f sharp g sharp a sharp c d' e', so that the whole chromatic scale, and even the Debussyan whole-tone scale, was known long before it came to any practical use. But all ancient Chinese melody continued to be made on the pentatonic scale; and this doctrine of twelve *lü's* or half tones remained entirely theoretical. The introduction of the *leading* tone B, and the *mediating* tone E (about 1500 A.D.) was in response to no Western influence, but was again (although more practical than the system of the twelve *lü's*) largely an invention of the theorists. For the pentatonic scale continues to this day to be the basis of that popular Chinese melody which is uninfluenced by Western music. It is possible, also, that the elaborate system of twelve *lü's* has been greatly predated.

The pentatonic scale, as we have said, is found in many other regions than China. Not only is it the basis of the Celtic music of Northwestern Europe: it is traceable also among the American Indians, in certain old German hymns (such as the early Easter hymn *Christ ist erstanden von der Marter alle*) and even, as Dr. Riemann maintained, in certain strains of the Gregorian chant. Indeed, it is supposable that the pentatonic scale represents a middle stage in the evolution of the more elaborate heptatonic.

The Earliest Greek Music—Its Relation to Poetry

We turn at once, therefore, to that ancient system which is definitely known to be the chief source of our own—that of ancient Greece. We have a considerable (if sometimes debatable) knowledge of the history, the technical system, and the aesthetic values of Greek music. The history, save for its illumination of the purpose of music to the Greeks, is relatively unimportant, and can be briefly told. The technical system, however, is of great importance for us, since it is linked at its beginning with types of music almost primitive, and at its culmination with the earliest music of Christian Europe. Many elemental features of our musical thought, like many words in our language, are of Greek origin. The aesthetic values of music, as they appeared to the Greek mind, seem to us strange and unusual; but they are of interest if only because they diverge so greatly from our own estimates, and show us in how many ways music can achieve ex-presssion.

The Greeks believed that their music, like their race, had a divine origin. Such mythical personages as Orpheus, whose journey to the underworld forms the theme of so many later operas, and Marsyas, whose contest in song with Apollo had such a distressful ending, have no more historic authenticity than Hercules or Theseus. But as Orpheus was said to have been a Thracian, and Olympus a Phrygian, the weight of foreign influence in the formation of the Greek musical system must be regarded as con-siderable. More positive influences from Egypt and Asia Minor are trace-able. The lute, the lyre, and an instrument like the oboe were imported from Egypt; the two latter, as lyre (or, in large form, cithara) and aulos, became the typical examples of string and wind instruments among the Greeks. The mathematical researches of Pythagoras, of which more will be said presently, may well have been stimulated by the Egyptians, who had also a hemitonic scale. Yet all these influences could have been effec-tive only up to a certain point. For as we shall see more clearly, Greek music was very intimately related to the Greek language, and no innova-tions incompatible with this relation could have been allowed. Because of this relation, then, it is well that we should have in mind a bare outline of the growth of poetic art in Greece. For the history of poetry in Greece is, in a loose sense, the history of its music also.

The Olympic games (begun 776 B.C.) show an established musical-poetic activity of wide popular appeal, whose foundations may reach far back into the earlier Minoan and Mycenaean civilizations. A special meter (dactylic hexameter), and a peculiar attitude of the poet (an impersonal, "prophetic" attitude, as of one inspired by the gods) characterize the poems of Homer and Hesiod. These are in the epic style—the only style, so far, to attain to popularity. These poems were sung, not merely spoken, and were accompanied by the lyre. But of course the melody of such song was in no way comparable to our own. The rhythm of the music was essentially that of the poetry. Therefore, the emergence of elegiac and iambic (originally satirical) verse, with a more highly varied rhythm, produced a correspondingly varied music, whose expression of the sense of the words was doubtless more subtle than in the case of the Homeric poems. And with the culmination of the poetic art in the many forms of lyric poetry, the union of music and verse was even more complete. A third vehicle of expression, the dance, was also represented.

Three tribes, the Ionians (from Asia Minor), the Aeolians (more partic-ularly from the Island of Lesbos), and the Dorians (of the Peloponnesus) contributed each a share to the development of lyric poetry. Inheriting these combined traditions, such supreme masters as Simonides and Pindar became (in a time when the danger of the Persian invasion had awakened a sense of Greek solidarity) truly Panhellenic figures. And with the founding of the Athenian empire came a fusion of earlier poetic styles in the supreme monument of Greek literature, the Attic drama. The great divisions of drama into tragedy and comedy have here their origin.

Tragedy (*tragos*, a goat + *ōdē*, song) began in the ceremonial of the sacrifice of a goat before the altar of Dionysus, and in the hymn which was sung thereafter. The essential feature for dramatic suggestion was the dialogue between the leader and the chorus. Comedy (*kōmē*, a village + *ōdē*) was originally a rustic jest. Aeschylus (born 525 B.C.), giving a part in the dialogue to a second leader or actor, and thus reducing the prominence of the chorus, was the founder of tragedy. Sophocles, only thirty years younger, brought tragedy to such ideal perfection that neither in the empire of Alexander nor in that of the Caesars could the dramatic poets offer any betterment. Certain principles of construction, the so-called *unities*, were observed (partly for reasons only connected with the open-air theatre in which the plays were performed). We shall see how in the sixteenth century this great achievement of the Greeks became the model for the founders of our modern art of opera.

Philip of Macedon, and more especially Alexander, whose empire was the vastest government known until then on earth, brought the culture of the city-states of Greece, whose population was numberable in thousands, into lands of East and West whose population was numberable in millions. These millions were not Greeks but foreigners—"barbarians," the Greeks called them. This diffusion of culture, accompanied by the inevitable turmoil of political and commercial interests, brought about a decline from the high perfection of Athenian art. Until the age of Augustus in Rome, the center of Greek culture was no longer Athens, but Alexandria, founded in 332 B.C. by Alexander the Great. During this epoch many changes in language and music came about; instrumental music became much more important than it had been in Athens; and ultimately a new idea of the scale emanated from Alexandria's most distinguished scholar, Claudius Ptolemy. These achievements contributed immediately to the music of the Christian Church, music which we shall find to be the direct forerunner of our own. With this meager sketch of the growth of Greek poetry we must be content, turning now to the technical side of Greek music.

The Evolution of the Greek Scale

Although there is a well-authenticated tradition of the existence of a six-note *scale of Olympus* (e f a b c′ e′), the essential scale form of the Greeks was that of the tetrachord (*tetra*, four + *chordē*, an intestine of which strings were made; hence, a string). The tetrachord was a group of four notes, always covering the compass of a perfect fourth of our scale, and thought of as tending downward. This interval of a downward fourth, it will be remembered, often characterizes primitive music. The highest note of the tetrachord (as E) was felt as the tone center. The lowest (as B) was fixed in relation to E because it satisfied the sense of concord, and formed the smallest concordant interval recognized by the Greeks. (The third, to the Greek and for long to the medieval mind, was considered a discord.) In the tetrachord, only the extreme notes stood in a fixed relation of pitch to each other. Between these, two *movable notes* were inserted. Although we do not use the term *movable*, we have largely the same condition in our own diatonic scale.[1] Only in our chromatic scale do we recognize four tones as possible between B and E. The Greek musician also conceived of only two variable tones in any one tetrachord; but some of these were tones not included in our own scale system. They will be understood from the following, which is a table of the three *genera* or types of tetrachord, classified according to the way in which the movable notes were inserted:

THE THREE GENERA OF THE TETRACHORD

I. THE ENHARMONIC

(The note *c represents approximately a quarter tone, between c and B.)

II. THE CHROMATIC

III. THE DIATONIC

It will be seen that the smallest intervals are always at the bottom of the tetrachord. This, indeed, is an invariable principle with the Greek theorists: that *taking the upper note of the tetrachord as fundamental, the*

---

[1] In B major, for instance, we insert c♯ and d♯ between B and E; in B minor, c♯ and d; in E minor (ascending) c or c♯ and d♯; in C major, c and d. The notes c and d, sharped or flatted as may be required, are thus *movable notes*.

lowest interval must be equal to or less than the middle interval, and less than the highest. The highest note was always the fundamental of the tetrachord, and the two fixed notes were invariably at the interval of the perfect fourth—the smallest *concordant* interval recognized by the Greeks, who felt concord as a relation of consecutive, not simultaneous, tones.

In these two facts of tone organization—the acceptance of the tetrachord as the scale unit (instead of the octave, as with us), and the placing of the smallest intervals at the bottom of the series—we see a fundamental convention of Greek musical thought. The earliest melody of the Greeks was confined within this narrow compass. But this melody was both less and more than a tune. It was less, at any rate to our comprehension, because it must have lacked the interest of extended and contrasted phrases; but it was also more because it was apparently designed to give immediate intensification to the words to which it was set. We shall see more fully, when we come to study the beginnings of musical rhythm, how the very nature of Greek poetry demanded subtleties of utterance, perhaps verbal as well as musical, which we can imagine only with difficulty. But we may here recognize that strange and unusual intervals, such as those of the enharmonic genus, can give qualities of melody which are impossible in our diatonic music; and that quarter tones, sung with fitting intonation, might intensify the meaning of words to a very great degree.

We often describe the tone qualities and the pitch changes which characterize a fine actor's enunciation as *musical*, although they suggest no really musical idea. It is possible that such *musical* reading—approaching more nearly than ours to actual song, but still lacking the complete self-intelligibility of our art—was what the Greeks cultivated as music. We must therefore view all the successive developments which we shall have to record as efforts toward the gradual emancipation of music from an original association with speech, and toward that condition of self-intelligibility which belongs to all our modern music.

In the three genera of tetrachords we have a positive step toward independent tone organization. To musical minds, such an achievement could not but evoke the imagination of a larger series of tones—a series employing the whole compass of the voice which, in those days and for long afterward, was regarded as approximately an octave. If we remember that the convention of the tetrachord was already firmly implanted in the Greek mind, we shall readily understand that this desired extension of the compass of melody would be brought about by joining two tetrachords together.

Two ways of joining them were possible. The extreme note of one tetrachord (for example, E in the diatonic tetrachord already illustrated) might be taken as the lowest note of another tetrachord, thus:

```
a g f e
      |
    e d C B
```

in which case the tetrachords were said to be conjunct, and the two together produced a scale of seven notes. Or the added tetrachord could
begin at the distance of a whole step from the extreme note of the original
tetrachord, thus:

```
e d C B
        A  G  F  E
```

in which case the tetrachords were disjunct, and the scale produced was
that of a whole octave.

The possibility of further additions at either end of the scale would be
immediately obvious, but the results which followed the exclusive use of
either the principle of conjunction or that of disjunction were confusing.
If the conjunct method were followed for every added tetrachord, the
following scale would be produced. (We now capitalize the notes of our
original tetrachord only, to show the additions on either side.)

THE SCALE INDEFINITELY EXTENDED BY CONJUNCTION ONLY

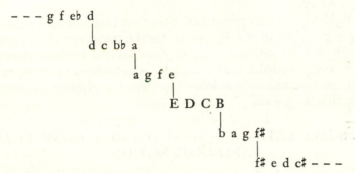

A scale of this sort was not a mere theorem, but was a musical actuality.
The term which the Greek applied to the joining of tetrachords was
harmonia—a word obviously very different in meaning from our own
derivative of that word. The above type of scale (whether or not its name
implied a geographical origin) was called the *Ionian harmony*.[2] And there

[2] The basis of the whole exposition here given is the doctrine of Aristoxenus, as
interpreted by Henry S. Macran. The older idea of the Greek modes (Dorian, Phrygian, etc.) as founded on tetrachords which placed the smallest interval in the middle
or at the top of the tetrachord, Macran shows to have been false. Some other statements, such as that just made with respect to the meaning of *harmonia*, and the evolution of the *harmonies*, are to a considerable extent hypothetical. Macran's exposition,

is one fact about this scale which we must realize clearly. In each added tetrachord, as in the original one, the upper of the two fixed notes would be regarded as the fundamental. (The word *tonic* seems too strong to apply, although something of the function of tonic is implied.) Therefore there would be as many fundamental notes as there were tetrachord segments in the scale; and, since these fundamentals are all different, no single note can function as fundamental or tonic for this whole, indefinitely extended Ionian scale.

If, on the other hand, the method or harmony of disjunction were employed exclusively, the following result would be obtained.

THE SCALE INDEFINITELY EXTENDED BY
DISJUNCTION ONLY

```
– – – f♯ e d c♯
        b a g f♯
                E D C B
                        a g f e
                                d c b♭ a – – –
```

This scale represents the *Dorian harmony*. It suffers from the same lack of a single fundamental for all the tetrachords which we observed in the Ionian harmony.

The rigid logic which prescribed either conjunction or disjunction as the single principle of the Ionian or the Dorian harmony is evidently responsible for the diffused sense of fundamental in those scales. But common sense revealed a third harmony as possible—a harmony of alternate conjunction and disjunction. This was the *Aeolian harmony*, and gave the following scale:

THE SCALE EXTENDED BY ALTERNATE CONJUNCTION
AND DISJUNCTION

```
    – – – e d c b

a g f e
      |
      E D C B

            a g f e
                  |
                  e d c b – – –
```

---

although disputed by more recent writers, gives a clearer idea than any other of the growth of the modern scale, and has been retained for that reason. Even Winnington-Ingram confesses that in certain important particulars, Macran is "hard to refute."

It is apparent that this Aeolian harmony is simpler than the others, since it involves no modulation and presents, in succeeding octaves, identical note sequences. It has also another superiority, which is of the greatest significance. It will be remembered that in any tetrachord the highest note is fundamental. In the Ionian harmony, above, G, D, A, E, B, and F sharp were the *tonics*, as we may call them, of the successive tetrachords; in the Dorian, the successive tonics were F sharp, B, E, A, and D. (Both series might be indefinitely extended, giving for each additional tetrachord a new tonic.) No single note, therefore, could possibly serve as fundamental for the whole extended scale. In the Aeolian harmony, however, only two fundamentals appear—A and E—and of these A takes precedence. For by the convention of tetrachord structure, A is tonic to the E below. But because of the obvious identity of octaves, A is also perceptible as tonic to the E above (which is almost identical in sound with the E below). E, on the other hand, cannot assume the function of tonic to the whole series. For it is, by convention, tonic only to B below, and secondarily to the B above. But the B above cannot be tonic to any note in the diatonic scale, but only to F sharp which is not in the Aeolian harmony. Therefore, since A is tonic to both the higher and lower E's, it takes precedence over E (which is tonic only to B), and becomes the central governing tone of the whole series. *It is thus the first approximation to a true tonic, governing an indefinitely extended scale, to be met with in music.*

We are not to imagine, however, that this note is at all the exact equivalent of our modern keynote. Indeed, its value to the Greek mind was so far different from the value we attach to the keynote that we have great difficulty in imagining how music really felt to the Greeks. These differences, however, are important, for they illustrate an essential step in the growth of that tonic centrality which is the essence of our system of tone organization.

In the first place, A, to the Greek, was the only possible tonic.[3] Our feeling that C is emphatically tonic in the series of *natural* notes was quite foreign to the Greek mind. In the second place, although A was felt as tonic, this did not entail the feeling that the whole scale should begin and end with A. Melodies as the Greeks composed them extended over the compass of about an octave. Some, of course, would use the octave A–a;

---

[3] That is, in the *natural* scale (the one we know as given by the white notes of the piano). The whole scale, however, might be transposed to any pitch. In such case, the note corresponding to A would become tonic; and this tonic was recognized as the note which (1) was highest in a properly formed tetrachord (with its smallest intervals at the bottom); and also as the note which (2) was followed in the upward direction by a disjunctive tone (i.e., a note a whole step distant) which was also the lowest fixed note of another tetrachord.

but others (with A still felt as tonic) would use the octave D–d, or B–b, or any other. This is as true of our music as of the Greek. The first strain of *Swanee River* uses the octave C–c. The first strain of the hymn *Adeste fideles* (if transposed to C) uses the octave G–g. We think of both melodies as in the major key. The Greek musician, however, would have analyzed the octave series G–g as quite another scale than the octave series C–c, even though both had the same tonic.[4] Since the average compass of a Greek melody was about an octave, it was natural to take each of the seven possible octave segments of the extended diatonic scale as a separate scale type. B–b, that is, or C–c, or D–d, or any similar octave group came to be distinguished as a separate scale, even though the tonic in every case was A. The differences here observed would appear insignificant were it not for the fact that the variable position of the tonic in the several scales gave a peculiar value of expression—a value which we shall examine in a moment.

The details of this scale structure must first be considered, however. Although the enharmonic and chromatic genera were gradually becoming obsolete, all the scales were still thought of as capable of being constructed in all three genera. Also, the seven different segments of the natural scale had each a name, indicating something, perhaps, of the geographic origin of types of melody which had become popular.

These seven different scales may be presented to the eye as seven diatonic octave-series, each one beginning a tone or semitone higher in the diatonic scale. It should be understood, however, that the Dorian scale does not necessarily begin and end with E, or the Lydian with C, and so on, but that the order of steps and half steps in each scale is merely represented in this way without accidentals, and hence more simply. Any scale could begin with any note. It is really the order of steps and half steps which gives each scale its individual character. Also, it must be remembered, the tonic of the scale, according to the Greek idea, is that *fixed* note which stands a perfect fourth above another, and at the same time is followed in the upward direction by a note a whole step distant. This tonic or *mese* (middle) as it came to be called, wherever it falls in the series, is always the governing tone of the series.

In the following table, the scales are presented in the simple diatonic succession. The interval distances which are their essential characteristic are marked above, using — for the whole step and ‿ for the half step. The essential tetrachord structure is indicated by brackets below the notes —complete for complete tetrachords, incomplete for those which are only

---

[4] This distinction was doubtless emphasized by the fact that an aulos, for instance, having the compass C–c, could play a melody like *Swanee River*, but could not play one like *Adeste fideles*.

partially included in any scale. The enharmonic and the chromatic genera are presented only in the last, the Hypodorian mode. (The word *mode* may be taken as practically synonymous with *scale*.) Fixed and movable notes are indicated by ♩ and ♪, respectively. The conjunctive tone which unites two tetrachords is shown thus: ♩

THE SEVEN PRINCIPAL MODES OF GREEK MUSIC

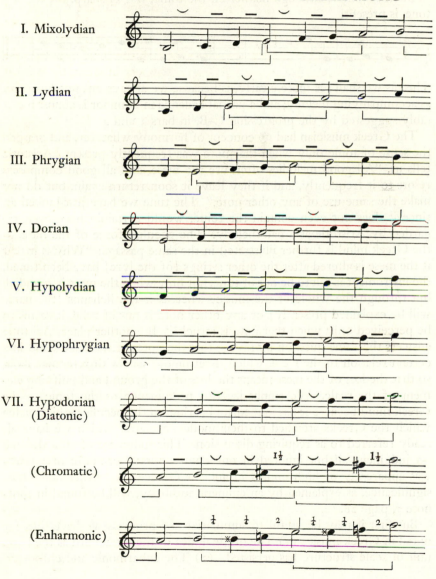

It will be seen, from scrutiny of these scales according to the definition of the mese given above, that the only note which can fulfill the function of mese is A. With our present convention of melody, which allows it to begin anywhere and end almost anywhere, while the tonic is still clearly understood, such an elaborate nomenclature and arrangement of scales would be quite useless. We shall almost inevitably feel the following tune to be in A minor, although neither A, the tonic, nor G sharp, the leading tone, is present:

This, as we shall see more clearly, is because we always imagine harmony as accompanying melody; and a partial cadence in A minor is almost inevitably suggested by the progression C–B, in bars 3 and 4.

The Greek musician had no concept of harmony whatever, and grasped the sense of tonic only when that note was frequently present. Aristotle tells us, "All good melodies often use the mese, and all good composers resort to it frequently, and if they leave it soon return again, but do not make the same use of any other note." The tune we have just looked at, since it does not even contain the tonic, would certainly have been regarded by Aristotle as a bad melody. The peculiar force of the mese to the Greek mind is further illustrated in the same passage: "Why is it that if the mese is altered after the other strings [of the lyre] have been tuned, the instrument is felt to be out of tune, not only when the mese is sounded, but through the whole of the music—whereas if the lichanos [the name will be explained presently] or any other note is out of tune, it seems to be perceived only when that note is struck?" In another place, Aristotle answers this same question by saying that the notes of the scale stand in a certain relation to the mese, which determines them with reference to it, so that the loss of the mese means the loss of the ground and unifying element of the scale. We emphasize this prominence of the tonic to the Greek mind because it has immediate bearing on the peculiar ethical value which the Greeks attached to their modes—a matter which we have already referred to as requiring discussion. This judgment of ethical value —a judgment all but ignored in our contemporary criticism of music— was apparently of high import in ancient Greece. A further hint of its significance, as explained by an eminent authority, will be found in footnote 7, page 28.

But first it may be useful to summarize the progress we have thus far noted in Greek music: (1) The original idea of the tetrachord as the basic unit of scale structure has persisted. (2) The enharmonic and chromatic genera are obsolescent. (3) The older fashions of combining tetrachords (the Ionian and Dorian harmonics) have been superseded by the Aeolian harmony. (4) By a perfectly natural process, a single note (A in the *natural* scale), has assumed the function of tonic for the whole series. (It is not the mere position of any note in the scale which gives it its meaning, but rather the function of that note in relation to the mese.) Finally (5) seven different modes or scales, each being a segment of the indefinitely extended Aeolian harmony, have been conventionally accepted. Since the one tonic or mese governs all these modes, it follows that Greek music, in the Aristotelian period, *had but one modality or sense of key.*

The Ethos of Greek Music

What, then, if there was but one modality, is the reason or sense in seven different modes or octave scales? The reason is to be found in the peculiar ethical and expressive character (*ethos*) which the Greeks felt to belong to these modes; and that character is in some degree explained by the comments of Aristotle, quoted above. The Greeks felt that modes of high pitch had a very different expressive sense from modes of low pitch. Aristotle probably expressed the common opinion in saying that musical forms are not mere symbols, but are an actual copy of the forms of moral temper. He agrees with Plato that the Dorian and Phrygian, representing the mean in pitch, are superior to the other modes which are either too high or too low. Aristides Quintilianus says that the ethos of notes differs as they are higher or lower; he says also that there are three kinds of composition, the higher, the middle, and the lower, corresponding to the three regions of the voice; and he speaks of the *nomic* (common) style in poetic-musical composition as related to *nete* (the lowest note of the scale), the *dithyrambic* style as related to *mese* and the *tragic* style as related to *hypate* (the highest note).

Now if the pitch of the seven scales above illustrated had been fixed, as we showed them, and not transposable to any desired degree, we should understand that the music of the different styles would be set, according to that pitch, in the desired mode for any given style. But the pitch of those modes was not fixed. The Dorian, that is, was not one step higher than the Phrygian. The mode represents an interval order, and no more; and any mode might be correctly sung either higher or lower than any other. How, then, are we to understand these modes as higher or lower in pitch? The answer is suggested in Aristotle's statement that "All good melodies often use the mese." For if the mese frequently recurs, the greater part of the melody will lie in the region of the mese. In our table of the modes, it will be seen that in the Mixolydian, for example, the mese lies one step from the top of the scale. In the Hypophrygian, it lies next the bottom. Therefore, "good" melody, as Aristotle describes it, would chiefly lie in the upper part of the Mixolydian mode, and in the lower part of the Hypophrygian. It is in this sense, then, that we are to understand the modes as higher or lower in pitch. The Dorian and Phrygian modes, representing a mean between extremes in pitch, were approved by Plato and Aristotle as steadfast and manly—the actual copies of courage and temperance. High pitch similarly implied excitement and passion, and low pitch softness and self-indulgence.

The Completed Greek Scale

During all this expansion of the artistic sense of music, the scale itself was, of course, undergoing expansion. It will somewhat clarify our idea of the growth of Greek music if we illustrate the essential stages in the enlargement of the scale. We have seen that the earliest melody was confined within the compass of a single tetrachord. The six-note scale of Olympus was perhaps the first expansion of the tetrachord. Although the two groups into which that scale may be divided (B–E, and E–A) are essentially based on the fixed notes of the tetrachord, there appears in each group but one note corresponding to the movable notes of the full tetrachords. The exact significance of the scale of Olympus in the evolution of the later scales is uncertain; but the tetrachord form is at least strongly suggested. And the next step—the addition of tetrachords by conjunction to form the Ionian harmony—seems like a filling out of the scale of Olympus. Names derived from the strings of the lyre were given to the seven-note scale of the Ionian harmony:

D   Nētē (*lowest* string—really the highest note [5])
C   Paranētē (next to the Nētē)
B♭   Trite (third string)

A   Mesē (middle string)
G   Lichanos (*first-finger* string)
F   Parhypatē (next to the highest [5])
E   Hypatē (*highest* string—really the lowest note [5])

The Dorian harmony, which combined tetrachords by disjunction, gave an octachord scale, necessitating the use of one more descriptive term, *paramese:*

[5] The terms *highest* and *lowest* applied to the strings of the lyre as it was held in playing position. The longest strings, or at any rate those lowest in pitch, as in our harp, were away from the performer, and held uppermost. We shall see that this peculiar use of terms may have resulted, much later, in a strange confusion of nomenclature for the modes.

{
E   Nētē
D   Paranētē
C   Tritē
B   Paramesē (next to the Mesē)
}

{
A   Mesē
G   Lichanos
F   Parhypatē
E   Hypatē
}

The Aeolian harmony, adding tetrachords both by conjunction and disjunction, gave an indefinitely extended scale whose octave sections were exactly symmetrical. Only two octaves, however, were required for the whole compass of Greek music. Melody for a single voice remained within a single octave; but the combination of lower and higher voices, such as men's and boys', was frequently employed. Those, of course, re-

THE PERFECT IMMUTABLE SYSTEM
COMPRISING THE GREATER AND THE LESSER
PERFECT SYSTEMS

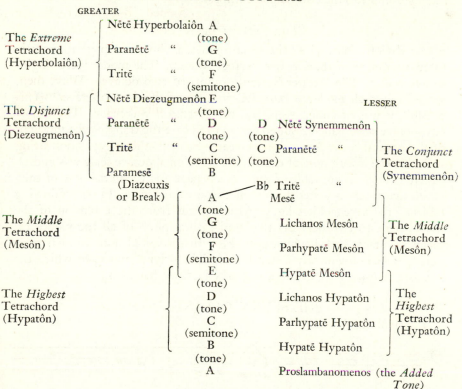

GREATER

The *Extreme* Tetrachord (Hyperbolaiôn)
{
Nētē Hyperbolaiôn   A
(tone)
Paranētē   "   G
(tone)
Tritē   "   F
(semitone)
}

The *Disjunct* Tetrachord (Diezeugmenôn)
{
Nētē Diezeugmenôn E   LESSER
(tone)
Paranētē   "   D   D   Nētē Synemmenôn }
(tone)   (tone)
Tritē   "   C   C   Paranētē   "   } The *Conjunct*
(semitone) (tone)   Tetrachord
Paramesē   B   (Synemmenôn)
(Diazeuxis   Bb Trité   "   }
or Break)   A   Mesē
}

The *Middle* Tetrachord (Mesôn)
{
(tone)
G   Lichanos Mesôn   } The *Middle*
(tone)   Tetrachord
F   Parhypatē Mesôn   } (Mesôn)
(semitone)
}

The *Highest* Tetrachord (Hypatôn)
{
E   Hypatē Mesôn   }
(tone)
D   Lichanos Hypatôn } The
(tone)   *Highest*
C   Parhypatē Hypatôn } Tetrachord
(semitone)   (Hypatôn)
B   Hypatē Hypatôn }
(tone)
A   Proslambanomenos (the *Added Tone*)
}

quired two octaves. Singing in octaves was called *magadizing*, a term derived from the *magadis*, an instrument on which it was possible to play in octaves. The complete two-octave scale was called the *Greater Perfect System*. Along with this, or rather within it, was included a *Lesser Perfect System*, in which the method of conjunction was alone employed, and which consisted of but three tetrachords in contrast to the four tetrachords of the Greater System. These two systems are exhibited in a single table on the preceding page. It will be seen from the names of the notes, as well as from the structure of the whole scale, that the tetrachord remains the unit of structure. The two together were called the *Perfect Immutable System*.

The Greater System contains only natural notes, and consists of the four tetrachords at the left of the table, the *Extreme*, the *Disjunct*, the *Middle*, and the *Highest* (which, as we have seen, is really the lowest in pitch). The Lesser System contains B flat, and consists of the three tetrachords at the right, the *Conjunct*, the *Middle*, and the *Highest*. The *Added Tone* at the bottom does not belong to any of these tetrachords, but merely completes the two-octave compass.

THE SYSTEM OF KEYS

It is obvious that each of the seven modes, as shown on page 19, constituted a segment of the Greater Perfect System. The modes were single-octave scales. The Greater System comprised two octaves. Why, then, should not each mode be extended to a compass of two octaves? This possibility was of course seen, and the extension was made. The whole two-octave scale which resulted was in each case the transposed equivalent of the natural scale, A–a, of the Greater System—the transposition being such that the lowest note of each mode or original octave scale was in each case the same. In our table of the modes (page 19) the initial note of each successive mode is a step higher in the diatonic scale. In the following table of the seven oldest keys (which result from the extension of the modal scale to two octaves) the fundamental pitch of all the modes remains constant, each beginning on F, with the initial note of each two-octave scale consequently a step lower. The original mode, of which the key is a two-octave extension, is marked off by bar lines.

THE SEVEN OLDEST KEYS

I. Mixolydian

* Mese.

II. Lydian

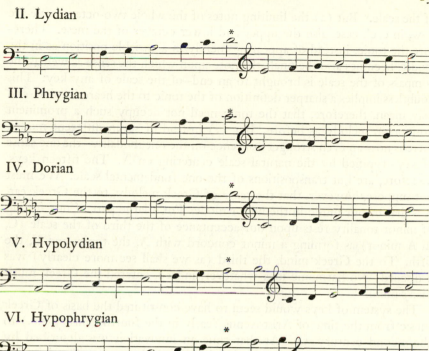

III. Phrygian

IV. Dorian

V. Hypolydian

VI. Hypophrygian

VII. Hypodorian

The total number of keys was increased later (probably by Aristoxenus) to thirteen by the obvious process of inserting another scale, of the above pattern, wherever the whole-step intervals permitted the half step between: that is, between Lydian and Phrygian, or Phrygian and Dorian. There were added, still later, two high keys, the duplicates in the higher octave of two lower ones, so that the total number of keys recognized by the Greek theorists was fifteen. All these scales could be constructed in the chromatic and enharmonic genera, as well as in the diatonic. They were written down in the two different systems of notation (one for voices, one for instruments) which were in use. The student will find a reproduction in Grove's *Dictionary of Music and Musicians* in the article on Greek Music.

What novelty in essential musical idea does this system of keys represent? It is to be noted that (1) the mese still remains as the governing tone of the scale.[6] But (2) the limiting notes of the whole two-octave scale are now, in each case, also the upper and lower octaves of the mese. Therefore the tonic, instead of appearing merely in a variable position as in the modes, becomes also the final—the note upon which the sense as well as the compass of the scale is brought to an end—of the scale of any key. This doubtless implies a sharper definition of the tonic to the hearer's mind, and may mean, therefore, that the tonic need not occupy such a prominent position in melody as before. But (3) instead of seven different modes, there is now an even stronger insistence on the one modality—the one sense of key—typified by the natural scale centering on A. The fifteen keys, therefore, are but transpositions of the one fundamental scale. We must not suppose, however, that the *sense* of Greek melody, to the Greek ear, was that of our music in the minor mode. For a large part of our feeling of minor tonality rests upon our acceptance of the third of the scale (C, in A minor) as forming a minor concord with A, the tonic, and E, the fifth. To the Greek mind, the third (as we shall see more clearly) was a discord. No harmonic idea whatever, indeed, entered the Greek musician's mind.

The system of keys would seem to have constituted the basis of Greek music from the time of Aristoxenus (early in the fourth century B.C.) to the second century A.D. At that time an innovation was described by Claudius Ptolemy of Alexandria, which seems to show some dissatisfaction with the monotony of tone relations allowed by the one modality. This is, in some respects, a return to the older idea of seven modes. But the new Ptolemaic modes are to be understood in a somewhat different sense. The names *hypate, parhypate,* and so on, which were applied to the eight notes of the disjunct Dorian harmony (page 23) are now applied in the same order to the eight notes of each of the seven old modes. That is, the "highest" note in *each* scale was now called *hypate,* the "lowest," *nete,* and so forth. In the older modes the names indicated the position of the notes in the tetrachords, and each note retained the same name, no matter what its position in the scale. The old order of names, however, which designated the notes "according to function" (that is, in the relation to the old fundamental mese) was also retained. The new order of names designated the notes merely "according to position."

Inasmuch as the function of a note in relation to its tonic is more important than its mere position in a given series, it may be doubted whether this new idea was as revolutionary as it may seem. Nevertheless, the placing of the mese at the beginning and the end of the scale, as well as in the

---

[6] It is identified, as before, as the upper note of a normal tetrachord, above which also appears a disjunctive tone. It is marked * in the table, and of course falls one note lower in each successive scale, just as in the table on page 19.

middle, which is characteristic of the system of keys, doubtless gave an emphasis to the extreme notes of the scale which, as we have said, sharpened the sense of the final as tonic in the key. And the new (Ptolemaic) designation of the final notes in every mode as *hypate* and *nete*, and the placing of the mese as always fourth in the scale series, doubtless gave to the finals of each mode a superiority in emphasis over the mese which tended to make of these finals the real tonic of the series. This new idea we shall find in full force in the music of the Christian Church. That stage of transition which is represented by Ptolemy's system will be sufficiently illustrated by two examples:

THE PTOLEMAIC MODAL SYSTEM

The notes are named

According to Function (Old System)		According to Position (New System)
The Mixolydian Mode		
Paramesē	B	Nētē
Mesē	A	Paranētē
Lichanos Mesôn	G	Tritē
Parhypatē Mesôn	F	Paramesē
Hypatē Mesôn	E	Mesē
Lichanos Hypatôn	D	Lichanos
Parhypatē Hypatôn	C	Parhypatē
Hypatē Hypatôn	B	Hypatē
The Phrygian Mode		
Paranētē Diezeugmenôn	D	Nētē
Tritē Diezeugmenôn	C	Paranētē
Paramesē	B	Tritē
Mesē	A	Paramesē
Lichanos Mesôn	G	Mesē
Parhypatē Mesôn	F	Lichanos
Hypatē Mesôn	E	Parhypatē
Lichanos Hypatôn	D	Hypatē

Observe that the names designating the function are exactly those applied to the scale of the Greater Perfect System (page 23); while those designating position are the same for each octave scale. The names *hypatē, parhypatē*, and so on, thus no longer designate the "highest" (really lowest), next highest notes, and so on, in a properly formed tetrachord, but only the "highest" note, and so forth, in an octave scale. Neither, in the new system, is the mese a single, fixed note for all modes, as in the old system. The Ptolemaic modes, then, are seven different octave scales like the old modes; but they differ in that the final has now come to be the distinguishing tone. Each scale has a different order of steps and half steps with respect to its final; and if the final is heard as governing tone (approximating to tonic) there will again be seven different modalities. The differences in modality, however, will be more striking to the ear, or rather to the mind (for the relation of the notes to the final has to be thought, in each mode); and, although this system is still a long way from our own, a distinct step forward in tonic-awareness, as well as a great advance in purely musical diversity and interest, has been made. A full table of the Ptolemaic modes is unnecessary. It would show the same scales, with the same names (Dorian, Phrygian, and so on), as the table on page 19. Only the sense in which these same scales are to be understood has changed, in the manner we have just described.[7]

The Researches of Pythagoras

It is evident that all this elaborate theoretical system of music, with its enharmonic and chromatic genera, would have been impossible without an exact basis of interval measurement on which to rest. That basis was provided by Pythagoras of Samos, in the sixth century B.C. Experimenting with a string stretched over a scaled sounding board (the monochord), he discovered that the ratios of all the intervals recognized as consonant could be expressed numerically by the figures 1, 2, 3, and 4. (He thought of his ratios in terms of string lengths; the modern physicist thinks of them in terms of the vibration rates; but the ratios, inversely, are the same.) Showing first that the octave is represented by the ratio 2:1, the fifth by 3:2, and the fourth by 4:3, he calculated the pattern of the whole diatonic scale approximately in the following way. A whole step is obviously the difference between the perfect fifth (as G–D) and a perfect fourth (as G–C). Therefore, if the ratio of the perfect fourth (4:3) be subtracted

---

[7] The first approach to the modal idea usually presents great difficulties. The following may help the student to grasp the essential point. The modes differ from each other in the order of their whole-step and half-step intervals with respect to the final. This is also exactly true of our major and minor scales:

Modern Major Scale	C–D–EF–G–A–BC
Modern Minor Scale	A–BC–D–EF + G♯A

(The – indicates a whole step; its absence, a half step; the + a step and a half.) We have also a descending form of the minor scale which is without the augmented second, F to G♯:

Descending Melodic Minor Scale	A–G–FE–D–CB–A

which has exactly the same notes as the scale of C, but is nevertheless understood as related to A. We have, that is, two scales, made of exactly the same notes, which center on different tonics. The Greek Modes centered upon one tonic only—*Mese;* but they formed seven different octave-patterns, according to the seven different positions which *Mese* might assume within the octave.

from that of the perfect fifth (3:2), we shall have the ratio of the major second (the whole step), thus: $\frac{3}{2} \times \frac{3}{4} = \frac{9}{8}$. The ratio of C to D, that is, is 8:9.

The third, to Pythagoras, contained two equal major seconds. His mathematical expression for the third, then, would be $\frac{9}{8} \times \frac{9}{8} = \frac{81}{64}$. This is relatively a very high ratio and represents a third so large as to be decidedly discordant when sounded as a harmony. (Theoretically, our modern third is tuned to the far simpler ratio $\frac{80}{64} = \frac{5}{4}$. But this is for harmonic purposes. The Greeks, as we shall see more fully, not only made no use of harmony, but had no use for it. The larger interval was perfectly satisfactory for melody, and would be so to us if we were ignorant of harmonic concord.) This gives the scale of C as far as the fifth. The other intervals can be readily calculated in the same way. The sixth consists of a fourth (4:3) plus a third (5:4 in the modern form) giving a ratio of 5:3. The seventh is a fifth (3:2) plus a third (5:4) or 15:8. (These latter figures approximate to our own scale rather than the Pythagorean, since they are arrived at by the use of 5:4 for the third, instead of the Pythagorean 81:64.) The great importance of the work of Pythagoras lay in the fact that for the first time it gave an absolute determination of the scale. Without such a foundation, disagreements could never be reconciled, for the ear alone would be the judge, and habit—especially in the absence of any harmonic test—might easily establish very different values for the intervals of the scale. Pythagoras, therefore, provided a stabilization of musical intervals which was as useful for music as is a uniform system of weights and measures for commerce.

We may add, as an illustration of the fine inflection of which Greek melody was capable, that the intervals of the chromatic and diatonic genera were of various *shades* or sizes. The *enharmonic diesis* (the word *diesis* means an interval of a half step or smaller) was calculated as three-twelfths of a tone. The smallest chromatic diesis (used in the *soft* chromatic genus) was four-twelfths of a tone; four and a half twelfths gave the diesis of the *hemiolic* chromatic genus, and six-twelfths, or half a tone, that of the *tonic* chromatic genus. There were also two *shades* of the diatonic: the *flat*, whose first two intervals from the bottom of the tetrachord were one-half of a tone and three-fourths of a tone, and the *sharp* whose first two intervals were one-half of a tone and one whole tone. Our description above, therefore, presented only the *tonic chromatic* and the *sharp diatonic* genera. These fine distinctions all disappeared at last, leaving the diatonic scale as we have described it.

A final summary of Greek achievement in the problem of tone organization will perhaps clarify the reader's impression of the whole (hypothetical) evolution. Two aspects of this evolution have been considered:

that of the scale itself, and that of the *ethos* or moral and expressive value of music.

From the simple tetrachord, with its three genera, a complete two-octave scale was built up—a scale which (in the diatonic genus) was nearly identical with our own *natural* minor scale, but which was understood in a very different way. This scale appears to have grown out of three different processes of joining tetrachords together: (1) that of conjunction exclusively (giving the Ionian harmony); (2) that of disjunction exclusively (giving the Dorian harmony); and (3) that of alternate conjunction and disjunction (giving the Aeolian harmony). In any tetrachord, the upper tone was tonic. In the Ionian and Dorian harmonies, none of these elementary tonics could govern the whole scale. In the Aeolian harmony, however, A almost automatically becomes tonic for the whole indefinitely extensible scale. This establishment of a single note as governing a whole scale is of the utmost importance for the extension of pure tone-relation as an element of music.

The sense of the identity of octaves, and an instinct to confine the melodic compass of a single voice within the octave, together with the recognition of A as tonic or *mese* in the scale, all now combine to produce the system of modes. Each mode is a complete octave scale. The pattern of each successive mode in the diatonic genus is practically equivalent to that of a series of white-note octave scales on the piano, beginning with A and using each successive white note as a starting tone. The sense of these scales, to the Greek mind, was not at all as it is to us. The one note A (or its equivalent if the scale were transposed) governed every mode. As the succession of starting tones ascends, in the series of modes, the position of the mese in relation to the initial will therefore descend. Since melody conventionally centered around the mese, the pitch of a mode in which the mese was near the top was felt to be high; that of a mode with the mese near the bottom was low.

As the total compass of music expanded to two octaves (the Greater Perfect System), the modes were similarly extended. The result was the Aristoxenean system of keys. In each key, the mese in the middle was reduplicated at each end of the scale; the value of the mode as a segment of the whole two-octave scale, with the mese in a variable position, was obliterated; and the distinction between the keys was now solely a distinction in the pitch of the *whole* scale, instead of a distinction in the high or low position of the mese as in the modes. The system of keys represents a distinct loss in melodic variety, compensated for, to some extent, by extended compass.

The Ptolemaic modal system attempted to make good this loss. It was in a way a combination of the older mode and the key. There were seven different modes, as in the old system; but the final of the scale was now (at least in one aspect) the chief note; and the mese (now always the fourth note of the scale) becomes a secondary tone, somewhat analogous to the dominant (fifth tone) in our modern scale.

The expressive purpose of Greek music was chiefly that of intensification of the poetic value of words. The meaning of music, then, to the Greek ear, resided less in the tone relations themselves, and more in the association of tone with word than is the case with us. The *ethos* of the older modal system lay in the suitability of high or low pitch to types of greater or lesser excitement. We shall see, when we come to study the development of rhythm, that other close associations—impossible today—existed between the poetry and the music of the Greeks.

In the emergence of the diatonic over the enharmonic and chromatic genera, and in the successive developments of mode and key, there is evident a gradual intensification of the purely musical impulse. The diatonic scale was itself almost ready-made for the production of harmony. Yet the Greeks, although recognizing consonance and dissonance (the basis of harmony), took no effective step toward the actual invention of harmony. It was not theoretical incompetence, however, or lack of artistic instinct, but the existence of certain ineluctable conventions (chiefly that of the peculiar relation between music and the Greek type of poetry) which made harmony useless and even unimaginable to them. Like Moses, the Greeks saw the promised land, but could not enter it.

CHAPTER III

Melody and Rhythm in Greek and Early Christian Music

THUS far, we have studied only the elaborate theoretical scheme of tone relations in Greek music, with little mention of the character of its melody. This is for the unfortunate reason that the quantity of Greek music which survives is so slight that it is impossible to gain from the existing examples any clear impression of the *meaning* of that music.[1] The mere characteristics of mode or key—even if we understood them thoroughly—would yield little insight into the impression created by the finished performance of a composition. But since Greek music was almost indissolubly bound up with poetry, we can derive a considerable addition to our theoretical understanding by a study of the relation between the two arts. A helpful illumination of the melodic design and a notion of the rhythm of Greek music can be gained in this way.

The Greek language had an accent different from that of English, and there was a different distinction between long and short vowels and syllables. Both these differences had important bearing on melody.

Instead of an accent of loudness, like that of English, the Greek had an accent of pitch. An accented syllable was pronounced: (1) at a higher pitch than the surrounding syllables, or with a rising pitch, later marked by the *acute* (´) accent; (2) at a lower pitch or with a falling inflection,

---

[1] From the ancient era there remain two tiny fragments of music for tragedy (one from the *Orestes* of Euripides); two Hymns to Apollo, cut in marble and therefore fairly well preserved; and the epitaph of Seikilos, quoted below. From the early Christian Era there are two Hymns to the Muse (also quoted), a Hymn to the Sun and another to Nemesis—the first certainly, the other possibly, by Mesomedes, a Cretan who lived during the reign of Hadrian, A.D. 117-138. Then there is a Christian hymn, found at Oxyrhynchus in Egypt, which dates from the third century. There are also a few other fragments, one of which gives three lines of instrumental notation.

or with "a condition of no accent," marked by the *grave* (`) accent; or (3) with both a rising and a falling inflection on the same vowel—the *circumflex* (^) accent. The Greek accentuation was as obligatory for proper speech as is our dynamic accent, and was thus not an emotional emphasis, such as pitch changes in our language usually convey. This does not imply that there were no emotional inflections in Greek, or that the language was spoken, aside from these syllabic accents, in a monotone. But it does imply that Greek speech was closer to song than is our own mode of utterance. The pattern of Greek melody was in some measure governed by the pitch accent of the words to which it was set, as we shall see.

The rhythm of Greek speech was likewise different from, and more nearly musical than, that of English. In our language, the distinction between long and short vowels is one of character, and not (as those words literally suggest) one of time. The *a* in *hate* is long; that in *hat* is short; but both words are normally pronounced in equally short time. In Greek the long vowels—or rather, long syllables, in which the vowel was long either by nature or by position (before two consonants)—were given about twice the time of short vowels and syllables. In consequence, the whole principle of Greek versification was different from ours. Our poetic feet consist of arrangements of accented and unaccented syllables, in which patterns the length or shortness of the vowels is immaterial. For example, the word *midnight*, whose accent is on a short vowel and whose weak syllable has a long vowel. Poetic feet, in Greek, were patterns of long and short syllables not marked by any dynamic stress, and the position of the speech accent in the foot was immaterial. (See the words *Kăllĭŏpēiă* and *prŏkăthāgĕtĭ* in the second Hymn to the Muse, page 36, where the acute accent falls on a weak syllable of the dactylic foot.) Greek speech, and especially Greek verse, had thus an intrinsic pattern of time—the primary basis of musical rhythm.[2] But the rhythm of that verse was quite independent of the speech accent. Indeed, if that accent coincided too frequently with the strong syllable of the poetic foot, the verse was held to be faulty.

Having thus a pattern of pitch (in its accent) and a pattern of rhythm (in the measure of its syllable length), the Greek language possessed the rudiments of an art of music. The actual music of the Greeks, therefore, grew out of their speech by intensifying or more sharply defining char-

---

[2] The leader of the chorus in the Greek drama wore on one foot a shoe with a kind of castanet attached, and marked time therewith for the choral dance and song. This was not intended to be heard by the audience, nor were the *theses*—the "foot falls" or strong elements of the poetic and musical measure—given any dynamic stress.

acteristics already present in their speech. In the light of these facts, many details of the theory we have studied become more significant. The tetrachord seems to us a scale of very narrow compass; but if the three genera were the musical equivalents of types of pitch accent, we may at least imagine that they offered enough variety, even within the compass of four notes, for the effective chanting of such "songs" as the long Homeric poems. The mese, likewise, might serve as a kind of tonic for *all* the modes, since Greek melody was hardly required to stand as a self-sufficient pattern of tone, and the high musical cohesion which our tonic provides might have been a hindrance to the understanding of music as primarily an intensifier of the sense of words. We can hardly expect, then, to find our kind of musical sense in Greek melody. But if the examples given below seem vague and aimless, and if we cannot grasp them as enhancements of poetic meaning, we must still remember that people do not habitually engrave on stone, ideas which they feel to be insignificant.

That, however, was the process by which our first example was preserved. It is from the tombstone of a certain Euterpe, erected by her husband Seikilos, at Aidin in Asia Minor, presumably in the second century B.C. The text consists of four homely little proverbs which offer a fairly cheerful "thanatopsis" or view of death. The music is notated by the letters which appear above the modern notes. The lengths of the notes correspond to the lengths of the syllables (the syllable *son*, in the first word, has a short vowel *omicron*, which, followed by two consonants, is long by position); but the four phrases of the text are not in any established poetic meter. In consequence, the rhythm is indicated by signs (— for what we should call two beats, —— for three) not shown in the transcript, and can therefore be translated precisely. (The bar lines are for convenience in reading, and do not imply the conventional rhythmic accentuation of 6-4 time.)

But the pattern of this melody is governed also by the speech accents. Except for the first syllable, every acute accent is set to a higher note or (as in *pha*í*nou*) to a rising progression; and every circumflex except that in *zés* has a descent of two (and at the end, of three) notes. This procedure is also followed, less precisely, in the second *Hymn to the Muse* (that part of the example which is in 2-2 time). This association of melodic contour with spoken pitch accent was an ancient convention, as is testified by a remark of a contemporary critic—that some of the melody for a play of Euripides did *not* follow the words in this respect. Although the convention was thus early defied, it must have had much vigor to survive into the second century A.D.

The prominence which Aristotle ascribed to the mese is not conspicuous, though the two notes—A and, especially, E—seem to dominate the line. The similarity of the endings of the second and third phrases (B–A, B–G, and C sharp–A, B–G) seems noteworthy. The general musical impression is hardly compelling to our ears, but a high measure of that satisfaction which the Greeks sought in music was doubtless offered.

THE INSCRIPTION OF SEIKILOS

Our next example, although we still print it as one composition, is now thought to be two separate hymns. In both, the versification in familiar iambic and dactylic measures unmistakably provides (without rhythm signs) the measure of the music. In the first hymn, in 3–4 time, the pitch implications of the accents are ignored; in the second they are again conspicuous. The chromatic coloring in the first hymn somewhat confuses what without it would appear to our ears a "natural" melody. In the second, although we must not interpret the frequent B flats as implying the key of F, the effect of melodic smoothness is much more in accord with our own notions.

TWO HYMNS TO THE MUSE*

"Ά - ει - δε Μοῦ - σά μοι　φί - λη　μολ - πῆς δ'ἐ - μῆς κατ - άρ -
A' - ei - de Moû - sá moi phí - le mol - pês đe - mês kat - ár -
("Sing, O Muse, dear to me, and begin my song;

χου· ἄυ - ρη δὲ σῶν ἀπ' ἀλ - σέ - ων ἐ - μὰς φρέ - νας δο -
chou; áu - re dè sôn ap' al - sé - on e - màs phré - nas do -
let a breeze from thy sacred groves stir my heart.

νεί - - το.　Καλ - λι - ό - πει - α　σο - φά, μου - σῶν προ - καθ -
neî - - to.　Kal - li - ó - pei - a　so - phá, mou - sôn pro - kath -
O wise Calliope, leader of the delightful muses,

α - γέ - τι τερ - πνῶν, καὶ σο - φὲ μυ - στο - δό - τα, Λα - τοῦς γό - νε,
a - gé - ti ter - pnôn, kaì so - phè mu - sto - dó - ta, La - toûs gó - ne,
and thou, wise giver of the mysteries, son of Leto,

Δή - λι - ε Παι - άν,　ἐυ - με - νεῖς πάρ - εσ - τέ μοι.
Dé - li - e Pai - án,　eu - me - neîs pár - es - té moi.
Delian Apollo, lend me your gracious presence.")

* Three notes (for molpês d'em-) are missing in the inscription. We follow
Macran's reconstruction here; but insert E♭ as the equivalent of H (which he omits)
for mous*ôn* and use only the notes A, C, for *Paián*, since only the characters C M
appear in Macran's reproduction of the original. Macran, and Wooldridge in the
Oxford History, Vol. I, p. 20, have the equivalent of A, C for *Pai-* and D for *-án*.

THE REPLACEMENT OF QUANTITY BY ACCENT

But even while this music was being composed, forces beyond the
control of the cultured Greeks and Romans were disintegrating those
refinements of their speech upon which, in considerable part, their conventions of melody were founded. The vast expansion of the Roman

Empire had brought the Latin tongue (as with the Alexandrian conquests the Greek tongue had also been brought) into contact with many alien peoples. These aliens spoke Latin only for practical purposes, and had little interest in the refinements which yielded poetry and music. Thus, many of the elaborate inflections through which the subtle syntax of the language was conveyed were abandoned, and along with them the discriminations of quantity upon which poetic meter had wholly depended. By the fourth century A.D., these changes seem to have been complete in common speech. The learned still wrote in quantitative verse, but the coincidence of speech accent (which has now become a dynamic stress) with the strong element of the poetic foot is such that the measure of the verse is felt as a dynamic ictus. "Irrational" quantities—long syllables in place of short—also appear with great frequency.

This change in poetic structure is of great importance for music. It will lead at length to a condition in which the poetic meter is wholly accentual; but even in this transitional stage, when the normal speech stress is becoming also the poetic accent, the rhythmic ictus may be vigorously marked without distorting the verse, and music set to such poetry may further enliven the accentual rhythm. The popular appeal of rhythm is as indisputable as that of musical tone. We shall find that not only in the early Christian Era but again in the time of the Reformation, fervent religious poems, set to simple rhythmic melodies, offer the most convincing embodiment of religious faith and the most cogent means for its propagation.

Because of this enlivening of its rhythm, music became in the Christian Era the property of common people. In ancient Greece, music was indeed the delight of young and old. It colored the lives of soldiers and artisans, as it pervaded the thought of poets and philosophers. But even though a considerable development of instrumental art was at last achieved, the preoccupation of the Greek composer was with the subtleties of poetry, and with the adjustment of his tones to those qualities. For the appreciation of his best efforts, intellect and taste were essential.

But intellect and taste had little to do with the essentials of Christianity. That doctrine taught the equality of all believers in the sight of God, no matter what their importance in the sight of man. Nobody had ever taught the Greeks to say, "Zeus is love"; but for the simple Christian the concept of divine compassion was the basis of a hopeful philosophy hitherto unknown in the world. Hence, the services in the earliest Christian communities consisted largely of spontaneous outpourings of reverence for the Universal Father. The procedure was largely without established ritual. It sufficed that the Spirit seemed immediately present, inspiring some to words and others to songs of praise—to songs, moreover, in the simple idiom of the unlettered and untrained. We know nothing, of course, of the detail of this music.

That it must have derived from existing idioms is incontestable. Christianity originated in the East, and for a time its propagation was far more rapid in the Eastern Roman Empire than in the Western. By the third century, it is said that nine-tenths of the population in the Eastern Empire was Christian. But (as the travels of the Apostles reveal) there was much intercommunication between the East and the West; and musical as well as doctrinal ideas were by this means spread abroad and gradually crystallized into liturgical convention.

The chanting of the Psalms had long been a feature of Hebrew worship. Hence, the Jewish practice of psalmody was from the beginning taken over into the Christian services. As the Liturgies crystallized, the Psalms and canticles of the Old and New Testaments were naturally kept as authorized texts for Christian song.[3] The Eastern communities, which sang these songs in their vernacular languages, developed for them many varieties of melody. But there was also a unifying force at work. Constantinople, founded by Constantine in 328, became not only the principal seat of the Eastern Roman Empire, but also of the Eastern Christian Church, which had at first been a kind of federation of the patriarchates of Antioch, Alexandria, and Jerusalem. From its foundation, the city was a point of convergence for oriental cultures of all sorts, and many of the religious observances which had developed in the neighboring regions underwent a kind of amalgamation there.

Syria, Armenia, Egypt, and Ethiopia all contributed something to the musical traditions that were forming; and from the fall of the Roman Empire in the West (476) until the Mohammedan conquests in the seventh century, a great activity was in progress. This had some effect on the Western traditions also, though the extent of the Eastern influence is hard to determine exactly. One of the most favored types of religious song in these communities was the hymn—a poetic ejaculation usually in a strophic form, with a simple and compelling rhythm such as the unlearned could understand. (The principle of quantity had also ceased to govern in Greek speech.)

Clement of Alexandria (*circa* 150–220) is the reputed author of a *Hymn to the Saviour*—the earliest extant hymn. From the third century also

---

[3] Among the canticles of the Old Testament are two songs of Moses (Exod. XV and Deut. XXXII), the song of Hannah (I Sam. II), Isaiah's song of confidence (Isa. XXVI), the prayer of Jonah (Jonah II), and the song of Habakkuk (Hab. III). Among those in the New Testament are the *Nunc dimittis* (Lord, now lettest thou thy servant depart in peace) in Luke II, 29, the *Magnificat* (Mary's song *My soul doth magnify the Lord*, after the Annunciation), and the song of Zacharias (Luke I:68).

comes a Christian hymn, in Greek, found recently at Oxyrhynchus in Egypt. It is in Greek musical notation, but is not necessarily an example of the contemporary Greek musical idiom. In Syria one of the most famous of hymnographers, Ephraim, wrote many such poems in Greek in accentual, not quantitative, verse; and his poetic form was reputedly taken over into Latin during his lifetime by Hilary of Poitiers (*circa* 300-367).

For the more stately portions of the Western ritual, Byzantine sources were also drawn upon to an extent which is still undetermined. In the earlier centuries, songs called *Kontakia*, with many similar strophes, were sung during the celebrations of the most solemn feasts of the year. The natural development of this art was disrupted by the iconoclastic disputes —controversies which in the end had no small part in the religious and political severance of the West from the East, and in the crowning of Charlemagne as Emperor in 800. In the eighth century, after these controversies had been settled, another sort of hymn, the Kanon, had taken the place of the Kontakion. This, however, had a text derived from Scripture. There were nine such odes, each based upon one of the nine canticles of the Old Testament. The persistence of melodic types or formulas—a notable feature of much of the music we are to study—is seen in the probable fact that the melodies of the Kanones were derived from those of the Kontakia.

Not only the practice but also the theory of Byzantine music had its influence in the West. Syrian music seems to have been based on a classification of melodic types into eight forms called the *oktoechos;* and in later times this classification seems to have become the basis of a division of the Byzantine scales into *authentic* and *plagal*—a division which we shall find to be elemental also in the theory of the Western modal scales. Detailed study of Byzantine music is, however, beyond the scope of this book, and we return therefore to our story of the evolution of the Western liturgical music.

In the East, as we have seen, Christianity developed among a large number of peoples speaking different languages.[4] In the West the long hegemony of Rome had made of the Latin a universal tongue; and although the Western Church at first used Greek as the liturgical language, the inevitable change to the Latin made for a uniformity in ritual and a unanimity in thought which the East has never known.

This, however, was somewhat tardily accomplished. Only after 313,

---

[4] Greek was indeed the liturgical language of the Byzantine Church, but it had no such universality as the Latin gained in the West. It was used, along trade routes and in commercial centers, for business purposes; but real life was lived in the vernacular.

when by the Edict of Milan Constantine countenanced Christianity, did the wealthy and cultivated Romans begin in significant numbers to enter the Church. When they did enter, they changed greatly the form and the condition of the service, contributing generously to the building of imposing places of worship, and also to the forming of appropriate rituals. In these rituals, music naturally had an important part. Even the reading of the liturgical words conformed to a kind of singing style which was meticulously taught; but many portions of the service demanded actual singing, and of this, according to the nature of the text, many varieties were developed. Most of the music was of necessity sung by trained choristers, but the hymns—at least at first—were designed for and sung by the congregations. We can deal but briefly with the various types of liturgical music, but will try to give some idea of the most important, beginning with the simplest—the hymns.

THE AMBROSIAN HYMNS

We have seen that the popular hymns of Ephraim had been adapted to the Latin by Hilary of Poitiers. But the most influential of the Latin hymnographers was Ambrosius, Bishop of Milan (340?–397). In spite of much opposition from the more doctrinal-minded clergy (the Council of Laodicea, between 360 and 381, had condemned all nonbiblical hymns as *psalmi idiotici*), such songs, either composed or fostered by St. Ambrose, were so enthusiastically chanted by his and other congregations that his Arian opponents reproached him with having bewitched his people. Only four texts, out of many formerly attributed to him, are now recognized as of his authorship; but these are the models for many others. The four are: *Aeterne rerum conditor; Iam surgit hora tertia; Deus Creator omnium;* and *Veni, Redemptor gentium.* They are all in strophes of four lines, and in a simple iambic tetrameter [5] (the antecedent of the English long meter), so that they yield a clear and easily rememberable musical phrase for each line. The melodies to which they are now sung, while possibly in the original meter, are of unknown origin. Being a man of education, St. Ambrose employed the quantitative versification, though with many "irrational" quantities. A hymn of later date, but made after the model of his verse, is given below with its traditional melody, and in a meter accordant with the accentual nature of the verse: [6]

---

[5] Technically, iambic dimeter, since each line contains two iambic *dipodies* (groups of two feet); but the designation *tetrameter* is in accord with the terminology of English poetics.

[6] Even this is nowadays interpreted as quantitative verse, though many of the weak syllables would be long according to classical reckoning: *Aēternā Christī mūnera.* Aurelian of Réomé, however, says that such a line has nothing of the

AETERNA CHRISTI MUNERA

Ae - ter - na Chris - ti mu - ne - ra Et mar - ty - rum vic - to - ri - as

Lau-des fe - ren - tes de - bi - tas Lae - tis ca - na - mus men - ti - bus.

"With joyful hearts, and offering due praises, we sing the everlasting gifts of Christ and the victories of the martyrs."

Comparison of this example with that of the Greek hymns already quoted will reveal not only a more natural and attractive musical rhythm, but also, in each of the phrases, a melodic progression far more akin to what we regard as good melody. (It is not in the key of G, however, as it may at first sight seem to be. The fundamental note is the E upon which the melody begins and ends; and the music is therefore in what the churchmen will call *Mode III*, and still later, the *Phrygian mode*. The modal idea will be more fully explained hereafter.)

VARIOUS TYPES OF LITURGICAL CHANT

In the elaborate ritual which was now evolving for the Mass and the Office,[7] the hymns played a less and less conspicuous part. Congregational

---

reckoning of the classical feet, but that its rhythm is discernible from the number of the syllables. (Gerbert, *Scriptores*, I, 33b.)

[7] The most solemn and exalted of the Roman ritual observances is that of the Mass. Like its offspring, the Protestant Communion service, this is a memorial of the Last Supper. In the Catholic service, the bread and wine are believed to be *transsubstantiated* into the actual body and blood of Christ. (Protestants regard these substances as merely symbolic.) Many details of the Protestant services are derived from the earlier observance of the Mass.

Appropriately to the occasion on which the Mass is said, various portions of this service—not only the Epistle and the Lesson, but also the Introit, Gradual, Alleluia, Sequence, Tract, Offertory, and Communion, as well as various Psalms—are chosen from the innumerable available texts. All these portions are called the *Proper* of the Mass (*proprium missae*).

But a considerable portion of the service is never changed, no matter what the occasion. These unchanging portions are called the *Ordinary* of the Mass (*ordinarium missae*). Five portions of the Ordinary—naturally, very significant portions—were chosen in later times as the texts for *polyphonic* music; and it is music to these texts which is nowadays thought of as a musical Mass. The five portions are (1) the *Kyrie eleison* ("Lord, have mercy")—a Greek phrase surviving from the time when the liturgical language was still Greek; (2) *Gloria in excelsis Deo* ("Glory to God in the highest"); (3) *Credo in unum Deum* ("I believe in one God"); (4) *Sanctus* and *Benedictus* ("Holy, holy, holy," and "Blessed is he that cometh in the singing, especially in the absence of instrumental support, tended to become disorganized and unsuited to the more solemn parts of the ritual. To the choir and the trained soloists, in consequence, was given the greater part of the ritual music. According to the character of the text, this music became more or less elaborate. The texts (which except for the hymns and sequences were in prose) yielded three types of chant: (1) *syllabic*—that is, chanted with one note (often the same note, repeated) to each syllable; (2) *neumatic*—with two or more notes (represented in the later notation by a cluster of note symbols called a *neume*) sung to many of the syllables; and (3) *florid*, where for most of the syllables many note groups were devoted to the utterance of each. These generic styles will be indicated in our description of the specific forms now to be studied.

PSALMODY

By far the greater part of the music for both the Mass and the Office is in *psalmodic* form. Three types of psalmody may be distinguished: (1) *responsorial* psalmody, in which the soloist sings the verses of the psalm, and is answered by a refrain in the choir; (2) *antiphonal* psalmody, in which the choir is divided into two groups, and the verses are sung alternately; and (3) *direct* psalmody, which has no refrains. (In antiphonal psalmody there is also a refrain—the *antiphon*—but in contrast to the responsorial usage it is sung only at the beginning and the end of the psalm.)

---

name of the Lord"); and (5) *Agnus Dei* ("Lamb of God that takest away the sins of the world . . ."). These polyphonic Masses—invariably set to the same texts from Machaut to Beethoven—are often thought of as comprising the whole of the Ordinary. In reality they form a relatively small part, the service in many portions being of such character that any music whatever would be inappropriate. The following will give some notion of the order of the service.

The priest approaches the altar with the words *Introibo ad altare Dei* (I will enter unto the altar of the Lord). Psalm XLIII in the King James Version of the Bible (XLII in the Vulgate), with various responses and prayers, leads to the Introit, which is followed by the *Kyrie eleison* and the *Gloria*. The Epistle is next, followed by the Gradual, together with a Tract, Alleluia, or Sequence, then the *Credo* (the Nicene Creed); and the Offertory. The immediate preparation for the offering of the Host (the consecrated and transubstantiated bread and wine) is called the Preface to the Communion; it may be said to culminate in the *Sanctus* and *Benedictus*. Then comes the actual rite (*Canon missae*) of the offering. It is followed by certain prayers (the Lord's Prayer among them), the *Agnus Dei,* and finally the dismissal—*Ite, missa est* ("Go, the Mass is ended").

The Office comprises those lesser services, obligatory for the clergy and some others, which occur frequently throughout the day (and, theoretically, the night). These are: Matins (properly for midnight), Lauds (for sunrise), Vespers (for evening), and Compline (*Completorium*—the completion of the day) together with the Day Hours—Prime (6), Terce (9), Sext (12), and None (3).

All these arose, in part at least, out of the processes which were devised to give impressiveness to liturgical reading. In such reading, vowels are often lengthened and their utterance thus approximates to a tone; the pitch of this tone, if fixed, can be given to the less important syllables also, thus raising them to the level of the singing utterance; and the punctuations or syntactical inflections can then be given their natural speech value by differentiating their pitch from that of the single *recitation tone* to which the greater part of the syllables have been chanted. The reciting tone was often called a *tuba*, which suggests a resemblance to the imposing sound of the trumpet. More than one tuba might be employed where length or especial significance demanded it; and since in the psalm verses a general form of antecedent and consequent phrases was originally exemplified (or was provided by punctuating more decisively the original text), a formula for the recitation or singing of these phrases was immediately suggested. There was a beginning, the *intonation* (*initium* or *inchoatio*), which ascended to the reciting tone; at the end of the antecedent phrase of words, there was a punctuation (*mediatio*), not, however, suggesting finality, before the consequent phrase was resumed (of course, on the tuba); and at the end of the whole verse there was a kind of cadence (*punctum* or *period*), invariably in a generally descending line, and often ending on the *final* or fundamental tone of the scale. The general formula will be sufficiently illustrated in the psalm verse *Deus in nomine tuo*, below; but while the *initium* was invariable, the other departures from the reciting tone were made in different ways.

Eight different formulas or *psalm tones* were recognized. The final notes and the reciting tones in these formulas we shall find to correspond closely to the finals and dominants of the eight ecclesiastical modes which, somewhere about the tenth century, will become the only authorized scales in which the liturgical chant may be composed. (Alterations were sometimes made—still later—in the older chants, to make them accord with the newly formulated modal law.) There is also an additional psalm tone, called the *tonus peregrinus* (wandering or, perhaps, strange), which has two reciting tones. Our two illustrations will be of the eighth and the fifth tones, or modes. The peculiarities of modal organization will be discussed later.

The psalmody of the Mass is ordinarily more elaborate and ornate than that of the Office. Two illustrations will suggest both this difference and that between the responsorial and the antiphonal psalmody. The following is one of the psalms that make up the third Nocturn of the Matins for Holy Saturday (day before Easter). The Antiphon, in the eighth mode, precedes the psalm and follows it. In both the antiphon and the psalm, the asterisk indicates the point at which the full choir answers the singers of the preceding section.

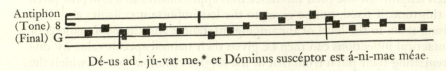

Antiphon
(Tone) 8
(Final) G

Dé-us ad - jú-vat me,* et Dóminus suscéptor est á-ni-mae méae.

Psalm LIII (LIV in King James Version)

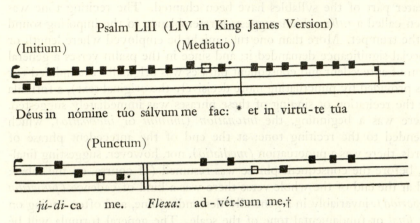

(Initium)   (Mediatio)

Déus in nómine túo sálvum me fac: * et in virtú-te túa

(Punctum)

jú-di-ca me.   *Flexa:* ad - vér-sum me,†

2. Déus, exáudi oratiónem meam: *áuribus pércipe vérba *óris* mei.

3. Quóniam aliéni insurrexérunt advérsum me,† et fórtes quaesiérunt ánimam meam:*et non proposuérunt Déum ánte con*spéctum* súum.

(The words *meam* and *oris mei* in Verse 2 obviously correspond to the syllables *me fac* and *judica me* in Verse 1; but the antecedent phrase in Verse 3 is punctuated so that an additional inflection—called *Flexa*—of the reciting tone —also called *tenor*—is made at the words *adversum me*, and the true mediation occurs on the word *meam*. The white notes are for the accommodation of such five-syllable groups as quo*niam* bonum est, at the end of a later verse.)

The more elaborate responsorial psalmody of the Mass may be illustrated by the following, from Verses 1 and 2 of Psalm CXI (CXII in the King James Version).[8] The first portion is the Respond, often indicated by the character ℞; the second, marked ℣, is the Verse, to which the Respond stands in the relation of a refrain. In both ℞ and ℣, the solo voice sings as far as the asterisk, the choir entering thereafter to finish the section. It will have been seen that the antiphon just quoted is essentially syllabic. Neumes (note groups) appear only on *ad*juvat and *est*. The fol-

<hr/>

[8] Psalm IX in the Vulgate comprises both Psalm IX and Psalm X as given in the King James Version. The numbering is thus at variance in the two versions until Psalm CXLVII in the Protestant Bible, which comprises Psalms CXLVI and CXLVII of the Catholic Version. Only the first eight and the last three, therefore, are similarly numbered in the two versions.

lowing Gradual, on the contrary, is florid; but if it were all in the manner seen at the words *qui timet* or *benedicetur*, it would be neumatic. (A few notes are still syllabic.) It is in Mode V (the F mode, later called *Lydian*.) For the gradual we now give the chant in the official square notation, together with a transliteration into modern notes. (The rhythmic signs, devised by the monks of Solesmes and printed in the *Liber usualis*—the "Book of Uses," or rituals of the Catholic Church—are, however, omitted.)

Following is a transliteration into modern notes:

The Gradual seems to have been so named from the fact that this chant was customarily sung from the steps *(gradus)* of the altar. Other *responsorial* chants found in the Mass are the Alleluia and the Offertory. The Alleluia (surviving, both as a word and a musical utterance, from Hebrew liturgical practice) is really a *versus alleluiaticus*—a refrain attached to a verse of Scripture. Its last syllable is extended into a long melisma. The

Offertory (sung during the preparation of the bread and wine) had originally several verses. It has now been greatly shortened, and consists of
the antiphon only; but this is sung responsorially. *Direct* psalmody in the
Mass is found only in the Tract. The Introit and the Communion are
antiphonal chants.

Of relatively slight importance in the scheme of the Mass, but of very
high musical interest as a burgeoning form, is the Sequence. It arose out
of the singers' practice of interpolating ornaments into the simple musical
declamations which were the primary form of the chants. (Even the
initium, mediatio, and *punctum* are ornaments of the single line.) Floridity, such as that in the Alleluia, was grateful both to sing and to hear, and
from the ninth century on was plentifully added. Such expansion was
called *troping*. (The word *trope*, familiar in rhetoric, implies an analogous
figure of speech.) Long extended, such ornaments became hard to remember, and the singers found that if words were added, this difficulty was
lightened.

The Sequence (implying an addition *following* an established form) was
a trope provided with rhythmic words. One with unrhythmed words was
a *Prose*.[9] A vast number of such pieces were composed and sung without
liturgical sanction. Of the Sequences, the Council of Trent (1545-63)
officially recognized but four—the Easter Sequence, *Victimae Paschali*;
the *Veni Sancte Spiritus* for Pentecost (Whitsunday); the *Lauda Sion
Salvatorem* for Corpus Christi; and the *Dies irae* for the Requiem Mass.
The *Stabat Mater*, for the celebration of the Seven Sorrows of the Virgin,
was admitted into the liturgy only in 1727, even though its text dates
from the thirteenth century.

There is a doubtful tradition that troping was invented, either by Tuo-
tilo or Notker Balbulus (the Stammerer), at the monastery of St. Gall.
It is not tradition but certainty that out of this practice grew a species of
liturgical drama—the enactment of scenes and incidents from the Scrip-
tures—that was the actual predecessor of the mysteries and miracle plays.
The Easter Sequence which begins, "Christians, offer praises to the Paschal
Victim," presently dialogues and dramatizes the visit of Mary to the tomb:
"Tell us, Mary, what thou sawest on thy way." "I saw the tomb of the
living Christ, and the glory of his resurrection, . . ."

The chants of the Ordinary of the Mass are later than the psalmodic
recitations of the Proper. The *Credo*, indeed, although the Nicene Creed
had been adopted (with less consideration than its dogmas proved later to
demand) by the Council of Nicaea, under the active sponsorship of Constantine in 325, was not finally admitted as a part of the Ordinary until

---

[9] But this term was also applied to the rhythmed forms. A more satisfying derivation is from *Pro s[equenti]a*.

1014. There are in the *Liber usualis,* the comprehensive service book of the Catholic Church, eighteen settings of these texts in the Gregorian chant. The music varies considerably in ornateness, accordingly as it is to be sung on the more or the less solemn occasions; but it is still true that the *Kyrie eleison* is florid, the *Gloria* moderately neumatic, the *Credo* very largely syllabic, and both the *Sanctus* and *Benedictus,* and the *Agnus Dei,* considerably florid. The form of the music varies with the nature of the text. Since the *Kyrie eleison* has three ejaculations of these words, with the *Christe eleison* and the following *Kyrie* also chanted three times, the words themselves create a repetitive musical form akin to the strophic pattern of the hymn. The *Agnus Dei,* also thrice repeated, is similar. The *Gloria* and the *Credo,* made up of long successions of brief, verbal phrases without repetition, are necessarily more recitational; but here, also, certain musical strains reappear to give a perceptible unity to the chant.

The florid chants, particularly, are in appearance extremely free in form. Yet within their fluid design one finds not only many purposeful repetitions of typical figures, but also a plan of total structure which could have been contrived by no other than an artist's imagination. Observe, for example, in the Gradual melody quoted above, that for the words *Beatus vir,* the descending minor third is used five times in succession, but that monotony is avoided by the skillful grouping of the notes into different figures of twos and threes; that the torculus (the three-note neume) for *ti*met, in high register at the beginning of the phrase, appears twice in low register at the end; that the pattern G, c, b, d, c, c, b, a for man*da*tis is amplified and varied on the syllable *tis* (G, c, d, c, c, c, c, b, a, b, a); and that at the word *cupit,* the verbal climax of the thought, the climax of the melodic phrase also occurs. Without any regularity of rhythmic beat, a greater flexibility of total design is achieved than is possible in our own regularly measured music. By comparison, even the florid excursions of vocal ornament in our operatic arias seem stiff and mechanical.

THE PROBLEM OF GREGORIAN RHYTHM

While it differs fundamentally from music in our familiar rhythmic scheme, this chant was not felt to be arhythmic. We are so accustomed to rhythms presented in patterns of regularly recurrent accent, and in strictly measured time, that we have almost come to believe that the word *rhythm* implies merely a succession of thumps. Properly, however, it means *motion*—motion which is indeed periodically intensified by propulsion of the moving body, but which need not be mathematically regular in time, or precisely symmetrical in space. The effort to escape such mechanical regularity is one of the most striking features of contemporary music.

Prose rhythms have been felt by every sensitive reader of our literature as one of its great charms. The rhythm of the Latin liturgy is equally noteworthy. The syllabic chants are for the most part so shaped as to exhibit this rhythm. The neumatic and the florid chants, however, while they by no means ignore it, contrive to superimpose upon this rhythm a musical expansion which not only decorates but also often exalts the verbal utterance to an extraordinary degree.

While this subtle art was in process of perfection, there existed no notation which could exhibit clearly either the time-values of the tones or their dynamic force. When harmony was applied to these melodies (as we shall soon see) exact time-measurement was obligatory, and a system of notation, exact as to both time and pitch, was devised. It appears that the chants, thus harmonized, were sung slowly and with no rhythmic variety; but this condition was only temporary, and could not permanently have obliterated the old rhythmic subtlety. The mensural notes, at length invented to show the rhythm as well as the pitch of the tones, were derived from older neumes (*virga*, /, *virga jacens*, —, and *punctum*, ·) to which different time-values had been generally but indefinitely ascribed by the contemporary writers. The relative time-values of the *mensural* notes (*longa* ⌐, *brevis* ■, and *semibrevis* ◆) were exactly determined for mensural music. But these same characters were used also for the notation of the Gregorian melodies, since they provided the only certain clue to the pitch of the notes. The rhythm of the chants, although free, and thus incapable of exact representation by mensural notes, may well have been approximately indicated by the mensural characters. The square notation, at any rate, preserves with meticulous fidelity the various compound groups or ligatures which had been in use before mensural notation was invented. But it is evident that no rhythmic certainty can be attained in the interpretation of the *chorale* notation—which presents the chants in mensural characters.

Hence, there are three schools of thought which today hold very different views as to the true rhythmic interpretation of the chants. The most widely accepted interpretation (which has received a certain official sanction by the Church) is that worked out by the long labors of the monks of Solesmes, headed by Dom Mocquereau. According to this theory (which is, of course, based on exhaustive study of hundreds of manuscripts[10]), the time-value of the short syllable is the unit of time-measurement for the music; and all the notes of the chant—whatever the character

[10] Especially the great collection presented in the *Paléographie Musicale*, where the doctrine now under discussion is expounded.

used to represent them—are of this length, unless they are elongated either by immediate repetition or by certain signs called *episemae*, some of which appear in the manuscripts, and many of which have been supplied by the editors. In addition to these (which are not so placed as to give a rhythmic design) there is also an *ictus* (always implied, but not marked) which divides the music into groups of either two or three notes. The ictus does not necessarily coincide either with the syllable accent or with the first (or any other) note of the neume. Neither is it marked by any dynamic stress or any lengthening of the note.[11] It is therefore a factor of extreme subtlety in the performance—recognizable, probably, as a characteristic quality rather than as a fact of the whole utterance. But when the chants are sung after this fashion by trained singers, there is no gainsaying the beauty of the interpretation.

That this is historically the correct rhythm is contended by the Solesmes school, but is disputed by two other parties. The "accentualists" (pointing to the liturgy as written in accentual—not quantitative—Latin put their stress on the tonic accent of the word where the chants are syllabic or neumatic, and on the first note of each neume when the chant becomes melismatic. The "mensuralists" (with considerable historic evidence for their opinion) contend that the *virga* and *punctum* had different time-values *which are still represented in the square notation (longs* and *breves* and *semibreves)*[12]; that the long and breve are indeed equal, but the semibreve of half this value; and that such a valuation yields groups of two to eight beats *(shorts)* called *measures*. The first note of each measure receives a stress, and the whole is varied by the differences in note length. Sung in these manners, the chant has also ineffable beauty. It is not for the historian to decide the dispute, but only to point out that the Solesmes doctrine is not historically incontestable.

The high organization of the Church made of the chant the universal musical language of Europe during the Middle Ages, just as it made Latin the universal speech of the learned. Because of this—and more because of its intrinsic beauty—the chant is a product of the highest significance for the whole later history of music. From it the art of harmony developed— even though that art was destined to engulf the chant which gave it birth. The theoretical basis of the art naturally became in time a matter of great concern to musicians. Our next chapter will set forth some of these theoretical problems.

[11] "Wedded to a tonic syllable the ictus is accent, to a note of impulsion it is élan, to the last syllable of a word or the last note of a rhythm it is thesis; but . . . it is always a footfall." Dom Gregory Suñol, *Textbook of Gregorian Chant*, p. 74.

[12] The *Virga jacens*, —, yielded the character ■, while the *Virga, /*, yielded the ¶. But these two, being both *virgae*, ceased, in the chant, to have any distinction. The *semibrevis* ◆, therefore, yields the only note which, in contrast to the others, is short.

<small>◦ॐ</small> *CHAPTER IV* <small>ॐ◦</small>

Modal Organization and Theory

W E have already studied what is of necessity a largely hypothetical account of the modes of ancient Greek music and their alterations in Ptolemy's time (the second century A.D.). The Gregorian chant is also a modal literature; but the continuity between the Greek and the Christian modes is less direct than would seem to be indicated by the fact that the Christian modes are also octave scales, and that they are widely known by Greek names. The Christian modes, like the Greek, are indeed "manners" of tone organization—manners in which the notes of a given melody are selected from the whole gamut of possible notes, and organized with relation to some one note which, in each mode, is fundamental to the rest. But the processes of selection and organization are very different from those of ancient Greece. The notion of the tetrachord is no longer of high importance; the scales are now thought upward instead of downward; and the mese—as a single tone, fundamental to all the modes—has disappeared.

The Christian system, in fact, is not in any direct way derived from that of ancient Greece. Instead, its source is really that vast literature of the chant which we have been studying; and, like the Greek system, it was formulated only after a great body of literature had been composed. Until the tenth century the system had hardly begun to receive recognition as a binding scheme of tonal organization; and as we shall see, by that time forces were at work in the actual process of musical thought which were to undermine and finally disrupt the modal theory altogether.

Yet it is clear that if rules can be derived from an existent practice, they must somehow have been obeyed in that practice—else they could never have been derived. The Gregorian chant proved itself a natural and effective type of musical utterance; and the modal theory—although its statement of principles is somewhat inaccurate—does greatly clarify our view of the process of composition.

This theory reduced the allowable framework of melodic composition to a system of eight modes. Of these, four were fundamental and four subordinate. The fundamental modes were called *authentic;* the subordinate, *plagal.* They were long known by number only, the old Greek names having been applied later, probably to reinforce the authority of the propounded theory. (The Church has never officially adopted the Greek terminology.)

The authentic modes are octave scales, each one a segment of the whole "natural" note-series (the white notes on the piano); but under certain conditions, B flat might be substituted for B natural. The whole tone-series is thus the combined Greater and Lesser Perfect Systems of ancient Greece (page 23); but it is extended one tone downward (this G was called *gamma*), and four notes upward, to e'. The four notes upon which the eight modes were erected were D, E, F, and G. These are the notes regarded as the proper final tones of ecclesiastical melodies, and in that respect resemble recognizably the tonics in our major and minor scales. These finals, however, govern far less extensively the behavior of notes within the melody than does our tonic.

Melody in each authentic mode lay between the final and its octave, with liberty of extension by one note either downward or upward. Melody in the plagal mode lay a fourth lower in total compass, but had the same range of one octave. The plagal mode had the same final as the authentic mode to which it was related.

Both authentic and plagal modes distinguish, within the scale, a Dominant. This is precisely that chief reciting tone we have already encountered. It may be said that the dominant bears a certain resemblance to the mese of ancient Greek music—if that note was actually as predominant in melody as Aristotle described it. The dominant resembles also the mese in the Ptolemaic modes "according to position," since it is in the middle of the scale. But whereas Ptolemy's mese was the fourth above the lowest note *(hypate)*, the dominant in the authentic Christian mode was originally always the fifth above the final. (After the invention of harmony, however, B, the original dominant of the E mode, was replaced by C, since in the natural scale the fifth above B—essential to the formation of a triad—is a diminished fifth, and therefore a discord.) The dominant in the plagal scale was originally always the third above the final (the sixth above the lowest note of the scale); but in the plagal E mode, for the sake of symmetry with the authentic, the dominant was also later raised a step—from G to A.

The following table shows the eight modes first recognized in Christian music, both according to their designated numbers and according to the Greek names which were later applied. The four added modes

(IX to XII) are not exemplified in the Gregorian chant, and were not recognized in extant theory until 1547, when the polyphonic composers had long since extended the basis of composition beyond the purely melodic thought of those who composed in the Gregorian tradition. The final and convincing exposition of the twelve modes was made by Glareanus in a book called *Dodecachordon* (*dodeka* = twelve; *chordon* = strings). The two added authentic scales are those of A and C—essentially, our minor and major modes. In their delayed recognition lies a considerable commentary on the difference between tonality as we know it, and the modality of the Gregorian chant. That modality was as satisfying to the medieval ear as our tonality is to us; and melody in the modes possessed many subtleties which have been drowned, for us, in the flood of harmony.

Here, then, is the table of modes, identified both by number and by their Greek names. Finals in each mode are in boldface type; dominants are in italics; and the intervals of whole and half steps are indicated by the space, or its absence, between the letters:

THE GREGORIAN MODES

I	Dorian	**D** EF G *A* BC D
II	Hypodorian	A BC **D** *EF* G A
III	Phrygian	**EF** G A BC D E
IV	Hypophrygian	BC D **EF** G *A* B
V	Lydian	**F** G A BC D EF
VI	Hypolydian	C D **EF** G *A* BC
VII	Myxolydian	**G** A BC *D* EF G
VIII	Hypomixolydian	D EF **G** A BC D

THE ADDED MODES

IX	Aeolian	**A** BC D *EF* G A
X	Hypoaeolian	EF G **A** BC D E
XI	Ionian	**C** D EF *G* A BC
XII	Hypoionian	G A B**C** D *EF* G

The note B does not appear as a final for the reason that its triad, as has been said, is diminished. Yet a mode—in the old sense of a "manner" for melody—might theoretically be constructed on this note also. This was recognized both as a theoretical possibility and as a practical error by Glareanus himself, who mentions the names Locrian and Hypolocrian as attached to these modes. Others included them—always recognizing their exceptional quality—and sometimes numbered them as Modes XI and XII, the Ionian modes then becoming Numbers XIII and XIV.

The order in which the Greek names appear in the table is at first sight perplexingly different from that which was used by the Greeks for their modes. This is usually explained by the fact that *nete* and *hypate*, meaning literally *low* and *high*, did not refer to the pitch of the notes they designated, but instead to the physical position, on the lyre when held in playing position, of the strings which sounded these notes. *Nete hyperbolaeon*, the lowest string (in this sense) was in pitch the highest note of the Hypodorian mode. But if you take the Hypodorian as the lowest mode, and proceed in order *up* the series, you will have: Hypodorian (A), Hypophrygian (B), Hypolydian (C), Dorian (D), Phrygian (E), Lydian (F), and Mixolydian (G)—exactly as in the table above. Boethius in Bk. IV, Chap. 15 of his treatise on music, names what he calls the Greek *modes* in this order, from *proslambanomenos* (the low A) upward.

But he also designates the intervals by which the successive scales are distant from each other, thus: T T S T T S (where T = tone and S = semitone). This is *not* the interval order of the white notes from A upward. If, however, you turn to the table of Greek *Keys* (pp. 24–25), you will see that this is precisely the order, both of intervals and names, in which the keys *ascend*. (Read the table backwards.) It is thus pretty certain that Boethius used the Latin word *modus* to refer to the Greek key, and not to the Greek mode, but that his later interpreters understood him to be speaking of that which they called a *mode*.

This table represents, then, a somewhat inexact epitome of what had for centuries been a practical method of musical composition. The literature of the chant, by the tenth century, was already vast. It did exhibit the distinction of authentic and plagal scales; but these had been conceived (as we have seen in the psalm tones) rather as distinctive formulas for certain portions of the melody than as binding limits of compass and organization; and their purpose—that of conveying the syntax and the spiritual meaning of the ecclesiastical texts—was somewhat defeated, both by the stricter modal regulations and by the floridity which was often brought to excess in the later chants. The modal theory had the great advantage of precision and compactness of statement—necessary for uniformity in the services throughout the now vast area of Christendom. But fixed rules both inculcate pedantry and incite revolt; and we shall see that the modal system will produce both these results.

The details of modal composition are too intricate for exposition here. Many of these details might well be called idiomatic—procedures in tone representing a widely accepted and living tradition of musical speech. The melodic formulas characterizing the eight psalm tones were idioms. The formulas for beginning, flexion, mediation, and closing conform in many ways, but not in all, to the later modal practice. The initial patterns are more precisely regulated, and the closes are less frequently on the conventional final than in developed modal melody. In simple psalmody, the dominant, as chief reciting tone, is so conspicuous that it becomes a *confinalis* or substitute final. But if it is recognized as a *new* final, a change of mode—a modulation—has taken place. This introduction of a new dominant is indeed a method of modulation within modal melody which yields great variety and subtlety in the more elaborated chants.[1]

Transposition was also made possible through the use of B flat— authorized by its existence in the lesser perfect system of the Greeks, and

[1] Suñol, *Textbook of Gregorian Chant*, p. 37.

often employed (with no implication of change of mode) to soften the harsh relation of the augmented fourth, F up to B natural. It was also used as a signature almost exactly in the modern sense. So used, it signified a transposition of the melody to the fourth above.[2] And since a whole tone obviously comprises two semitones, the possibility of far more extensive modulation was perceived, even though authority for it was rigidly withheld. The *chromatic* half step (not the natural semitone E–F or B–C) was shunned, however, in all Gregorian melody. Even the approach to the final by a diatonic half step from below—as in the Lydian mode—was long disliked, while that approach by a whole step—as in the three other authentic modes—was a favorite close. The conspicuousness of the half-step approach in the C mode was the chief ground of the persistent opposition to the admission of this scale into the modal system.

Some idea of the propagation of Gregorian chant and of the theoretical literature in which it was expounded remains to be given.

The first foundation of a school of church singers in Rome is attributed (with considerable uncertainty) to Pope Sylvester I (died 335). Boys trained as *lectores*[3] grew up to be not only cantors but often occupants of high positions in the clerical organization of the Church. But liturgical procedure—partly transplanted from the East—was at first by no means uniformly developed. The ritual observances at Milan, under St. Ambrose, were very distinctive, and other procedures, widely various, developed in Gaul (the Gallican liturgy) and in Spain (the Mozarabian). But all these, save to some extent the Milanese, seem to have been wholly superseded by the Roman rite, as established by St. Gregory (Pope from 590 to 604), and as later added to and emended. His unification of Western Christian worship meant the foundation of the Roman Church as the one stable institution surviving from the ancient world into the modern; and the value of that institution for Western civilization hardly needs to be emphasized.

What Gregory actually did for music is uncertain. He did *not*—any more than did St. Ambrose—"invent" the modal system and impose it upon the Church. His biography was first written by John the Deacon nearly

[2] The Dorian mode (D–d) has the interval order T S T T T S T. The Mixolydian mode (G–g) has the order T T S T T S T. But if a B♭ is persistently used in the G mode, the intervals will be T S T T T S T—exactly those of the Dorian mode; and it is evident that a Dorian melody may thus be sung with G as final. But since incidental modulation was also possible, a B♭, in certain progressions, might imply what would have required an unauthorized E♭ or F♯. A B♭ in the Hypodorian scale (A–a) would give the equivalent of an E mode with F♯, etc.

[3] i.e., readers in the prescribed manner, which reading was a kind of chanting, taught by chironomic gesture. This method survives in present-day methods of teaching the chant.

three hundred years after his death, and was thus compiled from tradition rather than from recorded fact. It tells us more about the rod with which he chastised unruly boys than about his actual codification of the ritual music. But it is certain that from his day a higher uniformity in ritual and music alike ruled throughout Christendom.[4] But this does not mean that the composers of that day were governed by a heavy theoretical hand. The only existing system of notation was alphabetic (it used the fifteen Roman letters from A to P, omitting J which was not then distinguished from I), and was quite unsuited to the notation of music to be read at sight by singers. Hence, the rapidly growing literature of that day had to be transmitted orally. Hence, also, the lack of general interest in theoretical ideas, which could be exchanged only between the learned, and were difficult to communicate in any practical form to the actual singers. Yet, among those who were interested, the problems of musical theory were seriously pondered. Beneath the surface of the sketches of personalities which follow, the reader can find a story of devoted effort toward perfecting the means of musical communication.

St. Augustine (354 to 430—author of the *Confessions*, the fervent vision of human well-being set forth in *De civitate Dei* ["Of the City of God"], and Bishop of Hippo in Algeria) planted the ideas of St. Ambrose, his spiritual adviser, in Africa. The *Offertorium* appears to have been the product of his institution of psalm singing during the offering of gifts. He wrote a treatise, *De Musica*, dealing mostly with versification and the relation between music and number, but containing a definition endlessly repeated by later writers: *Musica est scientia bene modulandi* (Music is the art of modulating well).[5] Pope Celestine I (422 to 432), Leo the Great (440 to 467), and Pelagius II, the immediate predecessor of Gregory, fostered the art in various ways. Gregory, before his elevation to the papacy in 590, had visited Constantinople and had found his musical interest much deepened by that experience. It was he who began the practice of sending emissaries to the frontiers of Christianity to establish both the proper ritual and the appropriate music for it. St. Augustine of Kent, who died in the same year as Gregory (604), was for that purpose sent by him to England

[4] Some pre-Gregorian ritual music seems to be preserved in certain "Old Vatican" MSS. at St. Peter's. Dr. W. H. Frere (*Oxford History of Music*, Introductory Volume) gives as illustration a Respond in the Gregorian, Ambrosian, and Old Vatican versions. The latter is palpably overornamented, and lacks the structural finish possessed by the other two versions—particularly the Gregorian.

[5] *Modus*, in classical Latin, means primarily a measure or standard. *Modulandi* therefore implies measurement according to rules or conventions—in music, the conventions of time and tune. The phrase may thus be freely translated: Music is the art of making good melody. The modern idea of modulation—*key change*—is, of course, not implied.

where he became the first Archbishop of Canterbury. From that center, Paulinus, his assistant, carried the burden to York, and became its first Archbishop. The Venerable Bede (made Bishop of Rochester in 689) and John, Archicantor of the papal chapel, working at Wearmouth, added such fame to England as a center of ecclesiastical music that in the seventh century St. Boniface was sent from there to Germany where his work was of like importance with that of St. Augustine. Alcuin likewise, until 804 the friend and adviser of Charlemagne in his project of reviving Latin culture among the Franks, was a native of York.

On the Continent the monasteries of Reichenau (on Lake Constance, at the source of the Rhine) and St. Gall (in Switzerland) were the chief centers for the dissemination of the chant. The story that Petrus and Romanus, emissaries from Rome, established the true tradition at Metz and St. Gall is too legendary for credence; but there is no doubt that Metz and Rouen—with the energetic support of Pepin, Charlemagne's father— were highly influential in spreading the one common tradition. This does not mean, however, that one inflexible rule of music-making was established. It means, rather, that a vigorous stimulus was provided out of which varied practices, healthily competitive, might arise.

The extent to which practice was governed by theory in the earlier time is as hard to determine as is the actual influence of Gregory the Great. Boethius (died 524) was not a Christian, but his great book *On the Consolations of Philosophy* was interpreted in a Christian sense throughout the Middle Ages.[5a] He left also a treatise *De Musica*, which was similarly revered by musicians in the later Christian world. He re-expounds, with few additions and sometimes with the reverse of clarification, the theories of Aristoxenos and Ptolemy, and is quoted at great length by most of the theorists of the reawakening. Cassiodorus (*circa* 495–*circa* 580) and Isidore of Seville (*circa* 570-636)—both, like Boethius, writers on a vast variety of subjects—add little, though they are both Christians, to our knowledge of the theory of the art. The theory expounded by these men does not derive from current practice, nor has it, visibly, any direct influence on the course of musical thought within the Church.

From the ninth century on, however, new concepts and new methods

[5a] Our statement that Boethius was not a Christian has offended a number of commentators. It is true that his treatise *De sancta trinitate* suggests adherence to the Christian doctrine, and the address of the treatise to Pope Symmachus appears to confirm it. But his conclusion—that the idea of the Trinity is implicit in the greater concept of Divinity—may also be interpreted as an effort to show that there is no essential conflict between the Christian doctrine and that which he later set forth in "The Consolations of Philosophy." In this, his last work, which was commented on, translated, and imitated throughout the Middle Ages, he neither mentions the Christ nor finds consolation in any specifically Christian tenet.

begin to be reflected in the theoretical writings. The first of these is by Alcuin, who describes the eight *tonos* as the agencies "through which all melody (*modulatio*), as if by a kind of glue, is seen to cohere." He numbers the four authentic modes consecutively, with Greek numbers (*protus*, *deuterus*, and so on), and describes the plagal modes as conjoined in a subordinate sense to the authentic.

Aurelian of Réomé (ninth century) in his *Discipline of Music*, following Boethius, divides the art into three genera: *musica mundana* (really, of the universe, since it embraces the "music of the spheres"[6]); *musica humana* (of the *microcosmus*, man's dwelling place; but, essentially, vocal music); and music *quae quibusdam constat instrumentis*—instrumental music. He repeats Cassiodorus and Isidore in defining *symphonia* as a mingling of high and low tones, but adds the qualifying adjective *concordans*, and makes further distinction between *symphonia* and *diaphonia*, which latter word means, to him, "dissonant or discrepant notes." The meaning is not beyond question, but the passage suggests that a new view of concord, implying a relation between simultaneous sounds (whereas the Greeks had applied the term only to successive sounds) is now recognized. (This view of concord is essential before harmony can be contrived—as it is to be in the near future of our study.) Yet he insists that his doctrine of music is fully fortified by Greek authority. He gives in addition, however, extended descriptions of the melodic formulas appearing in various types of chant in all the eight modes—matter which has definitely to do with contemporary music-making.

Few other ninth-century treatises offer much that is new. Remy of Auxerre merely comments on a fifth-century treatise by Martianus Capella; and Hucbald, whose name loomed large in all the histories of music until it was shown that most of the important work attributed to him was not his own, presents in his *De Harmonica institutione* a cumbrous system of notation which will be described in our chapter on that problem. The treatise called *Musica Enchiriadis* ("Handbook of Music") was long supposed to have been Hucbald's work, but while that can now be denied, the true author is unknown. The book is, however, a most important contribution to our knowledge of early experiments in harmony.

That new science—one of the most extraordinary discoveries in the history of art—is indeed "just around the corner." It is hardly hinted at in all the theory and practice we have so far perused; yet, as we shall immediately see, it was in no small degree prepared for, quite unconsciously, by those who were perfecting the essentially monodic chants.

---

[6] Boethius, contemplating the majestic march of the stars across the sky, had asked, "How is it possible that the vast machine of the heavens should move so fast, and yet in silence?" Aurelian is similarly perplexed.

The Beginnings of Harmony

COMPARED to the music of ancient Greece, the Gregorian chant—departing from immediate association with the actual text to express its emotional implication rather than its verbal sense—marks a definite advance toward that independence of purely musical ideas which is familiar in our instrumental compositions. But a far longer stride in that direction was taken with the invention of harmony.

The perception upon which that discovery depends is obviously that of consonance between simultaneously sounded *dissimilar* tones. (Octaves are obviously similar tones.) The Greeks had pleasure in the sound of men's and boys' voices singing in octaves. (The practice was called *magadizing*—from an ancient instrument, the *magadis*, upon which it was possible to play in octaves.) They also perceived concordance in the intervals of the fourth and fifth—as their determination of the *fixed* notes of their tetrachords proves; but they had no more than the most rudimentary notion of these intervals as harmonic concords.[1]

Neither in the Roman adaptations of Greek music (which were mere borrowing), nor in the first great expansion of musical art represented by the Gregorian chant, is more than an inkling of the possibility of harmony to be found. Boethius, Cassiodorus, and Isidore of Seville, the last writers before the long literary silence of the seventh and eighth centuries, de-

---

[1] Aristotle, in one of his "Problems" (XIX, 18), asks why magadizing is performed only with the consonance of the octave. His answer, emphasizing the identity of impression given by octaves, implies that a consonance which actually gave the impression of two dissimilar tones sounding simultaneously would be unpleasant to the Greek ear. And what we have seen of the close relation between music and speech in ancient Greece suggests that such consonances would have obscured that sensitive adjustment of tone to word.

scribe and justify music as a Greek art, and have the same notions of consonance as Aristotle. But with the resumption of literary effort in the ninth century, the new concept of consonance is almost at once discoverable. Aurelian of Réomé still defines *symphonia* (as did Isidore) as the mingling *(temperamentum)* and coming together *(convenientia)* of high and low tones. But he recognizes six "symphonies"—the fourth, fifth, octave, octave plus fourth, octave plus fifth, and double octave. Though his definition of *harmonica (musica)* is ambiguous, the meaning of *symphonia* seems pretty certainly to imply the new concept of consonance. However, neither he nor Remy of Auxerre—nor Regino of Prum nor the famous Hucbald (though the last two make vague mention of organum) —describe any systematic use of consonance in what we should call harmony.

The first treatise to exhibit such a practice unmistakably is also from the ninth century—the *Musica Enchiriadis* ("Handbook of Music") long ascribed to Hucbald, but since 1884 regarded as anonymous. Here, *symphonia* is described as "the pleasant combination of disparate sounds," and various combinations are set forth in *daseia* notation.[2] The common name for such combinations is given as *organum*.[3]

The first illustration of the process shows voices singing at the unvarying interval of the perfect fifth, the *organal* voice being the lower. The next is a similar process at the interval of the perfect fourth; then, by doubling each voice at the octave, we have the composite organum of the fourth, and that process is also shown in conjunction with the perfect fifth. The following example will sufficiently illustrate all these types, the single principle of which is parallel motion at the primary intervals of the fourth or fifth. Taking the two voices on the middle staff alone, we have the simple organum of the fifth. Taking the two highest voices, or the two lowest, and giving the name *principal* to the higher voice, you have the simple organum of the fourth. Grouping three—or all four—voices together by reduplicating one or both of the middle voices at the octave (as indicated by the braces), you have combined organum. And since the intervals are invariably perfect fifths, fourths, or octaves, it is natural to call this kind of music *strict* organum.

[2] (See Chap. VIII.)

[3] *Organon* is the Greek for a tool or instrument. The Latin form originally had the same meaning, but was also applied to the water organ, familiar to ancient Rome. Isidore, speaking of instruments which, "filled with the blown breath, are made to give forth tones—trumpets, reeds, pipes, organs, *pandoria* and similar instruments," says that *organum* is a general term for all wind-blown musical instruments. Whether the word has any reference, in the ninth century, to the instrument of that name which was beginning to be familiar (as *magadizing* refers to the *magadis*) is uncertain. Organum, as described in the *Enchiriadis*, is sung.

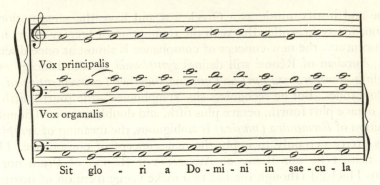

Observe that this harmony can be produced from memory, without any preliminary training, by singers who know the given melody (here, a familiar phrase of plainsong). For aside from the difference of pitch, *the two melodies are identical*. The only requisite is the recognition of fifths or fourths as *harmonic* concords. Indeed, it may be that the singers themselves are unaware of the interval. In schoolroom singing, it is often noticed that the less musical children, although they can carry the tune, begin at the fifth below the proper pitch and yet imagine themselves to be singing in unison. This could have happened in a ninth-century church choir as easily as in a twentieth-century schoolroom. It was probably often corrected—by directors who strove for the conventional; but it may sometimes have been encouraged—by directors of an inquiring mind.

But while the practice could hardly have been developed into a science of harmony by other than trained musicians, it need not have originated in groups directed by such men. There are ample proofs that primitive and more advanced peoples have also, in various ways, contrived a similar kind of harmony on other intervals. One such process is called *heterophony*—the simultaneous singing, by a number of voices, of a melody which is variously known by those individuals, and to which the more imaginative add ornament, as pleases them.[4] The product as harmony is unsystematic, and little benefit in its higher organization is to be expected from analytical study. But improvisers often grasp ideas more rapidly than analysts, and heterophony does sometimes exhibit a curious harmonic interest. What may be imagined as a product of such effort was described by a twelfth-century writer, Gerald of Cambrai, in Wales and northern England. His not very precise remarks seem to indicate a common prac-

---

[4] The song will presumably begin on the unison in all voices. Divergence from the unison will appear as the individual notions of the tune are presented. A similar divergence is seen in the example *Rex Coeli*, page 62. It is thus imaginable that harmony itself originated in that practice of *free* organum which, in another light, seems the product of an effort to avoid dissonance in *strict* organum.

tice of singing in thirds.[5] And there is preserved an English composition of the early thirteenth century—an apostrophe to St. Magnus, patron saint of the Orkney Islands—which is almost continuously in thirds, and may be a finished product of the practice recorded by Gerald. (It is, however, a much later product than strict organum.)

All this suggests that harmony originated as an "unpremeditated art," and that it was *not* primarily the invention of the churchmen. But its progress did accrue through meditation; the churchmen, not the hetero-phonists, were the meditators; and the first fruits of that effort are already chronicled in the *Enchiriadis*. It is evident at once that progression in perfect fifths or fourths cannot be carried out over the whole extent of the diatonic scale. F up to B is an augmented fourth; B up to F is a diminished fifth; and you cannot "cure" these dissonances unless you alter one or the other of these notes by using either B flat or F sharp. Each of these will of course distort the interval pattern of the diatonic modal scales. B flat, which had been admitted into the Lesser Perfect System of the Greeks, had ancient authority for its existence, and had been found useful in mitigating certain harshnesses in the Gregorian chant in which B was in close juxtaposition to F. To admit this note, indeed, was at worst no more than to effect the transposition of a mode; but to multiply "accidentals" was obviously to endanger the whole modal system. The author of the *Enchiriadis* managed to avoid all danger of dissonant fifths by adopting a scale of eighteen notes (from low G to c), made of four tetrachords and two extra notes, with the tetrachords disjunct, and all in the pattern, T S T. It is here shown, combined with itself at the interval of the fifth:

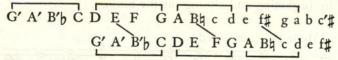

Upper line—*vox principalis;* lower—*vox organalis*

The tetrachords, bracketed, are in the described pattern; the fifths arising from the combination of the scales are perfect; but the augmented fourths cannot be avoided. (They are shown, by the diagonal lines, as they would appear if the scales were combined at the fourth.)

Organum with this scale is precarious at other intervals than the fifth. There are not only three augmented fourths, but three (much harsher) augmented octaves—B' flat–B natural, F–f sharp, and c–c' sharp. These

[5] This interval was dissonant to the trained ears of the ninth century. It was recognized as an *imperfect* concord in the twelfth, but was not employed until the fourteenth in long successions, such as appear in organum at the fifth.

irrational octaves seem to be ignored—or rather, not implied—in the description of the combined organum (compare the octave B′–B, twice, in our preceding example, which, if the notation were interpreted literally, would be B′ flat–B natural). But the augmented fourths cannot be ignored, and the author (representing, of course, the practical musicians) is forced to a vital (and for the future, most fruitful) alteration of the whole procedure of parallel motion. He perceives that the augmented fourth must arise whenever the second note of a higher tetrachord (as E, B, or f sharp, in the diagram above) is combined with the third note of a lower tetrachord (B′ flat, F, or c). He therefore states the practical rule that the organal (lower) voice must not descend below the "fourth sound" (the highest note) of the lower tetrachord. But this must frequently forbid parallel motion altogether; and the following examples will show the procedure when that condition arises:

No. 1 (Mode III)

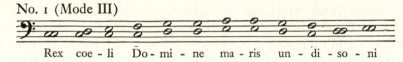

Rex coe - li   Do - mi - ne   ma - ris   un - di - so - ni

Since the E of the rising *initium* (C, D, E, F, G) would be "organized" by a lower B flat, the organum begins at the unison and maintains the bass-note C until the regular progression at the fourth is possible. Both the second, C–D, and the third, C–E— frankly dissonant—will be heard; but the beginning at the unison and the arrival at the goal of the consonant fourth make the discords *intelligible*—which is the criterion of admissible discord in any music. The close on two unisons is the only logical solution for the two notes D–E.

In the second example, the E is the only troublesome note, and can be managed by beginning and closing on the unison:

No. 2 (Mode IV, transposed)

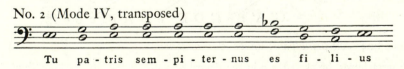

Tu   pa - tris   sem - pi - ter - nus   es   fi - li - us

The higher B flat is the permissible alteration appearing when a modal melody is transposed.

But with this melody sung in Mode I, the skip from D to F seems to justify the beginning of the organum on A (the *second* sound of the lower tetrachord). The close, however (F–E–D), compels the given alteration, and introduces the *occursus*, a progression *by contrary motion of the voices to the final.* Here, indeed, is the rudiment of our familiar perfect cadence.

No. 3 (Mode I)

Tu   pa - tris sem - pi - ter - nus   es   fi - li - us

Strict organum could be—and was—improvised. This, which is usually called *free* organum, must be premeditated, even though it was intended to be sung at sight, and by reference to the principal melody. The occasional beginning at the unison may suggest heterophony as a possible source for the whole idea of organum[6] (a suggestion not strongly supported by the carefully considered beginnings in our other examples), but the art is now reaching a stage in which accident can no longer yield a tolerable result. Harmony, although manifestly impossible on the *symphonious* intervals exclusively, has become so interesting that it is pursued even when it involves the discomfort of occasional discord. This discomfort is submerged in the higher interest of combined *dissimilar* melodies. Neither in the *Enchiriadis*, nor in a schoolbook of questions and answers on its subject matter which is called *Scholia Enchiriadis*, is the musical interest of the dissimilar melodies very great. But the essentials of such combinations are all present: oblique and contrary motion (as well as parallel) and the actual employment of dissonance.

For about a century after the *Enchiriadis*, the record of progress in harmony is no clearer than the record of its beginning. That manual, describing organum as "a kind of surface of musical art, devised for the ornamentation of ecclesiastical song," feels obliged to insist that this surface does not render less worthy of thought the inner substance of the art. And it does not appear that organum was by any means as yet a universal art. The next important account of organum appears only after about a hundred years, in the *Micrologus* ("Little Discourse," or "Brief Account" of music) by Guido of Arezzo. And this book, for another hundred years and more, was the most authoritative treatise on musical theory. Guido's contributions to the problem of notation and to the art of singing at sight were perhaps even more important; but the *Micrologus*, by comparison with earlier treatises, appears as the work of an independent and original mind.

Most of the book had still to be given up to the time-honored descriptions of the notes and intervals of the scale, the modes, and similar material; but the treatment is more penetrating and less dependent on antiquity than in the older books. Guido's scale is no longer the irrational sequence of the *Enchiriadis*, nor is any great stress laid on the tetrachord as a unit of

[6] For a brief summary of the evidence and of various opinions on this subject, see Reese, *Music in the Middle Ages*, p. 256f.

scale structure. The word *Diaphonia* which to the sixth-century writers implied dissonance, is now defined as the "disjunction of notes sounding concordantly together," and hence as a synonym for organum. The fundamental harmonic interval is now the fourth, to which, if the lower voice is reduplicated in the higher octave, the fifth will be added; but the fifth is not allowed as the *organal* interval. Indeed, the stricter organum seems now a little old fashioned. Guido calls it *durus* (hard, rough) in contrast to "ours" which he calls *mollis* (gentle).

The intervals available between the voices are the whole step, the minor and major third, and the perfect fourth, of which the minor third is the least desirable, the perfect fourth the most. The distance between the principal and organal voices cannot now exceed the fourth (the fifth appearing only with the doubling of the lower voice at the higher octave), and there is great care needed at the *occursus*, for, as Guido has earlier remarked, it is only at the end of the melody that the final, and therefore the true mode of the music, can be definitely perceived. The possible cadences are either on the fourth (in the F mode, with C below) or on the unison. Contrary motion to the unison is best, but a close cannot thus be made on C, since neither the minor third (as $\frac{D}{B}$ to $\frac{C}{C}$) nor the minor second (as $\frac{CC}{BC}$) is allowed.

The following will give an idea of the method recommended by Guido:

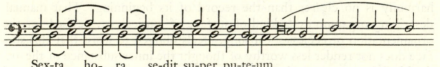

Sex-ta　ho-　ra　se-dit su-per pu-te-um
(At the sixth hour she sitteth at the well.)

Even at Guido's death (in 1050) the acceptance of organum was by no means universal. Two of his great contemporaries, Berno of Reichenau and Hermannus Contractus (The Lame) do not even describe the process. It was nevertheless widespread in what appear to be little islands of interest. At Winchester, in England, two *tropers* have been preserved (one dating from the eleventh century), in which the troping of various kyries, alleluias, and other melodies in two parts is exhibited. The notation is without staves, so that the exact intervals cannot be determined; but it is certain that contrary motion appears at other points than the *occursus*.

But by the twelfth century the picture comes into sharper focus. Organum (now called *discant*[7]) is well enough known to be described in the

---

[7] *Discantus* (double or divided song) is the Latin equivalent of the Greek *diaphonia* in the later sense of that word. We shall soon find that *discant* also acquires a more precise meaning.

vernacular (Old French) as well as in the conventional Latin of the learned. The opinions of its value vary, but its progress, at the hands of enthusiasts for the method, is considerable. The two most significant treatises are the *Musica* of Johannes Cotto (John Cotton), and an anonymous treatise, *Ad organum faciendum* ("On Making Organum").

Cotton, although he has no very high opinion of the art, gives information which shows that the two voices are rapidly growing in independence. Diaphony, he says, "is a congruous mingling of voices, in which at least two singers participate, in such a way that while the one maintains the proper melody, the other circles aptly about it, and both come together either on the same note or the octave." Contrary motion between the voices is preferred, and two or even three notes in the organal part are sung against a single tone of the plainsong. (Note that in our example from Guido, the organal voice has one note against the florid principal part.)

The author of *Ad organum faciendum*, unlike Cotton, is most enthusiastic for the new methods. His exposition of five "modes" according to which organum may begin or end is of little value; but his practical illustrations of the whole process reveal definite and important advances since Guido's time. Concords only appear between the voices, but among the concords the third, either major or minor, finds a place. It is inferior to the perfect concords and is infrequently used, but its admission is significant of a change in the harmonic consciousness that is definitely in the trend of later harmonic thought. Contrary motion—which means complete independence in melodic progression—is evidently preferred to parallel or even oblique. And the freedom of the organal voice to move above, across, or below the principal voice is evidently granted without reservation.

The two melodies still combine, for the most part, note against note, with floridity only at the end of the sentence. But there is here a latent sense of vigor which cannot long be restrained; and while the restriction of the available intervals to concords only is reactionary in appearance, it is doubtless true that the occasional discords appearing in the free organum are endured as inevitable rather than appreciated as contributory to melodic activity. The third, on the other hand, not only adds greatly to the thin and meager vocabulary of concord, but stands in such a position that transition, by means of intervening discord, must soon come to be musically meaningful. For the goal of discordant progression (when discord, inevitably, is reintroduced) is not now the rather distant interval of the fourth, but is only the very next step beyond the discordant note.

The following examples will show considerably more melodic freedom than was apparent in Guido's rather restricted method. Even though concords only appear, the interest of the upper voice is comparable to

that of the lower. And since the bass—the principal voice—is the same in
the two examples (and, in the manuscript, in two others), the idea of the
cantus firmus has been born:

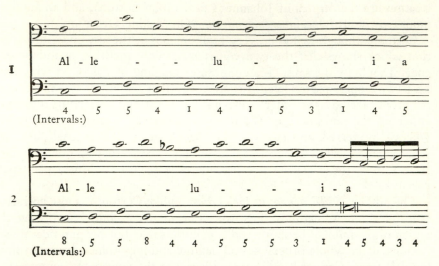

Note that with the exception of three thirds, the intervals are all concords
(the third is still so "imperfect" as to be regarded as nearly discordant); that
the upper voice in No. 2 has a florid figure of five notes against the last note
of the theme; and that the upper voices in the two examples are quite different
from each other. In each example the voices sometimes "cross"—i.e., the higher
sometimes goes below the lower.

These, of course, are exercises, rather than efforts at actual composition.
They hardly justify the author's panegyric on the art:

> *Organum acquirit totum sursum et inferius . . .*
> *Qua de causa applicando sonat multum dulcius.*

("Organum enhances everything, both above and below . . . for which reason,
when it is applied [music] sounds much sweeter.")

He does present a trope on the *Kyrie eleison* which is more extended than
our example, but differs not at all in method. The text offers the following
amplification of the sense of the word *Kyrie:*

> *Cunctipotens genitor Deus omnicreator eleyson*

("Father Almighty, God the universal creator, have mercy upon us")

with similar apostrophes to the Christ and the Holy Ghost. It is evident
that these experiments, like the strict organum, were regarded as decorations of the plainchant, and hardly as essays in independent musical composition; yet that independence is gradually being won.

The surviving literature in this style is meager, but is less observant of the letter of the law respecting dissonance, as may be seen from the following—an early twelfth-century piece. The alphabetic notation in which the music is preserved is shown along with the transcription into modern notes. The dots between the letters apparently indicate either a pause or a lengthening of the note. They are transcribed by bar lines which, of course, have not here their usual meaning.

UT TUO PROPITIATUS

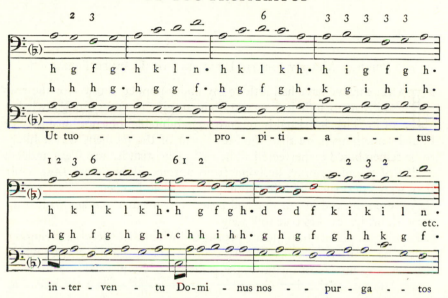

May the Lord, propitiated through Thine intervention, [unite us,] purged of our sins, [with the dwellers in the skies.]

The dissonances (seconds, and the tentative concords, thirds and sixths) occur with far greater frequency in this example than in the last. The added melody (above) is thus more fluid and interesting. It is also largely in the pentatonic scale (F, G, A, C, D), which suggests that it may actually be a popular melody; and if the supposed pauses are ignored, except at the third, fifth, and last bar lines, and the tune is sung in a rhythm of four beats, this impression will be heightened. The melodies still combine note against note, but with so much of freedom in the relations between the voices, it is evident that this restriction will soon be overridden. Organum has almost completely outgrown its simple method.[8]

[8] Please turn to Appendix I, p. 631, where a further important step in the organization of rhythm and harmony is described.

❧ *CHAPTER VI* ❧

Discant, or Measured Music

Popular Melody and its Influence on Learned Forms

THUS far, we have had little to say about popular music—for the reason that no sufficient records exist to give us any clear knowledge of it. That it existed is, of course, indubitable; but not until it celebrated something more than the excitement of the moment was it likely to be remembered or perfected. The early Christian hymns were, indeed, a kind of popular music, deriving from untraceable sources. But, while they were concerned with something deeper than momentary excitement, they were removed in purpose and practice from that contact with ordinary life which evokes true folk song.

Popular song is set to popular speech; and when that speech is changing, song is necessarily unstable. We have already observed the change which made accent, instead of quantity, the principle of Latin versification. This was by no means the final change in that language. When the decaying Roman Empire could no longer maintain schools in which the classical language was taught and spoken, illiteracy naturally increased; dialects multiplied; and out of these (which collectively were known as the *lingua Romana*) emerged at last the various Romance languages—French, Spanish, Italian, and Rumanian—which survive today. They were for long too unorganized for literary effort to be possible. Such popular song as remains from the period of their growth is therefore set to Latin—mostly classical Latin—words. There are "tunes" for six of the *Odes* of Horace (one of which, set originally to the *Ode to Phyllis*, is that of the hymn to John the Baptist on which Guido of Arezzo was later to found his process of solmization); several settings of Martianus Capella and Boethius; some to fragments of Vergil's *Aeneid*. There are also several *planctus* (laments) on the deaths of monarchs, such as Charlemagne. Most of these survive only in untranslatable notation.[1]

[1] St. Augustine, in his *De Civitate Dei* (Of the City of God), translates into Latin,

In the less cultivated Latin which in the tenth century was being super-seded by the *lingua romana,* a host of songs were written by a curious poetic fraternity, the goliards. These were wandering students who pos-sessed, as learned "clerks," certain ecclesiastical privileges. They were, however, mostly prodigal sons of the Church, whose intellectual curiosity was deeper than their faith. They criticized bitterly the misbehaviors of the priests, and even dared to inveigh against the Pope. But they were also zealous for a better life and, although their topics were most fre-quently wine, women, and song, they were also, as J. A. Symonds has described them, forerunners of the Renaissance. The universities, which from the early thirteenth century began to multiply, offered a better meeting place for such minds, and a certain restraint upon their grosser activities.

The descendants of the goliards were the *jongleurs* (compare our word *jugglers*), who made little pretence to intellectuality but served well the troubadours when their time came. Instrumental music doubtless owes an incalculable debt to these humble scrapers and tootlers. One of the goliard tunes, a song in unmeasured praise of Venus, survives at Cambridge with its original text, and at Monte Cassino with the more seemly words, "O noble Rome, mistress of the world, most excellent of all the cities," and so on.

Songs in the Vernacular—Troubadours and Trouvères

The earliest poems in the vernacular were written in old Provençal, a dialect spoken in southeastern France. This became the principal cultured tongue until the thirteenth century, and survives as a dialect of French to this day. In this pleasant region, blessed with a favorable climate and —from the end of the eleventh century until the Albigensian Crusade (1209–1229)—singularly free from the devastations of war, "finders" or "inventors" of poems appeared and were called in their own tongue *trou-badours.* (The word *trobar,* like the French *trouver*—to find—has ap-parently some relation to the word *trope.*) These artists entertained their princely patrons with poems (which were incomplete without accom-

---

from a codex owned by the proconsul Flaccianus, what was in the Greek an acrostic on "Jesus Christ, Son of God, Saviour." He had some difficulty in turning the acrostic into Latin, but gives it in hexameters which can be suggested thus:

Judgment's sign: the whole of the earth with sweat shall be moistened.
Everlasting, the future King shall descend from the heavens,
So, in the very flesh, to become the judge of the world.
Under that sign they shall see Him, both unbelievers and faithful,
Seated on high with the saints, God's self, at the end of the ages.

To this text a melody was set which is preserved in many later versions, some of them polyphonic.

panying melody) on a great variety of subjects, all consecrated by courtly convention.

There were, for example, *sirventes* (songs of service), sometimes religious, but often political—scurrilous diatribes against the patron's enemies

A l'entrade del tens clar

(When the springtime comes—*eya*—to bring renewed joy—*eya*—and annoy the jealous—*eya*—the queen desires to show how lovable she is. *On your way, on your way, jealous one! Let us all, let us all dance together, together.*)

which, if they caught the popular fancy, were of great value as propaganda. There was also the "debate" (*partimen* or *tenso*) on some nice question of courtly love or knightly behavior; the *pastorale*, describing the overeager wooing of a shepherdess by a passing nobleman who is usually discomfited; the *alba* (dawn), sung by one who is concerned lest the two lovers he is guarding from intrusion be forgetful of the approaching day; the *escondich*, an appeal for absolution from blame (by the mistress rather than by the Church); the *descort*, a "discordant" and usually satirical mingling of incompatibles in thought or language. There is also the *dansa*, a dance song with refrain, of which the above is a typical pattern.

The most highly regarded form of all was the *canso* (compare French *chanson*, Italian *canzona*) addressed to the poet's mistress (often his patroness) whose indifference to his plea is the almost invariable theme of his inspiration—and thus the actual source of his courtly favor. While some models may be said to exist in earlier Latin poetry, the technique of these pieces was far more finished than in any known sources, and their lyric intensity was quite unexampled. Something of this quality may perhaps be seen in the following, which we have translated as nearly as we were able according to the measure and the rhyme scheme of the original. It is by Bernart de Ventadorn,[2] probably the most gifted of all the troubadour poets. The poem has seven stanzas and an *envoi* of four lines, all made in the same measure and with identical rhymes, throughout:

> When I see how the lark, in song,
> Goes winging 'gainst the sun's bright ray:
> Forgets himself, and falls headlong,
> His heart to sun-sweetness a prey—
> Ah! then, of him whose joy I see,
> What envy doth my soul inspire!
> I marvel that not instantly
> My heart should melt for sheer desire.
>
> Alas! I boasted all awrong
> How skilled I was in love's soft way:
> I cannot cease for her to long
> Who love with love will not repay.
> My heart, my mind she takes from me,
> My very self, my world entire,
> And taking, doth to me decree
> But longing and a heart on fire.

But the troubadour was not merely a poet—he was also a singer; and

Can vei la lau-ze-ta mo - ver   de joi sas a-las contr' al rai, que

s'ob-lid' e's lais - sa cha-zer   per la dous-sor   qu'al cor li vai,

[2] Appendix II, p. 632, gives a brief sketch of Bernart de Ventadorn and his influence.

ai! tan grans en-vey-a m'en   ve de cui qu'eu ve-ya jau-zi - on, me-ra-

vil - has   ai car des-se   lo cor de de-sir-er no'm fon.

the above is, to our mind, the most satisfactory of the several extant
versions of the melody which Bernart de Ventadorn probably composed
for this verse. The rhythm is not indicated in the manuscript. Hence,
the notes are left without stems. The slurs indicate note groups which are
to be sung to a single syllable.

The problem of rhythm in this music is perplexing. A majority of
modern scholars adopt the opinion of Beck and Aubry who, early in the
present century, propounded the theory that all troubadour and trouvère
melody was measured according to one or another of the rhythmic modes
which, as we shall soon see, governed the learned music of the churchmen.
The author belongs to the minority which dissents, at least as far as troubadour music is concerned.[3]

The language of the troubadours was superseded by the dialect of the
Isle de France (Paris) in which, from the end of the twelfth century, a
still more extensive literature than that of Provence was at length developed. These poets of northern France were called trouvères—obviously,
a term equivalent to troubadours. Their poetic forms were borrowed,
both as to style and substance, from the southern types, and need not be
separately described. The rhymes, while often elaborately arranged within
the stanza, did not persist throughout the poem as in Provençal; but other
beauties of versification took their place. And the influence of the trouvères
in the world was great in proportion as the fortunes of the French monarchy—considerably ebbed during the last half of the twelfth century,
owing to the ineptitude of Louis VII as an antagonist of Henry II—were
retrieved under Philip Augustus. Paris was becoming not only a great
political capital, but a great musical center.

The work of the trouvères is preserved in far greater volume than that
of the troubadours. Of their melodies, also, about 1400 are preserved, as
compared to 264 of the earlier poets' works. A far closer association between these men and the learned musicians was thus established. That
they may have both drawn from the learned and contributed to their art is
thus a wholly reasonable supposition, presently shown as indubitable fact.

[3] The problem is too intricate for debate here, but the student will find some
defense of our position in Appendix III, p. 632.

The Minnesinger

Just as Eleanor of Aquitaine brought troubadour influence into England, so a French princess, Beatrix of Burgundy, by her marriage to Frederick Barbarossa, brought trouvère ideas into Germany almost at the same time. The results were more immediate and significant. The German poets who now began to imitate the trouvère models were called *Minnesinger* (*Minne* is an old German word for love). The German language was more vigorously accentuated than French or Provençal. The poetic principle of German verse was therefore more definitely accentual, and the rhythms of their music apparently reflect this condition. Both duple and triple time are dependably represented in the transcriptions of their music into modern notation.

A few of the Minnesinger—Walther von der Vogelweide, Wolfram von Eschenbach, and Tannhäuser—are more familiar to us (largely through Wagner's dramas) than are their French colleagues. The forms in which their poems are cast are mostly after French models—for example, the *Tagelied* ("Song of Day") from the *Alba*, the *Streitgedicht* ("Strife Song") from the *partimen* or *tenso*, and the *Lied* or *Minnelied* from the *Canso*. The devotion here expressed, however, is often quite unworldly. The Lied had conventionally the form of two stanzas *(Stollen)* and an *Abgesang* or refrain. This pattern we shall find copied by the later German poet-singers, the Meistersinger. The Minnesinger seem to have preferred the G mode (the Mixolydian) where the troubadours in general preferred the Dorian.

The troubadour influence spread also into Italy. Dante greatly admired certain of these poets, notably Arnaut Daniel, the most accomplished technician of all. Petrarch was likewise an admirer of his amazing skill. But there was in Italy no movement of strength comparable to that in France. Owing, in some measure, to the example and influence of St. Francis of Assisi, penitence, rather than courtly love or worldly interest, seems to have been the most inspiring theme. Bands of Flagellants (fanatics who beat their bodies fantastically to rid their souls of sin) traveled about in processions, singing songs called *laudi spirituali*, which name we shall encounter again in a more appropriate application. The Germans sometimes followed the same practice, their songs of castigation being called *Geisslerlieder*. Some of these suggest the later form of the Protestant chorale.

The Rhythmic Modes

Whether or not we can reconstruct its actual rhythms, there can be no doubt that this popular music possessed high interest for its hearers. The learned musicians must have been not only aware of, but sensitive to, its general appeal. But they were confronted, in their attempts at polyphony, with a difficulty greater than that of the monodists whose problem was to make melody appropriate in style and rhythm to the texts. Harmony, as soon as it outgrew the swaddling clothes of strict organum, was the product of combined dissimilar melodies; and it required no more than the timid experiments we have so far encountered to show that the interest of harmonic music grew greater proportionately as the combined melodies differed from each other, not merely in pitch but in rhythm.

These differences were limited—in pitch, by the ear's tolerance of discord; in rhythm, by the need of a common measure which could govern all the parts and yet allow each to appear free and spontaneous. Our present system of notation can deal with almost any imaginable combination of rhythms. The twelfth-century musician could neither imagine such complexities as are familiar to us, nor had he any system of notation in which to record such complications. Since Guido's time, music had indeed been written on staves and with clefs, so that the pitch of the notes was not in doubt. But this notation had been devised primarily for the Gregorian chant (essentially as it appears in our examples); and for the flexible line of such melody, precise time-measurement was not even desired. The first experiments in organum were made upon these melodies, and, even in the free style, made no new rhythmic demands. In the hymns and sequences, however, imaginary "feet" were in motion—as were actual feet in the dance—and when music required measurement it was thus the rhythm of verse which provided both its propulsion and its mensural basis.

Until the twelfth century, then, the verse was the actual indicator—the system of notation—for musical rhythm. It was imperfectly adapted to this purpose. Some poetic feet naturally suggest duple time and some triple, and the combination of duple with triple measure is not suggested by verse. But such a combination of duple- and triple-rhythmed melodies would certainly be attempted as soon as the practice of harmony had attained any perfection. To attain it, however, some adjustment of the one measure to the other would be necessary—an adjustment which would best be discovered in practice. Out of the large number of poetic meters which were found in the classical poetry of Greece and Rome, six came to be especially favored by the musicians. Four of these are by nature triple; two are duple; and the manner in which the incompatibles were accommodated to each other may be seen in the following table, which, with negligible variants, exhibits the rhythmic scheme of the learned music of the twelfth and most of the thirteenth centuries:

THE RHYTHMIC MODES

I. Trochee	‿ ⌣	=	𝅗𝅥 ♩
II. Iambus	⌣ ‿	=	♩ 𝅗𝅥
III. Dactyl	‿ ⌣ ⌣	=	𝅗𝅥. ♩♩
IV. Anapaest	⌣ ⌣ ‿	=	♩♩ 𝅗𝅥.
V. Molossus	‿ ‿ ‿	=	𝅗𝅥. 𝅗𝅥. 𝅗𝅥.
VI. Tribrach	⌣ ⌣ ⌣	=	♩ ♩ ♩

Only in Modes III and IV is there any departure from the natural poetic meter, and that is slight enough so that the rhythm of the foot is unmistakable.[4] The theorists, indeed, do not tell us that the triple rhythm here exhibited was adopted for these reasons. Indeed, they give no reasons at all, but only a kind of justification. They assert that triple time is *perfect* because the three beats of the measure show a marvelous correlation with the three Persons of the Holy Trinity. Duple rhythm, in fact, is alluded to by Walter Odington, and an anonymous writer who was somewhat earlier, as having existed in earlier music;[5] but no examples of such music remain, from which the origin of the triple-time convention might possibly be deduced.

The technique of rhythmic combination illustrated in the table of the modes was, of course, not the composers' only problem. Two melodies combining diverse triple rhythms would still be incompatible if they did not harmonize acceptably. The limit of exclusive concord, set by Cotton and his contemporary, was impossible to maintain if any real freedom was to be achieved; and the composers had no disposition to obey such a restrictive rule. Discord could not be wholly excluded. Yet neither theorist nor composer could find a wholly satisfactory formula for the relation

---

[4] If the iambus and the trochee had been reduced to duple time, so that they might be accommodated to the dactyl and the anapaest, each would have had to assume the form: ♩ ♩. Since it was usual to place the short syllable of the iambus on what we should call the strong beat of the rhythm, these two feet would thus have become indistinguishable from each other. The molossus, represented as 𝅗𝅥.𝅗𝅥 ♩, would not have lost character; but the tribrach—a favorite measure for sprightly melody—would have been incommensurable.

[5] "The 'long,'" Odington says, "among the older 'organists,' had two beats, as in the [poetic] meters." This was still true of the "imperfect" long in Odington's own time, when it was combined with a "breve" to express the trochaic or iambic meter; but in his day the long had primarily three beats. The *Discantus positio vulgaris* (Exposition of Common Discant") says that notes which contain less than one beat, or more than two, are *ultra mensuram*—beyond the measure.

of discord to concord. Both agree, however, that concord must appear on what we should call the strong beat of the rhythm, and that discord might appear on the weak.[6] That such discords were tolerated rather than enjoyed is indicated in the usual defense—that after discord, concord sounds more sweet. A sound *rationale* of discord was still far in the future.

THE FIRST POLYPHONIC FORMS

Neither was the composers' problem solved when they had discovered processes for combining rhythms and had devised a rule-of-thumb method for relating discord to concord. They had still to construct a coherent musical discourse. Even the musical sentence had, as yet, a rather indefinite syntax. The *initium, mediatio,* and *punctum* of the Gregorian sentence —clear enough in the earlier psalmody—had been obscured by the dissolution of the reciting tone into florid passages; and this obscurity was only heightened when melodies were combined into harmonies. The *occursus,* as a harmonic device, did indeed mark the end of a musical thought; but as polyphony developed, it often appeared at a point where musical continuity rather than conclusion seemed desirable. Nor was there any clear relation between one sentence and the next. The notion of a theme as the basis of a musical discourse was as yet embryonic.

The idea of form, that is, was by no means a purely musical idea. The verbal text seemed to the theorists to be the basis of a musical form, just as the poetic foot seemed the basis of musical rhythm; and the greatest theorist of the thirteenth century, Franco of Cologne, founds his discrimination between musical forms on the relation of the music to the text. So complete was the acceptance of his theoretical ideas (he also devised a most important system for the notation of rhythm) that music historians, until recently, adopted the name *Franconian* for the whole period of triple-time discant. Research has so far clarified the work of this period that it is now possible—and preferable—to speak of the forms in terms of actual musical procedure, and to designate the period as the era of its leading composers—Leonin and Perotin, or of the schools of musical thought—St. Martial and Notre Dame, which were then dominant.

Franco's descriptions of form are of interest, however, if only for comparison with the more modern classifications. He divides music into three types: (1) those in which not all the voice parts have words; (2) those in which all the parts have the same words; and (3) those in

---

[6] "All uneven notes in Mode I [i.e., the first, third, fifth, etc.] are longs, and should concord with the tenor. The other even notes [the weak third beats of the Trochaic meter] may be placed indifferently." Anonymus IV: Coussemaker, *Scriptores, I,* 356b.

which all the parts have different words. Something of the results of recent study may be seen by a comparison of Franco's descriptions with the following brief account of twelfth- and thirteenth-century efforts.

Out of a stage of experimentation, the process of organum emerged into a consistent art form at St. Martial, in Limoges. The first great advance is seen in the device of troping, where the upper voice—in contrast to the sedate little flourish with which our second example from *Ad organum faciendum* concludes—becomes highly adventurous. The tenor, on the other hand (whose model might perhaps have been found in the one reiterated note which appears in the *free* organum), becomes really the *holder* (the word is from Latin *tenere*, to hold); for it is obliged to sustain single notes during very extended excursions of the upper voice. The spontaneity of florid solo singing is thus preserved, while at least something of the richness of harmony is acquired. The effect is obviously very different from that produced by the note-against-note construction of the harmony in strict organum, or in such pieces as *Ut tuo propitiatus*, above. An early example of this sustained-tone style is found in an inexactly notated manuscript from St. Martial—a Christmas *Benedicamus* with the trope-text *Jubilemus, exultemus, intonemus canticum*, in which the tenor sings one note to each syllable of the text (two to the last), while the upper voice, which we may now call the *discant*, has for the first three words ten, twelve, and twelve textless notes, respectively, and for the final trisyllable has four, five, and nineteen notes. Another St. Martial manuscript, with the liturgical text *Benedicamus Domino*, has eight notes for the word *benedicamus*, and the discant has eighty-five.

Music of this type, according to Franco, was called *organum purum* (pure organum). It was the oldest of recognized harmonic forms, and the most highly revered—perhaps because it departed least from the character of the Gregorian chant.

Long melismas of this kind were as difficult to remember as the Alleluias to which, as we have seen, the singers added texts and so produced what were called *proses* and *sequences*. The same tenor for the text *Benedicamus Domino* is found in the same manuscript with a still more elaborate discant, to which the text *Stirps Jesse florigeram* (with single notes or short note-groups for each syllable) has been added.[7] Here, then, we have a type of music in which the parts have different words. Franco, under this heading, mentions only the *motet*, which has other distinctive features as well as this; but it is evident that the technique of combining different melodic lines, with their rhythms determined by the different

[7] Both of the preceding examples, and many others to which we have made reference, are included in the interesting collection *Examples of Music Before 1400*, by Harold Gleason (F. S. Crofts, N. Y.).

texts—the sort of combination which seems to have given rise to the system of Rhythmic Modes—is a practical method of composition.

The influence of the St. Martial musicians is seen in the fact that similar examples of organum are preserved at Santiago de Compostela in Spain, and at Conques in southern France. But the efforts at St. Martial were eclipsed in the later twelfth century by the brilliant achievements of the musicians at Notre Dame in Paris. A new style—or a new form: it is difficult, in these days, to distinguish between a style and a form—grew up at Notre Dame and was most fertile in its contribution. This was called the *conductus*. The word, as we have seen, had been used long ago for music which accompanied the ceremonial approach of the priest to the altar, and for exits and entrances in the old ecclesiastical drama. In the twelfth century this association is quite lost, and the music is acquiring high interest in itself.

The *conductus* is described by Franco as belonging (along with *organum purum*) to that class of forms in which not all the parts have words. He distinguishes it also from all other forms as one in which the tenor, instead of having been taken from the plainsong, is itself invented by the composer. Some apparent inexactness in Franco's description will emerge in the following account of the form.

Organum was by no means abandoned at Notre Dame after musical leadership was assumed at that center. An anonymous (possibly English) theorist (called Anonymus IV, since his treatise is so designated in Volume I of Coussemaker's *Scriptores*) names the two great figures whom we have already mentioned—Leonin and Perotin. He speaks of Leonin as "the best 'organist' " that is, composer of organa—and of Perotin as "the best 'discantor,' and better [in this field] than Leonin."

Leonin wrote a great book of Organa for the Graduals and Antiphons of the whole church year. This book, called the *Magnus Liber*, has itself been lost, but many excerpts from it have been preserved—some in manuscripts from St. Andrew's in Scotland, some in a French manuscript now in the Laurentian Library in Florence, and some in Spain. John Cotton's somewhat apologetic defense of organum as giving a new surface to ecclesiastical chant is no longer needed. Anonymus IV praises unreservedly the abundance of "colors," and it is evident that the musical part of the service is becoming of absorbing interest for the congregation. Leonin's music elaborates the Intonation (the beginning) of the Gradual or Alleluia, leaving the close to be sung in the original Gregorian monody. The more syllabic portions of the chant are "organized" by extending greatly the length of these single notes; but a grateful contrast is also achieved by giving to the tenor, in the more melismatic passages, a definite and undeviating modal rhythm. These latter, in contrast to the organal passages, are called *discant.*

Leonin excelled (as Anonymus IV asserts) in organum rather than in discant—whether from discomfort at the close confinement of strict rhythm or for some other reason. Perotin excelled where Leonin was less successful. Hence, he partly remade the *Magnus Liber,* composing what the theorist calls "better *clausulae* or *puncta.*" [8] Though he sometimes shortens and even alters Leonin's organa, it is in the passages of discant that his great emendations appear. But his skill is by no means exhausted by such two-part writing. He adapted the process to compositions in three and even in four parts. Of these, the three-part organa seem artistically to have overtopped those for four voices. That they were preferred in the thirteenth century is shown by the fact that of the several manuscripts which exist, the latest are written in the measured notation of the late thirteenth century, whereas the two- and four-part pieces are found only in the modal notation.

Technically, however, the four-part pieces are astonishingly contrived, considering the early stage of harmonic art. Three *organa quadrupla* are known, two of which are by Perotin—the *Viderunt* and the *Sederunt.* In the *Viderunt,* after a long initial chord (a kind of "tuning up"), the three upper parts—above the always sustained F of the tenor—plunge at once into the highly active discord B flat–e, and dissonance rules until the end of the two-bar phrase. The leading voice, with its buoyant melody, e, f, e, f, d, c, is imitated thereafter by the device of exchanging parts, essentially as in the rondel to be described later, but more freely. Other phrases are similarly exchanged. Sixty bars of what we should call 6–4 time are sung above the one note F, to the first two syllables of *Viderunt.* The harmonic effect may be inferred from the following reduction:

(Sung an octave lower)

Originally, only the lower voice had words. As with the organum *Stirps Jesse,* however, a text was often supplied later for the *duplum* (the voice above the tenor), thus suggesting the motet.[9] But if the motet was

[8] *Clausula* in classic Latin, and *punctum* in medieval Latin, may both mean *close* The *clausulae,* however, are not "grand finales" but sections—largely, those passage' which we have called *discant*—which are more or less complete in themselves.

[9] The whole passage of sixty bars (which is only the beginning of the composition) may be studied in Gleason, *op. cit.,* p. 36. The motet text is also given. It

thus germinating, the conductus, as Franco described it, was already in being. Indeed, the three upper voices of *Viderunt*, without the tenor but with the added text for the *duplum*, which will now be the lowest voice, would give an example of the conductus if only the harmonies on the strong beats were concordant. Franco says that the composer desiring to write a conductus must first invent the most beautiful melody possible as the tenor, and add the other voices in such a way that one, at least, will always be concordant with the tenor. Sometimes, however, a tenor part was taken from a popular song. The Florence manuscript already mentioned contains a conductus whose tenor is none other than the melody for the dansa *A l'entrade del tens clar*, given above.

The conductus was not, in its employment of musical devices, a form wholly distinct from others. The contemporary materials of music were plainsong, popular song, and organum in all its species, together with such modifications of any of these as the growing art of harmony might suggest or necessitate; and the composer of ingenuity put together such of these materials as might serve his purpose. The addition of a text to the *duplum* of the conductus was not a novelty but a useful expedient. The interest of music thus set to different texts for tenor and *duplum* lay not in the confused jumble of words, but in the sharper definition of rhythm and line given by verbal accentuation. It was natural that this process should be extended.

The product of its extension—the most elaborate and popular of thirteenth-century forms—was the motet. But the distinguishing mark of this form, in spite of Franco's classification, was not its polytextuality. It was rather—as Franco also says—in the pattern of the tenor. This, unlike the tenor in the conductus, was drawn from the plainsong; but in its adaptation to the motet it lost all the appearance of plainsong. A passage of the chant—usually melismatic—was given an arbitrary and very unmistakable rhythm in one or another of the rhythmic modes; and this pattern of rhythm was adhered to, with slight modification, throughout the piece. The same phrase of plainsong might be adapted to different modes by different groupings of the notes of the original. The mode itself would be the conventional trochaic, iambic, and so on, of the table given on page 75; but the mode was also said to be perfect or imperfect accordingly as the characteristic note group ended with a note of the same value as that with which the group began, or with one of different value.

---

means "Behold the fulfillment of the prophecy; darkness flees before the day, since the light of the Prophet was born with Mary," etc. Whether the tenor—surely a most uninteresting part to sing—was taken by voices or instruments is a question recently much debated. The evidence is, of course, inferential and was held unconvincing by the great German scholar Friedrich Ludwig.

The whole pattern, thus arbitrarily rhythmed, was called the *ordo* of the mode.[10] The first *ordo* of any mode was that in which the characteristic figure appeared but once before a pause—the pause itself being of the same value as one or another of the notes. The second *ordo* was that in which the figure of the poetic foot appeared twice, complete, before the pause. Third, fourth, or fifth *ordines*, "as many as you please," might be constructed analogously. The following will sufficiently illustrate the point:

Changes in the mode sometimes occurred as when, after a pause, Mode II took the place of Mode I; and in later times, as the complexity of the texture increased and rhythm began to be in some degree independent of poetic meter, *mixed* modes appeared, the changes then being made in the course of the rhythm, not after the pause.

The tenor had but one or two words of text—those which belonged to the ecclesiastical melody from which the notes of the *ordo* were drawn. Whether or not these words were sung is much debated. The rhythm of the *ordo* is often quite at variance with the normal accentuation of the original text—a distortion never found in Gregorian chant and seldom in the other voices of the motet. Thus, it seems probable that the tenor, when sung, was merely vocalized. It appears, however, that this part was often played on instruments.

[10] This type of rhythmic pattern was perceived to be implied in what is known as *modal* notation—the intermediate stage between the indefinite rhythm of the chant notation and that of Franco of Cologne, which was precisely rhythmic. The intricacies of this system are too great to be included in our present study.

The next higher voice (corresponding to the *duplum* of the conductus) was called *motetus*—whence the name of the form of composition. The term is apparently related to the French *mot* (word). This derivation perhaps gains credibility from the fact that in the earlier examples of the motet in three voices, the *motetus* was the only part to have a complete text. (In the motet in two parts, this is obviously the case.) Since the motet form grew out of the *discant clausulae* of Perotin, the earlier examples often present a *motetus* in the same rhythmic mode as the tenor. The phrases, even, are sometimes of the same length as the *ordo*, which causes both voices to pause simultaneously. More often, the phrase of the *motetus* is extended to cover two or more of the figures of the *ordo;* and variety is enhanced by casting the *motetus* in a different rhythmic mode from that of the tenor.

The valuations of syllable length in dactyl and anapaest which are exhibited in the table of rhythmic modes were, of course, essential when normally duple rhythms were combined with those normally triple. So far as the *motetus* was concerned, it was generally assumed that at the strong beat of the rhythm it would be concordant with the tenor. Discord was allowed, and even encouraged, on the weak beat, not because of the intrinsic interest of discord, but because it seemed to enhance the smoothness of the following concord.

The highest voice, the *triplum* (literally, *third;* but compare the modern word *treble*), was livelier in motion. Later virtuosos in composition added a *quadruplum* (fourth voice), but the normal structure of the motet was in three parts. For the triplum, the sixth rhythmic mode was often used. In the earlier examples this part was textless, like the upper voices in the conductus. If such parts, as is readily imaginable, were played on instruments, and if the tenor was likewise instrumental, the *motetus* would then appear as a solo song with polyphonic instrumental accompaniment. But in the later examples the upper voice had a text, differentiated from that of the *motetus* not merely in rhythm but in meaning. Indeed, these texts were sometimes in different languages. Particularly during the third quarter of the thirteenth century, the triplum was often in French, with the *motetus* in Latin. Such tripla were borrowed, with as little alteration as possible, from familiar trouvère melodies. The contempt for the motet, implied in the quotation from the *Leys d'amors* (Appendix III, page 632) was evidently not felt in Paris, where the association of "popular" with learned composers was closer.

The ecclesiastical modes were often ignored by the popular composers, who followed what seems to have been a natural instinct in casting their melodies in a close approximation to major tonality. Harmonies suitable to these melodies could hardly be contrived without giving the flavor of tonality to the whole fabric of the composition; and in this way there began a loosening of the bonds of tonality which prepared the way for our major and minor keys. The following brief excerpt will illustrate most of the points just observed:

MOTET: POVRE SECORS—GAUDE CHORUS OMNIUM

The *ordo* is arranged from an Alleluia verse for Easter Monday. The text for that portion of the chant which forms the *ordo* is *Angelus Domini descendit de caelo: et accedens revol* [*vit lapidem et sedebat super eum*] ("The angel of the Lord descended from Heaven, and came and rolled back the stone from the door and sat upon it.") The notes are with negligible exceptions as they stand in the *Liber usualis*. The rhythmic pattern is the first perfect *ordo* of Mode II. After twenty-eight bars the whole *ordo* is repeated; but during the repetition both *motetus* and *triplum* are entirely different. The *motetus* ("Rejoice, choir of all the faithful; the flaming rose . . .") is in Mode II, like the *ordo*, but pauses less frequently. The triplum, in Old French ("Meager reward have I had as yet from my lady, whom I have served according to her will") is essentially in Mode VI. Its phrases are mostly longer than those in our quotation, and the pauses are never with those of the *motetus*, though they sometimes coincide with those of the *ordo*. Of the sixty-two bars, fifty-six begin with perfect concord; four with the third; two with actual discord. The tempo was doubtless lively, so that the discords on the weak beats were rapidly passed over.

RONDEL AND ROTA—SUMER IS ICUMEN IN

The motet was by far the most popular, and for the future the most important, of thirteenth-century forms. Technical progress, however, is notable in one of the forms described by Franco as that in which all the parts have the same words. He includes in this category the *cantilena* and the *rondel*. The *cantilena* is not clearly described, and there are no examples, so entitled, which would yield a precise definition of this word as the name of a particular musical form. It seems rather a generic than a specific term. Within the genus, however, three more or less definite forms are distinguishable—the *rondeau*, the *virelai*, and the *ballade*.

All these are polyphonic elaborations of what were originally monodic songs. The rondeau was a dance song with a refrain. The words of the refrain were repeated at intervals in the course of the poem, and the phrases of music set to these recurrent words were sung by the chorus of dancers, and were interspersed with strains sung by a solo voice. (We shall see, long hence, that the instrumental form of the rondo displays this recurrence of a principal strain.) The charming song *Robins m'aime*, from Adam de la Halle's pastoral play *Le Jeu de Robin et Marion* is a later homophonic example of the form.[11]

The homophonic virelai and the ballade are in a sense expansions of the form of the rondeau. The virelai has a third musical strain, interpolated between the two first strains of the rondeau and their first repetition: *AB, cc, ab, AB*. The ballade omits the central repetition (*ab*) and substitutes still another new strain for it, so that the original strain appears only at the beginning and the end. In the polyphonic treatments of these forms, the voices all sing the same words. The borrowed melody is sometimes assigned to the tenor, and sometimes to the middle voice.

The form of the *rondel*, in its original homophonic state, was strophic, with a refrain; it is thus not unrelated to the rondeau. In its polyphonic form, its musical structure becomes its most interesting feature. The form is named by Franco, but is described in some detail by Walter Odington, whose *Speculum musicae* ("Mirror of Music") dates from about 1300. The technique of this composition is a kind of imitation, made by the exchange of parts by the participating voices. Three harmonizing strains

[11] It is printed in Gleason, *op. cit.*, p. 16, and Reese, *Music in the Middle Ages*, p. 223.

of melody are contrived, all of which begin together. When the end is reached, the lowest voice takes up the strain just sung by the middle voice, and the middle, that of the highest. A similar exchange takes place when this strain is finished. The form can be clearly seen from the following diagram:

Upper voice:	C A B	F D E
Middle voice:	B C A	E F D
Lower voice:	A B C	D E F

The effect, with equal voices, would be that of three repetitions of the same music, though a sense of imitation might be felt if the voices were of different quality. With mixed voices, the imitative hint would be clearer; and if the soprano sang an octave higher than the tenor, what is called *double counterpoint*—the inversion of two simultaneous melodic voices by the transposition of one of these to the higher (or lower) octave—would result.

This species of imitation (which is illustrated by Jean de Garlande, to whom Ludwig assigned the tentative date, 1240–50, as occurring in triple and quadruple organa, and in conductus) is employed as a kind of foundation for what is doubtless the most famous musical composition of the whole medieval period—the *Rota, Sumer is icumen in*. The foundation is not perhaps exceptional, but the superstructure, which is a strict four-part canon, has been an amazement to historians ever since its discovery in 1709. The piece is included in a manuscript now in the British Museum [12] which also contains a calendar dating almost certainly from about 1240. A rather hurried but long-unquestioned assumption that the music of the *Rota* (which is not written by the same hand as the calendar) was of the same date has recently been vigorously disputed by Dr. Manfred Bukofzer of the University of California. He contends that the piece could not possibly have been written before 1280, and that its most probable date is *circa* 1310.[13] A curious twinge of nostalgia, together with a sigh of relief, is the historian's reaction to this study which removes from the story of musical development the last of the many miracles—such as that of the invention of the modes by St. Gregory—that have long adorned that chronicle.

But even when this piece is placed in intelligible historic perspective its technique is still astonishing. Throughout the thirteenth century, four voices had taxed the extreme of the composers' ingenuity. This piece has six voices. The device of imitation, accomplished fictitiously by the interchange of parts, as in Odington's *Rondel*, was still a remarkable feat. But in this piece that kind of imitation is used only for the *pes* (the two-part

[12] Harleian MS. 978, folio 11, *verso*.
[13] See University of California *Publications in Music*, Vol. 2, No. 2, 1944.

foundation); the four upper voices sing a melody of forty-seven bars, strictly imitative throughout. (The song may continue until the last voice, emerging solo, has completed the melody; but the intention seems to be that all the voices should cease with the final note of the first voice.) The joyous lilt of the tune—in no ecclesiastical mode, but frankly in the major key, swinging along in its straightforward rhythm of four bars—is nothing less than captivating.[14]

SUMER IS ICUMEN IN

[14] This and many other pieces either in this text or in the collections referred to can be very tolerably performed, with little preparation, by any average class. Sing the melody once through in unison. Then divide the group into four female voices and two male, instructing the men to begin with the melody, and each group of women to enter when the preceding voice has reached the :S: at the fifth bar.

One more "form" was included by Franco among those in which not all the parts have words. This is the *ochetus*. The lack of words implies vocalization; and indeed the *ochetus* (which word the popular ear turned into *hoquet* in French, and *hocket* in English—a "hiccough") was not a form at all, but a kind of vocal trick. One voice suddenly ceased (the hiccough) and another filled in the silence. In general, one voice would rest for the time of a long, another for a breve, and the effect was also produced with the semibreve. If three voices were involved, two would sing while one rested.[15]

The achievements of the twelfth and thirteenth centuries, looked at in the perspective suggested by John Cotton's treatise and the *Ad organum faciendum*, are impressive. The wholly novel invention of harmony, groping throughout the tenth and eleventh centuries for an intelligible technique, had arrived at only the most elementary principles of organization. At the end of the thirteenth, the body of harmonized music has already become highly articulated, and its function as an expressive agent has been recognized, not only within the Church but by the world at large.

The framework of its structure—devised by rule-of-thumb, out of the sensitivity to discord and the rhythmic impetus of verse—has now become inadequate. A new and much more flexible system, not only of rhythmic structure but of harmonic tone relations, is urgently needed. How this need was met will be related in our next chapter.

[15] There are many indications that the eagerness of the musicians for new effects was greater than their reverence for the service. John of Salisbury, in the twelfth century, had complained that music defiled the service "by the riot of the wantoning voice, by its eager ostentation, and by its womanish affectations in the mincing of notes and sentences." And Ailred, a contemporary, was thus impressed by the execution of the hocket: "sometimes thou mayst see a man with an open mouth, not to sing, but as it were to breathe out his last gasp, by shutting in his breath, and by a certain ridiculous interception of his voice to threaten silence, and now again to imitate the agonies of a dying man, or the ecstasies of such as suffer." Nor does the complaint cease as time goes on. In the fourteenth century we find that Jacques de Liége, the author of the huge treatise *Speculum musicae*, which is attributed by Coussemaker to Jean de Muris, writes a whole chapter "On Inept Discantors," the tenor of which is indicated by the one ejaculation: "Oh, if those of the olden time who were skilled in music could hear such discantors, what would they say—what would they do?" (The translations of John of Salisbury and Ailred are from Wooldridge.)

The Fourteenth Century—Ars Nova

THE indefiniteness of the musical forms of the thirteenth century—forms which the theorists themselves described only in terms of the manner in which music and text were related—was in no small measure attributable to that dependence on poetic meter which is manifest in the system of rhythmic modes. A great lack of rhythmic variety, inherent in the triple time which was the inevitable product of those modes, must have been apparent to the composers; yet the theorists, up to the very end of the thirteenth century, seem to have accepted the restriction without any protest or any effort to escape from it. The frequent justification in the analogy with the Holy Trinity had doubtless more force in that day than we can readily recognize. The system of notation, however, perfected during the thirteenth century for the representation of triple time, must have operated much more forcefully than any theology to confine musical thought within that narrow frame. Yet the perfecting of that system by Franco of Cologne (accomplished apparently about 1280) may also have pointed the way to a more liberal rhythmic thought. It established a precise valuation of the time of every note, even in the ligatures; and such precision must have made at least thinkable a proportional valuation of time in duple measure.

The recognition of duple time as an acceptable musical rhythm is at any rate the first sign of a fundamental change in musical thought at the opening of the fourteenth century. Petrus de Cruce, described by Jacques de Liége as a follower of Franco's system, is said by him to have been the first to divide the breve into four semibreves—obviously a step in the direction of duple rhythm; and a further enlargement of rhythmic vision is set forth by Philippe de Vitry (1291-1361) in his notable treatise *Ars nova* ("The New Art"). This book, written about 1320, describes what proves to be a considerable forward step in the whole process of notation.

The Italians, however, were evidently at work on the same problem.

Marchetto of Padua, writing his *Pomerium in arte musicae mensuratae* ("Approach to the Art of Measured Music") probably at about the same time as Vitry, says that the breve—which by that time had replaced the long as the unit of musical measure—was divided by the Italians either into three semibreves (*divisio ternaria*) or into two (*divisio binaria*), and that the semibreve might be similarly divided into three or two minims (*minima*—"least" notes). Even these he can imagine as thus divisible "if the voice is capable of such a feat." He claims, indeed, that the French are backward in using the binary division; but Philippe de Vitry nevertheless describes clearly the time signatures illustrated on page 120 below, as well as the use of various combinations of red and black notes for the same purpose.

With so fundamental a change in the rhythmic basis of music, a "new art" indeed became possible. The implications of the new art were indeed far deeper than they at first appeared. Not only was rhythmic— and therefore melodic—design transformed; harmony, likewise, found new uses in accommodating itself to the new melody. And behind the whole endeavor of the musicians lay social, political, and religious ferments which were continuously to affect the purpose of artists of every sort.

The French, Italian, and Spanish tongues had long since emerged from the chrysalis stage of the *lingua Romana,* and were now assuming definitive literary form. Norman French and Anglo-Saxon had likewise been amalgamated in the speech which Chaucer (who died in 1400) was to model into verse whose wild-flower fragrance no later poet has ever been able to match. The thirst for understanding—awakened, in opposition to the older scholasticism, by the new interpretations of Aristotle offered by Averroes, and intensified by the keener thinking of Abelard, Albertus Magnus, Thomas Aquinas, and the incredibly progressive Roger Bacon— had prompted the founding of the great universities and was beginning to be manifest in many quarters far outside the walls of those institutions.

The troubadours and trouvères, writing for aristocratic patrons, reflect but a fraction of the general interest. Long before them, indeed, in the days when literature was still communicated by speech more than by writing, the *Chansons de geste*—rude epics celebrating the exploits of Charlemagne and his associates against the Saracens and other enemies— had been fabulated. The *Lais* of Marie de France and the Romances of Chrétien de Troyes, in the twelfth century, had instigated the forming of the great Arthurian cycle; and in the thirteenth century had appeared the *Roman de la Rose* (a part of which Chaucer translated) which is a conspicuous landmark in a long tradition in the style of the allegory. The popularity of this poem, which endured for three centuries, evidences the rapid spread of both literary interest and moral inquiry. The *fabliau*, a short tale in verse, almost always in the vein of satire or raillery, also grew to overwhelming popularity in the thirteenth century, and became an important vehicle for the descent of literary interest from aristocratic to bourgeois levels. These are but bare suggestions of the general invigoration of thought which the musicians were to interpret in their own way; but they may serve as a background for the new endeavors in composition, to which we must return.

Philippe de Vitry, who was a composer as well as a theorist, seems to have inaugurated the first practical modification of musical form to supplant the designs based on the triple-time system. Somewhere about 1314, and thus before his theoretical treatise was written, he gave to the motet a higher rhythmic organization than had hitherto been devised for that popular form. This was the device of *isorhythmic* structure. Its process is quite clearly an outgrowth of the rigidly patterned tenor *ordo* of the thirteenth-century motet.

In isorhythmic compositions, not only the tenor but also the upper voices (wholly or in part) are cast in sections having a certain rhythmic pattern, and that pattern of rhythm, *but not the contour of the melody,* is immediately several times repeated. The rhythm of the upper voices, for reasons of textual meter or harmonic compatibility, may deviate from the established patterns; but it is often maintained as precisely as is the given scheme of the tenor, which is usually inviolable. The following will show how the principle was applied in the case of a composition which is isorhythmic throughout:

The sections marked Ia, Ib, Ic are the beginnings of three consecutive strains of music, each of which is 24 bars long. In all three strains, observe that the *rhythms* in each voice are identical. The melodic patterns differ, although in Ib the curves are generally similar to those in Ia. Sections IIa and IIb are analogous.

Comparison with the fragment from *Gaude chorus omnium*, above, reveals here a considerably expanded technique of composition. Spontaneity such as that in the French triplum (*povre secors*) is gone, but a far more highly organized design has appeared. The rhythm of this triplum (*Rachel plorat*), if this were a thirteenth-century piece, would probably have been throughout in Mode I (as with the words *suos, Christi nuncios*, etc., it still is); but the modal rhythm is obviously dissolved at bars 4 and 5 of each section. Melodic design here predominates over verbal rhythm. Again, the motetus *Ha fratres* is less highly contrasted with the triplum than is *Gaude chorus;* but unity of structure is more apparent. (Observe that a misaccentuation of *domini* is allowed.) The tenor is no longer a modal *ordo*, and is indeed of little interest in itself. It takes part, however, in the hocketing which is the chief musical feature of Isorhythm II.

Of this device, and of the cultural inheritance at which we have hinted, the musicians of the fourteenth century made full use; and it was natural that one of the greatest figures in musical composition should also be a poet of high accomplishment. Such a man was Guillaume de Machaut. He was born in 1300, and after taking orders (quite early in life) became secretary to John, King of Bohemia and Duke of Luxembourg, whose warlike exploits he accompanied and from whom he received many favors. He at length became Canon of Rheims, and died there in 1377. His poems and compositions survive in many manuscripts, not only in France but in Italy and Germany. His compositions range from the monodic *lai* through the polyphonic motet to the Mass, and celebrate, though Machaut was a churchman, worldly more often than religious themes. Since his work thus offers in itself the whole perspective of composition in fourteenth-century France, we may observe a few typical pieces.

The *lai*, with Machaut, is almost always monodic—perhaps a survival of the art of the trouvères to whose company he has often, not altogether correctly, been said to belong. The verse is elaborate—twelve strophes, of which the first and the last are formed alike (even with identical rhymes), the others varied. Each strophe has two similar sections or stanzas, so that the melody for the first section is repeated for the second. The rhythm is of course not modal, but the melody is by no means loosely constructed. In the first (and last) strophe of a *lai* from the *Remede de Fortune*,[1] the first five of the seventeen bars of melody have the following pattern:

Not only is all the rest derivable from these; even the melodies for the other strophes (all in 6–4 time, though the lines are of great variety) are largely rhythmed out of these patterns, which are conjoined in many different ways. There is, indeed, a kind of melodic rhyming, sometimes simultaneous with, sometimes independent of, the poetic rhymes. (The note groups marked *a* and *b* are often used for this purpose.) Such rhythmic variety as this, together with such cohesion, was unattainable either in the Gregorian chant with its melismatically adorned prose rhythm, or in the persistent regularity of modal melody. Evidently, there is here an important stride in the direction of self-sufficient melodic ideas.

Other monodic compositions from the *Remede* are a *Complainte*, a *Chanson roiale*, and a *Chanson baladée*. Only the last form (which is equivalent to the virelai) appears elsewhere than in the *Remede*; but there are also two *Balades*—four-voiced compositions in which the text is apportioned to a solo voice, with the tenor, contratenor, and triplum appar-

---

[1] This is a long poem (4,298 lines) on the theme of courtly love, and on the role of Fortune in the affairs of men. The various songs mentioned in the text are tributes to the beauty and virtue of the loved one, or are expositions of the duty of the lover—largely in the manner of the trouvère poems, but on a grander scale and more impersonal in tone.

ently instrumental. Another *Ballade* in three parts (not from the *Remede*) has similar structure, and a few bars will serve to illustrate the texture:

BALLADE, De TOUTES FLEURS

Guillaume de Machaut

The sense of the text is: ‖: "Of all the flowers and all the fruits in my garden [there remained but a single rose. :‖ Despoiled and destroyed were all the rest, heavily oppressed by the hand of fate. ‖ Against this sweet flower, to enjoy its color and its odor, and even to pluck it, one sees them strive. But I shall never seek to have another."] The whole form is suggested by the double bars and the repeat sign just shown, the words *Despoiled . . . hand of fate* being the text of the first strain when it is repeated.

Independence of poetic meter is complete (three whole bars are sung to the preposition *de*). The punctuation of the melody by the cadences in bars 4 and 8 is more decisive than is called for by the text; but the problem of punctuation, as a fact of musical design, is nevertheless more fully recognized than in the thirteenth-century motet. Discord is perhaps less carefully regulated, since it appears at the first beat in bars 4, 6, and 8. Yet the lower (probably instrumental) parts combine to more consistent effect than in any piece we have so far quoted.

Of the *chanson balladée*, in which a recurrent refrain is a conspicuous feature, specimens may be seen in the *Oxford History*, Volume II, page 36, and in Gleason, in the work cited, page 80. It is obvious that in such occasional compositions as these, isorhythmic structure is not to be thought of. Other ingenuities appear, however, in the *Rondeau* whose poetic pattern, with several recurrences of the same line or lines, has already been described (page 84, above). An extreme of such ingenuity is reached in Machaut's enigma-rondeau whose text, without repetitions, reads: "My end is my beginning, and my beginning my end, and this holds ever true. My third song thrice must retrace its course, and thus ends." The music of this extraordinary piece is in three parts, the tenor (the middle voice) alone having the text. The words are indeed true, for the highest voice played backwards has the same notes as the tenor sung forwards; and the third voice (the contratenor), when it reaches the middle, goes backwards over what it has just played.[2]

In the more learned types of composition such as the motet, of which twenty-three examples by Machaut survive, isorhythm is almost always employed. Gleason, on page 88, prints a specimen (*De Bon Espoir, Puis que la douce*) in which the isorhythmic sections are conveniently disposed so as to exhibit the structure.[3]

Somewhere about 1300 was written the first known polyphonic setting of the Ordinary of the Mass—the so-called *Mass of Tournai*. This is apparently a composite work (by unknown composers), and is in different

---

[2] The old French text, complete with repeated lines, is as follows:

> *Ma fin est mon commencement*
> *Et mon commencement ma fin.*
> *Et teneure vraiement*
> *Ma fin est mon commencement.*
> *Ma tiers chans trois fois seulement*
> *Se retrograde, et ensi fin.*
> *Ma fin est mon commencement*
> *Et mon commencement ma fin.*

The music may be found transposed in Gleason, p. 81, and at its original pitch in Reese, *op. cit.*, p. 351.

[3] The tenor, with the text *Speravi*, has only four notes—F, G, A, B♭ which are disposed in three groups of six notes each to form three *melodic* sections, *a, b, c*. The *isorhythmic* sections, however, include but two of the three melodic groups. The content of the isorhythmic sections, therefore, is as follows: Ia has *a, b;* Ib has *c, a;* Ic has *b, c*. The whole scheme is then repeated in diminution, giving IIa—*a, b;* IIb—*c, a;* IIIa—*b, c*. The upper voices, with negligible exceptions, are also isorhythmic. The three divisions of the diminution are enlivened by a brief passage of hocketing.

styles, suggesting different periods. The *Gloria* and the *Credo* are in duple time. The technique is generally that of the thirteenth century motet, notably in the *Ite, missa est* (included along with the conventional portions of the Ordinary), which has the liturgical melody for those words in the tenor with a *motetus* in Latin and a *triplum* in French.

That Machaut may have been stimulated by this composition is possible; but his one great work in this form is far more advanced in technique. The motet technique partially survives (the *Kyrie*, for example, has the liturgical melody from Mass IV, freely treated, in the tenor) but without foreign texts, and there is also a melodic figure of seven notes which, in one rhythmic shape or another, appears in every section, and gives a certain purely musical unity to the whole structure. The mystic significance of the virgin birth is emphasized by a great broadening of the music at the words *Et incarnatus est*, and harsh dissonance brings home forcefully the sense of the ensuing *Crucifixus*. The *Sanctus* and *Agnus Dei* have as foundation the corresponding plainsong melodies from Mass XVII. The first two portions of the *Agnus Dei* are conveniently accessible—one in Gleason, on page 97, the other in the *Oxford History*, Volume II, page 26.

Music in Fourteenth-Century Italy

We have seen that France and Italy each claimed precedence in the innovations of the *Ars nova*—at least in the problems of notation. In the thirteenth century it was certainly true that St. Martial and Notre Dame had placed France far in the lead. Against the organa and the conductus of Leonin and Perotin, Italy could set only the *laudi* and the Sequence *Dies irae*, probably by Thomas of Celano. But this backwardness was overcome in the fourteenth century, when many indigenous forms were developed, and when one great composer, Francesco Landino, rose to heights disputable by no one save Machaut.

Although dancing is practiced everywhere and is peculiar to no nation, national dance-forms do develop. Such forms emerge in Italy as the *istampita* (French, *estampie*, Provençal, *estampida*—jongleur-tunes, provocative of stamping), the *trotto*, and the *saltarello*, the latter, at least in later times, distinctively an Italian dance. The tunes are given in the manuscripts as monodic, and without other titles, save that two are called *La Manfredina* and *Lamento di Tristano*—this last, surely, a curious association for a *saltarello*. In this one, the dance has three main parts in triple time, and each part has a *rotta* or refrain, in duple time, which states in simple form the outline of the more florid principal strain.

A disposition to floridity, notable in the dances just mentioned, is characteristic also of the Italian polyphony of this period. In this work the use of borrowed themes (as in the French motets) is unusual. That is, it would appear that the conductus rather than the motet is the model; and since the conductus was long since outmoded in France, the Italian forms are at least in some measure new, and have new names. The chief Italian polyphonic forms of the fourteenth century are the *madrigal*, the *caccia*, and the *ballata*.

The etymology of the word *madrigal* is obscured by its variable spelling. As *matricale* it suggests *mater*, and hence a song in the mother tongue; as *mandriale* (*mandra* = a herd) it implies a pastoral poem. The musical form had ordinarily from two to four stanzas (sometimes only one) of three lines each, with a *ritornello* of two lines, sung only at the end, however, like the *envoi* of the (poetic) *ballade*. Although it is not a primary feature, canon, of which the Italians will be found to be very fond, often appears in the madrigal. An excellent example of the form as we have described it will be found in *Fenice fu*.[4] There is no canon, however, but only a few incidental points of imitation.

Canon, on the other hand, is the distinguishing feature of the *caccia* or "chase," in which the liveliest motion and even tumultuous scenes of the hunting field are depicted. Examples of this form from France, in the first half of the century, cast doubt on the Italian claim to priority in its invention. The Italians, however, contrive a more complex structure, providing a lower, instrumental part as a supporting accompaniment for the imitative voices, and extending the pattern by adding a refrain which is itself another canon, in a somewhat contrasting rhythm, as a coda. Reese[5] quotes an extraordinarily vivacious example of the French *chace*, and an Italian specimen, *Tosto che l'alba* (As soon as the dawn of the fair day appears, the hunter awakes. Up! up! for now is the time! . . .)

The *Ballata* is the counterpart of the French *virelai*, or, as Machaut called it, the *chanson balladée*. (Both these words—*virelai* from *virer*, to turn, and *ballata* from *ballare*—suggest the dance.) Interest, however, seems in the thirteenth century to have been transferred from the feet to the ears. The form has two sections of nearly equal length, but not (as was the case with the *ritornello* of the madrigal) in a definitely contrasted rhythm. The text is ordinarily assigned in the manuscripts to only one voice, which would make of the other two, as in the French *ballade*, an instrumental accompaniment. An example of this form by Francesco Landini—*Gram piant' agli occhi*, which Friedrich Ludwig described as "the most precious pearl among the rich jewels of Francesco's *dolci accenti*," is printed in Gleason, page 104.[6]

---

[4] Gleason, *op. cit.*, p. 99.
[5] *Op. cit.*, p. 355.
[6] This piece was highly appreciated in its own time. It was copied into all the

Apparently, the Italians of the fourteenth century were little interested in sacred music. How much of this indifference may have been due to the deplorable conflicts within the Church, and the ultimate descent of the papacy to a very low level in the estimation of thinking men, would be hard to determine.[7] Yet, as compared with France, interest in new methods is equal and—doubtless because of the rivalry between the Italian city-states—is more widespread. The Italians did not follow that fashion of anonymity which seems still to have ruled in fourteenth-century France. Whereas only a few French composers, aside from de Vitry and Machaut, are named in the manuscripts (among them, Andrieu, Vaillant, J. Césaris, Molins, Trebor—about whom hardly any other information

---

great manuscript collections—two of those now in Paris, one in Padua, one in London, and two in Florence, of which one is the sumptuous Squarcialupi Codex, from which Gleason's copy is taken. F. Ludwig in 1923 published this piece for the first time in the *Zeitschrift für Musikwissenschaft*. In the accompanying article, he notes that the variants in the different manuscripts are negligible. However, where Gleason prints the tenor as instrumental, Ludwig not only applies the text simultaneously to this and the *superius*, but (surely with good reason) distinguishes the tenor as the leading part. He thus makes of the piece a vocal duet, with only the contratenor (which he prints as a middle voice) instrumental.

[7] The fourteenth century saw a striking overthrow of the almost unlimited power which the Church had attained under Innocent III and his successors in the first half of the thirteenth century. Struggles with Frederick Barbarossa and his grandson Frederick II had reduced the Empire to insignificance. The cities of Lombardy, which the emperors had failed to subdue, had emerged into powerful if diminutive states, quarreling with one another, but united in opposition to either Pope or foreign king. France and England were growing rapidly into firmly organized nations whose monarchs, Philip the Fair and Edward I, began to tax church property heavily. Although Pope Boniface VIII in 1300 still seemed the indisputable sovereign of the world, he proved but a feeble antagonist against the French king whose envoy Nogaret, with the support of the Estates General, entered the papal palace and heaped such insults on the aged Boniface that he soon died in a frenzy of despair. Philip thereupon proved influential enough to have the Archbishop of Bordeaux chosen as Pope, under the title of Clement V. The seat of the papacy in 1305 was transferred to Avignon in France, where it remained until 1377. During this period of the "Babylonian Captivity," the suspicion of other nations that the Church had come wholly under the influence of France was intensified by various malpractices of the churchmen—notably the sale of benefices. The founding of the Franciscan and Dominican Orders whose members seemed, by contrast with the regular clergy, to practice far more truly the essential Christian virtues, only intensified the general distrust of the Church itself. Heresies multiplied. The crusades begun by Innocent III against the Waldensians and Albigensians in the thirteenth century had led to the establishment of the Inquisition. In the fourteenth century John Wycliffe began in England a more fundamenal opposition which, continued by John Huss in Bohemia in the early fifteenth, was to culminate in the sixteenth-century Lutheran revolt.

If one adds to this unhappy picture the pleasanter background of the emergence of an independent middle class out of former conditions of serfdom, and also the fermentation of new ideas and desires in worldly matters which the travels of the Crusaders had awakened, an Italy indifferent to religious composition seems easy to understand.

exists), the list of Italian composers is long, and the volume of their work is great. Jacopo da Bologna, Nicola da Perugia, and Maestro Piero from the second quarter of the fourteenth century; Francesco Landini (1325-1397) of Florence (where worked also Ghirardello), Donati, and Lorenzo, Niccolo da Perugia, and Guglielmoda Santo Spiritu from the middle of the century; and Zacherio, Antonello and Filippo da Caserta, and Bartolomeo da Bologna at the end, are some of the more conspicuous names. The towns of their residence show how extended was their activity.

Landini's fame—perhaps because he was a skilled organist as well as a composer—seems to have been even more romantically great than that of Machaut. There is a story of a vast, spellbound audience, assembled for an organ "recital" at St. Peters; and another tells how his hearers at the villa of the Alberti family in Florence were so charmed by his love songs that "their hearts almost burst from their bosoms." Although blind from about his ninth year, he learned several instruments besides the organ, and once won the laurel crown for his poems.

Spain and Germany were less conspicuous for their musical creations, but each was active. French pieces were abundantly copied in the Spanish manuscripts, and in what appear to be indigenous pieces, at least rudimentary suggestions of the use of binary rhythm, in the French fashion, appear. The French *chace*, or possibly the Italian *caccia*, seems to have been widely imitated. There is a curious *Dance of Death* (monodic) which was the first of many art works to be inspired by the dreadful plague which swept Europe from 1347. The King of Aragon, John I, was himself both a poet and a composer of *lais*, *virelais*, and *rondeaux*.

The German *Minnegesang*, still monodic, continued to flourish, though the social transition from feudal to bourgeois economy was in progress. And the Meistersinger, with their quaint rules, were beginning toward the end of the century to show how deeply planted in the German heart was the reverence for music. The typical form of the *Meistergesang*—three *Stollen* (stanzas) and an *Abgesang* (refrain)—was becoming crystallized. Two Minnesinger—"Frauenlob," whose real name was Heinrich von Meissen, and Witzlav von Rügen—carried the thirteenth-century tradition into the fourteenth. Another Minnesinger—Hermann, the Monk of Salzburg—made some rather ineffective attempts at polyphony; but by comparison with French and Italian composition, German work is not seen in a very favorable light.[8]

[8] For a more complete sketch of German music in this period, see Reese, *op cit.*, p. 376f.

New Fourteenth-Century Techniques

Musica ficta

We noted at the beginning of this chapter that the introduction of duple time was more provocative of change in musical structure than it at first seemed. Many results of that innovation have been seen in our study thus far; but certain details of technical procedure, affecting what may be called the growing vocabulary of music, remain to be described. Doubtless the most important is that process of chromatic alteration which, as its use increased, tended to change the basis of musical syntax from the modality which has underlain all Christian music thus far studied, to the tonality which is familiar today.

That a whole tone was divisible into two semitones had been obvious even to the Greeks. Both B flat and B natural—existent in the diatonic scheme of their Perfect Immutable System—were present also in the earliest Christian scales. But the Christian modes, distinguishable from each other only through the location of the final with reference to the two semitones of the natural scale-series, could permit the use of B flat only as an agent of transposition. Certain melodic progressions, however—those involving the tritone—were felt as harsh, and might be softened without effecting transposition by the use of B flat written with our present character (♭) and called either *round* B or *soft* B. B natural, indicated wherever necessary by ♮ (whence the present-day letter name of that note, *H* in German) was called *square* B or *hard* B. These alterations, made even in the monodic chants whether for transposition or for the avoidance of harshness, were thus described as occurring either *causa necessitatis* or *causa pulchritudinis* (for the sake of necessity or of beauty).

Harmony so greatly intensified the unpleasantness of the dissonant augmented fourth (F–B) or diminished fifth (B–F) that, as we have seen, the procedure of the Free Organum had to be invented to avoid it. But the ensuing evolution of Discant greatly increased the number of cases in which alteration, whether for need or for beauty, might occur. When the interval of the sixth was to expand stepwise to the octave, it was felt that the minor sixth must be made major; and the same was demanded when the third was expanded to the fifth (that is, E–c to D–d becomes E–c sharp to D–d; d–f to c–g becomes d–f sharp to c–g). Though these were called *necessary* alterations, it is likely that their pleasurable value was also considered. Certain melodic progressions also were felt to be made more beautiful by alteration. F between two G's, or C between two

D's would be sharped; and B between two A's would be flatted.[9] This practice became so conventional that the singers made the alterations both without written indication and without reference to the harmonic result that might accrue.

Music thus altered was called *musica ficta* (artificial) or *musica falsa* (false); but the theorists, recognizing necessity, often qualify the latter term by the phrase *non tamen falsa sed inusitata*—"not so much false as unusual." A great many passages in medieval music must therefore be provided with accidentals if our performances are to reproduce correctly the originals. Naturally there were—and are—differences of opinion as to where these may be placed, and certainty in our interpretations is thus impossible.

The total effect of the procedure, however, is not in doubt. If a B flat is at all persistently applied to a melody in the Lydian mode, the melody will appear to us as in F major. Similarly, an F sharp in the Mixolydian mode will produce G major, and C sharp in the Dorian will approximate to D minor. The "leading" of the seventh note of these scales cannot but emphasize the finality of the eighth note; the harmony of that final will thus appear solidified; and since the Lydian and the Mixolydian modes will have become, by this alteration, identical in pattern, the two will thus have to be grouped together as a type in which the final chord is major —that is, as *major* modes. Since there are but two consonant triads, the major and the minor, it is evident that these two types of mode must inevitably emerge as the only types.

That they did so emerge is a fact so obvious to us that we hardly see why it should have taken more than two centuries to complete the evolution. But that is because we have lost the feeling of the older progressions out of which our tonality grew. Valiant efforts have been made during the last thirty years to substitute a more liberal basis of tone relation for the tonality which underlies our classical musical literature. Since progress in this direction—at least with the general public—is notably slow, the parallel between the contemporary movement and the medieval may appear inexact; but it has at least a certain illustrative value.

Faux Bourdon

Another alteration in tonal syntax which was much furthered during the fourteenth century is that which effects the recognition of chords as homogeneous, self-existent, and self-intelligible tone clusters. While the

---

[9] *Una voce super la semper est canendum fa* (Always sing the note above *la* as if it were *fa*) was the familiar rule. This rule, applied in the soft hexachord, would produce E♭, as well as the B♭ above the *la* of the natural hexachord.

richness of harmony was a delight not to be foregone, whether or not discord resulted, it is evident that in all the polyphony up to the fourteenth century, the chief consideration of both composer and singer was the melody of the individual part. Concord was expected at certain rhythmic points, just as discord was allowed at others; but there was no perception either of dissonant tone groups as possessing any intrinsic sense, or of the consonances themselves as representing—unless at the final—any particular region within the whole area of the mode (as our chords represent the dominant or subdominant regions), or as having any obligation to proceed toward any other region. The consonances, like the dissonances, were merely incidents in the progression of the whole musical fabric, and were judged as appropriate or not accordingly as the individual voices pursued agreeable melodic lines. A "logic" of harmonic sequence—what was regarded until the end of the nineteenth century as harmonic "propriety"—was essential before a purposeful treatment of discord could exist. The discrimination of chords as chords had obviously to precede any perception of harmonic logic.

The gradual admission of the third as a tolerable concord, and its more frequent admission into combination with the interval of the fifth, has been evident up to the end of the thirteenth century; but the triad had not yet appeared as a recognized harmonic fact in the process of polyphony. It did so appear during the fourteenth century; yet the manner of its appearance was not as a triad but as the first inversion of a triad. How this came to be has been a much debated question, for the process appears to have arisen both in France and in England; the dates in both countries are somewhat uncertain; and the medieval theorists seem to have been unusually slow in describing the process. The origin of the device in France may have been due to English influence. It may also have been due to a most uncomfortable jolt delivered to the musicians in France by Pope John XXII, resident at Avignon and eighty-four years old, when in 1324 or 1325 he administered it. Finding the existing polyphony highly inappropriate to the service,[10] he not only denounced the practice, but proposed—and imposed—a remedy:

The music of the divine offices is now performed with semibreves and minims, and with these notes of small value every composition is tortured. They cut up their melodies with hockets; they degrade them with discants; they even fill them out with trebles [*tripla*] and *motetus* of the vulgar sort [made on secular songs] . . . Wherefore . . . we command that no one shall presume to attempt such things in the said Offices or in the canonical Hours, or in the solemn celebrations of the Mass . . . Yet it is not our intention to forbid the use of some concords, such as the eighth, fifth, and fourth, which enhance the beauty of the melody; and intervals of this sort may be sung

[10] See footnote, p. 87, for a justification of his opinion.

above the plain ecclesiastical melody, but in such a way that the integrity of the melody may remain unaffected. (Translation from Wooldridge, *Oxford History*.)

This announcement must have seemed to the church musicians a dismaying demolition of the elaborate harmonic structures which, even from the time of the *Musica Enchiriadis* had been reared "for the ornamentation of ecclesiastical song." How far the papal command was obeyed is uncertain, though it appears to have been in force at Notre Dame in 1408. Plausibly, but without supporting evidence, it has been argued that a device which appears in French music toward the end of the fourteenth century was invented as an evasion of the Pope's decree, and was called *faux bourdon* (false bass) in recognition of the evasion. The process is described (as an English practice) by Guilielmus Monachus, a late fifteenth-century theorist, as follows:

"The English have a fashion which is called *modus faulxbordon,* and which is sung by three voices, viz., soprano, tenor, and contratenor. The soprano begins at the unison [with the cantus], which unison is taken as the higher octave, but thereafter at the third below, which thirds are understood to represent the sixths above; and afterward it reverts to the unison, which is to say, the octave, as appears in the example. The contratenor takes as its first consonance the fifth above the tenor, and thereafter takes thirds above [the cantus] until the end, where it takes the fifth above."

This is the example:

Cantus noted as ◻. *Supranus* noted *below* the *Cantus,* but *sung* an octave higher. The C♯'s would be sung according to the rules of *musica ficta.*

This example is much later than the invention of the device, since Guilielmus Monachus wrote his treatise about 1480. It explains very clearly, however, the title *false bass,* and since there would have been, under normal circumstances, no need for any kind of falsity, it appears also to describe such a method of filling in the parallel fifths of strict organum as would have conformed tolerably to the papal decree. But there is no longer any doubt that a similar process of stringing chords in sequence was invented in England about the end of the thirteenth century. In the collection published as *Worcester Mediaeval Harmony* there are various settings of tropes for the Mass, motets, and other pieces, among which is a conductus [11] which displays a similar technique. A Cambridge manu-

[11] Partly transcribed in Grove, Volume II, page 209.

script of still earlier date (the end of the thirteenth century) has a motet, *In te Domine speravi,* in which the same device is conspicuous. This style, which gives no hint of subterfuge, is described by Manfred Bukofzer as "English Discant"; and this rational acceptance of two methods goes far to clear up a confusion which has long existed with reference to this important addition to harmonic resources.

A device similar to *faux bourdon,* but consisting merely of parallel thirds, was called *gymel* (probably from French *jumeaux*—"twins"). No subterfuge is implied in this name; the value of *faux bourdon* as a method of composition could indeed be but slight, since the hearer's interest would as soon be exhausted by long successions of chords of the sixth as by any other persistent formula. It had its value, however, as a contribution to improvised harmony of the kind which Tinctoris (a fifteenth-century theorist) calls *contrapunctus supra librum*—"counterpoint on the book," where the book contains only the plainsong melody. For it is evident that with a little practice, three singers might execute a harmonization in false bass as easily as the ninth-century singers could improvise organum. This was at any rate a favorite practice among fourteenth-century amateurs. It was expanded by the more adventurous, who "broke and flowered" the simple notes which strict observance of the process would produce. In this way, no doubt, the consciousness of melody as having a possible substratum of harmony *not* produced by the conjunction of melodic voices must have been considerably augmented. And chords were thus beginning to be recognized as chords.

The Hexachord System

Although it had its origin in the eleventh century, and was widely known in the thirteenth—after its practical value had caused it to be greatly expanded—description of the hexachord system has been delayed until this point, since that system had doubtless a certain contributory usefulness in clarifying the harmonic consciousness we are now studying. Guido of Arezzo was the originator of the idea. Being greatly troubled by the tedious task of teaching the liturgical melodies by rote, he noted that in a familiar hymn to John the Baptist:

UT que-ant lax - is RE - so-na - re fi - bris MI - ra ges-
to - rum FA - mu - li tu - o - rum. SOL - ve pol - lu - ti

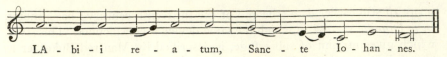

LA - bi - i   re - a - tum,   Sanc - te   Io - han - nes.

So that with liberated voices [literally, slackened strings] thy servants may sound forth the wonders of thy works, do thou, Saint John, absolve the sin of their polluted lips.

the first note in each successive line of the stanza fell on the six notes of the scale, C, D, E, F, G, A. The six syllables sung to these notes—*ut, re, mi, fa, sol, la*—he took as the names of the notes in that sequence, which was a sequence of whole steps save for the half step in the middle—TTSTT. The musical pattern and the note names being firmly established in the minds of his singers, he found that he had discovered a mnemonic by which, in a few days, his boys could learn what had hitherto taken them many weeks to master. He wrote of his discovery to a friend, and the system began forthwith to be spread abroad. Just how it underwent its final expansion is not recorded; but by the end of the thirteenth century the whole compass of vocal music (then two octaves and a sixth) had been organized by an ingenious overlapping of the fundamental six-note pattern or *hexachord*. Seven hexachords were required, and these were of three different types. The hexachord C–A which did not contain the note B was called *natural;* that which contained B natural (G–E) was called *hard;* and that which contained B flat (F–D) was called *soft*.

THE HEXACHORD SYSTEM

7. Hard

$\qquad\qquad\qquad\qquad\qquad\qquad\qquad\qquad$ g a b♮c′ d′ e′
$\qquad\qquad\qquad\qquad\qquad\qquad\qquad\qquad$ *ut re mifa sol la*

6. Soft

$\qquad\qquad\qquad\qquad\qquad\qquad\qquad\qquad$ f g abb c′ d′
$\qquad\qquad\qquad\qquad\qquad\qquad\qquad\qquad$ *ut re mifa sol la*

5. Natural

$\qquad\qquad\qquad\qquad\qquad\qquad$ c d ef g a
$\qquad\qquad\qquad\qquad\qquad\qquad$ *ut re mifa sol la*

4. Hard

$\qquad\qquad\qquad\qquad\qquad$ G A B♮c d e
$\qquad\qquad\qquad\qquad\qquad$ *ut re mifa sol la*

3. Soft

$\qquad\qquad\qquad\qquad$ F G AB♭ c d
$\qquad\qquad\qquad\qquad$ *ut re mifa sol la*

2. Natural

$\qquad\qquad$ C D EF G A
$\qquad\qquad$ *ut re mifa sol la*

1. Hard

Γ A′ B′C D E
ut re mifa sol la

The lowest note was called *gamma-ut*, whence our word *gamut*. The French use these syllable names (with the addition of *si* for B♮—said to have been de-·

rived from the initials of Sancte Iohannes) as the actual names of the notes C, D, E, etc. Elsewhere, and especially when the names are applied as in tonic *sol–fa* to the notes of any scale, the syllable *ut* is replaced by *do*. (Fétis believed this substitution to have been made by a famous Italian scholar named Doni.) The French *si*, likewise, has been replaced in the *movable do* nomenclature by *ti*, which allows *si* to signify a sharpened *sol*. The reader will perhaps remember that the hymn-tune from which the whole system was derived is an early Latin melody set to the Horatian *Ode to Phyllis*.

The singer "solmized" his melodies thus: Confronted with a melody of the compass D–f, and with B natural within it, he would name the D as *re* in the *natural* hexachord. But since the melody ascended beyond the A which was the limit of this hexachord, he would call G, not *sol* in that same group, but *ut* in the *hard* hexachord. (If the B had been B flat, he would have called F *ut* in the *soft* hexachord.) Similarly, c would be called *ut* in the higher *natural* hexachord, since the high f lies outside the compass of either the hard or the soft groups. This renaming was called *mutation*. The process will be clear from the above table.

A convenient graph of the whole system was devised by naming the joints and the tips of the fingers after the syllables. The general scheme is shown below. It was called the "Guidonian Hand." (How widely the hexachord system was known may be inferred from the fact that Walter Odington speaks of the chromatic notes produced by *musica ficta* as lying *extra manum*—outside the hand.)

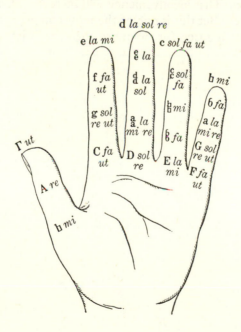

Note that the scale of two octaves and a sixth was "read" on the hand as beginning with the tip of the thumb (*Gamma ut*). A and B♮ (re and mi in the "hard" hexachord) are associated with the two joints of the thumb. The scale then continues by moving to the roots of the four fingers, locating C, D, E, and F. G is then found at the next joint of the little finger. The next octave (represented by small letters) continues to the tip of the little finger, and then, by way of the tips of the other fingers, reaches g (*sol, re, ut*) at the second joint of the first finger. (Note that "round b," *fa*, and "square b," *mi*, are both represented by the tip of the little finger.) This completes the second octave. The remaining, higher notes are represented by doubled small letters, the highest note (ee, *la*) being placed on the ball of the "big" finger.

The practical usefulness of the hexachord system for sight singing is obvious. It has, indeed, little other practical value, nor any great significance for musical theory. But it may have contributed somewhat to the growth of the tonal, as opposed to the modal, idea; for the three notes, C, G, and F, which are the initial notes of the three hexachords, are also the tonic, dominant, and subdominant of our scale, and their conspicuousness in the singers' minds may have enhanced their valuation as the foundation notes of the key.

The reader has doubtless been inconvenienced by the lack of any but the merest hints of the notation in which the music he has been studying was written down. That inconvenience will be removed, as far as possible, in the next chapter. But this is one of the most complex problems in musicology, and there is space for no more than the briefest outline of the tangled tale.

CHAPTER VIII

The Development of Musical Notation

I. The Notation of Pitch

I MAGINE a primitive singer into whose mind a melody has come un-bidden—a melody that will surely be lost unless he can somehow write it down. What conceivable characters can symbolize the fragile substance of his thought? The alphabet (if he has one) will be of no service, for alphabetic letters indicate definable facts of utterance—perceptibly different efforts of tongue or lips or palate. But the tones of melody are all produced by the same kind of effort—a varied tension which even the most skillful singer does not measure as a muscular effort. Nor does he remember the detail of his effort as we do—or at least may—with speech, but only repeats it by remembering the result. Even Isidore of Seville, who was not exactly a primitive singer, remarked that unless tones are preserved in the memory they will perish, for they cannot be written down (*quia scribi non possunt*).

Instruments, however, provide an empirical measure of tonal interval; and by naming the strings of his lyre or the holes in his flute, our primitive musician could acquire at least the rudiment of a notation for his melody. This might well be an alphabetic notation, if it had to symbolize merely the individual notes of a scale or melody. It sufficed for the Greeks, as we have seen; for their music was monodic, and its rhythm was almost invariably provided by the verse.

Our notation of harmonic music is obviously a more difficult matter. Our symbols must indicate not only the precise pitch but also the precise relative time-value of many simultaneous tones; and it is indispensable that both pitch and time be indicated by the same symbol. Our notation gives, in addition, a fairly graphic picture both of a whole melodic curve and of the character—incisive, ponderous, flowing, or whatever—of the whole musical substance. Such a notation cannot but be the product of a long history of feature added to feature, as the complexity of musical thought increased. We shall try to describe this accumulation of detail.

CHIRONOMY

The Greek notation, whether for instruments or voices, was essentially alphabetic, even though two different sets of symbols were used. Close association of vocal with instrumental music made this possible. But for centuries the music of the Christian Church was wholly without instrumental accompaniment. The only instrumental aid to their singing was the monochord, which merely demonstrated the dimensions of intervals, but did not support the song. The intervals, then, were what the singers learned; and these were named according to their audible dimension—semitone, tone, ditone, and so on. Boethius did use—perhaps for the first time—alphabetic names for notes; but these were merely the equivalents of numbers—at best, *note names*, not *tone signs*. They did not even imply the essential ideas of tone, ditone, and such. Hence, the singers made no attempt to read music from such signs, but learned their songs by rote. The choir director doubtless sang and stamped and made uncomplimentary remarks, as he often does today, to enforce his meaning. But he found that the most useful gesture was a movement of his hand that would represent the upward and downward course of the melody. This art of direction by hand movement was (and still is) called *chironomy* (from the Greek *cheir*, hand, and *nomos*, law or regulation). Such gestures had long been used, not for musical intervals, but to suggest the proper inflections of the voice in liturgical reading, and the translation to musical symbolism was an obvious possibility.

The first writing-down of Christian music was a representation of these movements. The three accents, acute (′), grave (`), and circumflex (^), which had been invented by Greek grammarians in the second century B.C. to indicate the proper pitch accentuation of Greek words, apparently retained enough of their original pitch-meaning to be adopted as the equivalents of the gestures. The earliest manuscripts which exhibit such notation are fragments from the eighth century, but many complete pieces date from the ninth. By that time, a considerable variety of characters had been devised, but they were all derived from the original accent signs. There is some evidence that a written notation existed earlier than the eighth century (the codification of the Gregorian chant, reported as having been made at the end of the fifth, hardly seems possible without some system of notation) but no trace of it has remained. The Byzantine church developed a notation from the same symbols, earlier than that of the Western church; and this system, related to the eight modes of the *octo-echos*, was somewhat more definite in pitch-meaning than the Western. The study of this system is, however, beyond our scope.

Collectively, these signs were called *neumes* (from the Greek *neûma*, a nod or command). They were written above the words, one or more characters to a syllable, but with no relation of space corresponding to either pitch or rhythm. Melismas were indicated by various conjunctures of the three simple characters derived from the accents. The following table will show the simple characters and their principal derivative combinations:

Signs for { 1. Virga or virgula ′ (acute accent) = ♩, used for a higher tone
a single { 2. Virga jacens (lying) —, = ♩, used for a lower or sustained tone
tone { 3. Punctum · (grave accent) = ♪, used for a low, short note.

(The Virga and the Virga jacens at length become indistinguishable, and when notation becomes definitely rhythmic evolve into the Longa. The Punctum becomes the Breve.)

Signs { 4. Pes or Podatus ✓ ✓ ∕ = ♪♩, ♩♩, ♪♩
for two {
tones { 5. Flexa, or Clinis, or Clivis ⌒ ⋀ = ♩ ♪

{ 6. Torculus ⋀ ∫ = ♪♩ ♪, ♩ ♩ ♩
Signs { 7. Flexa resupina or porrectus N = ♩ ♪ ♩
for three {
tones { 8. Climacus ⁄· ⁄= = ♩ ♫♩, ♩ ♩ ♩
{ 9. Scandicus ∕ ⁄ = ♫♩, ♩ ♩ ♩

It is fairly obvious that the *pes* is a combination of the grave with the acute accent; that the *clivis* (like the circumflex from which it came) is acute + grave; and that the neumes of three notes are similarly constructed. There is, indeed, a general hint of pitch relation; but there is no clear implication of distance, the intervals being anything from a minor second to a sixth. Obviously, such notation could not convey melodic ideas with any exactness. It served only as a reminder of what had already been learned by heart. Although its indefiniteness was complained of by writers as far apart as Hucbald in the ninth century and John Cotton in the early twelfth, it was still of great value. Many melodies exist in both this and the later *diastematic* notation (which measures the intervals exactly), and in the light of this later precision the older neumes can be seen to have represented the same thought; but they cannot be read without such aid. It is possible that there existed clues to their meaning which cannot now be found, for Peter Wagner observes that the neumatic notation persisted for many years even in localities where the diastematic notation was already practiced. Different styles of handwriting, both early and late, of course greatly complicate the problem of the interpreter.

The first step toward a more precise measurement of intervals was the spacing of the neumes at elevations generally proportional to the distances in pitch of the notes which they represented. These "heighted" neumes can be interpreted with some accuracy, but not with certainty. Indeed, nothing less than the precision that belongs to alphabetic letters could really suffice. And it is apparent from the fact that our present note symbols have alphabetic names that a kind of assimilation of the alphabetic idea to that of the diastematic representation of interval-distances was the ultimate goal of all the efforts we are describing. The alphabetic names for the notes which to Boethius were only a theoretical convenience, do at length appear in a more practical application. An anonymous writer[1] uses for the notes of the Greek Perfect System the Roman alphabet from A to S; and another, a certain Oddo[2] uses, to indicate the longer scale written below, the letters which accompany the notes:

Γ A B C D E F G a ♭ ♮   c d e f g α β ♮ κ δ

(The B in the lowest octave is apparently B natural. The initial gamma, and the round and square B's in the higher octaves have already been explained. Capital, small, and Greek letters signify clearly the different octaves in which the notes lie.)

A practical application of the alphabetic idea is seen in the following:

A CD F GD C FED E CD
Dic nobis Maria, quid vidisti in via.

It can be interpreted precisely as to pitch, but it is less graphic than the heighted neumes, and of course tells nothing about the rhythm. The following is more graphic, but equally unrhythmic, and is very wasteful of space:

```
                              F
          E    E E       E    E
       D        D D        D D
                    C    C
```

Qui tol-   -lis pec-ca-ta

The assimilation of alphabetic to graphic representation, however, is here clearly beginning.

A so-called *Daseia* notation in which a tetrachord TST (instead of

[1] Gerbert, *Scriptores*, I, 330.
[2] *Ibid.*, 265.

the octave) is the unit, but within which the symbols have alphabetic accuracy, was used by the writer of the *Musica Enchiriadis* for his examples of organum. The symbols are combinations of the Greek "rough breathing" sign, ⊦ (the equivalent of our aspirate, *h*) in combination with the letters C or S which, attached to the stem of the breathing sign, give what appears to our eyes as a variety of F's. Just as the Greeks indicated the chromatic and enharmonic genera in their scales by placing the letters horizontally or inverting them, the four primary characters in this system are reverted, inverted, or both, to represent lower or higher repetitions of the original tetrachord, which was the second in the given order: D EF G. The four notes in the respective tetrachords were called *graves*, *finales*, and so on, and those in the primary tetrachord were named *Finales* because they are the finals of the four authentic Gregorian modes:

Graves	Finales	Superiores	Excellentes

𝄞 𝄢 𝄡 𝄠   𝄢 𝄢 𝄡 𝄠   𝄢 𝄢 𝄡 𝄠   𝄢 𝄢 𝄡 𝄠

Γ A B♭ C	D E F G	A B C D	E F♯ G A

This is the scale mentioned before on page 61.

The lines and spaces of our modern staff were actually used, *but without anything of their present meaning*, by the same writer. In the spaces between the lines, which were essentially six in number, though several groups of six were juxtaposed, he placed the letters *t, t, s, t, t,* to indicate the interval-distances between the notes. There is here a curious, but evidently unperceived, anticipation of Guido's hexachord, notable also in that it is used, in the *Enchiriadis*, along with the *daseia* notation just described. (*Daseia* is the Greek word for *rough*—hence, the "rough breathing.") For the tetrachord pattern, primarily designated by the four *daseia* symbols (TST) is sometimes altered through the placing of the half step in the hexachord elsewhere than between the second and third symbols. In this system, the notes are indicated by the syllables of the words to be sung, placed in the appropriate spaces. The sense of the system is sufficiently illustrated by the following:

t		-ita li-	in quo		lus	
t	Ec-	isra-		-o-	no-	
s	ce	e-		do-	-on	
t	vere				e-	
t					-est	

which means:

Ec - ce   ve - re   is - ra - e - li - ta,   in quo - do - lus non est.

Although the lines, in this system, had no pitch-meaning, the letters signifying interval spaces were precise and clear. Larger intervals than the tone (whose names were familiar to the singers through their instruction according to the monochord) might be similarly designated. The first musician to make this enlargement was Hermannus Contractus (The Lame), a monk of Reichenau, in the eleventh century. All the intervals from the unison to the major sixth were designated by the following letters:

e (equaliter)—the unison
s (semitonium)—the half step
t (tonus)—the whole step
ts (tonus et semitonium)—the minor third
tt (ditonus)—the major third
d (diatessaron)—the perfect fourth
Δ (diapente)—the perfect fifth
Δs (diapente et semitonium)—the minor sixth
Δt (diapente et tonus)—the major sixth

and the example below will show how they were applied to the generally familiar neumes:

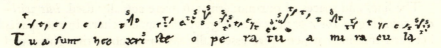

The neumes are themselves pretty carefully heighted, but their meaning is rendered unmistakable by the addition of the *litterae significativae* (signifying letters), as they were called. Indeed, taking note of one deviation from the table of letters above (the use of the long ſ for the semitone, and the round s for the *semiditonus* or minor third) we may even attempt a translation of the first phrase in this example. The neumes themselves are: a *virga*, a *pes*, and another *virga* sung to *Tua;* two more *virgae* for *sunt hec;* a *torculus* for *Chri-* and a *scandicus* for *ste.* The t shows that the *pes* covers a whole step (of course, upward); the following *virga* is shown by the t, and by its lower position, to be a whole step downward; the e's between the *virgae* following signify "no change in pitch"; the *torculus* begins a tone higher (t), its second note is a minor third above the first (s), and the last note a perfect fourth below the preceding (D = the d of the table). The *scandicus*, as is indicated by the low s, begins a minor third below the end of the *torculus;* it proceeds by a semitone (ſ) and then by a tone (t) to its highest note. Now, if we assume that the melody involved no accidentals, it will prove inevitably to begin on G; for no other starting tone will place the half step rightly without an accidental. (If we begin on C, the half step in the *scandicus* would have to follow an A, and this could be done only by flatting the B.) The whole line transcribed reads:

Tu - a sunt hec Chri - ste o - pe - ra

tu - - a mi - ra - cu - la

Thine, O Christ, are these thy miraculous works.

The slurs indicate the compound neumes of the original.

Exact though it is, this notation makes laborious reading. Alphabetic names would be simpler, if they could be attached to the neumes—as the reader will see from the following, which he will have little difficulty in transcribing for himself. This is from a manuscript of Montpellier, dating from the eleventh century:

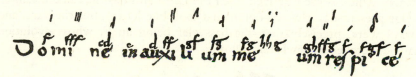

The text, *Domine in auxilium meum respice*, means "Lord, see thou to my assistance."

Here, although there is equal exactness, the neumes are a mere auxiliary to the letter names, and seem almost superfluous. There is still, in spite of the close conjunction, no real assimilation between the two, though the heightening of the neumes is an additional hint of the letter meanings. Apparently the value of heightening is not yet fully perceived.

More precision in this measurement was gained by drawing a line, with the uninked stylus, across the page in the space for the notes, and measuring their distance with the eye in relation to this not wholly imaginary line. (A similar scratch served for the alignment of the text.) To ink in the line would be to give the reader the same basis of measurement as that which the scribe had used; and this was sometimes done, even in the tenth century. To color the line, and assume that all neumes on that line had the pitch assigned to that color, was to give an alphabetic name first to the line, and secondly to the note on that line; and this is really the final imaginative step in the devising of our present system. The following steps are by comparison merely mechanical.

To determine the pitch of the first neume of a *new* line of music was, particularly before the invention of the staff, something of a problem. It was solved by writing, at the end of the completed line, a tiny character called a *custos* (guide), which stood, in relation to the last neume, in the position of the first neume of the new line. When lines and spaces came into use, it of course stood on the line or space to be occupied by the first note of the next line of music. The *custos* is still used in the notation of Gregorian chant, and will be found in our examples. A device similar in purpose is often seen in eighteenth-century books—the printing of the first word of a left-hand page below the last line of the preceding right-hand page—that is, the page that is about to be turned.

Guido of Arezzo, who was evidently a very practical musician, seems to have used more lines and to have colored them more meaningfully than his contemporaries. In his *Antiphonary* (1027) he also used a more practical method of naming the lines. Instead of coloring the F line red, and the C line yellow or green, he left the lines black and put the letters F or C (sometimes both) on the appropriate one. These "key letters" were called *claves* (keys); and our word *clef* is directly adopted from the French, which is itself derived from the Latin and has the same meaning.

Our present-day clefs do not at first look like letters, but they are, and always were, precisely that—the bass clef being an F, whose evolution may be sketched somewhat as follows:

The treble clef is similarly an ornamental G, which took these and other recognizable forms on its way to the present character:

Nowadays, these two clefs always stand on their one appropriate line—the F clef on the fourth line, the G clef on the second. This was not always so. Originally they might stand on any line, and there was indeed no fixed number of lines, the staff containing as many as were needful for the melody. Four, since they can exhibit the compass of a ninth without leger lines, were enough for almost any Gregorian chant; and that number is still used in printing that music. We still employ the C clef, and it is also still movable. It *may* stand on any line, but only in very old music will it be found elsewhere than on the first, third, or fourth lines of the five-line staff. On the first line it is called the soprano clef. (It was used for that voice in choral music until about 1850.) On the middle line, it is called the alto clef, and is in everyday use in music for the viola. On the fourth line, it is called the tenor clef, and is used for the celli, the bassoons, and the trombones in their higher registers. The following notes, it will be seen, are all middle C's:

Treble   Alto   Tenor   Soprano   Bass

II. THE NOTATION OF RHYTHM

The invention of the staff created a new environment for the neumes —one to which their form had gradually to be adapted. The *virga*, which had originally been written with an upward stroke of the pen—a mere light line—had come with the heightening of the neumes to be written downward, with the top perceptibly heavier than the bottom. To fit on to the staff, the top was still further enlarged—into a square, black note-head, with a stem or *cauda* descending from the right side: ◥. In measured music, this character was called the *longa*. In a similar way, the *virga jacens* and the *punctum* merged in a single character—the same note-head without the stem (■)—which was called the *brevis*. These two characters sufficed for the notation of music in the six rhythmic modes, but were added to, as polyphony developed.[3]

[3] The question as to the implied rhythmic significance of the neumes from which the long and the breve were derived has interest in itself, and bears pointedly on the vexed question of rhythm in the Gregorian chant. The substitution of accent for quantity, which was complete in common Latin speech by the end of the fourth century, reduced the originally long syllables to the same time-value as the short, as is the case in our English pronunciation. (This last word is a sufficient example.) It is contended by the Solemnes school that the Greek accents, from which the neumes were derived, had thus no reason for representing different time-values, and that since the *virga jacens* (theoretically, at least, a long) and the *punctum* merged, the *punctum* itself became the equivalent of a long, at least in that kind of music which was set to Latin prose, the form of the liturgical texts. It is in part on this assumption that the Solemnes school believes the equal valuation of all the neumes to have been the convention, not merely of the later centuries of the chant, but of the very earliest.

It appears probable, however, not that the *punctum* was assimilated to the *virga jacens*, but the *virga jacens* (which has something of the same form) to the *punctum*. The differentiation between long and breve is directly related by Walter Odington (Coussemaker, *Script.* I, 235) to the *virga* and *punctum*: "That note is called a long

The evolution of modal rhythm, which provided an exclusively triple beat for the learned polyphony of the twelfth and thirteenth centuries, has not been traced. That the system was completed in a single stroke is unthinkable. The curious distortion of the dactylic and anapaestic meters, represented in the table of rhythmic modes, would hardly have occurred unless some prior scheme of triple time had existed to which, as polyphony became more complex, these measures had to be adapted. The trochee and the iambus (Modes I and II), triple rhythmed by nature, are doubtless the most "natural" meters, and may well have been the first to appear. To represent them, the long and the breve with two beats and one, respectively, are clearly adequate. A remark of Walter Odington, near the passage quoted in the preceding footnote, seems to refer to the period of evolution. "Among the older organists," he says, "the long was valued at two beats, and the breve at one." And the *Discantus positio vulgaris*, 1230-1240 (the period to which Odington may refer), calls the long of three beats *ultra mensuram* (outside the measure) which, for that note, seems then to have been two beats.

Since rhythm was conceived in terms of poetic meters, the square notes designed for the staff were first conceived, not as representing precise mathematical time-lengths, but as representing—for the most part in combinations called *ligatures*—the familiar rhythmic patterns of the modes. The deciphering of notations thus conceived (which were often ambiguous) is a process too complex for study here. We shall pass over the stage of "modal" notation, accordingly, and describe only the main features of the truly "mensural" notation which was perfected toward the end of the thirteenth century, and was set forth with great clarity by Franco of Cologne.

The whole scheme must be understood as devised exclusively for the representation of triple time. Groups of three beats were invariably to be looked for, whatever the complex of notes confronting the reader. Such a group was called a *perfection*. The notes involved, at the end of the thirteenth century, were the long and breve already described, together with the *semibreve* (♦), now frequently used, and the *maxima* or *duplex longa* (■▬), which was becoming rare. The reader interpreted his text according to the following rules:

I. A long, followed by another long or its equivalent, contains three beats or *tempora* (times), and is therefore called *longa perfecta*.

---

which was formerly called a *virga;* that is called a breve which was formerly the *punctum.*" This may be, to be sure, merely the history of the form of the notes, and not the history of their value. But it is hard to see why so elaborate a distinction of form should have been so meticulously maintained, if it had been from the beginning no more than a distinction of form.

II. A breve, following or preceding a long (in case it is to be grouped with the long) has a primary value of one beat (*unum tempus*). Such a breve was called *brevis recta* ("proper" breve). But its combination with the long reduced the value of the long to two beats, since these two notes together made up one perfection. Therefore,

III. A long followed (or preceded) by a single breve, or its equivalent, when that breve is to be subtracted from the long, has the value of only two beats, and is called *longa imperfecta*. Its shape differed not at all from that of the *longa perfecta;* its difference was determinable only from its position in relation to other notes.

These two characters will thus suffice to represent rhythmic Modes I and II: ♩ ◾ ♩ ◾ being the equivalent, in modern notes, of ♩ ♪ | ♩ ♪ |, and ◾ ♩· ◾ ♩ of ♪ ♩ | ♪ ♩· But for the latter, to prevent the breve following the first long from being combined with that note, the dot or *punctum divisionis* was employed.

But Modes III and IV, with their peculiar distortion of the weak syllables of the dactyl and anapaest, could not be represented by these means without confusion. The dactyl's six beats were grouped as $3 + 1 + 2$. The notation ♩ ◾ ♩, interpreted according to the rules just given, would mean ♩ ♩ ♩., which is neither dactyl nor anapaest, nor any other mode. Even with the point of division after the first long, which would indeed give the proper time-division, there would be uncertainty; for the first long would then appear to be isolated, and the breve-long to represent Mode II. A solution, at first sight confusing, but really wholly rational, was found by giving the breve a second or supplementary valuation, as has been done with the long. The rule may be given first, and its explanation afterward:

IV. Two breves between two longs make up a full perfection, and are to be valued as $1 + 2$—*unless* the point of division is placed between them, in which case, each breve is grouped with its adjacent long, as in Rule III. The second breve, having the value of two beats, is called *brevis altera*. As with the imperfect long, it differs not at all in shape from the other breve, and its value is determined wholly by position.

Two dactyls with the time-value of ♩· ♪ ♪ | ♩· ♪ ♪ | would thus be represented by ♩ ◾ ◾ ♩ ◾ ◾; and there is this advantage—that the general rhythmic form of the dactyl is unmistakable. The same would be true of the anapaest, which need not be illustrated. A point of division, placed between the first two breves, would of course change the rhythmic meaning of the first four notes to ♩ ♪ | ♪ ♪ |.

V. Semibreves (which appear only as rhythmed melody becomes more

florid) may be grouped in either twos or threes, either group being equal
to one brevis recta, ■.

This is a grouping so similar to that of the breve as to require no
explanation. The semibreve which was the first of two, and which equaled
one-third of the breve, was called *lesser* (*semibrevis minor*). The second,
which equaled two-thirds of the breve, was called *greater* (*semibrevis
major*).

Pauses, which had indefinite value in the notation of the Gregorian
chant, were now measured and were represented by vertical lines drawn
across the staff. A pause of three beats covered three spaces, and others
were proportionately shorter.

When two or more notes were sung to a single syllable, the notes were
conjoined into groups called *ligatures*. These were derived, like the simple notes, from the old neumatic forms. The resemblance may be seen
in the table below.

Ligatures of two notes	Pes	♩♩!	▪	♪♩
	Clivis	⌐∧	▪	♩♪
Ligatures of three notes	Torculus	∧♪	▪	♪♩♩.
	Porrectus	N	◄	ρ♩ρ·
	Climacus	⌐. /=	▪	ρρρ·
	Scandicus	!	♪	ρρⱼ

A ligature was said to be *ascending* if its second note was higher than
the first; *descending* if the second note was lower than the first. The
length of the involved notes depended on this distinction. *Ascending*
ligatures *without a stem* attached to the first note, and *descending* ligatures *with a descending stem* so attached (at the left), were said to be
cum proprietate (with propriety); in such ligatures the first note was
always a breve. On the other hand, ascending ligatures *with* a descending
stem at the left of the first note, and descending ligatures *without* a stem,
were said to be "without propriety" (*sine proprietate*); in such ligatures
the first note was a long.

The length of the last note of the ligature was similarly determined, but
always by its position, not by means of a stem. If the last note was lower
than the preceding note, or was placed perpendicularly above it, the ligature was said to be *cum perfectione* (with perfection), and the last note
was a long. If the ligature consisted of an oblique bar (which in itself
always represented two notes only—those named by the line or space on
which the bar began and ended), or if a higher note at the end was

written at the right of the preceding note (instead of directly above it), the ligature was "without perfection," and its last note was a breve.

All the intervening notes between the first and last were breves, unless the semibreve also appeared. Whatever their number (at most, three, in a single ligature of six notes), semibreves always appeared at the beginning of the ligature. Their appearance was signified by an *ascending* stem at the left of the first note of the ligature; and this figure was then said to be "with opposite propriety." A few examples will sufficiently illustrate the various types of ligature:

Various combinations of propriety and perfection in the single ligature are shown by the small letters beneath the ligatures. The *c* stands for *cum* (with); the *s* stands for *sine* (without); the *o* stands for opposite. The first of the two letters indicates the "propriety"—the length of the first note of the ligature; the second indicates the "perfection"—the length of the second note.

When at last duple time was recognized and employed, as it began to be when the foregoing system was reaching its final exactness, the confusion it entailed was great. Various devices were invented—particularly, many different ways of using red and black ink--to indicate whether a given note was divisible into two or three of the next smaller denomination. This complexity is beyond our space to describe. We shall indicate only the main features of the system which survived and brought about our present system.

To the former complement of notes a still shorter note was soon added —the *minima* or "least" note, ♦. This, however, proved to be by no means the "least," for its modern counterpart is the half note, which in England is still called the *minim*. Signs rather than colors were at length devised to indicate how the longer notes were to be divided. To each of the three longer notes still current (the *duplex longa* was now obsolete), a kind of time signature was devoted. If the long was divided into three breves, the fact was indicated by the sign [Ⅲ]; if into two, by [Ⅱ]. These two divisions were called *mode perfect* and *mode imperfect*, respectively. If the breve was divided into three semibreves, the time signature was a complete circle: ◯; if into two, the signature was a broken circle: ◖ ; and these two conditions were called *time perfect* and *imperfect*, respectively. Finally, if the semibreve was divided into three minims, three dots were placed within the complete or broken circle which designated the time; if it was divided into two, two dots were used, or sometimes a vertical line. This condition was called *prolation*, and it was qualified as either *major* or *perfect* if the division was into three, and as *minor* or *imperfect* if the division was into two.

This system was cumbrous by comparison with our own, but it was capable of indicating with equal exactness any of our normal rhythms. The divisions of time and prolation were by far the most frequently used, and we shall confine our illustrations to those. Let us take first *time perfect* with *prolation imperfect*, indicated by ⊘ or ⊙. The breve will be divided into

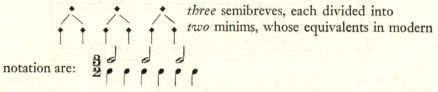

three semibreves, each divided into *two* minims, whose equivalents in modern notation are:

With *time imperfect, prolation perfect*, indicated by ⊙, the breve will be divided into

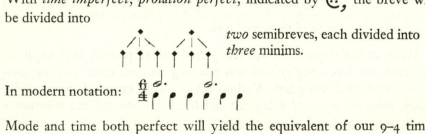

two semibreves, each divided into *three* minims.

In modern notation:

Mode and time both perfect will yield the equivalent of our 9–4 time; Mode and time imperfect will yield the equivalent of 2–2 or 4–4 time.

The square forms of the notes, with breve, semibreve, and minim black, survived into the fifteenth century, when for these notes the open or "white" were substituted, and all the note-heads for the smaller values became round, as we know them. The characters in the white notation, and their modern equivalents are as follows:

Brevis ▢   Semibrevis ◇   Minima ◊   Semiminima ⸙   Fusa ⸙   Semifusa ⸙

Breve |Ⅱ| Semibreve ◦   Minim ♩   Crotchet ♩   Quaver ♪   Semiquaver ♬

In our modern notation we have dispensed with the whole principle of mode, time, and prolation perfect—the division of a longer note into three shorter ones. Nevertheless, we have not lost that division. If we wish to make a note *perfect* we merely lengthen it by one-half its *imperfect* value by placing a dot after it. This single dot had been used, instead of the three dots, to indicate *prolation perfect*, so that the newer use was already prepared for. The dot, however, had many other meanings. In addition to that of a *punctum divisionis*, which has already been described, it was used to signify *alteration* (by doubling) of the value of certain notes; *imperfection*, where the ruling principle was that of perfection; *syncopation*, over an extended series; and also *augmentation*.

We have seen that graphic representation of a melodic idea was continually striven for in the whole course of evolving notation. This was chiefly for the advantage of the singers. For instruments, another kind of graph was desirable—one which would represent what to do with the hands in order to produce the notes desired. For keyboard instruments such as the cembalo or organ, and for fretted stringed instruments such as the lute, many such graphs were devised. Though they appear unwieldy to our eyes, these *tablatures*—as they were called—were almost universally used for the indication of instrumental music until the fifteenth century, and sometimes far beyond. Indeed, they are not yet obsolete. The little diagrams for the fingers of the players of popular music, printed above the notes, are simple tablatures.

CHAPTER IX

The Fifteenth Century

THE *Ars nova* proved more fertile in musical possibilities than Philippe de Vitry or even any of the later composers of the fourteenth century had imagined. In spite of the narrow range within which the modal rhythm of the thirteenth century had confined it, the melody of that era had possessed a healthy impetuosity which was temporarily lost in the more elaborately calculated rhythms and harmonies of the fourteenth century; but this loss was more than made up by the breadth and solidity of the new rhythmic structures. Isorhythmy seems to us a bare and mechanical process of composition; but whether or not an ordinary hearer perceived the similarity of the isorhythmic sections, that method did make for a solidity of structure hitherto unknown. Only by some such means could music attain to independence of either the sense or the rhythm of words, or to any real coherence in extended forms.

Remarkable as they were, the achievements of the fourteenth century still made but a distant approach to that vividness of expression, through the tonal substance itself, which is for us the highest attribute of music. Competency in expression could be gained only by amalgamating something like the old impetuosity and freedom of melody with a structural design more closely knit and more appropriate to its expressive purpose than mere isorhythmy could provide. The achievements of the fifteenth century in this direction were amazing.

The problem of the composers was the more complex in that the world that their compositions had to reflect was itself rapidly expanding. Although it was not until the end of the century that the "new" world was discovered, the old world was itself emerging—mostly by the painful process of war—from its older traditions. Economic stability was being won by men whose fathers had hardly hoped for freedom from degrading feudal obligations; education was becoming available to the children of those who were economically independent; and even monarchs were beginning to think of the welfare of their subjects as a kind of obligation imposed upon them by the divine power from which they supposed the title to their thrones to be derived. However slight their real regard for their subjects, their patronage of the arts was a contribution to the widening interest of living; and the attempts of several rulers to win regard as artists is a sign of more than a merely political recognition of the value of the arts.

It is needful to remember something of the tangled political history of the period if we are to understand the impulses which are reflected in the music. The quarrels of the Italian city-states, and their background—the animosity between the Guelphs and the Ghibellines—are so confused that a brief summary of their story is impossible. But the center of musical activity in the fifteenth century not unnaturally remained in the north of Europe where the *Ars nova* seems to have originated; and while the political conditions there were by no means simple, it is possible to grasp in a rapid glance the outline which is essential to our understanding of the musical achievements.

England and Burgundy in the first half of the century, and the Netherlands in the second, were the musically fertile regions. Toward the end of the fourteenth century, the dukedom of Burgundy (which hitherto had alternated between complete independence as an actual kingdom, and almost complete dependence on the French monarchy) rose to great prominence and power. Philip the Bold, who inherited the duchy in 1363, added rapidly to his dominions and was soon strong enough to threaten even the throne of France. This threat became the more possible because the Hundred Years' War between England and France, which began in 1337, had at first gone very favorably for the English. The Battles of Crécy (1346) and Poitiers (1356) gave England actual sovereignty over about a third of the territory of France. But the French king, Charles V, soon won it back, and England, which had lost half its population in the terrible outbreak of the bubonic plague which devastated Europe in 1348–49, was temporarily too exhausted to attempt its recovery. Charles VI, who came to the French throne in 1380, soon lost his mind, and the government fell into the hands of the nobles. The dukes of Burgundy and Orléans were the chief contenders.

Philip's son, John the Fearless, in 1407 caused the assassination of Louis of Orléans, the King's brother. Henry V of England, taking advantage of this strife, invaded France in 1415, won the amazing victory of Agincourt, conquered Normandy, and marched on Paris. In 1419, John of Burgundy, kneeling to kiss the hand of the Dauphin (Charles VII, as yet uncrowned), was murdered in cold blood, and his successor, Philip the Good, made common cause with the English, who once more laid claim to the throne of France. Henry V and the mad Charles VI both died in 1422. Henry VI was then but nine months old, so that the English dominions in France were governed by the Duke of Bedford, the new king's uncle. The Dauphin, still uncrowned, was too weak and indifferent to resist the English claims to the French throne which Henry V had again put forth, and which were recognized by the Treaty of Troyes in 1420.

But Joan of Arc, perhaps the most indisputably miraculous personage in history, aroused the conscience of the French, and achieved the coronation of Charles VII in 1429. Delivered to the English by the Duke of Burgundy, she was burned as a witch; but the French nation had been reborn. Philip the Good renounced his alliance with the English, joined forces with Charles VII, acquired the Netherlands, and thus became one of the most powerful rulers in Europe. The Duke of Bedford died in 1435; and thereafter the English cause was lost. By 1453 she had ceded every vestige of French territory save Calais, and had given up her claim to the French throne.

The distressful condition of the Church, which was notorious enough during the Babylonian Captivity, was intensified by the Great Schism, which began after the return of Pope Gregory XI from Avignon to Rome in 1377. Two Popes were elected in 1378—Urban VI and Clement VII—and Christendom was in doubt as to who was its true spiritual head. A general council at Pisa in 1409, instead of settling the difficulty, increased it by electing a third Pope. The Council of Constance, 1414 to 1417, finally deposed all three claimants and elected Martin V who was generally recognized; but the Schism had proved a strong provocation to heresy, and the burning of John Huss in 1415 was but the beginning of the Lutheran revolt of a century later.

Even this hasty sketch will serve to interpret some of the peculiarities as well as the more significant characteristics of the music of the fifteenth century, to which we may now turn. The incessant warfare we have just noted affected the life of the ordinary man far less than the "total" warfare of our own day, and was a less insuperable obstacle for the creators of music than we should at first infer. Music, indeed, was often of high interest to warlike princes. Henry V of England, the Duke of Bedford, and Philip the Good of Burgundy maintained "chapels"—companies of music-makers, headed by composers of note—and we know that Henry V, three years after the Battle of Agincourt, summoned his chapel to join him in France for the celebration of Christmas. Musical establishments more directly patterned after the papal chapel were similarly fostered in the great cathedrals. Intercourse was free among these institutions, and it is natural to find traditions communicated and methods of composition more rapidly perfected than had before been possible. We shall first study the work of the composers who were members of the Burgundian chapel, or who lived in Burgundian territory.

The detail of their earlier work is not clearly recorded. A poem by Martin le Franc called *Le champion des dames*, and dedicated to the Duke of Burgundy, gives us, however, a popular estimate of their importance. "Tapissier, Carmen, Cesaris," it runs, "not long since sang so well that they astounded all Paris; but never did they discant in melody so choice (those tell me who heard them) as did Guillaume du Fay and Binchois. For they have a new fashion of making fresh concord in high and low music, with feints and pauses and nuances; and they have taken something from the English manner, and have followed Dunstable, wherefore marvelous sweetness makes their music joyous and notable." We shall find this a tolerably accurate sketch of the course of Burgundian music.

The form most popular among the earlier members of the Burgundian school was inherited from Machaut—the three-voiced *virelai* or *chanson balladée*. Prevalent also is Machaut's vice of "arbitrary" discord (that which is allowed to appear without direct relation, as passing note or suspension, to the surrounding harmony); but this fault, as the poem suggests, was soon remedied, and there is progress to be noted even before this remedy was discovered. The general model of the *virelai* or song with refrain is, however, assimilated to that of the *rondeau*, in which the poetic text compels the repetition of specific musical phrases at precise moments. These phrases also become more definite in design, and are punctuated by conspicuous cadence formulas—very often on the successive scale degrees 8–7–7–6–8, which had been a trade-mark (but not altogether the invention) of Landini and his school. And as the definiteness of phrase design becomes clearer, imitation (already familiar in Italian and French *caccie*) is more and more frequently employed. Instrumental preludes and interludes are retained, and gradually the substance of the whole composition is made richer by the descent of the contratenor (formerly in the same register as the tenor) toward the region of a true bass.

The emergence of a courtly type of dance music is another sign of the times. Older dances such as *A l'entrade del tens clar*, quoted above, were dance *songs* devoted to no particular class, and danced as pleased the participant. In the fifteenth century, on the other hand, the courtly dances begin to be differentiated from the popular. Some of the manuscripts, indeed, indicate along with the music the number of steps to be taken to a given musical phrase. An old and apparently universal habit of associating an initial slow step with a faster and more sprightly gait is, however, retained. An *estampie*, in slow 4–4 measure, is followed immediately by a *saltarello* (*saltare* means to jump); and a *bassedanse* and a *pas de Brabant*, similarly rhythmed, are similarly related. Particular instruments, which are not specified for those earlier songs in which instruments are apparently indicated, are now sometimes identifiable. The *schalmei*, the ancestor of the oboe, has the melody, and the *bombard* (ancestor of the bassoon) or the trombone, the bass. Flute and harp or lute, sometimes with little drums, are other combinations. The music of the dance is often written without rhythmic differentiation. The performer therefore supplied the rhythm from the nature of the dance that was desired; and the faster *saltarello* was likewise made on the same melody as that of the *estampie*. Improvisation was also often resorted to for the coloration of the melody itself. It is evident that music is adapting itself rapidly to secular life.

We must turn now to a study of those English methods which, as Martin le Franc indicated, were adopted to such great advantage by the Burgundian composers. As we have seen, Henry V and the Duke of Bedford each maintained a chapel—the one in England, the other on the Continent. The insular group appears to have worked largely independently of the continental school. Three groups of manuscripts preserve this work. The Douce and Ashmole collections show, among simple examples of the ballade form and some rather mechanical pieces in parallel thirds and sixths, a little two-part song, *Alas, Departynge*, in which the expressiveness so much admired by the French is realized with great vividness. The Selden manuscript contains chiefly sacred songs for two voices. But there are also two secular songs, one of these the jocular *Tappster, Dryngker*,[1] and the other a wonderful paean in praise of the victor of Agincourt. This last deserves to be quoted in full:

THE AGINCOURT SONG

De - o gra - ci - as - - - An - - - - gli - a red - de pro vic - - to -

[1] *Alas, departynge* is printed in the *Oxford History*, II, 132; *Tappster, Dryngker* in the *Harvard Anthology*, p. 89.

- - - ri - - a.   Owre Kynge went forth to Nor-man-dy, with grace and might-

chy-val-ry;   ther God   for   hym wrought   merve-lus-ly,   wherfore Eng-

Londe   may   call   and   cry: Deo   gra - - - - - - - - - - ci - - - as.

De - - - o   gra-ci-as   An - - - - - - - - - - - gli - -

a   red-de   pro   vic - - - - - to - - - - - ri - - - - a.

The introductory phrase is a kind of invocation, its unison D's being an anticipation of the main melody, set to the English words. This, in the pure Dorian mode,
sweeps downward from the insistent high D's in two successive curves: one which
reaches only to the fourth below, the other spanning the whole octave to reach the

convincing cadence. The verse itself is concluded on two less vivid phrases, but only in order that the final ejaculation *Deo Gracias* may be the more exultant.

The harmonization, which one can hardly believe to be by the author of the melody itself, is ineffective; and the application of *musica ficta* distorts the melody intolerably. It seems to us that an adequate harmonization of this noble melody is impossible.

The third and most important source is the so-called *Old Hall Manuscript*. It contains, for the most part, settings of the Ordinary of the Mass, but there are also a considerable number of motets and antiphons. The book appears to have been used for services in St. George's Chapel at Windsor. Whether it was written during the reign of Henry V or of Henry VI is uncertain. Two pieces by "Roy Henry," a *Gloria* and a *Sanctus*, are included. If the book was written before 1422, the "Roy" must have been Henry V; but if these pieces are by Henry VI (which until recently has been supposed) the date must be considerably later. Bukofzer brings strong argument for the earlier date.

Only in this one of the three sources are the composers of the given works named; and of these names, only a few appear elsewhere. The most important are (Thomas) Dammett, Leonel (Power), and Forest. John Dunstable, by far the most significant figure in the English music of this period, is represented in this collection by one motet, but that work is here given as anonymous. Power and Forest, however, are represented in the continental collections which preserve the known compositions of Dunstable. For comparison with those works, we give the fragment of a *Gloria* by Leonel:

One vocal line, supported by one instrumental part, alternates with passages in which two vocal lines and two instrumental parts appear. The close (*cum sancto spiritu*) has three vocal and two instrumental lines. The four descending notes for *Domine* are sung to the initial *Et in terra pax*, and are more conspicuous in the rest of the *Gloria* than in our quotation. There is no parade of learned devices; but the vocal phrases are eminently singable, appropriately rhythmed for the sense, and in a certain degree directly expressive.

The external history of the English continental school, established at Paris under the patronage of the Duke of Bedford (brother of Henry V), is no more clearly recorded than is that of the insular group. It was headed —musically, and perhaps officially—by John Dunstable, whose genius far exceeded that of his insular countrymen. Although he was apparently born in England, and was buried there, little is known of his life. A treatise on astronomy belonging to his library is inscribed as belonging "to John Dunstable, musical companion to the Duke of Bedford," which proves that he was a member of that regent's chapel; and this explains why no more of his music than the motet *Veni sancte spiritus* (the supposedly anonymous work mentioned above), and a few other compositions were found in England. Most of his fifty-odd works are preserved in seven *Trent Codices,* and these have been transcribed in volumes VII and XL of the *Denkmäler der Tonkunst in Oesterreich.* If Dunstable was less prolific than other composers of his time, that fact may have been due to his preoccupation with mathematics and astronomy, in which sciences his epitaphs praise him as having been profoundly versed. He is also mentioned by Gaforius as having written a treatise on measured music; but this has not survived.

Dunstable's extant works have been exhaustively studied by Dr. Manfred Bukofzer,[2] who distinguishes seven types of structure. These include the "English Discant" already described (p. 103 above); the Ballad type of song form; the isorhythmic motet; the "colored" plainsong style; and a kind of "declamatory motet" in which the words, almost always sung simultaneously by all the voices, are clearly intelligible and are set to appropriately expressive melody. Of this last style an admirable example, *Quam pulchra es,* is accessible in Grove's Dictionary. The isorhythmic

[2] A summary of his findings is given in *Proceedings of the Musical Association* (London) LXV, 19.

motet, of which Dunstable has left twelve examples, shows in his hands a more elaborate structure (sometimes for four voices) than that of *Ha, fratres,* illustrated above; but the principle remains the same. The following, which is the tenor (complete) from his motet *Albanus roseo, Quoque ferendus,* will show how the foundation of such compositions was laid:

TENOR OF MOTET, ALBANUS ROSEO

From *D. T. Oe,* XL. 32. Note that the sections I, II, and III are identical in melodic design, and that the divisions a, b, and c in each section are isorhythmic. The increasing animation of the tempo is here more marked than in *Ha fratres,* though the process is the same.

This, although the most learned form of motet, was evidently less favored by Dunstable than a freer type, in which the notes of a plainsong melody were "colored" by the interpolation of ornamental tones. This coloration, a process akin to troping, was still popular on the Continent. The process may be illustrated by the first bars of *Regina coeli,* whose plainsong foundation begins as follows:

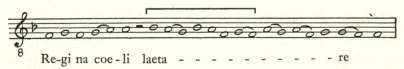

Re-gi na coe - li laeta - - - - - - - - - re

After the first phrase, sung in plainchant, the motet begins as follows. The notes of the plainchant, in the more ornamental upper voice, are marked +. Only that portion of the plainsong which is bracketed is here presented:

Observe that many "first inversions" (marked 6) are introduced, often emerging out of the progression of the melody against the more sustained lower voices. The sweetness of such harmonies was one source of the enthusiasm of the Burgundian court.

The important harmonic implications of *faux bourdon* were suggested in our discussion of the origin of that device. The significance of English discant is similar; and our last illustration shows to what an extent the chord idea—without as yet being actually a recognition of chord structure—was coming into being.

That Dunstable was also intrigued by the mathematical puzzles which are suggested by the arithmetical terms in which musical intervals and rhythms are conceived may be seen from his treatment of the following theme:

which, presented along with the accompanying voices in a very enigmatic form, is directed (in two Latin hexameters) to be taken first in the Dorian mode (final, D) and successively thereafter on the three other modal finals, E, F, and G. A portion of the whole composition runs as follows:

We may now return to the Burgundian school. Although the motet and the smaller song forms were by no means ignored by the continental composers, the more serious efforts of the Burgundians soon began to tend toward the enrichment of the noblest of the liturgical services—the Mass. We have seen that the Ordinary of the Mass was first set to polyphonic music in the fourteenth century. Machaut's great work itself is unified by the persistence of a single phrase, and is altogether a far more imposing work than the *Mass of Tournai*. The Burgundians, now attacking this problem in considerable numbers, do not at first attempt a co-ordinated setting of the five essential portions of the Ordinary. Instead, they seem satisfied to set only one or two portions, allowing the others to be sung in the usual liturgical plainchant. (Several individual and detached settings of the *Gloria* by Dufay attest to this practice, as may also the arrangement of the *Old Hall Manuscript*.) And even when the whole Ordinary was set, the basis of the structure in each section was the liturgical melody for its text, so that no organic unity in the whole composition was as yet aimed at.

The value of such unity was apparent, however, and it soon became the practice to build all the divisions of the Mass on a single, fundamental theme. This theme, curiously, was often not even a sacred melody. Popular songs, sometimes with very unecclesiastical words, were taken as *canti fermi*, cast in various rhythms, and sometimes somewhat colored; such a theme then formed the tenor nucleus of the whole composition. Often the theme was presented in what the Germans call "pound notes"—longs or double longs—with the other voices exhibiting all sorts of devices— sometimes melodically engaging, more often contrapuntally learned— above the tenor. Probably the most popular of all the secular tunes thus used was that of *L'Homme armé*. Tinctoris gives that theme as follows:

Lom - me lom - me lomme ar - mé et ro - bi - net tu

m'as la mort don - né —— quand tu t'en vas

Soldier, soldier, soldier boy, Ah, Robin, dear, you dealt me very death in leaving me.

Different texts, and variants of the tune, naturally appear, such as the following, used by Dufay:

FINE

D.C. al FINE

with a text filled with the terror of war.

On this theme every composer of consequence, from Dufay in the fifteenth century to Carissimi in the seventeenth, composed the Ordinary of the Mass—among them, Ockeghem, Obrecht, Josquin, Pierre de la Rue, and Palestrina. Another theme almost as popular was *Se la face ay pale*:

SE LA FACE AY PALE

Se la face ay pa - - le la cause est a - mer c'est la

prin - ci - pa - - le e tant m'est a - mer a - mer qu'en la

mer   me vol-droy-e vo-ir.   Or sect ben de -voir   la bel-le a qui

suis   que nul bien a-voir Sans el-le ne -   -   -   -   - puis.

If my face is pale, the reason is a bitter one. It is the real one, and is so bitter that I would gladly see myself cast into the sea. (A play on the words *amer*, bitter, and *en la mer*, in the sea, is untranslatable.) Now she to whom I am devoted knows that I can possess no good thing without her.

But countless other tunes, sacred or secular, were similarly employed—for example, Hermannus Contractus's melody, which the child in Chaucer's *Prioresses Tale* "coulde al by rote," and the beginning of which is as follows:

Al - - - - - - - - - - ma   Redemptoris   Ma - ter,

quae per - vi - a   cae - li por - - - ta .ma - - - - nes

Gentle Mother of the Redeemer, thou who remainest ever the portal of heaven; [and Star of the Sea, that dost rise to succor thy fallen people: thou who, as Nature wondered, gavest birth to thy holy Lord: Virgin ever before and after, do thou through that greeting taken from the lips of Gabriel, have mercy on all sinners].

The secular titles *Cucu, Le serviteur,* and *Gentil madonna mia* will suggest the endless variety of these themes. An additional unifying factor, besides the persistent tenor theme, is the frequent device of using the same musical substance (of course, rhythmically varied) at the beginning of each division of the Mass.

Masses thus composed on popular tunes are nowadays called "Parody Masses." No parody of the text, of course, was dreamed of in such works. But ribald churchmen sometimes did paraphrase the text itself, as in one example which begins, *Introibo ad altare Bacchi* (I shall enter unto the altar of Bacchus).

The unquestioned leaders of the Burgundian school from the second third of the fifteenth century were Gilles Binchois and Guillaume Dufay. Both were born about 1400 in the Belgian province of Hainaut, and each was conspicuous in the chapel of Philip the Good. That each was aware of the interest of Dunstable's work is strongly indicated in another phrase than that already quoted from Martin le Franc's *Champion des dames:* "You have heard the English play at the court of Burgundy. . . . I have seen Binchois ashamed and silent . . . and Dufay spiteful and frowning, because he had no melody so beautiful." Though each has some distinctive characteristics of style, the student will not be misled as to the general purport of the Burgundian movement if we confine our discussion, as space demands, to the work of Dufay.

His earlier work displays much of the harshness of the fourteenth century. He seems at first to have been hardly more sensitive to discord than Machaut, whom he also resembles in his fondness for imitation. This device he employed with increasing skill all his life, and found in it not only the delight of ingenuity but also a means of giving unity to large musical designs. Later composers shared this interest, and elevated the device into a feature of design that was developed, as we shall see, to almost incredible intricacy. Two brief extracts from Masses by Dunstable and Dufay will show the difference between the English and the Burgundian methods. In that by Dunstable:

EXCERPT FROM DUNSTABLE GLORIA

there is no attempt at learned edification; but an expressive purpose is discoverable. Both tenor and bass have long, upward leaps—the tenor, actually a major seventh—in the full-voiced music for *Laudamus te* ("We praise Thee"); the two higher voices, close together, and in more gentle melodic progression, sing *Benedicamus te* ("We bless Thee"); and the middle voice is omitted while the bass and discant (the latter in its low, soft register) suggest a kind of fervency for *Adoramus te* ("We adore Thee").

The example from Dufay is called *Et in terra ad modum tubae* ("In the manner of a trumpet"):

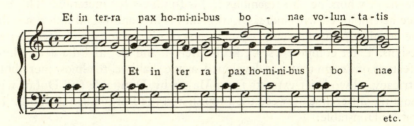

Above the persistent bass, which only much later makes any alteration in its trumpet-like pattern, the two upper voices begin and similarly maintain a *fuga duorum temporum*—a canon at the distance of two measures or "times." (*Fuga* had not yet acquired its modern meaning.) The ingenuity of this piece is greater, but its expressive interest far less, than that of Dunstable's.[3]

Dufay makes large use of the process of *faux bourdon*, both in his "free" (non-isorhythmic) motets and in many settings of texts from the Proper of the Mass, which he seems to have composed as if they were of equal importance with the texts of the Ordinary. In the motet *Supremum est mortalibus* (set to a text celebrating the peace signed between Pope Eugene IV and the Emperor Sigismund in 1433) the first nineteen bars and three shorter sections are in that style, while the greater part (with the same text for the two upper voices, and none for the tenor until the end) is without conspicuous imitations, and moves in smooth lines, with careful management of dissonance, very much in the manner of Dunstable. The declamatory style is especially marked at the end with the words, "Let this be our eternal Pope, Eugenius, and our King, Sigismund."

[3] A much more elaborate procedure will be seen in the third *Agnus Dei* from Dufay's Mass on "L'Homme armé," printed in the Harvard *Historical Anthology of Music*, p. 72. The legend, *canon: cancer eat plenus et redeat medius* means "Let the crab go forward full, and return half"; and this, in turn, means that the theme (which varies greatly from our quoted version) is sung, at first crab-fashion (backwards) in long (full) notes, and then forwards in notes of half the original length.

After Dufay's death in 1474, leadership in music in this region descended to Johannes Ockeghem, whose name proclaims him a Fleming, and whose birthplace is reputed to have been Termonde. He may have been a pupil of Dufay—or possibly of Binchois—but had also his early training at the Antwerp Cathedral, where he was a choirboy in 1443. In the early 1450's he entered the service of Charles VII of France, and continued to serve that throne for forty years, chiefly as treasurer of the Church of St. Martin in Tours. Although his associations were more directly with France than were those of Dufay, he is nowadays spoken of as the founder of the Flemish school. (The older distinction between three "Netherland schools," headed by Dufay, by Ockeghem and Obrecht, and by Josquin des Près, is thus superseded, with great advantage in perspective, since the sixteenth-century followers of the Flemish tradition thus fall into a single, long line.)

The distinction between the Flemish and the Burgundian styles is chiefly in the adoption of a norm of four voices instead of three, of a consequent expansion of the whole compass of polyphonic music downward, to exhibit a true bass (whereas the tenor had formerly been the lowest voice), and in a departure from the tendency we have already noted in Burgundian music for the melody to be chiefly set forth by the highest voice.

The compositional device most conspicuously employed in the shaping of this new technique is doubtless that of imitation. This process is by no means new. It was attempted as early as the twelfth century, but its possible significance had as yet been by no means fully revealed. It will be desirable to study the factors which must be implied in this process if it is to be fully effective.

The theme itself must be sharply and effectively designed if the imitation is to be perceived. A theme so vague in outline that it cannot be recognized when it is repeated cannot be of value in such a construction. Sharpness may be given by a distinctive rhythmic pattern; but such a pattern may also be wholly unsuited to the expression of the thought or feeling which is the composer's topic—for example, some condition of quiet religious exaltation. In addition to, or in place of, distinctive rhythmic design, some other resource must be at the composer's disposal.

A theme whose tone center is clearly evident is more rememberable than one whose center is uncertain. In plainsong, this center (which was the *final* of the mode) is often not clearly discernible until the end of the melody, and must be perceived by observing the succession of the melodic tones. Harmony—at any rate of the modern kind—can give this suggestion of the tone center long before the end of the phrase is reached. But since the modes all consisted of segments of what we may call the "white note" scale, and since modal harmonies, strictly constructed, could consist only of those same notes, pure modal harmonies could not exhibit with any distinctiveness the peculiarities characteristic of any one of the modes.

Musica ficta was the apparently inevitable product of the desire to make harmony appropriate to modal melody; but it was at first merely an alleviation of harmonic distress, and was only gradually perceived as a possible means of attaining clarity in harmonic syntax. The more clearly this possibility emerged, the more blurred became the distinctions between the modes. The music of the fifteenth century takes rather positive, but by no means final, steps in the direction of major and minor tonality.

Faux bourdon, likewise, must have revealed the interest that can inhere in chords as such, and in their ordered succession; but it did not, in its original simple form, suggest the basis of a clear harmonic syntax, nor could such an idea have emerged as long as the modal scales were assumed to be the only true bases of melody. Almost a hundred years will elapse beyond the period we are now studying before Glarean's *Dodecachordon* will give theoretical approval to Modes IX to XII—the *natural* minor and major modes; but it is well to realize that all the innovations with which we are now dealing are tending almost unconsciously in that direction.[4]

[4] The idea of progress in art—an idea strongly suggested by what has just appeared in the text—is an idea in great disfavor among present-day historians. (The idea of retrogression, logically just as indefensible, is not apparently considered opprobrious.) That the blissful state of music in the nineteenth century was the goal toward which all earlier musical effort had tended was indeed a belief generally shared by nineteenth-century historians.

The tendencies of the twentieth century, violently opposed to those of the nineteenth, could not but appear as anarchic if that particular theorem of progress were accepted. But it does not seem to us necessary, in defense of our own time, to deny the whole theorem of progress. Perfection, which is not easily achieved, surely represents progress beyond the imperfection out of which it must have grown. The music of the thirteenth century "advanced," along the general line of thought suggested by organum, to a perfection which could hardly be surpassed so long as modal rhythm and its attendant textures were accepted as final limitations. The *Ars nova*, indeed, did not further perfect this perfection. It merely advanced, along lines hitherto unopened, toward another stage of perfection, similarly conditioned and similarly capable of supersession. Perfection, however, begins in this light to be a dubious term. It merely represents a stage of completion within the framework of a given complex of conventions; and the question of advance or retrogression is one to be judged in a perspective which compares, not the artists' work, but the conventions themselves by which their art was conditioned.

But if, as may be possible, the objective of the artist is not merely to attain to technical perfection, but is to express, in a way that may be called truthful, the widening horizon of human understanding and sensibility, then the theorem of positive advance is no longer absurd. It is true that the criteria of perfection are altered, and that an odor of morality—highly offensive to the "purely" artistic nostril—begins to taint the aesthetic air; but as long as the conditions (and conventions) under which we live appear as better or worse than others, analogous judgments of good or evil will continue to form in our minds, and will embrace also the works of art which express those conventions.

Our study of Ockeghem and his contemporaries will appear as important steps toward that goal.

Until recently, the world has been taught to think of Ockeghem as essentially a "learned" composer. He was indeed that, for he developed the processes of imitation to a degree unattainable by his predecessors. Dufay, for the most part, had been content to confine his imitations to the first notes of the imitating voices. Ockeghem pursues them, in his stricter works, to the very end, and sometimes multiplies the difficulties until the results are astounding. But preoccupation with these marvels seems to have blinded the older commentators to the presence of a more natural musical impulse in many, at least, of Ockeghem's works. This quality can be seen in the following, the conclusion of a secular song, *Je n'ai deuil*, where, although the harmonies seem sometimes without clear objective, a decided gentleness and intimacy of expression can be felt:

The text, except for the words of the title, is not given either in this or other extant songs by Ockeghem. "I do not grieve," is, however, evidently not the purport of the song, a considerable dolor being implied by the music. Imitation is inconspicuous. At the opening (not quoted) the cantus (soprano) imitates immediately the four opening breves of the tenor (alto); but this phrase never recurs. The brief descending figure imitated in bars 38 and 39 and elsewhere in our excerpt appears four times in the opening portion, but only once in direct imitation.

Observe the evasions of the expected cadence in bars 36 and 46. This device is frequent in more elaborately imitative compositions, where it is often effected by the new entrance of an imitative phrase, and so makes that entrance conspicuous. The general effect is that of an *and* or a *but*, interjecting a new clause into a sentence. Note that the voice-leading avoids the apparent parallel octaves in bars 37 (D–E) and 40 and 41 (C–D).

Of Ockeghem's larger compositions, extraordinarily few remain, considering his great reputation. There are some fifteen Masses, seven motets, nineteen chansons, and four canons, of which only one Mass and five smaller pieces were printed by Petrucci and his contemporaries. That Mass is the enigmatic *Cujusvi toni* (literally, in whatever mode you please) which is without clefs, and can therefore be read only by supplying such clefs for the various parts as will bring the notes into proper harmonic relations in the different modes. In each case, certain accidentals must be supplied according to the general principles of *musica ficta*. A similarly clefless *Fugue for three voices in the fourth above* exists. This is a strict canon throughout, notated in a single line and with the entrance of the successive voices indicated as occurring *post perfectum tempus* (after a bar of three beats). The notation has the following enigmatic appearance:

The three sharps and three flats indicate the chromatic alterations necessary accordingly as the music is played in one mode or another.[5]

The motets show perhaps most clearly the artistry with which Ockeghem handles the polyphonic substance. The method pursued by Dunstable in *Regina coeli* is expanded in Ockeghem's *Salve regina* by a much more extended use of the floreated plainsong subject which appears in all the voices, sometimes almost without ornamental tones, sometimes with many, and with occasional brief points of imitation. These latter, however, are not obtruded, and the texture is varied by the use of more or fewer voices, with the same delayed cadences, and the same fluid continuity of melody as that illustrated in *Je n'ai deuil*, above—of course, on a vastly greater scale.

[5] For an illuminating discussion of these pieces, see Levitan, "Okeghem's Clefless Compositions," *Musical Quarterly* XXIII, 4.

That there was reason for Ockeghem's great fame as a maker of canons is proved by an astounding work in this form for thirty-six voices. This piece was printed anonymously by Petrejus in 1542, by which time the first mention of it (in a *Complaint* on Ockeghem's death) had become a legend. It was identified as Ockeghem's work by Robert Eitner. Although thirty-six voices take part, there are four separate phrases, assigned to nine altos, sopranos, tenors, and basses successively. The two higher voices soon drop out, leaving tenors and basses to finish. Consequently, no more than eighteen voices are heard simultaneously. Since each voice enters only one bar after the preceding, the harmony is even more closely confined than in *Sumer is icumen in.* Only the color of the dominant relieves the persistence of the tonic chord.

Doubtless the invention of music printing was in a curious way responsible for the preservation of so little of Ockeghem's work. The process was first perfected by Ottaviano Petrucci, a skilled typographer of Venice, who devised a way of printing the staves and the notes in separate, but very precise and clear, impressions. He put forth great numbers of Masses, motets, and songs; but the taste of his patrons was evidently for new music rather than older, so that Ockeghem, who died six years before Petrucci's first publication, was represented by no more than a few chansons. Many other music printers either copied Petrucci's method or devised others: Jacob Anton Junta, in Rome; Gardane and Amadino in Venice; Peter Schöffer in Mainz, Worms, and Strasbourg; Petrejus (who printed Ockeghem's Mass *Cujusvi toni*), Grapheus and others in Nürnberg; Plantinus, Susato, and Phalèse in the Netherlands; Attaignant in Paris; John Day in England; and Didacus de Puerto in Spain. Day and Susato were both composers, and great composers in the sixteenth century —such as Claudio Merulo and Claude Goudimel—were associated with, if not primarily engaged in, the printing business.

Jacob Obrecht, born about 1430 and therefore some ten years younger than Ockeghem, was at the height of his career when this process of printing began to revolutionize the musical practice of the world. His works were published much more extensively than the older master's, and show a further completion of the technique of polyphony. Five Masses of his were published by Petrucci in 1503 in a single collection—a distinction so far offered only to the great Josquin. These are all, as the custom now was, on familiar songs: *Je ne demande, Fortuna desperata,* and others. One, founded on Ockeghem's setting of the popular song *Malheur me bat,* is made, not of the tenor part of that song, but of the discant, of which a separate phrase constitutes the musical subject of each section. The *Christe eleison,* however, is not thus derived; and in the *Crucifixus,* Ockeghem's tenor is kept complete as a tenor, and the other parts are thus added, just as were Ockeghem's, with what Ambros pronounced to be even greater mastery. Another instance of the device of beginning the different sections of the Mass with the same melodic phrase is found in Obrecht's Mass *Sine nomine* ("Without a title"—that is, not on a known theme) from which the first *Kyrie* and the second *Agnus Dei* are printed in the *Harvard Anthology*. In all these, the feeling for choral sonority seems superior to that of Ockeghem.

Many motets were included in Petrucci's collections, among them the *Ave regina coelorum* with which the *Canti cento cinquanta* ("A Hundred and Fifty Songs"—but there were only 136) opened.[6] The introduction —*Ave, ave* ("Hail, hail")—is deep in register and very impressive, and the phrases for *Salve radix*, in three broad descending curves, seem almost modern in their direct and intense utterance:

Notable among Obrecht's pieces in motet style is his setting of the Passion according to St. Matthew. Plainsong music had been used for quasi-dramatic presentations of that story along with other dramatizations (compare the Sequence *Victimae paschali*, mentioned on page 46). And polyphony had been used in Obrecht's time for the utterances of the people (*turbae*) along with monodic recitation for the narrative. But Obrecht's version, which dates from about 1500, makes no distinction of characters and presents the story polyphonically throughout.

---

[6] Petrucci's arithmetic seems to have been persistently deficient. His first collection, the *Odhecaton* ("A Hundred Songs"), contained only ninety-six, and the second, *Canti cinquanta* ("Fifty Songs"), was one short of that number.

Ockeghem and Obrecht may be said to have perfected the Netherlandish methods; but it was their successor, Josquin des Près who imbued them with full artistic life. He was born about 1450, probably at Condé; was for some time a pupil of Ockeghem; became in 1471 a member of the papal chapel where he remained thirteen years, winning the highest distinction; was in the service of Lorenzo the Magnificent some time between 1484 and 1490 (when Lorenzo died); served at the court of Louis XII of France who reigned from 1498 to 1515; was probably for a time in the chapel of the Emperor Maximilian I; and returned to his birthplace, Condé, to end his days in 1521. His renown during his lifetime was fabulous. Baini, the biographer of Palestrina, calls him "the idol of Europe." He said, "They sing only Josquin in Italy, only Josquin in France, only Josquin in Germany, in Flanders, in Hungary, in Bohemia, in Spain—only Josquin." Martin Luther was similarly amazed: "Josquin is the master of the notes. Other masters do as the notes will, but Josquin makes them do as he wills."

Historians are indeed at one in praising not merely his mastery—which was gained at so early an age that the effort did not dry up the founts of inspiration—but the extraordinary power he possessed of finding the appropriate musical phrase for the text he was setting. This is no mere external fitness or representation. His phrase seems to come from the full implication of the text, and to set it forth in such terms as to make into a reality of meaning that which is ordinarily but dimly felt. It is true, of course, that he performed, like every other composer of his time, the "tricks" of counterpoint which were the outward and visible sign of technical mastery. He wrote two Masses on *L'Homme armé*—both, according to Ambros, printed by Petrucci in his first book of Masses by Josquin (1502). One of these, called *Missa l'Homme armé super voces musicales*—that is, with the theme, in successive movements, based on the notes of the hexachord—is a brilliant essay in technique—perhaps, Ambros thinks, the most brilliant composition in the old Netherland style. A hint only of the manner in which the old song is incorporated will be found in the following quotation from the *Sanctus:*

The theme is first in the soprano (bars 1 to 6), then, augmented, in the tenor. The version is that mentioned above as forming the tenor of Dufay's Mass.

The other Mass on the same theme is in the sixth mode, and presents no ostentation of learning. The same variety of treatment is found in the other Masses, of which there are thirty-two. One is actually contrived, rhythmically, by various combinations of the six spots on the dice! The

Missa sine nomine, likewise, is a display of canonic art, and little else. But others are deeply earnest, and even when the learned devices are used, they are submerged in a warmth of musical feeling that seems wholly devoted to its subject. This is true of earlier Masses, such as *Ave maris stella* (in which the charm does sometimes make the hearer forget the sense), and *De beata virgine*, but more particularly of later works such as *Da pacem* and *Pange lingua*.

Aside from one example—a canon for twenty-four voices (in six four-voiced choirs), *Qui habitat in adjutorio*, which really outdoes Ockeghem's monstrous creation, since all the voices are at last engaged—Josquin's motets are truer revelations of his genius than are his Masses. He uses no more than six voices, and usually prefers the four-voiced texture. If the Masses seem to fulfill the technical promise inherent in the Flemish methods, the motets go beyond his own time into a future which—since Josquin's music falls gratefully on our modern ears—is still beyond the limits of our vision. It is impossible within our space to discuss the great variety and high individuality of these works. One quotation, however, from one of the most universally admired creations—*Absalon, fili mi*, the lament of David over the death of his son—may serve to show both the high artistry and the quick sensibility of the composer:

The text, from II Samuel, XVIII, 33, "O my son Absalom! would God I had died for thee, O Absalom, my son, my son!," is amplified by the words of the excerpt, "I shall live no longer, but shall descend, weeping, into hell." Observe the imitations in all the voices for the phrases set to *sed descendam;* but note also both the appropriateness of the melodic design and the darkening of the harmony. The augmented fifth in the last bar but one is, for the time, a daring essay in intensity. (Josquin's pupil, Adrian Coclicus, speaks of many rules which Josquin laid down as absolute, "But Master Josquin did not obey them." This is perhaps an instance.)

We mentioned, without especial comment, a few of the lesser contemporaries of Dunstable and Dufay. The later members of the Flemish school, aside from the three great figures we have studied, were more numerous and more important, since it was through them that the high skill of the greater masters was established as the accepted style of composition, not only in the region where it originated, but over practically all Europe. Even though Josquin was as popular as Baini reports him to have been, his fame would have proved ephemeral if his methods had not been imparted to and practiced by a large number of highly gifted men. Of these, space will permit the mention of only a few; but it will be seen that the area in which they worked soon extended far beyond the Netherlands.

The most accomplished of all was Pierre de la Rue (*circa* 1460–1518), whom Ambros calls the only possible rival of Josquin. He worked apparently all his life at the court of Burgundy, or at that of Charles V, and in the Netherlands. He died at Courtrai. Actual rivalry with Josquin is suggested in his setting of the Mass on the perennial theme *L'Homme armé,* in which he discovered a great variety of rhythmic complications that are quite different from the brilliant and apparently exhaustive schemes of Josquin. Although the theme is maintained inexorably throughout (whereas Josquin varies it) the value of the text is not forgotten, and a just (if somewhat unyielding) expression of its sense is achieved.[7] In less pretentious works, however, there is a kind of simple fervency that is

[7] Kyries I and II are printed in the *Harvard Anthology,* pp. 95-96.

most appealing, as in the Masses *De Sancta Anna, De Sancta cruce*, and *De Sancto Antonio*. In the first of these, the *Osanna* preceding the *Benedictus* is replaced by an apostrophe to the Host (the transubstantiated bread and wine) in which Ambros found a full anticipation of the Palestrina style. A brief extract will justify that opinion, as far as a few notes can:

The text is: [*O salutaris hostia quae coeli pandis ostium bella premunt hostilia da robur fer auxilium*]. The beginning will be found, up to our quotation, in the *Oxford History*, II, 241. There the smooth, broad harmonies are almost wholly chordal. Fluidity begins in our excerpt, and is continued in the nine concluding bars, with a broadening of the simple descending phrase of four notes seen in the alto at bar 3, above, and elsewhere in several different rhythms. The Eb's in bar 7 are not in the original.

There are also many fine motets, psalms, and secular songs.

Some twenty years older than de la Rue, but living until 1514, was Caspar van Weerbecke, who served many years in the family of the Sforza at Milan. He was more enamored than de la Rue of the proportional rhythmic intricacies (which only gradually disappear in the work of this school); yet in spite of these he attains a high dignity of religious contemplation, as in his motet *Virgo Maria, non est tibi similis*. Anton Brumel, not less accomplished than van Weerbecke, seems to have been invited to enter the service of the Duke of Ferrara as chapelmaster; but whether he actually did so is not known. His sense of harmonic logic is said by Wooldridge to compare favorably with that of Josquin.

There were others—Alexander Agricola, who worked in Brussels, in Milan, and in Spain; Johannes Ghiselin, whose works appear in the collections of Petrucci and other publishers in considerable numbers; Mabriano de Orto, chiefly engaged at the court of Philip the Fair of Burgundy; Loyset Compère, of St. Quentin, whom Ambros describes as a romanticist and as a kind of younger brother of Josquin; François de Layolle, the music master of Benvenuto Cellini; Anton de Fevin; Eleazar Genet, called Carpentras. These and many more composers of high ability and thorough training spread the Flemish style over all France and Italy. Somewhat younger was Jean Mouton, a pupil of Josquin, who so far benefited by his instruction as to develop a rather distinctive style of his own. Indeed, it is this possibility of adaptation, by varieties of genius to varieties of problems, which proves the soundness and the significance of the Flemish methods. A continuation of these traditions will appear in the sixteenth century.

England and Germany, on the periphery of that widening circle of renaissance music which we have been observing, offer little contribution to the stream of musical thought during the second half of the fifteenth century. Although the English methods during the first half of the century seem to have fertilized those of the *Ars nova*, the political influence of the English on the Continent largely ceased with the end of the Hundred Years' War; and the immediately ensuing, even more disastrous Wars of the Roses, which ended only with the accession of Henry VII, were a continuing impediment to musical progress.

This decadence was noted by Tinctoris who, after praising Ockeghem, Régis, Busnois, Caron, and Faugues for their development of the art of counterpoint which they had largely learned from "Dunstaple," Binchois, and Dufay, begins his book on Proportion by remarking that while the Burgundian masters are pursuing new methods, "the English (and this is a sign of deficient genius) still compose in their one old way, . . . and are either wholly ignorant of the musical proportions used so ingeniously and with incomparable suavity by the moderns, or else set forth the little they do know quite wrongly, doubtless owing to their defective arithmetic, without which nobody can attain to eminence in music." (This was written about 1470, in the heyday of proportional intricacy. We have seen that even in the later years of the century this valuation of intricacy was revised.)

The English music of this period shows little distinction. A good many composers are represented in an Eton manuscript of the time. For example, Richard Davy, with a polyphonic Passion, treats the text in the general manner of Obrecht, but without elaborate devices. A Mass by Robert Fayrfax, from another source, possibly suggests by its almost ostentatious avoidance of such structure a conscious opposition to the Flemish methods. At any rate, actual adoption of those methods will hardly appear in England before the second decade of the sixteenth century.

A similar independence in musical thought is apparent in Germany. Just as the songs of the Minnesinger, although modeled after those of the troubadours, showed distinctive traits of melody and rhythm—partly, no doubt, deriving from the different accentuation and sonority of the German language, but also reflecting a very different national temperament— so the German adaptations of Flemish methods reveal an expressive purpose—and hence a way of life—different from that implied in the music of the Flemish masters. Neither England nor Germany took as kindly to the ancient classical traditions which are the background of the Renaissance as did Italy and France. There is in German music, from the time of the Minnesinger on, a kind of sturdiness too healthy to expend itself in mere courtly amiabilities: a rooting of the imagination in the soil of everyday life such as forbids excursion into the regions of mere tonal fancy.

How deep were these roots is to be seen in three collections of German songs, the first evidently dating from the twelfth or thirteenth century to as late as 1452, and called the *Locheimer Liederbuch*. Similar to this are the Glogau (or Berlin) and Munich songbooks—collections in which monody as well as two- and three-part harmony are found, the harmonies as simple as the tunes, and often remarkably appropriate to them. As evidence of the possession of music by other than the privileged classes, and of the deep affection with which this possession was cherished and cultivated, these books are priceless. They contain also many dances and other instrumental pieces, whose significance will appear more clearly when we come to a discussion of the development of instrumental music. The somewhat awkward but purposeful harmony, adapted to religious melodies and designed for domestic as well as congregational use, appears in a collection of sacred songs published by Oeglin in Augsburg in 1512— before the posting of Luther's famous theses. How the musical thought of the fifteenth century was expanded until the art became indeed a "universal language" will be seen in our next chapter.

CHAPTER X

Sacred and Secular Song
in the
Sixteenth Century

THE fifteenth century had endowed the sixteenth with a process of composition perfectible beyond the imagination of its inventors—just as the achievements of the *Ars nova* had been beyond the imagination of Franco of Cologne. Melodic lines of almost incomparable fluidity were combined into polyphonic textures in which the structural steel of syntactical coherence had largely replaced the wooden frameworks of the *cantus firmus* or of isorhythm. And the forms of music, now almost independent of the rhythms of words, began to show that relation to vital experience which—however difficult it may be to define—is perceived by the intuition of the common man as an unmistakable fact of expression.

The problems of expression which the sixteenth century posed were themselves unimaginably greater than those of the earlier era. Irreconcilable differences of religious opinion—known in the fifteenth century and before as heresies, and stamped out with little awareness of their meaning—now had to be acknowledged, and the opposed attitudes had to be expressed. Changes in the social structure, brought about by the emergence of a middle class possessed of independent means, a corresponding leisure, and a culture deeply rooted in the soil of everyday experience, likewise demanded musical utterance. And for all of these the methods of the Flemings, modified and adjusted as circumstances required, proved an adequate vehicle.

The assimilation of the Netherland methods to the cultural peculiarities of Italy, France, Spain, Germany, and England yielded in each case a distinctive, artistic product. The sharpest distinctions, however, appear between those regions in which the religious cleavage was sharpest, and between those whose general culture was most diverse. It happened, however, that the countries in which the classical literary traditions were most generally accepted—the Latin nations—were those most loyal to the Catholic faith, while England and northern Germany, where the classical traditions had been less influential, were more ready to adopt the Protestant belief.[1] They were also, for reasons already considered, less active in music than the Latin nations at the beginning of the century.

Even for Josquin, the motet rather than the Mass had become the most congenial musical form. Shorter and more flexible, adaptable to a greater variety of subjects, it was more stimulating to the imagination which was now beginning to concern itself definitely with the problem of expression. The proportional and imitative devices, displayed profusely in the parody masses, were losing their interest—or rather were beginning to assume their proper, subordinate place in the scheme of musical structure. The sense of words—of humanistic as well as of liturgical texts—was Josquin's strongest incentive to composition, and became, throughout the sixteenth century, the increasing concern of composers. The general purview of this period which we must now attempt will properly begin with a study of the spread of the Flemish style, and in the classical-minded Latin nations.

THE EXPANSION OF FLEMISH METHODS

The immediate successor of Josquin was Nicolas Gombert, whom Heinrich Besseler calls the founder of the "classical" Netherland school. As a classicist, he was more conservative than Josquin himself, even though he was a pupil of that master. He was born about 1490, and was from about 1530 in the service of the Emperor Charles V, thus working for a

[1] That this distinction is a mere coincidence seems to us unimaginable; but to prove a relationship would tax the resources of a philosophic historian. One item, however, may be suggested. Aristotle, who expounded the laws of classical drama as they were studied during the Renaissance, also provided through Thomas Aquinas, his most influential interpreter, the accepted authority upon which the logic of Christianity rested. It is a plausible supposition that scholasticism, which thus bound together ecclesiastical and literary tradition, became the indirect but efficacious support of the literary conventions.

It seems less plausible to argue that the absence of the literary tradition may have entailed a weakness in the armor of ecclesiastical faith. Humanism, which was at least an antischolastic attitude, was also essentially the attitude of the Renaissance. But in practice, humanism was accepted as a liberal interpretation of Catholic doctrine rather than as an opposition to it—a shining plate, indeed, in the armor of the Church. The slower acceptance of humanism in the Northern regions may have left exposed a spot as inconspicuous—and as vital—as the heel of Achilles.

considerable time in Spain. He holds firmly to the ideal of a true polyphonic texture, keeping all the voices of equal interest (in contrast to the
tendency in lighter songs to allow the upper voice to predominate). He
uses almost no passages of plain harmony such as occasionally appear in
Josquin; but he is no devotee of the more elaborate compositional devices.
Imitation is frequent, but is largely confined to the opening notes of a
motive—where it is most noticeable; symmetry is carefully avoided between sections, its only conspicuous appearance being in the similar closes
of the two parts into which the motet, in accordance with French taste,
was now ordinarily divided. Of illlustrative tone painting, and indeed of
any immediate expressive adaptation of music to text, Besseler discovers
none, but observes a certain warmth and refinement of tone and structure,
accordant with the general mystic purpose of Netherland polyphony.
Ambros, on the other hand, remarks in the motet *Miserere nostri* appropriate emphasis on the half step or major seventh, and similarly the rising
progressions in *Ad te levavi oculos* ("Unto Thee have I lifted up mine
eyes"). Perfect texture, however, rather than expressiveness, was Gombert's primary objective in his very numerous works.

Gombert's reactionary tendency was counterbalanced by the progres-
siveness of a brilliant contemporary, Jacobus Clemens, known as Clemens
non Papa (not the Pope).[2] Historians from Ambros on have been at one
in praising the skill and the vividness of Clemens non Papa's music. His
polyphony is not less sound than that of Gombert, although he is more
ready to use passages of plain harmony, and sometimes even tends towards
homophony. It appears also that he may have been a vastly more "progressive" composer, in the direction of chromatic harmonization, than has
hitherto been supposed.

A recent study by Edward Lowinsky,[3] if its findings are accepted, will
show that chromatic tendencies, more extensive and more destructive to
the modal system than any that appeared in actual notation until toward
the end of the century, were practiced by Clemens non Papa and several
of his contemporaries. He finds one example in Gombert, a great number
in Clemens non Papa, a lesser number in Hubert Waelrant, and a few

---

[2] It was long accepted that this phrase was added in order to distinguish Clemens
from the actual Pope, Clement VII (*reg.* 1522-34). Aside from the fact that the composer's works began to be published only in 1539, it was unnecessary to make such a
careful distinction between a Pope and a composer. Bernet Kempers suggests that
the phrase distinguishes the musician from one Jacobus Papa, a contemporary Netherland poet, and that it was probably applied with a humorous intent. The date of
Clemens's birth Kempers thinks about 1510; of his death, before 1557. He seems to
have lived all his life in the North, chiefly at Ypres and at Dixmude, at which latter
place he was buried.

[3] *Secret Chromatic Art in the Netherlands Motet*, Columbia University Press, 1946.

elsewhere. These alterations, which are in a sense an expansion of the principle of *musica ficta*, and were similarly without actual indication in the score, were understood and practiced only by a kind of inner circle of musicians, and thus constituted a really secret art. Since such transformations could not have been practiced in the Church, it was not in the Mass but in the motet that the supposed alterations were to be found.[4] The purpose of the chromatic alterations, as Lowinsky sees it, was primarily one of intensified expression for the sense of the words. There is usually possible a return to the normal diatonic reading of the notes; but in one instance—the motet *Qui consolabatur me*—this astonishing technique brings about a close for the whole motet in what we should call the key of G flat major. This is certainly startling, and will doubtless require scholarly confirmation, although Lowinsky has marshaled strong evidence in its favor.

Seventeen Masses by Clemens non Papa, partly on secular themes, partly on sacred songs, are described by Joseph Schmidt.[5] They follow the contemporary trend in giving little emphasis to continued imitation, and in using the major third in the final chord of the cadence; but there is no suggestion of the secret chromatic art. Seven of the Masses are in the Ionian and seven in the Dorian modes—a close approximation to our major and minor keys.[6] While the Masses naturally adventure less boldly into

[4] The music as written conforms in every respect to proper modal composition, and might be sung as written without giving rise to any suspicion of the possibility of another reading. The alterations are suggested, in most cases, by a superfluous accidental appearing (where it would have been supplied by the principles of *musica ficta*) in the score. Often, also, the "secret" transformation begins where a motive, already several times heard in its proper form, is written in a distorted form on another degree of the scale. See, for example, the motet *Vox in Rama*, *Harvard Anthology*, p. 134. The motive for *noluit consolari* at bar 54, alto voice, is E E E D C F E. It is repeated at once in the soprano on A, precisely transposed; but it appears in the tenor, bar 59, as D D D C B♮ E♮ D C—with B and E instead of B♭ and E♭. Lowinsky substitutes B♭ for B♮ and calls this a "code" note, since its use will entail E♭ (to avoid the augmented 4th) and this, in turn, several other flatted notes. (Bars 60–62 inclusive, and also 68–70, if the motive is precisely maintained, will yield "secret" chromaticism.)

[5] *Zeitschrift für Musikwissenschaft*, IX, 129 (1926-27).

[6] The Dorian is nearly as "minor" in feeling as the Aeolian; the Ionian is precisely the C scale. These two modes—the Ionian and Aeolian—with their plagal correlatives were about this time established on a basis of authority in the great theoretical treatise, the *Dodecachordon* (literally, "twelve strings," but implying twelve modes or keys) published by Glarean in 1547. This book, the solidest theoretical treatise since that of Tinctoris, not only sets forth the completed modal system shown in our table (p. 52) but analyzes with keen discrimination the music of Josquin and the earlier sixteenth century. The book was nevertheless accepted with many misgivings by the more conservative musicians.

It was not, however, the first attempt to bring to order the confused ideas engendered by the conflict of modal and harmonic ideas. As early as 1482, Bartholomeo

new regions of harmonic experiment, they are in keeping, expressively, with the more progressive form of the motet.

Confirmation of the idea of secret chromaticism may possibly be found in another as yet not clearly defined concept: that of *musica reservata*, first described in that phrase by Adrianus Coclicus (or Coclico)—mentioned above as a pupil of Josquin—in his brief *Descriptive Compendium of Music*. The idea is exemplified in certain settings of Psalms by Coclicus, which he says are in that style. As opposed to *musica communa* (music of the older, more conventional type), *musica reservata* is that in which the composer's first aim is "to give meaning to the words"—that is, to compose expressively rather than formally. The general concept is somewhat clarified by other writers, notably Vincentino and a Dr. Samuel Quickelberg who says of Orlando di Lasso's Seven Penitential Psalms that they express the text so vividly that it is "as if you saw the experience before your very eyes." The Psalms, although written in 1560, were "reserved" for Lasso's patron, Duke Albert V of Bavaria, and withheld from publication until 1584. This suggests a more obvious meaning for the word *reservata;* yet the term can still relate to composition in the intense and theoretically unorthodox manner of di Lasso's Psalms. Secret chromaticism, if employed, would likewise produce "reserved" music. Private, not public, performance; expressiveness which exceeds the boundaries of modal convention; and possibly the presence of secret chromaticism —these would seem to be the characteristics of *musica reservata*. We shall see, however, that chromaticism does not long remain secret.

THE VENETIAN SCHOOL—ADRIAN WILLAERT

We must now somewhat retrace our steps and describe the rise of the very important Venetian school whose work, by the middle of the century, had assumed distinctive characteristics, and was to pursue thereafter the most advanced methods.

Until the discovery of America and of a sea route around Africa, Venice had held, among the Italian city-states, a unique position, both geographical and political. The relation of Venice to the other cities is too tangled a story to be briefly told. Its great wealth and its cosmopolitan culture caused it to assume a proud isolation which was not without effect on its architecture and its art. As the first commercial city of the world, it

---

Ramis of Bologna, in his *De Musica tractatus*, had not only proposed the substitution of the complete octave-scale for the hexachord, but had recognized the difference between the "major tone" (9:8) and the "minor tone" (10:9). This, in effect, proposes a major third (5:4) more consonant than that recognized by Pythagorean theory (81:64), and is a probably unconscious step toward equal temperament.

had long since established business relations with the Netherlands—a fact of some import when the influx of Netherland composers into Italy began.

The earlier musical traditions of the city were not exceptionally exalted. Byzantine influence was great in many fields, but not in music; for Constantinople in the fifteenth century was (according to Ambros) "the most unmusical place in the world." The highly autocratic government of the Doges was unfavorable to any but the most conservative methods in composition, even though music, like the other arts, was cherished as a decoration of the city. From about 1400, it was the custom to celebrate the election of a new Doge by the performance of a specially composed, laudatory cantata. But in such music as this there was no room for the homelier spirit that animated the folk songs or chansons or *canzone* so popular in other regions; and the fear of secret denunciations—shared by citizen and noble alike—was hardly conducive even to private concerts, where veiled insinuations against the ruling powers might be uttered.

To orthodox church music, however, there could be no serious opposition. There had been, even before the sixteenth century opened, a feeble school of Venetian composers, and its activity naturally centered in the great Cathedral of St. Mark—that amazing edifice whose ground plan, in the form of the Greek cross, and whose mosque-like superstructure were designed in imitation of the Church of the Holy Apostles in Constantinople. The church records show that as early as 1318 the organist had been chosen with care, and that from 1403 the choir had been similarly selected and expensively maintained. In the eastern arm of the Cathedral there are three apses, the central one for the great altar, the others for the singers. From 1490 the records show the appointment of two organists—of course, for the two organs for which the structure of the church was adapted, and which the somewhat purse-proud Venetians were happy to provide. In 1527, the position of chapelmaster, which had been established in 1491, fell vacant; and for the first time a non-Venetian musician was appointed to the post. This was Adrian Willaert (*circa* 1485–1562), a native of Bruges or of Roulers, who had been sent to Paris to study law, but had there become a pupil either of Josquin or of Mouton, and like many another later composer gave up the legal profession for that of music. His mental horizon was nevertheless widened by his legal studies, which he remembered gratefully in later days. The earliest recorded incident in his Italian sojourn is his discovery that the papal choir had long admired and performed, under the impression that it was by Josquin, Willaert's motet *Verbum bonum et suave*. (The singers were put out by the revelation of their blunder, and would never sing the motet again.)

In a place so suited to antiphonal effect as St. Mark's, it was natural that Willaert should amplify the ancient practice of antiphonal and responsorial psalmody. Settings of *Confiteor tibi* (Psalm CXI in the King James Version), *Laudate pueri* (CXIII), *Lauda Jerusalem* (CXLVII, from v. 12), *De profundis* (CXXX), and *Memento Domine* (CXXXII), as well as a *Magnificat* in the sixth mode, employ this technique. There is also a *Magnificat* for three choirs. Zarlino noted the care with which the harmony for each choir was composed, and the rich effect of their combination. The "echo effect," which was at length looked on as a kind of trade-mark of Venetian music, is by no means obtrusive in Willaert's work, however grossly it was overdone by later composers. Whatever the device he used, it is evident that his aim was not to overwhelm his congregation, but to give fitting expression to his text. His mastery of the Netherland polyphony was complete.[7] But the sternness natural to this style was soon overcome by a singular sweetness, so engaging that one of his contemporaries spoke of his music as *aurum potabile*—"drinkable gold."

A few bars from a *Pater noster* (the Lord's Prayer) will illustrate both this general euphony and the manner in which each phrase of the text, set to its appropriate musical strain, is treated in imitation—not pedantically carried out to the end, but pursued far enough to make impressive the musical interpretation of the verbal sense:

[7] He wrote one motet which could be sung with the parts held upside down—i.e., in retrogression and inversion.

Note that the alto does not continue (at the words *qui es in coelis*) the phrase set to those words for the tenor, but has another strain, imitated by the soprano in bar 13. The bass begins on an independent line. *Sanctificetur*, on the other hand, is imitative in all the voices, as is *adveniat regnum tuum* ("Thy kingdom come"); but both are continued freely. The two instances of "false relation" between F♯ and F♮ (bars 10–11 and 21–22) show that this effect was less shunned in the sixteenth century than in the nineteenth. (Both F♯'s are in Gardane's edition of 1545, but not in that of Petrejus, 1538.)

As in all the music of this and earlier periods, the very careful adjustment of the note lengths to the natural emphasis of the words is obscured by the inserted bar lines. (These were not used by composers until the seventeenth century. They should *not* be understood as implying that the *one* in the measure has any rhythmic stress whatever.) Each part is sung with the emphasis proper to its text; no two voices coincide on predominantly *strong* syllables; and the result is a fluidity of motion seldom experienced in our modern music.

Antiphonal writing, which was a feature of Willaert's Psalms, sung at Vespers in Advent, is often spoken of as if it were a frequent detail in all his compositions. Its effect in the great church was striking, and was much imitated by other composers, so that it came to be regarded as typically a Venetian device; but Willaert was too fine an artist to overdo such tricks. Comparatively few of his compositions have survived. Many were doubtless lost in two disastrous fires (in 1574 and 1577), along with priceless paintings of Titian and Bellini, and others may have been carried off by Napoleon's soldiers in 1797. But even what remains justifies the high esteem in which he was held. Since the Venetian composers before Willaert were by no means outstanding, he is properly regarded as the founder of the Venetian school. We shall presently see something of the work of his pupils and followers; but for the moment we must turn to the study of a new form, in which the Netherland technique is grafted onto a humble Italian stock to produce a vigorous and fruitful musical organism. This is the *madrigal*.

The Madrigal in Italy

The parent stock of this new type of secular (and occasionally religious) song was not the fourteenth-century madrigal, cultivated by Landini and his school, but the *frottola*—in its first stages a far less learned type of music. (Landini's form of madrigal was now all but forgotten.) In 1504, Petrucci published a collection of frottole which gives us not only a fair idea of the general character of such songs but shows the extent to which the musical public was becoming interested in the practical cultivation of the art. The unambitious polyphony of these songs suggests, as Ambros says, that the composers had not actually gone to the Netherlands school, but had sat outside the door. The melody, definitely in the upper voice, is accompanied by a bass which moves largely in skips of the fourth and fifth—that is, in a harmonic rather than in a contrapuntal fashion—and by inner voices which enrich the harmonic substance without much attempt at continuous melodic interest. Yet these songs are not the work of amateurs or bunglers. They are set to poems by recent or contemporary authors, and seem frankly designed to give musical expression to the feeling and interest of the day. The intention is evidently that of performance by four voices; but the frottola might readily become a solo song, the lower parts being taken over by appropriate instruments, or arranged for the lute.

Two frottole from Petrucci's first collection may be found in the *Harvard Anthology*. A few bars from an earlier example by Alexander Florentinus will perhaps show the beginning of this popular style:

From Ambros, Vol. V, 531. This example is textless.

It will be recalled that the fourteenth-century madrigal had as text either two or three three-line stanzas, followed by a two-line conclusion called a *ritornello*, which was sung only at the end and was therefore *not* a refrain such as was found in psalmody, or in the fourteenth-century ballade or *virelai*. In the sixteenth century the verse has no strict form, and the music, although carefully fitted to the text, is similarly free in design. The ostentatious learning of the contrapuntists, however, was felt to be inappropriate to the subject and was largely avoided.

Of the Netherland composers (of course, resident in Italy) who lift the madrigal above the level of the frottola, the most important are Willaert, Philipp Verdelot (*circa* 1500–1565), and Jacob Arcadelt (*circa* 1505–1557). Costanzo Festa (died 1545), the first Italian madrigal composer, is represented in the *Harvard Anthology* by an example—*Quando retrova* (page 140) which is hardly distinguishable from the frottola save that the melody—such as it is—is in the tenor in keeping with the older Netherland tradition, and the sense of the major key is more evident than in the example just quoted, whose final cadence is on the G major chord. Verdelot, although he was reputed to be very prolific, is known today by relatively few finished works on a large scale. His madrigals, however, were printed not only in Venice but in Paris and Lyons, and Willaert himself arranged a number of them in tablature for lute and solo voice. (Verdelot was for some time one of the singers in the chapel of St Mark's.)

Arcadelt was earlier a member of the papal chapel, and later went to Paris where a great number of his works were published. His Masses are often on the songs which formed the traditional bases of such works—*Ave regina coelorum, De beata virgine*, and others—but the motets treat the chosen *canti fermi* with great freedom. His first book of madrigals (fifty-three pieces, published in Venice in 1538) went through fifteen separate editions, the last in 1617. Five other collections were composed. Ambros believed that in the madrigal *Il Bianco e dolce cigno* ("The White and Sweet Swan"), the first appearance of sentimental feeling in music is to be found. Another fine example, *Voi ve n'andat' al cielo* (given in the *Harvard Anthology* page 141), if not sentimental, is at least purposively expressive in a way immediately recognizable.

The rapidity with which the madrigal developed into a highly intricate, yet directly expressive, work of art is illustrated in the work of Cipriano de Rore (1516–1565?), a pupil of Willaert and his successor for a year or so in the position of chapelmaster at St. Mark's. Ambros felt that Cipriano stood in the same relation to Willaert as Mouton had stood in relation to Josquin—and, one might add, as Josquin to Ockeghem—absorbing rapidly that which the master had accomplished by more original effort, but using it also for independent and original work.

In his short life, Cipriano produced many eight-voiced antiphonal choruses after Willaert's manner; and his motets for four, five, and six voices were eagerly accepted by publishers in Venice and Paris, as were two Passion settings and countless madrigals. These included five books of chromatic madrigals which were the wonder of his day, and remained a perplexity to later musicians for two centuries. Even Ambros—so amazingly perceptive of the significance of Renaissance music that, aside from a more scientific classification of styles, contemporary historians find little to rectify in his judgments—felt that Cipriano's chromatic experiments produced only uninspired music. The chromatic progressions do depart strikingly from the usual quiet progressions of triads and first inversions in the modal harmony, but as intensifications of the text they seem justified.[8]

The further evolution of the madrigal, at any rate in Italy, will be inferable except for some details, from a view of the larger works of the great composers whom we have yet to consider. We have seen how the Netherland tradition, extended over all northern Italy, rose to especial significance in Venice, and how it elevated the frottola into the madrigal. This, however, implies not merely the sophistication of a popular form by a learned method. It means also that the horizon of the learned composers was widened by their frank recognition of this new field of popular interest. Their effort toward perfect structure was not lessened, but their contribution to what may be called humanistic literature was greatly enriched.

THE LATER VENETIAN SCHOOL

The story of the Venetian school during the remainder of the century may now be completed.

The successor of Cipriano de Rore as chapelmaster at St. Mark's was Gioseffo Zarlino of Chioggia (1517–1590), who was also a pupil of Willaert. Although he was a composer of significance, he is more famous as a theorist. His *Istitutioni armoniche* is an exposition not merely of the theory and practice of composition, but also of the philosophy of music as a humanistic art. (He wrote on religion and philosophy, as well). The *Istitutioni* looks definitely forward (as few theoretical treatises do) and

---

[8] See, for example, in the madrigal *De le belle contrade*, the passage A, A, A, B♭, B♮ for *sola mi lasci* ("Thou leavest me alone"); the C minor triad, following a pause after a cadence on the dominant of D minor, for *Ahi, crud' amor!* ("Ah, cruel love"); and the wide range (as far as the D♭ triad) of the ensuing modulations down to *finisc' in pianto* ("should end in weeping"). The madrigal is printed in the *Harvard Anthology*, p. 142. Observe that these modulations sound more decisive than those which are produced by "secret" chromatic art. They stem from a different purpose, and seem to point more definitely toward the future.

even poses, more than a hundred years before its solution, the problem of equal temperament. Another pupil was a Minorite monk, Costanzo Porta. Most of his work—Masses for four, five, and six voices, motets and psalms —shows a somewhat reclusive devotion to the older mechanics of Nether-land composition; but five books of madrigals reveal a lively interest in the world.

The great figures are Claudio Merulo and the two Gabrieli, Andrea and Giovanni (uncle and nephew), all of whom were organists at St. Mark's and whose compositions for that instrument will be described in a later chapter. Merulo's compositions for voices are of high skill (a *Bene-dicam Domino in tempore* is for twelve voices). He left Venice in 1584 at the behest of the Duke of Parma. De Rore had likewise gone to Parma —for what proved the last year of his life—and both he and Merulo are buried there. Andrea Gabrieli (*circa* 1510–1586), who became a singer under Willaert in 1536, added to his sound Netherland technique even more than his master had taught him of that brilliancy toward which the Venetian disposition had always tended. Not only "state cantatas" such as we have mentioned, but motets and psalms were enriched with effects hitherto unattempted. A setting of Psalm LXVI, for example, is for three choirs—one of high voices above the usual four-voice group, and one of low voices below. Like di Lasso, he gave especial care to the setting of the Penitential Psalms; and this effort his nephew praises, not for its brilliancy, but "for his discovery of the tones which will express the force of the words—of the thought."

Giovanni Gabrieli (1557–1612) was even more gifted and more accom-plished than his uncle. With him, indeed, the Venetian school reached its summit. To the polychoral combinations initiated by Willaert and—as pure choral music—perfected by Andrea, Giovanni added the luster of instruments, and became thus the "father of orchestration." (This does not imply that he would have countenanced the garish, concerted Masses which we shall meet with in the seventeenth century.) Such compositions he called *Symphoniae sacrae*. Among these are an extraordinary setting of the text *In ecclesiis benedicite Domino* ("Bless the Lord in the Churches") and an Easter piece, *Surrexit Christus* ("Christ is Risen"). But these are exceptions, not the rule. He does, indeed, seem to disdain to write for a mere four-voiced choir. The majority of his vocal works—even the madri-gals—are in six or more parts, and often for antiphonal choirs.

It can hardly be denied that the Venetian tendency—backgrounded by the worldly interests of the city-state itself—was always favorable to im-posing dimensions and brilliant surfaces. But these characteristics in them-selves are neither virtues nor vices. They may become either the one or the other; but the test is the purpose to which they are put. As Giovanni

Gabrieli employs them—for the expression of earnest thought—they can hardly provoke condemnation.

Elsewhere than in Venice the Netherland traditions, cultivated by composers no less skilled, pursued courses which perhaps preserve more truly the intrinsic qualities of the parent school. The forms of Mass, motet, and madrigal are everywhere current; but each, according to the genius of the composer or the disposition of his audience, takes on a somewhat altered character. The sharpest antithesis to the Venetian style we shall find in the Roman; but before we deal with that, the more general continuation of the Netherland tradition must be studied.

The Later Flemings—Philippe de Monte and Orlando di Lasso

Aside from Clemens non Papa, the most important composers of the mid-century who lived either in the Netherlands or on its French borders were Thomas Créquillon (died 1557) in Namur, Termonde, and Béthune, and Pierre Manchicourt (died 1564) who began in Béthune but worked also in Spain. Jacobus Vaet (died 1567) spread the tradition further, being a member of the imperial chapel at Vienna. There are countless others who contributed much to the deepening stream of musical thought, but of whom we can take no individual notice. However, of one great figure, who has but recently begun to be judged at his true value, an account must be rendered.

This was Philippe de Monte. He was born in 1521 at Malines in Flanders. He appears to have had his early training at his native city, and to have been tutor to a wealthy family at Naples where he remained until 1553, and where he first met his great contemporary, Orlando di Lasso. His first book of madrigals was published in Rome in 1554. He visited Antwerp, and journeyed to England where he met William Byrd, of whom we shall presently speak. In 1555, he was recommended as chapelmaster to Duke Albert of Bavaria (di Lasso's later patron) as "a quiet, self-contained man, as modest as a maiden, who has lived for the most part in Italy, knows Italian like a native, as well as Latin, French and Dutch, and is besides, beyond contradiction, the best composer in the country, especially in the new music, and in *musica reservata*." In spite of this recommendation, de Monte failed of appointment and returned to Italy. There he lived without definite patronage until 1568, when he became chapelmaster to the Emperor Maximilian II, and served both him and his successor, Rudolph II, until his own death in 1603.

He began publication, as we have seen, with the madrigal, and retained his interest in that form throughout his life, composing some forty-one books. The French chanson was also a favorite diversion. But in his later years he turned to larger and more serious forms—Masses, motets, and spiritual madrigals—and of these also a very large number were published, and more remained in manuscript. His style is very similar to that of di Lasso, whose acquaintance de Monte cherished, and whose career is very similar to his own—save for the fact that di Lasso is nowhere described as being "modest as a maiden." The high value of de Monte's work was recognized, however, both by his patrons and by the world of music; Elizabeth Weston, an Englishwoman resident in Prague, wrote in Latin a panegyric on de Monte which is typical of many similar appreciations. It describes him as "the prince of musicians in our age"; compares his musical powers to those of Amphion and Orpheus; and attests his fame in Rome, all Italy, Gaul, and Spain.

Since de Monte and di Lasso are largely similar in their activities and their style, we may first give a brief account of the latter's life, and a summary of the characteristics of their style thereafter. The genius of Orlando di Lasso was doubtless more comprehensive than that of de Monte, if only by reason of his extraordinarily energetic disposition. He was born at Mons—in 1520, according to older historians; in 1532, as more recent biographers believe—and was a choirboy in the church of St. Nicholas there. Like de Monte, he learned and worked in many places—Naples, Milan, Florence, and Rome; returned for a time to his native land; visited England and France, and settled for a while in Antwerp. In 1557 he joined the chapel of Duke Albert of Bavaria (to which de Monte, two years earlier, had been recommended), and became chapelmaster in 1562. He married a daughter of the ducal family, and his two elder sons were zealous propagators of their father's music. His position gave him time both for composition and for travel. He visited Paris, where he was received with unprecedented acclaim. Ronsard, the founder of the group of seven poets called the *Pleïade*, saluted him as "the more than divine Orlando."

If the volume of de Monte's work is great, that of di Lasso is incredible. The *Magnum opus musicum Orlandi de Lasso*, published by his sons, Ferdinand and Rudolph, in 1604, contains 516 motets for two to twelve voices. The catalogue of his compositions in Delmotte-Dehn's biography listed 189 collections of printed works and 194 in manuscript. Many of the collections contained whole books of Masses, motets, madrigals, and magnificats. Number 75 alone, for instance, is divided into nine parts and has sixteen Masses, twenty-one motets, a Passion, music for the Office for the feast days of half the church year, four magnificats, and many other works—enough to require from any competent composer a lifetime of effort.

Altogether there are something over 2,000 compositions. The earlier works are often on very worldly themes—French chansons set to gay and sometimes ribald texts, and madrigals that reach a high tide of passion; but the later years brought a change of disposition. Of all his works the most renowned, in his day as in our own, are the seven Penitential Psalms. These, as we have seen, were "reserved" at Munich—in a wonderfully inscribed and richly bound volume testifying to the regard in which the composer was held by his patron.[9]

Distinctions in style or character between two composers as alike in skill as di Lasso and de Monte are hard to draw without resorting to elaborate technical analysis. Such a competent critic as Peter Wagner, however, finds that in the form of the Mass, de Monte shows a certain restraint in the use of debatable tone progressions, and thus achieves a dignity more appropriate to that form than is the freer manner of di Lasso. In the motet, on the other hand, and even more in the madrigal and the chanson, di Lasso's boldness is notable. Each, whether consciously or not, is progressing away from the modal idea toward the tonal—the idea of key. Each, also, often approximates to the homophonic manner. Chromaticism, however, is infrequent in de Monte, who uses no more than the two sharps (F and C) and the three flats (B, E, and A) sanctioned by contemporary theory. Di Lasso, on the contrary, does not scruple to write such a progression as B natural–C–D–E flat (involving the diminished fourth) in the motet *Tristis est anima mea*. And in the song *Alma nemes* he writes what Burney believed to be the first A sharp in history. These, however, are exceptions. Di Lassos's idiom is fundamentally diatonic.

[9] The Penitential Psalms are (in the King James Version), Nos. VI, XXXII, XXXVIII, LI, CII, CXXX, CXLIII. The *Harvard Anthology* has three verses from the third of the seven (Ps. XXXVII in the Vulgate). What is there given as verse 20 is, in the Protestant Version, v. 19.

Do not expect to perceive the beauty of this music by pecking out the notes on the piano. The singers read their parts without bar lines, and found the appropriate emphasis for each phrase suggested by the sense and accentuation of the text. Take, for example, the phrase *Cor meum conturbatum est*. In each voice, the initial emphasis on *cor* is followed by diminution of stress on *meum;* and the word *conturbatum* (disturbed) is "illustrated" by the more rapid, rising motion to a peak of tension, and in alto and tenor by an immediate repetition and intensification of the same word. This is not harmonized melody, but three melodies in harmony.

We do, of course, hear harmonies—simple triads and first inversions. But they were not conceived as such. They were instants of consonance—and occasionally of dissonance—in the flowing combination of melodies. The consonances themselves are often unexpected, and in their simple succession the relatively infrequent dissonances acquire significant tension. The dotted quarter F in the alto (bar 6) is not actually dissonant at all; but it pulls strongly toward the E and has all the value of dissonance. The actual discords in bar 9, in consequence, take on a vividness quite unsuspected in our everyday experience of these chords. Only when you can apprehend these subtle values and their high appropriateness to the text will you realize that this music deserves its reputation.

The fame of de Monte during his lifetime was great, as is attested by the high praise bestowed upon him and his music by contemporary musicians and poets. The end of his life, however, coincided with the eruption of a new style so much more immediately attractive that it marks a new epoch in music history. It was deplorable, but not wholly strange, that so unassuming a personality should be forgotten.

Di Lasso's fate was somewhat happier, although he, too, had his detractors. Burney thought him much inferior to Palestrina, "for what is unaffected dignity in the Roman is little better than the strut of a dwarf upon stilts in the Netherlander." Baini, also, the later biographer and panegyrist of Palestrina, found di Lasso "sterile in imagination [!], lacking in grace and fire." But Proske, the editor of the great collection of ancient church music *Musica divina*, comes near to the present-day estimate of him as one who had so far assimilated the national characteristics of all contemporary European music that all these became, in his work, a simple whole. His epitaph, indeed, seems wholly just: *Hic ille est Lassus, lassum qui recreat orbem; discordemque sua copulat harmonia* ("Here lies that Lassus who refreshes the lassitude of the world, and whose harmony reconciles its discord").

THE ROMAN SCHOOL

In the music we have just been studying, worldly influence was not only manifest but was becoming predominant. The Mass, although composed with sincerity, was no longer the form of highest interest, whether to composer or public. The madrigal, although it had far outgrown the dimension and the significance of the frottola and had approached the dignity of the motet, was really the popular form of the day. With the chanson, it was leading the musical thought of the world in the direction, not only of homophony and major-minor tonality, but of music drama, as we shall soon see. The current of this secular thought was strongest in Venice; but it flowed over all Christendom, and was being fed in no small measure by the Protestant Reformation. Even the Church of Rome at the Council of Trent (1545–1563) took cognizance of it. But within the Church itself, which was sorely shaken, there were many whose opposition to the new trends took the form of increased devotion to the old faith; and the sincerity of this faith is nowhere more manifest than in the music which gave it expression.

A Roman school therefore developed. It was composed chiefly of those who lived and worked in the Eternal City; but it embraced also those of like belief in many other regions. Its technique is essentially a refinement of the long-established technique of the Flemings. It is not really new, except in its perfection. But this perfection, although it is analytically visible as a rejection of liberties or licenses practiced elsewhere, is fully perceptible only in relation to the religious thought which it was the purpose of the music to express.

These rejections seem few and slight. Chromaticism, which was everywhere recognized as appropriate only to secular music, is of course excluded. Dissonance is more guardedly treated, though such "idioms" as the *cambiata* and the *escape note* are allowed.[10] Also, some melodic figures which seem irreproachable to our less sensitive ears are scrupulously avoided (see No. 3 in footnote 10)—at any rate by Palestrina. The texture of the polyphony presents always a decorous surface; yet in spite of the restrictions, the individual parts, invariably accordant with the natural accentuation of the words, move with what seems like complete individual freedom. Imitations, although sometimes strictly canonic, are often abandoned after the initial phrases—the object being, not to exhibit learning, but to express a musical thought appropriate to the text.

Since the comparison will be inevitable between the kinds of music which reflect the Catholic and the Protestant points of view, we may here emphasize the fact that to the Catholic, the Church is an institution of no mere human origin, but one which exists by divine and exclusive sanction, and that its sacraments are not mere conventional observances, but acts of devotion and submission, participation in which is essential to salvation. The words of the ritual are thus charged with meaning beyond the burden bearable by ordinary linguistic symbols, and require, for appropriate utterance, no extraordinary emphasis, but only a certain elevation of tone, suggestive of their high function. The conservatism of the composers of the Roman school reflects this attitude. The rejections noted above were avoidances, not of tonal excess, but of spiritual error.

Ever since the time of Gregory the Great, the papal chapel had been

---

[10] The cambiata is a note foreign to the harmony against which it sounds, and taken in the same direction as that of the main melodic motion. The escape note is similar, save that it moves in the opposite direction to the main melodic line:

Cambiata   Escape note   Avoided by
       (*Échapée*)   Palestrina

the center in which the musical traditions of the Church were kept inviolate. The "Babylonian Captivity" of the fourteenth century had doubtless confused these long and exclusive traditions; but forced contact with Burgundian and Flemish musical ideas had not been detrimental. After the healing of the Great Schism, the chapel became the melting pot in which the "ore" of contemporary musical ideas, gathered from all Christendom, might be refined. Musicians of distinction from every corner of Europe sought membership in the chapel, and often, on leaving, served as propagators and unifiers of the central idea in their own lands.

Many conspicuous members of the chapel were Spaniards. One of the earliest of those who established the Roman, as opposed to the Venetian manner, was Cristobal Morales (1512–1553). He served five years in the chapel, from 1540, and then returned to Spain to finish his work, probably in his native Seville. Morales would have no traffic with worldly music, and thought such art a degradation of a divine gift. "The purpose of music," he said, "should be to fortify the soul in a stern and noble manner; if it serves otherwise than to praise God or to celebrate the memory of great men, it fails utterly to accomplish that purpose." His greatest works, the Magnificats (composed twice throughout on the eight psalm tones) and the Masses, hark back to the technique of Josquin, even to the use of the proportional devices. But his Mass on *L'Homme armé* is reckoned among the most beautiful of the countless works on that theme; and the *Missa pro defunctis* (Requiem), in spite of the restricted technique, is strangely tinged with the pallor of death.

Other Spanish composers who were members of the papal chapel were Francesco Guerrero (also of Seville), a friend of Zarlino, Bartolomeo Escobedo, Didaco Ortiz, Francesco Soto. Greatest of all was Tomas Luis de Victoria (Vittoria), *circa* 1540–1611, whose work is less learned than that of Palestrina, and—perhaps on that account—comprehends a narrower range of expression; but it possesses—again by virtue of his lesser absorption with the devices—an intimacy of expression which is felt by many to be unmatched. Among Victoria's greater works—Masses, motets, and magnificats, in considerable but not astounding numbers—his Requiem Mass, published in Madrid in 1605, is the most highly praised, and serves in the opinion of many critics to rank him next to the great leader of the school, Palestrina. Victoria published also, in 1581, a book of hymns for four voices "for the whole year"—a collection which may have stimulated Palestrina's similar and more famous collection published in 1589. We quote a portion of one of these for the sake of comparison with the Protestant hymn.

Victoria, *Hymnus in Ascenscionem Domini* (from Proske, *Musica divina*, III, 374). The beginning is the Gregorian strain on which the hymn is constructed. Observe that each voice begins imitatively with this strain, and that the soprano presents it in augmentation.

We have spoken first of the Spanish members of the papal chapel since some of their efforts antedate the high achievements of the Roman school proper. Their efforts at home, conditioned by a similar religious attitude to that in Rome, and unopposed by Protestant movements, continued the Roman tradition more purely than was the case in France, Germany, or England. Of the Italian members of the chapel, Giovanni Animuccia is the only older figure who demands attention before Palestrina. He was master of the chapel from 1555 until his death in 1571. He was apparently a prolific composer, in full accord with the Roman ideal we have described; but his works, eclipsed by those of his successor, remain largely in manuscript.

Both Animuccia and Palestrina were friends of Filippo Neri, who, at his new church, the Oratory of Santa Maria in Valicella, had instituted the custom of singing, after the Office, simple congregational songs called *Laudi spirituali*. These songs may be regarded as a kind of counterpart of the hymns that were already becoming the most distinctive musical utterance of the Protestant faith. Animuccia and Soto contributed enthusiastically to the movement. It appears that more elaborate texts, some in dialogue form, presently yielded types of spiritual madrigal, and that these are the germ of the seventeenth-century oratorio. The line of descent is not wholly clear. It may be only by one of those freaks of semantics that are more frequent in the field of music than elsewhere that the name of a place of worship (oratorio) comes to be the name of a musical form.

Animuccia's successor was Giovanni Pierluigi da (John Peter-Louis of) Palestrina, a village in the Campagna of Rome. He was born probably in 1525; seems to have studied at Rome in the private school of a Fleming called Gaudio Mell (confused with Goudimel by early biographers); served as organist and teacher in his native village from 1544 to 1551, when he was appointed master of the Cappella Giulia at the Vatican; and entered the papal chapel in 1555. Since he had for some years been married, this appointment was at once an infraction of the general rule and a recognition of his high merit. But he was dismissed by a new Pope, Paul IV, on that ground in the same year, and took posts of chapelmaster at the church of St. John Lateran and at Santa Maria Maggiore. In 1571 he was reappointed a member of the papal choir—really, as composer to that body, for his singing voice was not good—and remained in that service until his death.

His works, like those of any other great composer, are unequal and some have been justly disparaged. Others have always been regarded as almost incomparable. The number is great. There are in the complete edition of Breitkopf and Haertel ninety-three Masses, sixty-three motets for varying numbers of voices—many of the latter in two sections which would by ordinary reckoning almost double that number. There are the hymns mentioned above, and in addition many Offertories, Lamentations, Litanies, Magnificats, and Madrigals. He was also commissioned by Pope Gregory XIII to revise the Gregorian Gradual and Antiphonary—a somewhat time-consuming and thankless task which he never completed.

Among all these, a few have won the especial regard of the world—for example, the Mass for Pope Marcellus (long erroneously supposed to have been one of the compositions through which the Council of Trent was induced to permit the continued use of polyphonic music in that service), the Mass on *L'Homme armé* (a miracle of ingenuity, reverting obviously to Flemish devices, and hailed as superior to that of Josquin), the Mass *Assumpta est Maria* (1585) which so favorably impressed Pope Sixtus V that he (unavailingly) proposed to make Palestrina the master of the papal chapel, and two Masses from 1591, *Aeterna Christi munera* and *Iste confessor*, written for Duke William V of Bavaria. The motets on the Song of Songs (1584) seem only to fulfill the promise of the eight-voiced *Improperia* and the hymn *Crux Fidelis*, dating from 1560, which had at once established Palestrina's fame. A *Stabat Mater*, from a volume dedicated to Pope Gregory XIV, was much admired (and somewhat curiously edited) by Richard Wagner. The student will find many examples of Palestrina's works in the various anthologies. Our space obviously cannot accommodate adequate illustration.

The exalted pitch attained by the Roman school in the last years of the sixteenth century could hardly have been maintained for long, even had the circumstances been favorable. Against the new trends, particularly in the direction of drama, such traditions had no more hope of continuing than had the methods of Sebastian Bach in the second half of the eighteenth century. The younger members of the Roman school—Palestrina's own pupils, Giovanni Maria Nanino, Dragoni, and Stabili, and the two brothers Anerio (Felice, died 1614, and Giovanni, died 1621)—were composers in lesser forms, especially the madrigal. Luca Marenzio (died 1599) was indeed a consummate madrigalist, but left only one Mass, a few motets, and no large works in other forms. His madrigals, however, published in England in 1588 in a collection called *Musica transalpina*, seem to have greatly stimulated the activity of the English madrigalists, of whom presently we shall have to speak. The conservatism of the Roman school, characteristic of a long line of later composers such as Gregorio Allegri (1582–1652), Domenico Mazzocchi (1592–1655), reputedly the first to use the swell $< >$ as a mark of expression, Orazio Benevole (1605–1672) the composer of the monstrous concerted Mass already mentioned, is continued by still later composers into the eighteenth century with Fux, Lotti, and Caldara.

SIXTEENTH-CENTURY GERMANY

We noted in the chapter on the fifteenth century the distinctively German tone of the songs in the Locheimer and Glogauer songbooks. Not only the peculiar sonority of the German language, but a feeling-character essentially belonging to that sturdy race seems imbedded from the beginning in the German musical idiom. The same traits appear in early sixteenth-century songbooks published by Oeglin and Schöffer—polyphonic settings of traditional children's songs; and it had been true of the Minnesinger also.

That character is less evident in the music of the Meistersinger who were their descendants—or, more exactly, their successors—in the changed economy which the rise of the middle class had brought about. The old tournaments of song, held by the Minnesinger under royal patronage, became with the Meistersinger contests between burghers. These were members of the guilds of bakers, weavers, goldsmiths, and what not, who organized their music-making as they organized their industry. The traditions followed by the Meistersinger were somewhat artificial. They believed that in the tenth century twelve poet-singers, headed by one Klingsohr, had sung before the Emperor Odo I and Pope Leo VIII, and had been commissioned by letter and seal to spread abroad their noble art "in the whole Roman Empire of the German Nation." This wholly apocryphal yarn was cited as authority for the self-imposed rules—singularly stiff and unimaginative—according to which the actual guilds, originating in the fourteenth century and flourishing throughout the sixteenth,[11] contrived their songs.

The mastersong, called a *Bar*, was indeed modeled after that of the Minnesinger—two similar stanzas and an *Abgesang*, or refrain. The rhymes, the poetic meter, and the melody must all conform to rule, and nothing in the text must offend against holy writ. "Markers" were chosen to judge the songs, and contestants or candidates for admission to the guild were allowed but few departures from rule. Each melody must have its *Ton* or *Weis*, the exact nature of which it is impossible to distinguish in a musical sense. But this was described, evidently from the text of the song, as a *red* or *blue* or *bloody* tone, or a *tailed monkey*, a *white paper*, a *warm winter* melody, or whatever. The whole movement is vividly and accurately represented in Wagner's inimitable comedy *Die Meistersinger von Nürnberg*. There, also, is made manifest what might escape the cold historical eye—an earnest desire to enrich the plebeian life with the universally available gold of art. The real hero of Wagner's comedy is Hans Sachs, a historic figure, from whose pen a considerable number of mastersongs remains.

The melody of the Meistersinger, however much it must have disposed the German people toward music, had little influence on the German composers of the fifteenth and sixteenth centuries. The learning which appears in that music was derived from the Flemish; but its melodic life was derived from that source which nourished the folk song mentioned at the beginning of this section.

The earliest of the German polyphonists was Heinrich Finck, granduncle of the great theorist Hermann Finck. Heinrich Finck was educated in Poland, and was in the royal service there from 1492 to 1506. No Masses (indeed, except for Isaak, German composers even before the

---

[11] The last guild of Meistersinger yielded up its "charter" and paraphernalia to a local singing society at Ulm in 1839.

Reformation seem seldom to have chosen that form) but smaller songs —often angularly designed, yet of a convincing earnestness—are his contribution. A Pilgrims' Song *In Gottes Namen* with a kind of refrain on *Kyrie eleison* is a fine expression of the sturdy faith of its composer. A somewhat younger contemporary, Thomas Stoltzer (died 1526), displays the same heavy but not unkindly hand. Paul Hofheimer (died 1537), more important as organist, wrote many four-voiced songs, one of which, *Meins trauerns ist,* is the source of the fine German hymn *Aus tiefer Noth schrei ich zu dir*—a theme very dear to Sebastian Bach.[12]

A startling advance is seen in the music of Heinrich Isaak, the first great German composer, who may have been born in Prague but of whose birth date no record can be found. A part of his work belongs to the fifteenth century, for he was the composer of a kind of spiritual drama on the theme of Saints John and Paul, the text of which was by Lorenzo the Magnificent of Florence, who died in 1492. In Florence, Isaak was acquainted with Agricola, Obrecht, and Josquin, and by this varied intercourse with musicians became the most cosmopolitan of the German composers of his day. Songs after both the Italian and the German manner —and very differently styled—appear among his works.[13]

But more than all else, Isaak is the Netherlander, with a large number of Masses and motets set forth with all the panoply of the Flemish technique—save only that he avoids the designation of his mysteries in Latin riddles. The usual themes—songs such as *Malheur me bat* or *Comme femme* —underlie the Masses; the motets have also the familiar types of text; and there is a setting, with the Gregorian chant in the bass, of the music for the Offices for the Sundays and feast days of the whole year. The Gregorian cantus is here in the bass, not in the tenor. Proske described this work as "one of the most precious monuments of the older time, containing a treasure of the most instructive examples for the study of Gregorian chant and figurated counterpoint."

[12] Hofheimer gave hearty support to a movement, led by Conrad Celtes of Ingoldstadt and Vienna, toward the re-establishment of the classic meters in both verse and music. The defeat of the movement is a mark of the indifference of the Germans to classic culture, which we noted in the last chapter. If this movement had succeeded —a most unlikely supposition—a much earlier emphasis on chordal harmony would have been notable, since the classic meters could not have been perceptible in any such welter of sounds as polyphony provided. But that classicism was still alive in the seventeenth century, and that it had a very considerable force, will be seen when we encounter the beginnings of opera.

[13] His song *Innsbruck, ich muss dich lassen* appears in the *Cantional* or *Songbook of the Augsburg Confession* of Johann Hermann Schein with the text paraphrased into *O Welt Ich muss dich lassen* ("O world, I now must leave thee"). Set to many other hymn texts, it is a favorite with J. S. Bach (it appears in both the St. John and St. Matthew Passions), and is once more turned to secular association with the words *Nun ruhen alle Wälder.*

A large number of lesser German composers appear during the earlier sixteenth century, but we have space for little more than the names of the most important—Sixt Dietrich and Arnold Bruck. Dietrich's setting of the Magnificat, and Bruck's many skillfully composed Latin songs are notable. Perhaps the most interesting as showing the literal attitude of the German mind toward biblical incidents is a six-part song of Bruck's, whose text runs: "O unfortunate Judas, what hast thou done that thou hast thus betrayed our Lord? Therefore must thou suffer the pains of hell, and must be forever the companion of Lucifer. Kyrie eleison."

The next really great German master of the sixteenth century is Ludwig Senfl, a Swiss, but whether of Zürich or Basel is uncertain. Neither are the dates of his birth and death known. But from his mature music on the death of Maximilian I, in 1519, it must be inferred that he was born before the century began, and he is mentioned in 1556 as *selig*—dead. He was in the service of Duke William of Bavaria in 1526, and was announced as *musicus primarius* to the same prince in 1534. While he supported to some extent the classical movement mentioned above, he was thoroughly grounded in the Netherland technique. This is to be seen in his one Mass —*Nisi Dominus*—his motets, magnificats, and psalms, and in his completion of that series of Offices which Isaak left unfinished. But the greater part of his work has a decided German accent, and his simpler songs reveal his sympathy with the healthy life of the German burgher. He is able to infuse with musical humor the drinking song "Landlady, if you don't want us about, then what you must do is to turn us all out." Senfl composed one motet at the suggestion or the solicitation of Martin Luther; but he was not of the Protestant faith, and his collaboration has often been over-emphasized.

The first emphatic effort to represent in music the Protestant ideal was made at Luther's desire and with his advice, by Johann Walther and Conrad Ruppich, chapelmaster to the Electoral Prince of Saxony. In 1524 these two were summoned to Wittenberg by the great reformer. There for three weeks they struggled "to set down in good order the notes for some of the Gospels and Epistles, whereupon the first German Mass was sung in the parish church." In the same year a *Geistlich gesangbuchleyn* in five part-books was published, containing thirty-eight German and five Latin hymns, many of which (such as *Through Adam's Fall* and *In Deepest Need I Cry to Thee*) have remained favorites ever since. Many of the texts are translations of Latin hymns (for example, "Come, Creative Spirit" from *Veni creator spiritus*). This collection is the beginning of an enormous literature of hymns, to the harmonic and figurated treatment of which the later composers (most notably J. S. Bach) devoted their finest efforts.

Walther's phrase, "German mass," is somewhat vague. Luther did not intend to do away either with the use of the Latin language in the service, or with many of the portions of the Mass itself. The Ordinary of the Mass, or at any rate that portion of it which formed the texts set by musical composers, contained no doctrinal statements to which Protestantism of Luther's stamp was opposed. The miracle of transubstantiation was indeed rejected, though the Protestant communion remained—with the bread and wine conceived as merely symbolizing the body and blood of Christ —a commemoration of the Last Supper; but while the *Sanctus* and *Benedictus* were often retained, the *Kyrie* and *Gloria* alone seem to have been regarded as sufficient to constitute the German Mass.

The real purport of the Protestant attitude, however, was more directly expressed in the simple hymns than in the more formal liturgical music. These were sung, not merely in the regular services (where the congregation participated, as in the service of the Mass it had not done), but at home and at social gatherings of all sorts. The simplicity and directness of these hymns doubtless helped to make more converts to Luther's belief than did all his sermons and writings—save, of course, his admirable translation of the Bible. Heinrich Heine rightly called his great hymn *Ein' feste Burg*, the "Marseillaise of the Reformation." One of Walther's simpler sacred songs is given below for comparison with Victoria's:

sein höchstes pfand drumb mag-stu wohl auff wa - - - - chen

sein höchstes pfand drumb mag-stu wohl auff wa - - - - chen.

"Awake, awake, thou German land, thou hast enough of slumber; bethink thee of God's loving care, and wherefore He hath made thee. Remember all God's gifts to thee, his highest pledge entrusting: to this do thou awaken."

The melody is still in the tenor. The other voices, although they occasionally indulge in ornamental flourishes, form for the most part a chordal structure. The key is pretty definitely F major, but a flavor of the Lydian mode remains.

It was hardly to be expected that the Protestant movement should achieve at once music in its own vein, yet reaching the high excellence of the older art. The hymns very soon shift the melody from the tenor to the soprano, and become even more chordal. Psalms, which are not conspicuous (unless by allusion in the text) among the earlier Lutheran songs, begin after the middle of the century to take their place—largely through the work of Lucas Osiander, who was doubtless following the method employed by Goudimel in Huguenot France. But psalmody is hardly a feature of Lutheran church music. The tendency is rather toward the motet; but even this is modified by the influence of the hymn.

Toward the end of the century, however, Hans Leo Hassler, a pupil of Andrea Gabrieli, imports into Protestant music something of the brilliance of the Venetian manner. He was born in Nürnberg of Bohemian stock about 1564. His year of study in Venice seems to have given him full insight into the Venetian manner, and some of his larger compositions, eight Masses, and some of the motets follow that style; but other and smaller works are thoroughly German. There are many hymns composed with the melody in the soprano "so that the people may sing together with the choir." One of his five-part secular songs, *Mein g'müt ist mir verwirret* ("My mind is all perturbed"—by an unyielding maiden) became the beautiful hymn *O Haupt voll Blut und Wunden*, harmonized with wonderful variety by Bach.

One more German master of the sixteenth century must be mentioned —Jacob Handl (*circa* 1550–1591), who in Latin was called Jacobus Gallus ("Cock" on the assumption that Handl was the equivalent of Hahn). Although he did not in the least deserve to be called "the German Palestrina," his sixteen Masses, many motets, and other songs often display both sound technique and an inquiring harmonic imagination. He worked at Olmütz and at Prague. Johannes Ecchard (died 1611), Seth Calvisius (died 1616), and Michael Prätorius (a voluminous and significant composer—today more honored for his great treatise *Syntagma Musicum*, which is not only a history of the art up to his time but gives priceless information as to all the instruments known in his day and before) complete the German effort of the sixteenth century and initiate that of the seventeenth.

MUSIC IN SIXTEENTH-CENTURY FRANCE

The story of French music in the later sixteenth century is seldom inspiring. Political history is in large measure the explanation. After the end of the Hundred Years' War, Louis XI and Charles VIII had greatly stabilized the monarchy. Francis I, who came to the throne in 1515, began his reign, like his rival Henry VIII of England, with much promise; but he ended it in severe persecutions of the Huguenots, and the whole century was so torn with religious wars that it is not strange to find music reduced to insignificance. The attitude of the nobility was characteristic: music, after all, was but a charming diversion. And to this attitude, the Calvinistic religion of the Huguenots did not foster any significant opposition.

Calvinists and Lutherans alike based their belief on the doctrine of salvation by faith; but Calvin was a much colder and more logical theologian than was Luther. Against so dire a threat to the soul as was offered by the total depravity of man (induced by Adam's original sin), only the most certain of spiritual shields could offer protection; and music seemed to him, unless safeguarded by a soundly orthodox text, more likely to act as a seduction of the soul than as a guide to its needful grace. Protestant music in France, in consequence, was a far less vital force than in Germany.

Neither did the Church itself, in the first half of the century, offer any great stimulus. The papacy was at its lowest ebb. Alexander VI (father of the unspeakable Caesar Borgia), Julius II, and even Leo X (a son of Lorenzo the Magnificent of Florence) were wholly worldly men; and their successors, Hadrian VI and Clement VII, were too much concerned with the fortunes of the papacy against the rising power of France, England, and even the Empire to offer much patronage to worthy music. The confusion over musical problems at the Council of Trent indicates the extent of the official understanding.

French music shows the lack, which this brief sketch will suggest, of any such serious purpose as is evident even in the rough and plebeian music of Germany. Elegance, cleverness, grace, and wit are plentiful; the greater musical virtues are rare.

Such censure, of course, applies variably to different composers. Claudin Sermisy (died 1562) and Pierre Certon (died 1572) show full understanding of the Flemish technique, and exhibit their considerable powers in well-turned examples of the Mass and the motet; but their work lacks the tone that bespeaks an inner imaginative compulsion. On the other hand, in such lighter works as Certon's chanson *Je ne fus jamais si aise*, the bubbling gaiety of the courtier is genuine and infectious.

The most brilliant genius in this genre, however—one whom we may take as representative of the French disposition of the moment—is Clément Jannequin, whose birth and death cannot be dated, but who appears to have been alive, though an old man, in 1560. He composed in the serious forms, like Sermisy and Certon, but with less devotion than they. In the lighter field, however, he surpasses not only them but all his contemporaries. His realism was astounding, as may be inferred from Ambros's description of one of his most famous pieces, *La Bataille* (the battle of Marignano, between the French and the Swiss in 1515). It begins, "Hear, ye gentle gaulois, the victory of the noble king of France." Ambros continues, "Then comes the drawing up of the troops, with drums and a lusty march of the fifers, the thunder of the cannon, the rattle of musketry, the clashing of sabers, the trumpet-signals, the shouts of command, and at last—as the Swiss take flight with the cry, 'All is lost, bigot'—the French shout, 'Victory, victory to the noble king of France!' And all this tone-painting is done with human voices." One of Jannequin's two published Masses is made from this same song.

The line closes more impressively with Claude Le Jeune (died 1603), whose Calvinistic Psalms compare favorably with those of Goudimel. But there is no French master to be named in the same breath with di Lasso or Palestrina—or, as we shall soon see, with several of the English composers of the end of the century. Goudimel's work, however, stands out with startling distinctness against the depressing superficiality of contemporary music. Many Masses, motets, and other works prove his thorough mastery of polyphony. But his interest in these forms has been obscured by the importance which accrued to his settings of the Psalms. Versified by Clément Marot and Théodore de Bèze, these had been sung to popular melodies, even in the churches. To avoid this secular association, one Guillaume Frank had provided other melodies, at any rate for fifty of the Psalms; and Le Jeune and Goudimel both made use of these as themes.

Goudimel's first collection (1562) was cast in motet form with the themes elaborated in all the voices; the second (1565) was simpler, with the melody persistently in the tenor. He averred that he had designed

these for use in the home, and they were so used, not only by the Huguenots but by the Catholics, for the publication was approved by the
Sorbonne. They were much used also in Germany. There is no proof
that Goudimel was a Huguenot. Yet he was a victim of one of the worst
outbreaks of intolerance in history—the Massacre of St. Bartholomew,
August 24, 1572.

SIXTEENTH-CENTURY ENGLAND

We have noted the disaster that befell English music with the close of
the Hundred Years' War and the ensuing Wars of the Roses. The accession of Henry VII (1485) brought peace, and an immediate revival of
musical activity; but there is evident a loss of contact with the methods of
the Flemish school. A manuscript in the library of Eton College, dated
about 1490, probably shows the existing state of musical affairs. It contains compositions by Gilbert Banaster (died 1487), William Cornysh
(died 1524), Richard Davy (or Davys), organist at Magdalen College,
Oxford, 1490 to 1492, and many others. There are motets, hymns, and a
Passion—all much more diffuse and improvisatory than the works of Josquin or his predecessors, and with no comparable thematic elaboration.
Yet there is often a spontaneous quality in the melody which is lacking in
any but the greatest continental masterpieces.

That this book may represent a conscious reaction against Flemish
intricacies is hardly likely, though the same tendencies appear in later
manuscript collections—notably in what is known as the *Fayrfax Book*,
since Robert Fayrfax (died 1521), who is represented there by five songs,
is supposed to have written the manuscript with his own hand. The
method is generally that of the Eton collection, with a greater beauty of
sound but no more elaborate imitation.

It appears, however, that the Netherland methods were beginning to
be followed in England about 1516—possibly through the interest of
Henry VIII who came to the throne in 1509, and who was himself a rather
amateurish composer. Although no music printing was to be done in
England until 1530 (by Wynkyn de Worde, the successor of Caxton),
the publications of Petrucci could hardly have remained unknown. A
manuscript in the British Museum, dated 1516, contains two motets by
Sampson, dean of the Chapel Royal, which for the first time show any
resemblance to the imitative Flemish style. The opening portion of *Quam
pulchra es*, given in the *Oxford History*, II, 323, if compared with earlier
examples by Fayrfax or Cornysh, shows how far the melodic line has
become cramped through the effort to appear learned.

The continental method soon became popular, however, as may be
seen from the Masses on *Westron Wynde* (a popular English tune) by

Christopher Tye and John Taverner.[14] Thomas Tallis likewise adopted the Flemish technique, and applied it with such distinction as to suggest that had the course of English composition run smoothly throughout the century, the English genius might have shown itself equal to the continental in all departments.

The English Reformation, however, caused a more violent disruption of musical composition than occurred in Germany until the Thirty Years' War in the next century. Henry VIII, married to Catherine of Aragon, had as heir to the throne only a daughter, Mary. Desiring a male heir, he sought to have his marriage to Catherine annulled. To this Pope Clement VII would not assent; and Henry then managed to induce Parliament to declare his marriage illegal, and himself the supreme head of the Church in England. A complete break with the Catholic Church of course resulted. (Henry married Anne Boleyn, who became the mother of Elizabeth; beheaded Anne, and married Jane Seymour, who gave him a son who succeeded him as Edward VI.) Yet Henry was neither a Lutheran nor a Calvinist—in fact, he seems to have remained an adherent of his original creed, as far as mere doctrine was concerned. However, he did not scruple to plunder the monasteries and to gain political advantage by giving church lands to his favorite nobles.

Thus no settlement of the issue of Protestantism was arrived at during Henry's reign. He died in 1547, leaving the throne to Edward, a sickly boy of sixteen. During Edward's reign of three years, Protestant doctrine —reduced to forty-two articles—was adopted as the fundamental creed of the English Church. "Bloody" Mary, an unwavering Catholic who had married Philip II of Spain, tried by harsh methods to re-establish Catholicism in England; but by this time Protestant feeling had become too strong to be overthrown. When Elizabeth became Queen in 1558, the Protestant faith (stated at last in thirty-nine articles) became the state religion. The Spanish Armada had to be destroyed (in 1588) before it was secure; but with that event the Elizabethan era was inaugurated.

With the liberation came, first of all, the adoption of English as the liturgical language, and a consequent transformation of the motet into the anthem (from *antiphon*). The essential features of this form are illustrated in Tye's *Praise Ye the Lord*.[15] As in the motet, each new phrase of text is set to a new strain of music, and the voices enter in imitation; but the texture in the sequel often becomes chordal, with the voices singing the final words of the strain sturdily together. The rhythm and accentuation of English speech are ordinarily well represented (the "tyranny" of

[14] See an excerpt from Tye's work in *Oxford History*, II, 326; from Taverner's in the *Harvard Anthology*, p. 115.

[15] *Oxford History*, II, 346.

the bar line must often be evaded to perceive this), and the harmony usually exhibits a strong leaning towards tonality. Solo passages also occur in what is called the *verse anthem*. That which is choral throughout is called a *full anthem*. In later years also the organ was almost invariably used for accompaniment.

The new ritual also evoked "Services"—settings, in various styles, of the canticles and other portions of the liturgical formula set forth in the *Book of Common Prayer*. Here, English equivalents of many details of the old Roman Rite are preserved—the *Kyrie* and other portions of the Ordinary of the Mass, as well as the Magnificat, *Te Deum, Venite exultemus*, and so on—varying accordingly as the music is devoted to Morning or Evening Prayer or the Communion.

The accession of Elizabeth was an event of profound reassurance to the English people. Although the bitter differences between Catholic and Protestant were by no means at once allayed, persecutions ceased, the Act of Supremacy (reaffirming the headship of the English Church in the Sovereign) was passed, and life began to feel secure. There was indeed little of physical security for thirty years. Mary of Scotland and Philip of Spain had both to be disposed of; but with the incredible victory of the Armada in 1588, as Green says, "the long struggle for sheer existence was over. What remained was the Protestantism, the national union, the lofty patriotism, the pride in England and the might of Englishmen, which had drawn life more vivid and intense than they had ever known before from the long battle with the Papacy and with Spain."

The product of this liberation was the most liberal music to be produced in the sixteenth century. With what looks like a single leap, English composers, hitherto fumblingly adjusting the methods of the Flemish to the vagaries of their tangled religious life, attained a sudden command over the processes of musical expression that is nearly as incredible as the victory of the Armada. Their medium was the madrigal—borrowed from Italy, to be sure, but handled with a daring beyond that of any Italian, and yet often perfected to an equality with any Italian's skill.

The Italian madrigal had become known in England as early as 1564. Works by Willaert, di Lasso, Arcadelt, and others appeared early in Elizabeth's reign, but without creating any immediate furore. William Byrd (1543–1623) began to adapt his own style to known examples of this form as early as 1581, and in 1588 he published some of these attempts and a number of others in a collection entitled *Psalmes, Sonets, and Songs of Sadnes and Pietie, made into Musicke of five parts*. In the same year, and probably later, Nicholas Yonge published under the title *Musica Trans-alpina* a large collection of Italian madrigals with the texts translated into English. To this book Byrd also contributed two five-voiced examples.

Byrd put forth another collection in 1589—*Songs of sundrie natures, some of gravitie, and others of myrth, fit for all companies and voyces.* Thomas Morley in 1593 printed a very popular book of *Canzonets or Little Short Songs to Three Voyces;* and in 1594 he used the Italian title for the first time in English works in his *First Booke of Madrigalls to Foure Voyces.* Thereafter, John Mundy, John Farmer, Giles Farnaby, Thomas Weelkes, John Wilbye, and many others follow suit, with works whose number and perfection are astonishing.

In 1601, Morley printed the famous *Triumphs of Oriana*—a collection of twenty-five madrigals by twenty-three different composers, so uniform in quality and yet so diversified in character that it may be doubted whether Italy, even before the death of Palestrina and di Lasso, could have produced its equal.[16]

It is certain that these songs were originally intended to be sung without instrumental accompaniment. That one or more of the parts might be taken by instruments was soon recognized, however, and many composers announce their pieces as "Apt for voyces or viols." It is evident also that the word *madrigal* had no very precise meaning. *Song, Canzonet,* and *Sonet* appear in the titles given above, and *Ballet, Fa–la,* and *Pastoral* are also frequent. The term *motet* was also used, but not exclusively for sacred pieces, and the more serious madrigals might have been called by some *motets.* The words *ballet* and *fa–la* apparently implied similar differences in lighter songs—the *fa–la* being a piece in which a long sucession of those or similar syllables forms the whole text of a kind of refrain, while the ballet (from the Italian *ballata*) was itself a kind of dance song in character. These, however, were not danced by the singers.[17]

The most remarkable feature of these English pieces is their daring in matters of melody and harmony. The range of the voices is commonly far beyond that allowed in continental polyphony, and the adventures in chromaticism are similarly beyond those of Cipriano de Rore, or—if we adopt the practice of secret chromaticism—of Clemens non Papa. Only Carlo Gesualdo (1560–1614) among the Italians is to be compared with the boldest of the English, Thomas Weelkes. Both Weelkes and Wilbye use progressions which would have confounded the Italian theorists; and even Byrd, the oldest of the madrigalists, warned the singers of his col-

[16] Thomas Whythorne in 1571 published 76 *Songes of three, fower, and five voyces,* the only work of this kind between Wynkin de Worde's publication of 1530 and Byrd's collection of 1588. It is far below Byrd's work, but indicates an awakening.

[17] See a *Balletto* by Giovanni Gastoldi (1556-1622) and Ballets by Thomas Morley and Thomas Weelkes—all with fa-la refrains—in the *Harvard Anthology,* pp. 179, 180, and 193.

lection of 1588 not to interpret certain "jarres or dissonances" as misprints.

The nature of these novel progressions can merely be suggested within our space. Weelkes, in *Cease, sorrows, now* (No. 6 in his first collection), sets the words "I'll sing my faint farewell" to six rising notes, E, F, F sharp, G, G sharp, A—an unheard-of progression in Italian polyphony—and maintains it imitatively with strikingly "modern" harmony in all three voices. He uses in the same madrigal a C sharp in the bass against which the upper voices, in half notes, progress from $\frac{A}{E}$ to $\frac{C \text{ natural}}{A}$—a "false relation" of the extremest sort, which is nevertheless of extraordinary beauty in its proper context. The more usual type of false relation—for example, that of an F sharp in one voice followed by an F natural in another—appears also in this piece, and is almost a commonplace among the English madrigalists.

Written like all polyphony of the time—without bar lines, and with the melody designed to exhibit with meticulous care the natural accentuation of the words—this music displays remarkable freedom of rhythmic design. Except that the texts provoke more "realistic" rhythms than would a sacred text in Latin, this is, of course, the usual practice; but the English composers, with their more difficult texts, manage their problems with amazing nonchalance.

It will have been noted that little mention has been made of instruments or instrumental music thus far. Both the fifteenth and the sixteenth centuries took long strides in the development of instrumental art, and our account of these periods thus remains incomplete. Before we enter upon that story, however, we shall offer a rather extended sketch of the evolution of the instruments themselves. This will take the chronicle down to modern times, but is in accord with that general design which has been adopted—that of horizontal rather than cross-sectional treatment.

The Evolution of Our Modern Instruments

INSTRUMENTS of many kinds accompanied the song of primitive man, long before the dawn of history. Because a few instruments of extreme antiquity have been preserved, and because players of instruments seem always to have been attractive as subjects to graphic artists of all ages, our knowledge of early instruments is somewhat less obscure than our knowledge of primitive musical ideas. Paintings, sculptures, mural decorations, and many fragmentary literary allusions contribute to the reconstruction of the instrumental achievements of the ancients. In these instruments it is striking to find in use every essential principle of sound production which underlies the instrumental art of today. But hardly any of the refinements which we now demand are to be found; for not only primitive instruments, but those of many more advanced peoples, were not merely devices for making music, but were vehicles for the utterance of sound which had other than purely musical meaning—sound which in many ways typified the emotional interests of the individual or the tribe.

The purpose of song we have seen (not only with primitive man, but with the Greeks) as an intensification of poetic speech—speech, that is, which had already served to express both idea and feeling. Similarly the main purpose of primitive instrumental music was to intensify the excitement of the dance—the dance being itself also an outlet for emotion significant to the individual or the tribe. Used merely to accompany song (especially such song as that of the Greeks which was already subordinated to poetry), instrumental music took a low place in the scheme of art. Plato, indeed, had no interest in instrumental music, because it contained nothing which he could *understand*. But instrumental music, used to accompany a significant dance, is of a higher order of interest.

183

For the dance has character, violent or subdued, ecstatic or grave, expressed through motion. That motion is marked chiefly by the periodic contact of the dancers' feet with the ground or of the hands with each other. These instants of contact, these moments of rhythmic stress, outline to both dancer and spectator the essential idea of the dance. To heighten our awareness of the rhythmic pattern is therefore to vivify our idea of the dance. Percussion instruments then, which can greatly magnify the sounds of stamping feet or of clapping hands, we shall find liberally used at a very early stage.

But sustained tone has also its place in this instrumental heightening of dance feeling. For both in its individual tone quality, in its inflection, and in its increase and decrease of intensity, it can represent something of the actuality of motion—the swaying and whirling—which takes place between the instants marked by the rhythmic pulses. Song, of course, would offer the most immediately available tone to the dancer; but instruments which could imitate or enrich the quality of the voice would also be welcome. Also, the primitive dance sometimes had meaning which could not be uttered by human voices. The voices of nature, weird and dreadful or soft and alluring, suggested to the primitive mind various attributes of Deity; and these sounds were to be uttered not merely imitatively but in a spirit of propitiation or of praise. Instruments can often suggest far better than voices the tones of nature, especially of nature in its more fearful moods.

In a very real way, then, instrumental music (although often of a character unrecognizable by us as music) had a value of meaning to the primitive mind. And in a sense it may be said that the history of the dance is the history of primitive instrumental music, just as we said that the history of Greek poetry was in a way the history of song among the Greeks. This history, however, need not be told in detail, but can be sufficiently inferred from an examination of the instruments and a consideration of the uses to which they could be put. The various types of instrument can best be studied by classifying them according to the principle of tone production employed. Perhaps the most accurate classification is that of (1) Idiophones (self-sounding instruments without mechanism, such as bells); (2) Membranophones (hollow vessels covered with a membrane); (3) Aerophones (wind instruments); and (4) Chordophones (stringed instruments). But it is simpler to merge the first two into a single class and to call them *percussion* instruments. We shall study, in their order, the percussion, wind, and stringed instruments, beginning with primitive types and tracing the evolution of our modern examples in a succession as unbroken as possible.

I. Percussion Instruments

To intensify the sounds of clapping and stamping, countless varieties of instruments were invented: castanets, jingling bracelets, metal discs; stamping pipes (to be struck on the ground) whose hollowness emphasized the thud of the feet; stamping boards, shield shaped, which gave a resounding floor for the dancer. Out of such primitive experiments came two important acoustical discoveries: hollow instruments make more noise than solid ones; and small instruments of a given kind are higher in pitch than large ones. Whole "orchestras," as we might call them, of percussion instruments were presently contrived. For to hollow a flat metal plate is to produce, in successive stages, a cymbal, a gong, or even a bell. Bells, like drums and metal rods, grow deeper in tone as they grow in size. The rhythmic beating and jangling of all these together is a brave addition to the shrieks and shouts and threatening growls which come from throats of all ages in an orgiastic dance. Such broad distinctions of pitch not only associate instruments with individuals of contrasting size and sex, but lead to a more careful adjustment of those instruments by which tone, as well as rhythmic impulse, can be produced. Sticks properly graduated in length, somewhat hollowed and carefully mounted so that their sonority

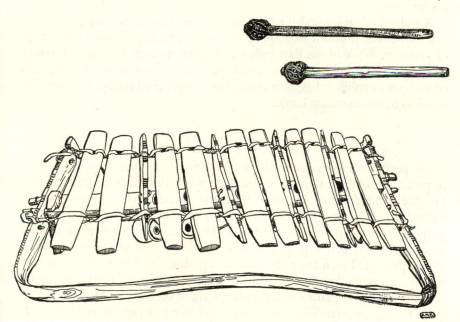

FIG. 1. AFRICAN XYLOPHONE, IN COLLECTION OF THE MINNEAPOLIS PUBLIC LIBRARY
(Drawn by Bernice Margaret King)

would not be deadened, gave an instrument upon which the songs of the tribe could be played. With but few refinements, this instrument becomes our modern xylophone; with a hollow resonator attached to each wooden plate it becomes a marimba; and with carefully tuned metal bars instead of wooden plates and with a keyboard mechanism it becomes an instrument much used for ethereal effects in the modern orchestra—the celesta. The glockenspiel ("play of bells") has also metal plates but is played with sticks. The triangle, cymbals, gong, rattle, and other instruments which orchestral players sometimes irreverently speak of as "the kitchen" are all adaptations and refinements of primitive idiophones.

The value of hollowness in a sounding body was further exploited by stretching a skin over a vessel of some sort. The result was a drum—whether the tiny finger-drum of some Eastern dancers or the big bass drum of the modern brass band. Here also pitch discrimination is possible, not only through variable size but through variable tension of the membrane. The modern orchestra uses three types of drum—the bass drum, the smaller side drum (whose association to us is chiefly military), and the tympani or kettledrums. The tympani have a mechanism for tightening the head which is capable of very precise adjustment; hence they can be exactly tuned, and are the only drums for which notes of definite pitch are written.

A hybrid of string and membranophone which utilizes the sonority of the skin-covered gourd to amplify the tone of strings is found in a type of primitive fiddle of the East Indies and other regions. For bowed strings, this type of amplification is so inadequate that no modern development of such an instrument has been made; but for plucked strings the principle survives in our common banjo.

II. Wind Instruments

All percussion instruments have the drawback that they are unable to produce sustained tone, or to increase their tone without repercussion. For the production of sustained tone the agency first suggested would naturally be the air. The breath of man is used for something like this purpose from the first moment of life. The breath of nature made strange tones as it blew across jagged rock or whistled around the rude shelter which protected man from the storm. The breath of man, blown against some sharp or hollow body, could imitate this voice of the Great Spirit. Imagine the consternation and delight pictured on the face of the first man who, testing his breath on some discarded horn of ram or antelope, suddenly blew a blast that ten times outdid the power of his own voice! No mere noise this, but a message in tone. To control this tone, or to discover a means by which this newly discovered instrument could be made to speak a variety of tones, might place the player among those purveyors of mystery who constituted the priesthood of the tribe.

Before we describe the many types of developed wind instrument, it will be necessary to discuss the various methods by which the air within a pipe can be set into vibration, and also, briefly, the behavior of the air within the pipe.

Three methods of blowing are in use. Essentially, each was applied to wind instruments of the most ancient times. These methods produce periodic impulses in the air column: (1) by breaking the stream of breath against an angular surface communicating with the column; (2) by actuating a vibratory reed; and (3) by substituting for the reed the tensed lips of the player.

The first, which is the simplest since it requires no special mechanism, is known to every boy who has made a tone by blowing across the top of a bottle. The physicist shows us how in this act the stream of breath is split against the rim of the aperture. A part of the stream is thus retarded. This part, on meeting the rim, is first compressed and then by its own elasticity is rarefied. Condensations and rarefactions succeed each other rapidly and are communicated to the air within the pipe, which has a natural capacity to vibrate at a rate corresponding to the length of the pipe. To a certain extent the pulses from the breath are controlled by and synchronized with the sound waves set up in the pipe.

Reeds (our second source of vibration) communicate their own pulsation to the air column—pulsation which has been set up in the reed under the impact of the stream of breath. There are three types of reeds: the double, the single or *beating*, and the *free* reed. The double reed is probably the oldest. Its prototype is the wheat straw, so compressed between the lips that its sides are brought nearly in contact thus: ◁▷ . Less perishable reeds are made of two slightly hollowed splits of bamboo bound together so as to give an aperture like that just described. Both edges vibrate, whence the term *double*. The single reed is larger. It consists of a single blade of bamboo laid against (but not completely in contact with) an aperture of the pipe which is so shaped that this part of the pipe, with its reed, can be held between the lips. The vibration (*beating*) of the reed alternately closes and opens the space between the reed and the pipe. Free reeds are tongues (usually but not necessarily of thin

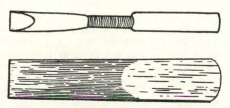

FIG. 2. OBOE AND CLARINET REEDS

metal) so set in an aperture that they perform a complete oscillation back and forth in response to the stream of air through the aperture which is very slightly larger than the reed itself.

The column of air within the pipe can vibrate either as a whole (which gives the *fundamental* tone of the pipe) or in successively smaller fractions of its whole length. Fractional vibrations (which can and do occur simultaneously with the fundamental vibration and with each other) give higher sounds, much less intense than that of the fundamental, which are called *upper partials* or *harmonics* of the fundamental tone. The succession of these partial tones, in order, is called the *harmonic series*. This series is also producible by the fractional vibrations of a string. The following table will show the tones produced by dividing an air column or a string successively into two, three, four, and more parts. Theoretically, the harmonic series is infinite; practically, it extends not far beyond the limits of the table. If we number the fundamental as 1, the successive figures thus show the number of parts into which the vibrating source is divided. They show also, in relation to each other, the vibration ratio of the interval between the notes indicated by the figures. The notes marked * are out of tune with our accepted scale built on the fundamental. Any note may be taken as fundamental; but for the sake of simplicity we choose the note C:

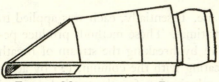

FIG. 3. MOUTHPIECE FOR BEATING
REED (Clarinet)

THE HARMONIC SERIES [1]

Fundamental		Partials								
1		2	3	4	5	6	7	8	9	10
C'		C	G	c	e	g	bb*	c'	d'	e'
Intervals:	8ve		5th	4th	maj. 3rd	min. 3rd			maj. tone	min. tone
		11	12	13	14	15	16			
		f'*	g'	a'	bb'	bʰ'	c''			
							half step			

[1] It will be seen that the ratio of the octave throughout the series is 2:1—i.e., the successive C's are numbered 1, 2, 4, 8; the G's, 3, 6, 12; the E's, 5, 10; etc. The major third c'-e' is 5:4, not 81:64 as Pythagoras determined it by adding together two "major tones." There are also two different major seconds: c'-d' (ratio 9:8) and d'-e' (ratio 10:9). The larger of these is called a *major* (greater) tone; the smaller, a *minor* (lesser) tone. We shall see what bearing this fact has on the problem of tuning when we come to study the problem of equal temperament. Diagrams of the first eight partials are shown in the text.

Pipes are classed as *open* and *stopped*. Stopped pipes are completely closed at one end. The column of air in an open pipe vibrates as a whole to give the fundamental tone of the pipe. When the pipe is closed, the obstruction forms a *node* (a point of no vibration) at the middle of the wave. Only half the whole wave thus forms within the closed pipe, and the pitch of a closed pipe is thus an octave lower than that of an open pipe of the same length. The bore of a pipe, whether conical or cylindrical, is of importance. For a pipe of conical bore with a double reed has the acoustic properties of an open pipe (that is, its length is that of the

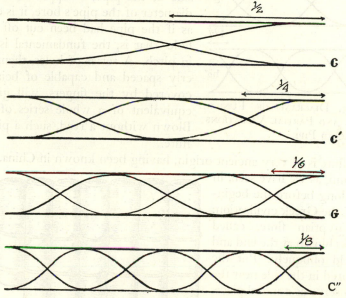

FIG. 4. DIAGRAM OF FUNDAMENTAL AND PARTIAL VIBRATIONS IN AN OPEN PIPE

fundamental wave); while a pipe of cylindrical bore with either single or double reed behaves like a closed pipe, and therefore sounds a note an octave below its fundamental. (A node is formed at the mouthpiece end.)

With so much in the way of necessary acoustical detail, we may return to our story of the development of the wind instruments. The simplest is the single pipe, blown by the method first mentioned: that is, across the end. Such a pipe can give but a single tone. To play a scale or a melody, then, several pipes of graduated length will be needed. These, bound together in a row or sometimes in a bundle, give the *Pan's pipe*, one of the most ancient of wind instruments. It is also one of the most modern; for anyone can see that our huge organs are only glorified Pan's pipes with, to be sure, a good many borrowed additions.

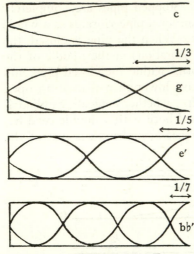

FIG. 5. DIAGRAM OF FUNDA-
MENTAL AND PARTIAL VIBRATIONS
IN A CLOSED PIPE

With the Pan's pipe a smooth progression from tone to tone was impossible, because for each new note the instrument had to be shifted. The great need was for a single pipe upon which all the notes of scale or melody could be played. The problem here presented was solved in very ancient times. It was discovered that if a hole be bored in the side of the pipe, of approximately the diameter of the pipe's bore, it is exactly as if the pipe had been cut off at the hole—that is, the fundamental is raised in pitch. A series of holes, then, properly spaced and capable of being uncovered by the fingers, will give the equivalent of a whole series of pipes. Blown without a reed, such a pipe is a flute.

The flute is of very ancient origin, having been known in China, Japan, India, and, as we have seen, in Egypt long before the beginning of the Greek civilization. The Egyptian flute, called *nay*, was blown at the end and was held obliquely. But the hole bored in the side near the end, to serve as a mouthpiece, is also very ancient. With such a mouthpiece the flute can be held transversely and the fingering is greatly facilitated. Transverse flutes were known to the Greeks and Romans, but found less favor than reed instruments like the aulos, which we shall meet in a moment. Hence the flute did not persist in the West after the fall of the Empire, but had later to be reintroduced into Europe from Byzantine sources.[2]

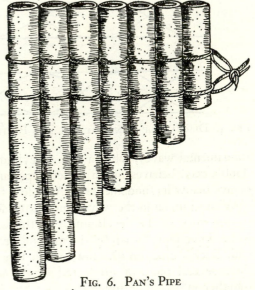

FIG. 6. PAN'S PIPE

[2] Our knowledge of this and other instruments during the early Christian period

By the time of Agricola, the flutes had come to be made in a complete family or choir of four voices; and *consorts* or concerted groups of flutes were much in demand. This variety in size has been much reduced in our day (the bass flute is the only large type to survive; but of the smaller

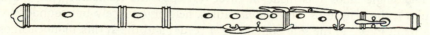

FIG. 7. FLUTE (18TH CENTURY)

types we have the piccolo and the military fife); and the design and the system of fingering have been much perfected. But the principle is still that of the earlier instrument.

The skill required for the blowing of the flute can be much lessened by contriving a *beak* or mouthpiece which will itself direct the stream of breath at the proper angle against the edge of the aperture. With the beak, however, the higher or *overblown* partials are not obtainable, since to produce these the breath must be directed at a flatter angle. The compass of the beak flute is

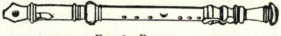

FIG. 8. RECORDER

thus small, but its tone is sweet and soft. The *recorders* of Shakespeare's day were a family of beak flutes. The instrument was called *flûte-à-bec* or *flûte douce* by the French, and sometimes *fipple flute* by the English. It survives today only as a *flageolet*, or *penny whistle*. But we shall find an important application of the principle of the beak in the *labial* of the modern organ pipe.

The favorite wind instrument of the Greeks was the *aulos*. The Romans, who also preferred it, called it *tibia* (literally, shin bone; for the primitive aulos was often made of bone). The aulos was primarily a reed-blown instrument, though the name in its wider significance included also the reedless Pan's pipe and flute. The reed aulos was made in many forms and sizes. Some apparently had single reeds, and some double. Some also (probably the earlier types) had the reeds exposed, to be held between the player's lips; some enclosed the reed in an enlarged bulb in the pipe. With

---

is gained chiefly from illuminated manuscripts and from a considerable array of paintings depicting musicians at their tasks. Verbal descriptions also begin to appear: for instance, in the *Garden of Delights* by a thirteenth-century authoress, the Abbess Herrad von Landsperg, where the flute is pictured and is called *tibia*. By the sixteenth century instruments had been brought to such a stage of perfection that systematic descriptions of them begin to be written. The chief authors of such books are: Sebastian Virdung (*Musica getutscht und ausgezogen*, Basel, 1515); Martin Agricola (*Musica instrumentalis deudsch*, Wittenberg, 1528); Marin Mersenne (*Harmonie universelle*, Paris, 1636); and Michael Prätorius (*Syntagma musicum*, issued in various divisions, 1615–1620).

the latter type, since the reed was not under the player's direct control, the production of harmonics was impossible. (But the process of overblowing was known to Aristotle.)

There were two main types of aulos: the single pipe and the double. The single aulos was made in three varieties—the monaulos (the single pipe); the plagiaulos (the *oblique* aulos, held transversely but sounded by a mouthpiece in the side containing a reed); and the syrinx monocalamos (syrinx is also the word for Pan's pipe; kálamos is a hollow reed). The double

FIG. 9. PLAGIAULOS

auloi were made in four sizes: the *maidens'*, the *boys'*, the *teleioi* (perfect, also called *Pythian*), and the *hyperteleioi* (lower than the perfect)—the four instruments being obviously in the pitch relation of the four natural human voices. There was also the *Aulos kitharisteros*—the aulos designed to accompany the harp or kithara. The representations of double-aulos players show a bandage called the *phorbeia*, which covers the mouth and cheeks and passes around the head. Whether this bandage served as a support for the too-distended cheeks, or merely for the instrument itself, is a question not yet answered. Neither, indeed, is the purpose of the double pipe certainly known. For without exact knowledge of the mechanism, one cannot tell whether the pipes sounded simultaneously (though from the absence of harmony in Greek music this seems improbable) or alternately (for with differently spaced holes two pipes could sound either a more complete scale or two scales of different genus).

The Greeks had still another type of aulos which was of less artistic value (it was merely a shepherd's instrument) but which employed a novel system of blowing. This was called the *askaulos*, and was essentially a bagpipe. It was not of Greek invention, but probably came from Persia or Chaldea. The bag, of course, was a kind of bellows; the pipes were double-reed auloi; and it needed but a little ingenuity to progress from this instrument to one which could insufflate a whole scale of pipes—that is to say, to the organ.

How early may have been the invention of the pneumatic organ (portable, with a leather bellows) is unknown. But the invention of a much more imposing instrument, the hydraulos or water organ, is definitely ascribed to Ctesibius of Alexandria in the second century B.C. Instead of bellows, this instrument had a submerged air chamber (communicating with the pipes) in which the pressure was maintained, as air was pumped in, by the weight of the water displaced by the air. Some sort of key and valve mechanism, now not clearly understood, controlled the admission of air to the pipes. The hydraulos attained to great favor in Imperial

Rome. Made on a very large scale it was placed in the arena, where it must have been comparable to the steam calliope of our present-day circus, and whence it acquired such evil association with pagan practices as to ban the organ altogether from the Church for many centuries.

This ban extended with equal force to other instrumental music. The chief development of musical thought, as we have seen, was carried on within the Church; and when at last in the ninth century the theorists began to describe church music in their treatises, secular music of all kinds (in which instrumental music was of course included) was referred to—for the most part contemptuously, but gradually with a kind of furtive interest—as *musica irregularis.* The direct line of instrumental descent from Graeco-Roman types was almost extinct; and variants of those prototypes, developed in the East, had now been imported into Europe from that source. Our story has thus perforce been broken off; and we must begin anew with the indirect descendants of the aulos.

Among modern instruments, that which most nearly resembles the aulos is probably the oboe. This instrument was known in the Middle Ages by

FIG. 10. MODERN OBOE

various names, all derived from the Greek *kalamos,* a reed. The Latin form was *calamus;* the French, *chalumeau;* the German, *Schalmei;* and the English, *shawn.* Virdung describes a larger variety of *Schalmei* which he calls *Bombardt.* Prätorius, a century later, sees the family increased to six instruments of graduated size, the lower instruments now being called *Pommer.* Of these, the *Discant Schalmei* becomes the oboe proper. It was first used at the performance of an opera *Pomone* by Cambert in 1671. The alto pommer, more slowly transformed, was called the *hautbois de chasse* in France and the *oboe di caccia* (both terms mean *hunting oboe*) in Italy. The English name for this instrument, *English horn* (*cor anglais*

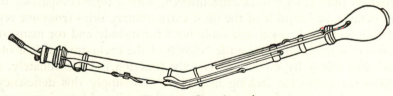

FIG. 11. COR ANGLÉ

and *corno inglese* in French and Italian) is often attributed to the similarity in appearance of this instrument to a hypothetical English hunting horn.

It is more probable that the name arose in France as a misunderstood version of *cor anglé;* for during the eighteenth century this instrument was made with a rather sharp angular bend in the middle. The English horn is a fifth lower in pitch than the oboe. In the eighteenth and early nineteenth centuries an instrument midway between these two in pitch was often used; its pear-shaped bell gave it a soft, veiled quality of tone, whence it was called *oboe d'amore.*

All the modern types of oboe have double reeds and conical bore. They overblow (that is, repeat their harmonic series) at the interval of the octave, as is natural to open pipes. The double reed gives to all the higher instruments of the family a peculiar quality of tone, far more vibrant than the smooth note of the flute. A very different group of partials also is present. The oboe is thus the most distinctive in tone of all the wind instruments of our orchestra. Its tone is also the most homogeneous throughout its compass. But the lower instruments of the family—the bassoons and contra bassoons—do not closely resemble the oboe or even the English horn in tone.

The predecessors of the bassoons—the bass and contrabass bombards—were at first made in one straight piece. The extreme inconvenience of this design (the contrabass bombard was over nine feet long) was remedied by laying two sections of the pipe against each other, and connecting them at the bottom. From its resulting resemblance to a bundle of sticks, the instrument came to be called *fagotto* in Italy and *Fagott* in Germany. The English and French names *bassoon* and *basson* more clearly imply the function of the instrument as the bass of the woodwind choir. Very dis-

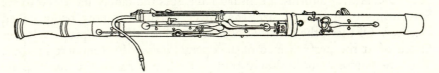

FIG. 12. MODERN BASSOON

tinctive in tone though somewhat uneven, with a total compass of over three octaves, and capable of the most extraordinary skips from one register to another, the bassoon is suitable both for melody and for many suggestions of humor. (It can be the "clown of the orchestra," as it is often called; but this is by no means its only function.) Unfortunately, the bassoons are somewhat lacking in power. To supply this deficiency a French bandmaster, Sarrus, invented a whole family of brass instruments, conical, with double reeds, which he called *Sarrusophones.* The lowest of these is much used, especially in French orchestras.

The single, *beating* reed, although probably known to the ancients, was certainly less in favor than the double reed; and that disfavor continued during the Middle Ages. Mersenne gives the earliest extant description of the single reed; but the instrument to which it was then applied (the *chalumeau*) which later developed into the clarinet, was not in his day clearly distinguished from double-reed instruments. Unless the true origin of the clarinet can be traced to the Netherlands, where instrumental manufacture was prolific from the fourteenth century to the sixteenth, it is probably correct to accept the statement of Doppelmayr that the clarinet was the invention of J. Christian Denner at the beginning of the eighteenth century. By adding to the old cylindrical chalumeau the *speaker hole* which makes possible the overblowing of the series, and providing the single reed (larger than the double) which was necessary for a pipe of larger bore, the essential characteristics of the clarinet were established. Since the scale of the clarinet proceeds for a twelfth before being repeated by overblowing, a larger number of holes and keys is necessary than for the flute and oboe, which overblow at the octave. The resultant difficulties in structure and fingering made the instrument somewhat slow of acceptance by musicians; not until Mozart's day did the clarinet become an indispensable member of the orchestra.

Because of its complex mechanism, the clarinet is difficult to play in keys having many sharps or flats. For that reason it is constructed in different sizes, especially in the two which give the instrument the fundamental scales of B flat and A, respectively. The clarinet in B flat, that is, when the natural scale (C to c) is played on it, sounds the scale of B flat. The natural scale played on the clarinet in A similarly sounds the scale of A. This is as if the pianist had a device by which he could shift his keyboard so that the key which he calls C would be made to strike the A string instead of the C string. Thus shifted, his instrument could play in A with the C fingering, in E with only one sharp, and so on, always subtracting three from the number of sharps in his signature. Shifted so that the C key would strike B flat, he could similarly subtract two from the number of flats in his signature. Such instruments are called *transposing* instruments. The English horn in F (sounding a fifth lower than it is written), the clarinets in B flat, in A, and that in E flat (sounding a minor third higher than it is written), and the French horns and trumpets (presently to be described) are the principal transposing instruments of the modern orchestra.

Aside from those mentioned, the only other clarinet now in general use is the bass clarinet, an octave lower than the usual one. But in the eighteenth century there was also a *basset horn*, a clarinet a fifth below the normal. The lower register of the clarinet is called *chalumeau*, the higher, *clarion.* There is a considerable difference in quality between the two, though the progression from the one to the other can be made nearly unnoticeable. The clarinet has enormous agility (far greater than the oboe, and nearly equal to the flute) and the greatest dynamic range of any of the wind instruments. It can play the softest pianissimo of any wind instrument, and can also cut through a considerable body of accompanying tone.

Although the organ, having a keyboard, might logically be included with other mechanical tone-producers like the clavichord, harpsichord, and piano, it may equally justly be described here, since it is the mechanical equivalent of all, and more than all, the woodwind choir. We have seen how the principles of Pan's pipe, aulos, and askaulos were combined to produce the portative and water organs of the ancients. The earliest record of the importation of the organ from the East (after the fall of the Western Empire) is that of an organ sent as a present to Pippin by the Byzantine Emperor Constantine Copronymos in 757 A.D. Charlemagne received another, with bellows of hide and pipes of bronze, whose "tone was as loud as thunder and sweet as that of lyre and psaltery." By the tenth century the instrument had been introduced into larger churches of both England and Germany; and the art of organ building continued to be cultivated thereafter, with a rapid increase in skill manifest in every feature of the structure.

The modern mechanism is so complex that no more than a sketch of its structure is possible here. We may consider first the pipes, and next the mechanism which makes them speak. Organ pipes are made of wood or metal. Wooden pipes are rectangular, and either stopped or open. The metal pipes are cylindrical or conical; are made of various alloys, according to the tone quality desired; and all pipes are of varying dimensions (according to the pitch they are to sound) and of varying ratio as to length and diameter (for the production of the partials tones desired with the fundamental). Pipes are also divisible, according to the method by which they are made to speak, into two general classes: flue pipes and reed pipes.

Flue pipes have an incision in the side, near the base where the wind enters. The upper surface of this incision is beveled to a sharp edge (the

Fig. 13. Flue Pipe

lip or *labial*); and an obstacle is placed within the pipe, in the path of the wind stream, in such a way that the stream will be directed against the lip at that angle which is necessary to produce pulsations. Flue pipes are thus blown according to the principle of the flute.

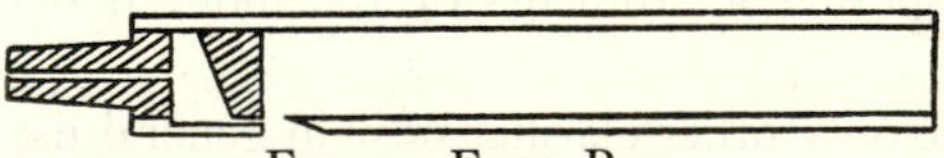

But being essentially *beak flutes* they cannot be overblown, and since the wind pressure remains constant and there is no agency for varying the tension or elasticity of the lip, each pipe produces only a single tone.

Reed pipes are mostly actuated by a beating reed, set within the pipe. Sometimes, however, the free reed is used. Reeds are tuned by a wire which slides along the tongue of the reed, altering its length and hence its pitch. All reeds should have the same fundamental vibration rate—that is, the same pitch—as the vibrating

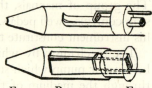

FIG. 14. BEATING AND FREE REEDS (in Organ Pipes)

column of air in the pipe to which they are fitted. All the pipes fed by a single wind chest must be so contrived as to speak at the wind pressure maintained within that chest. Hence, except in the rare cases where free reeds are used (and these, to vary their volume, must be provided with variable wind pressure) the loudness with which any pipe speaks is always the same.

The quality or *timbre* of a pipe's tone depends not only on whether it is a flue or a reed pipe, but also on the material of which the pipe is made,[3] and on the ratio between the diameter and the length of the pipe. For variation in these factors gives variation in the upper partials which sound with the fundamental; and timbre is essentially a product of these partials. A great variety of tone character can thus be produced, variety which somewhat makes up for the inevitable lack of dynamic responsiveness in the organ. All the wind instruments of the orchestra, both woodwind and brass, can be closely imitated; and even the string quality can be strongly suggested.

A whole scale-series of pipes of a given timbre is called a *stop*. Each stop can be either silenced or made ready to play by means of a handle or an electric switch which can close or open the section of the wind chest which admits air to its pipes. These stops are named according to their character and their pitch. Conventionally, a stop which gives notes of the pitch of the keys on the keyboard (named just as on the piano) is said to be an 8-foot stop. Some stops have pipes of twice this conventional length, and sound, in consequence, an octave lower than is indicated by the keys which make them speak. Such a stop is said to be of 16 feet; one two octaves lower, of 32 feet; one an octave higher than the keys, of 4 feet, and so forth. A whole group of stops connected to a single manual (keyboard) is in itself an organ. But so great is the variety of producible stops that

---

[3] The supposition that the material of the pipe has no influence on the tone is disproved both by scientists (see Helmholz, *On Sensations of Tone*, and D. C. Miller, *The Science of Musical Sounds*) and by the careful practice of organ builders.

several of these organs are combined in the whole instrument, each having its own manual. The usual names for these manuals (or organs)—*great, swell, choir, solo*, and *echo*—describe fairly clearly the character of each. The group of manuals, the pedals (another keyboard), and the various stop controls, swell pedals, and so on, through which the organist manages his instrument constitute the *console*.

The mechanism by which the pipes are made to speak consists of the bellows or pump which supplies the wind pressure, and the action which, through the medium of the key, admits the air to the desired pipes. A leather bellows, worked by hand or in larger organs by the feet, was familiar to the ancients. The ingenious mechanism of the hydraulos was capable of maintaining a far larger volume of compressed air than any manageable bellows. It may be thought of as the counterpart of the large electric blowers which can now be made adequate to any demand. A later employment of the smaller, hand-operated bellows was seen in the Bible Regal illustrated below. The pressure in any single organ (which must remain constant) is kept at the desired level by an escape valve which opens when the pressure becomes too great.

The problem of the key mechanism was much more difficult. The ancient portative organs appear to have had some sort of balanced key, not too unwieldy to be depressed by the finger. But the larger the instrument the larger the key had to be; so that for long, a handle which had to be

FIG. 15. BIBLE REGAL (German, seventeenth century)

drawn out several inches, or a lever which could be depressed by nothing less than a blow of the fist, was the only known key mechanism. These were direct levers, from key to pipe valve. So long as this simple mechanism was in use, the dimensions of the instrument were very limited. For large modern organs a variety of devices has been used. A sort of bell wire connection between key and valve, capable of being strung around corners, was the most important factor in the "tracker" action—a mechanism which came into universal use before the advent of pneumatic or electric communication. With the tracker action, when more stops were turned on more wires had to be pulled by the same key. Hence, with the "full organ" the action became very heavy. The electric action of course removes this difficulty entirely.

It is impossible to contrive a blowing mechanism which will give variable wind pressure such as is at the disposal of every flute or clarinet player. Hence, although its many stops give the organ a palette of color as rich as that of the orchestra and even more varied, the instrument suffers from a lack of dynamic sensitivity. The whole volume of tone can be increased or decreased, however, either by using more or fewer stops or through operation of the "swell." This is a large box with a folding shutter in the side, enclosing a whole section of the organ. The shutter can be opened or closed by means of a pedal, thus allowing greater or lesser volume of sound to escape and making possible a general crescendo or diminuendo. Emphasis of individual notes has been made possible in electric actions by an adjustment of the electric contacts such that a heavier pressure causes additional pipes to speak.

Through the electric action, also, all sorts of mechanically operated drums, percussion instruments, and even a whole piano can be controlled from the organ console. The complexity of the modern instrument staggers the imagination; and it sometimes seems to be used chiefly for that purpose rather than for sounding the noble music which great masters have written for the true organ. But in spite of this exuberance, and with due reservation for the shortcomings of majesty, it is certainly with reason that the organ has been called the *King of instruments.*

With the necessarily constant wind pressure used in the pipe organ, the peculiar value of the free reed—its capacity to vary the intensity of tone with varied pressure—cannot be exploited.[4] The *harmonium,* however, which operates by bellows under the foot of the performer, and which blows the air outward through the reeds, makes full use of this value.[5]

[4] Some German organs have a group of free-reed pipes operated through a separate wind chest in which the pressure is variable.

[5] The prototype of the harmonium is the Chinese *cheng.* This has a gourd or hollow vessel to serve as wind chest, into which are fitted small bamboo pipes, having

The *reed organ* (called in England the *American organ*) is a modification of the harmonium, gaining its wind pressure by producing a vacuum instead of the outward pressure of the harmonium and pipe organ. This difference involves the loss of almost all the dynamic control possessed by the harmonium. Common derivatives of the American organ are the accordion and the mouth organ.

Wind instruments which employ our third method of actuation, the use of the tensed lips in place of reeds, are probably of equal antiquity with the simplest reed instruments. These are all horns, of one kind or another; and the animal horn is their prototype. Like the hollow river reed, the easy source of the Pan's pipe, the animal horn constitutes an almost ready-made musical instrument. Such horns as the Hebrew *shofar* (ram's horn) or more refined copies in metal, were used by all the ancients. Their great power and coarse tone made them suitable as instruments of announcement; but their inability to produce any but a very few tones of the harmonic series made them ineffective for melody.

The Greeks had the *keras* (the word means, primarily, *animal horn*) and a straight metal trumpet which they called *salpinx*. This purely military instrument was adopted by the Romans for use as a cavalry trumpet, and

FIG. 16. SALPINX

was called *lituus*. In addition, they had several varieties of *cornu* (this word also has the primary meaning animal horn). The most important of these were the *buccina* (from *bucca*, a cheek) and the *tuba*. All three names survived in later speech; but the Roman instruments disappeared with the Empire and their later successors are again modifications of Eastern models.

The *buccina* of the Romans was a long metal pipe bent into the form of a great C, braced across its arch and provided with a mouthpiece. But the art of bending metal pipes was presently forgotten, so that the medieval instrument, which kept the name in a recognizable form, lost the curved shape of the original. It was called *busine, busun, pusun* in a variety of forms, and came at last to be called in

each a reed inserted in the base. These pipes do not serve as resonators, as in the organ, but as keys. In each pipe, near the plate into which the pipes are fitted, a hole is cut, which must be covered by the finger before the reed can speak. The instrument is mostly made so that tone is produced by drawing in, not by expelling, the breath. Imported into Europe during the second half of the eighteenth century, the cheng stimulated experiment which resulted in the invention of the harmonium.

modern German *Posaune*, which means *trombone*.

The Roman *tuba* was straight, like the Greek *salpinx*. It was the infantry trumpet, as opposed to the *lituus*, the cavalry trumpet. Through some etymological confusion the word *tuba* came later to be rendered *trumba*. This becomes *tromba* in Italian; and with the diminutive ending *etta* becomes *trombetta*, with the French and English equivalents *trompette* and *trumpet*. The augmentative Italian ending *one* (dissyllabic), gives *trombone*—a big *tromba* —whence our similar English term. From

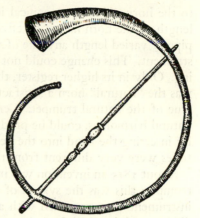

FIG. 17. BUCCINA

buccina through devious Spanish channels comes *sacabuche* which in English becomes *sackbut*. (The reader will not miss the interesting suggestion of geographic dispersal revealed in these etymologies.) The sackbut, although necessarily made of straight pipes, was exactly a trombone—a pipe made in sections which slid into each other like a telescope. Extension of the slides gave for each new position a new length of pipe and a new fundamental, the harmonic series becoming different with each shift. The modern trombone with its curved pipe employs the same principle and is much more convenient in form. In their cup-shaped mouthpieces and their cylindrical bore, trumpets and trombones are alike; and they are consequently much alike in tone. The slide has sometimes been applied to the

FIG. 18. SACKBUT

trumpet since the sixteenth century; but the device is not very practicable on the smaller instrument. Trombones are made in alto, tenor, and bass sizes, thus forming with the trumpet a complete choir; but the alto trombone is now rarely demanded.

The modern French horn (which musicians usually speak of merely as *horn*) is a descendant both in name and form of the Roman *cornu*. Its principal use in the Middle Ages was as a hunting instrument. It had then no proper mouthpiece, but only the finished opening of the pipe itself. The tone therefore was wavering and of rough quality. Extended in length, narrowed in bore, and provided with a long, conical mouthpiece, the number of available harmonics was greatly increased and the tone became very mellow. The possible compass of the horn of today is over three octaves. The slide mechanism of the trombone, however, was not applicable to the horn, which was conical in bore. Hence, changes in fundamental length of the horn had to be effected by the use of "crooks"—sections of pipe of varied length any one of which could replace the other on the instrument. This change could not be made while the instrument was playing. Only in its higher register, then, where the partials are close together, was the "natural" horn a satisfactory melodic instrument. The same was true of the natural trumpet. Certain "stopped" tones, in addition to the natural harmonics, could be produced by blowing in a certain manner, or by inserting the hand into the bell of the instrument; but in quality these tones were very different from the "open" notes.

About 1815 an invention was made which revolutionized both horn and trumpet; this was the system of valves or pistons. Crooks built into the instrument were provided with a piston having two holes of exactly the diameter of the pipe. In their natural position the lower holes in the pistons do not affect the natural length of the pipe. Depressed, the higher hole in the piston communicates with a built-in crook, thus instantaneously lengthening the whole column of air exactly as if a new crook had been inserted. A complete chromatic scale of open notes is thus made available—an improvement of incalculable value for orchestral music. Valves have also been applied to the trombone; but this instrument suffers considerably in tone quality from the addition, and is too low in register to require the rapid execution which the valves make possible; hence it is used only in military bands.

These are the principal lip-blown instruments of our day. A few of the many related types often mentioned in older books, or serving other than orchestral uses, may be described. The word *cornet* (obviously *cornu* with the Italian diminutive *etto*) meant in the later Middle Ages a straight or slightly curved wooden pipe of conical bore with a conical mouthpiece cut into the pipe itself. The pipe was pierced with finger

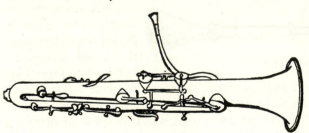

FIG. 19. OPHICLEIDE

holes like a flute. The Germans called this instrument *Zinck*. It had a very sweet tone without great power. Our contemporary cornet (properly *cornet à pistons*) is practically a small valve trumpet, conical in bore for a small part of its length. It is easier to play than the trumpet but much inferior in tone.

The bugle (Latin *buculus*, a young bull) was primitively a bull's horn.

Later metal copies have always retained the wide conical shape of the
primitive instrument. This shape, together with a less angular opening
from the mouthpiece into the tube,
gives the bugle a mellower tone than
that of the trumpet. More satisfac-
torily than with the trumpet (on
which the experiment was also tried)
the bugle can be fitted with keys
(not valves) covering sound holes
like those of woodwind instruments.
Enlarged, the key bugle became the
ophicleide, the predecessor of the
modern tuba. This strange word is
from the Greek *ophis*, a serpent, and
kleides, a key. But the application
was false; for there was a large derivative of the Zinck, made for practi-
cability of fingering in the shape and
given the name of a serpent, with
which the ophicleide had no real
relation. Inferior in tone and awkward for the performer, serpent and
ophicleide have disappeared from
the modern orchestra.

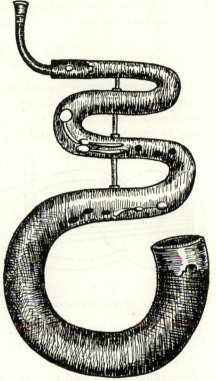

FIG. 20. SERPENT

Two important derivatives of the bugle are the saxhorns and the tubas—
both being fundamentally bugles with valves (not keys). The difference
between the two is that the bore of the tuba is larger than that of the saxhorn, a fact which gives to the tuba both an additional octave in compass
and a great superiority in quality of tone. The tubas are almost universally used in orchestras as the bass of the brass choir. The euphonium and
helicon of the brass band are also tubas; and there is another variety of
tuba, with rotary valves, much used in Germany under the name *Flügel-
horn*. For his great tetralogy *The Ring of the Nibelungs*, Richard Wagner had a medium-sized tuba constructed, to give a tone quality between
that of the horns and the trombones. These are generally known as
"Wagner tubas." The saxhorns are chiefly used in French and Belgian
military bands. They were invented by Adolphe Sax, who also invented
the saxophone. The saxophone is a hybrid, having a conical metal pipe of
wide bore to which is fitted the single reed mouthpiece of the clarinet. It

is thus a far cry from the bugle, but is mentioned here to avoid possible confusion between saxhorn and saxophone.

III. Stringed Instruments

To an ear sensitive to musical tone, the twang of a hunting bow would be enough to suggest a possibility of making music from stretched strings. Rested on a hollow log or on any more vibrant resonator, the bow would reveal its musical value unmistakably. To substitute for the log an attached

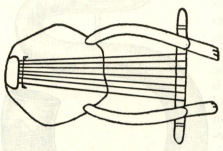

and carefully made resonance box would be the next step. This, of course, is only speculation. The Greeks had a legend that their favorite instrument, the lyre, was discovered by Hermes, who, walking on the banks of the Nile, happened to strike his foot against a tortoise shell in which remained some tendons which had dried and stretched in the sun. The shell

FIG. 21. SEVEN-STRINGED LYRE

gave forth a tone, and the hint was sufficient. This, too, is only legend. We know nothing of the origin of stringed instruments; they existed before history began.

Four types of stringed instruments exist today: (1) those which have one string, or more than one string, for each note they produce; (2) those which have few strings and produce many notes from each; (3) those which are sounded with a bow; and (4) those which have a keyboard. We shall observe them in that order.

The simplest of devices for producing tone from strings is doubtless that expansion of hunting bow and resonator which is found in the lyre. This tiny harp originated in Asia—perhaps in Assyria or Babylonia—and seems to have come into Greece by way of Egypt and Thrace or Lydia. It was mostly called *lyre* (λύρα), although it had another name, *chelys* (χέλυς), which is the Greek word for tortoise and which recalls the legend mentioned above. The sound box of the lyre was indeed often an actual shell; but when made of wood it preserved the same shape. From the upper shoulders of the sound box projected two slightly bowed arms (animal horns, in the more primitive instrument) which were bound together near the top by a crossbar. From this bar the strings were stretched to a sort of tailpiece or bridge, fixed near the bottom of the sound chest. The strings were at first four in number, corresponding to the four notes of the tetrachord, which leads some authorities to find the origin of the tetrachord in the lyre. The tuning was in any of the varieties of the three genera. As the compass of Greek music expanded the number of strings was increased, first to seven, in an oft-mentioned reform of Terpander, and later to eight or ten. The seven-stringed lyre, as depicted on a vase in the British Museum, is shown in Fig. 21. This small instrument was used in the home, and by those whom we should now call amateurs. Its Greek name was *phorminx* (φόρμιγξ).

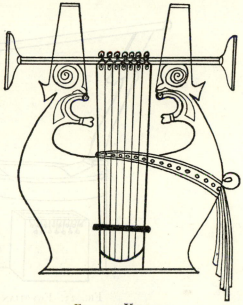

FIG. 22. KITHARA

A larger type of harp, the *kithara* (κιθάρα), was the instrument of the professional musicians. Aside from its greater size the chief structural difference from the lyre was in the sound box, which in the kithara was rectangular rather than convex. The Egyptians knew the kithara for centuries before the Homeric era, as is proved by actual specimens preserved at Berlin and Leyden. The Egyptian example, here drawn in outline, had fifteen strings stretched between a sloping crossbar and a notched bridge on the sound box. Another type, approaching to the harp in shape, was held over the shoulder. The Greeks used the kithara as an accompanying instrument for either song or dance. It came later to be used as a solo instrument, and also with the aulos as we have seen. The strings were twanged, either with the fingers (which gave a finer gradation of dynamics) or with a plectrum which alone could give the volume necessary for festival use.

The kithara was popular also in Rome. Nero, indeed, is depicted as a kitharodist. The instrument had a numerous and a very diverse progeny; but this was only after it had contracted a sort of union with another Egyptian instrument which as we shall see was a kind of lute. Most of these descendants were finger-board instruments, and so belong in another group than that which now concerns us.

The harp, although known to the Greeks, was held in far less favor than the lyre and the kithara. In Egypt, however, where it attained a remarkable development, it shared with the lute that highest place in popular regard which was held in Greece by the lyre and the aulos. The harp was

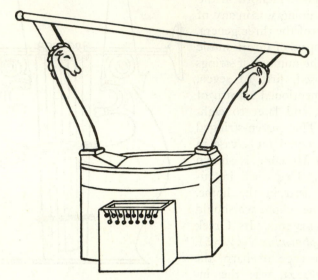

FIG. 23. EGYPTIAN KITHARA

FIG. 24. EGYPTIAN SHOULDER HARP

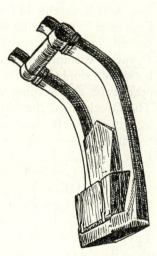

FIG. 25. ROMAN KITHARA
(from a statue of Nero as
kitharodist)

Fig. 26. Egyptian Harp or "Nanga"

not invented in Egypt; but a long series of Egyptian representations of the instrument in various stages of advancement seems to show clearly its derivation from the hunting bow. An early type called *nanga* had a boat-shaped sound box from which rose the bow-shaped arm to which the strings were stretched. The later instruments were very large (apparently over six feet in height) with a beautifully ornamented sound box. Neither type had a supporting pillar from the base to the tip of the string-arm; hence both the number and the tension of the strings were limited.

Both the name and the form of the modern harp come from northern Europe. The Anglo-Saxon term *hearpe* and the old Norse *harpa* are from some Germanic source. The Celtic races developed several types of harp, the earliest of which, depicted as without a supporting pillar, suggests a derivation from the Egyptian type. By the fourteenth century, however, the pillar seems to have been supplied; and the rest of the story is one of improvement in detail.

Modern chromatic music presents great difficulties to the harpist. If he has a string for each chromatic semitone (as on the piano) the strings must be placed in parallel rows (as in the Welsh triple harp). This makes the execution cumbersome, and the large number of strings deadens the tone. The modern harp, perfected by Sebastian Erard at Paris about 1810, reverts to the diatonic stringing. But each string is fitted with an

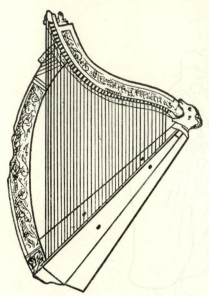

FIG. 27. IRISH HARP

ingenious mechanism operated by a pedal, which tightens the string and raises its pitch a half step or a whole step, accordingly as the pedal is depressed for half or all its possible distance. There are seven pedals, one for each note of the diatonic scale. The instrument is tuned in the key of C flat. The C pedal, then, if half depressed, raises all the C flat strings to C natural; if fully depressed, it raises them to C sharp. The other pedals perform a like function for the other strings. Even so, it has not been possible for the harp to keep pace with the rapid modulation of modern music.

A modification of the fundamental harp idea was to be seen in the instrument known as the *psaltery*, the sound box being here extended so that it underlies the whole length of the strings. In the ancient type, the strings were plucked. A medieval and nearly obsolete modern variant of much larger size, called the *dulcimer*, was played by little hammers in the hands of the performer. The German zither (the word is one of the countless derivations from κιθάρα) is the only direct survivor of the psaltery type; but we shall see that the piano is a keyed dulcimer.

Whatever the advantage of an instrument which has an individual string for each note, it must lose both in rapidity of execution and in certain characteristics of tone quality by comparison with an instrument so made that one string can sound many different tones. To give higher tones, a string must be either tightened or shortened. Tightening being impracticable (save in the limited manner of the Erard harp) shortening must be resorted to. This is, of course, accomplished by placing under the strings a finger board against which they can be pressed. The points at which the fingers will produce the conventional notes of the scale may be marked on the board—perhaps by *frets*, which are little metal bars fixed into the finger board.

To the convex sound box suggested by the tortoise shell, the Egyptians, Assyrians, Persians, and other ancient peoples affixed a long neck (the equivalent of the arms and crossbar of the lyre) bearing a finger board above which the few strings were strung. Instruments of this type, however, seem to have been popular everywhere but in Greece and Rome.

The medieval instrument which retained this pear-shaped sound box came into Europe from Arabia in the time of the Crusades. The Arabic name for it was *al'ud,* which means "the wood" or "the stick," but by reference to the long neck came also to mean the instrument. *Al'ud* became in Spanish *laud,* in French *luth,* in Italian *liuto,* in German *Laute,* and in English "lute." In the sixteenth century especially the lute was the most popular of instruments. It was made in many sizes, so that the whole family formed a consort; and the literature written for it was, as we shall see, an important element in the foundation of the great literature of the piano. The larger instruments had a number of strings, strung not over the finger board but beside it, which gave a bass to the fingered strings. Three types of large lute were recognized: the archlute, the theorbo, and the chittarone; the differences in structure did not involve any essential difference in principle.

As we have said, the kithara and the lute formed a liaison. The result was the fixture of the neck onto the rectangular sound box which chiefly distinguished the kithara from the lyre. The later history of the word χιθάρα (which itself came from the Assyrian *chetarah*), is very suggestive of the popularity of the instrument, though the derivatives do not always convey strictly the meaning of kithara as opposed to lute. The Latin word *cithara* was an almost exact transliteration; this became in Italian *chitarra,* in Spanish *guitarra,* and in English "guitar." And the guitar is, indeed, the flat sound box of the kithara with a finger board attached. But *chitarrone* (literally, a big *chitarra*) meant, as we have just seen, a large lute with a pear-shaped sound box.

But these are by no means the only derivatives of the word *kithara.* The Italians made of it another form, *cetera* or *cetra;* and this became in French *cistre* or *cithre,* and in English "cittern." The cittern kept the pointed oval sound box of the lute, but gave it a flat back and used four pairs of unison strings (like the modern mandolin) in various tunings. The cittern was reputed to have been invented in England. It was often called "the English guitar." The German word *Zither* is obviously related, the cittern being in fact a *Zither mit Hals* or zither with neck.

So popular an instrument as the kithara would be likely to acquire a popular name. From the Latin word for string, *fides,* came a diminutive, *fidicula,* which presently was associated with the instrument itself. Isidore of Seville says that *fidicula* was in his day another name for kithara. In the vulgar tongue which presently developed into the Romance languages, *fidicula* became *vigola* or *vihuela;* and this in turn became *vielh,* *vielle,* *vial,* and *viol.* This etymological approach to our *violin* (which is a diminutive of *viol*) is in some degree an outline of the genesis of the queen of instruments.

But before we take up that story we must mention another descendant

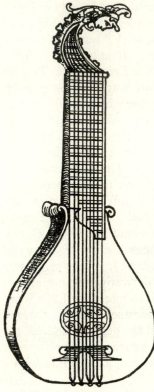

FIG. 28. CITTERN

of the kithara—one of the "poor relations" of the family—which became popular in Wales and was there known as *crwth* or *crowd*. This was essentially a lyre whose branching arms and crossbar had been made a part of the sound box, and which had a finger board erected between the upright arms. The finger board, that is, extended down the middle of the opening between the arms; and the player's left hand thus gripped through the opening to stop the strings, which were plucked by the right hand. The word *crwth* is originally suggestive of a bulging form of some sort—here, of course, the rounded back of the instrument. But there is a similarity between this word and the late Latin *chrotta,* a name for the then existing form of the lyre. In Old High German this word becomes *chrota,* which is the parent of *Kröte* (a toad). And *Schildkröte* (tortoise), which is an obvious compound, thus suggests an extraordinary persistence of the association which in Greece gave the name *chelys* to the lyre.

The crwth proper, although it came at last to be played with a bow, underwent no further development than that just described. But the chrotta, whose name presently became *hrotta* or *rotta,* had a most important addition in the shape of a neck which protruded beyond the sound box. The sound box, too, was flat backed like the kithara (from which rather than from the lyre the rotta was derived); and instead of being rectangular with rounded corners like the crwth, it was curved in at the sides and spread again toward the top where the neck protruded—the design being thus similar to the outline of the combined body and arms of the kithara. We have already seen how the word *fidicula* (another name for the kithara) became *vihuela.* There were three kinds of *vihuela* in Spain in the Middle Ages: one played by the fingers (*da mano*), one played by a quill (*da penola*), and, most important of all for the future, one played with a bow (*da arco*). This last is the *guitar fiddle* or *troubadour fiddle*—a not very remote ancestor of the viol and the violin. To make the act of bowing possible, the body was narrowed at the waist and the strings were elevated by a bridge.

But the bow itself was no part of the fiddle; nor was any use of a bow suggested by any of the various forms of lute, kithara, or lyre which we have observed. The great value of the bow as a device for producing sustained tone from a string was probably suggested to European musicians by Arab invaders, who had two different bowed instru-

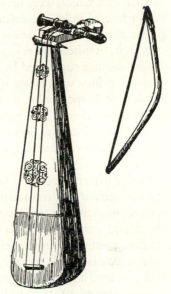

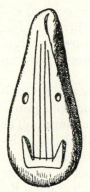

FIG. 29. BOAT-SHAPED REBAB   FIG. 30. SPOON-SHAPED REBAB   FIG. 31. REBEC WITH BOW

ments. One, the *rebab* (apparently of very ancient ancestry in Asia Minor, India, and Persia), was made in two shapes: either long and narrow like a very slim boat (see Fig. 29) or after the pattern of a half pear or a very short-handled spoon. (See Fig. 30.) It appears that in its earliest stage the rebab was not played with the bow; moreover, it is not known when the bow came into use. The earliest known representation of a bowed instrument is a fresco in a monastery at Bawit in Egypt, where Orpheus is depicted as playing a rebab by that means; the date of this may be as early as the sixth century A.D. The other bowed instrument was a development of the rebab, and was called *rebec*. It had the same boat-shaped or pearshaped forms as the rebab. A narrower type had two strings, a wider, three. The instrument was held vertically, like our violoncello. There is little structural relation between these instruments and the violin; but they are of extreme importance as having been the means through which the bow was introduced to the West.

The successor of the rebec was the guitar fiddle; the successor of the guitar fiddle was the viol, the derivation of which term we have already seen from *fidicula;* and it will be seen that *fiddle,* as well as the older English form *fythele* and the German *Fiedel,* have the same source. In order to give as clear an idea as possible of the development of these instruments into the viol and the violin, we have emphasized especially those features of structure which were preserved. But the reader will realize that no very direct line of influence existed, many examples of older types continuing in use along with the newer. For instrumental music was still *musica irregularis*, despised and rejected by the churchmen, possessed of no written literature, and supported by no strong social influence save that of an occasional prince who chose to reward occasional courtly entertainment by fiddlers or harpers who, to retain the interest of their audiences, had also to be mountebanks and jugglers. Under such conditions, there could be no established convention or standard, comparable to the carefully regulated practice of church music, in instrumental manufacture or performance.

In the fifteenth century however the spirit of the Renaissance has sufficiently secularized the learned music so that the association with instrumental musicians is no longer wholly contemned by churchmen. The royal and princely chapels also begin to offer established places to instrumentalists; and with such a stimulus the perfection of the instruments themselves is much more rapid. The viols, then, soon outdo all other stringed instruments in popularity, even though they are structurally the descendants of a relatively isolated type of guitar fiddle—that used by the Minnesinger of the thirteenth and fourteenth centuries. This instrument had a flat back and shoulders which sloped in a gradual curve to the neck; and these same features characterize the true viols. Like other instruments they were made in many sizes to correspond to the various registers of the human voice. No instrument as low in pitch as the bass voices could be made small enough to hold against the shoulder or under the chin, as the guitar fiddle had been held. Hence, the two great divisions of the viols into *viole da braccia* (arm viols) and *viole da gamba* (leg viols—those which are supported by the knees). Many sizes existed in each division.

As we shall see, the viols entered the precincts of learned music through their usefulness as supporting instruments for choral voices. Compositions were soon written for either voices or viols; and when these were played by the instruments alone, not only was the interest of purely instrumental music made manifest, but the failure of purely vocal part-writing to call forth all the capacities of the instruments was also strikingly revealed. This led, in turn, to a discovery that the viols themselves were by no means ideal in brilliancy of tone or in volume. A very ingenious but not highly successful attempt was then made to improve the sonority of the viol by the addition of more strings, both on the finger board and under it. Under the finger board, that is, were strung several fine wire strings so tuned as to sound sympathetically with the bowed strings. These instruments, also made in many sizes, were called *viole d'amore*. But the experiment produced just what was not wanted: an instrument of no appreciably greater sonority; of thicker and less variable, although of richer, tone; and of a still more unmanageable technique.

The viol, therefore, had to be corrected; and the instrument in which these corrections were perfected was the violin. But the violin is not, structurally, a viol. The sloping shoulder of the viol was abandoned for the square shoulder which had characterized the guitar and the troubador guitar fiddle. The back was made arched; the thickness (from back to top) was made less; the whole frame was cunningly and firmly braced, so as to give the strings a greater possible tension; the number of strings was reduced to four; and frets, which had frequently been used on the finger board of the viol, were abandoned. These are the most obvious differences between the viol and the violin; but the superiority of the violin rests also upon many minute details which were gradually introduced into the structure by a long series of violin makers, mostly Italians, whose names are almost as famous as those of the composers of their time. Cognoscenti discuss the merits of various violins in tone and in design, as connoisseurs discuss the bouquets of rare wines, so that the lore of old violins seems almost a mystic cult to the uninitiated. We can make but brief mention of the most famous of these makers.

The highest of the viols, the *discant viol*,[6] was not a soprano but an alto instrument. It was natural, then, that the earliest known example of the violin form should be, not the *violino* but the *viola*. (It is called *alto* in France, and *Bratsche*—evidently a transliteration of *braccia*—in Germany; but because of the great upward increase in compass of the violin, the viola is now the tenor instrument in the quartet of strings. The alto part is taken by a second violin, identical in compass with the first.) This early viola is labeled "Pietro Zanure, Brescia, 1509." But the true pioneer in violin making is generally recognized in Gasparo da Salo, also of Brescia. He also began with violas, turning to the violin about 1555. The chief successor of da Salo, probably his pupil, was J. P. Maggini. His instruments are somewhat more finished in design,[7] and are rather somber and melancholy in tone. The Brescian school led in violin making until about 1620.

[6] It had six strings tuned (after the manner of the lute) so that the extremes were two octaves apart, and the inner strings in fourths, except for a third in the middle, thus: D, G, c, e, a, d'.

[7] Every dimension of the violin has been minutely studied by the great makers—the size, the height of the sides, the degree to which back and top are arched, the thickness (always carefully graduated) of top and back, the pattern of the f-holes, and even the scroll. The necks of these old violins have all been replaced, to give the instrument greater compass.

From Brescia the center of the art was then removed to Cremona, a city whose name is almost synonymous with violin. Here a school had been founded by Andreas Amati (1520–1580), originally a viol maker, who turned in his last years to the making of violins. A whole orchestra of his instruments (twenty-four violins, six violas, and eight basses), made for Charles IX of France, was kept at Versailles until the Revolution, when all but two were destroyed by the mob. A more brilliant tone was achieved by the two sons of Andreas—Antonius and Hieronymus Amati—who worked together but produced instruments of considerably different pattern and size. The son of Hieronymus was the greatest of the family. He was called Nicholas, and his later violins—held by some to be the equals of any—were often called the "grand Amatis." They were more brilliant in tone and more perfect in design than any earlier instruments. A son of Nicholas, another Hieronymus, was far inferior to the father, and was also overshadowed by several of his father's pupils.

Of those who are considered pupils of the Amati school, the best known are Andreas Guarnerius, Francesco Ruggieri, Paolo Grancino (whose two sons, Giambattista and Francesco, excelled their father), and Sanctus Seraphin, perhaps the most finished workman recorded among the craft. The sons of Guarnerius, Peter and Joseph (each designating himself as *filius Andreae*), worked along very original lines; and the son of Joseph, called "Peter of Venice," carried his namesake's work to still greater perfection, having the advantage of a Venetian varnish which was used also by another Venetian maker, Montagnana. Toward the middle of the seventeenth century, the principles of the Amati school were adopted by a German maker, Jacob Stainer, who made a large number of instruments of very excellent quality and became the founder of the German art of violin making.

The Guarnerius family produced still another master, Joseph Antonius, called "del Jesu" because of the letters IHS which he placed on his labels, and also to distinguish him from his cousin, Joseph Filius Andreae. The originality of the Guarnerius family found its highest expression in this master, who went back to Gasparo da Salo for his model (rejecting that effort toward external finish and proportion which had too much absorbed the makers of his own day) and produced instruments of greater power and brilliancy than had ever been made. In the estimation of many, indeed, they have never been excelled.

But a still greater name is associated with the Amati school—that of Antonius Stradivarius who, though for a time a pupil of Nicholas Amati, was too great a genius to be reckoned a member of any school. Like the works of a great composer, Stradivarius's violins are recognized as belonging to various periods—the greatest of these being about a decade beginning with 1700. (He was born probably in 1644, and died in 1737.) He continued to produce until his death; and only the last decade of his ninety-three years of life shows any material deterioration in his work. His models have been copied endlessly, without approach to his mysterious excellence.

Stradivarius's best pupils were Domenico Montagnana who worked mostly in Venice, was especially skillful as a maker of violoncellos, and whose varnish rivaled that of his master; and Carlo Bergonzi who in his later years developed a model—somewhat different from that of his teacher —which is regarded as only second in value to those of Stradivarius and Guarnerius del Jesu. Two sons, Omobono and Francesco Stradivarius, were far inferior to their father but excellent makers nevertheless.

Another famous family at Cremona was that of the Guadagnini, of which the first violin makers, Lorenzo and Giambattista, claimed to be pupils of Stradivarius. The work of the latter is very much after the Stradivarius pattern, and is remarkably fine. Descendants of the family continued in the profession well into the nineteenth century.

French makers such as Nicholas Lupot and Jean Baptiste Vuillaume, and English craftsmen such as Barak Norman, Benjamin Banks, Thomas Dodd, and William Foster were all, in various degrees, copyists of the Italian masters, producing many fine instruments but none to compare with the masterpieces of the Cremonese.

Indispensable for the production of sustained tone from a string, and hence as essential a factor in our modern string music as the violin itself, is the bow. As we have said, its actual origin as a musical adjunct is obscure. From the arched form of the earliest depicted bows, it seems wholly natural to suppose that the source of the musical utensil was the hunting bow. Substitution of hair for the thong of the hunting bow necessitated some means for controlling the tension of the hair. This device, called *crémaillère*, assumed various shapes in the course of its perfection—perhaps notches in the stick into which a loop, holding the hair, could be strung; or round knobs serving the same purpose. Virdung describes a bow having the hair bound to the stick with waxed thread and with a movable wedge between hair and stick to vary the tension. A nut to which the hair was attached, and which nearly resembled the nut moved by a screw which is now universal, was in use in Mersenne's day (1636); but the screw was probably absent from this device, and the hair was therefore tightened by pressure of the player's thumb. This is the type of bow which Bach knew. A considerable relaxation of the pressure gave a loose tension very desirable for the playing of chords. Such an effect as *spiccato*, however, was quite impossible, and was unknown to Bach.

The present form of the bow with its curvature toward the hair (not away from it as in the older hunting-bow shapes) was largely suggested by Tartini in the second decade of the eighteenth century, who provided a lighter stick, a straighter shape, and a shorter head to give better balance; but it was perfected somewhere about 1780 by François Tourte whose models have not been improved upon.

One very important group of instruments remains to be considered. These are stringed instruments, but mechanically actuated; and since some are plucked and some have hammers with which the strings are struck, the classification as percussion instruments is not exact. The modern survivor of all these is the piano; but that familiar instrument has a very numerous ancestry. The main outline of its genealogy is probably as follows:

The monochord, which in the day of Pythagoras was a piece of physical apparatus rather than a musical instrument, came in the Middle Ages to occupy a higher plane. With its movable bridge, set upon an exactly designated scale, it served to establish the intervals of the musical scale for the singers in the choir. Made with four strings instead of one, it began to assume something of the character of a musical instrument. The division of the strings into various lengths (each, of course, giving a different pitch) was the principle of the clavichord (Latin *clavis*, a key, and Greek *chordē*, a string). This is a stringed instrument with keys; and the movable bridge is an extremely rudimentary form of key. Keys, as we have seen, had been applied to the organ but not as yet to the strings. The first recorded application of keys to strings occurs in the medieval instrument known as *organistrum*, which survived as the *hurdy-gurdy*. This, however, bore no resemblance to a piano, but was more like an ungainly fiddle. Beneath the strings near the tailpiece a rosined wheel was placed, to be turned by a crank projecting at the back. Above the strings on the finger board were placed keys which, when depressed, both stopped the strings at the point necessary to produce the pitch desired, and at the same time lowered the string itself so that it came in contact with the wheel and was thus made to vibrate. Here, indeed, were keys applied to strings; but these keys did not cause the strings to sound. Little progress is suggested toward a true clavichord.

If, however, a key instead of a movable bridge could be made to effect that necessary division of the string which would give the desired pitch, and would also actuate the string, the problem would be solved. Virdung says he could never learn who had solved it. The word *clavicordium*, evidently used in the sense under consideration, occurs as early as 1404, along with *monocordium* and *clavicymbolum* in a book of rules for the Minnesinger. Early in the sixteenth century, the term *a pair of clavy-cordes* occurs—the word *pair* (applied also to the *virginals*, to organs, and to *regals*—a species of organ) being used to imply a series, as in the expression *a pair of stairs*, and obviously referring to the row of keys.

The clavichord had a rectangular sound box over which were strung a number of strings all of even length—an obvious application of the monochord principle. Beneath the strings, on each key, was a blade of brass called a *tangent* (Latin *tango*, to touch or strike) extending upward, so that when the key was depressed the tangent struck the string. (Two or three unison strings were also sometimes provided.) All the strings were damped at one end by soft cloth interwoven among them; when the tangent left a string, this damper silenced the vibration of the whole string, so that the key had to remain depressed as long as the tone was desired to sound. The pitch of the note was determined by the point on the string at which the tangent struck. If it struck near the damper the pitch was low, since all the string, from tangent to pin, vibrated; while if it struck nearer the pin the pitch would be higher, for the damper would silence the vibration between it and the tangent. The tangent was thus both an exciter and a fret. And it was quite possible to construct the instrument in such a way that more than one key would bring its tangent into contact with but one string. In such an instrument, there were thus fewer strings than keys. Such clavichords were called by the Germans *gebunden*—that is "fretted"; only later were they made *bundfrei*—"without frets," with one string for each note.

The tone was very feeble, so that the instrument could be used only in small rooms. Within its dynamic limits, however, the clavichord was very sensitive to variations of force in the key stroke, so that it became the favorite of those players whose chief concern was expression. It possessed also one capacity which it has been impossible to retain in later keyboard stringed instruments: since the player's finger, through the key, maintained actual contact with the string, varied pressure during that contact produced a sort of vibrato in the tone somewhat analogous to that affected by players of the *steel guitar*. The Germans called this effect a *Bebung* (trembling) and were very fond of it.

Since the strings of the clavichord were struck (not plucked) this instrument is clearly a forerunner of the piano, although in the piano the hammer is only for an instant in contact with the string. Plucking rather than striking was, however, the mode of actuation most familiar, since it had been employed for all stringed instruments until the advent of the bow. But a plucked string can produce but one tone. Hence, any mechanically plucked instrument must have as many strings as tones. Essentially, then, the sound box to which plucking might be applied was that of the psaltery, not that of the monochord. The plucking device (called a *jack*) was a thin wooden upright with a little oscillating tongue set within it, from which tongue projected a little spine of crow quill. This upright was so placed on the end of the key lever that when the key was depressed the upright ascended close beside the string. The quill projected just far enough at the side of the jack so that it made contact with the string and, being forced past it, gave it a twang. When the jack descended, the oscillating tongue allowed the quill to pass the string without plucking.

The tone of the plucked instrument (whose many names we shall rehearse in a moment) thus differed altogether from that of the clavichord. For the whole string vibrated; it was actuated by a device which both caused a momentarily forced vibration and made a slight noise in itself; and, since the force applied to the string depended rather on the stiffness of the quill than on the speed with which the jack rose, the volume of tone did not vary with the stroke on the key. Neither the variable dynamics of the clavichord nor the *Bebung* was thus available. But the strings could be heavier, longer, and more tensely strung, so that in tone volume this instrument was vastly greater than the delicate clavichord. It was therefore available as a concert instrument, and with many variations in size and structure remained the chief of the keyboard stringed instruments until the advent of the piano.

The earliest name applied to this instrument was *clavicymbolum*, occurring in the Minnesinger rule-book above mentioned. *Cymbolum* or *cembalo* was the name for the psaltery. *Clavicembalo* thus means *keyed psaltery*. *Gravecembalo* etymologically is not very clear; *clavecin* (French), and *clavisinbanos* (Spanish) are obvious relatives. But from the quill which plucked the string, called in Latin *spina*, came another name, *spinetto* in Italian and *spinet* in English. Another name was *virginal* (putatively by association with the virgin queen, Elizabeth of England, but preferably from *virginalis*—suitable for a girl). There was also an upright spinet called *clavicytherium*. And from the triangular shape of the sound box of the larger instruments, recalling the shape of the harp, the instrument came to be called *harpsichord*. Properly, the harpsichord has two or three strings (even, rarely, four) to each note. The volume of tone thus provided made the instrument suitable for use in the orchestra; and in the eighteenth century it was a practically universal custom for the conductor to sit at the harpsichord, filling in when necessary the substance of the harmony from the figured bass part or *continuo* of the score.

The harpsichord's lack of expressive resource in tone, compared with the flexibility of the clavichord, caused much debate both as to relative superiority and as to the proper finger technique to be used by the player. Johann Sebastian Bach is reported as having preferred the clavichord; his son Karl Philip Emanuel, who wrote a very interesting book entitled *An In-*

vestigation as to the True Way to Play the Clavier,[8] insists that a good performer must be able to play both instruments, but again gives the palm for expressiveness to the clavichord. It was apparent that expressiveness (that is, dynamic variety) could be attained only in strings that were struck; and that power could be gained only through long, tense strings each of which must have its own key. The later harpsichords were provided with two manuals, one of which operated a set of stiff, one a set of weak, quills; so that the gross values of *piano* and *forte* could be obtained from the same instrument. But only swell boxes or similar devices could give any gradation between the two intensities. A combination of clavichord and harpsichord was thus much to be desired; and early in the eighteenth century a tolerable solution of the difficult problem was attained.

The actual invention of the pianoforte has been claimed for several men; but there seems little doubt that the honor belongs to Bartolommeo Cristofori, a Paduan harpsichord maker in the service of Prince Ferdinand dei Medici. As early as 1709 he seems to have completed four of the new instruments; but these were experiments, not complete in the design of the action. Two more finished examples have been preserved, dating from 1720 and 1726. These show, in a somewhat immature development, all the essential features of stringing and action which have been perfected in the pianos of today. Minute description of these features would require too much space; but a general idea of them may be conveyed.

The strings of the clavichord were very light and thin. Having to be struck by the tangent and maintained in vibration by the continuous contact of the tangent, the strings, if too long or too heavy, could not be completely stopped at the point of contact. Harpsichord strings, having only to be plucked, could be made much longer. But the strings of the pianoforte, to withstand the varied blows of the hammers, had to be still thicker; so that one of the first problems was that of bracing the body of the instrument (far more sturdily than was necessary for the harpsichord), to withstand the continuous tension of the strings and the added shock of the hammer blows. (The strings in Christofori's day were of brass; but later iron and at last steel strings were used which could endure a far greater tension.) The frame, as construction progressed, was reënforced by metal braces—in modern pianos, a large casting which extends over the whole surface of the sounding board and the block into which the tuning pins are set—so that the enormous tension of the strings (in a concert grand piano, about thirty tons!) is borne without danger of buckling the frame.

The conditions which a perfect action must meet will be easier to understand than the complicated mechanism itself. First of all, the hammer

[8] The word *Clavier* means, in German, any keyboard instrument.

must rebound instantly from the string after the stroke; for continued contact would cause the hammer to act as a damper. Therefore, the end of the key lever cannot itself serve as a hammer, but only as the actuator of a hammer which must be free from the lever. Moreover the actuator, or *jack* as it is called, must not follow the hammer shank throughout its passage to the string, else the hammer cannot rebound. The jack, therefore, is made to strike a little rounded knob on the shank near the point at which the shank is hinged; and since the jack thus moves but a short distance, an *escapement* must be provided which will shift the jack out of the way of the little knob as the hammer rebounds. This is accomplished by arranging to have the jack strike the knob a glancing blow, so that the jack moves behind, not under, the knob as the hammer rebounds. But now, if the shank rebounds to its original position of rest, the key will have to return also to its position of rest with the jack under the knob before another blow can be struck. Rapid repetition of a note would thus be impossible. Hence a *check*—a kind of little prop against which the hammer head falls midway on its rebound—must come into position while the hammer is ascending. With the shank thus held much nearer the string than in its normal position of rest, the jack can return beneath the knob sufficiently to give the shank another stroke before the key has completely returned to its normal rest position. Repetition, that is, can be much more rapid. All this complex adjustment must be accomplished, practically instantaneously, by a mechanism so light in operation that the finger will not be fatigued. (A part of the effort is obviated by placing lead weights in the descending arm of the key lever.)

Still another operation has to be accomplished by the single finger stroke. If the long, heavy, tense string of the modern piano were left to vibrate after the stroke, its tone would continue almost undiminished for many seconds. The player must be able to silence this string at will by releasing the key. Thus the key lever must operate still another device: a damper of felt, which lies against the string while the key is at rest, but is lifted off the string by the key stroke and remains lifted as long as the key is depressed. But again, it is often desirable to continue the vibration of a string while the finger which has sounded it is attacking another, perhaps very distant, key. Hence, a pedal is provided which lifts all the dampers at once.[9] The *damper* pedal gives to the piano a peculiar tone-capacity which is not possessed by any other instrument. For if all the strings are left free, and a single note is struck, the partial vibrations of the struck string set up sympathetic vibrations in those higher strings which are of

[9] A selective or *sostenuto* pedal is often supplied in addition, which, if depressed while any key is also depressed, will prevent the damper's return even though the key is released.

like pitch with the partials of the struck string.[10] The sound of the one string is thus not only amplified but is also enriched. For, as we have seen, timbre or tone quality is a matter of the presence, in a fundamental tone, of many upper partials.

A *soft* pedal is also provided. In upright pianos this moves all the hammer heads nearer the strings, and so lessens the speed and consequently the force of the hammer stroke. In grand pianos the soft pedal shifts the whole keyboard slightly to the right, so that the hammer strikes only two of the three unison strings which are provided for each tone. This, of course, lessens the volume; but the unstruck string also vibrates sympathetically with the two struck strings, and thus to a certain degree alters the character of the tone.

The piano thus offers to the performer, through its key mechanism, an enormous dynamic range absolutely corresponding to the speed imparted to the hammer by the finger stroke. Consideration of the mechanism will suggest what science has amply proved—that no other resource than that of varied intensity can be exploited by the fingers alone. The pianist's touch, so far as it is a finger act, is therefore wholly a matter of dynamic control. To this completely controllable intensity is added the value of quality given by the pedals. Contrary to most popular opinion, the pianist has no other resources. The extraordinary variety of touch exhibited by pianists—a fact palpable to the dullest ear—must thus be explained in terms of what seems an absurdly small variety of resource; but the explanation is entirely possible.[11]

Long as it is, this chapter has dealt with only a small number of the names and even of the actual instruments current in the Middle Ages. Our present-day instruments are very few in number by comparison. But this, as the student will have seen, is because instrumental music, in our day, is no longer *musica irregularis*. Composition and instrumental structure have gone hand in hand to effect a selection of those instruments and those principles of structure which give the finest results. No others than the most

[10] A simple experiment will interestingly reveal the presence of these partials. Gently and silently depress middle C, and hold the key down. While holding it, strike sharply the C an octave below, hold it for a beat or two, to allow its partial vibrations to be taken up by the higher string, and release it. Middle C, still depressed, will now be clearly heard. Others notes of the harmonic series can be similarly produced. Bb, out of tune with our scale, will be very faint. But the difference between the Bb of our scale, and that seventh partial can be heard, as a partial tone of the fundamental string, if the fundamental note (as low C) be silently depressed, and the Bb an octave and a seventh above be sharply struck. The partial will be faint, because not exactly in tune with its source, but yet audible.

[11] For a thorough scientific proof, see the *Physical Basis of Piano Touch and Tone* by Otto Ortmann. The author printed a less scientific but somewhat more inclusive explanation of the whole phenomenon in an article "The Secret of the Pianist's Beautiful Touch" in the *Musical Quarterly*, July, 1924.

perfect of instruments are now adequate for the rendering of our endlessly rich instrumental literature; and perfected types are naturally few in number.

The following table will perhaps help the reader to see the derivation of our modern instruments from their ancient or medieval sources. Some names are included which are not mentioned in the text but are clearly intelligible; the table, however, makes no pretense of completeness.

THE DERIVATION OF OUR MODERN INSTRUMENTS

I. PERCUSSION INSTRUMENTS

ANCIENT	MEDIEVAL	MODERN
(a) *membranophones*		
Drums	Drums, tabors.....	Bass drum / Side drum / Kettledrum
	Tambourine	Tambourine
(b) *idiophones*		
Cymbals	Cymbals..........	Cymbals
Sistra	Castanets	Castanets
Gong	Gong	Gong
Bells..........	Bells	Bells / Glockenspiel / Triangle * / Xylophone * / Marimba * / Celesta * / Music box (mechanical) *
Rattle	Rattle	Rattle
(c) *chordophones* (see also under stringed instruments)		
Monochord	Monochord.......	Clavichord * / Piano *

II. WIND INSTRUMENTS

(a) *without reeds*		
Pan's pipe	Pan's pipe	Organ * / Harmonica *
Nay..........	Flute (transverse) .	Flute / Piccolo
(Aulos) (Plagiaulos) ..	Recorder	Flûte à bec / Flageolet / Organ *

* The asterisk indicates that the derivation is indirect. The parenthesis, for ancient or medieval instruments, indicates that the instrument is a remote ancestor of the medieval or modern correlative. It seems impossible to indicate at all exactly the devious derivations; but the table may have some clarifying value.

ANCIENT	MEDIEVAL	MODERN

(b) *with double reeds*

Aulos, Tibia.... ⎰ Shawm .... → Oboe
⎱ Bombard .... → Bassoon
Pommer
Oboe da Caccia... → English horn

Askaulos....... Bagpipe .... ⎰ Bagpipe
⎱ Organ *

(c) *with single reed*

(Aulos) .... Chalumeau .... ⎰ Clarinet
Basset horn
⎱ Saxophone

(d) *with free reeds*

Cheng .... (no medieval ⎰ Harmonium
example) .... Reed organ
Harmonica
⎱ *Orgue expressif*

(e) *lip-blown instruments*

1. *simple tubes*

Animal horn
Shofar
Keras
Cornu .... ⎰ "Cornet" ⎰ Bugle
⎱ Zinck .... Ophicleide *
Serpent *
⎱ French horn

2. *with side holes*

"Cornet" .... Key bugle
Oliphant .... ⎰ Ophicleide
⎱ Serpent

3. *with slides*

(Buccina) ...... Busine .... Trombone
Sackbut

4. *with valves*

(Salpinx) ...... (Tibia)........... Trumpet
⎰ French horns
(Cornu) .... (Hunting horn) ... Cornet à pistons
⎱ Saxhorns

(f) *mechanically actuated (keyboard)*

Hydraulos ..... Positive organ..... Pipe organ
⎰ Reed organ *
Harmonium *
Portative....... Regal .... Melodeon *
Reed organ *
⎱ Accordion *

* See footnote p. 222.

THE DERIVATION OF OUR MODERN INSTRUMENTS—*Cont.*

III. Stringed Instruments

ANCIENT	MEDIEVAL	MODERN

(a) *plucked, strings free*

Lyre		
Kithara ⎫ ...	Harps	Harp
Nanga ⎭	Psaltery	⎧ Harpsichord * ⎨ Clavichord * ⎩ Piano *

(b) *plucked, strings stopped*

	⎧ Lute	⎧ Guitar
Al'ud	⎨ Theorbo, etc.	⎨ Mandolin
	⎩ Cittern	⎩ Banjo *

(c) *mechanically actuated (keyboard)*

1. *plucked*

(Kithara)	Psaltery	Harpsichord

2. *struck*

(Kithara)	Dulcimer	⎧ Clavichord ⎩ Piano

(d) *bowed*

	⎧ Rebec	
	⎪ Rebab	
(Kithara)	⎨ Vielh ⎬	Viol family
	⎪ Crwth	
	⎩ Guitar fiddle	
(Monochord) ..	⎰ Marine trumpet ⎱ Pochette	Violin family
	Organistrum	Hurdy-gurdy

* See footnote p. 222.

CHAPTER XII

The Beginnings of Instrumental Music to 1600

THREE agencies—ears, voices, and limbs—built into our bodies, make possible that stimulation of the brain which we call music. They are not only the agencies of creation but the means of musical appreciation; and our common possession of these resources, and their common pattern of behavior, make music the universal language. By the refinement of the tones and rhythms which the human body can create, music becomes an art; and through our understanding of these tonal and rhythmic creations as symbols or representations of the vastly more complex patterns of experience, music becomes an expressive art.

Words, included in the musical patterns of tone and rhythm, may often clarify the expressive sense—the relation to experience—of those patterns. But unless the sense made by the music is patently related to the sense made by the accompanying words, the combination of words and music yields a confusion. We detect such inappropriateness—and can only detect it—through our awareness of what the music, all by itself, is *saying* —that is, through our awareness of its character, which is really its meaning as a symbol of experience. The real meaning of music is thus always independent of the words which accompany it—even when the two are appropriate to each other. It cannot be created by those words. It can at best be illuminated by them, or can illuminate them.

Thus, music without words is not only possible, but may be more widely and more subtly expressive than when it is constrained to fit itself to verbal thought.[1]

---

[1] Such music does indeed become "pure" by virtue of its disassociation from the *substance* of words. But the notion—very generally prevalent today—that music, to become pure, must also be disassociated from all hint of verbal *meaning*, is not a logical consequence of that theorem of purity. The real meaning of words is not

Musical instruments, even of primitive kinds, greatly expanded the variety of available tone, and were valued accordingly. The ancient world perfected large numbers of musical instruments, and its instrumental art came—as also in our modern world—to stand at least on a parity with vocal music. But a peculiar condition prevented the Christian world from inheriting, along with the purely tonal system of ancient music, the elaborations and refinements of the ancient instrumental art. The associations —the expressive meanings—of the ancient instrumental music were all stamped with paganism; and because Christianity would have nothing to do with such art, Christian music for a thousand years was vocal.

Instrumental music was not unknown to Christendom, however. Even in the theory of Christian music it possessed a kind of anomalous status, for it formed one of the three genera (*mundana, humana,* and *instrumentalis*) recognized by Boethius; and Boethius, who was not a Christian, was nevertheless the chief instructor in music to the Christian Church during the first millennium of our era. Gradually as the taint of paganism evaporated, instruments began to find a place even in the music of the Church. Mostly, however, it grew up outside the sacred precincts, for jongleurs and goliards continued to give it a bad name.

Yet these gentry, however disreputable, were often imaginative-minded men, as absorbed with their instruments as we are. They taught each other a little—by example chiefly—but most of their skill came from improvisation. This faculty, which has been possessed by most composers, was a source of achievement both in technique and in formal structure, and we shall find it a partial determinant in many forms of later music.

Voices, the indubitable first source of music, can produce forms—and also by improvisation—as they did, often amazingly, with the Gregorian chant. Only when voices are feeble do they require, in monody, the help of instruments. The troubadour poets needed such help, and we shall see

---

merely objective and definitional, but lies in their total reference to experience, known or imaginable. The meaning of music (or of anything else) lies also in its reference to experience—but other media of expression refer to another aspect of experience than that which words, with their piecemeal evocation of details, can portray. Our minds, which summarize these piecemeal suggestions in what we call ideas, embrace these ideas not merely with understanding but with feeling. And we are generally interested in proportion as we feel (rather than know) the idea to be significant or, as we usually say, true.

This feeling—like any other—appears in us in the shape of emotions—nervous tensions and motor impulses which we recognize as appropriate to the idea. They are indeed the *enactment* of the idea within us; and an idea not thus enacted makes little impression. Similar tensions and motor impulses are palpably represented or embodied in the substance of music; and as music thus enacts the feeling-aspect of our ideas, we recognize it—by that same faculty which forms the criterion of our ideas— as either significant or trivial: essentially, as either true or false.

that the assistance they received from their jongleurs illuminated considerably the path of those who were presently to contrive harmonic instrumental music. But for the most part, voices singing polyphonically are those which need instrumental help, either for power or for accuracy of pitch, and it is from serving as aids to or substitutes for such voices that many forms of polyphonic instrumental music emerge.

The limbs of man, enacting his enthusiasms or his fears, often move rhythmically. That is, they dance; and the patterns of their movement, once recognized as patterns, may be elaborated and idealized—conceivably to a point where they lose all association with the emotion from which they sprang. But a thin thread of association is all that is needed to relate patterns to experience. We perceive readily the grace of the minuet; and though we cannot dance it, we can reconstruct the courtesy of manner that is implied in its measure.

Songs, dances, and improvisations are thus the activities that generate instrumental music; and to refer instrumental compositions to these sources helps sometimes to illuminate their meaning. Song and dance are of course the original facts. Because song was devoted to the more exalted emotions of religion, its notation preceded that of the dance. Not until the thirteenth century does any recorded instrumental music appear, and by that time the instrumentalists were already discovering polyphony for themselves. Monophonic dance songs however survive, one of which, an *estampie* (the name is a common term for dance and poem among the troubadours), seems to have been invented by two French jongleurs, and to have been turned into a song by one of the earlier troubadors, Raimbault de Vaquiras (who died in 1207). He set to that tune a wonderful jingle of similar end-rhymes.[2] Other homophonic dances surviving from the thirteenth century seem to have been formed after the pattern of the sequence (where again, as will be remembered, words were fitted to existent music) with several sections, each repeated, and each having a first ending (open) before the repetition, and a second ending (closed) thereafter. With only three or four such sections, the dance was called *ductia;* with more, *estampida*. Examples in both duple time (English) and triple (French) appear in the *Harvard Anthology*.

As to the use of instruments in the motets and other polyphonic com-

---

[2] Whether by accident or design, the rhymes for the first stanza, in *–aya*, are essentially the same as the ejaculation *eya* in the dance song *A l'entrada del tens clar*, quoted earlier; and like those, are so fitted to the melody as to hint vividly at recurrent antics in the dance. (The other four stanzas end in *–ia, –uda, –ira,* and *–ida*—fourteen similar rhymes in each stanza, with several inner rhymes.) But the rhythm of the music plagues the transcribers, as may be seen from the two alternative versions in triple time in the *Harvard Anthology,* and the one in duple time in Gleason, *op. cit.*

positions of the thirteenth century, little need be added to what has been said above.[3] No independent instrumental forms immediately arose from this practice, but the idea of the instrumental ensemble and of the instrumentally accompanied song was born. Polyphony, indeed, became an indeterminate genre, either vocal, instrumental, or mixed; and this remained true of many types of song up to the English madrigals, which, as we have seen, were announced as suitable for either voices or instruments. It does *not* apply, however, to Masses and the more sober liturgical forms, nor to the Italian motets and madrigals of the later sixteenth century.

The instrumental ensemble was first used independently for dance music. The elemental form of any dance is created by the feet of the dancers, both the speed and the character of the individual steps and, to some extent, their number (for set figures) being thus established. A curious habit of the medieval dancers helped greatly in the stabilization of the musical forms. The medieval dances were conventionally cast in pairs —a slower, beginning measure in duple time followed by a faster, in triple time. The two were called by the Germans *Tanz* and *Nachtanz* ("Dance" and "After-dance"), with the faster measure often described as *Hupf-auf* ("Hop-up"), *Sprung* ("Jump"), and also *Proportz* or *Tripla*, from the triple proportion of the mensuralists. In Italy and elsewhere, familiar dances in the same duple-triple relation were conjoined: the *Padovano* ("of Padua") or *pavane* (the French equivalent) with the *gagliarda* (French, *gaillarde*, or *galliarde*); the *passamezzo* (moderate step) with the *saltarello* (jump); and later the *allemande* with the *courante*.

The music of the faster dance was usually derived from that of the slower—often by improvisation. The players knew from the usual conventions when to strike into the faster motion, and—since the music was seldom elaborately polyphonic—were able to pursue the general scheme of the harmony (mostly one chord to a bar) by readjusting the rhythmic sense of their parts. The *after-dance* might also have its own theme, however. And in these successions of dance-with-variation or dance-with-complementary-dance lay the germ of the later *dance suite*, a form of the highest importance for our instrumental literature. For dance tunes, merely listened to instead of danced, may be idealized (as the Chopin Waltzes mostly are) without loss of their rhythmic interest, but with a great gain in their "purely" musical appeal.

When the instrumentalists began to form groups independent of the singers, one of their first efforts was to produce successions of dance pieces—two together, or two and two—so related and contrasted (in the

---

[3] See, for example, footnote 9, Chap. VI; the discussion of the Motet, p. 82; footnote 1, Chap. VII; the discussion of the *Ballata*, p. 96, and footnote 6, *ibid*.

old scheme of slow and fast) as to give interest to the succession as a whole. In the early sixteenth century many such collections were published, notably by Attaignant in Paris, and by Susato and Phalèse at Antwerp. Some of these are for wind and string groups; some for lute or clavier.[4] Thus emerges a solo instrument, capable of producing complete harmony under the fingers of a single player, and inexpensive enough to be owned by persons of moderate means. The ultimate consequence will be apparent from a mental glance at the literature of the piano. For the moment, however, the purpose is that of "domesticating" the dances, and idealizing them. A folklike character in many of these tunes often recalls the unlearned source from which the original music came. As the process of refinement went on, a differentiation arose between the simple dances of the people and the more courtly types, which latter will presently evolve into the ballet.

The transcription of dance music from groups of wind or string instruments to the lute and the virginals appears earlier in England than elsewhere. This was doubtless owing to the peculiar course of the Reformation in England, where the fluctuant religious currents greatly disturbed the older processes of composition. A large part of the effort of the best composers was thus deflected toward secular forms. But the treatment of the dance-pair by the process of variation is less frequent than a kind of variation *within* the dance movement itself. This is notable in Hugh Aston's *Hornpipe*, in which the "variation" consists of the addition of an extraordinary variety of fresh melodic figures (all vitally rhythmed) over a persistent alternation of tonic and dominant chords in the bass. *My Lady Carey's Dompe*, a mournful Irish air, has similar structure, its accompanying figure strongly anticipating the eighteenth-century Alberti Bass.

This type of variation was cultivated also in Spain in the early sixteenth century. Since the Spaniards had no religious disagreements comparable to those of the English, their interest in the lute and its music must be attributed to another cause. A remarkable example by Luis de Narvaez—*Diferencias* (Variations) on *O gloriosa Domina*—in which the theme is not a dance at all, suggests that high courtly tradition and the perfection of the methods of such Spanish members of the Roman school as Morales may have determined the style.

Altogether, the process of maintaining a short theme, intact or somewhat figurated, throughout a composition is the process we shall find in

---

[4] These arrangements for solo players often depart extensively from the originals, omitting polyphonic parts, or merely suggesting the more essential notes in the provided harmonies, but adding, as if by improvisation, a great amount of ornamental figuration, suited to the instrument itself.

the later *chaconne* and *passacaglia,* both of which are names pretty certainly associated with dances, and in which the technique of the *ostinato*
—the obstinately persistent idea—is often amazingly worked out. (Both
the persistent figure and the trick of adding improvised upper voices are
familiar in contemporary boogie-woogie.)

The English virginal pieces, whether in the form of dances or variations, show remarkable ingenuity. Collections appear as early as 1565
with *Mulliner's Manuscript;* and *Queen Elizabeth's Virginal Book* contains the work of twenty composers. *Lady Nevile's Book* has forty-two
pieces, all by William Byrd; and Benjamin Cosyn's Book, Will Foster's,
and a collection called *Parthenia* (Greek for *virgin,* and therefore doubtless implying Queen Elizabeth) containing works by Bull, Byrd, and Gibbons, and suggesting the *Triumphs of Oriana,* are other high examples of
a varied and living literature for domestic keyed instruments. These books
contain many pavanes, galliards, *correnti,* and *allemandes;* some arrangements of vocal pieces; [5] many fantasias with imitative portions suggesting
both the technique of the old motet and the coming fugue; and many
variations as above described, often on popular songs. An interesting survival of older contrapuntal practice is found in the frequent elaborations
of *ut, re, mi, fa, sol, la,* dealt with in all sorts of rhythms and proportions.
Fancy is a frequent name for such variation on what is essentially a *cantus
firmus.*

In France toward the end of the sixteenth century, groups of instruments rather than the clavecin were the medium through which the dance
was developed. And it was the French who, by grouping dance pieces
in attractive alternation, and abandoning gradually the thematic relation
between *dance* and *after dance,* produced the suite sequence which comes
to be so universally followed in later days. During the first half of the
seventeenth century the lute began also to be used for the form of the
larger suite, and the charming work of such French clavecinists as Couperin and Chambonnières contributed greatly to the final fixation of the
suite form.

In Germany likewise, at the beginning of the seventeenth century a
rudimentary orchestra came to be the chief vehicle for the development
of the dance. Variation is more extensively practiced there than in
France. The four dances which in Italy had originally been grouped into
a suite (*passamezzo* or *pavane, galliarda* or *saltarello, allemande,* and
courante) now appear in different successions and with other names, yet
forming a conventional group. In some cases, the whole suite will be a

[5] See, for instance, Peter Philips's arrangement of di Lasso's *Bon jour, mon coeur*
for keyboard, from the "Fitzwilliam Virginal Book," in the *Harvard Anthology,*
p. 159.

kind of variation—or rather transformation—of the theme of the first dance, each number, of course, retaining its characteristic rhythm. The following will show the process:

Peurl's four-movement form was later extended to include other dances. Johann Hermann Schein, for example, used five movements; Johann Neubauer, six. The dance-pair was often retained, especially in the succession *allemande-tripla*, where the *tripla* was a variation of the *allemande*. The *Paduan*, too, by expansion of its own substance, sometimes became a sort of *prelude*—a feature of great importance in later suites. Wolfgang Ebner of Vienna in 1648 writes the sequence *allemande, courante, gigue, sarabande*—almost that of the later French suite. Each dance is a variation, in the German style just illustrated, of the *allemande;* while in all the variations (which are for clavier) many figured ornaments in the English manner appear. The term *intrada* in Peurl's suite is irrational, at least in its position. The word frequently occurs in the developed French ballet, clearly in the sense of *entrance*, together with *retirada* (retirement) for the conclusion. Since the ballet was not without dramatic implications, the orchestral intrada suggests the later overture.

The organ, although at first shunned like all other instruments in Western Christendom, was never forbidden in the Eastern Church, and first made its way into the West from thence—as an imperial rather than an ecclesiastical instrument, the famous gift of the Emperor Copronymos to Pippin, the father of Charlemagne. The instrument remained a terror rather than a solace to most of its auditors for many centuries. But about

1300, when balanced keys had replaced the slides, the organ at last found its place in the church.

Some tablature notations of organ music survive from the fourteenth century, but the first true organ music is contained in Conrad Paumann's (the blind organist's) *Fundamentum organizandi* (1452)—a remarkably progressive instruction-book which contains, besides, many fine arrangements of German songs. The Buxheim Organ Book (1470) contains similar arrangements of Burgundian chansons. Paul Hofhaimer, already mentioned, was a famous organist, but most of his works are lost. Arnold Schlick was the last and greatest organ composer before the Reformation. His work brings to a culmination the instrumental treatment of the Catholic hymn, using the hymn-melody as a *cantus firmus*, with contrapuntal voices woven about it. In principle, a good deal of Bach's later practice is here anticipated, even to the use of preludial phrases. But since hymns held no such important place in the Catholic service as in the Protestant, the organ literature in this field is scanty.

It should be mentioned, however, that "Organ Masses" were composed to supplement, and in a sense to supplant, the choir in some parts of the rendition of the Ordinary of the Mass. The Gregorian strain (for example, of the *Kyrie*) after being chanted once in the usual manner was continued by the organ in a paraphrase of at least the first few notes of the vocal phrase. Whole Masses were thus composed for the organ. The practice goes back to the fifteenth century; but significant examples appear with Girolamo Cavazzoni (1542) and Claudio Merulo (*circa* 1590).

Other early organ pieces of great import for the future were the *canzone* and the *ricercare*. Cavazzoni (in an effort faintly similar to that of Peter Philips, noted above) paraphrased various French songs for organ, subtracting from and adding interestingly to the originals.[6] Later composers, instead of adapting earlier works, embodied the general style in original compositions. The imitative beginning, often at the fourth or fifth, presents essentially the technique of the opening or exposition of the fugue. (The word *fugue* was sometimes used by older German composers as a synonym for *canzona*.) We have here, then, one root of a vastly important musical form. Another is not far to seek.

The organ *ricercare* (the Italian word means "to search") developed simultaneously with the organ *canzona*. This same term, however, was applied to ensemble pieces as well—pieces which were designed, like some of the later madrigals, indifferently for voices or for instruments. The immediate implication of the title is that the player will find "sought out" effects or devices similar to those contrived by the ingenious in Masses

---

[6] See his arrangement and the original of Josquin's *Faulte d'argent* in the *Harvard Anthology*, pp. 126 and 93.

and motets; but the term appears also to have been understood as referring
to the technical difficulty and brilliancy of the composition. In this character it approaches to the toccata; but the word *ricercar* also appears as
a title for pieces for violin and even for voices, where the word *toccata*
(to touch) would be out of place. The instrumental *ricercar*, whether for
organ or ensemble, was usually a rather lengthy piece, displaying not
merely the imitative opening of the *canzona*, but many of the more rec-
ondite tricks of the contrapuntists. The learned aspect was not so much
cultivated by the earlier writers—Jachet de Buus, Willaert, and others, in
ensemble pieces and Cavazzoni in pieces for organ—but with Andrea
Gabrieli *research* becomes and remains the distinctive feature of the form.
How this elaboration of the themes (or theme, since the later pieces are
often monothematic) contributed to the middle or development section of
the *fugue* will be evident when we come to study that form.

We must return now to the Protestant development of the organ chorale or hymn. The great difference between the Protestant and the Catholic usage lay in the fact that in Protestant churches the congregation
always took part in the singing of the hymns, and was guided in its singing by the organ. To play the hymn with its harmonies before the congregation began to sing was needful in order to recall the tune (which
at that time was all that most of the congregation dared attempt) and to
show the harmonies against it in order that the singers might not be
thrown off their precarious hold of the tune. But when a hymn had
become thoroughly familiar such precaution was unnecessary, and the
organist—according to the time allotted him—might indulge his musical
imagination. How Bach utilized that privilege we shall see in its place.
We have here only to note that the earlier composers—particularly Samuel Scheidt, the greatest German organist of his day, with such a fantasia as *Ich ruf' zu Dir*—laid solid foundations for that pinnacle to which
Bach, in this field, was to climb.

A few other names—whether for other pieces or for those already mentioned—must be considered before our sketch is finished. The word
fantasia we found applied a moment ago to what was ostensibly a chorale
prelude. That sort of confusion is not uncommon in musical terms in the
sixteenth century. The title *Fantasia* would seem to suggest a liberated
imagination. Yet in most compositions so named we find what appears
as no more than a free kind of *ricercare*—often on one theme, and displaying considerable learning. The English *fancy* during the sixteenth century
is essentially similar but, as elsewhere, becomes more free during the seventeenth century. The word *tiento*, whose etymology is unexplained, is
a Spanish equivalent for *ricercare*. But again, the word *ricercare* is used
for lute pieces where no shadow of contrapuntal learning appears, and

must thus be held to refer to the technical problems posed for the per-former.

There is also the familiar word *sonata;* but it has at this time only the general meaning "played" (as *cantata* means "sung"). It thus refers to any kind of instrumental piece; but it will soon become more specific, with the *sonata da chiesa* (church sonata) and *sonata da camera* (chamber sonata). The word *symphony* is still quite indeterminate, having no more than its literal sense of a "sounding together," whether of voices or in-struments or both.

Instrumental music is still adolescent; but its health is sound and its con-stitution vigorous, and we may shortly expect great achievements from it.

ఆ *CHAPTER XIII* ಜಿ

Retrospects and Prospects

I N the period upon which we are to enter, the earliest music which is now at all commonly heard will begin to be produced. Even in the seventeenth century we shall find relatively little which is familiar to the general public of today. It is true that many groups, whether of scholars or of performers, have recently cultivated the publication and rendition of the madrigals, operas, and instrumental works of the sixteenth and seventeenth centuries and have revealed the remarkable maturity of the music of that period. These activities, however, only show that in many respects the seventeenth century was one of direct preparation for the great work of Bach and Handel. But we must not suppose that because our concert programs seldom present anything earlier, the art of music itself began with Bach and Handel. The untiring labor of generations of men contributed to their art as fully as theirs contributed to that of Beethoven and Wagner. Nor is the mere awareness that much had gone before sufficient for any true understanding of this great outburst of musical imagination. We must have a tolerably clear idea of the whole foundation of musical thought upon which this enduring structure was built. All our preceding study has been concerned with this foundation. It will be well, perhaps, to summarize the results of that study; to see in a single, rapid glance the most essential steps in musical progress; and, by such a survey of the foundations, to forecast the general character of the superstructure which is to be the object of our study in the pages to come.

In one sense, the most important elements in this foundation are those which have hardly been mentioned. These are not characteristics of purely musical thought, but rather influences upon music from that world of feeling which music is trying to represent. It often appears that these outside influences retard rather than promote the progress of purely musical thinking. But this is because purely musical thinking is of no great use to the world, which insistently demands that music shall be more than a mere combination of pleasing sounds. In every age men have cared for art because it gave expression to the greatest thoughts and the finest emotions of life; but they have often forgotten that it is precisely these thoughts and feelings which are the reasons for the existence of art. The influence of music on the world is great; but the influence of the world on music is equally important.

From the very beginning, a worldly factor is present in musical thought. Music arose out of a sense of pleasure given by rhythmically ordered pitch relations. Pitch relations alone give almost purely abstract pleasure; they appeal to a region of the mind untouched by any other sort of impression. Rhythm on the other hand, although its pattern can be mathematically described and abstractly thought, is a palpable feature of the motion which characterizes all life. To almost any region of the mind which commonly deals with life, rhythm can suggest some reality of life. Without the enlivening factor of rhythm, music would never have become an art of any importance. But since rhythm is in many ways a representation of life, the world has had from the outset an influence upon music.

We can fairly clearly distinguish the two essential factors of musical thought—its pure tone relations and its rhythm—in any piece of music or, in a more general way, in any period of musical development. To do so will give us perhaps the clearest view both of the progress of the art itself and of the influences of everyday life upon the art. Our summary will be made in this light.

The mere pleasure in tone relations was great enough among the Greeks to account for the evolution, out of an original two-note group, first, of the various types of tetrachord, and finally of a two-octave diatonic scale. Within this two-octave scale there appeared both the mese as a central, governing tone, and also the modes or octave scales, whose extreme notes or finals were subordinate to the mese. Altogether, the two-octave scale was so nearly like our own that both the suggestion and the actual materials of harmony existed centuries before harmony itself became a fact. But the mere tone substance of music could not develop alone. Rhythmic organization was necessary; and for the patterns of rhythm, music had to borrow from poetry and the dance. Dance rhythm is the epitome of bodily motion. The rhythm of poetry is far more abstract. It is nevertheless *alive;* and since its suggestion of life is joined to the almost limitless range of verbal idea, the whole meaning of poetry is both more exact and more inclusive than that of the dance. Verbal meaning and verbal rhythm are inseparably united in poetry; and verbal meaning thus becomes combined with musical suggestion in that strange and to us almost incomprehensible music of the Greeks. Dance and poetry, the sources of that rhythm vitality which was needed to give form to the mere pitch relations of music, were continuous influences in the first evolution of our musical thought. But it happened that the poetic meter of Greek verse was based on quantity, not on the normal speech accent of the words as with us. Quantitative verse could allow but little intensity of rhythmic accentuation. Hence a convention of language, in its essence unrelated to musical thought, both supplied and at the same time restricted the development of rhythm in music.

A profound revolution in the speech habits of men—a revolution beyond the power of any mere musician to instigate—was thus necessary before music could enter upon a free evolution. Vast projects of war and colonization—projects not in the least concerned with music—brought about this revolution in speech. And another revolution of equally profound significance, the triumph of Christianity, brought to life a new ideal of human relationship and hence a new field of emotion for music to express. The Greek musician had been preoccupied with the setting of tones to words whose poetic perfection he must not disturb. The value of thought or feeling in this poetry was hardly his concern. The Christian musician, on the other hand, dealt largely with prose texts in which the verbal organization was relatively unimportant. Not artistic but human sensibilities—feelings of humility, of tenderness, of religious exaltation—gave him his themes; and for the expression of these feelings the substance of music, as he had learned it from Greek or oriental sources, had to be remodeled.

The first changes in pure tone organization are slight, involving hardly more than the rejection of the harsher melodic progressions such as that of the augmented fourth. More conspicuous are the changes in rhythm; for the substitution of accentual for quantitative verse demands a new type of rhythm movement in music. At first, however, this naturalness (as we see it) of rhythm plays a relatively small part in musical organization. Religious sentiment is too ecstatic and too contemplative to be represented by any very vital motion suggestion. Even the rhythmic hymns are soon overshadowed by the imposing ritual music, set to the prose texts. But the accentual principle of poetry-making is nevertheless firmly established; and when other than the most exclusively religious emotion comes to demand expression, its force will be more fully apparent.

But, though the rhythm element is more conspicuous, so great a change in expressive purpose as that which Christianity brought about must have its influence on tone relations also. Christian expansion of the inherited system of pitch relations includes (1) the abandonment of the centrality of the old Greek mese; (2) the establishment of the extreme notes of the modal scales as finals, supplanting the mese and foreshadowing our tonic; (3) the addition of the plagal to the authentic modes; and, partly as a result of the new rhythm basis, (4) the gradual evolution of a considerably florid style of cantillation. The high organization of the Catholic Church, largely completed by Gregory the Great on the eve of the Dark Ages, makes possible the preservation of such progress as has been made toward the musical expression of the Christian ideal. No further steps can be traced until the beginning of new literary effort at the opening of the ninth century.

Now occurs the great expansion, first in pitch relations and later in rhythm, which marks the very beginning of modern music. Harmony, dreamed of but rejected by the Greeks, becomes a reality; and through this vast unfolding of musical possibilities, the world of the Renaissance is able to find musical expression. The simple steps in the early evolution of harmony are easy to grasp: strict organum with its inexorable parallelism of fifths and fourths is modified (because of the very structure of the diatonic scale) into free organum.

Next, the complete individuality of the combined melodies is achieved in the new discant; and with the twelfth and thirteenth centuries music begins to show all the essential impulses—but by no means the finished characteristics—of our own art. Rhythms, still directly derived from verse, are combined in the various voices in such a way that at first a scheme of exclusively triple rhythm is the rule. From accent marks and chironomic signs, a system of notation is evolved. As the influence of secular feeling (already strong in the thirteenth century) grows, duple rhythm, with a corresponding complication of the system of notation, takes its place in the scheme of music beside the triple rhythm of the preceding era.

Now at last musical rhythm loses its original dependence on poetic meter; and in the fourteenth century the ideal of a purely musical form, dependent on nothing external to the musical substance, becomes dimly perceptible. The emancipation of the substance of music from domination by the substance of verse is accompanied by a more vivid expression than ever before of emotion which words cannot express—of the essential feeling quality not only of religious but also of secular emotion. *Musica ficta* adds chromatic tones to the vocabulary of the modes. *Faux bourdon* and *gymel* give the first concrete suggestion of the chord idea which at last is seen to underlie all harmony. Cadences, essential for the punctuation of the musical sentence, become more definite. Arbitrary discord is abolished, and clear musical syntax becomes a fact. Musical rhetoric—the building up of a continuous musical discourse—follows naturally the attainment of a clearer syntax. Imitation is the basis of the first rhetorical structure; but this somewhat mechanical basis is at length superseded by a more inclusive and more rational principle of structure—the relating of harmonies to each other within the mode, under the domination of the final. But it will be long before these harmonic relations emerge from confusion. For the identity of the modes can be maintained only when chromatic alteration is forbidden; and the rapid increase of the use of accidentals (begun in the practice of *musica ficta*) is persistently confusing that identity. Out of this confusion will come the opposition of major and minor tonalities as the only clear distinction between the modes, but that distinction will not be finally established until late in the seventeenth century.

Every new discovery in tone relation or rhythm, interesting as it may be in itself, marks also a closer approach of music to the expression of new and vital interests in the life of the time. The music of the troubadours plays an important part in the structure of the motet; but such secular song is even more vividly suggestive of the emotional purpose which the motet fulfilled. The frequent use of such secular tunes as *L'Homme armé* in the Masses of the fifteenth century is as clear an indication as could be desired of the manner in which secular interest is coming to pervade even the most solemn religious feeling. And the madrigal and the dance forms, with their growing utilization of instrumental support, are but the natural products of an age in which worldly concerns are becoming paramount. The Renaissance, half unconsciously, has unleashed the spirit of individuality. Colonization and discovery are outlets for, as well as strong incentives to, individual effort; nationalism, and most of all the growth of the middle class as the mainstay of the nation, offers greater reward to the aspiring individual than the feudalism which it supersedes; cultural and scientific study are but expansions of the individual mind; Protestantism is the emphasis of the individual's right to his own way of worship. For all such individual impulses, music, if it is to survive, must somehow find expression. And as Christianity was the force which, by persistent effort, achieved out of the materials bequeathed to it by paganism the essentially congregational expression of polyphony, so now the Renaissance, out of materials bequeathed by the Christian Church, will achieve a new, homophonic style suited to that sentiment of individuality which in increasing measure will come to rule the world.

The Seventeenth Century—
The Monodic Revolution

The Beginnings of Opera and Oratorio

At the very opening of the seventeenth century a great change occurred in the method, the character, and the purpose of musical thought—a change so far-reaching that the new movement which resulted is generally called the *Monodic Revolution*. The effect of this revolution was the overthow of the old ascendancy of counterpoint and the substitution of a simpler kind of music. At first this simpler music was in the form of musical recitation rather than melody, sung by a single voice throughout and accompanied by instruments. The accompaniment was not in the elaborate contrapuntal style but was at first a simple succession of chords. And even when this accompaniment became more varied and interesting, as it soon did, it remained subordinate to the leading part—that of the solo voice. This new style was first employed in the opera; but it soon came to be used for instrumental and vocal music of many types.

A simple tune with a chord accompaniment is so familiar to us, and seems so entirely natural, that we can hardly understand how a revolution should be necessary for its establishment in popular favor. Indeed, it was only the trained musicians of the time whose ideas needed to be, and were, revolutionized. For the actual materials of the new music already existed; and it was only a simpler way of looking at these materials rather than any discovery of new musical elements which brought about the revolution. Once again a convention is to be overthrown.

The Opposition to Polyphony

How deeply the convention of polyphony was entrenched we have seen in all the elaborate development of music since the beginnings of harmony. Combined, co-ordinate melodies formed the substance of practically all the learned music—the really artistic music—which we have studied. Both the Mass and the madrigal were artistic products of a very high order. They expressed a very wide range of religious and secular feeling; they satisfied in church and aristocratic society the demands for expression which existed within those circles. But their style was too abstruse to appeal to the average man—to the rapidly growing middle class which lived on the fringe of aristocratic society. One force which brought about the revolution came, then, from *outside* the circle in which the polyphonic convention was respected.

From the beginning of the sixteenth century there had been a considerable opposition to the Netherlanders and their invasion of Italian music. The frottola and other popular types of song which we have described were not merely the sources of the learned madrigal, dropped from use as soon as the madrigal form was perfected; they remained the native musical expression of the Italian people, to whom the elaborate intricacies of the madrigal seemed a useless and destructive refinement. Such opposition as this was of course unorganized. It was nevertheless very real, and ready to follow any leadership which offered itself against the foreigners. This leadership, we shall now see, was provided from *within* the cultured circles which had also produced and fostered the madrigal.

The study of Latin and Greek had become, since the days of Erasmus, an essential element in the education of every cultivated man. We have already mentioned as instances of such interest the cultured groups which surrounded Conrad Celtes in Germany and Cardinal Bembo in Italy. As a result of this study almost all literary effort was colored by the influence of classical models; and, especially in the field of the drama, the ancient masterpieces appeared so perfect by comparison with any contemporary productions that the great ideal of the time was not merely to imitate the drama of the ancient world, but so far as was possible to reconstruct it. The native dramas (those which had followed the mysteries and the miracle plays of the early days) were mostly in the vein of comedy and dealt with the manners, customs, and desires of ordinary people—people who might be very amusing, but were by no means of heroic stature. By comparison with the high dignity and the profound philosophy of the ancient tragedy, such productions appeared, to the enthusiastic students of the classical tongues, trivial and coarse.

But as an element in this drama, especially that of the Greeks, it appeared that music was of essential importance. The close association of music with Greek verse seemed to suggest that the impressiveness of the ancient tragedy was due in no small measure to the fact that the lines were musically declaimed; and that consequently the solution of the problem of a contemporary drama which might rival the ancient could possibly be attained through the use of music as an adjunct.[1] The idea of this association, however, originated in the study of the classics, not in any directly musical impulse. It is evident that the elaborate polyphony and the discursive expression of the madrigal style would be quite unsuited to the purposes of drama.

THE FLORENTINE CAMERATA

Cultivated literary taste, and uncultivated but eager musical appetite, wide apart as their objectives were, thus combined to condemn the learned polyphony as sterile. The real leaders of the opposition were a group of enthusiasts for the ancient culture who formed a little circle at the house of Giovanni Bardi, Count of Vernio, in Florence. Among this group, which included the most renowned poets and philosophers of the city, were a few musicians—notably Vincenzo Galilei (a pupil of the great theorist Zarlino and father of the famous astronomer) and Jacopo Corsi, a rich and influential patron of the arts and himself a composer. To this group were presently attracted Jacopo Peri and Giulio Caccini, two of the men to whom the actual creation of opera is to be attributed, and Emilio del Cavalieri, the reputed discoverer of recitative and author of the first oratorio. This group of enthusiasts is often spoken of as the *Florentine Camerata*.

The nature and function of music speedily became the chief topic of interest. Classical study had revealed much that had been hitherto unknown of the relation of music to Greek drama; and the most profound speculations were engendered as to a style of composition which could

---

[1] The idea of introducing music as an incident of dramatic pieces was not at all new. Adam de la Halle (d. 1297), a famous trouvère, had written a comedy, *Robin et Marion*, into which a consideraable number of incidental songs had been inserted. The charming tale of *Aucassin et Nicolète* also had some fragments of music connected with it, and may have been presented in some quasi-dramatic form. The earlier attempts in the tragic style in Italy, such as the *Orfeo* of Politian (Mantua, 1471), and religious plays such as *The Conversion of St. Paul* (Rome, 1480) had had many musical numbers. Claudio Merulo and Andrea Gabrieli had each composed music as an incident to drama; and the *favola pastorale* (shepherd fable—a simple type of drama on popular themes) appeared as early as 1554 in the *Sacrifice* of Alfonso della Viola, where an actual monody occurred, repeated for three stanzas of text. Instrumental interludes and ballets were extensively employed. But in all these cases the music was purely incidental, and was not adapted to the essential dialogue of the play. Nor, of course, was the music in any very elaborate style.

make modern music as impressive as that of the ancients. Not realizing the enormous differences between the very substance as well as the purpose of music in ancient and contemporary times, these eager students took the doctrines of Plato as fundamental and evolved from them a new theory of musical art. Giovanni Bardi (reported by Doni, who wrote endless discussions of the proceedings of this little group) conceived the whole purpose of music to have been stated in a passage from the third book of Plato's *Republic* which he (Bardi) interpreted as follows:

"Music is nothing else than the art and fashion of giving to words their proper time-value; since they should be sung either fast or slow, accordingly as they are short or long; and practical music is an arrangement of the words (which have been set by the poet into verses of various measure, according to their long or short syllables) such that the words, sung by the human voice, shall move, now fast, now slow, now in high tones, now in low, the song being either entrusted to the voice alone, or accompanied by instruments. This is Plato's definition, with which Aristotle and other learned men agree." After reciting in the most credulous fashion a list of miracles worked by ancient musicians (such as that of Orpheus, who moved the stones with his art), he went on to disparage contemporary music. "Our music divides itself, today, into two great divisions: to the one belongs the so-called counterpoint; the other we may call 'the art of singing well.' In counterpoint [that is, in the madrigal] Mr. Bass parades about the ground floor of his palace in semibreves and minims, Mme. Soprano scampers around the roof-garden in minims and semiminims, while Messrs. Alto and Tenor trot, in varied dress, through the middle storeys. Our contrapuntists would hold it a mortal sin if they allowed all the voices to be heard at once on the same syllable, having the same time-value."

This complexity was all very well for instrumental music; but that again was precisely the style of music which Aristotle condemns as artificial. The remedy was, not to spoil the verse. "For, as much as the mind is superior to the body, so far superior are the words to the counterpoint; as the soul must guide the body, so counterpoint must take its rules and laws from the words." The same attitude was expressed by other writers —by Galilei in his *Dialogues*, and by Caccini in the preface to his *New Music*. Galilei thought the rules which forbade consecutive fifths and octaves had been invented only to make the art of composition harder; and Caccini averred that he learned more about music at the house of Bardi than he could have learned in thirty years of application to the study of counterpoint.

The Florentine Monody and the First Opera

The first tangible result of all this agitation was the so-called *Florentine Monody*. At an evening assembly at the house of Bardi, Galilei sang *sopra un concerto di viole* (to the accompaniment of a group of viols), a setting which he had composed of the scene of Ugolino from Dante's *Inferno*. "Some people were pleased and some laughed," says Doni; and the scorn was doubtless a spur to Galilei's determination, for he followed this production with a setting of some of the Lamentations of Jeremiah. Caccini, in 1589, composed other monodies "in a more beautiful and agreeable style" for the celebration of a wedding in the family of the Medici. And in 1594 he and Peri collaborated in a setting of the story of Daphne by the poet Rinuccini, which was privately performed at the house of Jacopo Corsi, who, now that Bardi had been called to Rome, had become the leading supporter of the new movement. This work has not been preserved, so that we cannot tell how far it approached to actual opera. The first public performance of opera was that of *Euridice* (text by Rinuccini), composed by Jacopo Peri for the celebration of the wedding of Henry IV of France and Maria de' Medici in 1600. The same text was also set by Caccini, and the two versions were published. Since Peri's work not only is the first real opera, but also quite clearly illustrates the theory of the new form, a brief description will be useful.

Although Rinuccini's verse is excellent, his handling of the dramatic theme is timid and rather uneffective. After an opening dance in celebration of the marriage of Orpheus and Eurydice, the nymphs are invited by Eurydice to continue their dance in a neighboring meadow. To Orpheus, voicing his delight in the marriage, comes Daphne, announcing that Eurydice has been bitten by a snake and is dead. Orpheus determines to follow her to the underworld. Guided by Venus he reaches the gates, and to the accompaniment of his golden lyre pleads for the restoration of his bride. Pluto, reminded of his affair with Prosperpine, is at last induced to relax the "law of iron" by which his kingdom is ruled. The scene reverts to the meadow, and the happy couple reappear to their delighted friends. (The episode of Orpheus's disobedience in looking back is quite omitted—perhaps because the tragic suggestion would have been unacceptable at the actual wedding which was being celebrated.)

The music is largely in recitative. The choruses are polyphonic, but there are no duets or concerted numbers by the principals. The orchestra, which played behind the scenes, consisted of a gravicembalo, a large tenor lute, and a bass viol. Behind the scenes also there were three flute players for shepherds' scenes. The so-called *Aria* is merely the repetition of a second strophe to the music of the first. The most intense parts are sung

—in accordance with the theory that the words must not be mutilated— to music in the "representative style," which is intensified speech rather than song. Natural emphasis in declamation is religiously observed; but the deeper psychological truth which music can reveal is as yet unimagined. A few instrumental dances and interludes relieve the monotony of the recitative. The scenery is described as having been of the most sumptuous order; and we have good reason to suppose that a large part of the success of the performance was due to its appeal to the eye rather than to the ear.

How meager the new style was in really musical resources may be seen from the following, a part of the Lament of Orpheus in Peri's *Euridice*. This is by no means the style of recitative in which the most of the opera is carried on, but represents the highest intensity of declamation of which Peri is capable:

"And you, ah, in pity for my suffering that shall dwell eternally in my heart, weep at my complaint, ye shades of Hell. Ah, me! ah, me! that to its dawning should be joined the setting of the sun (of my eyes)."

The original notation gives on one staff the melody for the singer. The fundamental bass, to which figures are supplied as an indication of the harmonies, is on a lower staff. This figured bass (which is familiar to all students of harmony) had originated, strangely enough, not in the simple practice of the new music, but in the most extreme developments of polyphony.[2] But since it gave a convenient method of indicating essential harmony, it was extremely useful in the new opera, which consisted of little else than a voice part with a few chords below it. The actual bass (together with the voice part) is all that is indicated by the composer in the illustration just given; the filling-in of the chords was understood by the gravicembalist (the pianist) and was readily executed at sight.

Operatic Experiments—Madrigal Operas—The First Oratorio

To the learned musicians, against whose practice the whole production was in a sense directed, such music must have appeared thin and feeble. The great richness of effect given by the madrigal was lost; and drama appeared to have been achieved, not through music but at the expense of music. For the madrigal had come to express, with far greater fullness than mere musical recitation could give, the vivid interests of secular life; and less pretentious songs like the villanella and the Moresca (a dance whose oriental rhythm recalled the Moorish occupation) had been used in carnival plays and masquerades for essentially dramatic purposes. Madrigals had even been used in a kind of sequence to relate a dramatic story. As early as 1567, Alessandro Striggio had contrived to tell a considerably dramatic story of love and intrigue in a sequence of madrigals entitled *The Chatter of the Women Over the Washtub*. Several similar collections

---

[2] The extent to which polyphony had been complicated by the sixteenth-century composers staggers the imagination. Canons for thirty voices or more, and compositions for four, six or eight complete choirs, were worked out with far more diligence than inspiration. The performance of such polychoral works was extremely difficult to direct. The organist, in consequence, had a heavy responsibility, for it was his business to keep the enormous groups together. Since several choirs could only be effective if some were silent, awaiting their turn to answer a statement of others, the single bass part for any one voice would not be continuous; and a "General Bass"— a part which gave the real bass of the whole music at any given instant, was provided for the organist. At points where fewer voices were engaged, the organist could supply useful harmony notes; and indeed at most times could duplicate the real harmony of the voices without attempting to follow their individual melodic curves. This general bass part or *continuo* (obviously so called because it was continuous throughout the composition, while the actual bass of the singer would be intermittent, or perhaps rise temporarily above that of the tenor and so not be the real bass at all) with its figures, was thus of the greatest importance in clarifying the harmonic idea of music, as opposed to the polyphonic idea which had underlain all composition up to this time.

are extant dating from the immediately following period; and in 1597—possibly in an attempt to show the insufficiency of the new monodic style—Orazio Vecchi, a composer of great attainment, produced his madrigal-comedy *Amfiparnasso*, a drama "addressed to the ear, rather than to the eye." It was long supposed that this work was a mere satire on the "new music," and was intended to be staged and acted like any opera—the parts for the singers on the stage being accompanied by the other singers (in place of an orchestra) behind the scenes. It appears however that the intention was merely to convey a dramatic idea solely through music and words. The music was far better than that of Peri; but the directness of recitative was of course lacking, and in the absence of scene and action, the work was without appeal to the new public which was attracted by the opera. But the very attempt to make out of a series of madrigals the equivalent of an opera, shows how great was the divergence of opinion between the musicians of the old and the new schools; and it is quite evident that the old idea could never survive if the new were shown to be capable of any solid results.

In addition to these conscious and learned efforts to re-create the ancient drama expressive of secular ideas and feeling, similar attempts were made to reanimate and re-establish the medieval religious plays by the addition of music. We have seen how the Roman priest, Filippo Neri, instituted the singing of simple spiritual songs called *laudi spirituali*. From such simple music in which the whole congregation could join, to *laudi* in dialogue form in which a particular episode of significance could be impersonated was a natural step. Animuccia and others had lent their aid toward the popularizing of the *laudi spirituali;* and in Rome in 1600, shortly before the performance of Peri's *Euridice*, Emilio del Cavalieri produced his *Rappresentazione di anima e di corpo*—an allegorical presentation of a moral theme in an extended style of dialogue, which is often called the first oratorio. The plan—that of the "morality"—is not however followed in the later oratorios; and it is rather in the use of current operatic types of recitative, and in the general dramatic form of the whole work, that the interest resides. In such pieces the chorus was far more frequently employed than in the opera; and to obviate the necessity of constructing the work wholly on a dramatic plan, an impersonal character called the *Testo* (Text) was introduced, whose function it was to carry on the narrative. This same "impersonality" we shall meet again as the "Evangelist" in the later form of the Passion. No immediate development of the form occurred after Cavalieri's work; so that we may turn again to the actual music drama.

The First Great Music Dramatist—Monteverdi

If the artificial and almost mechanical process of rendering speech in terms of recitative had not been at once bettered, it is probable that the new dramatic movement would have foundered at the outset. That the new style was in its first manifestation only shallow and lacking in real vitality is seen in the fact that no further efforts of importance were put forth in Florence, its birthplace. It was therefore most fortunate that a man of genuine musical imagination should have appeared almost at once, to show that the true function of dramatic music lay, not in a slavish imitation of the spoken inflection of words, but rather in an emotional expression of their sense. This man was Claudio Monteverdi. And it is due to him that Venice, the natural home of all that was rich and cosmopolitan in art, becomes the first real center of operatic development.

Monteverdi was born in Cremona in 1567. Under the tuition of Ingegneri his talent was so rapidly developed that in 1583 he published his first book of *Madrigali spirituali*. This was rapidly followed by more striking and popular works in the same style. He presently entered the service of the Duke of Mantua, where his ability as a viol player was much admired and where he became chapelmaster in 1601. Already his freedom of style had excited the condemnation of the graver theorists. His treatment of discord especially aroused their ire; for he deliberately disobeyed the rule that all discord must be both prepared and resolved. The following example of a cadence, from one of these madrigals, will illustrate this point:

The ninth above the bass (A), following a rest, is quite unprepared. Moreover, it skips to another discord (the seventh, F) and is thus also unresolved. "Is this a joke, or is it intended?" asked the theorists who, even at that time, probably enjoyed the sound but could not endure the infraction of a rule. To us, of course, the passage is altogether natural. But we hear both A and F as belonging to a single harmony of the dominant; and in a day when the very idea of a chord had hardly progressed beyond the concept of a triad, and when the idea of key was still confused so that the term *dominant harmony* was itself unknown, such discord may well have been somewhat confusing. But the vividness of discord for the expression of intense feeling was obvious to any ordinary hearer. It had exactly the quality which was needed for the immediate suggestion of passion in dramatic music. It was not strange that Monteverdi was attracted to the new form.

His first music drama was based, like Peri's, on the story of Orpheus. The poem, however, was not that which Peri had set, but was the work of Alessandro Striggio, the son of the madrigalist mentioned above. The enormous forward stride which was here made in adapting music to drama can be but lamely described in words; but even such comparison with the work of Peri is striking. Monteverdi wrote rather fully developed *Symphonies* (introductory orchestral pieces) and *Ritornelli* (interludes) for instruments alone, and mingled instruments and voices in many interesting ways. In his choruses he by no means abated from his high achievements as a madrigalist. He introduced a wealth of new musical figures, employed a type of chromatic harmony which in expressive power equals that of a Marenzio or a Gesualdo, had a style of recitative whose impressiveness and pathos has hardly been surpassed, and, last but not least, used an orchestra whose sonority already represents the summit of orchestral art of the first half of the seventeenth century.[3]

The first act is wholly joyous—an idyl whose theme is the wedding of Orpheus and Eurydice. This mood also dominates the opening of the second act. Orpheus and the shepherds are still singing the praises of Eurydice. Suddenly comes a messenger announcing the death of his beloved. Compare the following lament of Orpheus with that by Peri quoted above. The text may be translated thus: "Thou art dead, art dead, my life, and I am living; thou hast departed from me, departed from me forever."——"And the softened heart of the King of Shades must allow you, with me, again to see the stars. Ah, if impious fate shall deny me this, I shall wed with thee again in the company of the dead. Farewell, earth; farewell, heaven; and sunlight, farewell."

[3] In *Orfeo* he calls for 2 gravicembali, 2 contrabassi di viole, 10 viole da braccia, a double harp, 2 small "violini," 2 chittaroni, 2 organi di legno, 3 bassi da gamba, 4 trombones, a regal, 2 cornetti, a little flute in the 22nd (i.e., 3 octaves higher than written), a high trumpet, and 3 muted trumpets—in all, 36 instruments, with some others added as the drama proceeds. Compare this with the meager orchestra demanded by Peri!

This concludes with the following extraordinarily vivid representation of Orpheus's grief:

rammi em-pio des-ti-no ri-mar-ro te-co in compagnia   di mor-te.

A-dio ter-ra,   A-dio cie-lo,   e so-le,   A-di--o.

A chorus of lament concludes the act.

The third act is in the underworld. Over the gate of Hell appears Dante's famous line, "Leave all hope behind, all ye who enter here." After a tremendous appeal to the powerful spirits of the underworld (the song has two alternative parts, one quite simple, the other very florid) Charon is induced to ferry Orpheus across the Styx. In the fourth act the appeals of Proserpine and the lesser spirits added to that of Orpheus, at last move Pluto to allow Eurydice to return, on the condition that she follow Orpheus unseen by him. He begins a song of triumph; but in the midst of it is terrified to think that he may have been deceived and that Eurydice is not following. He turns to look; and with a plaintive lament, "Ah, vision too sweet," she fades from his sight. In the fifth act Apollo, descending in a cloud, gives him assurance that although Eurydice cannot return to earth, "in the sun and the stars he shall see her fair semblance."

This work was produced in 1607. In the following year, as a feature of the celebration of the wedding of the crown prince of Mantua, a still more remarkable work was produced. This was *Arianna*, with text by Rinuccini. The music, except for a few fragments, has been lost. The famous "Lament" of Ariadne, deserted by Theseus, has been preserved however, and this, together with some later scenes, was made into a madrigal sequence by the composer himself. The "Lament" is given, both in its original and its arranged form, in the *Oxford History*, Vol. III, pages 47 and 49. In directness and intensity of expression this music, written only eight years after the performance of Peri's *Euridice*, shows a profundity of musical imagination as remarkable as any to be discovered in the operatic music of far later periods.

THE OPERA AND THE PUBLIC

Although Monteverdi's genius was apparent to a few of his finer-minded contemporaries, the really imaginative qualities of his work were not generally rated at their true worth. Many other composers were producing operas founded on the somewhat mechanical principles followed by Peri and Caccini rather than on the more psychological and suggestive style of Monteverdi. These works were successful, if only because they were in the new and popular form of the *dramma per musica*. So great was the enthusiasm for the new style that in 1637 the first public opera house, the Teatro San Cassiano, was opened in Venice. Others rapidly followed, so that before 1700 no fewer than sixteen opera houses had been opened in that one city!

Thus opera, in its early infancy, became the ward of a paying public. At first, as we have seen, operatic performances had been devised for aristocratic entertainment and had attracted the patronage and the criticism of cultured circles only. Now the basis of criticism as well as of financial support is changed; and the effort of the composer must be directed toward the satisfaction of a larger and much less discriminating, though not less eager, audience. In the works designed for public performance, scenic display was as elaborately prepared and as keenly enjoyed by the unthinking as in our own day; action gained in spectacular interest rather than in dramatic truth; and the music similarly was designed to appeal to the superficial ears rather than to the deeper sensibilities of the public. The classical ideals which had inspired Peri and Caccini were unknown to this public, which was equally unable to perceive the expressive subtlety of Monteverdi's art. The opening of public opera houses thus complicates still further the vexed problem of music drama—a problem which still remains one of the most disputed of musical questions. It is necessary that we should perceive some of the difficulties which confront any writer who sets about producing a music drama.

The mere substitution of recitative for ordinary speech cannot transform drama into opera, because it cannot provide complete musical satisfaction. The opera composer's task is to unify the suggestions given by word, action, and tone against a scenic background which in itself demands a certain share of the observer's attention. Unity of speech and action is hard to maintain in the spoken drama; but with the addition of music the problem is far more difficult. For the satisfaction which comes from following the intricate course of a truly dramatic action is altogether different from the satisfaction which comes from following the intricacies of a competently written piece of music.

Music can often express even better than words the various states of feeling which are developed by a dramatic action. But really interesting music can seldom be made to move at the same rate as drama. Exposition and narrative, which are essential to intelligible action, can seldom be couched in words which require or even suggest musical expression. The narrative moves so fast and includes such varied ideas that no music could keep up with it and at the same time be musically satisfying. Hence, no thoroughly musical embodiment of the narrative or expository portions of a drama is possible. Musical form, which is essential for the conveyance of the most vivid musical expression, is thus available only at moments of crisis. But these crises of feeling which, in the spoken drama, often require but brief instants of time, will require in the opera minutes of elaboration. During such "purple patches" the action will stop, and the hearer's interest will become musical rather than dramatic. There is thus an inevitable conflict between the two technical processes of musical and dramatic construction—a conflict which becomes only more confused when the opening of public opera houses interjects into the problem the new and incalculable element of the general public taste. This last consideration, indeed, becomes paramount; for without public support the opera could not exist.

In the period immediately following Monteverdi's death, there began a long course of musical experiment which finally resulted in the establishment of a simple form—that of the aria—as the chief feature of the opera. At the same time the construction of the dramatic text underwent great modification—the problem of the librettist coming to be that of conveying some continuity of dramatic idea through the medium of a succession of verses which, so far as possible, could be set to music in the aria form. In spite of the degradation which popular taste was forcing upon the drama, considerable accomplishment is to be noted, if not in the ideal, at least in the practical solution of the musical problem.

In the period from 1640 to 1660 the orchestral element was extensively enlarged, a *symphony* in which plain chord-harmony is the most characteristic feature being used as introduction or interlude, and sometimes showing definite relation to the matters at issue on the stage. Here Monteverdi's influence is unmistakable. The recitative, partly in imitation of Monteverdi's style and partly because of the growing preponderance of interest in the musical side of the drama, became considerably diversified and began to divide itself, accordingly as the text was of narrative or more purely emotional character, into corresponding styles of declamation and *arioso*. Still further emphasis on musical values is seen in the development (from about 1660 to 1680) of a more intricate instrumental music, approaching the style of the fugue. The distinction between the recitative and the aria became still clearer. The aria form begins to show a definite organization, consisting either of two sections, A–B, or of three, A–B–A, which is the most usual of all song forms in our own day. The A–B–A form may be seen in embryo in the "Lament" of Ariadne referred to above; but the brevity of this piece—far more in accord with the natural current of dramatic action than the longer form now developing—is such that the form organization is hardly noticeable, and the hearer has no time to forget, in his absorption with the music, that he is listening to a play.

It is evident that in these newer developments the concern for drama is becoming submerged in purely musical interest. It is natural, then, to find that the fugal style for the instrumental pieces was still further cultivated during the last twenty years of the century, being applied not only to the longer instrumental pieces but also to the introductions and interludes for the arias. This no doubt took the place of the choral numbers which in the earlier operas were frequent and were written largely in the current polyphonic style of the madrigal. So important had the aria become, however, that it had all but banished the chorus from the stage, and even concerted numbers (duets, trios, and so forth) for the principals were becoming rarer. Elaborate execution, corresponding in a way to the prodigious scenic display which was demanded, was growing to be the chief characteristic of the vocal music. All this shows to what an extent the musical element was gaining predominance over the dramatic.

The Beginnings of Comedy Opera—The *Intermezzi*

Musical interest is even more exclusively to be found in those lighter forms which ultimately led to the distinction of the comic opera from the *opera seria*. In the intervals between the acts of serious plays it had long been the custom to present little comic scenes, which served to lighten the rather heavy impression of the larger piece and to beguile the time during which the scenes were being changed. These *Intermezzi* were often plentifully supplied with music, and gradually acquired a continuity of action which enlarged them to the status of a play within a play. As a result, either the scope of the serious opera was so broadened as to permit within itself the introduction of comic characters, or a true comedy opera was evolved as a separate species from the serious opera.

For the comic opera a considerably different style of music is demanded. Long and stilted recitatives are out of place; the action itself, more vivacious if not more logical, must be reflected in music of a more sprightly tone; characterization (often overdrawn to the point of caricature) is striking enough to suggest, more readily than in the serious opera, an appropriate musical idiom; and the development to suitable proportions of types of popular song or dance is an opportunity hardly offered to the writer in the serious style.

Among the hundreds of Italian opera composers after Monteverdi, only a few stand out as actual contributors to the perfection of the art. The first and probably the chief was Monteverdi's pupil Cavalli. (His real name was Caletti-Bruni, but he took that of this patron out of gratitude for grants which gave him his education.) Far less imaginative than his teacher, Cavalli was nevertheless a competent composer, and very clear in his practical vision of what was necessary to make opera a success. He learned, as well as taught, a great deal during visits to France in 1660 and 1662; and it is to him that the first clear distinction of aria and recitative is due. He died in 1676. Marc' Antonio Cesti, a pupil of Carissimi (whom we shall meet in a moment), and twenty years younger than Cavalli, was another important contributor to that higher organization of the musical substance of the opera of which we have already spoken. Ambros tells us that "At the performance of Cesti's *Il Pomo d'oro* ('The Apple of Gold') at Vienna in 1666 a special theatre seating 1500 persons was built in the castle courtyard; the scenery included landscapes and a harbor view, the open sea with tritons, the nether world and the Olympian heaven, each with its respective divinities, and the number of characters was bewildering. In the Prologue appeared the personified divisions of the Empire [the performance was given to celebrate the marriage of the Emperor Leopold I]—Spain, Austria, Hungary, Bohemia, Germany, Italy—even America! There were five acts and sixty-seven scenes. The cost of the production was said to the 100,000 thalers." No very vivid dramatic impression would be likely to be carried away from such a spectacle.

Probably the most significant music in the new style was written by Giacomo Carissimi, who was not an opera composer, however. It was in the then closely allied field of the oratorio that he chose to work—possibly because he perceived that the true musician was likely to be smothered in the detail of spectacle and action which made up the opera. His great power as a choral writer found far more scope in the soberer form. The *cantata* (a short work sometimes for one, sometimes for several voices, presenting a theme not without dramatic interest) was but the precursor of the larger oratorio, which now came to differ widely from that of Cavalieri. The earlier oratorios had been presented as dramas with scenery, acting, and even dancing. Carissimi did away with the stage presentation; continued the part of the "Testo" in that of the "Narrator"; and—strangely enough, in our view—did more than any other writer of his century to bring into favor that brilliancy of vocal execution which has ever since been characteristic of the Italian stage.

By all odds the greatest of the Venetian writers of comedy opera was Giovanni Legrenzi (*circa* 1625–1690), a musician of conspicuous attainment in religious and instrumental forms as well as in opera. His music is far more vigorous and independent than that of his predecessors, and shows, perhaps more clearly than any earlier work, that the sense of key is becoming sharply defined in the musical mind of the world. He also wrote many *cantate a voce sola*, on the same plan as those of Carissimi; but his powers in choral writing were far inferior to those of Carissimi.

Although Venice held the leadership in opera during the whole of the seventeenth century, the new art spread rapidly not only throughout Italy but into France and Germany as well. Rome, in 1700, had seen the foundation of but three opera houses. Giovanni Bardi, whose efforts in Florence we have described, had been ready when he became a Roman citizen to support Cavalieri's production of the *Rappresentazione di anima e di corpo;* and this early contact with the new style was continued in the strictly operatic works of Michelangelo Rossi, Luigi Rossi, and Domenico Mazzocchi. In Florence, Marco da Gagliano and Francesca Caccini[4] (the daughter of Giulio Caccini and perhaps a greater talent than her father) produced important works. Bologna, Turin, and other Italian cities soon took up the new art; and so rapid was the growth of interest in Naples that at the end of the century that city actually took from Venice the position of leader in the operatic world. How opera fared in France, England and Germany, and how the Neapolitans influenced its course will be seen in another chapter.

It is clearly to be seen that, in the century since its introduction, the monodic style has largely overthrown polyphony in popular favor. Unfortunate though it was in attracting and therefore having to propitiate so generous a measure of popular favor, its achievements must not be underrated. It is not monody which degrades opera, but opera—with its many interests external to music—which degrades monody. We shall see that in due time this monodic revision of the fundamental substance of the old polyphony will make possible the greatest of purely instrumental forms, the sonata. Already in the opera itself the instrumental portions are com-

---

[4] With the exception of the Abbess Herrad, Francesca Caccini is the first woman whose work we have had occasion to mention. Compared to the number of women who have attained eminence as poets or novelists, the number of creative feminine minds in music is remarkably small. Fortunately, this disability does not extend to the field of interpretation. And one result of the "revolt of modern youth" may be the appearance of a woman as a composer of the first rank.

ing to be the most solid and characteristic of all the work; and already the one germ of musical idea which will make possible an extended, coherent instrumental form—the idea of clear tonality and key relation—is coming into being. The first great instrumental works, for reasons which we shall see, will still be polyphonic; but their polyphony is of a different order from that of the madrigal and the Mass which the monody overthrew. And that which makes possible this new and more vital style of Bach and Handel is the sharp definition of musical thought which comes of individual, monodic melody, and the clear establishment of the idea of the keynote.

CHAPTER XV

The Beginnings of Opera in France, Germany, and England

OLD FRENCH PLAYS. THE *Mascarades*

W E have seen that the opera in Italy by no means remained a mere academic attempt to revive the ancient tragedy, but rather became an institution of wide popular interest because the monodic idea, the essential musical innovation required for musical-dramatic expression, was amalgamated with existing and already vital dramatic and musical types. Similarly in other countries, existing traditions are conspicuous factors in the various national types of opera which, stimulated by the Italian successes in this form, appear before the end of the seventeenth century.

Like every other nation in Christendom, the French had their early religious plays. These were somewhat less closely associated with the Church than in other countries; and it is certainly true that the element of comedy was more finely and intellectually developed in France than elsewhere. The *Play of Adam* dating from the twelfth century has, for example, a scene between Eve and the Serpent in which her pride, curiosity, and jealousy, and her marital inferiority complex are played upon with extraordinary cunning to induce her to taste the fruit. There was no music in connection with this piece. But as early as 1140 there was produced a dramatization of the story of Daniel in which there were many short strophic songs. And with the rather rapid secularization of the drama many popular forms of comedy appeared, ranging from the broad and gross types of carnival celebration to the *Jeux-partis* or *Debates* and the *Pastorales* of the troubadours and trouvères. Even more modern in tone is the extraordinarily witty farce, *Pathelin*—the story of a piece of swindling more ingenious than any of the exploits of Raffles. Adam de la

Halle's *Robin et Marion*—a dramatic elaboration of the poetic form of the pastorale, in which a courtly suitor for the temporary affection of a common shepherdess is comically repulsed—has a considerable number of songs interspersed throughout its dialogue, and is often spoken of as the first comic opera. In none of these works, however, is there any sign of an intention to make music an essential factor of the drama; the songs are simply incidents of the action.

The most direct impulse toward the creation of opera was given by the *Mascarades*, courtly entertainments presented with every luxury of scene and costume, in which a thin thread of action was maintained while songs and dances frequently colored the impression. Records of such entertainment appear as early as 1392; but the form attained no inordinate popularity until the middle of the sixteenth century. It then attracted the attention of a group of poets (called the *Pléiade* because they were seven in number) whose leading spirit was Pierre Ronsard and whose chief aim was the perfecting of the literary language of France. By these poets the study of the classics was as eagerly pursued as by the Florentine enthusiasts; but the artistic horizon of the Frenchmen was wider, and their aim in general was more progressive. One of their number, Antoine de Baïf, was a musician as well as a poet. His devotion to the classics was so great that he attempted to introduce the principle of quantity into French verse. He founded in 1570 an "Academy of Music and Poetry"—this being in a sense a predecessor of the famous *Académie française*—with the idea of establishing a closer relation between the two arts, and with somewhat the same idea of reviving the ancient drama which we have already seen in Florence. The dance also was included in this program of regeneration.

Catherine de' Medici (who acquired great political power after the death of her husband Henry II of France, and who was one of the prime instigators of the Massacre of St. Bartholomew in 1572) had brought to the court of France something of the Florentine tradition in matters of art. Here she gave generous support to the performances of elaborate mascarades, ballets, and intermezzi, whose themes were not merely mythological but were often related to the many political problems and religious wars of the time. Four days before the Eve of St. Bartholomew, for example, a great ballet was given in the Tuileries to illustrate the exclusion of the erring knights (the Huguenots) from Paradise. And in 1582, for the marriage of the Duc de Joyeuse, Catherine's ballet master Beaujoyeulx arranged the famous spectacle, the *Ballet Comique de la Royne*—an elaboration of the fable of Circe—in which every earlier achievement of brilliance and expense was eclipsed. Among the musical pieces for this ballet there were several choruses with echo effects (remember, here, the antiphony which was so largely employed by Willaert) and two really monodic solos for Jupiter and Glaucus.

A visit of Rinuccini and Caccini to Paris seems somewhat to have enlarged the importance of music in the mascarade, but to have done little to establish the Italian style of monody in popular favor. The incessant religious wars, which ended temporarily with the Edict of Nantes in 1598, had left little time for elaborate courtly entertainment; and it was not until the monarchy began to be stabilized by Richelieu, the incomparably astute minister of Louis XIII, that so costly a form of art could be cultivated. Indeed, it was only in 1645, after Louis XIV had come to the throne and Mazarin had succeeded Richelieu as minister, that Italian opera was at length imported into Paris. The Italian recitative made a very unfavorable impression. One courtly lady complained that she thought the audience would die of cold and boredom. Nevertheless, opera was seen to be a more truly dramatic form than the mascarade; and the French were moved to try their own hand at its composition. But literary and social institutions were already in existence whose influence upon French dramatic taste was very great; and in order to understand the characteristics of French opera these influences must first be observed.

LITERARY INFLUENCES—THE *Académie*

In 1618 the Marquise de Rambouillet founded the famous *Hôtel* which is known by her name—a salon, frequented by Richelieu and all the brilliant men of letters of the time, which had the greatest influence in all matters of literary and social taste. It speedily became a center of literary inspiration as well as of social elegance. Preciosity—a style of speech and writing which by its conscious effort at distinction soon degenerated into a weak and squeamish avoidance of all that was natural and forceful in language—was an unfortunate by-product of the conversations at the Hôtel Rambouillet. It was ridiculed by Molière in a famous comedy,[1] just as the Euphuism of Sir John Lyly in England came to be satirized by later writers who "wrap it in the more rawer breath" of their scorn. But as a refining influence in an early period of style development, both preciosity and euphuism had real value.

A still more significant institution was the *Académie Française*, founded by Richelieu in 1635. This was soon established as a fountain of authority in all matters concerning the literature and language of France. It consisted of forty of the most eminent literary men of the time, who sat as judges and gave incontrovertible opinions on all matters. The *Académie*

---

[1] *Les Précieuses ridicules.*

has been continued to this day. No other people has attempted to establish, or perhaps would have been willing to suffer, such official guidance of the national taste. And while the influence of this body was directly exerted on language and literature, its effect was also to be felt in the subtlest features of musical style. Neat and concise expression was as eagerly sought in music as in language; prolixity was shunned; emotional outbursts, not clearly related to real causes of feeling, were generally avoided; and as a general consequence, a greater insistence on form is apparent than in any earlier or contemporary work. In the drama itself, the classical tradition of the "unities" was more rigidly observed—at least in tragedy—than by any other nation. Here the influence of the *Académie* was very marked. "Tragedy," as Mr. Saintsbury observes, "was practically confined to a dexterous manipulation of the unities; the interest of a plot attenuated as much as possible, and intended to produce, instead of pity a mild sympathy, and instead of terror a mild alarm." This official viewpoint was also significant for opera; for although opera, like the spoken comedy, was under no such rigid restrictions as poetic tragedy, the serious opera was the nearest possible parallel to the tragedy and was governed to a great extent, if not by the same rules, at least by the same general dramatic taste.

The Crystallization of French Operatic Form—Cambert and Lully—The French Overture

The greatest of the French poets were not above providing texts for music. Corneille's *Andromède*, a *pièce à machines*, with music by D'Assoucy, was given in 1650. Benserade wrote a text for *Cassandra*, a *ballet de court*, in 1651, in which Louis XIV himself danced. The music was by various composers, among whom was Jean Baptiste Lully, later the dominant figure in the world of French opera. Fifty years after the first production of opera, that is, the French are maintaining their conventional forms of Ballet and Mascarade. The more strictly dramatic form was not attempted until the first French comedy with music, the *Pastorale d'Issy*, was produced in 1659. The poem was by an adventurous churchman, the Abbé Perrin, and the music by Robert Cambert who thus earned the title of the earliest French opera composer. The music of this piece is lost, so that we cannot tell what may have been the influence of the Italian methods which had more or less frequently been exhibited in Paris since 1645.

In 1660 Cavalli, now the most renowned composer of opera in Italy, brought his greatest success, *Xerxes*, to Paris. This work was coldly received by the French. Cavalli thereupon composed a new opera, *Hercules the Lover,* especially for the Paris stage; and this new work was given with great applause, apparently because it made very considerable concessions to French taste. Frequent ensemble numbers, imposing opening choruses, and of course the ballet are all employed, surrounded by the most sumptuous scenic display; and the imposing development of climax in stage effect is typically French.

In 1669 there was issued to Perrin a royal patent giving him the exclusive right to establish throughout France "operatic academies, or representations of music in the French language, after the plan of those in Italy." The dominance of Italy in opera, that is, was now fully recognized. Cambert again worked with Perrin, producing *Pomona* as the first work to enjoy the new royal privilege. Here we have a typical "French overture"—a form which is copied by practically all French writers during the whole eighteenth century, and which even became an important instrumental form quite without relation to opera. This form begins with a slow introductory movement, in a pompous rhythm which stamps about in dotted notes (♩.. ♪♩.. ♪ or its equivalent in notes of shorter value). Next there is a rapid fugue (that in Cambert's overture is somewhat feebly worked out) and an ending in massive style. A brief designation of the form of the French overture could thus be given in the words *slow, fast, slow.* We shall see that the Neapolitan school in Italy developed another type of overture, called the *Italian,* whose movement order is exactly the converse of this; namely, *fast, slow, fast.* And since the instrumentation became more and more imposing, these forms each had something to contribute to the symphony which, in less than a hundred years, came to be the dominant form of instrumental music.

The dramatic element in *Pomona* is slender, but the treatment of declamation is good, and the tunes—in the French style rather than in the Italian manner of the aria—are both frequent and fairly attractive. The high development of French opera which ensued was not due to Cambert however, but to Lully—an Italian by birth who, since his performance in *Cassandra,* had played an increasingly conspicuous part in the organization of the court ballets, and who is probably far more responsible than Cambert for the invention of the French overture as a form. Financial difficulties preventing Perrin's further direction of opera, Lully bought his privilege and became for the rest of his life the dictator of the French operatic stage. The *Académie Royale de Musique et de Danse,* as the Opéra was called,[2] was soon brought to a state of unexampled brilliancy. From 1673, when after Molière's death the Opéra was established in the

[2] The reader will not miss the suggestion, conveyed by this title, of the importance of the dance in French opera. We shall meet with a remarkable instance of its survival in connection with the Paris performance of Wagner's *Tannhäuser.*

royal palace, Lully wrote a great tragic opera every year until his death in 1687.[3] Under the direct patronage of the court, his work suffered less than did that of the Italians from the degrading influence of general public taste. The texts of Lully's works, with the exception of three, were written by Quinault, a poet of considerable gifts. He had made a dismal failure of tragedy, but his talent was quite suited to the slighter task of opera; and he was of course conversant with, and carefully followed, the literary fashions of the period. Patronized by the court and enjoying the highest social and literary associations, French opera thus maintained high dignity as a national institution. It was largely for the same reasons that its formality became almost as absolute as that of the poetic tragedy. The rigid tradition established by Lully suffered no modification; and as a consequence the opera in France made no further progress until the time of Rameau. His work, falling wholly within the eighteenth century, will be considered in a later chapter.

Opera in Germany in the Seventeenth Century—The Singspiel

The early association of music and drama in Germany was very much the same as in other countries, the forms of religious drama being generally similar. The literary background, however, soon became different from that of France or Italy, being, until the coming of the Meistersinger, far more intensely and darkly religious. The great Minnesinger Walther von der Vogelweide summed up in his work the lyric impulse of the age of chivalry. In the thirteenth century, also, the epic (in which field the *Nibelungenlied* is the crowning achievement) and the many versions of the Arthurian legends reveal a national and intellectual awakening, much of whose stimulus arose from the Crusades. The chivalric ideal, however, was opposed by a wandering singer who called himself *Freidank* (free thought) and who voiced that independence of mind of the German middle classes which, in the Reformation, came to show itself as a national attitude. The fourteenth and fifteenth centuries saw the decadence of romantic literature, the growth of the guilds of the Meistersinger, and a vast outpouring of popular feeling in the Volkslied.

The drama itself, emerging slowly from the domination of the Church, began with popular representations of biblical events proper to Christmas and Easter, of which the Passion plays of Oberammergau and Freiburg are the direct continuation into our own day. Legends of the saints formed the basis of the later plays which followed those based on scriptural incidents; and to these were added in the sixteenth-century festival per-

---

[3] An excellent description of one of Lully's most mature works, *Roland* (1685), is given in the *Oxford History*, Vol. III, p. 233 ff.

formances of a spirited nature, the subjects of which were similar to the *Schwänke* (comic anecdotes) which had been freely circulated in the preceding century. (*Till Eulenspiegel*, which forms the program of the inimitable symphonic poem of that title by Richard Strauss, is an example of the *Schwank*.) This popular narrative drama remained largely uninfluenced by the classical movement which in Germany seems to have been more completely restricted to the educated classes than in Italy. As elsewhere, music was freely introduced into the popular plays; but there was little disposition to effect a revival of ancient tragedy through musical declamation. We have already noted that under the influence of the celebrated Viennese scholar Conrad Celtes, the ideal of quantitative verse as supplying a basis for musical rhythm had been exemplified in musical settings of the *Odes* of Horace. The same idea was even applied to Celtes's Latin drama *The Play of Diana* (*Ludus Dianae*) which was given in 1501; but such attempts had no interest for the general public, nor were they in any way applicable to the popular drama; so that they represent no forward step toward the solution of the problem of the opera.

The tendency in Germany, then, was to ignore the classical influence and to use music merely as an adjunct to the spoken drama. Such plays with incidental music, when the music grew to form a considerable portion of the whole work, were called *Singspiele* (sung plays); and the Singspiel remained the only true type of German opera until the nineteenth century. The song itself, partly because the classical influence was thus slight, began to be a significant form early in the seventeenth century; but the style of this song, which quite vividly foreshadowed the romantic song of the nineteenth century, was too contemplative, too personal, and too subjective to be well suited to the stage. Hence, the beginnings of true opera, when they finally did occur in Germany, were almost wholly in imitation of the Italian style.

One very significant reason for the lack of interest in abstruse dramatic theory was doubtless the general preoccupation with religious problems. Almost from the beginning of the sixteenth century the struggle of Martin Luther against certain practices and doctrines of the Catholic Church had occupied in increasing measure the minds of the German people. We have already seen something of the extent to which the Protestant hymn became a sort of national utterance. Such individuality of feeling as was inculcated in the Lutheran doctrine required, of course, a correspondingly individual musical speech, even though the sentiment to be expressed was general or congregational. Both the music and the words of the Protestant hymns were far more personal, far more individually contemplative, than the remote and exalted style either of the Gregorian chant or of the Masses or other polyphonic compositions used in the Catholic service. But this music was too contemplative and too introspective for drama. There-fore, both the most absorbing popular interest, and the equally absorbing musical language—that of the hymn and of church music in general—in which that great religious interest was expressed were of a type hardly likely to stimulate music drama of the rather esoteric sort which was the aim of the first Italian opera writers. Neither was life in the German towns at all comparable to that in the rich and rather purse-proud city-states of Italy, where to uphold an artistic tradition and to excel in devel-oping new artistic forms were accepted civic obligations.

THE FIRST GERMAN OPERA WRITERS—HEINRICH SCHÜTZ

In 1627, Heinrich Schütz, the first important writer of opera whom Germany produced, set to music a version of the story of *Daphne* whose text was an almost literal translation of the poem of Rinuccini which Peri and Caccini had set and produced at the house of Bardi in 1594. Schütz' music is lost; but it appears that there was much emphasis on the chorus, and that the recitative was largely in the free, unaccompanied, highly ex-pressive style common in the Passion music of the time. The work thus apparently shows a considerable divergence from Italian methods, even though its text is directly borrowed. But there is no indication that Schütz was founding a true German school of opera. The Thirty Years' War was now raging, so that the time was not propitious for opera, especially of native origin. Sigmund Staden produced the first German opera which is still extant, at Nürnberg in 1644. This is *Das Geistliche Waldgedicht, Seelewig*. It is sung throughout (in contrast to the more purely German style of the Singspiel); but recitative is sparingly used, and strophic and dialogue songs are frequent. There is a Nightingale aria; and echo effects and other imitations of nature, together with much of the colorization common to the madrigal style, are freely used. Even hymn-tunes appear, showing that the style is less purely Italian than the composer perhaps supposed.

Into Catholic Germany, on the other hand, direct importations of Italian opera were extensive. Because of the interest of the Emperors Ferdinand III and Leopold I, Vienna was visited by Monteverdi, Cavalli, and Cesti. In Regensburg, once the capital of the Empire (the name Ratisbon may be more familiar) and in Munich, where the imperial court paid visits of state, performances were given which like those in Vienna were for the most part wholly in Italian. The German style was not wholly un-cultivated, however. The famous Munich organist Johann Kaspar Kerll produced there four operas. This music is lost; but that it was no mere slavish imitation of the Italian manner may be inferred from the fact that

Kerll's later work *The Legend of St. Nathalie,* produced at Vienna in 1677, is distinctly of the Singspiel type, the music being merely an incident to the spoken drama.

Gradually however, as Germany began to recover from the ravages of the Thirty Years' War, the Singspiel was largely thrust into the background, although it represented German taste far more truly than did Italian opera. The reason seems to lie in the diffidence of the courts with respect to their own taste, and in their disposition—not uncommon elsewhere—to regard importations as superior to domestic products. German court life, which was beginning to find its model for both art and manners in the court of Versailles, was thus much farther removed from contact with popular thought and taste than was the case in the more liberal atmosphere of the Italian cities. The consequence was that Germany was overrun by Italian musicians almost to the end of the eighteenth century, and guided at least in its higher social strata by Italian taste, just as Italy in the later fifteenth and sixteenth centuries, had been dominated by the Netherlanders. Even the Hamburg opera, founded in 1678 for the purpose of presenting German works, was unable to resist the foreign influence. In 1689 Lully's *Acis and Galatea* was given, and was followed by increasingly frequent performances of Italian operas. Siegmund Kusser, director of the Hamburg opera from 1693 to 1695, adopted many Italian features. Reinhard Keiser, who was by far the most brilliant figure as yet to appear in German music drama and who was called by some of his contemporaries the greatest opera composer in the world, began his career showing a strong emphasis on German subjects and German methods; but so great was the appeal of the foreign manner that he was soon reduced to the expedient of introducing arias, in the Italian style and even with Italian texts, into the mainly German substance of his dramas. It was at this stage of operatic development in Germany that Handel appeared in Hamburg. The later relations between German and foreign influence we shall study shortly, as introductory to the reforms of Gluck.

The Beginnings of Opera in England—The Masques

We have already seen that the monodic idea was not wholly a product of the Florentine camerata. The madrigal style was at least as highly developed in England as in Italy; and that love of straightforward tune which was evinced in the frottola and the villanella of the Italians had its similar expression in types of popular song which not only appear in characteristic turns of phrase in the English madrigal but affect the church music as well. Clear tunes, simple harmonies, and definite rhythms had considerably supplanted the vaguer modal melody, the indefinite harmony, and the generally unrhythmic flow of contrapuntal music in the older style. Instrumental music similarly direct in character had been produced, as we have seen, in greater profusion in England than anywhere else. In 1600, the year of Peri's *Euridice*, Thomas Morley published his *First Book of Aires or Little Short Songs to Sing and Play to the Lute with the Base Viol.* The importance of such work for the growth of instrumental music has already been seen. But the monodic nature of the music is of greater general significance, for it shows the crystallization of popular musical thought into those forms of key clarity and rhythm directness which are to govern all the music of the future until our own day. The melodic impulse here, it is to be noted, is wholly natural and musical. It contrasts sharply with the artificial, learned impulse out of which the Italian monody arose, and is more akin to the musical thought of Germany. Nor, in the precise association of music with the drama, is the case the same as in Italy; for the great English dramatists had not conceived that exaggerated respect for the traditions of antiquity which was upheld by the Latin races.

In one respect, however, there is a strong resemblance between the foundations of opera in England and in France. Masques, the correlative of the French mascarades, had been popular at the English court from early Tudor times. Dances and solo songs were thus as much in demand as in France. The musical composition for the masques was at first the work of amateurs rather than of recognized masters, so that there was nothing in the development of the English masque to compare with the famous *Ballet Comique de la Royne* either in magnificence of setting or in musical interest. The masque, also, was by no means strictly dramatic in nature, and hence bore little resemblance to the tragedy which the Italians were attempting to revive; it therefore shows no strong impulse toward that high style of declamation which was aimed at in the recitative.

The masque rose to its greatest popularity in the time of the earlier Stuarts, before the Commonwealth. The most famous of English poems in that style—Milton's *Comus*, which is of course a far different product from that of the earlier times—was set to music by Henry Lawes for a performance at Ludlow Castle in 1634. Only fragments of this music survive. In these few examples the tuneful impulse is conspicuous, and nothing so directly declamatory as the Italian recitative is to be found. The Italian style was not unknown however. Thomas Campion, a physician who was also both poet and musician, produced many masques, such as *The Masque of Lords, Mercury Vindicated, The Golden Age Restored,* and *The Vision of Delight* (1617), in which the express direction *stilo recitativo* is used. Such attempts appear, however, to have been the exception rather than the rule. No direct invasions of Italian opera into England are to be noted, and the influence of the "New Music" is relatively slight.

The establishment of the Commonwealth put a stop to theatrical perform-ances of all sorts, though the prohibition was rather easily evaded by the devising of spectacles which could not technically be called plays.

HENRY PURCELL

The singular effervescence of courtly gaiety which came with the Restoration and which is so vividly described in Pepys's *Diary* was marked by a decided change in musical style. The older style of the madrigal had gone out of favor with the deaths of the great madrigalists Byrd (1623), Gibbons (1625), and Dowland (1626).[4] The trend towards lyrical song was now stronger, and dance suites had taken the place of older forms of instrumental music made in imitation of choral forms. The graver style in church music was altogether unwelcome to the frivolous Charles II and his court; and though several composers of the old school, such as Cooke, Lawes, Christopher Gibbons (son of the madrigalist, Orlando Gibbons), and Benjamin Rogers (who had been prominent in Charles I's time) still survived, their only recourse was to write in a style for which neither their age nor their training fitted them. Pelham Humphrey, a choirboy under the Royal Chapelmaster Cooke, was sent to France to study the methods of Lully, the great master of dramatic music, "in order," as Parry remarks, "to learn how to compose English church music." The declama-tory style thus received the full approval of royalty, and became the irresistible fashion of the time in England. John Blow, another member of the Chapel Royal, and Michael Wise, a somewhat less esteemed organist and composer, did their share to establish the new manner in England; and thus the youthful Henry Purcell, who was apparently a pupil of Cooke, Humphrey, and Blow, and probably the greatest genius among purely English composers, had ample opportunity to add to his own na-tive gifts whatever was of value in the methods of contemporary music as his preceptors had learned it.

Purcell's earliest work was in the form of anthems (the word is a cor-ruption of *antiphon*); and these he seems to have written, in a style as mature as any, at a very early age. He was also prolific in instrumental compositions. His first printed work is a set of twelve *Sonnata's of III parts: two viollins and basse: to the Organ or Harpsecord*. In a preface to this work he avers that he has "endeavour'd a just imitation of the most fam'd Italian Masters"; and it appears that the chief of these masters was Vitali, between whose work and Purcell's a close resemblance in form may be traced. These sonatas were published in 1683, by which time he

---

[4] John Bull, more renowned as an instrumental composer and virtuoso than as a madrigalist, died in 1628. Thus the greatest of the old school of Elizabethan com-posers passed within five years; and there were few to take their place.

had already supplied incidental music for four plays. Several similar attempts—none of them demanding great exertion—followed almost yearly until 1688–1690 when, apparently with no other preparation for true dramatic writing, he produced *Dido and Aeneas*, a full-fledged drama with music, which in sheer dramatic power far outshines any earlier opera of the seventeenth century. The French Overture and the Prologue are lost. The drama itself has three acts and four tableaux. Choral passages are frequent and highly characteristic, following Lully in their simple, homophonic type of melody. Both the trained church composer and the artist capable of feeling the force of popular melody are evident in these numbers. The famous "Witches' Scene" has four choral numbers, together with five accompanied recitatives, a duet, and a closing chorus with a dance of the Furies. For the mocking laughter of the witches, a series of echo effects proves highly realistic. But the crowning moment of the whole is perhaps the scene of Dido's death, at the end. (Note that the English stage convention demands no god in a machine to soften the bitterness of the catastrophe.) The vividness of Purcell's melody may be seen from the following (from the first act; Dido's death scene is too long to quote) which is the "Lament of Dido" over the tortures which her passion for Aeneas is causing her. Belinda is Vergil's Anna—the change of name being made out of consideration for some canon of contemporary taste which is also suggested in the emendations of Shakespeare to be mentioned below.

This example shows something of Purcell's power of direct and forceful expression. It also shows how his command of purely musical form is exemplified in passages which for the voice are dramatically just. Note that the bass consists of a single strain four bars long, repeated throughout. This plan of *ground bass* or "divisions on a ground" was, as we have seen, one of the most popular forms of instrumental music.[5] Here, however, there is more than mere composer's ingenuity; the persistent repetition, as well as the sturdiness of the bass melody itself, has a suggestion of inexorability about it which is dramatically as well as musically effective.

Even more remarkable than *Dido and Aeneas* is *King Arthur*, the text of which was by no less a poet than Dryden. Dryden had made one earlier effort in the direction of opera—*Albion and Albanius*, a remarkable allegorical laudation of Charles II and his brother, which had been set by a French composer, Louis Grabu, in the manner then in vogue at the French court. Purcell's music to *Dioclesian* (an adaptation of *The Prophetess* of Beaumont and Fletcher) had attracted Dryden's attention, and he commended, in his preface to *Amphitryon*, "the excellent composition of Mr. Purcell; in whose Person we have at length found an English Man, equal with the best abroad." At the suggestion of Purcell he even made considerable changes in the verse of his already completed version of *King Arthur*, to which work *Albion and Albanius* had at first been intended merely as a prologue. No operatic music until the time of Gluck, nearly a cenutry later, can compare with this for *King Arthur* in dramatic directness or in truthful characterization. Here Purcell proves himself to be the only music dramatist of the seventeenth century who is worthy to stand beside the great Italian Monteverdi.

King Arthur, however, instead of being the first mature work of a genius who in age and capabilities was only at the threshold of a possibly long and illustrious career, was the last of Purcell's real operas. His later dramatic work was again all in the form of incidental music for spoken plays. The evident implication is that the English public, unlike that of France or Italy, was as yet unready to accept the opera as a form of art equal in interest to the spoken drama. The reasons appear somewhat obscure, since the Elizabethan tradition had been sorely weakened by influences of style emanating from the Continent. Dryden himself was willing to join in the universal practice of revamping Shakespeare's verse, in order that certain peculiarities of diction might be avoided and more flowing "numbers" might result. The following variants of a passage from *The Tempest*, quoted from Dent's admirable study *The Foundations of English Opera*, will show how far the taste of the time had changed in

---

[5] We shall presently see the culmination of this form pattern in the *chaconne* and *passacaglia*.

verse itself, and will illustrate the difficulties of the directly and powerfully imaginative Purcell in trying to appeal to the great public of his time:

Shakespeare

Where shou'd this music be? i' th' air, or th' earth?
It sounds no more;—and sure, it waits upon
Some god o' th' island. Sitting on a bank,
Weeping again the king my father's wrack,
This music crept by me upon the waters,
Allaying both their fury, and my passion,
With its sweet air: thence have I followed it—
Or it hath drawn me rather,—but 'tis gone.
No, it begins again.

Dryden

Where should this Musick be? i' th' Air, or th' Earth?
It sounds no more, and sure it waits upon some God
O' th' Island, sitting on a Bank, weeping against the Duke
My Father's Wrack. This Musick hover'd o'er me
On the waters, allaying both their Fury and my Passion
With charming Airs; thence have I followed it (or it
Hath drawn me rather) but 'tis gone;
No, it begins again.

It is no wonder that so vivid a piece of dramatic writing as the "Frost Scene," in *King Arthur*, should have remained unvalued in a time when such taste as is here displayed was universal. It happened, too, that shortly after Purcell's death (in 1695, when he was only thirty-seven years old) Handel brought over to England his strange mixture of Italian and German styles—styles which he was able to amalgamate with certain characteristics of English music in so remarkable a way as to capture wholly the English public. The resultant deflection of truly English taste was disastrous for English music; and from Handel's day until our own no English music dramatist of the first rank has appeared.

One reason why the discussions of the whole problem of opera in the English language have arisen, which are so prevalent in our own day, may be seen in this instance of Purcell's work. The opera expresses in a rather artificial way the subject matter of drama. To the continental, accustomed to the classic tradition in drama, the high formality of opera and of operatic music is more readily acceptable than to us, for our reliance on the classical models is slight and we prize naturalness far more than formal correctness. Even Purcell in his day was constrained avowedly to imitate the Italian manner. Being himself unable to impose upon the public the more natural type of expression for which his genius was most perfectly fitted, it was not to be expected that greater things could be done by the far lesser men who followed him.

CHAPTER XVI

Forms of Instrumental Music at the Opening of the Eighteenth Century

THE ESTABLISHMENT OF TONALITY

Not only was the monodic idea firmly established by the end of the seventeenth century, but one characteristic of musical thought which is essential in monodic writing had come to pervade all musical production. This essential is of course the harmonic as opposed to the contrapuntal way of thinking; and an inevitable consequence of this emphasis on the chord idea is the firm establishment of the modern concept of key. The growth of this harmonic viewpoint is difficult to follow. Any polyphonic composition must present, by the combination of its voices, many instances of the grouping of simultaneously sounded tones which we now recognize as chords. It is not easy to tell at first sight whether these chords and chord sequences—perfectly clear to us—were thought of by the composer as constituting the ground plan of his structure, or were merely incidental results of the combination of the melodic parts.

That chords were at first merely an incidental result of the combination of melodies is of course certain, and we have noted the most important of those steps which indicated that the chord idea was beginning to take shape in musicians' minds. The cadence itself, even in its first rude form of the occursus, has a possible harmonic suggestion, and in its later, more definite forms indicates an increasing clarity of harmonic conception. *Musica ficta*, with its destructive effect on the modal scales, sharpened the consciousness of tonality and, by implication, of the harmonic idea; and *faux bourdon* and *gymel* seem to indicate a dawning consciousness of chord structure. By 1500 the triad (but not its inversion, considered as the same triad in another aspect) was recognized as a fact, and passages of plain chords appear in the midst of the purely contrapuntal fabric. Instrumental music, especially the music for the lute, greatly sharpened the consciousness of chord identity. And, since the increasing use of chromatic music was continually undermining the individual character of the modes, the consciousness of major and minor keys and of the centrality of the tonic in those keys was coming to be recognized as the only solid fact of tone relation upon which the musical fabric could be built.

The final steps in this process seem to have been two: the shift of the attention from the old *cantus firmus* to the melody itself, in the highest voice, as the leading element in the thought; and the introduction of unprepared discord, first daringly championed as we have seen by Monteverdi. Purcell, in a revision of Playford's *Introduction to the Skill of Music*, showed that he was conscious of the first of these changes: "Formerly they used to Compose from the Bass, but Modern Authors compose to the Treble when they make Counterpoint or Basses to Tunes or Songs." Even Monteverdi, who showed little disposition to maintain a single key-center, had quite a modern sense of the emotional characteristics as well as the structural differences in major and minor tonality; and never introduced an unprepared discord without having a fairly clear fundamental tone at hand to which the discord is palpably related. His process of modulation was of course indefinite, at least in so far as the total form of the music is concerned. He used modulation largely for emphasis, introducing it when some word or phrase of his text required especial stress. But with Lully and Purcell, the case was different. Purcell especially used extreme care in his key relations. The range of his tonality (that is, the number of different keys to which he modulated in a given composition) was rather small. Neither the musical understanding of his time nor the commonly accepted system of scale tuning would have permitted such sudden modulation to extreme keys as delights us nowadays. But it may be said that by the end of the seventeenth century the key idea was not only fully accepted but had come to be an essential factor in the construction of all the important musical forms.

It was in the field of instrumental music that the problem of form was naturally most acute. Vocal music cannot, of course, be really formless; but the words often demand and justify peculiarities of form which in purely instrumental music would be confusing. If we had never heard any version of Schubert's *Erlking* other than Liszt's piano transcription, and were completely ignorant of the poem, the recitative at the end (to the words *In seinen Armen das Kind war tot*) would appear but a lame ending to so wild and stormy a piece. A musical discourse carried on by instruments alone cannot hang together unless some principle of rhetorical cohesion can be made to operate throughout. A musical sentence of some sort is possible as soon as a formula of cadence can be devised which will let us know that the sentence is ended. But successive sentences will not appear to have anything to do with each other unless a single principle of connection binds them all together. We have seen that the older polyphonic forms relied chiefly on the repetition and imitation of a single theme. But in the more directly expressive and longer-extended melody of homophonic music, this elaborate imitation would be impossible. The sense of definite key, then, and the possibilities of definite key relation, offer a valuable means for achieving rhetorical unity.

THE SYSTEM OF EQUAL TEMPERAMENT

With the clear recognition of major and minor tonality, the sense of key came to be relied upon by composers for structural features of the most fundamental order in the composition. Obviously, also, if modulation to closely related keys[1] had proved valuable for certain types of expression, modulation to remoter keys would be useful for more vivid contrasts. But an obstacle to such remoter modulation existed in the accepted tuning of the scale—an obstacle which was removed only after the most painstaking study. The result of that study was the establishment of the system of *equal temperament*. The meaning of that term and the process by which the system was perfected may be explained in detail only by elaborate mathematical discussion. The nature of the problem however will be understood from a less intricate exposition, and this must precede our study of expanded musical form.

The Pythagorean system of scale structure gave, as we saw, a major third whose ratio was 81:64. With the acceptance of the third as a concord, this over-sharp third was slightly flatted, its ratio then becoming 5:4. With such a third the triad C–E–G is a very smooth concord. The other major triads (G–B–D, and F–A–C) must, however, be made to conform to this pattern, if continuous smoothness of harmony is to be attained. The Pythagorean scale then must be further altered in the following way.

It is clear that if the third C–E be tuned at the ratio 5:4, while the second C–D remains at the old ratio of 9:8, then the second D–E will be smaller (by $\frac{81}{80}$, the so-called *comma* of Didymus) than the sec-

---

[1] Closely related keys may be loosely defined as those whose scales differ from the principal key only in one or two notes. E.g., F major with one flat, and G major with one sharp, are closely related to C; while E major with four sharps, or G flat with six flats, are distant keys.

ond C–D. To make the two major triads G–B–D and F–A–C correspond with this fundamental triad, the thirds G–B and F–A must be similarly made to contain each a *major* (greater) tone (9:8) and a *minor* (lesser) tone (10:9). Both B and A, that is, must be tuned at the ratio 5:4 in relation respectively to G and F. The calculation for such a diatonic scale, made by multiplying the mathematical expression for each successive note by the fraction representing its proper ratio to the preceding tone, would then appear as follows, taking C as 1:

$$1 \times \frac{9}{8} = \frac{9}{8} \times \frac{10}{9} = \frac{5}{4} \times \frac{16}{15} = \frac{4}{3} \times \frac{9}{8} = \frac{3}{2} \times \frac{10}{9} = \frac{5}{3} \times \frac{9}{8} = \frac{15}{8} \times \frac{16}{15} = 2$$

C (major   D (minor   E   (half   F   (major   G (minor   A (major   B   (half   C
tone)   tone)   tone)   tone)   tone)   tone)   tone)

The three major triads are exactly alike. The minor triad D–F–A, however, differs from the minor triads E–G–B and A–C–E in that the minor third D–F contains a minor tone plus a half tone, while the thirds E–G and A–C each contain a major tone plus a half tone. This variation, in the diatonic scale, is of little moment.

For any modulation, however, half steps must be introduced between the notes which are a whole step apart. But these whole steps, as we have just seen, are not alike. Some are major tones and some are minor. Moreover, F♯ and G♭ are not identical, and F♭ and C♭ are not exactly equivalent to E and B. If all the notes required to give all the accidentals needed for perfect smoothness in every key were thus to be provided, the keyboard would become cumbrous beyond any practicality. In the diatonic scale figured above, even F♯ cannot be made perfectly satisfactory. Demonstration of this fact will sufficiently illustrate the difficulties which would be involved in adding more accidentals.

To be consonant in the triad D–F♯–A, F♯ must stand to D as 5 to 4. Its mathematical expression, in relation to C, will then be the product of the ratios 9:8 (C:D) and 5:4 (D:F♯); that is, $\frac{9}{8} \times \frac{5}{4} = \frac{45}{32}$. But the major triad D–F♯–A must consist of a perfect fifth, made up of a major third plus a minor third. In our diatonic scale, if we subtract the major third from the perfect fifth we have $\frac{3}{2} \div \frac{5}{4}$ ($\frac{3}{2} \times \frac{4}{5} = \frac{6}{5}$) as the expression for the minor third. It should be a minor third from F♯ to A. But if we subtract our ratio for F♯, $\frac{45}{32}$, from our ratio for A in the diatonic scale, $\frac{5}{3}$, we have the following: $\frac{5}{3} \times \frac{32}{45} = \frac{32}{27}$. This third is slightly flatter than the proper minor third 6:5, as we may see by subtracting it from the larger interval:

$\frac{6}{5} \times \frac{27}{32} = \frac{81}{80}$, exactly the *comma* of Didymus. Calculated according to our formula then, F♯ makes the A of our diatonic scale sound a comma flat in the D major chord. Further addition of sharps (and of flats, which would be calculated by a similar process) would soon produce an intolerable out-of-tuneness. Evidently, the theorem which gives a practically perfect diatonic scale cannot yield even a tolerable chromatic scale, if that scale is to be used for harmonic purposes.

We shall not lead the reader further into the labyrinth of mathematics which underlies the present scale, but shall merely describe the two most essential steps taken toward a solution of the problem. The first was the so-called *mean-tone* system, which attempted to leave the major third at its truest value (5:4) by evening the distance between the major tone (9:8) and the minor tone (10:9). By a little exercise of his mathematical powers, the reader may demonstrate to himself that such alteration as this is insufficient. For the half steps E–F and B–C, which we found to be reckoned as 16:15, are larger than the half steps which would divide either the major tone or the minor tone into two equal intervals. It is evident, then, that a major third such as E♭–G (containing the natural half step) would be larger than a major third such as C–E or F–A; and that major triads based upon such different intervals would have decidedly different values. It was thus found impossible to introduce satisfactory half steps between the whole steps of the mean-tone scale. Only those keys having few sharps or flats could be made tolerable. The farther one went from the natural scale, the worse the discordance became. The simpler keys were, indeed, very smooth; and for music which was of a sober order, the mean-tone system served well enough. It was in use in organs even well into the nineteenth century. But adventure into remoter keys was so obviously desirable that the problem was energetically attacked. Indeed, the theory of a more usable scale had been studied long before any great demand for freedom in modulation existed.

The first really penetrating studies of interval measurement since the days of Pythagoras were made by Guiseppe Zarlino, whose *Istitutioni armoniche* (1558), together with two later works, laid the foundations of modern musical science. He was unable, however, to formulate a sound theory of temperament. The first real solution was propounded by Andreas Werckmeister who in his *Musikalische Temperatur* (1691) formulated the principle of a twelve-tone octave scale in which the half steps were to be exactly equal. This scale was welcomed by the more progressive musicians of the time, although its confessed impurity was roundly objected to by the conservatives. The new tuning was applied to the clavichord and harpsichord rather than to the organ. Even Bach, who championed the new system by writing the *Well-Tempered Clavichord*, did not attempt to extend the use of the system to the organ, but wrote for that instrument within a narrower range of keys than that used in "The Forty-eight" (as the *Well-Tempered Clavichord* is often called).

It seems at first glance quite an easy matter to divide the octave into twelve equal half steps. The actual achievement of such a division, however, is simple neither in theory nor in practice. The mathematical formula for such a half step is $\sqrt[12]{2}$; and this root is not exactly easy to determine. Neither is any human ear acute enough to judge whether this value is being exactly observed in tuning. A set of twelve tuning forks, scientifically made at the calculated intervals, would give the only certain base for the central octave of the piano. From this, of course, the higher and lower octaves of each note could be tuned by ear. But no tuner possesses such a set of forks. He has only one or two, for judging the pitch of a single A, for instance, as having 435 or 440 vibrations per second. Getting the proper pitch for the single note from this fork, he works thereafter by an entirely empirical, though ingenious, method. He tunes the middle octave (or, as he calls it, "sets his temperament") by tuning the perfect fifths slightly flat and the fourths slightly sharp. The degree of this flatness or sharpness he measures, not by a judgment of pitch, but by a judgment of the number of *beats* which, as the interval is altered, occur within a given time.[2] This judgment is necessarily somewhat inexact. It may nevertheless have a distinct musical value; for it seems probable that the peculiar differences of color or character in different keys—differences which are often clearly apparent to ears not possessed of that peculiar keenness of judgment or memory which is called "absolute pitch"—may arise out of the slight inaccuracies inherent in this empirical method of tuning.

Whether or not this conjecture is sound may soon be determined; for an electric apparatus has recently appeared (called the "Stroboconn") which measures precisely the twelve equal half steps which the tuner strives to produce in setting his temperament. It also provides a kind of visual gauge (a stroboscope) by which the intonation of the piano strings can be tested and brought into conformity with the established measure. There can be no doubt that this temperament is more accurate than any that can be set by ear. Yet it appears that the extensions, above and

[2] Beats are periodic intensifications of the volume of sound produced by two (or more) tones of different pitch sounded simultaneously. They appear when the crests of the sound waves from both sources coincide; and their loudness is made more apparent by the fact that in the interval between these coincidences the crest of the one wave tends to neutralize the trough of the other, weakening the total intensity of the combined sounds. Two tones, produced respectively by 200 and 203 vibrations per second, will give three beats per second.

below the original tempered octave, still require adjustment, and that scientific accuracy thus somehow fails to give complete musical satisfaction.

The emergence of clear tonality, the consequent perception of possibilities of modulation, and the establishment of the system of equal temperament are all, therefore, essential to the attainment of extended, purely musical form. By the end of the seventeenth century many such forms had been perfected, out of those tentative beginnings which we have already observed in the fields of the dance and the polyphonic or homophonic song. The most important of these forms we shall describe in some detail as they existed in 1700. For they are the forms which Johann Sebastian Bach knew and in which he worked. Several of these are forms which either persist until our own day, or are soon developed into forms with which we are confronted in every concert program. In relation to each form we shall attempt to summarize the essential stages of its growth, out of the rather confused and tentative conditions of thought described in the earlier chapter on instrumental music. The most important of these forms is

THE FUGUE

This form, which retains its resemblance and relation to vocal music even in its most elaborate developments, derives from the old motet. We saw how this was at first composed upon an *ordo* (a phrase taken from the Gregorian chant) and how, as the form grew in complexity and interest, this fundamental part came to be invented by the composer instead of being taken from the chant. In the fifteenth century the motet lost that relation to secular music which allowed the use of popular melodies (see page 83), and became the most severe type of musical composition, with the exception of the Mass. In the sixteenth century the motet, having largely adopted the imitative principle of structure, assumed the following form: each separate section of the text had its own characteristic melody, which was announced successively by all the voices as in the later fugue; after this "exposition" the section was soon brought to a cadence; for the second division of the text a second theme was introduced and similarly set forth, and so on throughout. The whole motet thus consisted of a succession of fugal expositions, without much development of the material. The patchy impression which resulted from combining such unrelated sections was avoided as far as possible, either by merely continuing the cadence note of the one section into the beginning of the next, or by beginning the theme of the second section while the cadence of the first was still being sounded.

Thus, neither the form nor the name of the fugue is brought into use until the seventeenth century. In the first stages of instrumental development the generic title *Sonata*, as indicating an instrumental composition distinct from *Cantata*, was still employed. The generic title later came to include the more specific designations *Ricercar, Tiento, Fantasia, Canzona,* and *Capriccio,* as we have seen. The first arrangements were for the lute, in spite of the fact that this instrument could not well suggest the true voice-leading of the vocal polyphony. Adrian Willaert, perhaps following suggestions given by the lutenists, made more effective transcriptions for the organ. In 1542 his pupil Cavazzoni published Ricercari, Canzone, and so forth, which Willaert followed in 1549 by works in the same form. Here, as in the motets, the theme was stated in one voice and was then answered, often in the dominant (a fifth above or a fourth below the original statement) and sometimes at the interval of the octave. In his work, as well as in that of Gabrieli, Merulo, and others, the structure was made more coherent by the gradual elimination of the many successive themes. The composition was then developed out of a single theme, the later sections, after the first statement of the theme by all the voices in turn, consisting of variations (augmentation, diminution, or ornamental figurations) of the one subject. Also the themes assumed a more purely instrumental character, so that the relation to the original vocal form was less conspicuous. The restriction to a single theme, however, was not universal. But when the older process of successive expositions of different themes was employed, the contrasts between the sections (in the absence of words which would justify the introduction of a new theme) were nearly meaningless unlesss made more striking than was compatible with any impression of unity in the whole piece. Hence, these two types of ricercar—the monothematic and the polythematic—are suggestive of two very different forms. The monothematic type resulted in the true Fugue; the polythematic, as Wilhelm Fischer thinks, at least anticipates the *Sonata da Chiesa,* where contrasts are intensified and the contrasted sections are expanded into separate movements. More directly, however, the succession of themes is also suggestive of the Double and Triple Fugue.

Two great musicians share the honor of having brought to a point of clear definition the formal structure of the fugue: Jan Pieters Sweelinck (1562–1621), the son of an Amsterdam organist, who studied in Venice under pupils of Willaert and especially with Zarlino; and Girolamo Frescobaldi (1583–1644), a pupil of Luzzasco Luzzaschi of Ferrara, who was likewise a follower of Willaert's school. Sweelinck's fugue structure differed somewhat from that of Frescobaldi. Sweelinck maintained the opening theme throughout the fugue, using the devices of augmentation, diminution, and so forth, but never the florid figuration of the theme

which was popular with earlier writers. In each successive division, however, he introduced a new counterpoint to the subject—perhaps in some
sense a substitute for the older fashion of new principal subjects—which
also is a step in the direction of the double and triple fugue. Frescobaldi,
although he also used the single theme with new counterpoints which is
characteristic of Sweelinck, frequently introduced in the successive divisions of the form a figured or rhythmic variant of the subject. Examples
of this type of variation may be seen from the following:

The pupils of Sweelinck and Frescobaldi who had most to do with the
further development of the fugue were Germans. Indeed, it was in Germany that the term *Fuga* was first used to designate this particular type
of ricercar. Johann Jakob Froberger (1616–1667), a pupil of Frescobaldi,
was a sufficiently commanding figure to introduce his master's principles
into favor in Vienna, and later in Héricourt in eastern France. Hamburg,
Lüneberg, and Lübeck in northern Germany; Halle, Dresden, and Leipzig in Saxony; and Nuremberg and Munich in Bavaria, all became
conspicuous centers of organ playing, in which the leading spirits were
Reinken, Georg Böhm, the great Danish organist Buxtehude; Zachau (the
teacher of Handel), Strunck, and Kuhnau (predecessor of Bach at the
Thomas Church); and Pachelbel (conspicuous also for his development
of the choral-vorspiel or hymn-prelude) and Johann Kaspar Kerll (whom
we have already mentioned in connection with the opera). The new
style spread rapidly; this was natural, since in Germany the questions
raised by the Protestant revolt were of commanding interest. For the
natural musical expression of religious emotion is polyphony; and we find
in Germany a very great development—along the new lines which the
establishment of key feeling has made possible—of that polyphonic art
which in Italy had died with the rise of the opera to popularity.

With so many diverse traditions contributing to the final form, it will
be readily understood that the fugue is not, as is often supposed, a rigidly
mathematical musical pattern. It is impossible to give a description of the

form which will fit every example; but the following will be found to give a general plan of the structure as it is found in Bach's usage.

THE FUGUE FORM

Exposition—Subject Entries in Tonic and Dominant

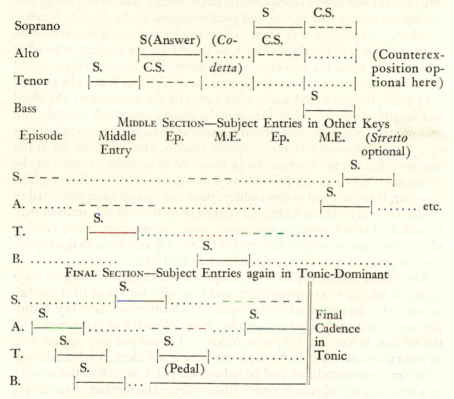

S. is subject; C.S., countersubject, indicated by short dashes. Dots indicate the continuation of the voice with free or derived matter; cessation of the dots, pauses.

The *subject* is a short, epigrammatic phrase of melody usually announced by a single voice, unaccompanied. Any voice may give this first announcement. The number of voices to participate may be from two to six or even more; but by far the greater number of fugues are for three or four voices. The *answer* is the subject itself, transposed usually to the dominant and entering therefore a fifth above or a fourth below the subject. If the answer is an exact repetition of the subject in the new key, it is called a *real* answer and the fugue is called a *real* fugue. Sometimes, however, the transposition of the subject is slightly altered, in which case the answer and the fugue are both said to be *tonal*. The *countersubject* is an accompanying figure made to combine interestingly with the subject, and also to have interest in itself. It must be so made as to sound well when placed either above or below the subject. Two voices which may be thus inverted are said to be in *double counterpoint*. Subject and answer are sometimes called *dux* (leader) and *comes* (companion), respectively. The short passage following the entrance of answer and countersubject in the diagram is called a *codetta*.[3] Its purpose is to form a convenient transition, if that is needed, to the point where the third voice is to enter with the subject, or to offer a little relief from the monotonous regularity of entrance which would otherwise occur in the successive appearances of the subject. The codetta is optional, however, and may occur between the entrance of the third and fourth voices instead of between the second and third. Subject and answer are successively taken by the remaining voices, the others keeping up a less conspicuous free counterpoint (that is, phrases which fill in the harmony, but are not intended to be observed as essential elements of the structure). When all the voices have entered, the *exposition* is complete; however, if subject and countersubject have not therein been presented in double counterpoint, an additional statement of them in this relation may be added. There is also in some cases a *counterexposition*, which consists of the statement of subject and answer by the voices which, in the exposition proper, had respectively the answer and subject.

The middle section begins with an episode which may be made of fragments of subject or countersubject, and is usually for fewer than the full number of voices engaged in the fugue. Modulation to a new key is usually accomplished during this episode. A *middle entry* or *repercussion* of the subject, in the new key, now follows. The subject may appear here in more than one voice, but a single entrance is sufficient. Varied relations of subject, countersubject, and added counterpoint, as well as the novelty of a new key, will appear in each middle entry. The number of successive episodes and middle entries is limited only by the composer's ingenuity in devising new forms of presentation. The various devices of augmentation, diminution, inversion, and so forth, are often used in the middle sections. *Stretto*, which is the sounding of the subject in a second voice before it has been completed in an earlier voice, frequently appears in this part of the fugue. A stretto which involves all the voices engaged in the fugue is called a "master stretto" (*stretto maestrale*).

The final section presents the climax of the piece. Here the subject is often (but not always) presented in stretto. Also the original key, which

---

[3] This term, absurd as it is in relation to the passage it indicates, is used by most theorists and is repeated here out of respect for convention. In reality the codetta is nothing but a brief episode.

is now returned to, may be given greater emphasis by the use of a *pedal point* or *organ point*—a single note (usually the tonic or dominant) sustained in the bass or other voices while the remaining parts sound the subject, or fragments of it, above.

Double or triple fugues are those which have more than one subject. The entrance of these subjects may be simultaneous, at the very beginning, or successive. In either case, the countersubject of the simple fugue is either omitted altogether or reduced to a position of little importance; for the several subjects must appear simultaneously, and the addition of a regular countersubject to a fugue which already had two or three subjects would be only confusing.

The great variety of possible treatments of the subject matter makes the fugue highly flexible; and the great coherence which can result from the use of these few essential materials makes it at the same time the most completely logical and unified of musical forms.

The *Sonata da Chiesa* (Church Sonata)

After the fugue, this is perhaps the most dignified of the musical forms of the period. Its derivation is also from those early types of vocal music without a *cantus firmus* which gave rise to the fugue. In this case, however, the originating form is not only the polythematic motet but also the *canzona*, which had its foundations in the popular song. From the opening of the fourteenth century, when the generic title *Cantilena* came to cover many different specific forms, such as the *Rondeaux, Chansons*, and *Chansons Balladées* of Machaut's day, a great variety of melodic types, expressive both of secular and spiritual sentiment, had been cultivated. As we have seen, the instrumental accompaniment for vocal music became a purely instrumental rendition of that music; and in the process the song types just mentioned were chosen as the materials for such purely instrumental works as the orchestral *Canzone* of Giovanni Gabrieli. These consist of two contrasted sections, several times alternated, with a lively coda.

Later composers increased considerably the number of different ideas, replacing thus the repetitions in Gabrieli's work, and producing what is really a succession of movements of highly contrasted character, even less closely knitted together than the sections of the motet which had a separate fugal exposition for each of its divisions. The form suffered a great lapse in popularity in Italy after the time of Frescobaldi; but became in Germany one of the most cultivated of instrumental types. In Italy the orchestral *canzona* gave place to the trio sonata—less imposing in the number of its instruments, and more homophonic in style than the *canzona*. The number of movements was gradually reduced; but each movement was extended. The growing art of fugal structure was incorporated, and the general order of the form became, even as early as 1613 in a trio sonata of Salomone Rossi, a clear foreshadowing of the later conventional four-movement group. The convention of four movements was established by Arcangelo Corelli (1653–1713), in whose hands the church sonata assumed the following form: (1) *Grave* (slow), either homophonic or imitative; (2) *Allegro*, fugal; (3) *Andante*, homophonic (Corelli usually wrote this movement in triple time); and (4) *Allegro* or *Presto*, either fugal or homophonic. The form as written by Bach offered no essential modification of the above outline. His treatment of it, however, was vastly richer than that of any of his predecessors. The instruments used were at first two of high register, with a *basso continuo*. With the coming into popularity of the violin, this instrument gradually superseded all others for the higher parts. When the harpsichord was used it was possible to take one of the higher parts, as well as the bass, on this instrument; so that the evolution of duet sonatas for harpsichord and violin was natural. The trio character was still maintained, however, even in the sonatas of Bach for violin and piano; for the piano takes two of the parts and the violin the third, and these three were all that were essentialy involved. A vast amount of ornamentation was used in the earlier examples, both by the player of the *continuo* and by the others. Bach's highly ornamental passages were but the careful working out, to a point of artistic perfection, of the earlier more improvisatory ornaments. Naturally, also, styles of phrase or ornament which had grown up in connection with one type of form were often found suitable for other forms. And even dance movements, directly borrowed from the suite, were freely used for the last movements of church sonatas by Bach and others. We shall see that it is a mixture of the movement successions, form outlines, and expressive characteristics of both the church and the chamber sonatas which gives rise to the later sonata form of Haydn and Mozart.

THE DANCE SUITE (*Sonata da Camera*)

But little description of the evolution of this form is required in addition to that which has already been given. The universal popularity of the dance itself gave rise to a vast unwritten literature of dance music whose general form, as we have seen, was almost universally that of the *Tanz* and the related *Nachtanz*. These dance tunes suggested at once the possibility of artistic elaboration. In England, where the sixteenth-century virginalists first worked out dance suites, the treatment of the tunes took the form of variations—highly figured elaborations of the simple melody of the dance tune. In France the first idealization of the dance took the shape of orchestral ensembles—this instrumentation having been chosen apparently because of the popularity of the court ballet, for which a large instrumental group was required. Four movements, together designated by the general term *Branle*, were derived out of the original dance-pair: (1) *Branle double* (the equivalent of the *Tanz*); (2) *Branle simple* (*Nachtanz*); (3) *Branle gai* (melodically unrelated to the others, in triple time); and (4) *Branle de Bourgogne* (also unrelated, in duple time). Out of this quadruple group grew the succession: (1) *Allemande* (common time); (2) *Courante* (variation, in triple time); (3) *Sarabande* (independent, in triple time); and (4) *Gigue* (independent, duple time). This succession was first written for the lute by Denis Gaultier, but was soon transplanted to the clavicembalo by Couperin and others and was destined to supersede other groups of dance tunes in all Europe.

In Germany the group of four movements was also accepted as most satisfactory. Peurl writes the succession: Paduan (common time)—Intrada (triple time, a variation of the Paduan), followed by Dantz (common time)—Galliarda (triple time, a variation of the Dantz).[4] This is obviously a succession of two of the original dance-pairs. The variation form maintained its popularity in Germany until after the Thirty Years' War, when the brilliant court of Versailles began to set a social example for all Europe and the French form of suite was adopted in place of the older variation type. The idea of variation was not wholly abandoned however; and even in the Suites of Bach occasional dances were followed by varied forms which are called *Les Agréments* ("The Ornaments") of the same dance, or *Double*. These two were by no means identical, however. The *Agréments* were figurated variations of the melodic line of the dance tune, and were conceived as taking the place of the original form when the section was repeated. The first part, that is, was played in its simple and then in its figurated form; and the second part in the same way. The *Double*, on the other hand, was a contrapuntal variation made by adding new melodic voices above the essential bass or harmony of the original, and was played wholly after the original dance form was ended. The original group of four dances was further expanded during the latter half of the seventeenth century, often by the addition of a Prelude, and still more frequently by the insertion of additional dances—often called, collectively, *Intermezzi*—into the dance sequence itself. The prelude was an extended form, not of the dance character, which was often of greater extent (especially in the orchestral suites) than the whole series of dances following. Indeed, Bach gives the title *Overture* to his orchestral works

[4] See the quotation of these themes, above, p. 231.

in this form, the succeeding dances then constituting merely a *Divertissement*.

The following, then, will give the order of the dances in the dance suite in its highest development, at the hands of Bach:

> (Prelude—optional)
> Allemande
> Courante
> Sarabande
> (Intermezzi—optional interpolated dances or pieces)
> Gigue

The various dances have certain individual characteristics which suggest either the old dance steps, or the conventional patterns of rhythm which in other ways had become associated with the dances. The Allemande was most frequently given a running figure of even sixteenth notes in 4-4 time, and began with the upbeat of a single sixteenth note, thus: ♪|♫♫. The Courante had two types of rhythm, the French, often in a mixture of 3-2 and 6-4, and the Italian in simple 3-4 or 3-8 time. The Sarabande was a slow and stately dance, possibly but not certainly of Spanish origin, in 3-4 time and having a characteristic accent on the second beat of the measure. The Gigue was the most lively of all; it was usually in some compound triple time—6-8 or 12-8—and often adopted the plan of fugal entrance for its subject, thus suggesting that the bystanders were infected by the joyousness of the dance and were moved to join in it.

It is hardly possible to describe all the dances of which a selection may be included in the interpolated group. Probably the chief of these was the Minuet—a courtly dance in 3-4 time, to which a second minuet, called a Trio, was often added. In the dances for varied instruments this second minuet was often composed for three instruments only—whence the designation *Trio*. That term came to be applied to the middle section of any such composition, whatever the number of instruments. The Gavotte was a graceful dance in moderate tempo in 2-2 time, and properly began with the upbeat of a half bar: ♩ ♩| or ♫♫|. The Bourrée was a very lively dance in 2-2 time, rivaling the Gigue in energy and vivacity. Like the Rigaudon, which it closely resembled, it was a fast Gavotte. Both Gavotte and Bourrée often had an appended *Alternative*, the equivalent of the Trio. The Trio of the Gavotte is often called *Musette*, after the *Cornemuse, Muse,* or *Musette*—the French names for the bagpipe—the drone of that instrument being often imitated by a single or double "pedal point." (*Musette* is also the name for a small oboe, without keys.) The Passepied, which likewise may have a Trio, was a sailor's dance in 3-4 or 3-8 time. The Loure was also originally a bagpipe dance, was generally in 6-4 time, and rather slow. In its later form it had somewhat of the dignity of the Sarabande. Still other dances were used, such as the Polonaise, the Anglaise, the Siciliano, the Canario, and the Hornpipe. There was also frequently an *Aria*, which was in the same musical form as the dances but without specific dance character. The most important of the forms not of the dance type is the Rondeau, which was in especial favor with the French. This had a main thematic idea which was presented several times unaltered, while different types of phrase were interspersed between the repetitions. We shall see that this form later underwent an important development.

All the dances in the suite were usually in the same key (with the exception of the *Alternatives* or *Trios*, which were usually in the relative major or minor); and all had exactly the same general form. That form has also a definite relation to the form of the later homophonic Sonata. It is therefore important to have its chief features clearly in mind. It may be clearly exhibited in a diagram:

SUITE DANCE FORM

‖.“S” .. Cadential Figures . ‖	. Modulations	Partial Cadence	Final Cadence .‖
‖.(in Tonic) (in Domi- .‖	. (beginning in	(in Rel. Minor	(in Tonic) .‖
nant, or Rel.	Dom. or Rel-	or Dominant)	
Maj.)	ative Key)		

S is *Subject*—the characteristic dance figure. It is by no means as definite as the subject of a fugue, but its pattern is very largely the foundation of the whole dance. It is of course at first presented in the tonic key; and the first section of the piece (which is repeated) is chiefly concerned with establishing this character and with effecting a modulation, either to the dominant, or often, if the main key is minor, to the relative major. Only slight excursions outside these two keys are made in the first section. The second section then presents the characteristic figure in a far wider range of keys (indicated in the diagram by *Modulations*). This section often has a definite cadence in a key closely related to the tonic. The rest of the section is taken up with the final cadence, which is similar in matter to the cadence of the first section and is usually not closely derived from the original figure. The essential elements of this form which are involved in later evolution are (1) the two repeated sections and (2) the essential key contrasts. We must remember that in 1700 the sense of definite key was a fact much more conspicuous to the hearer than it is now; and that key contrasts therefore were more vital form elements than they are with us. We shall see that this key contrast is later intensified by the use of subject contrast. But the problem of introducing essentially different and important subject matter into the one movement is as yet only barely pre-visioned. Much labor will have to be expended on the rhetoric of homo-phonic composition before the later sonata form can come into being.

VARIATIONS

We have already seen that there were two very distinct types of varia-tion: that in which the melodic line was ornamented or otherwise altered, and that in which the essential bass, preserved unvaried, was provided with ever new counterpoints above it. The first type is naturally that which will survive when—as will presently happen—the polyphonic style is super-seded by the monophonic. The unaltered bass gives in reality a type of *cantus firmus;* and of variation on this persistent subject we saw an exam-ple even in the time of Dunstable (see pages 131 and 136). Two types of dance—the Chaconne and the Passacaglia—kept this form of variation; but its musical possibilities were so great that in the later examples the dance character is hardly apparent, and our interest is rather in the many ingeni-ous additions of upper parts which the composer can contrive. In the polyphonic period this type of variation is naturally preferred to the fig-urative type. Bach has left marvelous examples in the famous *Chaconne* for violin solo, in the *Goldberg Variations* for harpsichord, and in the *Passacaglia* in C minor for organ. The term *Folia* (of uncertain origin, like the others) was also used to designate the same form. Corelli wrote an admirable set of such variations for violin, known as *La Folia* or *Les Folies d'espagne.*

OVERTURE AND CONCERTO

Different as these two forms ultimately came to be, they had a common origin in the instrumental *canzona.* The *Symphonies*—introductory or intermediary orchestral pieces in the music dramas—were patterned after the instrumental *canzone,* but they often borrowed from the current dance types as well. The already described *French* Overture of Lully can be considered as an expansion of the first two or three movements of the *Sonata da Chiesa,* the fugal second part bearing close resemblance to the second movement of the sonata. Alessandro Scarlatti, leader of the Nea-politan school of opera writers which we have still to consider, at first used the full four-movement group of the church sonata as overture. The fugal element was much flimsier than with Lully; and in the cantata *Olim-piade* (1697) Scarlatti omitted altogether the introductory *Grave* and wrote the first movement in a homophonic style. Thereafter, with the large substitution of homophonic for polyphonic writing, the order became fast—slow—fast, the last three movements of the *Sonata da Chiesa* being the apparent foundation.

It was out of instrumental experiments of this sort that the Concerto arose. The literal meaning of the word—retained in English (a "concerted" effort)—implied, at first, not the form of the music but the fact that it was produced by a concerted group of players.[5] Naturally in such a group some people played better than others, and the better players took the most prominent parts. They could not do this effectively however if the music they had to play was merely that which the *tutti*—the "whole" group—had announced. Hence, not only figurations of the *tutti* themes but distinctive *solo subjects*, in which the individual instruments had opportunity to display their especial powers, were added. The players were thus grouped into two divisions—the *Concerto grosso* or big (*tutti*) group, and the *Concertino* or little group of soloists. Sometimes, as in some of the Brandenburg Concertos of Bach, there was no concertino. Sometimes on the other hand the concertino is reduced to a single person, whereupon we have a solo concerto. The distinction between solo and *tutti* subjects was maintained, however. The general form of the music was at first chiefly that of the church sonata. The relation between solo and *tutti* was not easily maintained in this form, and a clearer distinction between the two groups was achieved by writing a sturdy opening subject for the *tutti* and an answering solo subject (each having several significant phrases, for later development), and by having the principal subject recur—somewhat as in the rondeau—either in *tutti* or solo, at fairly regular intervals.

The greatest *Concerti grossi* are those of Corelli, Bach, and Handel. The first Concertos for solo violin are by Torelli and by Albinoni (of whose work Bach made intensive study); but the form of the solo Concerto just described was chiefly fixed by Antonio Vivaldi. As was natural for an Italian, Vivaldi seldom exerted himself to provide a polyphonic texture for the accompaniment or for the *tutti* subjects. In this respect he differed from Bach, to whom polyphonic thought was utterly natural and who, both in his elaborations of Albinoni's works and in his original Concertos, used a polyphonic style throughout.

The most familiar examples of Bach's work in this form are probably the Concerto for two violins and the *Italian* Concerto for piano. The latter presents, by means of a single keyboard instrument, practically the transcription of a concerto for violin and orchestra. In studying the Concerto for two violins, the student should note that the solo instruments do not properly take part in the opening *tutti*. The whole substance of the

---

[5] The primary sense of *certare* is "to strive"; of *concertare*, "to strive together." The idea of competition is not absent, in the Concerto; but that of concerted effort (obviously, the word *concerted* has the same origin) is more clearly evident.

tutti, however, is so difficult to play on a single keyboard that the solo instruments usually take the *ripieni* parts, thus obscuring the identity of the solo subject when it enters after the fugal opening of the first movement. In the *Italian* Concerto the *tutti* is represented by the first thirty bars. The supposed solo enters immediately after with a simple phrase which appears at first sight almost insignificant—as is to some extent the case with the solo subject in the Concerto for two violins. There is no single predominant theme for the solo, but rather several phrase types; and the solo itself often takes up matter which has been first sounded by the *tutti*. The *tutti* also occasionally gives the solo a short rest, punctuating the lighter texture of the solo passages with occasional outbursts of vigor. There is no prescribed order of entrance of the materials, the nature of the subjects themselves being allowed largely to dictate the form after the entrance of the solo; the movement ends, however, with an emphatic restatement of the opening *tutti*, complete. The fugal type of *tutti*, of course, has less of variety in thematic material to offer. The slow movements, in Bach's works especially, are almost invariably marvels of profundity in feeling. Often in the solo concertos they resemble the older polyphonic variations on a ground bass. The E major Concerto for violin solo, the D minor Concerto for piano (which was originally a concerto for violin), and the *Italian* Concerto have such movements. The solo part, of course, is in no sense a variation of the bass theme, but takes the form of an amazing improvisation above the reiterated figures of the bass. The final movement has practically the same structure as the first, the matter being usually more vivacious.

In the contrasts of solo and *tutti* subjects, and also in the use of several thematic ideas in the *tutti*, the concerto may be said to foreshadow the later form of the sonata as perfected by Haydn and Mozart. The concerto was a far more significant form than the overture, which was used merely to give warning that the opera was about to begin, and was but little heeded as a musical piece by the not too well-behaved audiences of the time.

CHORAL-VORSPIEL (HYMN-PRELUDE)

This is the only important descendant of the old vocal forms with a *cantus firmus*. The elaborations of *canti fermi* taken from the Gregorian chant dwindled rapidly in importance during the second half of the sixteenth century. But in Germany the Protestant hymn, which became the universal congregational expression, took the place of the older type of song and became the basis of elaborate schemes of variation, performed by the organist before the singing of the hymn itself. The development of the form was begun by Sweelinck (who to some extent was following the lead of the English virginalists in their variations); and in his work we find the *cantus firmus*—a line or phrase from the hymn-tune—always present in one voice or another in long notes. Sweelinck's pupils and successors introduced all the elaborate types of figuration which we have seen developed in other variation forms. The organist was expected in those days to possess unlimited powers of improvisation. Hence, the stricter manipulation of the theme itself was later lost in free, fantasia-like elaborations in which all the art of the organist as well as that of the contrapuntist was exhibited. From the example of works in this form by Reinken, Buxtehude, and especially Pachelbel, which introduce many of the characteristic features of other musical styles, Bach created Chorale-Preludes such as those in the *Klavierübung* and the *Orgelbüchlein*, and the Canonic Variations on the Christmas song *Vom Himmel hoch, da komm' ich her*.

TOCCATA, FANTASIA, AND PRELUDE

Originally devised as a *touch piece* to exhibit the player's command of his instrument, the toccata soon adopted the imitative or fugal style for one or more of its varied sections, while retaining the brilliant passage work which in the earliest examples had alternated with simple chord successions. Even the dramatic style was represented in recitative-like introductory or intermediate passages. The result is a form which is distinguishable from the Fantasia only by its greater completeness and by its usual conclusion in a free style of fugal movement. The division of the preliminary matter from the closing fugue, if made absolute, resulted in the Fantasia and Fugue, or the smaller and still more familiar Prelude and Fugue of the *Well-Tempered Clavichord*.

These preludes are generally divisible into three types: (1) the *arpeggio* prelude, in which there is no thematic line but rather a succession of chords elaborated into more or less intricate arpeggio figures (for example, Nos. 1 and 2 of Book I, W. K.); (2) the thematic prelude, in which a thematic idea is developed in a free contrapuntal style (as in No. 4) or even in the manner of the toccata (as in No. 22); and (3) those which in form exactly correspond to the pattern of the suite dance, given above, but of course without the dance character. In the first volume of the *Well-Tempered Clavichord* (1722) there is but one Prelude in this latter form; in the second volume (1744) there are ten. Some of these approach rather closely to the later sonata form: No. 5 in D has a complete recapitulation, but of course lacks the second subject which we shall presently find added when, as the sonata evolves, key contrast comes to be intensified by subject contrast.

It is beyond doubt that Bach generally intended the prelude to suggest something related to the character of the fugue which followed. Even a similarity of figure is sometimes to be noted between the two pieces. Such resemblances are hardly possible, however, when that which follows the prelude is not a fugue but a succession of dances, as in the English Suites and the Partitas. Here the variety of names given to the introductory movements is bewildering; the six Partitas (the latest of Bach's collections of Suites for the piano) have each a long introduction, to which he gives the successive titles: *Praeludium, Sinfonia, Fantasia, Ouverture, Praeambulum,* and *Toccata.*

It will be apparent that in this as in all the other forms we have described there was the greatest latitude allowed to the composer's imagination. Nothing is farther from the truth than to suppose, as many seem to do, that the music of Bach and his contemporaries is a mere filling-out of pre-established patterns of form. On the contrary, the frequent great dissimilarity even in compositions bearing the same form designation is the best possible evidence that it is not the form itself which is the composer's chief concern, but—as truly as with any later music—the musical ideas themselves and their emotional character.

❧ CHAPTER XVII ❧

The Forms of Vocal Music at the Opening of the Eighteenth Century

T HE word *form* as applied to vocal music must be understood in a
somewhat different sense from that which it conveys when applied
to instrumental music. For instrumental music must be completely
self-intelligible; while vocal music is of course governed, almost wholly as
to its character and to a considerable extent as to its form, by the words
to which it is set. So far as its purely formal structure is concerned, vocal
writing naturally follows the same plans of organization as instrumental
music; but in its more elemental details, and particularly in the design of
homophonic melody, instrumental music copies and reproduces the types
of phrase which are most natural to the human voice. In reality then, so
far as pure structure is concerned, we shall find no other essential form
outlines in vocal music than those which have just been described as
instrumental forms. The fugue is obviously as suitable for voices as for
instruments; and the simple or figurated homophonic melody, and even the
recitative frequently occurring in instrumental music, are really of vocal
origin. Vocal forms, therefore, will require discussion only as to the manner in which the musical structure is governed by the words.

Aside from the opera, the most important vocal forms of the early
eighteenth century were religious in character. The most vivid religious
interests were of course those aroused by the rise of Protestantism. It is
Germany, therefore, with its wealth of popular religious song rather than
France (whose Calvinistic faith was much less friendly to the emotionalism
aroused by music) or England (where religious thought had been greatly
confused with political issues) which offered the most varied and inter-

esting vocal music. Some of the forms, like the cantata and the Passion, had direct relation to the forms and observances of the Lutheran service. Others, like the oratorio and the motet, had a more general (but not less profound) application to the religious thought of the time. All were interpenetrated with the essential musical idiom of Germany, which we have seen to have its source in that studied form of popular song bequeathed to the nation by the Minnesinger and the Meistersinger.

The Cantata

We have seen that this word was originally used, in a very general sense, to distinguish that which was sung from that which was played (sonata). The term acquired a more specific meaning during the early years of the seventeenth century, when the "new music" of the monodists was taking the form of the opera. The cantata then became a rather extended solo piece, partly narrative but chiefly lyrical in character, in which a more individual emotional attitude was expressed than could be achieved in the polyphonic madrigal. It was the reduction of the opera to the proportions of the drawing room, and was called *Cantata da camera* or *Cantata a voce sola*, since it was at first for a single voice. Gradually it superseded the madrigal in favor, but not without borrowing something from that form. The *basso continuo*, used as the foundation for the monodic recitative or aria in the opera, was applied to the cantata; and the other accompanying instruments, like the middle voices of the madrigal, pursued a much more significant melodic course than in the simple chord harmonies of the operatic recitative. Voices and instruments, that is, were concerted exactly as were the instruments in a concerto. In this concerted *madrigal-cantata* form the voices became more numerous and the manner somewhat more dramatic. Yet in the absence of stage setting the musical element, as in the oratorio, remained more significant than in the opera. The peculiar problem of the vocal duet, musically highly organized and at the same time definitely expressive of the sense of its text, was solved with astonishing mastery by Monteverdi, Carissimi, Cesti, and others.

Transplanted to Germany, the cantata became chiefly (but not solely) religious in character. The Protestant service, conducted of course in the vernacular, gave large prominence to music both for the choir and for the congregation. Each Sunday in the calendar had its special commemorative meaning, and to emphasize this significance the music as well as the lessons and the sermon were designed. The cantata texts were composed partly of scriptural words, partly of added verses or prose phrases, to suggest a distinct emotional attitude toward the main idea of the service of the day. Soli, choir, and orchestra combined to make the cantata the moment of highest emotional realization in the service. And since each Sunday had its peculiar meaning, a cantata of especial character would be suitable for only one performance during the year. Hence arose the custom of composing cycles of cantatas, one for each Sunday of the year.

Bach wrote five complete cycles of church cantatas. He wrote also several secular cantatas, two of them (the *Peasant* and the *Coffee* cantatas) being comic, and the *Strife Between Phoebus and Pan* being as near an approach to opera as Bach ever cared to make. In his earlier works the solo parts are extraordinarily direct and vivid in expression; in the later, the growing influence of the Italian opera is seen in the more frequent use of the *da capo* aria, with a considerable measure of that floridity of ornament which had come to such popularity in the more elegant world toward which Germany was beginning to turn longing eyes. But in spite of the loss of that direct musical expression which reveals so lucidly the literalness of the Lutheran faith of the time, these later works show no essential derogation from the high dignity and the complete devotion which marks the more youthful productions.

THE PASSION

The events which lead to the tragedy of the Crucifixion naturally engender the most profound contemplation of the believer. The Passion (that is, the suffering) of Christ as related by the four Evangelists forms the substance of the commemoration celebrated during Holy Week. In the old Catholic service, the narration was recited in the style of the Gregorian chant, while the comments of the people or *Turba* were either sung by the choir in energetic unison or were set to polyphonic music.[1] Obrecht was the first to provide a polyphonic setting of the whole gospel text. This, however, remained an exceptional treatment of the theme. The Latin text and the unaccompanied, chanted rendition were at first taken over into the Lutheran service. The German version in Luther's translation was for long similarly treated. It was Heinrich Schütz whose wealth of dramatic and musical imagination bore fruit, not only in the opera as we have seen, but in an essentially dramatic type of music for the Passion. For the old chant he substituted a style of declamation which is strongly colored by the manner of the recitative. The completely polyphonic settings, after the manner of the *St. Matthew* Passion of Obrecht, had found less acceptance and disappeared altogether during the first half of the seventeenth century. The oratorio of the Italians however, which was at first hardly other than a type of religious drama, offered the suggestion

[1] For further detail, see Grove's *Dictionary*, articles "Passion," "Oratorio," and "Noel," where examples of the music will be found.

of a combination of the monodic and polyphonic settings. Thus, not only in his settings of the Passions themselves but also in a similar treatment of the theme of the Resurrection, Schütz gave the task of carrying forward the story—fulfilled in the oldest Passions by the chant—to a narrator called the "Evangelist"; used other solo voices to impersonate the characters involved in the story; and gave to the chorus the reaction of the people to the events, or the moral comment incident to the action.

This is essentially the method of Bach, who like Schütz indulges in no mere music-making but contrives everything so as to vivify to the utmost the meaning of the story he is relating. The German manner is still more evident in the settings by Keiser, Mattheson, Telemann, and Handel, of texts by Menantes and Brockes. These texts, however, are unfortunately more didactic than biblical; and Bach shows great discernment in reverting as far as possible to the scriptural words. He wrote five Passions, of which two (the *St. Matthew* and the *St. John*) are preserved. (A *St. Luke* Passion in Bach's hand is extant, whose authenticity is much doubted.) The *St. Matthew* Passion is by common consent regarded as the greatest example of this form. It opens with a majestic chorus for two choirs, "Come ye daughters, share my mourning," which provides the atmosphere of expectant solemnity with which the coming narration is to be heard. The Evangelist then takes up the story, singing only the narrative portions. The words of any individual character are sung by other soloists, and the chorus impersonates any group—for example, the Apostles at the Last Supper who, being told that one of their number is about to betray the Christ, ask "Lord, is it I?"—or represents the crowd which demands the release of Barabbas. At appropriate moments familiar hymns are introduced, in comment on pointed incidents of the story; and at the betrayal the sense of disaster is expressed in a tremendous chorus of outrage and horror. The treatment of the hymns is as notable as any feature of the work. The familiar tune *O Haupt voll Blut und Wunden* (considerately translated, "Dear Head, how art thou wounded") occurs five times to different texts and with different harmonizations—the last, in comment on the Crucifixion, being in a lower key and strangely pitiful in tone. The recitative is always clearly related to the words. Sometimes it rises to extraordinary vividness and even literalness of expression, as in the Evangelist's description of the weeping of Peter after the third crowing of the cock. Of similar interest to the hymns are commentatorial arias for various solo voices, set to verse written by the arranger of the Passion text. These, like the hymns, are interpolated at appropriate moments in the course of the drama. They ordinarily assume the ABA form and are often of comparable floridity to the operatic arias which are their model.

ORATORIO

We left the story of the oratorio where Carissimi had brought the form to a point of equality of interest with the opera. The history of the oratorio in Italy thereafter is not of great significance. Alessandro Scarlatti, a disciple of Carissimi and the most prominent figure in Italian opera until the year of his death (1725), was as skilled in oratorio and in the cantata as in opera; but the operatic element so far overshadowed the religious in his oratorios that it is difficult to judge them fairly when the more significant works of the German writers are placed in comparison. Neither is the work of his chief contemporaries, Caldera, Colonna, and Stradella, of greater importance for the later history of the form.

It was with Heinrich Schütz (often called the father of German music) that the German oratorio, like the Passion and the German opera, began to show true independence of the Italian models. Both in his *History of the Happy and Triumphant Resurrection* and in the later *History of the Joyous and Gracious Birth of Jesus Christ* there is evident a truly individual genius, accepting existing works, whether of Italian or German origin, not as models to be copied but as efforts to be improved upon. The attitude toward problem and model alike was that which Bach himself assumed half a century later. Reinhard Keiser, at Hamburg, came much nearer the free and intense expression which Bach later achieved.

There are but three works by Bach which bear the specific title *Oratorio* —a succession of six cantatas, intended to be performed on six holydays from Christmas to Epiphany, which he called the *Christmas Oratorio;* the *Easter Oratorio,* which is more nearly in the Italian manner than the former, being set not to biblical words but to a succession of poems in madrigal form; and the *Ascension Oratorio,* which again is founded mainly on the biblical narrative. Only the Easter piece has the quasi-dramatic style which is characteristic of the Handelian oratorio. Handel's manner (though by no means his vigor and depth of meaning) is more directly suggested in the works of the incredibly prolific Telemann, a contemporary of Bach who was far more famous in his lifetime than the great master, but whose work is shallow and formal, lacking the breath of life. Since many of his works were published, while those of Bach remained in manuscript, Telemann's influence on religious composition in Germany was far more immediate; and since religious interest was becoming doctrinal rather than vitally spiritual, the easier and less significant style of Telemann was followed in Germany rather than the more difficult manner of Bach. Hence, the greatest achievements in the form of the oratorio are those of Handel in England where, as we shall see, various conditions combined to make this form more popular than the opera.

The Mass

The high perfection of Palestrina's treatment of the Mass was soon forgotten when, after his death, the opera began to reflect the vital interest in worldly concerns which the Renaissance had brought about. During the whole seventeenth century there was a continual decadence in Italian religious music. To this the growing rage for opera contributed. One feature of this later religious work, although it was not a direct imitation of any feature of operatic work, was nevertheless a palpable outcome of operatic influence. This was the tendency toward an altogether spectacular complication of the musical fabric, seen in the multiplication of the choirs and in the use of a large body of accompanying instruments. Palestrina of course wrote for an unaccompanied choir. But the brilliant effect of an added orchestral accompaniment was an attraction not to be resisted. Hence *concerted* Masses—sometimes on an enormous scale, such as that written by Orazio Benevole for the consecration of the Cathedral of Salzburg in 1628, which is for eight choirs with a corresponding instrumentation—succeed to the purely vocal forms of the Golden Age. At the great Church of St. Peter in Rome the same fashion was adopted, some of the many divisions of the choir being grouped on the main floor while others were stationed in the galleries which surround the ascending dome. It is obvious that this magnificence, while profoundly impressive, suggests a far different mood of contemplation from that awakened by the ethereal music of Palestrina.

The same tendency is to be remarked in Catholic Austria and southern Germany. Even Johann Joseph Fux, "the Austrian Palestrina of the Eighteenth Century," whose tendencies were mainly conservative and whose *Gradus ad Parnassum* remained one of the principal texts for the study of the older counterpoint until Beethoven's day, produced concerted Masses. J. K. Kerll, whose connection with the beginnings of opera in Munich has already been noted, adopted the same style. It is only when the aim is spectacular rather than expressive, however, that the use of the concerted style is to be regretted. It is clear that the opposition of solo and *tutti* which constitutes the concerto can be made the vehicle of profound expression as well as of mere magnificence. And since the greatest of German religious music is based on the fervent melodic idiom of the Protestant hymn, the gradual adoption of the concerted style is altogether commendable. It is in Protestant rather than Catholic Germany, however, that the greatest achievements are to be expected; and it is in other forms than the Mass that the greatest interest will naturally be manifested.

But in spite of the fact that Protestantism denied the miraculous transubstantiation of the bread and wine of the sacrament into the actual body and blood of Christ—that miracle which forms the supreme moment in the Catholic service—the liturgical text itself offered no real ground of doctrinal dispute. It was therefore not merely because Bach served two masters—the Protestant Thomaskirche in Leipzig and the Catholic Prince August III of Saxony—but because it gave opportunity for the fullest expression of his religious convictions, that he chose to produce what is probably the greatest choral work ever written, the Mass in B minor. He wrote four other Masses, of such dimensions that they might be used in the service; but this one is so vast as to be practicable only when sung independently. It is an idealization of the whole meaning of the service, rather than a direct liturgical setting of the service; and offers the most comprehensive view of the religious soul of the composer to be found in any of his works. The choruses are mostly for five voices. Heaviness is avoided by the judicious interspersion of solos or duets, Bach's favorite obbligato instrument, the violin, being given in several of the solos a most significant part. The orchestra, in spite of the intricacy of the voice parts, is largely independent, giving a richness of polyphony which is almost incomparable. Yet there is here no thought of the mere piling up of intricacies, since every part, orchestral or vocal, has its definite purpose in the expression of the idea. In its sheer mastery of the technique of composition the whole work is marvelous; but it is evident that the display of musical science is a matter of small concern to the composer. The religious attitude to be revealed is really Bach's only concern. This, by comparison with the attitude of Palestrina (or, as we shall see, of Beethoven) is extremely interesting. We have noted the unworldly, mystical feeling with which Palestrina imbued the whole service. His music is so exalted as to be almost removed from the plane of worldly emotion. Bach, on the other hand—a Lutheran, of course, and sharing to the full that awareness of immediate personal relation to God upon which Luther chiefly insisted —interpreted the Catholic text in the light of his own belief; while abating nothing in reverence he suffused the whole Mass with a sense, now profound, now almost childlike in its literalness, of the human meaning of the Christian mysteries.

It is only in the remotest degree, for instance, that the sense of sin can be said to be suggested by Palestrina in the opening phrases of the Mass (*Kyrie eleison*—"Lord, have mercy"). But Bach, the Protestant, without a preparatory note, makes his chorus and orchestra burst out with an impassioned plea, terrible in its intensity and bitter beyond belief in its consciousness of sin. The great five-part fugue which follows is similarly weighted, although phrases are not wanting, in the episodes, to suggest the assurance that grace is attainable.

The most vivid expressions of joy or grief are alternated in the following minute discussions of each phrase which goes to make up the text.
The *Gloria* begins with a swift and joyous movement underneath whose
gladsome exterior a tone of true fervency is apparent; while *et in terra pax*
is equally vivid in its sense of the blessing of peace. *Qui tollis peccata
mundi* is set to music of indescribable tenderness, and the *miserere nobis*
in the same movement is pitiful in its dejection. The opening of the *Credo*
has as subject a phrase from the Gregorian chant, to which the words
Credo in unum Deum had been sung from time immemorial. Against this,
which he reiterates in the most bewildering array of imitations, Bach
makes in the orchestral bass a firm and stately counterpoint, mightily
assured in its tone of unwavering faith. *Et incarnatus est* is sung in strange,
hushed harmonies which reveal how deep was the hold upon Bach's unquestioning mind of the mystery of the incarnation; and the *Crucifixus*,
with its tortured accents of pity and awe, stands almost alone in the literature of human agony. The joyousness of the *Et resurrexit* which follows
is in complete contrast, but its tone is equally direct and literal in acceptance of the contemplated fact. The *Sanctus* is perhaps the crowning glory
of the work. The Chorus (now in six parts) has strains of the utmost
exaltation against an almost homophonic orchestral accompaniment, its
sense of high adoration again contrasting with the pathos of the *Agnus
Dei* which follows. Some of the movements are borrowed from cantatas:
the *Qui tollis*, for instance, being taken from the cantata *Schauet doch
und sehet*, and the *Crucifixus* from *Weinen, Klagen, Sorgen, Zagen.* But
although the original application of the music was sometimes to words
not closely related to those of the Latin text, Bach manages to make the
music fit so perfectly the new meaning that it is difficult to imagine that
it ever had any other association. Thus, even more than the *St. Matthew*
Passion, the Mass in B minor—since it is not cumbered with narrative nor
with physical illustration, but deals with the very essence of religious
feeling—offers the clearest revelation of the devout mind of its composer
and his age.

THE MOTET

This form is a direct inheritance from the preceding age. The unaccompanied chorus was becoming infrequent, owing to the gradual adoption of the concerted style; but the motet remained unaccompanied, only
borrowing from the more complex forms something of their intricacy of
substance. That division of the old form into sections, each having a new
fugal exposition of its subject matter suggested by the new phrase of the
text, had evolved into a succession of separate movements as in the analogous instrumental form of the church sonata. The large number of

voices (usually eight) for which it was written gave opportunity also for the use of structural features analogous to those of the concerto. Thus the motet may be regarded as a sort of concerto for unaccompanied voices. Bach wrote many examples, as did all his predecessors and contemporaries. Only a few of Bach's motets have survived; but these, like his other great works, show the singular individuality of his mind. They were among the few of his compositions to remain in favor immediately after his death. Their performance became a tradition with the choir of the Thomas Church; and it was due to this practice, and to his few published compositions, that Bach's name was not completely forgotten during the sharp transition of style that followed his death. The motet *Singet dem Herrn ein neues Lied* ("Sing unto the Lord a new Song") is perhaps the greatest of Bach's works in this form, as it is certainly the supreme test of the abilities of an unaccompanied choir.

THE SONG

Since singing is the most immediate and natural of musical expressions, the song, in the largest sense, is at the foundation of all the history of musical thought. But the term *song* is more properly applied to music set to an independent lyric poem, with a subordinate accompaniment; and of such compositions but few examples can be found before the present period of our study. That great contributions to the ultimate literature of the song had been made by the troubadours and by their German musical brethren the Minnesinger and the Meistersinger is not to be doubted. But for these the art of accompaniment was lacking. Hence, it was not until the monodic Revolution, which brought with it the concept of the figured bass with its attendant harmonic suggestions, that the song in the modern sense could come into existence. It was not in Italy or France, where social and artistic conventions of an elaborate sort governed the development of monody, but in Germany (and to some extent in England) where local and national traditions remained more natural and unaffected, that the song had its origin.

That strong impulse to individual utterance which found voice in the Protestant hymn was not far removed from the impulse which naturally gave rise to the song. The rendition of madrigals and similar compositions by a single voice, the other parts being supplied by instruments—a frequent occurrence during the sixteenth century—needed only to become simplified by the reduction of the polyphonic accompaniment to simple harmonic proportions to give a sufficient hint of the necessary technique in song composition. But in Italy this technique remained the property of musicians whose interest was largely devoted to the music drama. Hence it was in Germany, where the new method was somewhat divorced from its immediate association with the opera, that the true song impulse—already expressed in the hymn—found outlet. It is not strange, then, to find Heinrich Albert (1604–1651), a cousin of Heinrich Schütz and something of a poet, devoting himself to the musical expression of his lyric fancy. His songs (or *Arias*, as the eight volumes are entitled) derive musically from the hymn and from the dance song, both of which were a product of natural, popular feeling. Perhaps because he had not before him the conventional A–B–A form of the operatic aria (which had not as yet become crystallized), his songs show a singular disposition to follow the natural course of the verbal idea, and to model their musical form after the pattern thus suggested.

In any case, the constantly changing *durchkomponirtes Lied* is clearly foreshadowed. Albert's initiative was followed by other German composers, especially in Hamburg where Johann Rist and Johann Schop, Scheidemann, Hammerschmidt, and Staden produced before 1670 a considerable literature of the song. In other cities also the form was popular —Dresden, Nuremberg, Cologne, and others showing a conspicuous production. The invasion of Italian opera and its methods, however, which took place toward the end of the century, seems to have swept aside the song as an important form. Singers now preferred to exhibit their powers in the cultivated arias of the Italians, or in imitations of them. The songs of Adam Krieger, Johann Wolfgang Franck, and Georg Böhm continued to reflect the simple German taste; but in this field as in many another, there was beginning to be felt the force of a musical tide which Johann Sebastian Bach himself was not able to stem, and which after his death almost obliterated the sturdy polyphony which had its deepest roots in German Protestantism.

In England, collections of solo songs appeared as early as 1600, Morley, Ford, Campion (also a significant poet), and others showing a clear sense of the musical suggestion inherent in the exceptionally rich lyric literature of the Elizabethans. In the ensuing period in which the Masque had its heyday, the amateur as well as the finished and schooled composer had his opportunity. Even the influence of the French style, brought to England in all its brilliancy by Pelham Humphrey, could not wholly uproot the typically English sentiment which had found expression in the earlier songs; and Purcell, the greatest musical dramatist of his time, left many examples which show not only his own incomparable musicianship but also the great vitality of popular sentiment which inspired them. Nor did the love of the song succumb, as in Germany, to the superior brilliancy of the aria. *The Beggar's Opera*, whose tunes were English, was popular enough to start a strong reaction against even so Anglicized a product as the opera of Handel.

The song is not necessarily for a solo voice. Duets especially are frequent in the compositions of Albert and other German composers. In England, from the very beginning of the development of the true song, there was produced a characteristically English product, the *Catch*. This was originally a round or canon for three or more voices unaccompanied. The trick or *catch* lay in the singer's problem of finding out where to enter, in imitation of voices already started; for the music was read from a single part. A later element in the catch was introduced through the use of words in which a double meaning or "catch" was involved. Something of the same character is to be found also in the later *Glees;* but this name applies properly to a later type of composition, less intricate in structure and more purely popular in sentiment.

This and the preceding chapter will give the reader a fairly comprehensive view of the range of musical thought at the beginning of the eighteenth century. There is here a far greater variety of musical forms than we shall find to be current at the end of the century—the "classical" period of Haydn and Mozart. Then, as we shall more clearly see, the earlier forms of overture, church sonata, chamber sonata, fantasia, and variation will all contribute to and merge in the more flexible and expressively inclusive form of the classical sonata. But the basis of this classical sonata is homophonic, not polyphonic. A second "monodic revolution," in the field of instrumental music, will then be found to have occurred. Some hint of forces tending in this direction has already been given in the description of the polyphonic forms. The directness and simplicity of melody in the aria, together with the principle of harmonic rather than purely contrapuntal structure, were adopted, as the sense of key became clearer and as far as the forms allowed, into the polyphony of Bach and his contemporaries. Bach, more fully than Handel, represents the culmination of the polyphonic tradition. The foregoing description of forms, therefore, has in several cases been made to lead up to a view of the particular treatment of the form which was peculiar to Bach. Handel, although he was in some respects as gigantic a figure as Bach, represented another phase of musical thought. He was essentially a musical dramatist, although at the same time he was a follower of the same polyphonic tradition as Bach, and had further to adapt his style to English ears. The following chapter will therefore present a comparative view of Bach and Handel, in so far as these two men are comparable, and will show the relation of Handel's dramatic work to that of the Neapolitan school from which it derives.

CHAPTER XVIII

Bach and Handel

O F Bach's life less is known than of the career of any other supremely great composer who may be called really modern. But
less needs to be known; for no other great man has had so little
of a career, or has left in his music so full a revelation of himself. Only
the most obvious of external circumstances—such as his residence in
Cöthen, where he was without religious duties—had any influence on his
work. He seems to have been remarkably unconcerned with success.
There was in him no envy, no shallow personal ambition, no possibility
of equivocal dealing which might bring him worldly advantage. To him,
as he said himself, music was "nothing else than the glory of God and
pleasant recreations. Where this object is not kept in view there can be
no music, but only an infernal scraping and bawling." To understand
how he conceived this "glory of God," and to enter into the "pleasant
recreations" in which he felt it justifiable to indulge, is to comprehend the
man; for in his view little else was of importance.

The greater part of his work was indeed made "to the glory of God"—
his vast literature of cantatas, Passions, Masses, and motets. In its utter
sincerity, this music is of course more than an expression of the mind of
Bach himself. It is a revelation of the religious spirit of his age: of the
literal and often childlike acceptance of doctrines and beliefs which no
man could hold unquestioned today. In this sense his music is a historical document of the highest value and authenticity; for it underlies and
antecedes all doctrinal squabblings, and reveals the very attitude of belief.
When we consider his secular music we find that the "pleasant recreations" of such a mind as Bach's are often startlingly severe. But they are
by no means always so, and this music reveals a gaiety of spirit and a
wealth of honest sentiment which could proceed only out of a mind profoundly human in its sympathies. Such universal understanding is the first
requisite of the great artist in any age; but to have given enduring expres-

sion to all this understanding in an age when the art of music had hardly come to maturity was an achievement of the very highest order. Schumann spoke but the sober truth when he said that the art of music owes almost as much to Bach as religion owes to its Founder.

Only the barest recital of the facts of Bach's life is possible here. His musical ancestry is doubtless important (though Handel's genius, nearly if not quite as great, is without hereditary explanation); but if we take genius for granted, as we must, the question of education becomes the first essential. Although he made no mark as such, Bach must have been a prodigy. Usually the prodigy is sufficient unto himself—inordinately apt at learning the few things which attract him, impervious to many ideas which he will later have to master. But this fatal indifference to other than natural interests was not in Bach's nature. One of the first certain facts with regard to his education (the episode of the music copied by moonlight) shows the boy's insatiable thirst for other musical ideas than those which doubtless came unbidden to his brain. During all his earlier years this desire to know how other composers made music was a passion with him. No effort was too great, no journey—even on foot—too long, to be undertaken if it could give contact with new musical ideas. Bach's genius was too healthy to be self-fertilized.

Outside music, his schooling was slight. Theology, Latin, and New Testament Greek, with a little rhetoric and arithmetic, seem to have been the only subjects regularly taught in the exceptionally good "Lyceum" at Ohrdruf, where the ten-year-old boy went after the death of his parents to live with his brother. Four or five hours a week were devoted to music; and Bach was one of the principal singers in the school chorus. He soon learned all that his brother could teach him of the art of organ playing; and in 1700, when he was fifteen, he obtained admission to the school of the Convent of St. Michael at Lüneberg. Here, his voice failing, he played organ, harpsichord, or violin as was needed, and was no longer a dependent. Both instrumental and vocal music then were objects of careful study. Here he met Georg Böhm, an organist who had worked at Hamburg under Reinken, and who was especially interested in the French music of the day. Böhm not only interested the boy as a composer; he made him acquainted with the French style (which, however, is scarcely traceable in Bach's extant work, the so-called *French* Suites having no relation to this style) and stimulated his curiosity with regard to the music to be heard in Hamburg and in Celle where there was a famous court band.

At eighteen, Bach took his first really professional position—that of organist at Arnstadt. Here he began to compose in earnest. At the same time, he continued his excursions to other musical centers—this time to

Lübeck, fifty miles from Arnstadt, where was the famous Danish organist Buxtehude, whose *Abendmusiken* (vesper services in Advent) were famous. His curiosity seems to have outrun his sense of duty, for he prolonged a four weeks' leave of absence to four months and had rather awkward explanations to make to the consistory of his church when he returned. Just what he did in Lübeck is unknown; but that he absorbed much from Buxtehude's music is evident, especially in the dark richness of his later chromatic harmony; for Buxtehude's chromaticism was remarkable. His stay in Arnstadt was short, as was also his tenure of the position of organist at St. Blasius's Church in Mühlhausen. Here he married a distant cousin, Maria Barbara Bach, and wrote a remarkable cantata *Gott ist mein König* which was performed early in 1708. The power and maturity of this work are striking. Already at twenty-two Bach seems to have acquired complete mastery of the problems of composition, and exhibits at the same time a sense of effect, both in the choral writing and in the instrumentation, which is altogether individual. But before a year had been lived at Mühlhausen, the position of court organist at Weimar (where Bach had been for a short time a member of the band and a personal servant of the Duke's brother) fell vacant. Bach applied for and obtained the position; and with this removal the preparatory stage of his work was ended.

THE WEIMAR PERIOD

Duke William, Bach's patron, was a man of earnest mind; and there were several musicians of distinction resident in Weimar, such as Walther, organist at the town church, and Drese, the court Kapellmeister. Consequently organ music and the church cantata occupied Bach's attention almost exclusively during this period. The smaller keyboard instruments, the harpsichord and clavichord, were not neglected, however; and it was doubtless the court band which stimulated him to the study of the concertos of Vivaldi—an interest which bore mighty fruit in the shape of the Brandenburg Concertos written later at Cöthen. Such mature and original works as the Toccata and Fugue in D minor for organ, or the wonderful cantata *God's Time Is Best*, show how rapidly the already notable powers of the Mühlhausen genius were expanding.

The Weimar cantatas are especially interesting. The manner is still altogether German, the Italian influence which was gradually seeping into all the musical life of Germany being as yet largely unfelt. The *da capo* aria, therefore, and the somewhat excessive use of ornament which Bach later adopted, do not appear; the music is direct and forceful in diction, and completely absorbed in the contemplation of the idea to be expressed. The solos are usually made out of the repetition of a few melodic phrases, set in a very expressive relation to the few phrases of text. The accompaniments similarly consist of definite figures, polyphonically combining with the voice, so that the whole song is closely woven. In both solos and choruses every opportunity for direct musical illustration is seized, the resultant suggestion sometimes provoking a momentary smile by its naïveté. In *God's Time*, for instance, the words "in Him we live and move and have our being" are set to music whose lively motion and apparently secular character are almost disconcertingly frank; but when we hear the tremendous admonition "And in Him we die," the earlier suggestion is amply justified by the vivid contrast. In many respects, the cantatas are adaptations to sacred purposes of the methods and styles of the opera. Neumeister, the author of many of the texts which Bach set, says that "a *cantata* seems to be nothing else than a portion of an *opera* composed of *stylo recitativo* and arie together." The Pietists opposed this introduction of worldly style into church music; but the Orthodox sect (the followers of Luther were already divided over doctrinal questions) welcomed it. Although his religious sentiments were with the Pietists, it was naturally to the Orthodox group that Bach officially belonged, as did Duke William and the Weimar court.

The Cöthen Period

In 1717, for uncertain reasons, Bach accepted an offer of the Kappellmeistership at the court of Prince Leopold of Anhalt-Cöthen. Here he had no relation to the church, and devoted himself almost wholly to the composition of instrumental music, largely exclusive of that for the organ. The smaller keyboard instruments, the violin, the violoncello, the flute, and the orchestra are all studied in their minutest detail; it might almost be said that the foundations of modern instrumental literature were laid by Bach during his six years' residence at Cöthen. One might think that he foresaw, for instance, the vast popularity which the piano was to attain. His children were beginning to grow up, and Bach began to think out a practical method of teaching the clavichord and the harpsichord, not only for them but for other pupils who eagerly sought his instruction. A more rational use of the fingers was first devised. The thumb had been avoided as far as possible in the systems of fingering in vogue until Bach's time, the longer fingers being passed over the shorter, instead of the thumb being passed under the hand. This Bach corrected; and although the great French clavecinist Couperin adopted the same attitude, it may be said that Bach is one of the founders of the modern system of fingering.

Technical problems were hidden under a musical exterior attractive to youth in the *Clavier-Büchlein* ("Little Clavier Book") written for his son

Wilhelm Friedemann. This contains little preludes, chorale arrangements, and dances which presently lead up to simple fugues. Out of this beginning grew the familiar *Inventions* in two and three parts (Bach called the three-part Inventions *Sinfonien*) which are usually the first pieces by Bach with which the modern student becomes acquainted.[1] The suite form was dealt with in three sets of six dance collections: the French Suites, the English Suites, and the Partitas. These latter are sometimes called *German Suites;* but geographical titles mean nothing as to the character of the music. The crowning achievement of the Cöthen period is the first volume of the *Well-Tempered Clavichord*, containing twenty-four preludes and Fugues, one in each major and minor key. The system of equal temperament is here vigorously championed; but this merely mechanical aspect of the work is of little significance in comparison to its musical value. It was not without reason that Von Bülow spoke of the *Well-Tempered Clavichord* and the Beethoven Sonatas as "the Old and the New Testaments of the pianist's literature."

Equally remarkable with the piano music is that for the violin. The six Sonatas for violin solo (three of them are church sonatas, and three are suites) still stand alone as marvels of composition for the unaccompanied violin. The technical demands—aside from the fact that the highest positions were never used in Bach's day—are as great and as diversified as in the later virtuoso literature, while the musical interest, as always, remains the first consideration. The *Chaconne*, which is appended to the Suite in D minor (usually listed as Sonata No. 4) is incredible in its reduction, to the capacity of four strings, of musical ideas worthy of any later symphony. Not even the Finale of Brahms's Fourth Symphony (which is also essentially a *Chaconne*) is more weighty in meaning. There are also six Sonatas for violin with accompaniment. These are essentially trio sonatas, the violin having one part, the piano, two. For the violoncello (or the *viola pomposa,* a large and sonorous viola which Bach is said to have invented) he wrote six unaccompanied Suites, and for the viola da gamba, three accompanied Sonatas. The three Flute Sonatas approach the concerto form, being in three movements instead of four, with plural subject matter; but the clavier is also a solo instrument, not the mere counterpart of the *tutti*. The true concerto form is employed in many examples for solo violin, one for two violins, seven for clavier (three of which were originally violin concertos), three for two

---

[1] Unfortunately these seem to be almost universally regarded as mere finger exercises. Their musical value, however, is very high; and it is a pity that such a marvel of construction and expression as the *Sinfonia* in F minor (No. 9) should not be used to give the student an introduction to the wonderful world of chromatic harmony in which Bach dwelt.

claviers, two for three and one for four claviers (the last being an arrangement of a Concerto for four violins by Vivaldi). An exceptional work is the so-called *Italian* Concerto for clavier alone—the characteristics of solo and *tutti* being conveyed by contrasting the two different dynamic powers of the two manuals of the harpsichord. Greatest of all Bach's works in the concerto form are the Brandenburg Concertos—*concerti grossi* all of them, and each written for a different instrumental group. Not all the works above referred to were written at Cöthen; but the later examples are obviously the result of the stimulus to instrumental composition which was so strongly aroused there.

The Leipzig Period

Partly owing to a decline in his patron's musical enthusiasm, and partly because Bach had begun again to long for opportunity to work out more fully vast projects of religious composition, he left Cöthen in 1723 and settled in Leipzig. Here he produced the major part of his great collection of cantatas, the B minor Mass, the *St. Matthew* Passion, the Magnificat, many motets, and some secular cantatas. Several of these works have already been discussed.

Gradual changes in style are apparent during the three periods represented by his residence in Weimar, Cöthen, and Leipzig. Some idea of the differences may be gained from a comparison of the two parts of the *Well-Tempered Clavichord,* dating from 1722 and 1744. In the earlier portion there is no immaturity; but a greater play of fancy and a more abundant romanticism (the word is entirely justifiable) are to be seen here than in the later collection. In this respect, there is nothing in the later book to compare with the Preludes in C sharp minor, E flat minor, or B flat minor; while on the other hand, there is a sterner maturity as well as a more tender grace and a more philosophic tone observable in such examples as the Fugues in G minor, F minor, and B minor from the second book. In a general way this same difference in the point of view is perceptible, not only in the *Well-Tempered Clavichord* but in all the earlier and the later music. Interest in freer instrumental design may be noted in the more frequent use of the two-part form of the suite dance or chamber sonata movement in ten of the Preludes of Book II, as compared with but one in the earlier work. On the whole, however, little concern is manifested with contemporary fashions or tendencies. The changes in style or character come from within, and not from without; yet they represent an ever clearer comprehension of the essential feeling qualities which it is the business of music to express, and consequently reveal the composer's complete contact with the world in which he lived.

To him more truly than to any other musician it is possible to apply the wise observation, "the style is the man."

If Bach transmuted all the experience of life into musical language which was largely of his own contriving, Handel's musical thought was both largely and subtly influenced by the great variety of experience which his active life provided. We do not mean to imply that Bach was a visionary. His circumstances compelled him to be practical, and his earnest desire was to give of his best in meeting his practical obligations; but he seems never to have been aware of the immediate advantages to himself which could be gained by propitiating his public. Handel, on the other hand, seems almost to have drawn the breath of musical life from his public. Such sensitivity to public desire—coupled of course with enormous creative powers—might be expected to produce a more enduring impression on public taste than Bach's attitude of unconscious indifference. Yet it so happened that while Handel's fame endured, at any rate in England, without much diminution, his work remained a monument of achievement rather than a stimulus to creation for succeeding generations. But Bach, forgotten for almost a century, was rediscovered at the beginning of the Romantic period; and so vital was the current of his thought that it became in many respects the source and inspiration of what was best in nineteenth-century music. He has again been rediscovered by the ultramoderns, who look to him as their model, just as did the once ultramodern romanticists.

HANDEL'S EARLY LIFE

Handel was the son of a surgeon who had begun life as a barber and had won, by his own efforts, the position of Groom of the Chamber and Private Surgeon to the Duke of Saxony. The musical propensities of little George Frederick were viewed with great disfavor by his father, who had no mind to allow the advantages which he had won to be dissipated by a son who had no more sense of worldly values than to choose the career of a musician. For this beloved child of his old age (the father was sixty-three when Handel was born) the career of jurist had been intended from the beginning. The boy's precocity was so great however that the father was forced to yield; but it is not unreasonable to suppose that something of his father's worldly astuteness was implanted, both by heredity and by instruction, in the mind of his son. Three years of incredibly intense study with Zachau (or Zachow), organist of the Liebfrauenkirche in Halle, gave Handel a thorough grounding in composition. Distrust of the favors of the great as well as awareness of their value had been developed in the father; and we find him refusing for his son an offer to complete his education in Italy and to provide him with a position at court on his return. The father died in 1697, when Handel was twelve years old. In 1702 he matriculated at the University of Halle as a student of law; but his interest in his studies was sadly diminished by his acceptance of the post of organist at the Schlosskirche, where his duties, as well as his attention to the work of a voluntary choir which he formed among the students, kept his mind fully occupied. He soon saw that neither his native village nor his reluctantly chosen vocation could give occupation for his greatest talents; and in 1703 he departed for Hamburg, where the wealth of the city as well as the already conspicuous achievements of the Opera seemed to offer the greatest opportunities for self-instruction and personal advantage.

Here he immediately made friends with the most active and important figures in the operatic world, especially with Mattheson, whose versatility as composer, singer, cembalist, and writer placed him in a position second only to that of Keiser, the talented but now dissipated director of the opera. From Mattheson, Handel seems to have learned much about the operatic style, for which his earlier contrapuntal training had scarcely fitted him. Already in the autumn of 1704 he had succeeded to the conductor's chair at the opera, in place of Keiser, and in January, 1705, produced the opera *Almira*, the libretto of which had been given him by Keiser himself, now too busy or too indifferent to set it to music. This and another opera, *Nero*, not only established his fame in Hamburg but suggested that Handel's talents might be welcomed in a larger field. Through a disfavored scion of the Medici family then in exile at Hamburg, Handel was given introductions to the Grand Duke, Cosmo III, and especially to the Gran Principe, Ferdinand, an ardent music lover, and traveled to Florence in the summer of 1706.

THE NEAPOLITAN SCHOOL OF OPERA

Here Handel produced his first real Italian opera, *Rodrigo*. The same rapid assimilation of a new style which he had shown in Hamburg was seen in this and in the other opera, *Agrippina* (produced in Venice in 1709) which, together with certain essays in the style of the oratorio, were written during his Italian sojourn. The ruling style in Italy in those days was that which had been developed in Naples. In our discussion of the beginnings of Italian opera we traced its development at the hands of Monteverdi, Cavalli, Cesti, and Legrenzi, only to a point where the original Venetian supremacy had waned in favor of the new methods of the Neapolitans. The Neapolitan style—which is largely that of Alessandro Scarlatti—must now be discussed; not only because it is the style which

Handel chiefly absorbed, but because it remained, throughout a long period of decadence, the ruling style in Europe (at any rate outside France) until the great "reform" of the opera at the hands of Gluck.

The importance of Naples as a center of music began in the middle of the fifteenth century when Johannes Tinctoris, an important composer and a still more important theorist, founded the first school of music in that city. This short-lived school was immediately succeeded by four "Conservatories," whose name suggests their original purpose—that of asylums for homeless orphans. Schooling as well as shelter was provided; and music, which at first formed but a small part of the instruction, came gradually to occupy a principal place. As time went on eminent musicians became associated with the conservatories, which became centers of discussion of musical principles as well as centers of training for brilliant performance.

The first Neapolitan to extend the current dramatic style of the seventeenth century beyond the limits reached by Cavalli and Cesti was Francesco Provenzale, the teacher of Alessandro Scarlatti. The original purpose of dramatic music—to render in musical terms the immediate sense of the text—had been supplanted, even by Monteverdi, and more extensively by Cavalli and others, by a more general purpose: that of giving through music intensification to the general emotional sense rather than to the words themselves. The gradual definition of the aria as distinct from the recitative was palpably a product of musical rather than dramatic thought; and this elevation of the musical element to a position of predominance was fully characteristic of the work of Alessandro Scarlatti. General emotional character, together with a higher degree of purely musical satisfaction, was given, at the expense of fragmentary musical emphasis of mere text-detail. And of course the satisfying of the musical desire of the operatic public could be accomplished only through a simple musical form, such as was exemplified in the highest degree by the aria.

With Alessandro Scarlatti, therefore, the A–B–A or *da capo* aria became stereotyped and was used without exception for the expression of the highest moments of feeling in the drama. It must not be inferred, however, that, because the arias had the same form throughout, they had also the same character. The most diverse passions can be embodied in the same general form, just as the most diverse types of dance measure can be cast in the form of the dance suite. This variety of expressive character indeed was the basis of distinction between such different types as the *aria cantabile*, tender or pathetic, and simply accompanied; the *aria di portamento*, in a more measured rhythm, dignified rather than passionate; the *aria di mezzo carattere*, including a great variety of not very definite emotional suggestions; the *aria parlante*, which, as its tone became more intense, was called *aria agitata, aria di strepito,* or *aria infuriata;* and, most brilliant of all, the *aria di bravura* or *d'agilità,* in which the singer's technical powers were fully displayed and which was always counted on to bring down the house. There was also the *aria d'imitazione,* in which the old ideal of music exactly suited to words was maintained in the shape of the imitation of natural sounds; and—almost the sole departure from aria form allowed by the conventions—the *cavatina,* which merely corresponds to the A-section of the aria without the following B–A.

To cast the poetic substance of a drama into such form that every significant moment of the action should be embodied in an aria was an almost impossible task. Yet the demand of operatic audiences for this type of singing was so insatiable that it became the rule that every scene throughout the opera should terminate with an aria. (A new scene, according to the continental conventions, begins whenever an actor comes on or leaves the stage.) Two arias of the same character might not succeed each other, nor might the same singer sing two in succession. The essential narrative connection between the arias was in the shape of recitative. Out of the old *stilo rappresentativo* of Peri and Caccini, Monteverdi and his successors had contrived a more moving sort of musical speech; and this was now diversified, especially by Scarlatti, into two styles: the *recitativo secco* or "dry recitative,"—accompanied by the harpsichord only—almost unmelodic and following as far as possible the declamatory accent of the words; and the *recitativo stromentato* accompanied by the orchestra, which had a middle place in musical interest between the dry recitative and the aria. The essence of these distinctions, as also the essential outline of the aria form, is to be found in the work of Monteverdi; but no such clearly organized or exclusive prescription for the use of the various forms would have been tolerated by him.

This whole convention, it will be seen, gave the composer and the singer very much the upper hand over the dramatist and the actor. That there might be agreeable variety in the voices, without too much confusion, the number of personages in the opera was conventionally established at six —three women and three men. The *prima donna* (first woman) was a high soprano, and one of the other two a contralto. The *primo uomo* (first man) was an artificial soprano no matter how masculine his role, the second an artificial contralto, and the third a natural tenor. It was allowable to have a seventh principal personage; in such cases the bass voice was generally employed. When we add to these restrictions whatever of existing convention was still borrowed from the highly artificial spoken drama of the time, it is easy to understand that the opera was moving in a direction quite opposite to that ideal of dramatic intensification which

Peri and Caccini had conceived. Yet in spite of the conventions Scarlatti and his contemporaries, Stradella and Francesco Rossi in Naples, Caldara and Lotti in Venice, and Bononcini in Bologna and later in London, produced operatic music which not only appealed to the multitude but which has many moments of true dramatic character. We have already spoken of the Italian overture, also to a large extent conventionalized as to form by Scarlatti.

This strange art form, the opera, which Handel learned to know in Italy, he proceeded to introduce, not to his native Germany, but to England. It will be seen that Handel's absorption with music is very different from that of Bach, who in 1710 was at Weimar making music to the glory of God.

Handel in London—His Operatic Ventures

Handel's cordial reception in Italy, and especially the unprecedented success of *Agrippina* which ran for twenty-seven nights in Venice, gave occasion for an offer of the Kapellmeistership at the court of Hanover. Permission to visit England was also involved in the contract; and after a short stay in Hanover Handel accepted the invitations he had received from prominent Englishmen in Italy and went to London late in 1710. After the failure of Purcell's efforts to make opera in the tradition of the English drama, the form had languished until, in 1705, Clayton's *Arsinoë*, produced "after the Italian manner, all sung," had revived the art. The first performances of Italian opera were sung either in English or, as was the fashion in Germany, with the recitatives in the vernacular and the arias in Italian. Just before Handel's arrival, performances entirely in Italian had been given—"the town," as Addison observed, "tired of understanding but half of the entertainment having determined to understand none of it." Handel was commissioned to write an opera, and produced *Rinaldo* in two weeks. In spite of the acid criticism of Addison and Steele the work was a huge success, and Italian opera was now firmly established in popular favor.

Handel's personal success was great. It is interesting to find him participating in the extraordinary Thursday concerts of Thomas Britton, "the small-coal man," which took place in his diminutive garret over the coal cellar. Duchesses crawled up the crazy ladder leading to his concert room, which was thus celebrated by the doggerel poet Ned Ward, a near neighbor and intimate friend of Britton's:—

> Upon Thursdays repair
> To my palace, and there
> Hobble up stair by stair;
> But I pray ye take care
> That you break not your shin by a stumble.

Thither Handel often went, as Hawkins tells us, playing both harpsichord and organ and directing the performance to the delight of the audience who, as Ward vivaciously observed, were "willing to take a hearty Sweat that they might have the Pleasure of hearing many notable Performances in the charming Science of Musick." Handel gave no other concerts during this visit; but this evidence of his geniality and independence of spirit is proof that his success in opera had by no means turned his head. He returned to Hanover in June, 1711, and remained in service to the Elector until 1712, when he again obtained leave of absence for another visit to England.

Opera, he found, was already beginning to languish; but Handel produced two works, *Il Pastor Fido* and *Teseo*, the latter of which was again a success; and he was asked to compose an ode in honor of Queen Anne's birthday and a Te Deum and Jubilate commemorating the Peace of Utrecht. The latter were performed on the 7th of July, 1713. The Queen gave him a pension of £200; and Handel was thus induced to prolong his already excessive leave of absence. In August, 1714, the good Queen Anne suddenly died; and the successor to her throne was no other than George, the Elector of Hanover, Handel's flouted and aggrieved patron. That Handel was restored to favor through the famous *Water Music* is doubtless a mere legend—but one that it is harmless to enjoy. At any rate, Queen Anne's pension was not only continued but was soon augmented to £600, and in 1716 Handel accompanied his sovereign on a visit to Hanover. Here he wrote the *Brockes Passion*, his last work in the German tongue. It is in the general style of the German Passion music; but the unquestioning sincerity which Bach infused into the subject is lacking, essentially in the text,[2] which is nonbiblical, and also in the music, which reveals the attitude of a man far more in touch with the world than was Bach.

Returning to England early in 1717, Handel found that interest in opera had again waned. At the invitation of the Duke of Chandos, he established himself at the Duke's magnificent palace of Canons in Edgeware (then just outside London) where he wrote the remarkable series of *Chandos Anthems*, his first English oratorio *Esther* (the text is an adaptation of Racine's drama), and the so-called serenata *Acis and Galatea*, from which comes the famous bravura aria *O Ruddier Than the Cherry*. But the longing for opera awoke again, and a stock company called *The Royal Academy of Music* was formed for the production of Italian opera at the King's Theatre in the Haymarket. Handel, Bononcini, and Ariosti were

---

[2] Bach's *St. John* Passion was also set to Brockes's text; but Bach made many substitutions of biblical words for the doggerel verse, and considerably emended the portions he retained.

the musical directors. Handel went to the Continent to engage singers, and left Halle, where he had gone to visit his mother, just in time to miss a visit from Bach who, unfortunately unheralded, had traveled the forty miles to pay his respects to his renowned contemporary.

HANDEL'S LATER LIFE—HIS ORATORIOS

Now began a time of feverish activity. Bononcini's graceful tunes captivated the English public more completely than Handel's weightier arias; rivalry was engendered between the supporters of the two composers and of the famous singers Faustina and Cuzzoni. As a result the Academy collapsed, its deathblow being dealt by the success of the *Beggar's Opera* in 1727. Handel, undaunted, took over the management of a new operatic venture which he kept alive for ten years in spite of even more vigorous opposition than the Academy had encountered—since it was headed by no less a composer than Niccolo Porpora, a Neapolitan rival of Scarlatti, and was supported by the glorious voice of Senesino, who had formerly been a member of Handel's company. His Herculean efforts were of no avail, however; and in 1737 he went to Aix-la-Chapelle suffering from brain trouble, with his right hand paralyzed, and with his comfortable fortune swallowed up in bankruptcy. He had found that the form of art in which he had most profoundly believed was, to the English public, no more than a social diversion. Recovering completely from his illness, he set about repaying his creditors. A kind of dramatic music which was neither opera nor oratorio was produced, the first two examples being *Saul* and the colossal *Israel in Egypt*. But these had no success. The fickle London public would have none of him, and he turned to Ireland, whence many cordial invitations had come.

For this visit he had composed, to the libretto of his friend Charles Jennens, the oratorio *The Messiah*. This was produced in Dublin in 1742, with such success that when he returned to England his fame was already considerably re-established. But *The Messiah* proved less successful in England than it had been in Ireland; nor did *Hercules*, a secular oratorio, and *Belshazzar*, a sacred piece of high rank, serve to restore his former position. Inexplicable enmity of the great who had once been his supporters frustrated every attempt to regain public favor, and in 1745 he was again declared a bankrupt. But the final defeat of the Jacobites at the Battle of Culloden gave to Handel an opportunity for its celebration in the oratorio *Judas Maccabeus*, which is really a celebration of the hero of Culloden, the Duke of Cumberland. It was not the aristocracy, however, but the overjoyed English public which acclaimed Handel's music with almost as much enthusiasm as it had the victory itself. The work was produced in April, 1747, and from that time on Handel's star was in the ascendant. *Joshua, Solomon, Susanna, Theodora,* and *Jephthah* followed each other with the usual rapidity. In 1751 his sight became seriously affected; three operations were submitted to, but in vain; and in 1753 he became totally blind. His misfortune naturally occasioned much sympathy. It interfered seriously with his composition but attracted ever larger audiences to the performances of the oratorios, which he still conducted and at which he often played interludes on the organ. He died suddenly in 1759, and lies buried in the Poets' Corner in Westminster Abbey.

A greater contrast could scarcely be imagined than that between the careers of Handel and Bach. In variety of human experience, few men of genius have been richer than Handel and few, perhaps, poorer than Bach. And this difference in experience is reflected in the music of the two men. Aloof from the world, in utter sympathy with the spirit of humanity but unable to understand its baser action, Bach wrote music which is an idealization of human experience. Mingling incessantly with the world and knowing to the core its vices as well as its virtues, Handel is almost invariably the realist, seeing things and people in their true light, and speaking, in the ideal language of music, the most remarkably unadorned truth. He is sometimes trivial, sometimes noisy, sometimes even merely dull, as a man working under such pressure must be. Neither has he that longing to achieve the ideal which makes Bach slave at the task of understanding and bettering the music of his contemporaries.

The opera was a far younger art than the forms of music in which Bach wrote; but Handel has no theories as to how it may be perfected. The form and organization which he learned in Italy serve him to the end; and it is only his towering genius which can reflect a reality of life in so stilted and conventionalized a form. That form, as the history of Italian opera suggests, was cunningly devised to appeal to the generally untutored public. Handel's success was due to his instinctive preservation of that in the Italian music which was immediately striking, while at the same time his fertility of imagination and his absolute command of technique enabled him to create a musical substance both true in character and solid in structure. Although his mastery of counterpoint is comparable to Bach's, he never lost himself in polyphonic intricacy. Rather, he devised his fugue subjects in such a way that they are easily perceptible, no matter what the complexity of development; so that in immediate clarity his style is almost unapproachable. The secret of this clarity is probably in the fact that his thought was based upon a simpler concept of harmony, taken as a framework for the whole composition, than that which ordinarily underlies the work of Bach. Bach's harmony is not less logical than Handel's, and to the musician is often more stimulating. But it is also more parenthetical. Bach's harmonies arise out of, and are to some extent disguised by, the flow of the individual voices. Handel's harmonies on the other hand mostly appear as pre-established facts, to which the pattern of the voices is made to conform. Massiveness, in Bach, is achieved (as, for instance, in the *Kyrie* of the B minor Mass) by an almost bewildering multiplicity of parts. In Handel's choruses it is largely achieved by granitic chord blocks, striking out rhythmic patterns of the utmost vigor and energy. Such structure is not really polyphonic in effect, although the actual leading of the voices is never faulty or broken. It is certainly true that Handel in this respect anticipates, far more than Bach, the harmonic practice of the later eighteenth century.

It is necessary to mention one feature of Handel's music which has caused a vast amount of comment and much adverse judgment of him, both as man and artist. This is his very extensive borrowing from other composers. He not only appropriated little scraps of tune which he worked up into fugues and other forms, but sometimes took whole movements from his distinguished and even undistinguished contemporaries. Such borrowing would be both reprehensible and illegal today. In Handel's time, however, neither convention nor law forbade the practice; and Handel seemed neither to have disguised his takings nor to have resented being himself a victim. It is beyond question that he was far more capable of invention than those from whom he borrowed; and there is probably no instance (when he was not merely transplanting) in which he did not improve upon his source.[3]

Competent criticism recognizes in Handel a musician of the first rank: one who used the language of music not merely as a vehicle for the exhibition of skill, but for the expression of a vast variety of human experience. The substance of his music is indeed considerably colored by the English idiom; but of this he was probably as unaware as of the possibility that opera was in need of reform. Yet in spite of the limitations which this

[3] The world is full of puny critics who, hearing a new work for the first time, and detecting in a few notes a resemblance to some known theme, solemnly wag their heads and mutter in mock regret, "*Very* familiar!" The use to which the composer put these notes is beyond their comprehension; only the superficial resemblance strikes their minds. Does anyone suppose, for instance, that César Franck stole the principal subject of his Symphony from the C sharp minor Fugue in the *Well-Tempered Clavichord*, or that Grieg took the somber theme of *Åses Tod* from the B minor Rhapsody of Brahms, or that Brahms copied the *Emperor's Hymn* of Haydn in the last movement of his piano Sonata in F minor, or that Wagner got Hans Sach's *Der Vogel der heut' sang* from the slow movement of that same sonata? Upon such prying and talebearing, the best comment ever recorded is that of Brahms, when unnecessarily reminded that his A major Violin Sonata began with a bar from Walther's Prize Song in *Die Meistersinger: "Das sieht jeder Narr."* (Every fool can see that.)

unquestioning acceptance of current conventions imposed, and in spite of the fact that he wrote in a form no longer capable of being acceptably staged, Handel is coming to be recognized as one of the most human and most penetrating of musical dramatists. Beneath the formal exterior of his *da capo* arias there is always discoverable exactly the emotional attitude which is suggested (beneath its equally formal exterior) by the text. This is to be seen in the familiar oratorios as clearly as in the largely unknown operas. Our modern rationalism will not allow us to feel the sense of gentleness with which Handel's concept of the Christ as the Shepherd is imbued, nor his implicit confidence in the resurrection of the body; but if we have the imagination to understand what these concepts meant to Handel, we can see at once that "He shall feed His Flock," and "I know that my Redeemer liveth" express as perfectly as language ever can, a religious attitude which was with Handel a reality. The case is the same with the operas, which after all were Handel's most natural expression. It was not because of his hard-won fame, but because of his great command of the musical tongue that Handel earned the reverent admiration of Gluck and Mozart, Haydn and Beethoven.

The Great Clavecinistes—Couperin and Scarlatti

We should here consider two great contemporaries of Bach and Handel who contributed materially to piano literature. The elder of these, François Couperin (1668–1733) came of a large family of famous organists and harpsichordists. François, who so far outshone the others as to win the title "Le Grand," developed the most distinguished style in playing that had hitherto been known. This style he expounded in his *Méthode, ou l'art de toucher le clavecin,* in which the same modernity in fingering is advocated as that proposed by Bach. But his influence extended far beyond the domain of performance. The dance suite—until his time largely a reflection of the rhythms and patterns of conventional dances—takes on at his hands something of the courtly character and refinement of the ballet. Indeed, he arranged some of the dances from Lully's operas for clavecin. He often retained the descriptive titles for these pieces (such as *La Flatteuse, La Voluptueuse,* or *Fureurs bachiques*), and thus imbued his clavier music with a somewhat dramatic character. Such poetic suggestion accorded with contemporary taste, and to condemn the work as unmusical because of it, is unnecessary.

Domenico Scarlatti (1685–1757) the son of Alessandro, was an even more remarkable virtuoso. He was well known to Handel. In 1709 in Rome, Cardinal Ottoboni arranged a kind of tournament between the two. Scarlatti was adjudged the peer of Handel on the harpsichord, but his inferior on the organ. Yet Scarlatti remained, all his life, a relatively inconspicuous artist. This is largely attributable to the domination of his father who guided too assiduously the steps of his son (as did later the father of Mozart).

Under his influence Domenico wrote considerably for the church and for the stage (one of his operas was a very un-Shakespearian version of *Hamlet*), but it was only after the death of Alessandro in 1725 that his really distinctive imagination began to develop. After holding various positions in Naples and Venice, and in Rome where he became chapel-master to the Portuguese ambassador, he was called to the court of John V of Portugal. Here he taught the Princess Maria Barbara the harpsichord. She became later the Queen of Spain, and as the King, Philip V, was also a sincere music lover, Scarlatti remained in their service until his death.

It was in Madrid that the greater part of his contribution to the literature of the harpsichord was written. Ralph Kirkpatrick, his most exhaustive interpreter and biographer, lists 555 Sonatas as his known output. Of these, only 30 were published by him. The rest were copied into some 15 beautifully bound volumes made for the Queen, but copies from these were circulated fairly widely.

The Sonatas (as he later preferred to call them) were almost invariably written in the binary (two-part) form already exhibited in the 30 published *Essercizi* (Exercises or Studies). This form had long been in favor as the over-all pattern of the Dance (see p. 287), and was therefore in itself not original. But whereas in the Dance the rhythmic and melodic character announced at the beginning ruled throughout the piece, Scarlatti not only ranged far beyond the conventional character of the Dance but introduced remarkably vivid contrasts of figure or theme. These he developed according to no pre-established plan but with an inexhaustible wealth of invention, achieving a novelty and freshness of interest quite unparalleled in the music of that day.

More than half of the Sonatas (as Kirkpatrick seems to have been the first to recognize) were intended to be played in pairs, the second being either the complement or the illuminating contrast to the first. There is thus an apparent anticipation of the Viennese sonata-form of Haydn and Mozart, both in the use (but not in the precise arrangement) of contrasted themes and keys, and in the coupling together of related movements. But since Scarlatti was so completely isolated, in Spain, there is no likelihood that the actual evolution of the Sonata (which took place far from Madrid) was at all directly affected by his example.

CHAPTER XIX

Gluck's Reform of the Opera

The Need for Reform—Later Neapolitan Writers

THE great popularity of opera is a striking indication of the trend of musical thought at the beginning of the eighteenth century. The spectacular and technical brilliancy of the performances had attracted a large public and was creating endless discussion. Opera was the most successful type of musical performance that had as yet been known, and the rewards won by composers and singers were the envy of musicians who had been trained wholly in the older polyphonic style. And aside from its material advantages, the homophonic style made possible a kind of forceful personal expression which could not be attained in any polyphonic form. Hence, the new style had begun to oust the old, even in Germany where religious preoccupation had preserved and fostered polyphony during a whole century of its gradual abandonment in Italy and France. The work of Bach, for instance, barely escaped oblivion, having enjoyed no more than sufficient general approval to make its production possible. Once Germany had emerged from the introverted religious consciousness into which she had been plunged by the Protestant controversies and the Thirty Years' War, her rapid and rather slavish adoption of the ruling continental attitude in matters of art is easy to understand—especially when we remember the imputations of backwardness and social inferiority which were leveled at her by her neighbors. Even in England, where the classical tradition had never gained great ascendancy, the new manner achieved a temporary, largely fashionable popularity. But that high cultural ideal which had prompted the invention of the *dramma per musica* had dwindled as the opera, with its increasing appeal to the senses, had created a paying public upon which it depended for support. The classical ideal was supplanted by ideals of propriety in manner rather than in matter; and the almost universal system of patronage gave to the opinion of a few social leaders a force which was quite out of proportion to the soundness of their ideas.

The condition of opera (and indeed of all music) in the eighteenth century is unintelligible except in the light of this system of patronage. Only a very rigid social formality could have bred the rigid conventions of operatic structure which were described in the last chapter. And no other condition could have brought about the general degradation of operatic art which followed the death of Alessandro Scarlatti in 1725. The serious opera became a spectacle whose absurdity can hardly be matched in the annals of art. Only in the field of comedy, where convention rules with a far freer hand, is any significant progress to be noted. It is inconceivable that opera could have continued indefinitely to exist without being in some measure reformed. But before we take up the matter of Gluck's reform we must see—in the work of a few of the vast number of composers who were courting favor with the operatic public—what it was that stimulated Gluck to revolt against the traditions.

With the exception of a few men in France, of whom Rameau was the greatest, the chief purveyors of opera were followers of the Neapolitan tradition. Alessandro Scarlatti had several important pupils—his son Domenico, more notable for his instrumental works than for his operas; Feo, the teacher of Pergolesi; Durante, most influential of all the teachers of the Neapolitan school; and Hasse, the greatest figure in German opera between Keiser and Gluck.

Francesco Durante (1684–1755) almost an exact contemporary of Bach and Handel, was not a composer of opera but devoted himself to church music and the oratorio. His solid contrapuntal knowledge was mingled with the graces of the Neapolitans. He was one of the first writers to give especial prominence to two soprano parts in the chorus—the ultimate result of which was the dreary succession of saccharine thirds (in lieu of any real part-writing) which occurs in so much of the later Italian opera. This is only one of the mechanical devices for giving pleasure to the unthinking through the use of conventional harmonies and figures which came to be characterized as the style of the Zopf (pigtail or peruke) by later historians.

Johann Adolf Hasse (1699–1783) began his operatic career as a tenor singer at the Hamburg opera. Showing promise in composition, he was sent to Naples in 1724, where he at once won the undying enmity of Porpora by deserting him, as teacher, for Alessandro Scarlatti. So rapid was his progress that he was selected to compose the new opera for the next year, Sesostrato, which won him fame throughout Italy. In Venice he married the remarkable soprano Faustina Bordoni (later a member of Handel's company in London), whose share in his success was very large.

His chief residence was Dresden, where he vanquished Porpora in popularity. In 1763 he went to Vienna where he collaborated with Metastasio. His fertility was incredible. He set all of Metastasio's dramatic poems to music, and produced in all over a hundred operas, besides oratorios, Masses, symphonies, and other works. In instrumental composition and in sacred forms his style is distinctly German; but in the opera it is purely Italian. Nothing could more clearly indicate the hold which the Neapolitan style had gained over the operatic taste of Europe; not only was Germany overrun with resident Italians who were regarded with the utmost favor by the socially important, but German composers themselves deserted their native style for the Italian.

Durante's pupils, even more than those of Scarlatti himself, were influential purveyors of the Italian opera throughout Europe. Eight of these pupils, at least, attained to great fame. Tommaso Traetta (1727–1779), after great success throughout Italy, produced two works (*Iphigenia in Aulis* and *Armida*—both subjects being later treated by Gluck, in more masterly fashion) at Vienna in 1759 and 1760; he was called to St. Petersburg as master of music to Catherine the Great, and had some success in London. He was a composer of rich and energetic imagination, much influenced by the style of Rameau and not unlike Gluck himself in his desire to make his music move hand in hand with the drama. Leonardo Vinci (1690–1730) was also famed in his day for his sense of dramatic expression. His close association with the great singer Farinelli seems to have brought about his expansion of the simple aria form of Alessandro Scarlatti. In order to give greater variety to the aria than the simple A–B–A form could contain, the A-section itself was expanded so as to include a contrasted phrase, and these two with their variants gave the following form for the A-division: A–B–A'–B'. The still more vividly contrasted B-section then follows, and the whole is completed by the *da capo*. This idea of thematic contrast is of great importance in the working out of the later sonata form.

Nicola Jomelli (1714–1774), after thorough study of counterpoint at Naples (his mastery exciting the admiration of the famous Padre Martini of Bologna), produced operas in Naples, Venice, Vienna, Rome, and especially in Stuttgart where for fifteen years he directed the court music. Here his work showed a distinct German influence, the earlier suavity of his melody being much strengthened by the use of richer harmony, freer modulation, and a far more competent handling of the orchestra. By the almost entire abandonment of the *recitativo secco* the solo scenes are much intensified in dramatic power; and the vivid declamation characteristic of Rameau is much used. Both of these improvements are to be seen in the work of Gluck, though it is not known that any definite influence is to be traced. Antonio Sacchini (1734–1786) according to Burney was "a graceful, elegant and judicious composer," whose masterpiece, *Oedipus at Colonna*, produced at Versailles in 1786, shows much of Gluck's influence. Niccola Piccinni (1728–1800) was a favorite pupil of Durante: "The others are my pupils; this one is my son." After many successes both in serious and in comic opera, he went to Paris in 1776 where, much against his own desires, his friends pitted him against the redoubtable Gluck. The results we shall see.

The comedy, which had begun in the Intermezzi and had suggested the introduction of comic scenes into serious opera as we have seen in the work of Legrenzi, was now gradually developed into a separate genre. The Italian term for such a piece was *opera buffa*. It was comic opera, with secco recitative. The distinction between comedy and farce is later applied to opera, the term *opéra bouffe* implying the farcical character while *opéra comique* (originally opera with spoken dialogue) becomes the antithesis of "grand" opera which is sung throughout. Giovanni Pergolesi (1710–1736) won a remarkable and apparently somewhat undeserved success with his Intermezzo *La Serva Padrona* which, although cast for only two characters, was one of the most popular light operas of the whole century. It was performed in Paris in 1746 without much success; but when a company of Italian comedians, the *Bouffons Italiens*, produced it again in 1752 it scored a triumph which was the beginning of the famous "War of the Bouffons"—a dispute as to the relative merits of the Italian style (upheld by the Bouffonistes) and the more stilted manner of classical French opera in the tradition of Lully (championed by the anti-Bouffonistes). This "war" merged into the still more acrimonious dispute between the Gluckists and the Piccinnists, of which more must be told in its place. Nicola Logroscino (1700?–1763?) showed so great a gift for comic characterization that he was called by the Neapolitans "the god of comic opera." He is often said to have invented the imposing concerted Finale which, combining the principal voices in several successive ensemble numbers, closes each act in the later operas; but this statement is refuted by the great English historian E. J. Dent, who finds no evidence to prove it. He places Logroscino in the first rank, however, in genuine comic feeling. This long list of Durante's pupils may be closed with the name of Giovanni Paisiello (1741–1816), whose setting of Beaumarchais's comedy *The Barber of Seville* was not without influence on Mozart (whose *Marriage of Figaro* tells the further adventures of the Barber) and was only superseded in popular favor by the incomparable *Barber* of Rossini. Paisiello was active in St. Petersburg, and in Paris where he was highly favored by Napoleon.

All the composers mentioned in the three preceding paragraphs were pupils of Durante. But the list of important Neapolitans has by no means been exhausted. Leonardo Leo (1694–1744) was a significant teacher (Jomelli and Piccinni owed much to him as well as to Durante), wrote many serious operas and scored an immense success with the comedy *Amor vuol soffe-renze* ("Love Loves to Suffer") in 1739. He also wrote much religious music. His mastery of modern harmonic counterpoint, free from modal influences, was complete. He did not travel outside Italy. Other Italians, however, transplanted the opera buffa: Giovanni Alberto Ristori, active in Dresden from 1715, and Egidio Duni (1709–1775) whose work at Paris is the direct antecedent of the famous Monsigny's. Antonio Caldara (*circa* 1670–1736) and Antonio Lotti (*circa* 1667–1740), pupils of Legrenzi, were both prominent in the musical life of Vienna. Baldassare Galuppi (1706–1785) deserves the credit for the expansion of the Finale formerly ascribed to Leo and Logroscino. He collaborated with the celebrated Italian playwright Goldoni, producing his comic operas as far from Italy as London and St. Petersburg.

Lully's Successors in Paris—Rameau

The only successor of Lully who added significantly to the substance of French opera was Jean Philippe Rameau (1683–1764)—born only four years before Lully's death, and contributing nothing to the literature of the opera until after his fiftieth year. In that long interval of nearly half a century no figure of commanding importance appeared on the French operatic stage. Lalande, chiefly a church composer, won some recognition with his ballets; Campra and Destouches and a few others, of whom Francoeur was perhaps the most significant, barely served to keep alive the interest in serious opera, in opposition to the popularity of the ballet and its related dance spectacles. The Lullyan tradition had become fixed; and although he proposed no very revolutionary treatment, the work of Rameau was at first only reluctantly accepted. He had been almost wholly self-trained; but so penetrating was his musical mind that he founded (with the works of Mersenne, Zarlino, and others as a starting point) a novel system of harmony, which he published in 1722 and in which is to be found the first exposition of the idea of the inversion of chords. A short sojourn in Italy had awakened no interest in Italian music. He at first devoted himself to the organ, church music, and clavier pieces. His theoretical works and his fame as a player gave him an assured position in Paris. One or two small essays in comedy revealed dramatic talent; and at length *Hippolyte et Aricie* (founded on Racine's *Phèdre*) was produced at the Académie. He was accused of having deserted the principles of Lully for those of the Italians; the work was almost a failure; but gradually, by unremitting industry, he won the favor of the Parisian public, and in the war of the Bouffonistes was set up as the champion of the Nationalists against the Italians. His work was really not in imitation of either school, but highly original. His arias were varied and showed a considerable vigor of declamation; his harmony was remarkably rich, his orchestration more musicianly and more highly colored than that of any of his predecessors; and his choruses were forceful additions to the dramatic scheme. The novelty of rhythm and color in his ballet music was striking. He was one of the few composers of the time from whom Gluck could derive any elements of his later reform.

The Degradation of Opera

We have spoken of that which was good rather than of that which was bad in the opera preceding Gluck. The extent to which interest had sunk in the problem of the true music drama is best seen in the popularity of the *Pasticcio* (literally, a pie), which was a collection of operatic airs strung together without any semblance of dramatic relation, and only designed to give the audience that delight in vocal execution or brilliant spectacle which had been growing to predominance in opera almost since its inception. These conglomerations were not unknown in the seventeenth century. Such a mixture of arias, by several composers, was performed at Naples in 1646 under the title of *Amor non a legge* ("Love Knows No Law"). In the eighteenth century even the most notable composers were not above collaborating in this way. Mattei (not Ariosti, as is usually stated), Bononcini, and Handel in 1721 each contributed one act to the opera *Muzio Scevola*.[1] Gluck also produced a pasticcio, *Piramo e Tisbe*, in London in 1746, made of successful airs from his earlier operas. The vogue continued until late in the century. Twelve composers were represented in a pasticcio produced in Vienna in 1789. Indeed, the growing isolation of opera from all that was real or even honest in sentiment seems to have been apparent to all the critical minds of the time—especially to the literary men. Only the closed circle of musical dilettantes were impervious to the new breath of scientific clarity which was beginning to blow in the contemporary world of letters. Voltaire is said to have remarked, "If a thing is too silly to say, people sing it." Saint-Evremonde says: "If you wish to know what an opera is, I answer that it is a strange production of poetry and music, where the poet and the musician, each bored by the other, take the utmost possible trouble to produce a worthless performance. A piece of nonsense packed with

---

[1] This, however, is really a collaborated opera, rather than a pasticcio.

music, dances, machines and decorations is magnificent nonsense, but nonsense all the same." La Fontaine chuckles at the mishaps which sometimes befell the mechanical apparatus: "Often the counterweight resists the weight of the loveliest flesh; a god dangles from a rope and shrieks for the machinist; part of a forest remains in the sea, or the half of heaven in the midst of hell." Dryden and Addison in England were equally caustic but showed a more kindly desire to improve the form. Yet the opera continued to fascinate enormous audiences; and since these people cannot all have been intellectually beneath contempt, there must have been some reason why its glaring absurdities were forgiven.

The essential unreality of opera is apparent to everyone. People do not normally express their passions in song or enact their quarrels to the accompaniment of a carefully synchronized orchestra. But neither do even the most heroic of men habitually speak in verse, nor is the brilliant and pointed dialogue of the prose drama often to be met with off the stage. To go to the theatre at all is to take for granted certain conventions of expression—certain condensations in action and speech which may heighten our imaginative understanding of those human situations which constitute the drama. Without imaginative participation in the represented conflict of will and purpose, we have no drama; but once a clear imaginative concept of this conflict is conveyed to us—through no matter what medium—drama is achieved. The great moments of drama—the moments toward which the whole action tends—are moments of emotion. Thus music, with its unparalleled emotional intensity, is a possible medium of dramatic expression. To the music lover, there is conveyed by music an imaginative reality of feeling more rich and full than can be conveyed by any other art. To the lover of poetry, the essentially unreal but sonorous and suggestive verse of the poetic drama has a similar value. But neither verse as verse nor music as music is in itself dramatic. If then either poetry or music is applied to drama, a double appeal is offered to the hearer; and there is constant danger that the merely poetic or the merely musical appeal may diverge from the original dramatic purpose. The point at which the sense of dramatic meaning is lost sight of will vary, of course, with various hearers. But it is an incorrigible love of music, rather than a state of mental depravity, which is exhibited in the popularity of eighteenth-century opera. The correction of this excess, and at the same time an attempt to provide opera with an appeal to critical minds more worthy of respect than those of the musical dilettantes, was Gluck's object in his so-called reform of the opera.

GLUCK'S EARLY WORK

Gluck was born in 1714, the son of a poor forester in the service of Prince Eugene of Savoy. His education, the best obtainable under the circumstances, included instruction in violin, 'cello, and organ. In 1736 he went to Vienna where he was befriended by Prince Lobkowitz, and whence after a year he was sent to Milan for study with the celebrated opera composer Sammartini. In 1741 he produced his first opera, *Artaserse* (poem by Metastasio). Although his work was criticized as "German" it was a success, as was likewise *Demofoonte* (also by Metastasio) in the following year. Altogether he produced eight successful operas in five years. In these works, entirely acceptable to Italian ears, there is no hint of reform but rather a facile adaptation of his natural German idiom to Italian taste, such as had been accomplished by Handel and Hasse. In 1745 he was invited to England, where occurred the unsuccessful performance of the pasticcio *Pyramus and Thisbe* above referred to. At the end of 1746 he went to Vienna, producing an opera in Dresden on the way. Neither this work nor the one he produced in Vienna for the Empress's birthday in 1748 shows any disposition to abandon the Italian manner. After a visit to Copenhagen, where he was very well received, he went to Rome where he produced *Telemachus, or the Isle of Circe*, the first of his operas in which signs of change in style are to be found. In the years which followed he was in demand at Naples and Bologna as well as in Vienna.

The French opera in the newer style of Duni and Monsigny became about 1759 all the rage in Vienna; and both in its more animated declamation and in the more graceful and concise turns of phrase in its arias Gluck found models which he imitated with great facility. His complete accord with the current dictates of fashion is also seen in his frequent use of imitations of natural sounds or similar realistic suggestions—a practice incessantly in vogue in the opera of the time. It seems certain that the directness and simplicity of the lighter opera, dealing with themes of contemporary interest rather than with the outworn mythology of the ancients, had much to do with clarifying Gluck's ideas as to the true purpose of music in relation to drama. He was beginning to seek definite characterization of his persons and situations through the music, and to avoid the merely musical appeal which satisfied most of his contemporary writers and their audiences. He was studying too in the cultured circles with which he was intimate, the general problems and principles of aesthetics which bore upon his art. Gluck was much like Handel in the sturdy self-sufficiency which, especially during his later years, made him independent of the vicious system of patronage. But he was much unlike

Handel in his disposition to consider the theoretical problems which his art presented in its relation to other arts.

The First "Reform" Opera—*Orfeo ed Euridice*

Doubtless the first object of his attention, when at length the possibility of a true union of music and drama appeared to him, was the text itself. We have already seen to what straits the librettist was reduced in conforming to the tradition which demanded the *da capo* form for every aria, the inclusion of two arias in every scene, and the suppression of dialogue. Not even a Metastasio (of whose libretti Gluck had set twelve up to 1760) could make a dramatic idea appear out of the perfunctory series of verses which constituted the established opera form. Hence, prompted alike by the general criticism and by his own common sense, Gluck cast about for a poet with whom he could truly collaborate. Such a one he found in Raniero di Calzabigi. The theme chosen for the new work was curiously enough that which had been treated in two of the most significant efforts toward the invention of opera: that of Orpheus and Eurydice. And it is perhaps just to say that in Gluck's work is to be found a realization of the ideals of both Peri and Monteverdi; though that ideal is more fully attained in Gluck's later works.

The story is here more succinctly told than in the earlier versions we have described. As the first scene opens, Eurydice is already dead, and shepherds and girls are mourning at her tomb. Soon Orpheus's voice pierces through the chorus in the thrice-repeated cry, *Euridice!* vivid and poignant against the somber song of sorrow. An aria which makes impassioned plea to Eurydice to return to him remains unanswered, though the strain is sung a second and even a third time. Thereupon Orpheus declares his resolve to take his petition to the gods of the underworld. Cupid appears, telling of Jupiter's sympathy and confirming Orpheus's resolve to use the magic of his harp to win back his wife. Cupid already knows and warns Orpheus of the conditions under which Eurydice may be freed: that Orpheus is not to look upon her face until they have ascended to the earth. The act ends not in any imposing ensemble but in a soliloquy by Orpheus, couched in highly characteristic accompanied recitative. As the second act opens, the horrors of the underworld are first impressed upon us. Lowering clouds and livid lightning form the background for an infernal ballet, interrupted by a chorus of the Furies, "Who is the mortal who dares approach this place of dread?" Orpheus, thus announced, appears and sings his entreaty; time after time the Furies answer "No!" Their rage is at last appeased by his words, "In my breast are a thousand torments; hell itself is within me" (so that this hell of yours daunts me not at all). Singing "What magic in him overcomes our rage," they allow him to enter. Their voices and the howling of Cerberus (which has been heard intermittently in the orchestra) die away, and the scene changes to the Elysian fields. The contrast of scene is heightened by a ballet of the happy spirits, among whom Eurydice is dwelling. Orpheus enters, asks for her, is told that she is approaching, and, after a charming ballet, seizes her hand and with averted face leads her away. The third act is in a dark labyrinth, on the way from Elysium to Earth. Orpheus, never looking back, tries to hasten her steps. But Eurydice cannot understand his constantly averted face. She becomes suspicious, thinking he does not share her delight in the reunion; for he will not embrace her nor even speak directly to her. There is an open rupture and Eurydice breaks free, unwilling to follow unless he looks at her. He cannot choose but yield; but at once she is again stricken with death. Orpheus's lament *Che farò senza Euridice?* leads to his determination to slay himself; but Cupid appears again, telling him that the gods are convinced of his fidelity, and the trials of Orpheus and Eurydice are brought to the happy issue which the convention of the time demands.

Although the music is by no means consistently strong in its representation of the scene, it was indeed a remarkable achievement. The overture itself is empty and unrelated to the drama; but the orchestral introduction to the opening scene is entirely in character, and in many places the orchestra fulfills the purpose of comment on the action which belonged to the chorus in the ancient Greek drama, and for which Wagner employs it in a much more elaborate way. The distinction between aria and recitative is by no means obliterated, but the accompanied recitative is singularly powerful in suggestion as well as musical in interest; and the aria itself is largely denuded of the senseless ornament which the feebler taste of the time demanded. (The mechanical deliverance from death at the end was absolutely demanded by operatic convention, and must not be regarded as any indication of Gluck's concept of dramatic values.) The *da capo* form of the aria—rightly objected to by many critics as impeding the action, since it returns upon itself—is sparingly used. In order to make the action proceed more naturally, he makes a less obvious break between the successive musical numbers and tries to have the later music grow out of the earlier. Thus the current conventions as to the number of principal characters, the occurrence of at least two arias in each scene, and the sacrosanct *da capo* aria itself are set at naught. Naturally the first performance was received with amazement; but five repetitions sufficed to establish it in an assured position. It made its way into Italy, and was engraved in Paris; but a single novelty could not overthrow so deeply rooted a convention as that of the current operatic style; and owing to the pressure of official duties Gluck was obliged to go on producing minor works of the old order for five years.

THE PREFACE TO *Alceste*

In 1767, however, the second of Gluck's dramas based on the new principles was produced: *Alceste*, the libretto again by Calzabigi and far superior to that of *Orfeo*. In 1769 the third, *Paris and Helen*, was given in Vienna like the others. Here the opportunity of giving expression to more purely lyrical feeling is remarkably realized. This is in spite of an avowed purpose of making the music always subservient to the drama. To the scores of both *Alceste* and *Paris and Helen*, Gluck wrote prefaces, in which the main principles of his theory were stated. His later work follows these principles; the abridged preface to *Alceste* follows:

I sought to avoid all those abuses which the misapplied vanity of singers and the excessive complaisance of composers had introduced into the Italian opera. . . . I sought to reduce music to its true function, that of supporting the poetry, in order to strengthen the expression of the sentiments and the interest of the situations, without interrupting the action or disfiguring it with superfluous ornament. . . . I have avoided interrupting an actor in the warmth of dialogue, to make him wait for a wearisome *ritornello* [instrumental interlude]. . . . I have thought that the overture should prepare the spectators for the character of the coming action, and give them an indication of its subject; that the instruments should only be employed in proportion to the degree of interest and of passion involved, and that there should not be too great a disparity between the air and the recitative, in order not to spoil the flow of the period. . . . I have avoided parading difficulties at the expense of clearness; the discovery of any novelty has seemed to me precious only in so far as it was called forth by the situation; . . . lastly, there is no rule I have not thought it my duty to sacrifice willingly in order to make sure of an effect. . . . Signor Calzabigi, . . . in the place of flowery descriptions, useless comparisons and cold and sententious moralizing, had substituted strong passion, interesting situations, the language of the heart and a continually varied spectacle. . . . The universal approbation of a city like Vienna has convinced me that simplicity and truth are the only principles of beauty in works of art.

The simplicity and common sense of Gluck's contentions are apparently disarming. One wonders at first why so obvious an idea should have had to be fought for. But closer examination reveals that Gluck to a certain extent is mistaken. For it is not the direct sense of the words which his music amplifies, but rather certain implications conveyed by those words. Actual union between the expressive purpose of music and words is only to be attained in short phrases of sudden passion, in exclamations, or in outcries such as the thrice-repeated *Euridice!* in the opening scene of *Orpheus*. The more general sense of grief—such as is there expressed by the chorus of shepherds and maidens—is conveyed by music whose words are almost unsuggestive in comparison with the harmony of voices and orchestra. Here, and in almost every other significant passage, the music brings us to a realization of emotional facts which are just as significant as those which can be expressed in words; but the music can do this only when it is allowed to proceed according to its own principles and its own nature. Gluck realized this instinctively, and often acted upon it. But his verbal argument blinded him to the fact that, instead of exalting words above music, he was really exalting the expressive power of music over its merely sensuous or decorative values. He supposed that his expressive suggestions resided primarily in the words and emanated from them; while as a matter of fact he, as musician, was constantly dictating to the poet, since only those passions may be dealt with in the opera which will allow the musical substance to be developed to a point of musical satisfaction. His "reformed" opera could never have succeeded if it had not been musically satisfying. His glory then resides in his rediscovery of the expressive powers of music, in an age when those values had been almost extinguished. He reformed opera through an exaltation of music; not, as he seeems to have felt, through its debasement.

THE WAR OF THE GLUCKISTS AND THE PICCINNISTS

Gluck now began to look toward Paris as the center in which his ideas must find approval. Together with the Bailli du Roullet, he made an opera out of Racine's tragedy *Iphigenia in Aulis*. Du Roullet had influence in Paris, and finally secured the acceptance of the work which, after great difficulties in rehearsal, was produced on April 19, 1774. It grew rapidly in favor, and its success created a demand for a revival of *Orfeo*, which was given during the following August in a somewhat altered form. Early in the following year Gluck traveled to Vienna. During his absence the Italian faction, in the war of the Bouffonistes, brought Piccinni to Paris as champion of the powerful opposition to Gluck and his theories. Gluck had received from the directors of the Opéra commissions for two new works, *Armida* and *Roland*, both on poems by Quinault. *Roland* was now also offered to Piccinni. Hearing of this offer, Gluck destroyed the work he had so far completed on the subject, desiring to avoid too open a conflict with the Italian. *Armida*, however, was completed, the text of Quinault being preserved just as Lully had set it, and was produced in Paris in September, 1777. It was rather bitterly criticized for its noisiness and for its lack of melody. Gluck was moved to reply to La Harpe (who had especially bewailed the lack of old-fashioned arias) in a sarcastic vein which can be suggested in a single sentence: "As I see that you are passionate for tender music, I will put in the mouth of the furious Achilles a song so tender and so sweet, that all the spectators will be moved to tears." The controversy that ensued grew to enormous proportions, Gluckists and Piccinnists quarreling in the streets, fighting duels, and going to every length of exaggeration in support of their favorite. Gluck retired to Vienna to write his greatest opera *Iphigenia in Tauris*, while the war of the factions still raged. Piccinni was induced to set virtually the same poem to music, being promised that his work would be produced before that of Gluck. The promise was not kept. Gluck's work, produced in May, 1779, was a great success; and the setting by Piccinni, not given until January 23, 1781, was quite unable to maintain its position against that of Gluck.

Iphigenia in Tauris proved to be the last of Gluck's great operas. A lighter work, *Echo et Narcisse*, had no great success. He returned to Vienna, laden with honors undiminished even by the disreputable incident of the opera *Les Danaïdes*, which Gluck tried to sell to the Opéra for 20,000 livres, although not he but his pupil Salieri was the author of the work. Even his old rival Piccinni proposed to found an annual concert in Paris at which nothing save Gluck's music should be performed. The proposal came to nothing; but Gluck's influence upon the later course of operatic history was indelible. The demand for music rather than drama was still too strong to be altogether ignored, as we shall see; but never again did the art sink to such depths as those from which Gluck raised it.

CHAPTER XX

The Evolution of the Modern Sonata

THE SOCIAL BACKGROUND OF THE NEW FORM

AMONG the great variety of forms into which the musical thought of the early eighteenth century was molded, none could aspire to any real universality of expression. The nearest approach to this condition was made by the fugue. Equally adapted to voices or to instruments, and maintaining the most undeviating coherence through the predominance of its one primary subject, it offered at the same time an endless variety through manifold variants of the subject itself or through new relations of subject and countersubject. From the purely musical point of view, no more perfect form is possible than that of the fugue. But there are many kinds of feeling which the fugue cannot effectively express. To be convincing, a fugue must be made upon a terse, epigrammatic subject, in which rhythmic vigor—even when the motion is slow—is almost indispensable. Thus, true lyric feeling is almost excluded from its expressive possibilities; and it is precisely in this lyric quality that music offers its most immediate and perhaps its highest appeal. Neither is the mental concentration which the fugue demands, nor the emotional preoccupation which it suggests, altogether suitable for the expression of lighter moods and gaieties. These are far more fitly embodied in the tunes and rhythms of the dance. Thus it is not merely fanciful to see in the great variety of eighteenth-century forms a true reflection of eighteenth-century life: in the opera, for instance, the shallow and rather isolated taste of exalted society; in the fugue, the contemplative spirit of the devout or the thoughtful; in the dances, the unaffected manners of the peasantry. Such social classes as are here represented were largely separated from each other in ideals and activities; and because of this isolation, no single form was conceivable which might embody within itself the expression of feelings or purposes common to all humanity.

But such a unification of emotional outlook—such a leveling of social barriers—as would make possible a universal form was fast coming into being. Although aristocratic conventions and tastes were abating but little from the high artificiality which had been imposed by the court of Versailles, a profound intellectual and social unrest was beginning to be felt. Especially in France, science and the rationalism which comes of scientific thinking were beginning to complete, in relation to all worldly institutions, that revolution which the Renaissance and the Reformation had worked in matters of culture and religion. The principles of modern scientific thought had been laid down early in the seventeenth century by Francis Bacon in England and by Descartes in France. These principles were soon applied not merely to mathematical or physical investigations but to larger problems of philosophy and religion. Beneath the all-enveloping cloak of religion, speculation as to the proper scope of human liberty began to arise. Questions as to the extent to which divine grace or forgiveness for original sin was attainable became, in the disputes between the Jesuits and the Jansenists, thinly veiled arguments about "certain inalienable rights" of man. At first, as in the writings of Pascal, the tone of the discussions was theological. But as the arguments became more involved and the true question—that of human liberty—appeared, the cloak of theological conformity was thrown off and the metaphysical method was discarded for the scientific. Locke's *Essay on the Human Understanding* (1690) and Pierre Bayle's *Dictionnaire historique et philosophique* (1696–1697) mark the definite inauguration of the age of reason. A thoroughly rational scepticism is evident in the writings of all the great literary men of eighteenth-century France, and especially in the *Encyclopédie* which, largely under the direction of Diderot, expounded the problems of the world in terms of advanced scientific thought.

The most extreme development of this long fermentation of ideas is to be seen in the *Social Contract* of Rousseau, the Bible of the Revolutionists. Founded as it was in sentiment, and appealing, in Pascal's phrase, to "those reasons of the heart of which reason itself knows nothing," Rousseau's doctrine was unscientific and contrary to the thought of the eighteenth century. Its main thesis—that man is good by nature, and is made evil by society—was also unchristian. But this was the natural form which the older philosophic and religious disputations would take when implanted in unphilosophic or irreligious minds. It was a doctrine easy to understand and very flattering to the individual reader, who of course supposed himself to have been exempt from moral evil while he was at the same time at the mercy of the evil institutions of society. The obvious remedy was to destroy the institutions, and to trust to the native goodness of man to repair the damage. Hence the Revolution—an incredible orgy of destruction, wrought out of the most tragic faith in the goodness of man.

But these ideals of liberty, equality, and fraternity implied the emancipation and emphasized the importance of the individual. A society made up of independent individuals had not the same ideals, tasks, or emotions as a society made up of divinely constituted classes. Whether for better or for worse, a profound change in emotional outlook had been brought about; and the artist could not escape the problem of representing that change.

The first stages of development in the sonata represented no high and noble ideals, but rather a reaction against the heaviness of polyphony. This reaction was strongest among those influential social groups whose chief concern was the cultivation of a polished exterior. Polished grace is not the most outstanding characteristic of polyphonic music. The eighteenth-century revolt against polyphony was thus largely similar in motive to that which gave birth to the opera; but it was far less acrimonious and less rapid. Opera had its rise in a cultured desire to re-establish the Greek drama; but much of the energy for its support was generated out of resentment against the cumbrous polyphony of the Netherlandish invaders of Italy. The homophonic sonata had its rise in a cultured desire for the pleasing expression of emotions which were outside the range of polyphony; but much of the energy for its support was generated out of a motive almost as powerful as resentment—the lofty sense of social superiority, mostly exhibited in a superior grace of manner. The first development of the sonata was concerned rather with external perfections than with the inner reality of feeling. But as the cloak of social conformity was thrown off, the essential impulse toward individual expression was revealed. Such generalizations as these are perhaps of little value; but they will point out the fact that the coming evolution of the sonata was not a process of purely musical thought.

The first stage of the sonata represented a reduction to the simplest possible terms of many features of the contemporary polyphonic types. Not only in its several movements, but also in the inner structure of its movements, the sonata is a composite form. Three main sources may be discerned out of which the sonata was to grow: (1) the operatic overture, (2) the older sonata (church or chamber), and (3) the concerto. From the overture came the movement succession (fast—slow—fast); from the suite dance (chamber sonata) came the structural division of the first movement (the real "sonata form") into two sections, of which the second was an expansion of the material of the first; and from the concerto (which also had the three-movement order, borrowed from the church sonata by a process of reduction) came the idea of thematic contrast. We must trace in some detail the influence of these older forms upon the new homophonic sonata.

The essential features of the sonata structure were occasionally hit upon long before the form gained that wide popularity which made it what the fugue could never have been—a vehicle for the expression of almost every variety of feeling. In order to understand more clearly the successive steps toward the completed form, it will be well to have in mind as exact an idea as possible of the structure as it was perfected, by Haydn and Mozart, toward the end of the eighteenth century. The essential features may be shown in a diagram; and since the form of the suite dance is that from which the sonata develops, the diagram of that form is here repeated for comparison. Key relations in the sonata form in major keys are indicated above the horizontal line; those in minor keys, below the line, except in the development section.

SUITE-DANCE FORM

‖. "S". .Cadential Figures.‖. Modulations   Partial Cadence   Final Cadence.‖
‖.(in Tonic)   (in Domi-.‖. (beginning in   (in Rel. Minor   (in Tonic) .‖
      nant, Rel.   Dom. or Rel-   or Dominant)
      Maj.)   ative Key)

FIRST-MOVEMENT FORM OF THE CLASSICAL SONATA

Exposition   ‖. S. I. (maj.) trans. S. II. Dom. trans.   Cl. S.   .‖
             ‖. S. I. (min.) trans. S. II. Rel.   trans.   Cl. S.   .‖

Development ‖(˙.˙)   Varied treatment, in distant keys,   Cadence
             ‖(˙.˙)   of material of the exposition

Recapitulation   S. I. Tonic maj. trans.   S. II. Tonic   trans. Cl. S. Tonic(˙.˙)‖
                 S. II. Tonic min. trans.   S. I. Tonic   trans. Cl. S. Tonic(˙.˙)‖
                                            (maj.)

S. I. is *first* or *principal* subject; trans. is transition; S. II. is *second* subject; Cl. S. is *closing* subject.

The first section of the dance form is expanded into the Exposition of the sonata. It will be seen that the antithesis of key is the same in both forms; and that the key contrast is heightened in the sonata by the use of a second theme. (This is to some extent foreshadowed in the suite dance by the use, at the cadence, of sequential figures which differ in pattern from the dance tune stated at the beginning.) The closing subject may be understood either as an intensification of these cadential figures, or as a new feature necessitated by the character of the second subject, which is usually gentle and lyrical in contrast to the sturdy and emphatic principal subject.

The development, while modulatory as in the suite dance, may now involve much more material—anything already used in the exposition, and sometimes even new material; but this is only a natural expansion corresponding to the already expanded exposition. The cadence which ends the development is not now in the related or parallel key, but is so arranged as to give full force to the resumption of the principal subject in the tonic. Recapitulation is now necessitated by the large development of the whole form. Its persistent reiteration of the tonic key is apparently monotonous; but experiment would show that a wider range of key relations would lack the necessary sense of finality.

It will be seen that the suite dance is really a three-part form, the second section, divided by the middle cadence, being really two sections united into one. The sonata, then, emphasizes this tripartite structure; and it assumes on a very large scale the general outline of the A–B–A aria: A being Exposition, B, Development, and A, Recapitulation.

Contributions from Overture, Prelude, and Dance

Having now a clear idea of the goal which was unconsciously before the minds of the sonata writers of the early eighteenth century, we may return to a consideration of the manner in which that goal was reached. The first steps were apparently taken in the field of the overture. Even as early as 1721, Francesco Conti, a court composer of Vienna, wrote a significant overture to his opera *Pallas Triumphant*. The first section has a clearly defined principal subject (B flat major); a transition to the dominant, with cadence; a brief second subject (subtheme is here a more accurate term) in F minor (not F major, as will later be the rule); and a short closing phrase or epilogue—all constituting the repeated Exposition. The second section begins with a Development in which the principal theme and the subtheme are alternated in a variety of keys. Then there is a condensed restatement of the three thematic elements of the first section by way of Recapitulation. Here, certainly, is the essential outline of "sonata form." [1]

---

[1] Two meanings, a generic and a specific, have unfortunately become associated with the word *sonata*. The generic implies a composition in several movements, at least one of which is written in "sonata form"—that having exposition, development, and recapitulation as just described. The specific meaning is that of the "sonata form" which, since the first of the several movements is usually in that form, is often called *first-movement form*. Classical and romantic *Trios*, *Quartets*, *Quintets*, etc., are all usually sonatas. The symphony, likewise, is a sonata for orchestra, and the concerto a sonata for a solo with orchestral accompaniment. (In the concerto, the opening *tutti*

This expanded structure was soon employed by Feo, Porpora, Vinci, and Leo—already mentioned as purveyors of the opera—and also was used for music not connected with the drama. It thus became an independent piece of concert music; and the overtures of Mozart and Beethoven will be found to preserve the essential features of sonata form. The same form was also employed in the early violin sonatas of Meneghetti and Veracini, and was the foundation of the *Exercises* (now called *Sonatas*) of Domenico Scarlatti. J. S. Bach himself quite frequently used it. The frequency with which it occurs in the second book of the *Well-Tempered Clavichord* has already been noted. The Prelude in D major (No. 5) of this collection even has a full recapitulation; and the same extension is to be seen in the Two-Part Invention in E major, and in the Fantasia in C minor where Domenico Scarlatti's characteristic cross-handed technique is freely used. Bach's structure, however, is naturally more polyphonic than that of Scarlatti.

But this reduction of the sonata to a single movement entailed a loss of one of the most striking values of the overture, the suite or the older sonata or concerto: the contrast of fast and slow movements. The expansion of the fast movement into the larger form naturally suggested the expansion of the other movements of the overture; so that out of the brief, slow section of the Scarlattian form we presently find developed a Siciliana, a Sarabande, or even a more imaginative type of slow movement, which had already its prototype in the slow movements of the church sonata. Pergolesi published in 1731 a set of twelve trio sonatas in which three movements appear, all in the expanded form just described. Karl Philipp Emanuel Bach, considerably later, applied the same organization to three-movement sonatas for piano solo; and symphonies began to appear which have the same dimensions.

Characteristics of the New Style—The Mannheim Group

A style transition was thus in progress. Not only was the form itself involved, but also the more difficult problem of contriving suitable subject matter and relevant types of transition from subject to subject. The types of subject suitable for the old operatic overture—mere vigorous figurations, bustling scales and arpeggios and the like, designed only as a conventional signal that the performance of the opera was about to begin—could not stand the scrutiny of concert audiences whose interest was centered on the music itself; and both the audience and the more competent per-

corresponds to the exposition; the solo thereafter has the repetition.) We shall hereafter use the term "sonata form" to designate the usual first-movement form just described.

formers naturally desired some exhibition of the technical graces of which the instruments were capable. This was particularly evident in the sonatas for piano and violin, whose solo character gave ample opportunity for the use of delicate ornamentation quite analogous to that which had already been produced in the operatic aria. For a considerable time, indeed, grace and elegance in the turning of phrases were cultivated at the expense of the vitality or meaning of the phrases. The sonatas of K. P. E. Bach seldom show any positively characteristic subject matter, and abound in turns, mordents, appoggiaturas, gruppetti, and other *Manieren* whose graceful execution constituted in that day the main interest of music.

But the style of the newer sonata swept rapidly into popularity in every country of Europe where music was cultivated. Sammartini, Pugnani, Durante, and the "reformer" of the concerto, Tartini, are among the leading composers in Italy; Wagenseil and Monn in Vienna; Czernohorsky (the teacher of Gluck) in Prague; most important of all were Stamitz, Richter, Filtz, Holzbauer, and Cannabich in Mannheim, where the most highly perfected orchestral ensemble in Europe was soon developed, and where the orchestral form of the sonata—the symphony—consequently received great attention. Riemann's high opinion of the contributions of the Mannheim school to the evolution of the symphony has been shown by later research to be exaggerated. Yet the vividness of the orchestra's performance delighted Mozart (who was there made aware of the value of the clarinet); and it is certainly true that careful dynamic gradations, the tremolo, the singing quality of the violins, and a kind of thematic design to which such effects are appropriate, were all cultivated at Mannheim.

Karl Philipp Emanuel Bach in Berlin and Hamburg; Johann Christoph Bach in Bückeburg; Wilhelm Friedemann Bach in Halle, and Johann Christian Bach in London—all sons of the great Bach—were leading spirits in the new movement, deserting the solid polyphonic style of their father for the lighter homophonic form. In France, Rameau, Gavinies, and others continued the development which Couperin, Daquin, and their school had initiated.

The popularity indicated by this wide dissemination of the new form shows that the sonata was appealing to the same taste as that which supported so lavishly the decadent opera of the time. No demand for profound or intense expression could be expected of audiences accustomed to listen to pasticcios of opera airs. Yet the large cultivation of *Manieren* had its value as training for the handling of musical ideas in an easy and fluent manner. And it is certainly true that the sonata up to 1760 shows a far more promising vitality than the contemporary opera. One thin thread of reality did indeed manifest itself, both in operatic and instrumental music. That was in the current passion for the musical imitation of natural sounds—birdcalls, thunder, marching feet, or the sighs, groans, or wailings of heroes and heroines in distress. Indeed, the idea of imitation went much farther than this. The lesson taught by all the scientific investigation, and the doctrine preached in all contemporary philosophy from Voltaire to Rousseau, was that of the "return to nature" as the solution for all the evils of life. But this kind of a return to nature, in instrumental music especially, becomes a weariness to the ear almost as soon as it is perceived. The original idea of the Camerata—that music must wholly occupy itself with intensifying the mere declamatory character of the text—had been abandoned for a more purely musical process of suggesting the reality of emotion which lay behind the words; and likewise the mere imitation of nature in music was now to be abandoned (not merely by Gluck in his reform of the opera but also by instrumental composers generally) for a more purely musical and at the same time more truly expressive style of writing. To express the inner reality of passion seemed to Gluck more important than to describe the superficial actions which indicate passion. His reform was in itself a more thoroughgoing return to nature, a perception of the futility of music which pleased the ear with caroling "while some necessary business of the play was then to be considered." Out of a similar futility of instrumental music it was necessary for a similar reality of expressive meaning to be suggested, if the sonata was to survive. Not the rejection of the new form, but the discovery of a clearer, more significant thematic substance in which that form might be embodied, was the real need. And it was the imaginative genius of Haydn and Mozart which in the next period of the sonata's history supplied that clarity. What these two men did can be realized only in relation to their personalities. Their work, therefore, will form the subject of the next chapter.

The Perfecting of the Sonata— Haydn and Mozart

ROM 1760 onward, the molding of the sonata into the form which was to be the principal vehicle for the expression of musical ideas for more than a century to come, was to a remarkable degree the work of Haydn and Mozart. Before Haydn began to write significantly, the form, as we have seen, had already become widely popular. Its main outlines had been accepted by public and composers alike as providing a plan of musical discourse both easy to follow and rich in variety of interest. As yet, however, the subjects chosen were mostly figurations—characteristic of the instruments involved, rather than expressive in any real sense—surviving from the conventional figures of the opera overtures and similar pieces. The problem of subject design in homophonic music was not unlike that which confronted the originators of the monodic style. In the opera stereotyped phrases, largely imitative of verbal declamation, had to be replaced by more imaginative, more expressive—in a word, more truly musical—melody. In the development of the homophonic forms of instrumental music, stereotyped phrases, lying naturally under the fingers of the players, had to be replaced by themes which were more purely musical, and by passages which, although still technically effective, were also expressively interesting. Moreover, the extended scale of the developed sonata form demanded a propriety of relation between the principal subjects, and an appropriateness of transition passages to these subjects, which was by no means easy to hit upon. The perfunctory filling-in of the formal outline was possible at a moment's notice; but the achievement of that subtle balance and perfection in the design and relation of subjects and transitions which would give an impression of continuous interest was a problem which only genius could solve. None but men of the stamp of Mozart and Haydn were equal to such a task.

Although Haydn (1732–1809) was much older than Mozart (1756–1791) the incredible precocity of the younger man soon placed him on a level with the older. Indeed, most of that work of Haydn's which is now commonly heard was written after 1782, by which time Mozart had settled in Vienna and the two were on terms of creative intimacy. It is during this decade that the final perfecting of the form itself occurred; but signs are not wanting that the form was also perceived as more than a gratification of the musical sense, and was making ready to withstand the rude breath of revolutionary feeling which during that decade attained cyclonic violence. Haydn was not at all, and Mozart was only slightly, of the revolutionary disposition. Their work therefore was largely an unconscious preparation for the vastly more inclusive expression which Beethoven was to attain; but the formal structure which they contrived was both strong and elastic enough to serve the needs of Beethoven and many of his followers.

Haydn's Early Life—His First Quartets

Josef Haydn's father was a poor wheelwright at Rohrau, on the border between lower Austria and Hungary. Max Kuhač[1] mistakenly felt that Slavic influences, both hereditary and environmental, had large part in shaping Haydn's musical idiom. The father, although unable to read notes, was a great lover of music, and his musical gift was inherited not only by Josef but by his younger brother Johann Michael (1737–1806), who became a composer of no mean powers. Josef's first musical instruction was given by a distant cousin, Johann Frankh, who took the boy under his wing at Hainburg. "Almighty God, to whom I render thanks for all his unnumbered mercies, gave me such facility in music, that by the time I was six I stood up like a man and sang masses in the church choir, and could play a little on the clavier and the violin." So well did he acquit himself in Hainburg that after two years he was taken into the choir of the Cathedral of St. Stephan in Vienna. Here he had regular studies in religion, writing, arithmetic, and Latin, and "learned singing, the clavier and the violin from good masters." He had no instruction in harmony or composition; but he could not resist the sight of a piece of music paper, which he economically covered with as many notes as the staves would hold. His fairly competent instruction in the practice of music, together with the neglect of all theory, is probably significant. His experience of playing and singing gave him sound ideas as to what he might demand of executants; and his freedom from compositional authority at least allowed a fuller play of fancy than would have been granted by Fux or other masters of counterpoint or composition. His natural musical

---

[1] See Hadow's *A Croatian Composer*, largely based on Kuhač's studies.

impulse was conserved, at any rate, at a time when it might readily have been stifled. A sturdy habit of self-dependence was soon added to his determination to get on; and this was sorely needed, for with the change in his voice he lost his position in the choir and was virtually put out into the street to shift for himself.

FIRST AND SECOND VIOLIN PARTS OF HAYDN QUARTET, Op. 1, No. 1

With little aid save that of his own energies he acquired pupils, learned the contemporary theory of Fux and others, made friends with such musicians as Wagenseil, Gluck, Dittersdorf, and Porpora (serving the latter as both valet and accompanist), and, above all, mastered the new homophonic style as it was exemplified in the clavier sonatas of K. P. E. Bach. Invited in 1755 to the country house of Karl Joseph Edlen von Fürnberg at Weinzirl, where a small orchestra was maintained, Haydn wrote, in the manner of K. P. E. Bach's sonatas, larger pieces for various combinations of instruments, called *Divertimenti, Nocturnes,* or *Cassations*.[2] Here also were written his first string quartet and his first symphony. The two violin parts of an early quartet, until recently supposed to be his first, compressed on a single stave, will show the extremely unpretentious organization of the sonata form as Haydn then understood it. It will be found on pages 344 and 345.

Simple as this is, its form clearly foreshadows the later structure. The principal subject—a vigorous arpeggio of the tonic chord, *forte,* followed by a brief turn of melody, *piano*—fills a phrase of four bars which is repeated. There follows a transition eight bars long, which pauses definitely on the dominant. The sixteenth-note arpeggio figure which follows does duty as a second subject (four bars) and there is a little cadential figure as epilogue. Observe that like the principal subject it has little definiteness of character. Each serves, however, to give a positive statement of the key in which it stands. Key contrasts, as in the suite dance, are still a main feature of the structure. This convention of making the principal subject, especially, around the arpeggio of the tonic chord persists for a long time. The development section has first the figure of the second subject (C minor) answered by the *piano* pendant of the principal subject. The rest of the development, though related rhythmically to the exposition, is practically new material. The imitative echoes from bar 31 on are interesting, particularly the darker quality of the B flat minor key in bars 35–38 and the last echo, *pianissimo,* followed by the sudden outburst of the B flat minor arpeggio downward in unison. This almost threatening gesture is immediately and charmingly quelled by the nonchalant figure (bar 39) which concludes the development. The recapitulation is both altered and abbreviated, although every essential feature of the exposition is recalled. No more extended restatement would be desirable here; but when the second subject comes to be more highly differentiated from the first, in later developments of the form, a fuller recapitulation will be necessary. This section, like the exposition, is repeated. The stark contrasts of *forte* and *piano* are the only varieties of

[2] The meaning of this last word is obscure. It seems to imply either a "farewell" or possibly a sort of serenade—from *Gasse*, a street.

"expression" used. They were the only usual demands for dynamic contrast in the music of the time, and indicate a great deal as to the players' capacity as well as to the expressive purpose of the music.

The Divertimenti—The First Symphonies—The Rondo

In this quartet there are five movements—the opening sonata form *Presto*, a *Minuet*, an *Adagio*, another *Minuet*, and a final *Presto* also in sonata form. Most of the quartets in this and the following opus have exactly the same order and number of movements. The third quartet of this set opens with a long *Adagio*, and there follow a *Minuet*, a *Presto*, another *Minuet*, and a long final *Presto* in rondo form. The fifth quartet, however, has but three movements—two *Allegros* with an *Andante* between; all three movements are in sonata form. This quartet is really Haydn's first symphony, the term still being applicable to a composition for three or more instruments. The dimensions of the sonata-form movements are here far larger than in the other quartets, which are really *divertimenti*, and which by their character and relative number seem to indicate that the possibilities of the larger development of the form are only beginning to appear in 1755.

A short period of service with Count Morzin saw the production, along with several *divertimenti*, of another true symphony in three movements which is often called Haydn's first symphony. During this period Haydn was married (most unfortunately) to the elder daughter of a Viennese wigmaker. Like Jacob, Haydn had preferred the younger daughter but at the father's instigation took the elder—a woman unsympathetic, cold, inartistic, and ill-tempered. In 1761, having by now made a considerable name for himself, Haydn was invited by Prince Paul Anton Esterhazy to take the position of second Kapellmeister at his princely seat of Eisenstadt. About thirty symphonies, many concertos, trios for piano with other instruments, and several cantatas, operettas, and incidental pieces were composed up to the time of his leaving Eisenstadt. In 1766 Haydn succeeded the Kapellmeister Werner, who had died; and in the following year Prince Nicolaus, who had assumed the title after the death of his brother Paul Anton, built on one of his estates at the end of the Neusidler lake a resplendent summer residence whose magnificence almost rivaled that of Versailles. Two theatres were built, one for drama, and one for puppet shows, and the "chapel"—consisting of a considerable number of singers in addition to the orchestra—was called upon at regular intervals during the week to give entertainment for the Prince and his guests. Since the Prince disliked traveling and hated Vienna, Haydn was practically immured here until the death of Prince Nicolaus in 1790. He produced not only innumerable symphonies and quartets, but also Masses and several operas. He had first essayed an opera in 1752, when *Der neue krumme Teufel* had been produced in Vienna. But he had little confidence in his dramatic powers. "My operas are calculated exclusively for our own company, and would not produce their effect elsewhere." A few were actually produced in Vienna but held no very conspicuous place in the repertoire.

Almost the only contact with the outside world was gained during Haydn's annual midwinter visit to Vienna; and it is probable that on one of these visits in the winter of 1781–82 he first met Mozart, now no longer a prodigy but a man of twenty-five years, with a vaster musical experience already acquired than could be attained by many an octogenarian. Mozart had then just quitted the service of Archbishop Hieronymus in Salzburg, and had determined to try his fortunes in Vienna. He had already known Haydn's music, especially his string quartets, some of which he had heard on a visit to Vienna eight years before. This meeting marks the beginning of a most remarkable artistic friendship between the two men. Their personal intercourse was slight; but the degree of their mutual esteem may be inferred from the often-quoted statement of Mozart that "it was from Haydn that I first learned the true way to write string quartets"; and from Haydn's declaration to Mozart's father, "I declare to you on my honor that I consider your son the greatest composer I have ever heard; he has taste, and possesses the most consummate knowledge of the art of composition."

Just in what way this mutual influence worked it would be impossible to say. Haydn's example could hardly have been of the pedantic sort. No eighteenth-century composer is more unconcerned than he about the precise conventions of form. He usually presents the pattern of the first movement in the binary division which we have shown to have been derived from the older dance form. But within the movement the detail is almost unpredictable. Whether or not he will introduce a second subject; how much of subsidiary matter may be included; how extended the development may be; whether there will be a coda, or merely the completion of the second part in the manner of the first—all these are questions which Haydn decides, conformably to no established rule, but according to his immediate judgment and desire. He once remarked that the rules of harmony "were his very humble and obedient servants"; and he has evidently little more regard for the rules of form. The slow movement, which had at first been made in sonata form, has now the simpler structure of a Romanza (a *da capo* form like the operatic aria, with a contrasted middle section) which gives greater scope for lyrical expression. The Minuet (which occurred twice in the *divertimenti* and not at all in the first symphonies) is now included in the symphony after the slow movement. The final movement, which in the earlier symphonies was always in sonata form, is now lightened by being cast in the form of the Rondo.

The Rondo had until now appeared but seldom in instrumental works. As a concluding movement in the sonata it soon became popular, so that its history must be recounted. This form was to some extent foreshadowed in the old *rondels* of Walter Odington (see page 85), and was more definitely related to the poetic forms of the *rondeau*, or the *rondel*, as developed by the French—little poems of thirteen or fourteen lines having but two different rhymes, and with a repetition of the initial couplet in the middle and again at the close. The following example by Austin Dobson will give an adequate idea of the form:

> Love comes back to his vacant dwelling,—
> The old, old Love that we knew of yore!
> We see him stand by the open door,
> With his great eyes sad, and his bosom swelling.
> He makes as though in our arms repelling
> He fain would lie as he lay before;—
> Love comes back to his vacant dwelling,
> The old, old Love that we knew of yore!
> Ah! who shall help us from over-spelling
> That sweet, forgotten, forbidden lore?
> E'n as we doubt, in our hearts once more,
> With a rush of tears to our eyelids welling,
> Love comes back to his vacant dwelling,—
> The old, old Love that we knew of yore!

We have found an older musical rondeau, related to the poetic, in the chansons of Orlando Lasso and in the rondeau en couplets of Couperin. The essence of the instrumental rondo is the repetition of a subject, A, after some less significant intervening matter has occurred, thus: A–b–A, where b is the intervening passage. (Compare the aria form A–B–A, where B is far more significant than the b of the primitive rondo.) If A is sufficiently interesting, it is possible to have it recur more than once, thus: A–b–A–c–A–d–A, etc., the only substance of real thematic interest still being A. But if b is now elevated to a position of thematic importance, B, we have nearly the same relation between A–B as between the first and second subjects of the sonata form. The second occurrence of A likewise may be followed by a third subject, C (derived from c as was B from b). But the importance of B will make it preferable to repeat it, after a third appearance of A, rather than to erect d into D. Thus the final rondo form came to be A–B–A–C–A–B′–A, to which a coda might be appended. The key chosen for B was usually that of the dominant or the relative major; that for B′ was usually that of the tonic. Since, with highly contrasted subjects, some transition is necessary between them, the rondo group A–B is very like the exposition section of sonata form; A–B′ is like the recapitulation; and the group A–C takes the place of the development section. The recurrences of A, however, are regularly all in the tonic. Thus, if there is any doubt about the form as we hear it, we shall be set right as soon as we reach the middle section; for hardly a sonata-form movement can be found whose development section begins with the complete statement of the principal subject in the tonic key.

The lighter forms of the sonata—such as sonatas for piano solo, piano and violin, trio—retain more of the *divertimento* character. Also, Haydn's melody was often largely colored by the idiom of Austrian or Hungarian folk song. In the use of these turns of phrase, indeed, he endowed his themes with an individuality of character, a naïveté, and a kindliness of humor which elevate them far above the rather labored technical figures which did duty for subjects in the earlier sonatas, so that they retain their charm almost unimpaired for contemporary ears. It is thus that Haydn escaped, as K. P. E. Bach had been unable to do, from the "galant" style of melody affected by the ruling social orders in the earlier day.

Another weakness of the "galant" style began also to be remedied, somewhat by Haydn but more extensively by Mozart. The graces and affected turns of the first "galant" homophonic melody had been concentrated in one leading part. To that part (from a figured bass, with perhaps a few additional indications) an accompaniment was provided whose interest depended largely on the powers of improvisation possessed by the accompanist. As mere mannerism gave way to a more definitely expressive melodic invention, the accompaniment could no longer safely be left to the invention of the performer, and was written out in full to be played exactly as it stood. Such a part was an *obbligato* (obligatory) part, in contrast to the *ad libitum* or improvisatory accompaniment. (The power of improvisation was more highly regarded, not only in Haydn's day but during the first half of the nineteenth century, than later. Beethoven speaks of his earlier violin sonatas as "sonatas for piano with violin obbligato.")

All this had Haydn accomplished, largely by his own efforts, before 1780. Then with the coming of Mozart to Vienna began that "Viennese Classical Period" which continued to the death of Schubert in 1828, although the classical aspect began to be highly colored by romanticism from 1810 on. The actual features of the sonata structure were fully germinated. The efflorescence, however, was immensely enriched by Mozart's influence and example.

Mozart's Early Life

No record exists of another such incredible genius as Mozart. Twenty-four years younger than Haydn, he yet made such strides that, by the time he reached ordinary maturity of age and when Haydn first came to know him, he had produced music in every current style, from opera, Mass, and symphony to *divertimenti* and smaller piano pieces; was the most famous pianist in Europe; was an excellent violinist; and had shown a keen intelligence and great ability in other fields. His father was court composer to the Archbishop of Salzburg, and a teacher of eminence as is proved by his excellent *Violin School*, which was a standard instruction book for long after his death. Aware of Wolfgang's gifts and fully cognizant of his own responsibility for the development of such a talent, Leopold Mozart gave his best energies to the training of his son, and soon found that he had indeed a prodigy to deal with. The sister Maria Anna (nicknamed "Nannerl"), four and a half years older, was also highly gifted. In 1762, when Mozart was six years old, the father took the children to Munich, and later to Vienna where the "little magician," as he was called, astounded the whole court by his playing and by his improvisations and writings. His absorption of courtly style-influences was highly significant for his later work. He played with all the little princesses, sat on the lap of the Empress Maria Theresa, and once announced that he would marry Marie Antoinette (a year older than himself) because she had been kind enough to help him up when he had slipped and fallen on the polished floor. All the court musicians were amazed, particularly Wagenseil, whom Mozart commanded to turn the pages for him while he played a concerto of Wagenseil's composition.

The visit to Vienna having been thus successful and profitable, a longer tour was planned. In 1763 they set out for Paris, visiting many minor centers on the way. There Wolfgang gave even more remarkable proofs of his genius, playing the organ, the clavier, and the violin, playing faultlessly—and even transposing—difficult pieces at sight, and improvising accompaniments to songs he had never heard. Four sonatas for piano and violin by the little master were printed when he was seven years old. The war of the Bouffonistes, which had been raging for nearly ten years, was still active. The questions at issue were of course beyond Wolfgang's interest; but his father's sympathies were strongly on the side of the Italians, and the natural emphasis of his opinions could hardly escape affecting at least the unconscious prejudices of his son.

The Paris success was soon repeated in London where they went in April, 1764, remaining until July, 1765. By way of The Hague, Amsterdam, and Paris they traveled slowly back to Salzburg which they reached in November, 1766. In London at the newly opened Italian opera Wolfgang for the first time heard singers of the highest rank. He also had singing lessons from Manzuoli, a remarkable male soprano, and was on friendly terms with Johann Christian Bach, the son of Sebastian Bach, who had recently settled in London where his operas were in considerable favor. From this experience dates Mozart's interest in the opera—perhaps the strongest of his musical passions.

A year was now spent at home in the most severe study of counterpoint and composition. One of the fruits of this work was an oratorio, of which the first part was by Mozart and the other two by Michael Haydn and Adlgasser. He wrote also a cantata and some incidental music for the annual Latin play at the University—this time on the myth of Apollo and Hyacinth. In January, 1768, Leopold Mozart took his family to Vienna where were encountered much misfortune in the shape of illness, and the first opposition in the shape of jealous intrigue. The Emperor Joseph was parsimonious, the court was indifferent, and the public dared not show any independent enthusiasm. Under the circumstances the musicians were jealous of any success won by the young prodigy. Yet the Emperor was at length induced to command Wolfgang to write an opera—*La Finta semplice*—which was so intrigued against that it was not performed. (No trace of Gluck's influence is as yet to be seen. His *Alceste* had been performed in 1767, making a most unfavorable impression upon Leopold Mozart.) A little German operetta, *Bastien and Bastienne*, was privately performed, however.[3] The style of the work is that of the Singspiel, and the music is in the German idiom in contrast to the Italian manner of the larger work. An important string quintet (afterwards expanded and re-scored as a serenade for wind instruments) and three Masses were also completed before 1770, when Wolfgang was appointed concertmaster of the Archbishop's chapel at Salzburg.

But the musical experience of the youth could not be considered complete without an Italian tour. Accordingly they set out late in 1769, visiting the principal Italian cities where Wolfgang's playing, and still more his composition, excited unbounded astonishment. Most remarkable of all was his writing out, after a single hearing, of the famous *Miserere* of Allegri,[4] which was performed in the Sistine Chapel only on three days in the year—Ash Wednesday, Maundy Thursday, and Good Friday. At Bologna he was warmly commended by the venerable Padre Martini, probably the greatest theorist and musical historian then living. His great-

[3] In this there is a little song which has been made far too much of as having the same phrase as the principal subject of Beethoven's *Eroica* Symphony.
[4] Mendelssohn's minute descriptions of this music—made in 1831, when he was twenty-two—are hardly to be compared to this achievement by a boy of fourteen.

est success was with the opera *Mithridates* (produced, after much intrigue against it, at Milan, December 26, 1770) which ran to twenty performances. Other operas for Milan were at once commissioned.

In the following year the Archbishop Sigismund of Salzburg, whom Leopold Mozart had served for so long and in whose chapel Wolfgang had been made concertmaster, died and was succeeded by the detested Hieronymus, whose brutality at last caused Mozart to quit his service altogether. Mozart was much abroad for a time, however, on visits to Milan and Munich, so that the new regime was not at first unbearable. In 1778 occurred the second visit to Paris, made this time in company with his mother since Leopold Mozart was refused leave of absence for the journey. On the way they stopped at Mannheim where Mozart heard the famous orchestra, made many friends among the musicians, and fell in love with Aloysia, daughter of Fridolin Weber, who was the uncle of Carl Maria von Weber, the great opera composer. Rumors of this passion caused the greatest consternation to the father, since Wolfgang was in no position to marry and nothing fruitful was to be expected from a long stay in Mannheim. Singularly, none of the compositions written at Mannheim were symphonies.

Urged on by the father they continued their journey to Paris; but the venture proved almost a fiasco. Mozart had failed to provide recommendations to the court, and without them his prospects were poor indeed. He failed to receive a commission for an opera—the main objective of his journey. The war of the Gluckists and the Piccinnists was at its height. Mozart, indifferent to aesthetic theories, not impressed by Piccinni, and not warmly enthusiastic for Gluck, was compelled to stand on the side lines during the conflict. To crown his misfortunes, his mother died. He returned empty-handed from Paris in September, 1778, visiting again at Mannheim and Munich and finding that Aloysia Weber had grown indifferent to him. At home he found welcome from his friends but could not endure his official life in the employ of Hieronymus. His only consolation was a commission to write an opera for Munich, to be produced in the season of 1781—*Idomeneo, King of Crete*. This, in spite of his apparent indifference to the Gluckian controversy, shows more direct influence of Gluck's theories than any other of Mozart's operas. It was produced January 29, 1781. Soon after, Mozart was summoned to attend Hieronymus who was then in Vienna. Here occurred the disgraceful dismissal of Mozart (June 8, 1781), which determined him to remain thereafter independent of such patronage no matter what the consequences.

Two objectives, especially, kept him in Vienna—the possibility of producing an opera, and a newly awakened interest in Constanze Weber, the younger sister of Aloysia. Both objectives were attained: *Die Entführung aus dem Serail* ("The Abduction from the Seraglio") was produced with great success, July 13, 1782; and he and Constanze were married in the Cathedral of St. Stephan on August fourth. But the conventional fee of a hundred ducats (about $250) which Mozart received for his opera was but a small help toward defraying the expenses of a family; hoped-for preferment at court was prevented by the hostility of Strack and Salieri, and Mozart was compelled to seek his livelihood by playing and by giving lessons—the latter an occupation he much disliked. Thus began a new period in Mozart's life. We may therefore observe the development of the sonata structure at his hands, comparing it with that of Haydn, the study of whose work we left off at about this period.

The Earlier Work of Mozart and Haydn Compared

Both men were children of the period of transition. The considerable likenesses in their work are referable to their natural absorption of the current fashions of musical thought; the differences are largely due to differences in education and musical environment. Folk life and folk music, almost without stylistic refinement, gave Haydn his first imaginative impressions. By his own exertions, and chiefly in the light of his own intelligence, he developed a technique of expression which never really dissevered itself from this background. Mozart on the other hand grew up in contact with what, in comparison to Haydn's background, was a highly learned style. The music and manners of the court, not of the folk, first stimulated his imagination. Watched and competently supervised at every moment he acquired, as if by instinct, not only the delicate airs and graces of courtly manner, but a command of contrapuntal technique which made his most intricate writing seem as transparent as the simplest homophony. The favor in which Italian music was held at every European court, Leopold Mozart's preference for it, and the culmination of Wolfgang's tours, at what for him was the most impressionable age, by actual successes with Italian opera in Italy—all this gave to Mozart's style an Italian flavor which it never lost and which is of course quite absent from Haydn's music.

The *divertimento* was for both men, as for the society of their time, at first the favorite form of instrumental music. Mozart's treatment, however, shows certain features which are not found in Haydn's examples: the cantabile subtheme recalling the tender, sighing phrases of Neapolitan opera melody, and the frequent use of the Alberti Bass—a simple arpeggiation of the essential harmony, effortlessly executed by the pianist's left hand and easily imitated on string instruments, which was profusely used though not really invented by Domenico Alberti, a popular Italian composer (*circa* 1717–1740). It must not be understood, however, that Mozart's style was wholly Italian. It was fundamentally German; and was derived by his own admission, as was also Haydn's, from Karl Philipp Emanuel Bach. "Bach is the father, and we are his children," Mozart once said. "Whoever of us can really do anything, owes it to him; and whoever refuses to admit that is a . . ."

It was Haydn who, through the use of the string quartet as the favorite instrumental group for the *divertimento*, came first to see the possibilities of a larger expansion of its more significant movements into the sonata; and it was from Haydn, as we have already seen, that Mozart learned the "true way of writing string quartets." The fugal finale, and especially the gradual adoption of the "obbligato" style were all begun by the older man, and carried, in the period now to be discussed, to an unexampled perfection by the younger. Mozart's first symphonies, like Haydn's, have only three movements, the minuet being but sparely introduced before 1772. As with Haydn, also, the second subject is often only slightly contrasted with the first, the closing subject (perhaps an expansion of the cadential figures in the suite dance) showing more contrast than the second subject. There is seldom any decisively expressive tone, animation and brilliancy contrasting merely with a kind of easy calm which is more complacent than expressive. It was only gradually that the symphony and the quartet in sonata form grew to greater popularity than the *divertimento*, or attempted expressive depths not welcomed by the lovers of pleasant diversion. The first of Mozart's quartets was written in Italy in 1770, and a set of six was begun in Milan in February, 1773, all of which have the older constitution of three movements only. In August and September of the same year—probably in emulation of Haydn—he wrote at Vienna another set of six which are far more mature in substance and have the four movements always thereafter characteristic of the form. There was apparently little demand for quartets in Salzburg, however; and no more appeared until 1784, after Mozart had removed permanently to Vienna. The concerto was a far more popular form, and many examples for violin and for piano belong to the last years of the Salzburg period. Haydn also wrote many concertos during this time, none of them of great importance. Until about 1780, then, the instrumental works of Mozart showed few important differences from Haydn's; and these were largely due to Italian influences by which Haydn was little affected.

MOZART'S MATURER WORKS

In 1780 Mozart was really only entering manhood; his artistic experience was already immense, but his human experience was slight. The foot of Count Arco which pushed him out of the antechamber of Hieronymus pushed him also into a world far less in accord with his idealistic visions than he could believe. This bitter experience reflects itself in a vastly deepened musical substance. The subjects have a sharper contour and a more vivid suggestiveness. The minor key is chosen with great frequency—and this, it must be remembered, had a degree of significance which is now lost for us. The whole formal pattern of the sonata structure is expanded, and its parts are knit together with a coherence hitherto unknown. The principal subject is designed on a larger scale. Its initial phrases (still closely adhering to the notes of the tonic chord) are no longer merely spun out into the transition which presently leads to the essential key contrast of dominant or relative minor, and to a second subject, often of no particular significance, in the new key. Instead, the principal subject is more sharply designed—often by giving its initial phrases a slight expansion, followed by a repetition, almost in the original form, of the terse and almost epigrammatic beginning. The following transition thus becomes more obviously different from the principal subject, and at the same time can contain subsidiary thematic ideas which it would have been impossible to insert if the principal subject had been merely spun out until the arrival of the second subject. But in such a scheme as this the second subject now demands similar definition, both in expression and design. It will be contrasted of course with the principal subject; but the contriving of just that degree of contrast which will be striking, and will at the same time maintain a clear relevance to the principal subject, is a problem which none but the finest musical instinct can solve. The second subject too, like the principal subject together with the transition which contains subordinate thematic matter, often consists of a thematic group. The epilogue or closing subject often refers back to the principal subject, to round out the exposition and to facilitate its repetition. After such an expanded exposition the development section may naturally be much intensified. The richness of the exposition in thematic matter offers endless opportunities for development; and the contrasts of character may permit the attainment of highly dramatic moments. (Indeed, with the later inventions of highly suggestive subject matter, especially by Beethoven, the enlarged scope and diversified character of the whole sonata structure often takes on a truly dramatic aspect.) The recapitulation can no longer be reduced to a mere passing reference (as in Conti's overture) to the main subject matter of the exposition. And that sense of anticlimax which is almost inevitably given by the full recapitulation is sometimes relieved, even in Mozart's work, by a coda in which further possibilities of development are exhibited.

Mozart's growing sense both of musical significance and of formal organization is seen in many works of diverse character: chiefly in the three wonderful symphonies (in E flat, G minor, and C major—the *Jupiter*) composed in the summer of 1788; the six quartets dedicated to Haydn (published 1785) and the four later quartets, three of them dedicated to Frederick Wilhelm II of Prussia whose offer of a position at his court, if it had been accepted by Mozart, might have given a considerably different turn to the later history of music; in the four string quintets of which the second in G minor, composed in 1787, is a remarkable example of intense and even bitter expression; in several of the seventeen piano concertos composed in Vienna, which were among the chief works upon whose performance Mozart's livelihood depended; and finally in the lesser works—sonatas for piano solo and chamber music with piano and strings or wind instruments. Here the coming instrumental art of Beethoven is clearly anticipated, not merely in the perfection of the sonata form but in many details of harmony, thematic development, and instrumentation.

Mozart's harmony, while generally simple and straightforward, especially in the faster movements, is often remarkably abstruse in slower passages. The extraordinary introduction to the C major Quartet:

in which the false relation of the A natural of the first violin following the A flat of the viola (note that the two phrases are otherwise identical) was for a long time a stumbling block to the theorists, is almost equaled in strangeness by many other passages in the symphonies and concertos. In thematic development his ingenuity is beyond anything which has as yet been introduced into the sonata form. The first movement of the G minor Symphony, whose principal subject probably represented in Mozart's day a far greater agitation than it immediately suggests to us, is throughout so impregnated with the rhythmic beating of its initial three-note phrase that a comparison with the famous C minor Symphony of Beethoven is readily suggested. The development of the last movement, likewise, has passages of the most abrupt and violent harmonic transition. And the famous contrapuntal finale of the *Jupiter*—not a fugue, but a sonata form in which the fugal technique is used almost throughout—is a far remove from the thin and affected mannerism which ruled the sonata in the early decades of the century. In instrumentation, Mozart makes no demands beyond the simple orchestra which Haydn knew. He adds the clarinet, after the example of the Mannheim orchestra; but it is in the grouping and the manipulation of his instruments, rather than in the increase of their number, that Mozart's exquisite orchestral instinct is seen. The choirs of wind and strings (there is as yet no complete brass choir) are opposed as distinct and complete groups, or single instruments stand as solo instruments against the background of the other, or the two choirs are combined in one energetic *tutti* outburst. Also the division of the phrases of a single theme occurs between the two opposed groups—a practice very frequent with Beethoven:

Mozart, G minor
  Symphony

Beethoven, No. 1,
  in C

Beethoven, No. 3,
  Eroica

Mozart offered us in his instrumental compositions no program or suggestive title by which we may be initiated into (or deflected from) his expressive meaning; but we shall see, when we speak of Mozart as an opera composer, how vividly he felt his music to be uttering the very essence of the emotion involved in the action, and it is only reasonable to suppose that the Mozart of the symphonies had the same expressive purpose as the Mozart of the operas.

Haydn's Later Achievements

While Mozart in the last decade of his life was thus perfecting the sonata structure, Haydn, still at Esterház, was quietly continuing his course, slowly adding to his command of the symphonic form, but, in his position of practical servitude, unstimulated to any epoch-making revolutions. The decade 1780–1790, indeed, shows many improvements which are more or less directly derived from Mozart; but only one which is at all particularly his own. This is the frequent use of the rondo for the final movement, and the approximation of the rondo to the sonata-movement form as described above. In 1790 Haydn's patron Prince Nicolaus died, and the musical establishment at Esterház was broken up. Haydn now felt free to accept the urgent invitations to come to London which Salomon had been frequently extending during the last few years. Mozart (who was likewise invited to come after Haydn's visit was ended) spent the day of Haydn's departure with him in Vienna. Moved to tears, Mozart exclaimed, "We are taking our last farewell in this world." Neither then imagined that it would be because of the death of the younger man that this prophecy would come true.

The twelve "Salomon" symphonies which Haydn wrote during his two visits to London (1791–1792 and 1794–1795) show a considerable influence of Mozart's later manner. But Haydn was by no means a mere imitator, and does not follow Mozart into regions uncongenial to his own nature. There is in all Haydn's works no parallel to the tragic intensity of the G minor Symphony, nor to the contrapuntal brilliancy of the *Jupiter*. Many quite individual features are, however, to be observed. The slow introduction (derived from the French overture) is far more frequently used by Haydn than by Mozart. In this there is sometimes (as in the *Clock* symphony) a thematic relation between the introduction and the principal subject of the following allegro. In the *Paukenwirbel* Symphony also the introduction is partly reintroduced after the recapitulation—a feature later used by Beethoven in the *Pathétique* Sonata. The remarkable finesse which Mozart displays in the designing of his principal and second subjects for contrast is seldom achieved by Haydn. His transitions are generally derived from the principal subject; and the repetition of that subject, which frequently occurs, sounds, not like the final summing up of the subject as in Mozart, but like a mere incident in the transition, intended to recall the material from which that transition is being derived. Haydn seldom points out the coming of his second subject by a sort of "present arms!" (as Parry describes it); for his second subject is still of secondary value and not on a parity with the first. Even in so late a work as the *Military* Symphony, the long transition to the dominant and the cadence in that key are followed by a repetition of the principal subject in the dominant; and the only true second subject comes in the place of the usual closing subject at the end of the exposition. Haydn's slow movements either are in the Romanza form already mentioned, or consist of sets of variations. His variation process is simpler than Mozart's, his treatment consisting usually in the application of successively more rapid figures of accompaniment (hardly polyphonic) to the original thematic line. An occasional transformation of the theme itself occurs, this being most frequent when the major theme is transformed to the minor. Sometimes also two contrasted themes, one or both varied, give greater intricacy to the form; and a coda, somewhat developed, is added as in the *Paukenwirbel* Symphony. The minuet more often retains the primitive dance character with Haydn than with Mozart. Sometimes, however, Haydn used the stylistic treatment in canon as Mozart did in his G minor Symphony.

It is doubtless because of the ideas Haydn wishes to express—ideas to some extent traceable to his first, simple musical impressions—that his technical methods thus differ from Mozart's. And indeed it is this difference which is most important and most interesting. Haydn's proverbial geniality and humor can be expressed in a less carefully considered rhetorical scheme than Mozart's more finely discriminated representations either of feeling or of pure artistic beauty. For Haydn to have attempted to follow Mozart into these regions would have been as great a blunder as for Mozart to have attempted to imitate the naïve and kindly discourses of Haydn. And the art which Beethoven learned, to some extent directly from both of these men, would have been dangerously narrowed in scope if the technical principles of its structure had been confined by convention to those exemplified in the supremely perfect patterns which Mozart drew. It is much easier to describe technical processes than the thing which is expressed through a given process; but we must not let our preoccupation with technical problems blind us to the fact that technique is itself the product of inspiration, and is in the last analysis no more imitable than inspiration itself.

The overture, as the form out of which to some extent the symphony grew, was also gradually expanded to the proportions of a symphonic movement, so that from the time of Beethoven the form is almost identical with sonata form. With Gluck's *Orpheus*, although its overture is musically disappointing, the old three-movement type of overture was abandoned. Thereafter in Gluck's hands the overture either became a simple sonata form, or was preceded by the slow introduction which belonged to the old French overture form. Distinct contribution to the later highly dramatic character of both overture and symphony was made by the association of the principal themes with persons, ideas, or emotions involved in the coming drama. The program music of the future, and even the leading motive of Wagner, are thus in some measure foreshadowed. Although Haydn adopted little of this type of suggestion for his works, the program tendency is marked in the three symphonies *Le Matin* ("Morning"), *Le Midi* ("Noonday"), and *Le Soir* ("Evening"); and many other titles, such as *Mercury*, *The Schoolmaster*, or *The Chase*, show that the disposition to see pictures or some other physical reality in music was not unknown in the period of high classicism. The introduction to Haydn's great oratorio *The Creation*, which is a depiction of chaos, is a truly remarkable example of tone painting. Mozart's overtures for his earlier operas are all in the three-movement form. With *Idomeneo*, however, Gluck's one-movement structure was adopted, although sonata form was not always adhered to. In the overture to *Die Entführung aus dem Serail* the opening aria, transformed into the minor key, takes the place of the development section; in that to *Figaro* a similar procedure was intended but was later abandoned, and a few energetic bars of transition or interlude take the place of the development. In the overture to *Don Giovanni*, however, the development is complete; and in that to the *Magic Flute* both main subject and development are presented in fugal guise. For the overture, also, Mozart demands a larger orchestra than for any of his symphonies.

Although Haydn, Mozart, and to some extent Gluck are the great leaders in this evolution of the symphony and the overture, we must not suppose that they were the only contributors to the widening stream of musical thought which was expressed in those forms. Mozart's grace and Haydn's humor, typical as they are, are by no means either their only qualities or the only ones which the music of the time was expressing. Lesser men, possessed of less striking gifts, nevertheless achieved occasional masterpieces of expression or structure, and according to the measure of their individuality enriched the art, or at any rate helped to give it the characteristic tone which represents the whole period. Some of the earlier symphonists have already been mentioned. Of the later contemporaries of Haydn and Mozart in Vienna the most important were Karl Ditters von Dittersdorf, Leopold Hoffman (who removed from Mannheim to Vienna in 1772), Wenzl Pichl, Georg Wagenseil, and two members of

Haydn's orchestra, Franz Anton Rössler and Paul Wranitzky. Luigi Boccherini, an Italian who worked chiefly in Spain, wrote chiefly in chamber music forms, though his symphonies are fairly numerous. From his numberless string quintets (which have two 'celli, whereas Mozart improves upon this grouping by using two violas) one little movement, the famous *Minuet*, still retains its charm.

The Sonata and the Revolution – Beethoven

THE French Revolution, which broke out only shortly before Mozart's death, probably meant to him little more than a popular uprising entailing the possible overthrow of a dynasty. Largely indifferent even to artistic controversies such as those of the Gluckists and the Piccinnists, he was completely unconcerned with those social theories which, after the fall of the Bastille, rapidly became the vital problem not only of the hour but of the future. Although he was strongly the individualist in his attitude toward the system of patronage, he conformed without thought of protest to the Imperial regime under which he lived, and had no thought that his attitude toward Archbishop Hieronymus might be expanded into a theory for the reorganization of society.

There is a vast difference in this respect between Mozart and Beethoven. A far more extreme individualist than Mozart, Beethoven saw his own individual convictions and aspirations idealized in the revolutionary principles of liberty, equality, and fraternity, and believed in those principles with all his heart. He was sensitive, proud, and suspicious of persons; but his faith in humanity was unbounded and incorruptible. His convictions are almost constantly perceptible in his work. It was only in the last decade of his life that Mozart's personal experience led him to the employment of more intense and bitter musical expression than he had hitherto cared to use. To the youthful Beethoven, on the other hand, the world was seldom gracious, and even his early music often voices a cry of pain rather than a carol of pleasure. Purely as a musician he matured more slowly than Mozart. As a man he matured far more rapidly. In early youth he was called upon to develop not merely his remarkable musical powers but also a sturdy independence of judgment and action. As a result he conceived a pugnacious opposition to all sham and falsity which was thoroughly in accord with revolutionary sentiment. He was no mere rebel, however. His purpose went beyond the overthrow of the old to the establishment of the new. Almost from the beginning he was occupied with the problem of a musical expression for his ideal.

What he had to do in thus expanding the existing technique of homo-phonic composition can be fairly clearly described. Not only had the dimensions of the sonata form to be enlarged: its thematic substance had to be made more solid and suggestive, while at the same time the coherence of each movement within itself, and of the successive movements with each other, had to be strengthened just in proportion as the design itself was enlarged. A fairly exact account of the detail of Beethoven's purely musical processes could be given in technical terms descriptive of features of melody, harmony, rhythm, period-structure, motive-development, and the like. But such description would fail to convey any idea of the most important fact of all—of the thought itself which it is the purpose of the expanded form to express. Nor was it Beethoven only whose purpose was thus represented in the new art; the whole succeeding generation of ro-manticists were animated by the same purpose of individualistic expression. We are therefore at the threshold of another musical revolution—not perhaps as complete as the earlier monodic revolution in its reversal of existing musical processes, but equally profound in its vision of new ex-pressive purposes.

The New Individualism—Its Effect on Classicism

The essence of the revolutionary attitude, toward art as well as toward social organization, lies in the new sense of the importance of the indi-vidual. Instead of supposing himself to exist for the benefit of the state, the church, or whatever social institution to which he may owe allegiance, the individual now conceives that the state, the church, and all social or-ganization exists for the ultimate benefit of his collective self. Such a complete reversal in the relative importance of individual and society implies a new emotional attitude which cannot but be reflected in works of art. For all serious art represents an attempt to "hold the mirror up to nature," not merely in externals but in the inmost recesses of emotion out of which all external action proceeds. Music, as truly as any other art, pursues the same ideal—the revelation, not merely of things, but of a fun-damental emotional attitude toward things. But since the expressive pur-pose of music, although palpable enough to the ear, is all but indefinable in words, it will perhaps help our grasp of the new attitude if we first observe its expression in a more easily intelligible form—for example, in the classical drama.

With such reservation as all generalized statement requires, it may be said that the classical dramatists of the seventeenth and eighteenth centuries attempted to submerge the thought or feeling of the individual as such in an expression of thought or feeling concurred in by all humanity. In his endeavor to make his characters into types, the dramatist often ceased to endow them with any but superficial personal traits; they became the embodiment of accepted conventional attitudes toward social or moral questions. Revenge, honor, miserliness, nobility, jealousy, wifely devotion, misanthropy—these and a hundred other passions were in a sense magnified and at the same time impersonated in the characters of the drama—not literally, of course, as in the old moralities, but in a larger, more philosophic sense. A sufficiently human exterior was provided to hide the abstraction; but the drama often consisted essentially of the conflict of these rather abstract passions, either with each other, or with a still more metaphysical abstraction in the shape of an implied moral principle (in some sense the counterpart of the old Greek idea of Fate) imposed upon humanity from without. The drama thus incidentally involved an exposition of the conventional moral code of the existing regime. Incidentally, also, the exalted code of manners of that regime was exhibited in the action and speech of the characters. Refinements and graces of manner which imply conformity to existing moral conventions often cloaked—at any rate for our minds, brought up in the nonclassical, English tradition—all ordinary reality of feeling.[1]

From the new point of view, the individual is no longer to be dealt with as an abstraction. He is a complex and somewhat unaccountable reality, swayed by contradictory passions, incapable of absolute analysis; a subject from which a tentative philosophy may be derived, not an object to which an absolute philosophy must be applied. Individual characteristics were negligible in the older view because they appeared as minor aberrations from the accepted norm. In the newer view they become vitally significant because they may represent one element, at least, in that great composite which constitutes the true norm. The individual is still striving toward contact with that abstract Power in which, according to the older idea, the conduct of human affairs resides. But he now conceives himself as imbued with a fraction of that power. Hence his visions of beauty or truth are not subject to revision upon abstract principle, nor are they the

[1] The conventional technique of eighteenth-century homophonic music was scarcely capable of representing more than these externals of manner. Cramped by its own conventions, this music lagged far behind contemporary literature as a revelation of the profounder feeling which was generating the Revolution. But this is not true of the polyphonic music of the time—particularly that of J. S. Bach—which seems a full revelation of both the religious and the social ideals of Germany of the earlier eighteenth century.

mere vaporings of an idle fancy; but all are possible contributions to ideal reality. Imagination, in short, becomes the most godlike of human faculties—the vehicle through which mere animal existence is transcended. Here, then, is the Romantic attitude, opposed to the classic.

The great logical danger of this attitude is of course not at once apparent—that it lacks any foundation for judgment as to what is truly imaginative, and is likely to mistake enthusiasm for clear perception. But the stimulus to individual effort is incalculable; and when creative imagination such as that of Beethoven is added to intellectual clarity of the highest order, it is unlikely that any more significant work can ever be produced than that which emanated from his brain. There is danger, of course, that the unfettered fancy of sensitive but unintelligent men may degenerate into mere effusions of sentiment, and that style may degenerate correspondingly into mere mannerism. But that degree of decadence in romanticism had not yet come. Beethoven was too ruggedly honest, too profoundly reverent toward humanity, too forgetful of himself in the absorbing interest of his own vision—in a word, he was too *imaginative*—to be often deceived into such superficialities.

BEETHOVEN'S EARLY LIFE

There is relatively little in the known detail of his life which seems to contribute greatly toward that vast imaginative resource which his work reveals. Some indications exist however of the native tendencies of his mind; and some facts show the direction in which it was forced by circumstance. These we shall try to select. Ludwig van Beethoven (the name recalls the family's Flemish origin; the *van* is not a sign of nobility) was the eldest surviving son of Johann van Beethoven and Maria Magdalena Leym (nee Keverich), daughter of the chief cook at Ehrenbreitstein. He was born at Bonn, probably on December 16, 1770. Both his father and his grandfather (Ludwig) were members of the chapel of the Electoral Archbishop of Cologne.[2] The family was very poor as is evidenced by the pitiful little room, now preserved as part of a museum, in which Ludwig was born. Five more children were born to the family during the years 1774–1786. Although but two survived (Caspar, 1774–1815, and Johann, 1776–1848), the frequent illness of the mother left her but little

[2] The Archbishops of Mainz, Cologne, and Trier, and four secular princes, the Count Palatine of the Rhine, the Duke of Saxony, the Margrave of Brandenburg, and the King of Bohemia had for centuries constituted a body of "Electors" who chose the successor to the throne of the Holy Roman Empire. Although the throne had come to be in practice a hereditary possession of the House of Hapsburg, the Electors were still important figures in the loose federation of German princes which constituted the Empire.

time for the care of the little genius; and he seems to have been a rather dirty, neglected boy. The father, by profession a tenor singer, had also some knowledge of both piano and violin. Perceiving signs of great musical interest in Ludwig, he gave the boy lessons on both instruments in the hope that another Mozart might be produced. Johann van Beethoven was no such competent teacher as Leopold Mozart, and was a still less competent father; but his early harshness toward his son has often been exaggerated.

Regular education in the schools, involving only the three R's and a little Latin, ceased in 1781, but seems to have been supplemented by some private instruction in Latin, French, and Italian. Having already at eight years exceeded his father's knowledge, he was sent for further (free) musical instruction to the court organist Van den Eeden, and in 1779 to Pfeiffer, then newly come to Bonn as a singer in the opera. Pfeiffer was an excellent pianist and apparently a competent teacher; but he shared with Johann van Beethoven a lingering affection for the bottle. Consequently, it was often not until the evening drinking bout was over that Ludwig was rudely awakened and taken to the piano for his lesson, where he was sometimes kept until early morning. Some work in theory was also included. He must have made considerable progress, for in the autumn of 1781 he went with his mother to Holland, where there is some unestablished reference to a public concert; but the only certainty about the visit is Beethoven's acquired opinion of the Dutch: "The Hollanders are penny-pinchers. I shall never visit Holland again." Shortly after this he was sent to Christian Gottlieb Neefe, Van den Eeden's successor as court organist. Neefe was a very competent musician, a skilled composer, and an able director. His comment on his pupil (one of a series of short notices which he frequently contributed to *Cramer's Magazine*) will give an idea of the range of his instruction and of the boy's advancement at this time (1783): "Louis van Beethoven, son of the above-mentioned tenor singer, a boy of 11 years,[3] and a very promising talent. He plays the piano very fluently and with power, reads very well at sight, and, to put the matter in a nutshell, he plays most of the Well-Tempered Clavichord of Sebastian Bach, which Herr Neefe put into his hands. He who knows this collection of Preludes and Fugues in all the keys (which might almost be called the *non plus ultra* of music) will understand what this means. Herr Neefe, also, so far as his other duties permitted, has given him some instruction in General-bass [harmony]. Now he is training him in composition, and for his encouragement has had a set of nine variations by him engraved in

[3] Through some confusion of birth registry, Beethoven for many years believed himself to have been born in 1772. He was 13 years old, not 11, when this was written. The spelling of his name is one of the many different versions then current.

Mannheim. This young genius deserves help, to enable him to travel. He will certainly be a second Mozart, if he goes on as he has begun."

In addition to the *Well-Tempered Clavichord*, the Sonatas of Karl Philipp Emanuel Bach, which Beethoven afterward used in teaching Carl Czerny, were diligently studied. It was not until after 1783 that Mozart's work is recorded as having come under Beethoven's eye. The theoretical work was based on Rameau and Kirnberger, and included simple counterpoint and the principles of strict musical sentence structure. The effect of this study is apparent in the compositions of 1785, especially in the piano quartets, which are far superior to earlier efforts. His practical abilities will be judged from the fact that when in 1784 Neefe took over the direction of all the court music, Beethoven was put at the piano during the orchestral rehearsals—a place which was then equivalent to the position of conductor. He was already able to read easily at sight from the orchestral scores, and gained in this way some acquaintance with popular French, Italian, and German operas.

The always precarious fortunes of the Beethoven family now began definitely to decline. The father lost his voice, and only became the more intemperate. A two-year-old brother died; and Ludwig had to assume, in the support of the family, a share which grew larger and larger as the father's intemperateness increased. A small salary was at length granted by the Elector, which Beethoven began somewhat to augment by teaching. Max Franz, Archduke of Austria, succeeded the old Elector, Max Friedrich, in 1784. The new Elector, the youngest son of Maria Theresa, was considerably trained in music and was interested in every sort of cultural effort. He gave liberal support to the newly founded University of Bonn and to the preparatory schools. He had met Mozart in Salzburg and hoped now to secure him as Kapellmeister; but Mozart was too much occupied with the production of *Figaro* to consider the offer. It is possible, but improbable, that it was Max Franz who provided Beethoven with funds for that journey to Vienna which took place some time in 1787, and which fulfilled Neefe's hope that the young man might be given opportunity for travel. Mozart, whose judgment of his powers the boy was seeking, was indifferent to his playing, doubtless comparing it unfavorably with his own at a similar age, or with that of young Hummel, eight years younger than Beethoven, then living in Mozart's house. Beethoven sensed Mozart's indifference, and begged him to give him a theme upon which to improvise. The evidence given by this far more decisive test was conclusive. "Pay attention to him. Some day he will make a name for himself in the world!" was Mozart's comment. Some few lessons, presumably in composition, seem to have been given; but Beethoven's visit was cut short by news of the illness of his mother. He returned to Bonn some time before her death in July, 1787, and never saw Mozart again.

Beethoven was now engaged as teacher in the cultured family of the Von Breunings, and began to enjoy what he had never hitherto known, the pleasure of intellectual association with people of refinement. The ancient classics as well as many contemporary English authors were discovered to him (in translation), and his literary sense had now a belated awakening. He also made the acquaintance of Count Waldstein, related to many of the most aristocratic families of Austria, who was then in Bonn preparing to take vows as a knight of the German Order. The Count was an enthusiastic amateur of music. Realizing Beethoven's genius, he gave him much material help and was instrumental in arranging for his later removal to Vienna. Both he and Stephan von Breuning were also afterward in Vienna, and assisted in introducing the young genius to the Viennese aristocracy. At the same time the father's intemperateness had reached such a pitch that the Elector was petitioned to have a part of his salary paid to the son, who thus became at nineteen the responsible head of the family. The sense of injustice in his position, and especially the high aspiration of his mind toward the solution of such social problems as his own case represented, is seen in the fact that at this time he was already deeply fired by the sentiment of Schiller's *Ode to Joy*, which he is mentioned as having determined to set to music. It has been said (apparently without authority) that it was not to Joy (*Freude*) that Schiller's *Ode* was originally addressed, but to Peace (*Friede*), or to Freedom (*Freiheit*). In any case, the joy which is here apostrophized is no mere exuberance of spirit, but is palpably that which is to come when men have recognized their universal brotherhood. Many other musical embodiments of the same thesis were completed before Beethoven finally achieved his lifelong purpose in the Ninth Symphony; but the ideal of this poem was one which guided and inspired his whole life.[4]

When Haydn passed through Bonn on his return from London in 1792, Beethoven was presented to him, and received his warm approval of a cantata (not now identifiable) which the young man submitted to him. This and other evidences of unusual talent which were accumulating appear to have determined the Elector to send Beethoven to Vienna for further study. Haydn was willing to accept him as a pupil; and in Novem-

[4] Such a concept of Schiller's *Ode* as that which is indicated in Mr. Robert Haven Schauffler's contemptuous phrase, "Schiller's drinking song *de luxe*," is lamentably out of accord, at least with what Beethoven saw in the poem, and with what it was evidently his intention to express, not only in the choral *Finale* of the Ninth Symphony, but in the whole work. A man of Beethoven's artistic mentality hardly ponders an idea for more than twenty years without having attained to tolerably firm convictions about it.

ber, 1792, Beethoven journeyed again to Vienna, thus escaping those more material manifestations of the Revolution which soon caused the Elector to flee from Bonn and which finally abolished Electorate and Empire altogether. But the finer spirit of the Revolution was already too deeply implanted in Beethoven's heart ever to be eradicated. The probable extent of his expression of this spirit could not be foreseen; but Waldstein's prescience of something significant is seen in his note to Beethoven on the eve of his departure: "...The genius of Mozart is still weeping and bewailing the death of her favorite. With the inexhaustible Haydn she found a refuge, but no occupation, and is now waiting to leave him and join herself to another. Labor assiduously, and receive Mozart's spirit from the hands of Haydn."

We are often led to infer that it was a mere novice in the art of composition who thus traveled from Bonn to Vienna. It was not indeed until 1795 (more than two and a half years later) that Beethoven began to publish his creations. Also, it is certain that it was rather his power as a pianist than any other quality which rapidly endeared him to the Viennese aristocracy. But it was his amazing improvisations, not his mere repetition of learned pieces, which most astonished his hearers; and this gift, in such measure as Beethoven possessed it, is unmistakable evidence of creative imagination. Vienna looked forward to the time when his inspirations could be recorded. And when active publication began, the stream of creative activity was so turbulent and full that it is completely inexplicable unless we understand it as fed by many smaller springs of youthful inspiration. The first period of Beethoven's work is generally accepted as extending from 1795, the year of the three Trios dedicated to Haydn, until the end of 1802, when the *Pastoral* Sonata and the String Quintet Op. 29 appeared, and the Violin Sonatas Op. 30 were in course of publication. Altogether, ninety-three works can be counted as appearing in ninety-six months—a quantity of production in itself amazing, and, in the case of the laborious and self-critical Beethoven, altogether incredible, unless a considerable part of the work was already at least largely formed. Among these works are thirty-two Sonatas for piano alone or with other instruments, three Piano Concertos, six String Quartets, nine Trios for strings or piano and strings, three Quintets, two Symphonies, the Septet, the *Trauercantata*, and the oratorio *Christ on the Mount of Olives*. The young man who soon after his arrival in Vienna won the enthusiastic support of the Viennese aristocracy was thus no mere student, but a musician of matured powers and distinctive originality. It is in the Bonn period, if at any time, that Beethoven was the mere imitator of Mozart and Haydn.

Even in his directed study we have many evidences of his independence of mind. He was one who could take nothing for granted, but must test everything for himself. He would not accept even the simplest rules of harmony until he had satisfied himself of their reasonableness.[5] In his notebooks appears one single theorem of harmony worked out seventeen times to disprove an accepted rule; and at the end the unflattering comment on the authority who had propounded the rule, *"Du Esel!"* This was done, not out of perversity or conceit but only because of his imperative need of understanding for himself the problems that confronted him. His demand for intellectual certainty was one of the most essential characteristics of Beethoven's mind. He had such inordinate facility as an improvisator and as a pianist that without this profound mental scepticism he might readily have degenerated into a complacent, public-courting virtuoso. But to him every attractive surface gave promise of still more attractive things to be found beneath. And as a consequence his originality consisted, not in the mere virtuoso's discovery of new tricks, but in his penetrating vision of the essence of the subject with which he was concerned. For the communication of this vision he often had to discover new turns of phrase; but in so far as he was able he used the conventional musical language of his day. It is desirable to have some concrete illustration of the working of this creative mind.

THE FIRST PERIOD

No great intrinsic interest attaches, perhaps, to the first of the Piano Sonatas (Op. 2, No. 1). But even in this simple piece we can see that coherence and justness of design are only the products of an inexorable pursuit of the idea itself, and are not at all an evidence of mere conformity to tradition. The principal subject is conventional, in that it is based (for definiteness of key suggestion) on the arpeggio of the tonic chord. But a stern purpose resides in that upward staccato march—a purpose manifested in the culminating A flat with its ensuing impatient twitch.[6] Greater

[5] On the fly leaf of the MS score of *Coriolanus* appears the number 24, set down 13 times and added up. It has been inferred that this proves Beethoven to have been ignorant of the arithmetical process of multiplication. But it might also be explained as a speculative test of the correctness of the usual method of solving the problem 24 × 13; and his usually correct notation of elaborate beat divisions into 32nds and 64ths, and even 128th notes, does not indicate quite this supposed degree of mathematical incompetence.

[6] Parry, in *The Evolution of the Art of Music*, draws a comparison between this theme and that of the finale of Mozart's G minor Symphony which is very interesting, though somewhat unfair in its disparagement of Mozart. So much is made, both here and in countless other cases, of mere similarity in note succession, that it seems necessary to point out the fallacy of regarding these two themes as in any real sense comparable to each other. The tempo of Mozart's phrase is nearly twice as fast as

point is given to the phrase by repetition on an unstable harmony. Thereafter the concentration is wholly upon the crisis itself, even the cadential
figure (in bars 7 and 8) appearing but as an enlargement of the briefer
curve of the earlier phrases:

The continuation of this terse, sensuously unappealing subject never loses
sight of the point at issue. It is palpably built throughout from the subject
matter itself, and is really a brief development of that matter. But there is
much difference between this transition and that (also to some extent
continued from the original subject) in the Haydn Quartet quoted above,
page 344. Here the tenseness of the idea is heightened by the use of relatively very harsh discord—discord perfectly in keeping with the suggestion
already given by the subject. The transition closes with a more flowing,
syncopated phrase which is a clear anticipation of the coming second
subject. The form of this second subject is likewise no accident. The
rhythm of its two-bar phrase is essentially that of the principal subject,
the last three notes being merely ♩. ♪ ♩ instead of ♩. ♬ ♩. The key is
almost A flat minor, instead of the orthodox A flat major; and the generally
descending curve of the melody, together with its rhythmic relation to
the principal subject and its peculiarly dark harmonic color, serves to give
a type of feeling suggestion very closely related to that of the principal
subject. Although the succeeding transition is more loose than the earlier
one, it never really loses character; and the brief closing subject again
exhibits the peculiarly darkened harmony already employed in the second

---

that of Beethoven's. The upward motion consequently, in Mozart, is light and tripping, and the culminating note B flat has no especial weight. The phrase is incomplete,
both because of its ending on the active note A, and because of its lack of any
decisively stated character. But the completion lies, not in any further continuation
of this thought, but in the sharp and humorous contrast, offered by the ensuing phrase.
This music admirably suggests its own object; but to condemn it because Beethoven's
object is more serious is both unkind and undiscriminating. The theme in question
is as follows:

subject. The external impressiveness of this music is not great; but the draftsmanship and the persistent musical logic are far beyond anything to be expected of a mere imitator.

Naturally, such austerity is not suited to every subject; and it is as much the range of Beethoven's imagination as the logic of his musical thought which impresses us in examining the work of the first period. Slow movements, especially, indicate the emotional disposition of the artist; and to follow a succession of these is to gain at least a fair idea of the growth of his imaginative power. The *Adagio* of this same Sonata, in both form and content, is indeed Mozartean; but it comes from one of the Piano Quartets of 1785. The *Largo appassionato* of Op. 2, No. 2 is far more intense and original; and the *Adagio* of Op. 2, No. 3 is really the salvation of that work, which is otherwise more interesting pianistically than musically. The *Largo con gran espressione* of Op. 7 is singularly poignant, its first detached phrases revealing a brooding concentration which is strangely colored by the major key in which they are presented. The ensuing contrast (bar 9) gives an exquisite lightening of the tension; but the slight lapse into floridity becomes almost ruinous when, in bar 14 and at the parallel passage in bar 64, it degenerates into a tripping figure quite incongruous with the general tone of the music. The interlude from bar 36 to the resumption of the principal theme is also more intense than intelligible, emotionally. But in the *Largo e mesto* of Op. 10, No. 3, not only are such momentary irrelevancies avoided, but the idea itself is of a depth not hitherto attempted in music since the days of Johann Sebastian Bach.

The first unmistakable revelation of the revolutionary Beethoven, however, is doubtless to be found in the ever-popular *Sonate Pathétique*, Op. 13. The *Grave* introduction (of course, a derivation from the French overture) is unprecedented both for its arresting intensity and for its orchestral sonority and color; and the ensuing *Allegro di molto e con brio*, twice punctuated by a recall of the introduction, maintains a nervous vigor and displays a concentration of purpose not to be found in any work of Mozart. Melodically the principal theme is hardly more than an ascending minor scale; rhythmically, however, and in the rapid alternation of its harmonies, it suggests a degree of tension almost unendurable, and a tenacity of purpose quite ruthless in the pursuit of its object. The second subject, entirely in character, is again in the minor, not the major key. Like the principal subject of Op. 2, No. 1, it begins with an ascending arpeggio figure which culminates in a vivid note of crisis—an instant of lyrical outcry which is remarkably vivid in the midst of the unimpeded rush of the whole musical substance. The closing subject with its impetuous diverging chord figures in octaves is terrible in its revelation of energy. The reminiscence of the principal subject at the close of the exposition, and the recall of the tragic introduction, although by no means unprecedented structural facts, are here expressively conclusive. After so rapid a succession of emotional crises, no discursive development would be possible. A hint of the principal subject; a recall of the tragic phrase of the introduction; a few figures made of the second and third notes of the principal theme as it first appears in the development; and the whole substance begins to sway and topple. It sinks rapidly into obscurity; and for a moment there is the strangest jumble of ultramodern harmony (bar 31 of the development) whose very incoherence is the fullest revelation of the expressive sense of the whole music. Familiarity has blinded us to the extraordinary originality of this work—an originality which, as will be seen, is but the rational outcome of the thought itself which is the theme of the music. The *Adagio cantabile* which follows is not less revolutionary in the nobility of its aspiration.[7] The character at least, if not the rather contracted development, of the following episode (bar 17) is perfectly in accord with the opening; and the whole piece, if somewhat perfunctory in its observation of formal procedure, is a fit complement to the first movement. The *Finale* was originally intended as a movement of a violin sonata—a fact which somewhat destroys the supposed significance of the resemblance between its opening phrase and the upward-tending figure of the second subject of the first movement. It was apparently beyond the composer's power to maintain the character already suggested; but it may equally have been that he did not choose so far to offend the current taste for happy endings as would have been necessary in a fully related *Finale*.

The two Sonatas included in Op. 14 are much slighter in texture, but the second, especially, is interesting for its delicate humor. Op. 22 in B flat follows after more than a year; and in that interval Beethoven had been doing great things. Most important of all are the six String Quartets, Op. 18—works in which such a sure hand is seen, and an imagination so wide in range, that there can no longer be question of any dependence on the past. The problem of quartet writing is in all probability the severest which can confront a composer. Even to master the technique would prove him ready to undertake any instrumental form whatever; but to exhibit at the same time such a range of vision as Beethoven here shows is to announce himself as a prophet. The certainty of mind which he had acquired gave him courage to attempt the more crucial but not more difficult task of writing a symphony. In Op. 21, then, we have the first of those nine immortal works which are the most universally accepted evidences of Beethoven's greatness. He had as yet written but little for

[7] The main curve of its melody, as Von Bülow pointed out, is repeated in the *Adagio* of the Ninth Symphony.

orchestra. Thus the substance of the First Symphony is less daring and original than that of several of the quartets; but his very first chord—a dominant seventh in F, while the Symphony is to be in C—was enough to set all the critical tongues in Vienna a-wagging. Two other features are notable as indicating the progressive mind of the composer: the mysterious passage for the basses, made from and shortly succeeding the second subject of the first movement; and the humorous absurdity of the *Adagio* which introduces the last movement—a succession of short scale phrases, each one note longer than the preceding, meaningless in themselves but uttered with elaborate "expression," which turn out to be no more than the mere upbeat of the jolly principal theme itself.

The next following works, from Op. 22 to Op. 31, are practically all sonatas—five of them being "with violin accompaniment" as the phrase then was, and eight for piano solo. Not only do all these show the maturity gained through the writing of the quartets and the symphony. But the later ones, especially the two *Fantasia* Sonatas, Op. 27 (the second of these is the *Moonlight* Sonata) and the three which make up Op. 31, are distinctly unusual in form and show a disposition to treat the formal element of music as decidedly inferior in importance to the element of expression. This emphasis on the idea remains throughout all the later work; and the compositions here under discussion therefore represent an important period of style transition—a final and conscious emancipation from the merely conventional canons of the past. "From today I will strike out a new road," he said; but the new road was not (as might appear from Op. 31) to be cut through the trackless wilderness of formless music. It is only in order that he may more clearly express his idea that he temporarily abandons the strict outline of form.

THE SECOND PERIOD

The second period of Beethoven's creative activity is generally held to begin with Op. 31. It includes by far the greater volume of his whole work, and represents him at the very height of his confidence in revolutionary principles. The Second Symphony (Op. 36) was finished before the end of 1802, and belongs to the period of transition. But the Third (the *Eroica*, Op. 55), finished in August, 1804, is wholly representative not only of the second period but of the prophet of the new faith. Throughout its then unusual length it maintains a rigorous logic of development equal to that of the older polyphonic forms; while at the same time it displays a wealth of material and a corresponding range of feeling never hitherto achieved by any musician within the scope of a single work. Its purpose (unless one is to deny that music has expressive sense) was to embody in music the ideal of heroism—not the cannon-shooting, flag-waving uproar with which the crowd acclaims a victory, nor the hollow apparition of the mere victor, but the very psychology of the heroic attitude itself toward life and death and all human aspiration. It was doubtless true that Beethoven saw in Napoleon Bonaparte the actuality of his ideal of heroism. He supposed it to be Napoleon's ambition to effect that brotherhood of all nations of Europe of which he was always dreaming and which he saw extolled in Schiller's *Ode*. So he dedicated the Symphony to Napoleon. But when he heard that his idol had had himself proclaimed Emperor, he tore off the title page in a fury, saying, "He is no better than other men." When he heard of Napoleon's death years later, his comment was, "I have already written the music for that event." That Napoleon proved unfit to fill the role of hero is of no consequence; he helped Beethoven to clarify his own ideas—which was doubtless one of the best things he ever did. For it is this heroic attitude, toward small things as well as great, manifested in the profoundest tenderness as well as in the most titanic strength, and related to almost an infinity of human experiences, which is the theme of all the work of Beethoven's second period.

Again we are blinded by long familiarity to the wonder of this symphonic achievement. Homophonic music, even in 1788 (the year of Mozart's three greatest symphonies), was but beginning to discover its expressive power. In 1804 it had become equal to the revelation of realities of feeling indescribable through any other medium, and hence hardly recognized hitherto as realities. It would require a volume to describe in detail the works of this second period, many of which are of an equal impressiveness with the *Eroica*, though none are quite its equal in dimension. The symphonies naturally take the highest place in our estimation; but it may be doubted whether their meaning is more significant than that of some of the solo and chamber works.

The Fourth Symphony, Op. 60 (1806), is less popular than the rest. But this is probably because its high serenity provides less excitement than is given by the others. Longer familiarity gives it an increasingly high place in the musician's regard. The Fifth, Op. 67 (begun in 1805, finished in 1808) is certainly the most popular orchestral work ever written. So far as it may be characterized in the few words which our space permits, it may be said that it represents an even more kinetic, affirmative sense of exalted human purpose than the *Eroica* itself. "Thus Fate knocks at the door," were Beethoven's words in answer to a question as to the meaning of the pregnant motive of four notes which occurs almost incessantly in the first movement and pervades significantly the scherzo and the triumphant finale. It is impossible to divine Beethoven's meaning from the words themselves; but from the music it is at least arguable that the Fate of which he spoke is that larger human destiny which Beethoven the revolutionist constantly envisioned.

The *Pastoral* Symphony, Op. 68 (1808), expresses Beethoven's love of nature—a sentiment so profound as to amount to a sort of pantheism. Endless discussion has resulted from his declaration that the five descriptive movements ("Awakening of Joyful Feeling on Arriving in the Country"; "Scene by the Brook"; "Peasants' Merrymaking"; "Thunderstorm"; and "Song of Thanksgiving after the Storm") were intended as "more the expression of feeling than painting." The discussion is chiefly academic. That sense of release from strain which came to Beethoven on his long walks through the mountainous suburbs of Vienna is the dominant theme. Incidentally we have more or less vivid pictures presented to us which are all to be seen from this emotional attitude—in the scene by the brook, for instance, a wholly imitative (if not wholly realistic) representation of the songs of cuckoo, quail, and nightingale; and in the peasants' merrymaking, a little German band, not altogether respectful of the niceties of time-keeping and intonation. But he who sees only the pictures, and not the soul of the painter, misses the whole point.

The Seventh Symphony, Op. 92 (1812), is the most enigmatic of all. Wagner calls it "the apotheosis of the Dance"; and in the light of that comment we are to understand the music as a representation of the most direct and literal of all human expressions of feeling—that of bodily motion. The first movement is preceded by a long introduction in which some hint (but no thematic anticipation) is given of the motive forces later to be unleashed—half-formed impulses to action, chiefly embodied in rising staccato scales, and a momentary glimpse of nude, unconscious grace in an exquisite fragment of melody: a march measure for the spirit rather than for the body. The introduction prepares us for the first movement proper—a movement whose exuberance is almost unrelieved, only a strange suggestion of elemental pain appearing, toward the end. The slow movement, one of Beethoven's most extraordinary conceptions, is strange and hushed—a sacrificial dance of death which contrasts remarkably with the funeral march in the *Eroica*. For it seems to suggest neither pity nor terror; its stately figures move inexorably, but not with overweighted grief, in a kind of solemn greeting from the force of life to the kindred force of death. The scherzo is a dance of daintiness whose flitting figures seem in the trio to form into tense, poised groups, swaying largely in sweeping gestures that imply a climax of ecstasy. The *Finale* is incredible. It may well be doubted whether any later composer, with all the modern resources of harmony and orchestration, has made music so madly abandoned. In its unmoral release of the most primitive of emotional forces, and in its perfect artistic control of these forces, this is a pagan symphony.

Its very strangeness of concept is evidence—plentifully corroborated by other work of the period—that the whole mental attitude of the composer is changing. The interest of the symphonies from the *Eroica* to the *Pastoral* is immediately human, directly related to familiar emotional experience. Indeed, the characteristic tone of the whole middle period may be described by an analogy with sentence structures as *declarative*. Similarly, the mood of the work of the third period may be hinted at in the characterization *subjunctive*. Forthright and sincere, the Beethoven of the second period speaks his mind, confident that his vision has embraced the whole of his subject, and convincing us by the very vehemence of his own confidence that he is right. There is great depth; but nothing appears beneath the surface which is not to some extent indicated on the surface. And there are few suggestions of the later cryptic, symbolic speech. Although he cannot be said to repeat himself, the same theme is sometimes dealt with in several different works—frequently in those written nearly at the same time. The serenity of the Fourth Symphony, for instance, is felt also in the *Waldstein* Sonata and in the G major Piano Concerto. The vibrant passion of the C minor Symphony is echoed in the wonderful *Appassionata* Sonata, in the *Emperor* Concerto, and to some extent in the *Thirty-two Variations* in C minor. The program symphony (the *Pastoral*) is followed in 1809 by the Piano Sonata, Op. 81a, whose three movements are entitled *Farewell*, *Absence*, and *Return*. Other phases of Beethoven's abundant spiritual energy are to be seen in the *Kreutzer* Sonata, in the *Rasoumoffsky* Quartets (Op. 59), in the Cello Sonata in A with its extraordinary *Scherzo*, and in the D major Trio (Op. 70, No. 1), whose mysterious slow movement has caused the work to be called (not very justly) the *Ghost* Trio. But the Seventh Symphony is not be summed up in terms of its direct statement. Its ideal dance rhythms can be understood only as high and almost cryptic symbols of an attitude toward life which has now become too visionary for expression in the direct and literal manner of the earlier works. And while it would not be expected that the same type of expression—the dance suggestion—would be found suitable for all the subjects in which the composer's mind was hereafter to find inspiration, it seems reasonable to infer that we have here an approach to a new change in style, far more profound than that which differentiates the second period from the first.

The Eighth Symphony (Op. 93, also written in 1812), while smaller in dimensions than any save the first two, bears out this supposition of a changed artistic purpose. The subject or idea of this work is no longer epic in breadth. On the contrary, it is almost diminutive. Its themes are not without the character of the dance, as is perhaps natural since this and the Seventh Symphony were produced in the same year. Its tone is less enigmatic. It seems rather to compress into its few miraculously chosen thematic fragments a simple kindliness and gentleness that are almost childlike. But a deeper familiarity reveals that these are the kindliness and gentleness that are possible only to a man who, having passed through the fire of life, can exhibit his comprehension in a mere glance, a gesture, a gentle pressure of the hand. The message is not in itself a great and vital thought upon whose expression the fate of the world may depend. Fate indeed is left to take care of itself; but in a few simple statements we are given implications from which we can fully infer a sense of character which, it has been wisely observed, is indeed Fate.

The actual technical complexities in all this work of the second period are extremely few in comparison to the results achieved. The sonata form has been inordinately expanded; but its main outlines have scarcely been changed. The subject matter, from the *Eroica* on, is so cunningly invented that its phrases are capable of endless development; and it is almost wholly through this process of development that Beethoven's innovations are accomplished. His harmonic vocabulary is not greatly enriched. Indeed, it is seldom that a great and vital effect is produced (as is often the case with Wagner) by the use of some new and original harmonic progression. He sometimes jumps bodily from one key to another without modulation, as in the opening of the *Waldstein* and the *Appassionata* Sonatas; and sometimes uses enormous masses of harmony without much detail of thematic line (as in the development section of the first movement of the *Eroica*, from bar 97 on, or in the development section of the *Waldstein* Sonata); but on the whole it is pregnant thematic material, and especially an altogether unmatched rhythmic vitality, which are his chief resources. Different as the spirit of the second period is from that of the first, its musical substance is but the natural expansion of that of the earlier period. Hardly more than two real innovations in sonata structure, save that of expansion, can be discovered. These are, first, the use of an extended coda after the recapitulation, which thus becomes a second, intensified development; and, second, the substitution of the scherzo for the minuet as the third movement of the total form. And these innovations are to some slight extent anticipated in the work of Haydn and Mozart. Contrapuntal study was pursued in Beethoven's youth rather as a general technical discipline than as a compositional method or resource. Hence, although he is never at a loss when it seems desirable to deal polyphonically with his themes, this style of writing is rather incidental than fundamental throughout the first two periods. Quartet composition, however, is almost necessarily polyphonic; and in this form we find more examples of true polyphonic writing than in the symphonies themselves. But altogether there is no other great work which is accomplished with so little of abstruse technical process as this of the first two periods of Beethoven.

THE THIRD PERIOD

The year 1812, enormously productive like the year 1808, marks a sudden, almost complete, cessation of creative activity. Various conditions of his life suggest reasons for the break, but do not fully explain it. His increasing deafness and his consequent inability to maintain his public position as pianist; his difficulties with the widow of his brother Caspar over the disposition of her son Karl; the disturbance of Austrian finances owing to the wars; and the awakening of a "Rossini fever" in Vienna which considerably dimmed Beethoven's popularity, all conspired to intensify his natural disposition to look inward upon himself, rather than outward upon a world with which, at least in the large, he was gaining increased sympathy. The Piano Sonata, Op. 90 (1814), again shows the gentle characteristics of the Eighth Symphony. The B flat Trio, Op. 97 (1811), has a slow movement whose elevation is above any imaginative height to which Beethoven had as yet attained. It is apparent that a profound change in form organization will soon be necessary in order to express the new attitude—that of seer and prophet—which the giant is gradually assuming. This form alteration had indeed already been necessary for the strangely novel Quartet, Op. 95, which had been written in 1810. And with the Piano Sonata, Op. 101 (1816?), the new manner is established.

This new manner is fully exemplified in the last five Sonatas for piano— Op. 101, Op. 106 (1818–1819), Op. 109 (1820), Op. 110 (1821), and Op. 111 (1822). The original outline of sonata form is generally preserved in the last movement of Op. 101 and in the first movements of Op. 106 and Op. 111; but the substance is often so strangely new that old canons of form seem to be unimportant. Fantasy seems to take the place of direct statement; but again this fantasy is only the cloak of a profound vision of reality. The student will most readily gain a first insight into the new manner through the study of the first and third movements of Op. 101. The almost diffident gentleness of the first movement may perhaps be a reminiscence of Beethoven's improvisation for Dorothea Ertmann on a day when, distraught over the death of her only child, she came to him for consolation. The brief *Adagio* is but an interlude; but it contains such intimations of immortality in its first eight bars as can seldom be found in all the literature of music. No two of these sonatas are alike in form; but one feature is common to all—the frequent use of a richly polyphonic texture. And this disposition to use the resource of counterpoint is characteristic of all the last period. It is by no means, however, the counterpoint of Bach or that of the textbooks, but is rather a new and free kind of many-voiced music, enriching beyond measure the sound value of the whole, and voicing a certain strangeness which is characteristic of all the more purely romantic music to come.

The completion of a lifelong project was attained in the Ninth Symphony, Op. 125 (1817–1823). The *Finale* of this work, for the first time since the symphony had become a purely instrumental form, employs a chorus; and the text is that of Schiller's *Ode to Joy* which Beethoven had already determined to set to music while he was yet a boy in Bonn. The first three movements are in the nature of a prologue to this imposing *Finale*. Probably the sense of tragedy has never been more grimly conveyed than in the opening movement. The *Scherzo* (which is unusual in following the opening movement) has a bitter and sardonic tone which is but slightly relieved in the *Trio*. The *Adagio* is similar to that of the Trio, Op. 97, in its lofty idealism. But after the terrible fanfare which opens the *Finale*, Beethoven quotes briefly from all these movements, and shows the purpose of this quotation in the words he gives to the baritone solo by way of introduction to the choral part of the work: "O friends, no more these sounds! But let us sing something more cheerful and more full of gladness." The chorus thereupon deals in various ways with the theme of the poem: "Joy, fair scintillation of godhood, daughter of Elysium, drunken with thy fire we tread, O heavenly one, thy holy realm. Thy magic unites what stern convention divides. All men become brothers where thy gentle wing is spread. . . . Embrace, embrace, ye millions! This kiss for the whole world! Brothers, above the starry heaven a loving Father must be dwelling." But the apostrophe to joy itself is far overshadowed in intensity by the passage, "Embrace, embrace," and especially by the following section, incredibly modern even to our ears, "Do ye kneel, ye millions? Dost not sense thy Creator, World? Seek Him above the starry heaven—above the stars He must live!"

There is much debate as to the success of this last movement. Undoubtedly Beethoven demands too much of his voices; undoubtedly the movement is too long. Possibly the union of word and tone is less effective in suggesting the composer's purpose than purely instrumental music might have been. But when all is said the symphony remains the most colossal symphonic effort of the nineteenth century, and a priceless revelation of the undying human sympathies of its creator.

Scarcely second to the symphony in general affection, and even more highly regarded by the composer himself, is the Solemn Mass in D. His interest is here again almost more human than religious. The sense of sin —so profoundly felt by Bach in the *Kyrie eleison* of the B minor Mass—

is less acute; the mystery of the incarnation is overshadowed in importance by the sentiment of the phrase *et homo factus est* to which Beethoven gives all possible emphasis. The *Sanctus*, with its wonderful interweaving of a solo violin among the voices, is the celestial vision of a seer; but the *dona nobis pacem* from the *Agnus Dei* is especially indicated as a "prayer for inward and outward peace"—an interpretation in itself scarcely orthodox; but this departure from convention is further emphasized by a strange interpolation of warlike clamor in the orchestra. The effect is repellent—perhaps designedly so—but it is again indicative of Beethoven's humanism.

But the noblest music of all is to be found in the last Quartets, Op. 130 to 135, in which the whole later development of nineteenth-century music seems to be foreshadowed. In the tone of the strings—to Beethoven always more eloquent than voices—he seems to find utterance for thoughts which are hopelessly beyond any attempt at verbal description. That freedom of form toward which Beethoven was striving in the last Piano Sonatas seems now fully attained. Each idea seems (as indeed it should) to create its own form; and while the listener's effort in adjusting his expectations to an ever-new musical order is at first so great that the music seems hardly intelligible, repeated experience only increases our certainty that in these Quartets Beethoven has attained the highest ambition of the creative artist—to make form and thought indissoluble.

With the last Quartets of Beethoven, then, music enters fully into that phase which we call the *romantic period*. Beethoven, as we have seen, links the classic feeling of Mozart and Haydn to that romantic freedom of imagination which is essentially an assertion of individuality and as such is a product of the Revolution. To have achieved such a change of style and attitude as made him in the second period the full exponent of revolutionary ideals, was a remarkable feat for any artist. To have gone beyond that point—deaf, and all but alone—and to have embodied the richest stream of romantic imagination in music which is as fresh as when it was written, is to have done what few other artists and no other composers have accomplished.[8]

---

[8] It will have been noted that we have ignored entirely one important phase of the work of both Beethoven and Mozart, their operatic music. This is because we prefer to follow the general development of opera from Gluck to Wagner in one unbroken succession.

CHAPTER XXIII

The Flowering of Romanticism— The Song and Its First Great Master, Schubert

THE designation *romantic* is generally applied to the period upon which we are about to enter. The word is derived from the term *Romancium,* signifying that derivative of the speech of the ancient Romans which ultimately branched into our modern Romance languages —Italian, French, Spanish, and so on. A vast number of narrative fictions or *romances,* displaying the current attitude of chivalry and tinged in large measure with superstition and magic, constituted the earliest literature in these tongues. It is from association with these tales that the word *romantic* has come to suggest a large element of fantastic unreality or overemotional sentiment; and this indeed is often taken as the only significance of the word. Such a definition, however, by no means connotes all the qualities recognizable in romantic art. Fancy and sentimentality are frequently to be found; but they are also often absent, or are submerged in a peculiarly intense and highly personal vision of the subject which is under the artist's hand. We, as observers, are asked to assume the romantic artist's attitude toward his subject—to feel with him, and through him, its peculiar appeal. We shall have to deal with many romantic writers; it will be necessary then to be sure of what we mean by the term *romantic art.*

Any artist's creation must first of all arrest our attention and appeal to us through its quality of beauty. But it will also convey, ordinarily, some expressive quality. That is, the work will be "about" something—will have a *subject,* which also has emotional interest for us. But the emotion aroused by the subject (let us say, some aspect of love or death or moral strife or religious contemplation) is of a different kind from the emotion which is aroused by the sheer beauty of the artist's tone or language or color or design. We may call the feeling reaction to beauty itself "aesthetic" (even though this is a somewhat narrow and literal definition of the word); while the emotion aroused by the subject, representing as it does some phase of the experience of life, may be called "experiential." The two kinds of feeling are so intimately blended that we can never absolutely separate or identify them; nor can we be sure that the two are making the same appeal to all observers.

Every artist attempts to make this double appeal to our sensibilities. But the romantic artist adds a peculiar quality to the presentation of his subject—that of his own personal reaction to it; and he asks us, from the beginning, to feel the subject with him. It is partly through this appeal to our sympathy with his own attitude that he gains our interest in the subject itself, and our admiration for the beauty of his creation. The classicist, on the other hand, disdains this appeal to our sympathy for his own feeling; he exalts his subject above the ground of personal interest as something generally or eternally true; and thus he conceives beauty itself as allied to eternal truth. Some interjection of the artist's personality is of course unavoidable even here; for if he has any significant power of imagination he cannot fail to develop an individual style, and hence to reveal something of himself in his work. But the attitude of the romanticist is confessed in every feature of his work; and his style, in consequence, may be colored by features which are even offensive to the mind of the classicist.

It may be inferred from all this that the classical attitude is likely to be assumed in those periods or situations in which formulas of belief or behavior have been accepted as unquestionable, and in which the general endeavor is to establish conformity to these formulas. Romanticism, on the other hand, proceeds out of indifference to, or revolt against, the rigid canons which generate classicism, and represents essentially the individualistic rather than the collective attitude. A period therefore in which great changes occur in men's beliefs or in their most vital interest is one in which some quality of romanticism is likely to appear in the work of its artists. The early nineteenth century is certainly not the first period of human history in which such ideals were conceived and propagated; we ought not to suppose, then, that the first characteristically romantic art is produced during this time. Every important release of new individualistic impulse should have found artistic expression in work which, in proportion to its subjectivity of attitude, is romantic in character.

The first of these impulses which is important for us is that involved in the doctrine of Christianity—the first fundamental attempt at the emancipation of the individual, since in theory it presupposes complete human equality in the sight of God. It is this sentiment of individual as well as collective communion with God which is implied in the words of the Ambrosian hymn quoted on page 41: "With joyful hearts, and offering due praises, we sing the everlasting gifts of Christ and the victories of the martyrs." But while the organization of the Church (militant as well as spiritual) widened the boundaries of Christendom, it narrowed the range of individual response to the example of Christ. An established ritual engendered similarly established music—music above and beyond the expression of individual sentiment. It is not altogether fanciful, then, to speak of the Ambrosian hymns as tinged with romanticism, or of the more highly organized Gregorian chant as the classical music of the early Church. This chant is far more noble, profound, and exalted than the hymns. Neither is it forgetful of the beauty or tenderness of the mysteries upon which the religion is founded; but in its tone the sense of individual or personal expression is submerged, and a high formalism takes its place.

Romantic feeling associated with secular life attains its first literary and musical expression in the work of the troubadours. This movement was soon suppressed by the Albigensian Crusade; but the earlier work sometimes displayed many of the qualities of later romantic poetry. It was also imitated by the trouvères, the poets of northern France who presently established the supremacy of the French tongue over the Provençal. In each case literary traditions grew up which tinged the work of the later poets with classicism; and the Renaissance, with its glorification of the ancient literary masterpieces, imposed from the outset a more rigid classical manner than perhaps would have resulted without that influence. English literature, however, from Chaucer to Shakespeare, is far less affected than the continental by the classical tradition of the ancients, and exhibits many qualities which are essentially romantic. The growth of simple musical expression was somewhat impeded by the great efforts which the development of harmony demanded, but in the association of the troubadour melody with the motet we may see the expression of such romantic impulse as the technique of contemporary music permitted.

Emotional impulses and musical expression far more closely approaching to that which is usually called Romanticism marked the great outburst of individualism called the Reformation. Among the many objectives of reform which Luther had in mind, not the least was that of making the Christian ideal generally intelligible. The formalism of the Catholic service was, in intent, an exaltation of the meaning of the Christian mysteries; in effect, the service was to many an ancient ritual whose meaning was beyond true comprehension, and of which therefore a merely mechanical observance was offered. It was precisely the emphasis of the individual's right to approach God in his own way which, for many strong-minded men, changed religious assent from an act of submission to an act of conviction. It is this immediate and personal belief which is voiced in the music of Johann Sebastian Bach. Discussion of his enormous technical mastery of musical processes has all but smothered our perception of the humanity of the man. He is called the great musical mathematician, when he should be regarded as the first complete human figure to be revealed through the medium of music. Even in his purely instrumental music (the most "formal," of course, of all his work) the tinge of romantic feeling is frequently to be found. But it is when we examine his religious work that we see that romanticism—in the sense of an immediately personal expression of his convictions and an appeal to his hearers to join in those convictions—is the very breath of its life.

These instances and many others, such as the growth of the madrigal in a tentative effort of the individual imagination to express itself through the uncongenial vehicle of polyphony, or the rise of the opera (especially with Monteverdi) as a direct expression of personal feeling, and the almost immediate submersion of that feeling in the borrowed formalism of ancient tragedy—these all point to the continuous existence of those types of impulse which assume either the "classical" or the "romantic" manner of expression accordingly as the stimulus is less or more individualistic in tone. And it is but the same impulse—generated out of interests which not only religious freedom but the discovery of the new world, the invention of printing, the founding of the universities, the rise of the middle class, the development of science, and a thousand other circumstances more immediately concerned with daily life had brought into being—it is but the same impulse of individual initiative which, after the Revolution, flowers more luxuriously than ever in romanticism. There is hardly a region of thought or action which surviving convention screens from its dissemination. But romanticism is not mere enthusiasm for principles of liberty, equality, and fraternity. It is rather the attitude of mind which is induced by the acceptance of these principles and by their half-unconscious application.

One of the terse phrases which have been found to define romanticism is Pater's "Strangeness added to beauty." This may be easily reconciled with our argument. The "beauty" which Pater conceives is doubtless that combination of aesthetic emotion with experiential feeling of which we have spoken. "Strangeness," obviously, will characterize the peculiarities either of form or matter which are so frequently to be met with in romantic art. But these irregularities are characteristic not so much of the subject with which the artist deals as of his personal vision of the subject. And not only Pater's phrase, but Goethe's sharp antithesis, "Classicism is health; romanticism is disease," or Saintsbury's "Classicism is method; romanticism is energy," seem clearer when "strangeness" or "disease" or "energy" are interpreted as manifestations of individual peculiarity in the artist's vision of his subject. Similarly, "beauty," "health," and "method" connote clear and impersonal vision of the subject, and a large respect for those canons of structure which have been founded in long experience.

The later work of Beethoven may justly be described as strongly tinged with romanticism. But the full tide of romantic feeling flows first in the music of Franz Schubert (1797–1828). Not unnaturally, also, it is in a new and vivid treatment of the song that romanticism is most fully revealed. The immediate emotional appeal of lyric poetry had already been heightened through the adoption of the romantic manner by all the principal poets of the time. Schubert's musical imagination was so susceptible to poetic appeal that the musical counterpart of a poetic idea seems to have been awakened in him by the mere exposure to poetic suggestion. And it was doubtless through this outlet of song that he found that means of larger expression which made possible his extraordinary contributions to symphonic and chamber music. This lyric element must now be more minutely studied.

SCHUBERT'S EARLY LIFE—MUSICAL AND LITERARY INFLUENCES

Music is so remote from contact with things that the outward aspect of a composer's life seldom contributes greatly to our understanding of his thoughts. This is more true of Schubert than of any other great composer; for no other ever lived so completely in the inexplicable world of the imagination. He seems indeed to have been born into that world rather than into ours; so that even the course of his early education affects but slightly the activity of his musical mind. His father, a most upright and conscientious schoolmaster, gave him his first music lessons. But these were intended merely as a part of the necessary equipment of a schoolteacher who was to follow in his father's footsteps; and there was no thought of fitting the boy for the career of a musician. His progress however was so rapid in both violin and piano (which he learned under his elder brothers, Ignaz and Ferdinand) that he was sent for further instruction to Michael Holzer, the choirmaster of the parish. Singing, organ playing, and harmony were now learned with equal rapidity, and apparently with little real discipline from the master, for Holzer was so amazed at the boy's gifts that he could devise no plan of instruction for him. Schubert's exquisite singing was the means by which he obtained admission, at eleven years of age, to the Imperial "Convict," a preparatory school for the University of Vienna, where in addition to their general education the boys were trained to take part in the performances of the Imperial Chapel. There was also an orchestra, in which Franz rapidly rose to the position of first violin. Here he had immediate contact with the larger compositions—symphonies, overtures, and so forth—of Mozart, Haydn, Méhul, Kozeluch, Cherubini, and sometimes of Beethoven. But composition rather than performance was his great passion. In other studies than music he seems to have done well, except in mathematics which he hated.

His shy confession to Spaun, the principal violinist of the Convict orchestra, that he composed almost every day—in fact, whenever he could get music paper—produced a supply of that needful article and also made the first of a slowly growing circle of admiring friends. But little encouragement was given by the school authorities. Salieri was connected with the school as chief examiner in music; but he seems to have done little besides correcting the boy's harmony exercises. After the performance of Schubert's first Mass in F (1814), however, Salieri was glad to claim the boy as a pupil; and even the father was so pleased that he made Franz a present of a five-octave piano. His earliest preserved composition is a long *Fantasia* for piano (four hands) in more than a dozen movements of varied character. There is also a long vocal piece, *Hagar's Lament*, in twelve movements, and a setting of Schiller's *Leichenfantasie* ("Corpse Fantasia") in seventeen movements, all, as in the other pieces, in strangely disrelated keys, and seldom ending in the key in which they begin. These works illustrate the lack of discipline but also the ready fertility of his mind, and his susceptibility to tragic suggestion. Naturally there is in his early work much evidence of the influence of his most-admired musical gods, Haydn and Mozart, and later of Beethoven. In the early symphonies, for instance, we meet with subjects which are palpably cousins to themes in the works of these men, although it may be doubted whether Schubert was aware of the fact. Even the great C major Symphony (1828) may be said to show the same unconscious influence of the Ninth Symphony of Beethoven.[1] In spite of his fertility in instrumental composition, however, it is in the song that Schubert first fully revealed his unique imaginative powers. We must review for a moment, then, the growth of that song literature which was Shubert's most immediate stimulus; and must consider the problem of song writing as a special type of musical composition.

---

[1] In a modification of the last part of the second subject, appearing as a subtheme at the beginning of the development section of the last movement, which bears some resemblance to the great main theme of the *Finale* of Beethoven's work.

THE PROBLEM OF THE SONG

While the song, as a poetic form particularly, had had a remarkable vitality during the fourteenth and fifteenth centuries in Germany, and even as a distinct musical form had had a beginning at the opening of the seventeenth century in the work of Heinrich Albert and his successors, the rapid development of the opera and of other forms of music, all largely affected by the classical ideal, had overshadowed the more tender romantic plant, which slowly withered and died. But the later anticlassical movement, marked by the famous "war of the ancients and the moderns" in France, was extended also to Germany. Klopstock and Lessing effectively championed the modern cause, and following them a transition to romanticism was achieved through the highly individualistic movement known as *Sturm und Drang* ("Storm and Stress"). The founder of this movement was Herder who, among his many contributions to the modernization of historical science, published a great collection of the folk songs of all nations (*Stimmen der Völker*) which was suggested by the similar collections of Ossian and Percy, and revealed, like them, a new aspect of the poetic spirit as belonging essentially to the people. Through Herder, Goethe was enlisted in the movement, his drama *Götz von Berlichingen*, his romance *The Sorrows of Werther*, and many short lyric poems being the result of the attitude which he had for the time assumed. (Goethe's later tendency to classicism, exemplified in the saying quoted above, was due to a reaction against the iconoclastic methods of the *Sturm und Drang* writers; but his classicism is not what it would have been if the earlier influence had been absent.) Out of the poetry of the *Sturm und Drang* period grew, then, not only the modern classicism of Goethe and Schiller but also the more truly romantic movement of which Tieck, the brothers Schlegel, Eichendorff, Chamisso, Rückert, Wilhelm Müller, Uhland, and Heine in his earlier years are perhaps the most important representatives.

Schubert's songs are set to the verse of ninety-one poets, among whom several of these greater names are either infrequent or altogether unrepresented. Tieck, Chamisso, and Eichendorff are absent; there is but one song by Uhland; and of Heine's lyric poems (the *Buch der Lieder* appeared only in 1827) Schubert's early death prevented his setting more than six. Of Klopstock, Schubert set thirteen poems; of Goethe, fifty-nine; of Schiller, thirty-one; of Wilhelm Müller, forty-five—all but one of these being included in the two song cycles *Die Schöne Müllerin* and *Winterreise*. Lesser poets provided the great body of his texts; and many of these poets, such as Mayrhofer (forty-seven songs), Schober (twelve) and Schubart (four) were his personal friends. The relative unimportance of much of this verse has less significance than might at first be supposed.

For any poem must necessarily lose something of its purely poetic value when it is uttered as a song. It is poetic imagination rather than poetic artistry with which the musician has to deal.

But the problem of writing a song is by no means solved by the mere making of a tune to which the words can be sung. The poem itself must be presented to the observer, while at the same time a new embodiment of its emotional character must be conveyed by the music. Not any tune, but the right tune, must be invented to convey this character; and the musician is often seriously hampered in its making by the very words which suggest the character. The melody will of course be chiefly carried on in the voice; it must respect the rhythm and the natural accentuation of the words, as well as their relative emphasis; and the emotional sense of the music must be continuously related to the idea which at any given moment is being suggested by the poem. And yet this melody must appear quite free and spontaneous! Although the successive stanzas of a poem may be symmetrical in length and rhythm, it is obvious that significant words can seldom occur in such positions of rhetorical emphasis (to say nothing of their emotional suggestion) as always to be justly rendered by the same melody repeated for each stanza. It is still more seldom that a poem of any interest will present in its successive stanzas such sameness of mood as can be properly embodied in the same music. Melody, however, takes such precedence over other appeals to our attention that we are often satisfied if the musical character is only generally suited to the words; and our sense of form demands a clear intelligibility in the tune itself, whatever may happen to the text.

Strophic and Modified-Strophic Forms

Hence the simplest type of song is the strophic—that in which the same melody is repeated for each successive stanza of the poem. This is the form in which the true folk song is found—that product of untutored imagination which, as fully as the popular lyric poem, reveals an unending source of inspiration in the race itself. Folk song, as the culture of the race develops, acquires instrumental accompaniment, and takes on some features of higher artistic organization in its form, while preserving its original strophic character. The Germans call songs in this intermediate stage *volkstümlich*—a word which may best be translated "in the style of the folk." Various arrangements of the successive phrases in the melody may occur, one of the most frequent being A–A–B–A—a scheme which will be found exactly to fit such geographically divergent examples as *Die Lorelei* and *Swanee River*, and thousands of other simple, popular tunes.

But it is evident that a greater degree of perfection in the structure of melody and accompaniment may raise the *folk-style* melody to the status of the true art song. Schubert himself has countless examples of this strophic art song. One of the noblest of all is the *Litany for All Souls' Day*. The verse itself in its successive stanzas being but a varied treatment of the one underlying emotion, the strophic form is perfectly suited to the musical expression of the whole poem; and no more elaborate musical scheme would be desirable. But although a lyric poem is almost by definition the expression of a single thought—or perhaps rather of a single predominant emotion—that thought or feeling may be presented in many varied aspects; and in such cases it may well occur that the repetition of the same melody for each stanza would be the negation of the sense of the poem. In such degree, then, as some new characteristic is suggested, the true purpose of the union of words and music can only be fulfilled by making music which varies its character in accord with the changing sense of the text.

It may be possible to produce a most remarkable intensity of suggestion by no more than a slight alteration of the form of the strophic song. Of this possibility a supreme example is to be found in Schubert's *Der Kreuz-zug* ("The Crusade"). This is a sort of ballad or narrative song, which tells of a monk who watches from the window of his cell the embarkation of a company of crusaders. Not the brilliancy of their shining armor nor the militant eagerness of the warriors is echoed in the music, but only that in the spectacle which stirs the monk's heart—the high nobility of the spiritual adventure. The music therefore partakes throughout of the character of the pious songs which he hears the company singing. From his iron-barred window he watches the ship vanish like a swan on the horizon, and consoles his loneliness with the thought that he can be with them in spirit if not in body; for life itself is but a crusade into the promised land. But Schubert's music for this last stanza is amazing in its subtlety and pathos. Instead of the voice, the piano now takes the melody; and to this the monk sings only a stiff and imprisoned bass. The suggestion is too subtle for the average audience; but it may be doubted whether anything more truly poetic ever came from Schubert's pen.

The strophic form may be more effectually disguised, either by the use of several varied phrases within the large unit of the form itself, or by the use of more or less extended instrumental preludes or interludes, or by the use of elaborate and suggestive accompaniment figures which may convey a considerable share of the whole meaning of the music. All these features may be found in the song *Auf dem Wasser zu Singen*. The form of the melody may be roughly described as A–A–B–C–B–C (pause) D (derived from A)–E–E (expanded). D and E together have the value of a sort of coda or refrain. It will be noted that the melody does not return upon itself as in the A–A–B–A or other simple forms. This is partly because the most conspicuous feature of its motion is persistently used in the rippling accompaniment, which provides the extended introduction and the interludes; and partly because the last two lines of the stanza have a different aspect of the whole picture to present. The three stanzas have, however, exactly the same music. Such an example as this may be regarded as intermediary between the strophic form and that of the *durchkomponirtes Lied*, or song composed to conform throughout to the sense of the words, which is the most elaborate and difficult type of song composition.

The Ballad and the *Durchkomponirtes Lied*

The type of poem which would seem most obviously to require this last style of treatment is the ballad. The oldest melodies for such song, in the pure folk-song style, of course had the same tune for each stanza. But with the melody unaccompanied, the singer had large liberty of variation as the narrative proceeded. Set accompaniment for such poems would sadly cramp the expressive powers of the singer. Harmony, however, is indispensable to the art song; and if its vividness and minuteness of suggestion are to be utilized it is evident that the problem already mentioned will arise, that of making music which varies its character with the changing sense of the text. The most perfect example of the ballad is Schubert's *Erlkönig*. The introduction gives us a sense of dread and of urgent haste, possibly even of galloping hoofs. Against this background incessantly maintained, we have not only the narrative itself but the actual voices of father and son, and of the Erlking, whose eerie song first coaxes and then threatens the child whom at the end the father finds dead in his arms. Here the form of the music is constantly created by the text; there is no exact melodic repetition save of the child's ever more frantic cry of fear, "*Mein Vater, Mein Vater!*" But the incessant motion of the accompaniment suffices to give an impression of entire musical unity to the song.

The thread of narrative which gives continuity to the ballad is lacking in more truly lyrical poetry which, with as little suggestion as may be of external fact, voices the immediate feeling of the artist. For such poetry neither strophic nor ballad music can suffice. The underlying emotion of the poem is often allusively rather than directly suggested; and these allusions are too significant to be submerged in music which, if it deals only with the underlying idea, must ignore their individual character. "Composition throughout" is here the only method which can prove adequate to the composer's task.

But merely to contrive characteristic musical phrases for each of these details is to ignore the greater necessity for continuity and unity in the whole song. Not only must the essential detail of the poetic idea be vividly represented but, like those of the poem, the details of the music must combine to produce the ultimate impression that they are all directed toward the expression of the one dominant mood. This is doubtless difficult for the poet; but it is still more difficult for the musician. For music must have its own symmetry, and its phrases must be developed to some degree of purely musical conclusiveness; else it will seem fragmentary and pointless. The poet must shape his thought into language which is rhythmed and rhymed; but he is under no necessity of developing any single image to any predetermined length. The musician can enjoy complete freedom from symmetrical phrase-structure only when he uses the declamatory style of the recitative; and of course no sense of high lyric feeling could be conveyed by the exclusive use of this device. "Composition throughout" therefore absolves the musician from none of the difficulties of purely formal composition, but only intensifies them.

Perhaps as perfect an example of this style of song writing as can be found is to be seen in the great song *Der Wanderer*, which was written in 1816, the year following that in which the *Erlkönig* was written. The essential feeling-character of the poem is that of homelessness. Verse of no great distinction embodies this feeling through various suggestions of immediate condition, memory, or desire. Music of extraordinary vividness manages to embody every essential feeling-suggestion without losing for a moment the clear thread of musical interest. The six bars of introduction, with no true melody but only a slowly expanding series of gloomy dissonances, suggest perfectly the sense of loneliness which is to dominate the whole song. The singer's first words, "I come here from the mountains," are in bleak recitative. His first impression of the scene that confronts him, "the valley steams with fog; the sea is moaning," is scarcely more melodically expressed; but its disheartened phrases are accompanied by bitter harmonies like those of the introduction. Now self-consciousness is aroused: "I wander still, am seldom gay; and always my sighs are asking, 'where?' always, 'where?'" The melody becomes gentle and almost winces with pain, while the rhythm of the accompaniment maintains, in less dissonant harmonies, the triplet motion of the whole music thus far. "Always 'where?'" has for its harmony the longing chord of the augmented sixth—so frequently found in Schubert for such expression as this that it might almost be called his *leitmotiv* of pain. The sense of isolation grows deeper: "The sun here seems to me so cold; the flowers seem faded, and life seems old; and what they say seems empty sound: I am a stranger everywhere." For the first time, now, we find really formal melody—eight bars of it, dejected and spiritless, robbed even of the spark of vitality which in the triplet figures was maintained in the earlier phrases. Suddenly the singer's real desire is clarified: "Where art thou, where art thou, my beloved land? sought for, dreamed of, and never found! The land, the land so green with hope, the land where my roses bloom, where my friends go wandering, where my dead arise again—that land that speaks in my own tongue: O land, where art thou?" The pain of loneliness is lost for a time in a vision of that happiness which can be found only in the undiscovered country—but it is lost only to recur with doubled force. "I wander still" returns; and to the reiterated question, "Always 'where?'" at last comes the answer: "In ghostly voice the sound comes back: 'There, where thou art not, happiness is there.'" This is again in vivid recitative; and a plaintive phrase in the accompaniment, unheard in the song, still serves to recall the predominant emotion.

More minute examination of the formal structure is impossible in our space, but the eight different musical phrases which were necessary to the full expression of the poetic idea have been in some measure indicated. No instrumental piece of this length would ever include so many diverse musical thoughts. Yet, while the words undoubtedly suggest and justify the variety of the musical material, the hearer has no impression of musical incoherence or discontinuity. And it is precisely this power not only of inventing the right phrase for the verbal thought, but of making the whole musical substance to seem naturally related that marks the musician's imaginative gift as supreme.[2]

Not only an imagination untrammeled by too great a respect for constituted form was necessary for the production of such songs as these. A great vocabulary of musical speech and a considerable flexibility of musical form had had to be brought into existence before any such work was possible. The actual novelty of Schubert's basic materials is not great. He had little contrapuntal knowledge (indeed, it was only a few weeks before his death that he arranged with Sechter to pursue a regular course of study in counterpoint), and his vocabulary was largely that which he acquired by contact with current music. Probably no chord exists in his music which cannot be found in Beethoven, or for that matter in Bach. His rhythms are certainly no more novel that Beethoven's. It is only in his fertility of melodic invention that he excels perhaps every other com-

---

[2] The student must of course examine the music itself in order to realize the values which we have attempted to suggest. The songs which we have especially noted: *Litanei* as an example of pure strophic form; *Der Kreuzzug* and *Auf dem Wasser zu Singen* as modified strophic forms; *Erlkönig* as a ballad form; and *Der Wanderer* as a full example of the song composed throughout, are types which will be found exemplified in many different forms in Schubert's work.

poser who ever lived—not even excepting Mozart. But Schubert's melodic phrases are almost as simple, on the whole, as those of folk song. It is not then in the novelty of his musical substance, but in his novel use of familiar musical substance, that Schubert's originality resides. Familiarity dulls that novelty for us, but to his contemporaries it was not only striking but perplexing.

Beethoven's delight was unbounded when he at last came to know a few of Schubert's songs, "many of which," he said, "contain ten others"—a reference doubtless to their singular inclusiveness of form as well as to their length. But the less imaginative musicians, in whom an orthodox musical education had engendered a bland self-confidence of judgment, were slow to apprehend the true meaning of Schubert's work. Their minds had been trained to conform to classical ideals; and Schubert's highly romantic utterances either were incomprehensible or were ignored as being in bad taste. He was reproached by the critics for trying to render too minutely the sense of the words in music, instead of rendering the whole meaning of the whole piece "which Mozart proves to be the only means to reach the highest object of Art." [3] But it was precisely this denial of generalizing classicism which was essential to the creation of the song; and it was only indifference to mere formula, combined with an extraordinary sense of meaning in musical phrases—both of which might have been destroyed by orthodox training—which made possible Schubert's sudden and almost unapproachable creations. In the larger operatic form his ideals were the same. Here, largely owing to his never finding a proper libretto, he was practically unsuccessful. But in the song at least he is fulfilling, more than any other composer since Gluck's day, that master's ideal of music as a handmaiden of poetry.

Schubert's Later Life and Works—The Symphonies

We have been deflected from the story of Schubert's life by a discussion of his work in the form which he most fully mastered. But there is little to tell. His friendship with poets like Mayrhofer and Schober, with singers like Vogl (a great favorite of the Viennese opera stage who did more than any other to popularize his songs), with a few families of cultivated musical taste, such as the Frölichs, where he was as fully appreciated as possible, contrast painfully with his failure to impress the managers of the opera houses, and with his occasional excursions into the lower strata of Viennese life which were doubtless responsible for the serious illness of 1822—an illness from which he never fully recovered, and which weak-

---

[3] This criticism related to Schubert's early opera *The Twin Brothers*, but it was directed in substance against the songs as well.

ened his resistance to the typhus which ended his short life. Various official posts were applied for but never attained. It was not until 1821 that
a composition of Schubert's (the *Erlkönig*) was published—by private
subscription. All the rest of his life the publishers were reaping rich
harvests from his works and paying him the merest pittance for them.
His average earnings for thirteen years were about $200 a year—enough
to exist on in the Vienna of those days, but unendurable to contemplate
in comparison to the $15,000 which Diabelli made in a few years out of
the sale of *Der Wanderer* alone.

But a man who writes not only some six hundred songs but also six
Masses, eighteen dramatic pieces (some only fragmentary, but *Alfonso
and Estrella* and *Fierrabras* fully developed operas), nine symphonies,
twenty string quartets and other chamber works, twenty-four piano sonatas, and a whole literature of smaller pieces—a man who writes all this
in something less than eighteen years can hardly have time for such tedious
business as the ordinary life of this world. Such contact with life as could
enable him to interpret so fully the pains and passions of ordinary men
seems impossible in the midst of such continuous creative work. But, the
marvelousness of that work being taken for granted, its development seems
to follow a perfectly natural course. His truest instinct was for the song;
and since that form demanded less of constructive power and more of
intimate imagination than any other, it was in this field that he first showed
complete command of his resources.

If we count the production of *Erlkönig* (1815) as marking a safe maturity in song composition, even though *Gretchen am Spinnrade* was written
in the previous year, we may fairly safely say that the production of the
Unfinished Symphony (1822) marks a full maturity in his development
of an instrumental style. Seven symphonies precede this one—compositions which show only occasionally the hand of genius, and none of which
compare in vividness with the songs. Yet the *Unfinished* comes not from
the mind of the youthful enthusiast who is compelled by the sheer glory
of musical sound to the act of composition, but from the mature artist
who has developed his powers from the original sources of musical inspiration rather than by study of the principles of composition which other
men have followed. Only a writer of song could have contrived the lyrical
thematic substance of this Symphony. Schubert's broader imaginative
vision here seems to suggest his perception that words, which can give
definiteness of meaning to music, may also hamper its development to full
reality of expression. Hence this Symphony is a larger song—a song more
rich in suggestion and more complete in exposition than any which could
be set to words. Nor is it, even to the untutored listener, much less definite in meaning than if it had a text.

More perhaps than any song he ever wrote, the *Unfinished* Symphony reveals the man himself. Its tragedy, if it were self-conscious, would be unbearable. The singular absence of the sense of protest, however, lightens the apparent pathos of the music. The introductory phrase in the basses, like the principal subject itself, lacks resistant energy. Its gloom therefore is always tempered with resignation. The lovely second subject similarly is unaware of all the charm in the vision it evokes.[4] The development, to be sure, is highly intense; but not even here is the sense of tragedy aroused. Pain is endured for the moment, since it cannot be evaded; but it leaves no rankling memory. Indeed it is the listener, not the composer, who suffers.

More and more after the making of this Symphony Schubert turned to instrumental forms. The later Sonatas (especially that in B flat), the String Quartets (the one whose slow movement is based on the song *Death and the Maiden*, the incredibly beautiful one in A minor, and the still greater but inordinately long one in G), the String Quintet in C, the Octet—all these display an instrumental insight quite amazing, and, like the *Unfinished* Symphony, fully informed with the expanded spirit of the song. Two more Symphonies also were produced in these few last years. One was dedicated in 1826 to the *Gesellschaft der Musikfreunde* in Vienna. It has been lost. The other, written in March, 1828, and therefore Schubert's last symphony, is among the most striking of all the works that have been written in symphonic form.[5] Its tone, unlike that of the *Unfinished*, is almost wholly joyous; but this joy, while clearly born of some earthly experience, is so idealized that all thought of the world is banished. Its great length makes it peculiarly susceptible to the disposition of conductors to "interpret" it in various distorted ways; but when the music is allowed to pursue its natural course there is no sense of tedium. No other man could have maintained an impression of utter spontaneity for so long a time; and this is precisely because his themes, while capable of truly symphonic development, are yet largely lyrical in character. Again, one feels, this symphony is a revelation of the mind of its composer. The tone is now that of elation rather than sorrow; but the abandonment to the

[4] The taste which could take this amazing melody out of its context and, by destroying every poetic allusion in it, turn it into a stupid, not even Viennese, waltz (*Blossom-Time*) beggars one's vocabulary of condemnation.

[5] Schubert's last symphony, that in C major, is usually designated as No. 8. We gave the number of his symphonies as nine. There may possibly have been ten. Sir George Grove, who believed this the true number, included in his reckoning a score, in his possession, which is sketched throughout but contains, after the 110th bar, no more than hints of the composer's whole idea. Grove was also convinced that a grand symphony was composed at Gastein in 1825; but it is doubtful that this work ever existed. Probably that which is now known as No. 6 was Grove's "Gastein" symphony.

feeling of the moment is as complete and as unself-conscious as in the *Unfinished*. Such ecstasy of joyous excitement as is reached in the final movement (a sort of march, expanded to full sonata form) has hardly been expressed by any other musician.

The song was by no means forsaken, however. Many settings of poems which came under his eye were made—usually with that complete absence of preliminary study which marked most of his writing, and mostly justifying in his case this most dangerous method of creation. Two great song cycles also belong to this period in which the trend is toward instrumental composition. These are *Die Schöne Müllerin* (1823) and the *Winterreise* (1827). The poems of each cycle were by Wilhelm Müller. *The Maid of the Mill* tells, in twenty songs, of the disastrous love of a young apprentice for the coquettish daughter of a miller with whom the young man finds employment. The *Winter Journey* is a tale, hinted rather than told, of the hopeless wandering of a rejected suitor about and away from the scene of his passion. Every guidepost shows him the way back to the town; but the one he sees is that which points out a road which no traveler ever retraces. The green garlands about the tombstones in a graveyard seem like the bush which announces that good wine is to be had at the inn over whose door it hangs. The last song *Der Leiermann* is a marvelous picture of desolation—an old organ grinder whose life has dwindled to the mere turning of a crank. One cannot but wonder how deep was Schubert's conscious irony in setting the last words:

> Wonderful old minstrel,
> Shall I go with you?
> Will you for my ditties
> Turn the handle, too?

There was never a writer to whom method meant so little. Beethoven's process of development, imposing and fluent as it appears in the music itself, was, as we know from countless sketches, the result of laborious and hesitant efforts. Of Beethoven's method Schubert adopted but little; for he could not labor over composition. To ponder a process was for him to wither inspiration. Consequently, there is no writer whose method is so inimitable. Of counterpoint, as we have seen, he had no technical command; yet many passages in the chamber works and symphonies show an easy and natural polyphony, adequate to that aspect of the subject which he chooses to present. Discursive as his treatment often is, it is never mechanical. Sometimes, on the contrary, it attains to unimaginable vividness through the simplest means. In the singularly uninsistent Piano Sonata in B flat, for example, the development section, instead of being the usual forceful intensification of the principal subject matter, is—altogether rightly—a quiet, almost inferential revelation of its unconscious pathos. The melody of the principal theme, accompanied by only the thinnest of harmonies, begins to rise in various keys into what might readily become an atmosphere of ecstasy; but after every beginning it falls back, broken-winged, to the same spot—a mere hushed harmony of D minor. There is no apparent compulsion, no hint of overwhelming force; yet the exquisite melody has not the power to resist or to escape this influence. In the *Finale* of the great C major Symphony, on the other hand, a march tune of elemental joyousness is made at last to rise to an incredible frenzy of excitement merely by the almost Rossinian device of presenting long stretches of it in a gradually rising succession of keys. The method of the *durchkomponirtes Lied* is, of course, largely suggested by its text; but enumeration of the analyzable details of the method, whether in song or symphony, gives but a woefully inadequate account of the results. We describe Schubert's vocal or instrumental melody as lyrical, and marvel at the profuseness of his invention. We remark the diffuseness of his structure, the freedom of his modulation, the peculiar warmth of his orchestral color (which comes from the warmth of his melodic lines as much as from any characteristic use of the instruments, though his combination of oboe and horn, or his treatment of the trombones, is unusual); but in none of the technically describable details can we find any adequate explanation of the palpable character of his music.

Yet, though he had no method to impart, his influence upon later writers, although perhaps chiefly indirect, was very great. In the particular field of the song, it is indeed Schubert's method (if that can be called method which varies with every example) which is followed and refined by Schumann, Franz, Brahms, and Hugo Wolf. But Schubert's song is not merely an adaptation of music to poetry; it is rather an intimate revelation through music of the latent meaning of words. It contributes greatly then to the closer association of musical and nonmusical ideas, or of music and human experience. Not all our experiences take verbally definable shape. Yet our awareness even of indefinable experience is an idea; and to reveal the essence of such experience in music is to contribute greatly to humanity's fascinating record of itself. We shall see that a still closer relation between music and experience is sought and found in the Wagnerian *leitmotiv*. Wagner may have found no direct intimation of his leading-motive idea in Schubert's songs; but he could have found endless justification for it. Thus Schubert was a very real contributor to the music of the future.

But it was in the realization of still other types of experience—of those flights of fancy to which we are all subject but which we have not the wit to crystallize into any lasting form—that Schubert was at his best.

These most indefinable experiences are far more important for all of us than they are commonly allowed to be. We all have poetic impulses, else we should never enjoy poetry; we are all poets in embryo whose wings have never sprouted. To awaken our poetic instinct is to enlarge our capacity for experience; and there is no music which probes so deeply in search of a responsive poetic sensibility as Schubert's. Liszt spoke with profound comprehension when he called him *le musicien le plus poète qui fût jamais* (the most poetic musician who ever lived).

CHAPTER XXIV

The Romantic Idealists— Mendelssohn, Schumann, and Chopin

EETHOVEN's last works, and those great instrumental compositions of Schubert in which the romantic attitude was most fully exemplified, remained practically unknown to the musical world for long years after their production. The romantic attitude, however, was almost universally adopted in the period which followed, as may be seen in the work of poets, painters, and other artists of the same period. Beethoven, like the Goethe of the last part of *Faust*, was almost more philosopher than poet: confronted with a vision of his subject so vast and so allusive that the actuality of his subject is almost lost in the maze of its implications. Schubert, on the other hand, was no philosopher but only a poet, whose subject was illumined for him by a "light that never was," and who is sometimes able miraculously to sensitize our literal eyes to that imaginative light. The expressive processes contrived by men of such extraordinary vision must remain forever inimitable. But their disposition toward their subject, once grasped, can be assumed by others in proportion to their vision; and a classification of romantic writers may be made on this basis. The distinctions will be difficult and not altogether clear; but they may be useful if not too literally interpreted.

One disposition—that already shown by Beethoven and Schubert—is to present the subject as the artist feels it: we are asked to share his feeling, and through it to grasp the nature and the significance of the subject. The other tendency is to present the subject as the artist sees it: we are to share his vision, and through it to grasp his feeling. The one method may be called idealism; the other, realism. Both may be thoroughly romantic, for each is the expression, through a different channel, of a personal interpretation of the subject. The realistic romanticist is the more akin to the classical artist, for with him as with the classicist the subject itself is the main object of attention. But he is also concerned (unlike the classicist) with the vividness of his subject rather than with its whole rounded proportion, and calls to his aid in presenting his subject every device which can intensify its vividness for the observer. Virtuosity, therefore—which may readily come to be employed for its own sake—is likely to characterize the work of the romantic realist.

The tendency of the German romanticists was generally toward idealism. Realism on the other hand was mostly characteristic of the French, whose traditions were more strongly classical. We shall deal first with the earlier German romanticists, the chief of whom are Mendelssohn and Schumann. Chopin, the first world figure among Polish composers, is also essentially of this group.

MENDELSSOHN

Felix Mendelssohn-Bartholdy, unlike most of the heroes of musical composition, was a child of fortune, the son of a wealthy banker. The grandfather, Moses Mendelssohn, had been eminent as a philosopher; the father, Abraham, was also a man of keen intellect and high purpose. (He assumed the name Bartholdy on the advice of his wife's brother, Salomon Bartholdy, to distinguish this branch of the Mendelssohn family from the rest.) Felix was born at Hamburg in 1809, and showed very early such talent as to suggest comparison with Mozart. The family escaped to Berlin during the French occupation of Hamburg in 1811, and founded the great banking house. The mother was musical and gave the first lessons both to Felix and to his elder sister Fanny (born 1805) who, like Mozart's sister Marianne, also showed precocious talent. Notoriety being financially unnecessary, the children's education was even more systematically ordered than was that of Mozart. They were tutored in general subjects by the father of Paul Heyse, the novelist; by Ludwig Berger in piano, and by Zelter (a composer whom Goethe preferred to Schubert) in harmony; they learned violin, drawing, and Greek with other masters. At nine years Felix played in public the piano part of a trio by Wölfl. At eleven he had begun to compose—sonatas for piano and with violin, pieces for organ, a cantata and a little operetta, to which were added in the following year symphonies for string quartet and three more short operas. He met Weber, then in Berlin for the production of *Freischütz*, and it was proposed that Felix should become his pupil; but nothing came of it. A vast amount of composition preceded the published work, and shows a rapid and very thorough assimilation of the principles, and a generally classical manner. Much of his music was performed at home on Sundays when a small orchestra was assembled, and Felix conducted even though he had to stand on a chair to be seen. Such experience was of course invaluable.

At fifteen he had some lessons from Moscheles, whom he speaks of as "the prince of pianists." During the same year he composed what is now known as his First Symphony in C minor (twelve earlier attempts preceded this work). At sixteen he was taken (for the second time) to Paris, meeting there a great number of musical celebrities. His impressions of French music were very unfavorable; but with Cherubini, whom he calls "an extinct volcano," he got on well. Back at home, he completed the two-act opera *Camacho's Wedding*, which was performed without much success two years later. In 1826 came the remarkable *Midsummer Night's Dream* Overture—a work so brilliant in substance as well as in promise that it has hardly a parallel in history among youthful compositions. It marks the beginning of Mendelssohn's maturity.

The range of his interests and talents was remarkable. His drawing was exceptional; his knowledge of languages was such that he was making translations into German verse of several of the Latin poets; at the same time he was hearing lectures at the University of Berlin in philosophy, geography, and music. His social affability made him welcome everywhere. Also his musical horizon was broadening. He became passionately fond of the later works of Beethoven. His musical memory was phenomenal. He played by heart not only such great works as the *Hammerklavier* Sonata of Beethoven, Op. 106, but also the Ninth Symphony. He never played in public from notes—a very unusual thing in those days. In 1829, against considerable opposition, he brought to performance for the first time in a hundred years the *St. Matthew* Passion of Bach—thereby inaugurating a general interest in Bach's music, later on to culminate in the formation of the *Bachgesellschaft*, which ultimately published every work of that master which could be discovered. He appears even to have known the *St. Matthew* Passion by heart.

In 1829, having finally decided to make music his profession, he began on his father's advice a long tour which was both to give him contact with the great world and to test his powers as a professional musician. He went first to England, where he conducted his C minor Symphony with great success, was elected an honorary member of the Philharmonic Society, and won unbounded social acceptance. A visit to Scotland in the summer gave him the inspiration for the later *Fingal's Cave* or *Hebrides* Overture. The Italian sojourn of 1830–31 was marked by a similar mingling of composition and social diversion. Both the *Scotch* and the *Italian* Symphonies were begun here, and the *Hebrides* Overture in its first form was finished. All his work underwent a ceaseless revision, the *Italian* Symphony being unfinished, to his mind, even at his death. At Paris again in 1832 he met many conspicuous musicians, among whom were Liszt, Chopin, Meyerbeer, Ole Bull, Herz, Kalkbrenner (who proposed to teach Chopin for three years in order to make of him a good artist), and many others. The Second Symphony in D (called the *Reformation* Symphony because it had been written in celebration of the tercentenary of the Augsburg Confession) was rehearsed but not performed; and he left Paris more than ever disgusted with its musical taste. Berlin, although his home, was similarly uncongenial to him in a professional way. He failed of election to the conductorship of the *Singakademie*, a disappointment which his happy family life was scarcely able to mask.

In Düsseldorf in 1833 he conducted the Lower Rhine Festival with such success that he was chosen permanent director of all the varied municipal music there, both sacred and operatic. He came to dislike the opera, however, gave up his connection with it, and in 1835 was invited to Leipzig as conductor of the Gewandhaus concerts. The manifold duties of this position, as well as his happy marriage to Cécile Jeanrenaud, considerably impeded his composition; but the oratorio *St. Paul* had been finished before the marriage, and several important compositions had been begun —notably the Violin Concerto, in regard to which he had the valuable advice of Ferdinand David, concertmaster of the Leipzig Orchestra. In 1839 he gave the first performance of Schubert's great Symphony in C, the manuscript of which Schumann had found in Vienna. He was thoroughly happy at Leipzig; but this pleasant life was somewhat disturbed by his having to accept the direction of the musical division of a great Academy of Fine Arts which Frederick William IV desired to found in Berlin. The Academy itself came to nothing, and he was at last able to return to Leipzig. The music for *Athalie* and *Oedipus* and the remaining incidental numbers of the *Midsummer Night's Dream* music were commissioned by the King and at length completed, together with the Violin Concerto, in 1845. In the following year *Elijah*, doubtless his greatest oratorio, was finished and was first performed in Birmingham, England.

The extraordinary activity of his life had begun to tell upon his health; and the death of his father and then of his mother had heavily increased his depression. At Frankfort, on his return from another visit to England in the spring of 1847, he learned of the sudden death of his deeply loved sister Fanny. It overwhelmed him; and he was never able to regain his strength or interest in his work. The String Quartet in F minor seems to reflect his state of mind, and a few other works, chiefly choral, were completed; but his health at last gave way altogether, and he died November 4, 1847, mourned by the musical world at large but especially in Germany and England.

Romanticism is less conspicuous in Mendelssohn than in any other of the important composers of his time. It will have been noted that his education, both in music and in other branches, was considerably tinged with classical interests. He greatly admired Beethoven; but it is the work of his middle period, not that of the last, which Mendelssohn most obviously took as his model. His love for Bach is manifested in his frequent choice of the form of the fugue; but it is seldom that the profoundly rhapsodic or contemplative aspect of Bach's imagination is reflected in his work. He had, too, but little interest in the greatest of his contemporaries. He could make nothing of Berlioz; was inclined to patronize Schumann; felt that Wagner was cold and heartless and "no true musician"; and gave his heartiest admiration only to men like Gade, Sterndale Bennett, and others who were palpably his inferiors. This was doubtless from no conscious unwillingness to measure himself with his equals. It was rather—in spite of his own mental brilliancy, or perhaps because of it—an inability to detect worth in that which was expressed in a manner irregular or inelegant by comparison with his own. The conditions of both his education and his musical experience doubtless tended to enhance the native artistic squeamishness which often characterizes such extreme sensibilities as his; and there was no force strong enough to penetrate the citadel of superiority into which he instinctively withdrew. His brilliancy as performer, composer, conductor, and social lion was so great that he could always find acclaim in some quarter; and he fled to such congenial circles (as from Paris or Berlin) whenever the recognition which he felt to be due him was not forthcoming.

"*Es bildet ein Talent sich in der Stille*" (Talent develops in isolation), said Goethe; and this isolation or refuge or retreat which Mendelssohn needed was the one thing which his fortunate circumstances did not provide. Such unrelieved and individual concentration is especially needful for the development of the romantic idealist. Hampered by a condition which Mendelssohn could hardly have been expected to correct, his work nevertheless shows many essential qualities of romanticism. If the *Songs Without Words* seldom show that insurgence of the poetic spirit which is to be found in the *Impromptus* and *Musical Moments* of Schubert or the *Nocturnes* and *Fantasy Pieces* of Chopin and Schumann, there is yet in many of them the pale reflection of that spirit, whose character is not to be mistaken. The two later symphonies, far less profoundly obsessed than the *Unfinished* and the C major Symphonies of Schubert, are yet palpably imbued with a romantic vision of the lands and peoples they represent. The larger piano pieces are sometimes notably and convincingly romantic in tone—especially the G minor Piano Concerto and the *Variations Sérieuses* (the latter doubtless being Mendelssohn's finest piano composition).

The Concerto for violin (far surpassing the Piano Concertos in vitality and still retaining a proud place among the greatest examples of that form) is thoroughly romantic in feeling, even if its brilliancy is more striking than its romanticism. The chamber music is less favored than the orchestral work; but the F minor Quartet and the Piano Trio in D minor display many qualities of romantic imagination as well as that certainty of execution which marks all Mendelssohn's work. The symphonies are less vivid than the overtures—an indication that the composer's imagination was natively more romantic than classical, since in this smaller and more flexible form it finds a more congenial and characteristic outlet. But for some reason, probably discoverable in his education and environment rather than in his natural talent, the untrammeled expression of the romantic spirit was denied him. He could not bear to be wrong; and this risk is one which must be run by any pioneer.

SCHUMANN

The romantic spirit found far more complete expression in the work of Robert Schumann, who was born a year later than Mendelssohn (in 1810) at Zwickau in Saxony. His father was a bookseller, editor, and author; his mother the daughter of a surgeon. Neither parent had any musical talent; but the father was sympathetic with all artistic endeavor, and if he had lived longer Schumann's life would have been made far easier. The boy's interest in music was shown very early. He began to compose before he was seven, and showed a peculiar gift for improvisation. No competent instruction was available in Zwickau; but he had lessons with Kuntsch, a local organist, until he outstripped his teacher. His general and literary education was more regular. He showed great love for poetry, and at fourteen published some small verses. This literary interest is important, not only because it gave a foundation for Schumann's later work in musical criticism, but because it established, during the years when the boy's imaginative powers were forming, a close connection between verbal and musical expression.

The father died when Robert was sixteen. The mother, anxious to see her son well established in life, insisted on the career of jurist for him. At eighteen accordingly he matriculated at the University of Leipzig as a *studiosus juris*, but studied instead of law the works of Jean Paul Richter —a fantastic romantic novelist of whom Schiller said that he would be worthy of admiration "if he had made as good use of his riches as other men made of their poverty." The ready susceptibility to feeling which marks all Jean Paul's writing was reflected in Schumann's personality, and was intensified in him by this reading. Thus Jean Paul, as he is usually called, became one of the most potent influences in the formation of Schumann's style. Aside from a few lessons in piano from Friedrich Wieck (an excellent teacher and the father of Schumann's future wife) he had no regular instruction in music. As in literature, his natural appetite was his guide, and the music he studied was chiefly that which awakened his romantic imagination. Strangely, the most appealing of all was the music of Sebastian Bach. It was a rare susceptibility indeed which, in 1828, could penetrate to the imaginative core of the mighty Leipzig genius of bygone days. It was not the contrapuntal ingenuity (almost all that was understood by the theorists of the time) but the richness and variety of Bach's polyphonically evolved harmony which appealed to Schumann. Thus a certain polyphonic richness of texture which is almost always apparent in Schumann's writing is the result, not of imitation, but of his understanding of one of the great secrets of Bach's style. Schubert also was one of Schumann's gods. The influence of this kindred spirit is seen not only in the later songs, but in the fluid, somewhat improvisatory form of many of Schumann's instrumental compositions.

He removed to Heidelberg in 1829, ostensibly for further study of the law; but so strong was his interest in music that even the lectures of Thibaut were but indifferently attended. Schumann was indeed hardly honest in thus devoting time, energy, and money to a pursuit so foreign to that which his mother had marked out for him. He was becoming neither a lawyer nor a practical musician. But he could not endure the law. Returning to Leipzig, he again had lessons with Wieck and became more determined than ever to make of himself a great virtuoso. It was Wieck who helped him to make up his mind, and who finally won the mother's tardy consent to the change in his plans. At first the career of pianist was Schumann's aim. He seems, even in 1830, to have been unsure of his creative powers. In order to hasten the perfecting of his technique he devised a mechanical contrivance for strengthening the weaker fourth finger of the right hand by holding stationary the third finger. The result was the crippling of the third finger, and the ruin of his prospects as a virtuoso. This misfortune was most serious. The career of pianist had seemed doubtful enough; but that of composer appeared almost hopeless.

His misfortune however was his ultimate gain—and ours—for it made him discover his own creative abilities, and at the same time corrected a possible excess of interest, natural to a young pianist, in virtuosity for its own sake. This interest was at first considerable. The *Abegg Variations* (Op. 1) show an obvious adoption of the rather superficial brilliancy of the technique of Moscheles, whom Schumann, when he was nine, had heard and admired at Carlsbad. The fascination was deepened when, in 1829 and again in 1830, he heard Paganini, "Wizard of the Violin," the first of the supreme virtuosi of the nineteenth century. Schumann began, like Liszt, to adapt Paganini's trickeries to the piano, making two sets of Caprices (Op. 3 and Op. 10) based on Paganini's works. But the crippling of his hand turned his mind away from this more superficial interest and gave rein to the far more significant qualities of his imagination.

He went to Heinrich Dorn, conductor of the opera at Leipzig, for composition. Wayward and undisciplined as his musical thoughts were, it was impossible for him to follow any regular course of study; but Dorn showed his wisdom in allowing the young man's originality as great freedom as was possible, and Schumann speaks of him later as "the man who first gave a hand to me as I climbed upwards, and, when I began to doubt myself, drew me aloft so that I should see less of the common herd of mankind, and more of the pure air of art." In spite of their peculiarities his early works were quite favorably received by the critics. The *Abegg Variations* (the theme is made of the notes A, B (flat), E, G, G, the letters spelling the name of a fictitious Countess, invented by Schumann) and the familiar *Papillons*—his first two published works—were noticed in the Vienna *Musikalische Zeitung* by the poet Grillparzer. The public, on the other hand, seems to have been repelled by their peculiarities; and this is perhaps not strange, for the *Variations* are somewhat vague in design, and the *Papillons* (a sort of miniature *Carnaval*) are so fragmentary in their first impression as to give little idea of continuity or constructive power. In 1833 his work showed a solider tone. The Impromptus on a theme of Clara Wieck, the first and third movements of the G minor Sonata, the beginning of the F sharp minor Sonata, and the completion of the *Toccata*, Op. 7—a most ingenious exemplification of technical brilliancy within the solid outline of sonata form—date from this year and mark an extraordinarily rapid development both of imagination and understanding.

Against the general insipidity of musical taste then governing in the complacent musical centers of Germany, little headway was likely to be made by such works as Schumann felt himself able to produce. With clearer insight than anyone could possess who had not his wider literary sense, he saw that the public needed not only to be provided with a better kind of music, but also with some tangible judgment of its value. A truly progressive critical journal of music was needed; and this Schumann, with the aid of several enthusiastic friends, proceeded to found. It was called the *Neue Zeitschrift für Musik* ("The New Musical Journal") and first appeared in April, 1834. In the following year Schumann became sole editor, and continued in that capacity until 1844. The vivacity and attractiveness of the articles were enhanced by the continued reference to an imaginary band of progressive-minded artists called the *Davidsbund* ("Brotherhood of David"), who were supposed to be in league against the Philistinism of contemporary music. Two of the imaginary figures, Florestan and Eusebius, really represented only the fiery and passionate or the dreamy and contemplative characteristics of Schumann's own nature. (They were suggested by two characters in Jean Paul's *Flegeljahre:* Vult and Walt.) Schumann's enthusiastic recognition of the talent of other artists was here given free rein. Indeed, it had been manifested even before the *Zeitschrift* was founded in an article, "An Opus ii," which dealt with a set of variations on *La ci darem la mano*, and announced the author of the work—Frédéric Chopin—to the German musical world as a genius. In the *Zeitschrift* itself, Mendelssohn, Taubert, Hiller, Heller, Henselt, Bennett, Gade, Kirchner, Robert Franz, and last of all, Johannes Brahms, were brought to the notice of the world. "Consciously or unconsciously," he wrote, "a new and as yet undeveloped school is being founded on the basis of the Beethoven-Schubert romanticism, a school which we may venture to expect will mark a special epoch in the history of art. Its destiny seems to be to usher in a period which will nevertheless have many links to connect it with the past century."

The amount of direct benefit which Schumann, as a composer, received from this literary effort is as nothing to the benefit it conferred on others and on the musical taste of the time. Indeed, it interrupted his own work seriously. The *Carnaval* and the magnificent *Symphonic Etudes* were completed in 1834; but the next year is a blank. From 1836 to 1839, however, having learned the routine of his editorial work, he was able to devote much energy to composition and produced what are probably his finest piano pieces; the great *Fantasia* in C, the F minor Sonata (called a Concerto without orchestra), the *Davidsbündlertänze*, the *Kreisleriana*, the inimitable *Scenes from Childhood*, and many small pieces. With the exception of an early symphony in G minor, recently uncovered, his only effort had been in the direction of piano composition. The extraordinary novelty of form in his earliest compositions somewhat prevented the immediate understanding of their imaginative content; but with the appearance of work after work, always in some new formal guise and related to some new and hitherto untouched subject, his unusual manner had come to be more widely accepted.

This was fortunate, for otherwise one great objective of his life would never have been attained. This was his marriage to Clara Wieck, the daughter of his old teacher. Clara was some ten years younger than Robert and had become, even in 1835, a very notable figure in the German musical world. Her father's crabbed opposition to the marriage had finally to be overcome in the law courts; but this difficulty apparently left no taint of soreness upon that most ideal married life which ensued. Clara supplied what Schumann had lost in the crippling of his hand—the direct influence of the performer upon the public; and he was only made the freer to express himself in the manner most congenial to him—that of composition. In order to establish himself as a self-dependent person, he had gone to Vienna in October, 1839, hoping to transplant thither the publication of the *Neue Zeitschrift*. This venture was a failure; but the visit was important in that it resulted in the discovery of Schubert's symphony; and some record of Schumann's impressions of Viennese life is to be seen in the buoyant *Faschingsschwank aus Wien*.

The year of his marriage, 1840, marked the beginning of a quite new creative endeavor. Hitherto he had written nothing but piano music. Now, possibly because of the approaching culmination of his romance with Clara, possibly because his visit to Vienna had intensified his already great interest in Schubert's works, he suddenly found inspiration in the song itself instead of in that instrumental counterpart of the song which he had hitherto almost exclusively created. In 1841, the symphony became his passion; and in that year alone he wrote three symphonies. The first of these, in B flat (known as the *Spring* Symphony) was completely sketched, as he has told us, in four days. The other two Symphonies are the one in D minor (now known as the Fourth, since its publication was delayed until 1851) and the *Overture, Scherzo and Finale* which, lacking a slow movement, is not altogether of symphonic proportions but is entirely of symphonic character. In 1842 his interest turned to chamber music. The three String Quartets and the Quartet and Quintet for piano and strings date from this year. Thus, in three years an imagination which had long been confined to expression solely through the medium of the piano had expanded so as to demand the voice, the orchestra, and the chamber group for its utterance.

Only two important fields of composition remained to be entered—those of choral music and the opera. Choral music was attacked immediately. In 1843 appeared a sort of secular oratorio or unstaged music drama, *Paradise and the Peri*, on a text from Thomas Moore's *Lalla Rookh*. Its success was so great that he immediately began work upon the similar choral treatment of a far profounder subject, Goethe's *Faust*. Only four numbers were completed, however, before he found that his health was breaking under the strain of such ceaseless production. Tours into Bohemia and Russia served both to relieve his mind of the strain of effort and to make his compositions more widely known—Clara, of course, being the interpreter. In October, 1844, he left Leipzig for Dresden, where there was much less music to be heard and where his health in consequence could more rapidly improve. He had given up the editorship of the *Neue Zeitschrift* in 1844, and by his removal relinquished a professorship in piano and composition at the Leipzig Conservatory.

In Dresden the desire to produce an opera seized him, and the result was *Genoveva*, the text of which he finally had to construct himself from dramatic treatments of that subject by Reinick and Hebbel. It was produced under Schumann's own direction at Dresden in 1850; but neither then nor since has it won any great approval from the public. It was not the penetration of the subject that was lacking, but the more external quality of stage effectiveness—a quality hardly to be expected in the music of so introspective and idealistic a musician. Those same characteristics however which made his opera unoperatic were exactly suited to the treatment of *Faust*, and especially of that last part which deals with Faust's salvation. This music had been finished in 1848, and was held by many to be not only profoundly philosophic but remarkably illuminating in connection with the text. Several scenes and an overture were later added, the whole work not being published until after the composer's death. Another stage work—the music to Byron's *Manfred*, the text of which Schumann somewhat rearranged for performance with his music—was produced by Liszt at Weimar in 1852. Here again a lack of instinct for the stage is manifest, although the music is remarkably fine as a reflection of the reaction aroused in the composer by the poem. *The Pilgrimage of the Rose*, a sort of companion piece to *Paradise and the Peri*, was completed in 1851. Two other large choral works, a Mass and a Requiem, were written in 1852. They are not intended for use in connection with the service, but are rather expressions of the sentiments of religious contemplation awakened in him by the words.

Two more Symphonies, the so-called Second in C, and the Third (really the last) in E flat, which is known as the *Rhenish* Symphony, complete his work in this form. This last work is intended in some way to reflect the impression made upon the composer by the sight of the Cologne Cathedral; and is also connected vaguely with his removal from Dresden to Düsseldorf. Many operatic projects were taken up, but none were brought to completion. Schiller's *Bride of Messina* and Goethe's *Hermann and Dorothea* suggested overtures which were completed; but the texts remained untouched. A species of concert drama in the shape of ballads set for chorus and orchestra, such as Uhland's *Der Königssohn*, *Des Sängers Fluch*, and *Das Glück von Edenhall*, was more congenial to his disposition than opera.

Although the first threat to his health was not alarming, he never recovered that power of incessant work which had marked his earlier years. In Dresden he had been somewhat active as a conductor, taking the relinquished post of Ferdinand Hiller as conductor of a men's chorus. With this beginning, he felt himself able to undertake larger projects and again succeeded Hiller as municipal director of music in Düsseldorf. This was a

mistaken effort, however, and the ultimate result was that in 1853 he had
to be replaced. His naturally retiring disposition was manifested in an increasing and almost distressing taciturnity. Hallucinations began to haunt
him, such as that he was surrounded by flying bats, or that a persistent A
was sounding somewhere, or that voices were whispering to him words of
praise or blame. Along with this came a decided weakening of his imaginative powers. He attempted suicide, was confined in an asylum at
Endenich near Bonn, grew intermittently but steadily worse, and died
in 1856.

Less indifferent than Schubert to practical affairs, as his ten years' editorship of the *Neue Zeitschrift* amply proves, Schumann was nevertheless
almost equally the idealist. Similarly also, the extent of his own powers
was somewhat obscured to himself by his high and sympathetic regard
for other musicians. For Mendelssohn, with whom he became intimate
at Leipzig, his admiration was unbounded—an attitude doubtless induced
by a comparison of his own desultory training and his feeble abilities as
a performer with Mendelssohn's brilliancy. In sheer originality and creative imagination, however, it can now hardly be denied that he surpassed
all his immediate contemporaries save only Richard Wagner. He attempted
composition in every important field, and was really unsuccessful in only
one—the opera. In almost every one of his works some novelty of form
is revealed—a novelty which is obviously the product of imaginative penetration into the subject with which he is dealing. "As if all mental pictures
must be shaped to fit one or two forms," he wrote, to confound an
impertinent critic who presumed to give him advice—"as if each idea did
not come into existence with its form ready-made; as if each work of art
had not its own meaning, and consequently its own form!" Distressing
as this attitude is to the professors of musical rhetoric, it is at once the
source of all their doctrine and the essential mark of the creative artist.
For it is not conformity to structural rules, but the reconciliation of
imaginative concepts with principles of general intelligibility which constitutes the artist's constructive problem; and the rhetorical doctrine of
form is only an abstract of artists' solutions of this problem. We have
seen how Schubert was fired by a poetic suggestion to the creation of
music which was the immediate counterpart of that suggestion. His first
really original utterance was in the form of the song, whose subject of
course was verbally stated. Schumann's first utterance was through the
medium of the piano; but his subjects, while not always verbally indicated,
seem to have been almost verbally vivid. And it is in this high absorption
with the imaginative vision that he resembles Schubert.

If it is the orchestra which Liszt's piano music almost invariably suggests, it is the more intimate character of the human voice or of chamber

music combinations which is largely represented in Schumann's piano writing. The earliest works—doubtless because the vision of the subject as yet fails to imply its corresponding form—are both fragmentary and diffuse. The *Papillons* (Op. 2) is only a collection of charming sketches. The *Carnaval* (Op. 9) is similar in purpose but much larger in design, and is unified by the use of the four-note groups already alluded to. The *Davidsbündler Dances* and the *Kreisleriana* are also extended series of detached pieces—somewhat akin to a song cycle but lacking either text or poetic title. Yet there is somewhere a true thread of relation which binds these discrete-looking numbers together, so that the total impression is one of a singular richness in detail, impossible to be conveyed by the more restricted and concise form of the sonata. Indeed, save for the *Toccata* (Op. 7) which is an unexceptionable example of sonata form maintaining coherence largely through the persistence of the rhythm of its principal subject, the sonata structure as a whole is uncongenial to Schumann. The F sharp minor Sonata is diffuse in the extreme; the G minor, much more coherent, is abrupt in transition and seems somewhat cramped in imaginative range; and even the F minor, doubtless the finest of the three, is lacking in that energy of development which carries conviction. It is in the great *Fantasia* in C (Op. 17) that the real virtue of Schumann's method of construction is at last seen. Its form scheme is peculiar to itself, recalling nothing pre-existent, and incapable of repetition. Its tone of immediate and inspired improvisation is maintained throughout, while at the same time no sense of vagueness in purpose appears; the passion, the buoyancy, and the poetic exaltation of its three movements are supreme; and altogether it must be regarded as one of the greatest extant feats in the recording of the untrammeled imagination. In an entirely different manner and in a more youthful vein of feeling, it is nevertheless an imaginative effort comparable to the last sonatas of Beethoven.

As a song writer, Schumann had the inestimable advantage of Schubert's achievements to serve him as a model. He was no mere imitator, however, save in the one primary feature of the poetic concept which must generate the whole musical expression. His sense of literary value was keener than that of Schubert; and in consequence partly of this fact and partly of the more ruminative study which he usually gave to his subjects, the whole substance of his song is likely to be more completely or allusively expressed. The accompaniment becomes more nearly an integral part of the whole suggestion, bearing in general a larger share of the burden of thought. This is intended as no disparagement of Schubert's work. We are only suggesting that Schumann, by taking thought, often managed to add a cubit to the stature of his song. Several poets whom Schubert knew but slightly or not at all are largely represented in Schumann's almost 250 songs. Heine provided him with the texts for the *Dichterliebe* ("Poet's Love"); Chamisso for the *Frauenliebe und Leben* ("Woman's Love and Life"), a cycle of eight songs which sum up the greatest moments in woman's life—early fascination, wonder at being loved, marriage, motherhood, and widowhood. Eichendorff provided a less connected but almost more poetic *Liederkreis* in which are such extraordinary examples of lyric fancy as *Mondnacht* and *Fruhlingsnacht* and the weird ballad *Waldesgespräch*. Almost any of his songs, chosen at random, will reveal Schumann's care in blending the sense of voice and instrument for the full realization of his subject; but *Mondnacht* and *Im wunderschönen Monat Mai* will show to what height his fancy could rise when stimulated by a thoroughly congenial subject.

His ideal of the symphony was apparently similar to Schubert's. Lyrical rather than philosophic expression seems to have been his aim. It is probably true that the C major Symphony of Schubert is a higher example of symphonic writing than Schumann could have attained. But only the *Unfinished* approaches this work in significance; while the level of Schumann's symphonies is more uniformly high. Uncongenial as the orchestra was to Schumann as a medium of expression, his work in the symphonic form is nevertheless far more fully representative of the romantic spirit than that of any of his contemporaries.

We have already noted that one of the most potent influences on Schumann's style was the music of Bach. From that he derived a new and vital type of free polyphony, represented since Bach's time only in the later work of Beethoven. This free intermingling of melodic lines—clearly seen even in so simple a piano piece as *Warum?* or the wonderful *"Kind im Einschlummern"* from the *Scenes from Childhood*—is productive of so much novelty of harmonic effect as to constitute a most important addition to the resources of musical expression. We shall see that it constitutes a large factor in the musical style of Richard Wagner, and is almost the guiding principle of structure in all the music to follow during the nineteenth century.

Another remarkable feature of Schumann's musical thought is the remarkable variety of his rhythm. Not only are new and unusual rhythmic figures of a normal sort to be found in abundance—figures which often constitute, as in the first movement of the *Faschingsschwank*, a cogent factor of unity in most diverse episodes—but abnormal accentuations, and especially unexpected syncopations, are almost invariably to be found in large or small instrumental works. Schumann has often been reproached for writing in this way, the claim being that the notation only is complex; that the effect to the hearer would be the same if the accents were placed on the beat instead of persistently off the beat, as we find them; and that the thought is therefore not what it appears to be. This frequently expressed judgment should be corrected. If we take as a single example the little piano piece *Des Abends*, we find a melody moving regularly in 3-8 measure, accompanied by a figure which has six sixteenth notes (two to each eighth note of the melody). This whole substance, it is argued, is thus really in the 3-8 time in which the melody appears to stand. Schumann however wrote the time signature 2-8 at the beginning. That means, if it means anything, that Schumann thought—and intended us to hear—not three but two main beats in the measure. The three eighth notes in each measure of the melody therefore are to be heard as a triplet against these two main beats; and the two main beats in consequence must be made conspicuous enough so that the melody will appear in this somewhat strange and irregular light. This is easily possible, if the performer will give the slight accent which the notation implies to the fourth sixteenth note of the bar (always appearing in the accompaniment). The difference in effect is at once apparent, not only to the player but to the uninstructed hearer. The music also, instead of being dully sentimental, becomes tense and fluid—a true expression of nocturnal fancy. It is true that other instances of this rhythmic complexity are more difficult to realize—notably the slow melody in the middle of the march movement of the C major *Fantasie*, and the second subject of the last movement of the Piano Concerto in A minor. A very subtle sense of relative accent value is needed in the interpreter for the realization of Schumann's actual musical thought in these passages. But to dismiss them as mere mechanical tricks of notation, needlessly complex, is only to confess one's inability to understand musical ideas. We shall see that this sort of rhythmic suggestion is a frequent feature of the music of Johannes Brahms. Instead of being condemned for his capriciousness, then, Schumann should be praised as an effective discoverer of one extremely valuable addition to the resources of musical suggestion.

CHOPIN

François Frédéric Chopin, the third of the great romantic idealists, was of course not a German, nor in any great degree a follower of German musical traditions. Neither, although he was partly by birth and wholly in nationalistic sentiment a Pole, did he remain exclusively devoted to the musical idioms of his native land. Nor, although his father was a Frenchman and Paris became his spiritual home for the greater part of his creative life, was he at all typically a French musician. All these nationalistic influences, passing through his highly sensitized mind, became so transformed as to be hidden in the final total impression of the artist's personality. He was in a sense the most cosmopolitan of all the romanticists. But his style is no mere eclectic jumble of nationalistic strains; it is rather a revelation of the sensitive nervous organization of the man himself. An extreme excitability (generally supposed to be characteristic of the Slavic temperament) was united with an equally intense dislike of all that was rough or angular in expression—an attitude largely in accord with French artistic taste.

Because of this extreme sensitiveness to the sheer sound of music, his imaginative vision was sharp and definite only within a comparatively narrow range. He was stimulated only by emotions which could be expressed in lyric strains. That large sense of nature, for instance, which suggested to Beethoven a *Pastoral* Symphony, aroused in Chopin no imaginative response. The idea of heroism likewise, which provided Beethoven with the substance of another whole symphony, found no expression at Chopin's hands, unless in some such work as the *Revolutionary* Etude—obviously a far narrower concept. Neither had he that immediate sympathy with the mind of the child which is revealed in Schumann's *Kinderscenen.* Chopin's *Berceuse* is a wonderful *tour de force* in pianistic composition: the cradle rocks incessantly amid the golden arabesques of figuration, but it is not a baby that lies within the cradle—only the phantom child of an artist's brain. Indeed, it was seldom any reality of experience which Chopin wished to suggest. Often it was an escape from the crude reality of experience—a dwelling upon emotion itself, exaggerated and refined to a point of ideal unreality. Moods then were essentially his theme; and more, perhaps, than any other composer he was able to discern and to express in terms of music fine shades and distinctions of mood. But our own moods, aroused by an infinite variety of experiences, are often far more vividly present to our consciousness than is the awareness of the experience itself which has given them birth. Moods are a kind of sublimation of experience; and to express them fully is to give an apparently complete expression of the truest reality of experience. Hence, George Sand was right in saying that there was more music in a tiny Prelude of Chopin than in all the trumpeting of Meyerbeer. Hence also the larger media of expression—chamber and orchestral groups and the chorus, and the largely extended forms which are suited to such groups—were both beyond his requirements for expression and beyond his technical powers.

Chopin was quite aware of these limitations. He once spoke of himself as being "like the E-string of a violin on a contrabass"—a most admirable simile. For the slight medium of his nervous organization was inadequate to the transmission of the grosser fundamental vibrations of feeling. His note sounds mostly but as the attenuated harmonic of the deeper throb from which it springs. Yet, because the vibration is forced, his honeyed tone is tainted with a most suggestive hint of bitter reality in its hidden source. He presents to us rather the refined essence than the gross reality of feeling. So it was not strange that Chopin should have appealed to sensitive natures, or to the more sensitive regions of bolder natures, with a force hitherto unrealized.

Because of this appeal he initiated many new enthusiasts into the mysteries of the language of music. Writing almost exclusively for the piano and evoking from that instrument sounds which had been hitherto unimaginable, he gave the whole substance of musical thought of the most appealing nature into the hands of that growing myriad of music lovers who, through the medium of the piano, were beginning to cultivate music at home, in that solitude where the imagination is freest. The piano had been, to Mozart and his successors, increasingly a vehicle of artistic expression. Yet it had remained rather a convenient substitute for the ensemble of voices or strings or orchestra than an instrument possessed of its own peculiar individuality. The earlier sonatas of Beethoven for instance, although they are pianistic enough, are still so palpably the counterparts of orchestral compositions that the first problems set to students of orchestration are usually the rearrangement of these works for the larger instrumental group. Relatively little needs to be done to the substance of this music to make it orchestrally "possible." But the piano compositions of Chopin, just in proportion as they become pianistically individual, become impossible to transcribe for the orchestra. He could not write well for strings or voices; yet he managed to make the piano into something which, in flexibility and vividness, almost transcends these more perfect utterances.

His acquisition of this unique power of expression is as enigmatic as is the growth of Schubert's genius. Nothing in his environment can account for even a tithe of his achievement. He was born at Zelazowa-Wola, a village some twenty-eight miles from Warsaw, probably on March 1, 1809. His father, a native of the Duchy of Lorraine, had entered business in Warsaw in 1787, had fought with Kosciuszko in the unsuccessful revolution of 1794, and had begun thereafter to earn his livelihood as a teacher of his native tongue. At the home of a Countess Skarbeck, whither he had gone as tutor to her son, he met Justina Krzyzanowska, a lady of noble birth but of no fortune, whom he married in 1806. After the formation of the Grand Duchy of Warsaw under Napoleon in 1807, Nicholas Chopin returned to Warsaw where he gradually attained to considerable distinction as Professor of French at the Lyceum. He also kept a private school. The mother was a woman of great gentleness and refinement, wholly devoted to her four children. The family was intimate with the most intellectual and aristocratic circles in Warsaw. Thus a fine sensitivity to culture and an instinctive discrimination in social manner, as well as a passionate love for his own country, were bred in the mind of François Frédéric from birth.

Systematic general education was pursued with distinction but was gradually subordinated to the study of music. Two men share the honor of having been Chopin's only real music masters: Adalbert Zywny in piano and Joseph Elsner in composition. Zywny was already an old man (he was born in the same year as Mozart), apparently a sound classicist and a lover of Bach. Little is known of his process of instruction save that he gave his pupil large assignments of Bach's music. Mozart was the lifelong ideal of the young man. With Beethoven he seems never to have attained any great familiarity. He thought the Finale of the Sonata, Op. 31, No. 3 "vulgar," and is not recorded as having played Beethoven's music in his relatively few public concerts. Yet in a letter dated October 20, 1829, he speaks of having heard Beethoven's last Quartet: "I haven't heard anything so great for a long time; Beethoven snaps his fingers at the whole world." Neither did he play Bach in public (indeed, he was notoriously weak in the interpretation of other music than his own) but always as a stimulant, for mind as well as fingers, before his concerts. Chopin's Twenty-four *Preludes* in all the keys were doubtless suggested by the *Well-Tempered Clavichord*. They show, however, almost no grasp of that polyphonic manner of thinking which, as we have seen, Schumann derived from his study of the same source. Yet it may well be that the peculiar subtleties of Chopin's harmonic progression derive, by a more circuitous route, from his study of Bach. There is little possibility that Zywny contributed directly to the formation of Chopin's pianistic style. The boy's gift for improvisation was marked from the first, and it was doubtless during the many hours of such communion with his instrument that the discovery was made of that highly distinctive manner which marked his playing and his writing alike.

It was Elsner's task to mold the creative technique of this remarkably individual nature. But again we have little information as to his method. He seems to have understood better than most teachers his peculiar responsibility: to develop his pupil's powers from within rather than to impose a rigid and inflexible method from without. The competency of Elsner's method was fully recognized by Chopin himself, who wrote, "From Zywny and Elsner even the greatest donkey must learn something." Liszt observed with great discrimination, "Elsner taught Chopin those things that are the most difficult to learn and the most rarely known: to be exacting to oneself, and to value the advantages that are only to be won by dint of patience and labor."

In the background of this conscious study there is the incessant and largely unconscious assimilation (probably chiefly from his mother) of the Polish musical idiom. The most characteristically Polish of Chopin's compositions are, of course, the Mazurkas and Polonaises which adopt, unaltered but refined, the rhythms of the folk music in these genres.[1] In other forms Chopin seldom employed these folk rhythms; but the peculiar nervousness of his melodic strain is perhaps not less truly Polish in source than the more frankly nationalistic utterances.

At the same time, as the earlier letters reveal, there was great interest in the opera. Chopin was himself a very clever mimic, his talent being often recognized by professional actors. He even made a childish attempt at playwriting in collaboration with his sister; but, although he was often encouraged by his friends to produce an opera, he instinctively recognized his inability to deal with so large a problem. The operatic performances in Warsaw were very inferior, and one of his most eager anticipations during his first visit to Berlin in 1828 was the hearing of finer performances: "It is good to hear first-class opera even once; it gives one a conception of fine technique." It was chiefly the lyric element which interested him, and this indeed he transformed into pianistic song the like of which had never been heard before. It is probable that his interest in opera was somewhat confused with his passionate interest in Mlle. Constantia Gladkowska, a young debutante on the operatic stage with whom he had fallen silently in love while the two were yet students at the Conservatory of Warsaw.

Two ventures into the greater world were made in 1828 and 1829—visits to Berlin and Vienna, at which latter place he gave two concerts which were well received. It was now time for him to be launched as a professional pianist. After three farewell concerts at Warsaw, in one of which he was assisted by Constantia, he set out in November, 1830, with Paris as his goal. He visited Breslau, Dresden, Prague, Vienna, Munich, and Stuttgart on his way, playing sometimes in concert, sometimes only

---

[1] The Mazurka had its origin in popular dance song. It is in 3-4 time, with the same type of harmonic accompaniment as that of the waltz. The first beat of the measure is mostly divided, suggesting a gliding motion whose crisis occurs properly on the third beat of the measure. Chopin's treatment is, of course, a high idealization of the simple original. The Polonaise has a more doubtful origin. It was known in the sixteenth century as a ceremonial processional march, for the opening of courtly festivities, and as the music of the opening dance of the evening. It was at first by no means as characteristic in rhythm as now, being (according to Matheson) either in 3-4 or 4-4 time. The vigorous rhythm which is now always to be expected is ♪♫ ♪♫♫ . Chopin's treatment is again a great amplification. Two styles of melody, one melancholy, the other fiery and martial, are clearly distinguished—the melancholy type being found in the C♯ minor Polonaise, Op. 26, or in the *Andante spianato and Polonaise* with orchestra; the fiery type is seen in the *Military* Polonaise, Op. 40, or in the extraordinary example in A flat.

privately, but always awakening much interest in his novel style. It was already apparent, however, that his physical energies were hardly equal to the task of frequent public appearance as a pianist, and his interests in any case lay more in composition than in performance. When he set out for Paris he had already composed the early Rondos (Op. 1 and Op. 5), the variations on *La ci darem* from Mozart's *Don Giovanni*, the posthumously published Sonata, Op. 4, the 'Cello Polonaise, and the Trio, Op. 8, most of which exhibit many immaturities in style. But to these he had also added the two Concertos—in E minor, Op. 11 (really the second), and in F minor, Op. 21, the *Adagio* of which he expressly tells us was inspired by thoughts of Constantia.

Many works even more characteristically in his mature manner were also finished, such as a large number of the Etudes and several collections of Mazurkas and Nocturnes. The variations had been published in Vienna in 1830; and in 1831 Schumann contributed to the *Allgemeine Musikalische Zeitung* a long laudatory article about them, the purport of which is comprised in the oft-quoted phrase, "Hats off, gentlemen, a genius!" The famous *Revolutionary* Etude was composed at Stuttgart, where Chopin heard the disquieting news of the unsuccessful Polish Revolution of 1830. When he reached Paris therefore he had ample material preparation for a successful career. He was well received, also, by the musical public since a considerable sentiment in favor of the Poles had been aroused by the Revolution. He soon attracted pupils who paid high fees, and was never really in serious straits thereafter. There is little of Bach, Beethoven, or Schubert to be discovered in his work, either now or later; but the influence of Mozart and his pupil Hummel may be traced, as well as that of John Field (1782–1837), an Irish musician and the originator of the *Nocturne*, whose delicate sentimentality is reflected in many of Chopin's finer works in that form. Spohr also, whose chromatic style lends itself admirably to the expression of a rather morbid mood, was often enthusiastically praised by Chopin and doubtless contributed much to that master's style.

An intention to visit Italy before settling in Paris was given up. Thus, one possibility of deeper immersion in operatic interest was removed. Also, a strong intensification of that introverted emotional sentiment which was already characteristic of the man was doubtless given by the news of the marriage of Constantia to a merchant of Warsaw. The rather showy virtuosity of the earlier manner was soon replaced by a far more significant and direct utterance. Undoubtedly the new experience of independence and the association with new artistic conditions and ideals in Paris had also its share both in energizing and clarifying his style.

The Paris which Chopin entered in 1831 was still the intellectual and artistic capital of Europe. Vienna, in the first decade of the century, had been the great musical center; but that position had not been fully maintained after the advent of Rossini and the Italian opera, and Paris, especially as an operatic center, still held its old supremacy. The Revolution had been by no means forgotten. The deposition of Charles X in favor of Louis Philippe in 1830 had been a move in the direction of liberalism, but the new government was as yet by no means fully established. In their contemporary aspect the political problems engendered by the Revolution were still matter for vigorous debate, and the effects of revolutionary philosophy on social life were now apparent not only in politics but in art, which was rapidly adapting itself to the expression of the new ideals. The romantic ferment was at its height. The romantic movement in literature had been initiated by Chateaubriand and Mme. de Staël, and the new attitude was now adopted by a host of enthusiastic and significant writers—poets such as Alfred de Musset, Théophile Gautier, and Lamartine, novelists like Victor Hugo and Balzac, and dramatists like Hugo, De Musset, De Vigny, and Dumas the elder.

French music, resting upon far flimsier foundations of popular song than that of Germany, far less universally loved, and because of its courtly associations far more stylistic in manner, had as yet hardly adjusted itself to the new romanticism. Berlioz was the only French musician who was thoroughly in accord with the romantic trend, and had himself hardly attained to a significant individuality of utterance. Thus Chopin—by instinct rather than by inheritance sympathetic with French taste—became an important influence in the development of French romantic music. But being exclusively a composer for the piano and unable to deal with symphony or opera, his influence upon the larger currents of musical thought was necessarily somewhat indirect.

He was himself subject to influences of current taste. At the opening of the nineteenth century the general reading public had begun to be rapidly expanded. This had its effect not merely upon literature but upon every region of thought. As individual opinion became more confidently founded, a far greater variety of tastes in art and of opinions in politics or philosophy became manifest. Questions arose as to what was good or bad, right or wrong, in art; for the old criteria—valid for the small groups of literati who in the older days constituted the only public to whom art was addressed—no longer sufficed. Thus criticism—the valuation (not the mere condemnation) of works of art—became an indispensable element in the whole expansion of artistic interest. And, instead of basing itself upon a few aesthetic axioms (such as the unities of the classical tragedy), criticism now had to seek a firmer, more reasoned foundation. Naturally, competent criticism first made itself felt in literature. The work of Cole-

ridge in England and of Sainte-Beuve in France is scarcely to be matched
for solidity and logic in any contemporary discussions of the plastic arts
or of music. But divergences of opinion are the bases of critical development; and these divergences, in matters of music, although difficult to
formulate in words, are as stimulating as in matters of literature. Musical
criticism consequently had a new birth. Largely unformed and even
largely unwritten—for the occasional critical work of Schumann and
Berlioz marks the first modern effort at a reasoned judgment of music—
criticism, or at least the critical attitude, was nevertheless a positive element of musical thought. A great division of musical opinion, involving
perhaps the most fundamental question with which criticism has to deal,
now came to be more sharply defined. We shall understand Chopin more
clearly if we examine for a moment this conflict of opinion.

We have already described as "experiential" and "aesthetic" the two great
categories of feeling which an art work may arouse. Pursuing this thought
we may readily see that the two great objects of critical attention must be,
first, the subject itself with which the artist deals, and second, the manner
in which he deals with his subject. Matter and manner, that is, or meaning
and the expression of meaning, or content and form—the terms are virtually equivalent—must be sharply scrutinized and valued. To be properly valued, also, they should be observed in isolation. Now, the subject
matter or the meaning or the content of music is far harder to distinguish
from the manner of its expression than is the case with other arts. Music
which appeals to us deeply seems to be so wholly beautiful that the question of its meaning—apart from its form—is hardly likely to be raised. It
is largely for its beauty that we value music. But it is not only music
which arouses in us this sense of beauty. The ecstasy into which we are
thrown by a compelling landscape or by a perfect example of lyric poetry
is very similar to the state aroused by music. Indeed, without some measure of this delight we feel that we have no art work. Forgetting, in this
absorption with its beauty, the other values which have contributed to
our pleasure, we may readily decide that art may be fully defined as that
which can arouse this condition of delight. We shall thus attribute to
purely aesthetic stimulation a special virtue not belonging to other kinds
of experience: the "goodness" of art will appear to transcend all other
kinds of goodness, physical or moral, and we shall become converts to the
doctrine of "art for art's sake." [2] The danger in such an attitude is, of

[2] It is perhaps noteworthy that this peculiar valuation of art is not made until
romanticism has become an established attitude, and that it is a doctrine readily asso-
ciable with that exaltation of remote and unusual aspects of personal feeling which
is characteristic of romanticism. Hanslick's little book *Vom Musikalisch-Schönen*
("On the Beautiful in Music") was doubtless intended as a counterblast to the effusive

course, that the subject of the art work will become a negligible factor, and the treatment all-important. Feeling—aroused by artistic deftness rather than by a larger appeal to emotion related to human experience—is then the artist's only objective; and novelty of appeal to the purely artistic sensibility is prized above novel revelation of emotional reality. Any minute study of artistic expression will show that matter and manner are so closely related as to be very difficult to distinguish. But the absence of significant matter is nevertheless fairly easy to perceive; and those to whom the matter as well as the manner of a work of art is still important will judge excessive emphasis on manner as decadent.

By his very sensitivity, his peculiarly pianistic imagination, his concentrated vision, Chopin was highly susceptible to the appeal of the ideal of art for art's sake. Almost from the beginning he had an ambition to found a new era in art. He had been taught by Elsner to study the works of other men as an aid to the solving of problems involved in his own writing; but little by little his interest waned in music other than his own. His letters up to the time of his removal to Paris often make mention of the music he had been hearing, and reveal the mind of the eager and absorptive student. After the first years in Paris this sort of comment becomes infrequent. We learn of his contacts with many musicians— Cherubini, Franchomme, Liszt, Hiller, Mendelssohn, Kalkbrenner, Field, Berlioz, and others—but we find him learning little by these contacts. We find, for example, nothing comparable to Schumann's enthusiasm, either for his fellow-artists or for their work. More and more his genius came to feed upon itself. Less and less is any reality of life his apparent theme. Art alone, and the preoccupation with ideal beauty, absorbed his interest. The G minor Ballade (No. 1, published in 1836) is permeated with elemental passion. In the Second Ballade in F major (1840), the scope, though not the violence, of that passion is already reduced. In the Third in A flat (1841) the artistic design is doubtless finer than that of the earlier works, but the theme itself is far less substantial. And though none can gainsay the still greater technical perfection of the Fourth (1843), it can hardly be denied that its greatest value lies in the artistic subtilization of the exquisite melancholy which is its theme. The case is the same with the four Scherzi and the two later Sonatas; and the same rather distorted perspective, enhancing the purely artistic suggestion and reducing the natural emotional character, is to be found in the *Berceuse*, the *Barcarolle* (Op. 60, 1846) and many of the smaller works of the later years such as the B major Nocturne (sometimes christened *The Tuberose*).

---

romanticism of the "realistic" order to be discussed in the next chapter. But its doctrine is no more defensible than the ideas it attacks.

The reasons for this artistic preoccupation are only partly to be found in the circumstances of his life or his health. He first visited England in 1837, arranging for the publication of his work. His health made outstanding public success impossible; but one might reasonably expect greater interest than was shown in the current of English music. In the same year he first met the novelist George Sand—an acquaintance which rapidly grew into an intimacy fruitful in the greatest extremes of delight and misery. The next ten years were full of the distractions which this remarkable passion occasioned. Intimacy with other musicians was gradually abandoned. His health, his liaison, his pupils (more frequently aristocratic ladies than talented and struggling artists), and an incessant social activity largely unrelated to musical interests—all this kept him from contact with the vital world of music and drove him in upon himself. But this indifference was founded more in his own nature than in his circumstances.

Yet his contribution to the current of musical thought is of the greatest significance. Although he was not at his best in the classical forms of the sonata and the concerto, the B flat minor Sonata remains one of the most vital examples of that form produced during the period. The Scherzi, as Niecks remarks, are without the humor which their titles lead us to expect; but there is instead a vein of sardonic cynicism which, in Chopin's day, was almost a new type of expression in music. The Ballades—but distantly suggestive of the vocal form—are really more like symphonic poems. These, the *Fantasia* in F minor, and the Scherzi are remarkable essays in expanded form, and fully exemplified Schumann's already quoted assertion that every real musical idea contains its own formal implications in accord with which it must be worked out. Slight as was Chopin's output when compared with the symphonies, oratorios, and operas of his contemporaries, his work shows such valuable additions to the harmonic and melodic vocabulary, such perfection in simple and direct statement, and such vividness in the delineation of emotion hitherto only circuitously expressed, that it becomes one of the most potent forces in the establishment of music in popular favor. The great works beginning with the B minor Scherzo are in many ways the very culmination of romantic idealism, and largely justify Schumann's generous estimate of Chopin as "the proudest poetic spirit of his time."

CHAPTER XXV

The Romantic Realists—
Berlioz and Liszt

THE distinction between idealists and realists—more tangible when applied to painters or novelists or poets than to musicians—is still intelligible in relation to composers, and serves to group such men as Berlioz and Liszt somewhat apart from the idealists of whom we have just spoken. The distinction was felt by the men themselves, and as it came to be more clearly expressed was at length manifest in a bitter controversy regarding "the music of the future." How complex were the questions involved we shall see when we come to study Richard Wagner—in theory a champion of realism but by temperament the most extreme of idealists. Realism will reappear in many guises, such as *impressionism* and *symbolism*—all designed to veil the direct relation of the music with nonmusical idea or experience, and it is all but impossible to draw a clear line of distinction between the vaguer kinds of realism and that more immediate expression of emotion which would ordinarily be called ideal. But the controversy, crystallizing at last into a drawn battle between *absolute* and *program* music, soon assumes such proportions that it is impossible to understand the whole of the music of the nineteenth century without reference to it. It will probably clarify our understanding if we study for a moment the rather abstract questions involved.

We have said that the realist exhibits his subject as he sees it, asking us to share his vision of the subject and, through that vision, his own emotional reaction to it. The idealist, on the other hand, shuns direct reference to his subject and asks us to enter at once into that region of feeling into which we are more circuitously introduced by the realist. Mere physical representation is hardly in question; since the realist is also concerned to awaken his hearer's emotion, and would regard the mere copying of natural sounds as a degradation of music. But the realist—agreeing that the mere illustration of some physical reality, such as thunder or flowing water or the songs of birds, is not music—contends that such physical suggestions as these, in music which is chiefly intended to awaken the emotions, may greatly vivify the emotional suggestion. And he points to the *Pastoral* Symphony of Beethoven, in which exactly these and many other physical suggestions are given, as an ample justification of his attitude. He contends that Beethoven's phrase of excuse for this adventure into reality (*Mehr Ausdruck der Empfindung als Malerey*—More the expression of feeling than painting) applies also to his own possibly even more realistic music. He insists that to know what the music is about is no hindrance, but is rather an aid to really musical perception. Beethoven's Overture to Goethe's *Egmont*, for instance, was not intended to be heard as mere music, but rather as a summation of the most important emotions aroused by the drama, and is only half intelligible without this dramatic association. He holds that to employ such nonmusical suggestion as this in a really musical way is legitimately to expand the range of musical expression.

Also, to admit this illustrative or descriptive purpose as legitimate is to give value and meaning to a great many types of instrumental figure or ornament which, used without such definite purpose, would remain mere tricks of virtuosity, sterile and really unmusical. Thus virtuosity itself acquires a purpose. Even the unimaginative explorer of virtuosity for its own sake may contribute greatly to a higher expression than he himself can understand; for the imaginative composer may find real meaning in his antics, and a really musical use for them. The distinction between legitimate technique and virtuosity is, of course, as vague as that between realism and idealism. Technical accomplishment of a high order is necessary for the execution of much of Bach's music. The last Sonatas of Beethoven bristle with difficulties, to surmount which real virtuosity is demanded. Yet there is always ample musical justification for these passages, and none of them can be properly called virtuoso pieces. However, observed by a composer or performer insensitive to this musical purpose but keenly alive to the quality of brilliancy itself, such passages may suggest technical feats still more brilliant and, to persons of like mind with himself, completely satisfying.

THE RISE OF VIRTUOSITY—PAGANINI

Such a figure was the first of the modern virtuosi—Niccolo Paganini (1784–1840). Extraordinarily gifted, and trained from his earliest years toward the mastery of his instrument, he made his first professional tour at the age of thirteen, playing compositions of his own in which the technical novelties were already striking. Prodigy though he was, he had no satisfaction in these easily won triumphs, but devoted his energies as no one before him had ever done to the devising and mastering of new and unheard-of technical processes. Not until after his fortieth year was he widely known outside the borders of Italy. In 1828 however his first concert in Vienna aroused such a furore that he was demanded in every great capital. An extraordinary agility over a greater compass than had ever before been at the command of any violinist, an entirely new treatment of artificial harmonics,[1] of left-hand *pizzicato* (plucking the string), of accompaniment either bowed or *pizzicato* to a sustained melody, and other similar devices hitherto all but unknown, were frequently used. By tuning the violin to other intervals than those conventionally in use, chords and other passages wholly impossible with the conventional tuning were played before the very eyes of trained violinists who, unaware of the trick in tuning, were inclined to believe the man to be a wizard. Indeed, he was once compelled to produce a birth certificate to prove that he was not the child of the Evil One!

He refused for long to publish his compositions, since his tricks would all have been exposed by being set down in print. But his extraordinary command not only of novel feats but also of all the legitimate technique of the violin fired not only all the violinists but other instrumental virtuosi to the emulation of his effects. We have seen that Schumann in

---

[1] The production of artificial harmonics is easily understood. Since the vibration ratio of the double octave (the interval of the fifteenth) is $4:1$ (i.e., twice the octave, or $\frac{2}{1} \times \frac{2}{1}$), a tone two octaves higher than any open string will be obtained by stopping the string at a point distant from the bridge by ¼ the length of the string. But the string may also be caused to vibrate in segments of a fourth of its total length by lightly touching (not stopping) the string at the same point, or a point ¼ of its length from the nut. For instance, if the G string of the violin is thus touched at a point representing the C a fourth above G, the contact of the finger prevents the vibration of the whole string but allows its vibration in segments of ¼ its length. Hence, the resultant sound will be a G two octaves higher than the pitch of the whole string. If, now, the string be stopped at any point (e.g., the E above the open G), and at the same time touched lightly at a point a fourth above this stopped note (i.e., at the A above this stopped E) the resultant sound will be two octaves above the stopped E. Many *natural* harmonics can be produced by touching the string at the various fractions of its length which represent the various partials—i.e., at fractions of ½, ⅓, ¼, ⅕, etc., of the total length, producing on the G string the notes G, D, G, B, etc. The artificial harmonics could be produced in as great variety if the necessary points of contact could be reached. But in practice, since one finger of the hand must stop the string (i.e., produce an artificial nut), only a few nodal points can be reached with the other fingers. Hence, the artificial harmonics of the third, fourth, and fifth partials (produced by touching the string lightly at intervals of a fifth, a fourth, and a major third above the artificial nut) are the only practicable harmonics; and that of the fourth is by far the most frequently used.

his early years wrote pianistic adaptations of his *Caprices*. Liszt not only did the same (the familiar *Campanella* is a transcription of the *Bell Rondo* from the B minor Concerto) but found in Paganini's originality the clue to that novelty of pianistic style which he had been seeking in vain while following the methods of his master Czerny. Nor are Paganini's compositions lacking in musical interest. The twenty-four *Caprices* for solo violin remain, after the solo Sonatas of Bach, almost the only important works for the unaccompanied violin. Brahms found inspiration in the last of these for an extraordinary addition to the technical problems of the pianoforte. Even the two Concertos in E and B minor, the *Witches' Dance*, and other compositions of Paganini are occasionally to be heard. Doubtless it was because his virtuosity had attracted to the concert room an almost new public—sensation loving, indeed, but eager and altogether honest in its affection for the new style—that his later influence was so great. But there is no denying that influence, which was far greater than could be accounted for by the purely musical interest of Paganini's work.

BERLIOZ

As Paganini had made the violin into almost a new instrument, so Berlioz now applied the idea of virtuosity to the orchestra; and Liszt—utilizing suggestions from both Paganini and Berlioz—made of the piano a striking if somewhat inferior rival of the orchestra itself.

Hector Berlioz, certainly one of the most extraordinary personalities to appear in the annals of music, was the first French musician to adopt uncompromisingly the realistic attitude toward romanticism. He was born at Côte-Saint-André, December 11, 1803. His father was a physician, bent from the first on having his son follow him in his profession. Hence, although the child betrayed an insatiable thirst for music, no systematic instruction was allowed. He learned to play a little on the flute and the guitar, but never attained any real mastery of these or any other instruments. Sent to Paris for the study of medicine, he found his interests so overwhelmingly attracted to music that he finally informed his father that he had determined to become a composer and joined the class in composition under Lesueur at the Conservatoire. His father was disappointed and angered by this resolve and refused to support his son, who had to make his living by singing in the chorus at a small theatre. The young man's musical progress did not show much promise. He failed ignominiously in a competition for the *Prix de Rome*, and was ordered by his father to return to Côte-Saint-André. Here he was so melancholy that the father at last consented to his return to Paris, but only for a limited time. Although he was completely out of sympathy with all his professors at the Conservatoire except Lesueur, nothing could stifle either his musical ardor or his self-confidence. Beethoven and Shakespeare were his idols; and in his own way he was forming concepts of the artistic significance of these men which were to be his guide all his life as against the academic precepts laid down at the Conservatoire. Lesueur indeed had been something of a revolutionary in his earlier days. He had produced at Notre Dame, Masses with full orchestra and even with an overture, avowing a purpose of making sacred music "dramatic and descriptive." It is hardly possible that Lesueur could have suggested any of the novel effects which Berlioz later produced; but the apparent kinship of their temperaments seems significant.

Essentially Berlioz's concept of the purpose and meaning of music was his own. He saw in the music of Gluck and Beethoven far more of descriptive or pictorial suggestion than had probably been intended by those composers, and followed this idea from the first. He was not content with small beginnings, but produced as early as 1825 a Solemn Mass with orchestra. The Overtures to *Waverley* and *Les Francs Juges*, eight scenes from Goethe's *Faust* (a theme which never failed to fire the imagination of Berlioz), a *Fantasia* on Shakespeare's *The Tempest*, and the first draft of the *Symphonie fantastique* (which was later worked over into one of his most important compositions) were all produced during the next five years. After five attempts, the coveted *Prix de Rome* was won with a cantata *La Mort de Sardanaple*. Performances of the earlier works had been few and unsatisfactory, so that he had as yet only the reputation of an erratic and even dangerous revolutionary.

Life in Rome proved uncongenial, and he was unable to endure the two years of residence prescribed by the terms of the prize. Little that reflects the Italian scene is to be found in the work of the year and a half spent abroad. The *Symphonie fantastique* was revised; a sort of sequel, *Lelio, or the Return to Life* (a Monodrame), was added; Overtures to *King Lear* and Byron's *Corsair* were sketched; and a very fine song with orchestral accompaniment, *La Captive* (revised in 1848), gave perhaps the only direct reflection of his feeling during the period of his travel. The program symphony *Harold in Italy* (suggested, of course, by Byron's *Childe Harold*) was completed in 1834. The prominent part for the solo viola was suggested by Paganini, though not played by him since it offered no opportunity for the display of his virtuosity; but it may be supposed that some of the color of this work, as well as the whole theme of the later overture *The Roman Carnival*, was suggested by the Italian sojourn.

His position as an artist in Paris was not greatly elevated by his foreign experience. Attending some representations of Shakespeare's plays by an

English troupe in 1832, he fell desperately in love with Henrietta Smithson, an Irish actress, whom he as yet had not even met. Although surprised at his ensuing urgent declarations of devotion she was not wholly forbidding, and in 1833 his impetuous suit was accepted. But the enlarged financial burdens involved could hardly be borne by the income from his unappreciated art. He was forced to turn journalist, and showed almost as great an originality in his criticisms and discussions of contemporary musical movements as in his compositions. In spite of the serious distraction from the work of composition which this labor involved, he went on producing one great design after another. Three symphonies, *Harold in Italy*, the *Symphonie funèbre et triomphale*, and *Romeo et Juliette;* a cantata on the death of Napoleon; his first opera *Benvenuto Cellini;* and the imposing *Requiem*, demanding in addition to the great main body of chorus and orchestra, four brass bands, one at each corner of the church—all this besides many songs and smaller works was written, sometimes with miraculous speed, before 1840. A remuneration of 20,000 francs for *Harold in Italy* (supposedly from Paganini but really given by Jeannin, the proprietor of the *Journal des Débats* for which Berlioz wrote), and other lesser sums for the *Requiem* and the *Symphonie funèbre*, at last gave him independence and made possible a tour in Germany, where much interest had been aroused in his compositions. Madame Berlioz, whose career as an actress had been cut short by an accident, refused to consent to his departure on this journey. A quarrel, as violent as had been the original wooing, resulted in a break between them which was never healed.

The tour was a vast success. Liszt, Schumann, and even Mendelssohn (who disliked Berlioz's music and had spoken of him in Rome ten years before as "a regular caricature, without a scrap of talent, groping in the dark and believing himself to be the creator of a new world") showed him every courtesy, and the public was amazed at the novelty of form and color which this fiery, red-headed Frenchman could produce. But neither this venture nor an equally brilliant tour in Austria in 1845 nor a Russian triumph in 1847 could awaken Paris from its apathy. The *Damnation of Faust*, completed in Austria, was produced in 1846 before a small and indifferent audience. After the Russian tour, undertaken partly because it might enable him to make up the deficit incurred in the production of the *Damnation*, he helped to secure the conductorship of the Opéra for a M. Roqueplan, who was to give him in return an official post and also to produce *Benvenuto Cellini*. But neither post nor performance was forthcoming. He went to England to conduct opera at Covent Garden; but Jullien, the manager of that theatre, went bankrupt. The Revolution of 1848, culminating in the short-lived Second Republic, all but cost him his post as librarian of the Conservatoire. The second part of Berlioz's only oratorio *The Childhood of Christ* was given in Paris with considerable success—because the music was announced as the work of an unknown eighteenth-century composer, Pierre Ducré. In 1852 he was engaged as conductor for the first season of the "New Philharmonic Society" in London (a rival to the old Philharmonic which had commissioned Beethoven's Ninth Symphony). The next year he conducted *Benvenuto Cellini* at Covent Garden, and in 1855 was again with the New Philharmonic and in some sense was pitted against Wagner, who was that year startling the English public by conducting excerpts from some of his works for the old Philharmonic Society.

These continued successes abroad inspired little but failure at home. In 1855, however, came a great Paris Exhibition. For this he wrote a great *Te Deum* (even more imposing in dimensions than the *Requiem*) and a cantata *l'Impériale*. A tardy membership in the *Académie* was the result. A comedy opera *Beatrice and Benedict*, written in 1860–1862, was successfully performed at Baden, and at Weimar under Liszt, but not at Paris. In 1863 *The Trojans*, his greatest dramatic work, whose text (like that of *Beatrice and Benedict*) he had made himself, was given in the new opera house in Paris, and after a short run was ignominiously driven from the boards. He could write no more. His health had always been precarious. Now it gradually broke down. He died in 1869, and was almost at once recognized by his countrymen as a genius.

His work will probably always continue to excite the most diverse of judgments. It is essentially the work of an overwhelmingly romantic nature.[2] Untrained in the orthodox principles of musical structure, and convinced that the value of music lay rather in its expression than in its form, he was largely unaware of that problem which Schumann and Chopin had

---

[2] His strange passion for Henrietta Smithson is only one instance. After her death in 1854, he married a singer of small ability, Mlle. Recio, who often nearly ruined his concerts by insisting on taking the prominent parts; yet he was desolated at her death. In 1848 while at Côte-Saint-André for his father's funeral, he made a visit to his grandfather's house at Meylan. Near by was the house in which had lived a young girl, Estelle, for whom in early youth Berlioz had conceived a boyish passion. Now all his childish sentiment returned to him. After long search he found that Estelle was living, and addressed to her a letter recalling their early friendship and signed "Despised Love." Fourteen years later he again visited Meylan. Again his old passion seized him. He learned Estelle's address at Lyons, visited her and established a rather desultory correspondence in which Estelle's part may be inferred from the last letter which Berlioz records: "I have always found that the best way to make children calm and reasonable was to give them pictures. I take the liberty of sending you one which will recall to you the reality of the present and destroy the illusions of the past." "It was her portrait! Adorable creature!" exclaims Berlioz; and goes on, ". . . True, she does not love me; why, indeed, should she? But she might have remained in total ignorance of me, and now she knows that I adore her."

solved in such varied fashions—the problem of discovering for each musical thought the individual form pattern which was implied in that thought. The result is very often a chaos of suggestions, vivid and even convincing in themselves, whose relation to each other or to any conceivable total scheme is so obscure that the hearer is frequently thrown quite off the track of normal continuity in the music. His melody, although frequently unsymmetrical in phrase balance, is generally easy to follow and remarkably convincing, especially when it is associated with words. His harmony is sometimes almost bald in its simplicity, sometimes extreme in its distortion and discontinuity. His rhythms are frequently novel and striking, and seldom banal. But for the enormous canvases he proposes to cover, these values, which are after all the evidence of creative imagination rather than of constructive power, do not suffice. For the production of effect, he can pile Pelion on Ossa—the most overwhelming volume of sound which a composer has ever seriously demanded. But he cannot develop a musical thought in the sense in which Beethoven, for instance, understood development.

This is probably because he failed to realize that the "program" which he always had in mind, and for which his music was in some sense the illustration, must necessarily be less vivid in other minds than his own, and that the hearer's task of reconstructing this program from the music itself was all but impossible. It is evident that from the beginning music spoke to Berlioz with a clarity almost verbal. His interest in purely musical ideas, correspondingly, was slighter than is usual. It is possible that a more orthodox training would have corrected in some measure his somewhat astigmatic vision, and that in such a case he would have met more directly the attitude of those to whom he wished his music to appeal. But he would also have lost something of that unique sense of orchestral color which—precisely because of his unusual sense of music's meaning—he possessed in a higher degree than had hitherto been known. This new concept of the value of tone color—a value recently exalted by some critics into a new element of music—is indeed his greatest contribution to musical thought. This contribution was so completely in line with the contemporary development of virtuosity in solo instruments that we may well doubt whether any learned correction of his somewhat aberrant ideas would not have been more harmful than valuable.

In both his symphonic music and his operas this extraordinary color sense is made to do duty in place of the formal structure of more orthodox music thinkers. Naturally it is less confusing in the operas, where the text itself or the action or the scenic spectacle gives the observer a clue—lacking in purely orchestral composition—to the intended meaning of the music. Possessed of the most scintillant literary style ever developed by a musician, he was able to construct his own libretti for *Beatrice and Benedict* and for *The Trojans;* and having, like Wagner, made his texts with a clear idea of the music in mind, the correspondence between music and text is singularly vivid and convincing. Yet his operas are by no means equal to those of Wagner in purely musical interest. Wagner, as we shall see, was able to devise a process of purely musical development which contrasts sharply with Berlioz's lack of this quality. Berlioz, moreover, had been always a devout admirer of Gluck, and had doubtless felt more fully the force of the classic tradition than had Wagner. Hence, the story of Dido and Aeneas appealed to him more strongly than to his more romantically emancipated contemporaries. Great as this last opera of Berlioz must be allowed to be, it has little currency outside France.

His orchestral compositions are naturally more widely known. Here his peculiarities of style are more exaggeratedly present. Everything is subordinated to the purpose of conveying the poetic idea. The *Fantastic Symphony*, for instance, subtitled *Episodes in the Life of an Artist*, is really a picture of his passion for Henrietta Smithson—a picture colored with all his own exuberance of imagination and involving dreams quite as much as reality. The first movement deals, quite in normal musical fashion, with the artist's love itself. Both in the slow introduction and in the *Allegro agitato* this passion is represented by a definite figure or theme —the *idée fixe* which obsesses the hero throughout—and this theme both in concept and treatment strongly anticipates the Wagnerian *leading motive*. Some semblance of orthodox symphonic form is maintained in both this and the following movement, which is called *A Ball*, and which corresponds to the minuet or scherzo; but the interjection of the *idée fixe* gives personal or dramatic suggestions not contemplated in the usual symphonic treatment of these forms. The slow movement is a *Scène aux Champs*, also only mildly pictorial. But now the artist dreams that he has been condemned to death; and the music becomes a *March to the Scaffold*, in which the fixed idea plays an extraordinarily vivid part. The last movement, *Songe d'une Nuit de Sabbat*, is still more reckless and exaggerated in its pictorial and dramatic suggestion. The same love of depicting the lurid and terrible is seen in the Brigand scene in *Harold in Italy*, and especially in the famous chorus of the infernal spirits in the *Damnation of Faust*, where, finding no human tongue raucous enough, he invents an "infernal language" in which to make his demons scream. It should not be supposed, however, that all Berlioz's work is conceived on this exaggerated scale. When his theme demanded it—as in the *Enfance du Christ*—he wrote with the utmost simplicity and in a vein of melody at once unique and charming.

Naturally a style and a concept of musical values so exceptional could suggest but little direct imitation. Hence, that work of Berlioz which was most usable by others was his remarkable *Treatise on Modern Instrumentation and Orchestration* to which, as if it were a musical composition, he gave the opus number 10. Here for the first time the art—or, rather, almost the science—of writing for the orchestra is set forth. The compass, character, executive capacity, and individual peculiarity of every important instrument is minutely described; and as much as could well be stated in words of the peculiar possibilities of instrumental combination is also given. This work is the counterpart of the countless studies in virtuosity which pianists, violinists, and others were now beginning to pour forth. Its value is perhaps best measured by the fact that Richard Strauss—certainly one of the greatest masters of orchestration of all time—instead of writing a new treatise on the subject, found it necessary only to revise the work of Berlioz in the light of modern instrumental improvements. (Even here, Berlioz's megalomania is amusingly seen in his suggestion for an ideal orchestra—242 strings, doubled and quadrupled wind, and in addition thirty harps and thirty grand pianos!)

As we have seen, necessity made of him a musical journalist. But his uncompromising artistic honesty, his irrepressible imagination, his quick sense of both indignation and humor, and a love of fairness almost incongruous with these other qualities, made this enforced labor an exceptional contribution to the newly developing art of musical criticism. His exposition of the hollowness of Parisian musical life is complemented by an admirable awareness of true musical values. He was the first of Beethoven's successors to attain to any true comprehension of that master's work; his studies of Weber and Gluck are equally sympathetic. If he failed to understand or admire his great German contemporaries as fully as was their due, the fact is hardly incomprehensible in a man passionately devoted to his own country. And his letters, and above all his *Mémoires*, are almost on a par with the greatest examples of correspondence and biography left us by any of his compatriots. It is perhaps only by way of these writings that we can approach to an actual understanding of his music.

Liszt

An almost equally interesting personality and a far more accomplished artist than Berlioz was the great Hungarian Franz Liszt. Like Berlioz in his predominantly pictorial imagination, in his love of virtuosity and color, and in his aptitude for verbal expression, he was unlike him in his sounder youthful training, his more diplomatic attitude toward contemporary music and musicians, and his more catholic musical sympathy. As perhaps the greatest pianist who ever lived, he contributed incalculably to the enlargement of general musical interest. As a composer, he helped materially toward that culmination of descriptive and expressive music which Wagner achieved; and in his almost selfless devotion to the music of all ages and to the artists of his own time, he was the idol of his friends, and remains a lasting example to later generations.

Liszt was born in 1811 at Raiding in Hungary, the son of a steward on the Esterházy estates. His father was a musical amateur of some accomplishment, so that he was able to give the boy his first instruction in music. Such inordinate talent was manifested at a first public appearance, in Oedenburg at the age of nine, that a group of noblemen combined to offer an annual guarantee to provide for six years of more advanced study. Liszt was first sent to Vienna where he was placed under Czerny (the pupil of Beethoven) in piano, and under Salieri (once Beethoven's teacher) in composition. In January, 1823, he gave two concerts, at the second of which Beethoven is said to have been present, recognizing the boy's gifts with a kiss and the oft-quoted words, *Gott segne dich, du wunderbares Kind* ("God bless you, you wonderful child!"). Through Randhartinger, also his teacher in composition, he was introduced to Schubert. His abilities as a composer were recognized in an invitation to contribute a variation to that famous set on a Waltz of Diabelli, on which Beethoven, as well as contributing the one variation requested, wrote a whole set of thirty-three.

From Vienna Liszt went in the same year to Paris. He was refused admission to the Conservatoire on the ground of his foreign birth, but continued his studies privately with Reicha and Paër. Here, as "le petit Litz," he soon became the favorite of the public; and in 1824 made his first artistic success in England, which was followed by other tours to Switzerland and England. In Paris he was intimate with many leading figures in French literature—Hugo, Lamartine, George Sand, and later with the Countess D'Agoult, who became the mother of his three children. The youngest of these was Cosima, who became the wife of von Bülow and later of Richard Wagner. He was of course well known to all the musicians of importance then resident in Paris. His admiration of Chopin was great, and there is little doubt that many features of Liszt's later pianistic style were absorbed from Chopin's already novel manner. In 1831 he heard Paganini. Here he found an actual embodiment of many of his half-formed technical ideas, and, while sharing the amazement of the whole world at that magician, proceeded to turn the experience into solid technical achievement. It was doubtless the new brilliancy derived from Paganini which gave him his undisputed position as the greatest virtuoso of his time; but his appeal as an executive artist rested upon far wider foundations of musicianship and intuition.

Liszt inaugurated the piano recital; and one has only to reflect on the vast popularity which that form of musical presentation has attained to realize something of the greatness of his contribution to general musical understanding. As an interpreter, Wagner called him a producer rather than a reproducer; no style or school of composition was unsympathetic to him; when the musical idea he wished to convey did not exist in pianistic dress, Liszt was immediately ready with an uncannily suggestive transcription of its effect. So, both as performer and as arranger, he brought within the grasp of the world the most significant of musical ideas in the simplest possible form—that which could be managed by a single player. We have now mostly outgrown the need for transcriptions and arrangements; but their value to the musical world in Liszt's day should not go unrealized. He arranged the nine symphonies of Beethoven, the *Fantastic* Symphony and other works by Berlioz, the *Tannhäuser* Overture, many songs by Schubert and Schumann, and that famous *Miserere* by Allegri which Mozart had written down, as well as countless arias and scenes from operas by Auber, Donizetti, Gounod, Meyerbeer, Berlioz, and Wagner.

In spite of the universal acclaim with which his playing was received, Liszt disliked the career of the virtuoso. Feeling, as his experience widened, that his abilities went beyond the scope of pianistic performance, he turned with growing enthusiasm to problems of conducting and composition. In 1842 he undertook the direction of a yearly series of concerts at Weimar. In 1847 he accepted the position of conductor of the court theatre there, and began to put into still larger effect that advocacy of contemporary music which had already shown itself so largely in his recitals and transcriptions for the piano. Although the resources of the theatre were small, his genius as conductor was great enough to obliterate all sense of deficiency. He gave, among many others, Berlioz's *Benvenuto Cellini*, Schumann's *Genoveva* and *Manfred*, and even *Alfonso and Estrella*—that work whose failure of acceptance in Vienna had gone far to break Schubert's spirit. Wagner's *Flying Dutchman*, *Tannhäuser*, and *Lohengrin* also were given, with such understanding as both to astonish the composer himself and to maintain the interest of the world in the greatest of all music dramatists when, after his exile, he was able only to look from afar at the distortion and misrepresentation of his ideas.

Original composition, hitherto not much cultivated, had nevertheless been largely prepared for by the long series of arrangements. He now added considerably to the list of piano compositions which had begun with such works as the *Consolations* and *Années de Pélerinage*. The Sonata in B minor, the two Ballades, the *Transcendental Etudes*, and other works show clearly the enlarged vision which he had attained. But the most important productions are the two symphonies (on the *Divine Comedy* of Dante, and on Goethe's *Faust*) and the twelve *Symphonic Poems*. The symphonies, like those of Berlioz, are definitely related to the subjects suggested by the titles, although they hardly go so far in the direction of narrative or direct description. The *Symphonic Poems* are practically of the same nature as single movements of the symphonies—musical illustrations, descriptions, mood pictures or characterizations of the themes indicated by the titles. The term *Symphonic Poem* was invented by Liszt, and implies the application of the processes of orchestral composition in the most developed style to a poetic concept. *Tasso (Lamento e Trionfo)*, *Hungaria* (a Hungarian march), *Prometheus, Mazeppa*, and *Die Ideale* (after Schiller's poem) are some of the titles. The most widely known is *Les Préludes*—a sort of meditation on this life as a preparation for the next, which was suggested by some of Lamartine's *Méditations poétiques*.

No pre-established form, such as that of the sonata, is available for the symphonic poem. The number of themes, the points at which they are introduced, and the nature and extent of their development will all be governed by the poetic, descriptive, or narrative idea—the "program"— which has suggested the music. But such music can be made as satisfying in form as the sonata itself, and offers many opportunities of striking and dramatic effect which are hardly possible in the sonata form. In addition to an extremely colorful treatment of the orchestra—doubtless derived in large measure from Berlioz, but also reflecting Liszt's novel pianistic effects—Liszt also employed in the symphonic poems another device which was not exactly new in itself, but which attained, through association with the poetic subject, a new quality of literal meaning. This was the so-called *transformation of themes*. Considered merely as a musical device, it is only a slight expansion of the ancient processes of augmentation, diminution, and so on, already exhaustively employed by the Gallo-Belgic composers of the fifteenth century. But in that time, when the only known plan of musical structure was polyphonic, such thematic variations were valuable rather for their rhetorical and formal interest than for any sharply expressive suggestion. Applied to the already highly developed homophonic style, such variations are capable of being presented in far more diversified forms, and with many different types of accompaniment which again can greatly enhance the varied and intensified meanings of the themes themselves. Even in compositions which have no stated program the themes, thus presented in various guises, will often appear to take on qualities of meaning and a definiteness of expression almost verbal in clarity. The symphonic poems of Liszt contain many instances of this type of expressive suggestion. The same values, equally vivid, will be found (unassociated with any expressed program) in the Sonata in B minor. Comparison with the Fugue in E flat minor from Book I of Bach's *Well-Tempered Clavichord* will show the similarity of Liszt's process to that of the more ancient practice. Nor is the use of thematic transformation in homophonic music unknown, as the many varied forms in which the Fate theme is presented in Beethoven's C minor Symphony will clearly show. But the association of theme with poetic idea not only adds to the vividness of expression, but also doubtless suggests many novel forms of transformation which would not have occurred to polyphonic writers or to homophonic composers who were chiefly concerned with formal construction for its own sake. Liszt thus added considerably to the accepted vocabulary of music, and doubtless supplied many hints which we shall find embodied in the still more highly expressive leading motive of the Wagnerian drama.

In addition to a vast correspondence, Liszt also found time to produce several literary works—a *Life of Chopin* (more rhapsodical than biographical, but extremely interesting as an appreciation of Chopin's genius), a discussion of the Gypsies and their music in Hungary, essays on Field's Nocturnes, on the songs of Robert Franz, and on Wagner's *Lohengrin* and *Tannhaüser*, and articles in the *Gazette Musicale de Paris* and the *Neue Zeitschrift für Musik* (Schumann's journal). In this work he was largely inspired and assisted by the Princess Caroline von Sayn-Wittgenstein, with whom Liszt lived after breaking with the Comtesse D'Agoult.

The Weimar sojourn is also notable as the period during which his influence as a teacher was firmly established. Von Bülow, later his son-in-law; Karl Tausig, almost a rival to Liszt in his amazing technical brilliancy; Eugen d'Albert, also a great virtuoso, perhaps the greatest of Beethoven interpreters, and a composer of distinction; William Mason, the dean of American musicians—these and many others in the later years, such as Joseffy and Rosenthal, received from Liszt instruction which has ultimately resulted in the almost universal acceptance of principles of piano playing which originated with him.

But probably the greatest significance of Liszt's residence in Weimar lay in his growing enthusiasm for the ideas of Richard Wagner and in the association of many artists, like-minded with himself toward Wagner, which became an actual party of "futurists." It was characteristic of his unselfish nature to devote himself to this furtherance of the work of another artist, even when such devotion meant the abandonment of his most cherished ambition—to express himself as a composer rather than as a virtuoso. For, as with Bülow, Hans Richter, and many lesser figures, true comprehension of the greatness of Wagner's genius only withered Liszt's faith in his own powers.

He gave up the conductorship of the Weimar Opera in 1859, and in

1861 removed his chief residence to Rome. Here the old religious fervor returned, which in his youth had all but made of him a priest. Although he still retained connection with the Weimar court and was officially occupied in Buda-Pesth, he pursued religious studies which ended in his assuming minor ecclesiastical orders, but he never became a fully ordained priest. His career was by no means abandoned, but there was little further composition in the forms so far developed. At Weimar he had already written several Masses (the most notable being that for the dedication of the cathedral at Gran), and he now produced a considerable series of religious works: the oratorios *St. Elizabeth* and *Christus*, and a *Requiem;* the cantatas *Die Glocken*, *St. Cecilia*, and *Die Kreuzesstationen,* and a thirteenth symphonic poem *From the Cradle to the Grave.*

In spite of his entire religious sincerity, these compositions show too much of that deeply ingrained love of effect to be altogether satisfying as religious compositions. And indeed the whole body of Liszt's original composition is marred, in the minds of most critics, by occasional irrelevant excursions away from the point at issue and into the region of virtuosity. There is here an essential resemblance to Berlioz, although the external appearance of the divagations of the two men is dissimilar. Berlioz introduced episodes, apparently because they offered opportunities of developing new types of orchestral color, which were doubtless related in his mind to some feature of the poetic idea he was discussing. But since that idea is less clear to us than it was to him, we see such episodes, as we see the long parenthetical cadenzas of Liszt, merely as superfluous ornamental passages, often irritatingly out of character with the whole composition. Both men lacked that rigid logic in construction which marks the work of the great master, whether in accepted or untried forms. No work of Berlioz or Liszt is more truly novel in form than the last Sonatas of Beethoven or the still more gigantic creations of the later Wagner; but neither Liszt nor Berlioz could resist the lure of brilliant irrelevancy. The pedants, who are always legion, condemned all such work on the ground of formal looseness, and thus set up false standards of criticism which are all the more dangerous in that they have an apparent show of logical justification. For to them all logic and continuity in music is a mere continuity and symmetry of form. They cannot analyze in any scientific terms the quality of emotional character which they find maintained throughout a significant composition; and they ignore in their account of the music's value this elemental quality of character suggestion—a quality often far more apparent to the nonanalytical hearer than to the formally learned (and blinded) critics. They cannot see that it is the larger revelation of this meaning (whether that meaning is embodied in a stated program or not) which is both the main object of the composer and the basis of his choice of formal development.

The sonata itself, as we have seen, had progressed from the simple structure of the earlier Haydn to the diversified patterns of the later Beethoven, largely in response to expressive impulses (characteristic of the *ancien régime* or of the Revolution) which were not in themselves directly musical. The same impulses were also the inspiration of poets, painters, and dramatists. And the rightness of the expanded sonata lay, not in the fact that it was a sonata, nor in the mere exaggeration of its dimensions, nor even in the ingenuity of its thematic development, but in the fact that its form was relevant to, and even conditioned by, its expressed or implied subject or content. The symphonic poem, considered merely as a form, was as justifiable as the expanded sonata. Its weakness lay far less in its reliance upon a poetic idea than in the incompetence of its first purveyor to conceive his subject in completely musical terms, and to maintain that continuous logic of emotional thought which had justified the formal aberrations of Beethoven's last Sonatas and Quartets. We shall see that the symphonic poem, deriving from Wagner's music dramas a certain process of direct expression only feebly imagined by Liszt, will grow at the end of the century into a form which threatens the supremacy of the symphony. Liszt's contribution then, like that of Berlioz, is the important contribution of a pioneer.

Lesser Romanticists

The romanticists whom we have studied in the last two chapters have emerged in our time as the great leaders of the movement. We must realize, however, that the very rapid expansion of the musical public could have occurred only if a host of lesser men had been devoted to the same end. We cannot stop even to mention the names of many men who, in their own communities at least, were often regarded as the equals of the greater figures; who thus helped (often involuntarily) to obscure the finer imaginations, but who nevertheless did significant service to the cause of music. Some brief notice of a few of these men is essential, however, to any account of the romantic movement. It would be difficult to classify them as definitely belonging either to the realistic or to the idealistic group; for their vision was hardly clear enough to give their work that positive stamp of character which, with a fair degree of definiteness, reveals to us the imaginative bent of the greater men. It will not be forgotten that our discussion so far lacks almost all mention of the operatic aspect of romanticism—a most important element which will be more fully discussed in the next chapter. Some of the writers now to be mentioned were significantly, and even predominantly, devoted to opera; but this feature of their work will be ignored for the moment.

Carl Maria von Weber, although essentially a dramatist in imaginative gift, was a brilliant pianist and made early contribution to the romantic literature of his instrument. The four Piano Sonatas (of one of which the famous *Perpetual Motion* forms the final *Rondo*) are somewhat diffuse but contain many novelties of effect and are clearly romantic in tone as well as in their structure. The variations are more remarkable for ornament than for that essential novelty of meaning which a great variationist like Beethoven can discover in every new transformation of his theme. The two rather early Concertos are forgotten; but the brilliancy of the *Conzertstück* was a definite contribution to modern virtuosity and retains something of its fire even today. The presence of a "program" in the composer's mind is often suggested by the character of the music, although none has been stated except in relation to the famous *Invitation à la Valse*, whose introduction represents the courtier's request for the favor of the dance and the damsel's somewhat reluctant consent. The two early Symphonies are less important than the Piano Sonatas.

Louis Spohr (1784–1859) began his musical career as a violinist, touring extensively in Germany and Russia. He had begun to compose (with but little formal instruction) from his earliest years. He studied Mozart's scores, and formed his early technique on that model. This knowledge sufficed until he attacked the problem of oratorio, when, feeling the want of more contrapuntal knowledge, he studied Marpurg, wrote a few fugues, and felt himself equipped to go on. This lack of conventional routine was largely compensated for both by his natural gifts and by his persistent industry; and it also accounts for the considerable originality of his style. Aside from his operas, his contributions to the symphony and the concerto were the most important. The first three Symphonies (from 1811) are without program. The fourth, *The Consecration of Tones*, is based directly however on a poem by his friend Carl Pfeiffer, which he directs to be either printed in the program or read before the performance. The form of the music is considerably altered from the classical standard by this adherence to a poetic idea. The sixth Symphony (*The Historic*) illustrates in its four movements the styles of four periods of composition— those of Handel and Bach (dated 1720), of Haydn and Mozart (1780), of Beethoven (1810), and of the (then) "Most modern period," dated 1840. This last he was content to write in his own manner. Two other program Symphonies, *Earthly and Heavenly in the Life of Man* (No. 7), and *The Seasons* (No. 9), show his predilection for poetic music. Fifteen Concertos for violin solo were his chief contribution to the literature of his instrument, though there are many sonatas (both with piano and with harp) and many string quartets. Spohr's style was notable for its chromaticism. It has been said that he never wrote a diatonic progression if a chromatic one could be found; yet, in spite of his many enharmonic modulations [3] and other devices, he is hardly to be counted with Chopin, Schumann, or Liszt as a harmonic innovator. His great *Violin School* still remains an important pedagogical work, exemplifying certain additions to the technique of the instrument not suggested by Paganini. Spohr was mostly indifferent to the music of his contemporaries. He thought the later Beethoven a madman; disliked Weber; was contemptuous of Rossini; yet he was the very first, and almost the only one, of the older school to understand Wagner. At Cassel (where he had been recommended to the post of conductor by Weber) he brought out *The Flying Dutchman* in 1842 and *Tannhäuser* in 1853. Spohr's reputation was great, both in Germany and in England where for a time he was ranked with Handel and Beethoven.

Several men should be mentioned who were ultimately much less influential but of great repute in their own day. John Field (1782–1837) was an excellent pianist, whose larger works are completely forgotten but whose eighteen Nocturnes gave to Chopin a model for his still finer expressions of delicate lyrical sentiment under that title. Ignaz Moscheles was one of Mendelssohn's teachers and a vast admirer of Beethoven; his compositions were very much in vogue both in Germany and in England. He has left an interesting volume of reminiscences. To the literature and technique of the violin important contributions were made by Andreas Romberg who, with his cousin Bernhard Romberg, a 'cellist, was a friend of Beethoven and conspicuous in Viennese musical life; Pierre Rode, upon whose style Spohr somewhat founded his own and whose concertos are still fundamental elements in the violinist's education; Charles de Bériot, the founder of the Belgian school of violin playing from which have come many later artists, such as César Thomson and Eugène Ysaye; and Kalliwoda and Molique, whose works still are to be found in the studio if not in the concert hall.

All these men belonged to the older generation of romanticists, and are often hardly significant in that aspect. When in the thirties the center of German musical interest shifted from Vienna to Leipzig, Mendelssohn's brilliant personality attracted a large circle—in some degree comparable to that which surrounded Liszt at Weimar—of whom several were of great renown and influence both in Germany and elsewhere. Ferdinand Hiller

---

[3] Two notes having the same pitch, but designated by different names (as C♯ and D♭) are said to be *enharmonic* (*en*, one; *harmonia*, tone). Enharmonic modulation is that which is effected by using one or more notes, in two successive chords, in this double meaning.

(1811–1885)—who is not to be confused with Johann Adam Hiller (1728–1804), the first conductor at the famous Leipzig Gewandhaus and an important pioneer in the development of the song—was a precocious pianist and composer. He was the friend of Schumann, Mendelssohn, and Berlioz, conductor at the Gewandhaus, and from 1850, when he founded the Cologne Conservatory, a leading figure in the development of musical interest in the region of the lower Rhine. Sterndale Bennett (1816–1885), coming to Leipzig from his native England in 1837, gained the esteem of Schumann and Mendelssohn, produced some compositions there, and helped materially to enlarge the musical horizon in England.

Scandinavia, likewise, felt its first impulse toward international significance in music through Niels Wilhelm Gade (1817–1890). After beginning as a violin virtuoso he rapidly developed a talent for composition; went in 1843 to Leipzig where he was recognized both as composer and conductor; and returned to Copenhagen, where he devoted himself to the furtherance of Danish music. While at Leipzig he was the teacher of Edvard Grieg. His eight Symphonies have disappeared from the repertoire; but smaller works, like the Sonatas for violin and a charming Trio, are still attractive. Karl Reinecke, as pianist, composer, conductor, and professor, maintained throughout his very long life a significant influence on German music. Although somewhat conservative, his work shows real vitality of impulse and some individuality of form. He wrote in every important form, religious, instrumental, and operatic. Together with Moritz Hauptmann, now chiefly remembered as a theorist, and Ferdinand David (1810–1873), a remarkable violinist for whom Mendelssohn wrote his famous Concerto, Reinecke helped materially to establish the great fame of the Leipzig Conservatory. Ferdinand David is not to be confused with Félicien David (1810–1876), a French composer whose Symphony *Le Désert* is one of the earliest attempts to introduce into Western music the color of the Orient.

As minor contributors to the development of pianistic virtuosity we should note, as pioneers, Muzio Clementi (1752–1832), author of the still valuable *Gradus ad Parnassum* and of many Sonatinas still current in the instruction books; Johann Dussek (1761–1812), a promoter of the singing tone, in contrast to the more brilliant but drier tone of Clementi; J. B. Cramer (1771–1858) like Clementi, the author of still-extant Etudes, and associated with him in the business of music publishing in London; and finally Joseph Wölfl (1772–1812), a remarkable virtuoso, whose hand could compass an octave and a sixth and who wrote some pieces which, though unplayable by anyone else, did to some degree show the value of pianistic chords in extended position as used by the later virtuosi, especially Chopin and Liszt. Extended notice of these men is of course beyond our space. Their significance for the spread of musical interest is greater than our account can indicate; and the student may amplify his impression by reference to the articles in Grove's *Dictionary*.

We now turn to the long-neglected subject of opera, taking up the promised task of tracing its growth from Gluck to Wagner.

CHAPTER XXVI

The Opera from Gluck
to Wagner

GLUCK had wrought his reform of the opera with little prevision of the coming romanticism. His subjects were chosen and treated very largely in accord with the principles of classic drama. His music surpassed that of his rivals, not only because it was finer in itself, but because it really embodied (as the decadent and merely conventional writing of his contemporaries did not) much of the true ideal of classical form and expression. He used as far as possible the current resources of homophonic music; but the reader will realize that the perfected sonata and the *durchkomponirtes Lied*—the two main types of homophonic music—were brought to completion only after Gluck's death. He had as a resource neither the flexible polythematic exposition, with its possibilities of free polyphonic development, which the sonata of Beethoven or even of Mozart offered, nor the still freer characterization and form of the Schubert song. These larger liberties were suggested by the romantic spirit itself; and that spirit engendered also a similar change in the forms and purposes of spoken drama. Both in drama and opera the classic ideal was waning; and the course of opera—a composite of contemporary tendencies in pure music and in drama—is thus very complex and hard to follow.

Even long before Gluck's period, opposition to the classic ideal was manifest. The popularity of the *intermezzi* is evidence. The classic attitude was essentially that of learned people, to whom literature offered a kind of high abstraction of the real problems and motives of life. The less learned—and the learned, too, in moments of relaxation—preferred a more concrete presentation of contemporary life. Gradually, then, there was a waning of the wholly dominant influence of the ancient literatures, so enthusiastically studied during the Renaissance. Toward the end of the

445

seventeenth century arose the famous "Quarrel of the Ancients and the Moderns"—a bitter dispute as to the relative virtues of the ancient writers and the moderns who, after having studied the ancients and imitated them, were held by some to have equaled or even bettered their instruction. The quarrel really marked the beginning of a sentiment of self-confidence and of progress in literature, and an antipathy to mere tradition; and this attitude was, of course, intensified by the growth of scientific thought and the spread of individualistic sentiment in politics and social consciousness which we have already noted. In France, the leader of culture in Europe, the classical drama, at its height with Corneille (1606–1694) and Racine (1633–1699), began to decline with Voltaire (1694–1778). But Molière (1622–1673), appealing to a somewhat more heterogeneous public than that to which tragedy was addressed, had already offered in his inimitable comedies a kind of challenge to the supremacy of tragedy. Marivaux (1688–1763) placed, as Molière had not done, the psychology of love in the foreground; and Beaumarchais (1732–1799), an amazing master of intrigue, was the real precursor of modern comedy. Two later types—the *comédie larmoyante* (weeping comedy) of La Chausée, and the *drame bourgeoise* of Diderot which sought as the basis of drama to substitute the conditions of life for the psychology of characters—these are but steps toward the modern type of play, distinguished as tragedy or comedy by little else than its sad or happy ending. Historical subjects, too, are often chosen in place of the legends and myths which formed the basis of all classic tragedy. In short, the modern drama obliterates most of the ancient distinctions between the two great genres.

In other continental nations and even to some extent in England spoken drama was consciously dominated by that of France. In Italy the eager cultivation of the *dramma per musica*, which of course required a text which could be fitted to the rapidly crystallizing forms of music, soon produced a separate genre of spoken drama. This "beautiful monster, the opera," as Voltaire called it, nearly extinguished tragedy in Italy at the end of the seventeenth century; but this decline perhaps made easier the adoption of a freer style in spoken drama by Maffei and Alfieri, the most important figures in the transition to romanticism. In comedy, likewise, a departure from the artificial and burlesque character which had characterized both the *commedia dell' arte* and the lighter opera was effected by Goldoni and Gozzi, the former an amazingly prolific and gifted writer. Germany, less affected by the classical tradition, had little native drama until Caroline Neuber and J. Christoph Gottsched established in 1727 in Leipzig a new school of acting and dramaturgy from which derived the great dramatist and critic Lessing; his *Miss Sarah Sampson* was the first tragedy of common life in German, and his *Minna von Barnhelm* is a great landmark in the progress of German drama. From Lessing's time, Shakespeare became an idol of the German stage; and his influence is to be seen later in the work of Goethe and Schiller.

The foregoing will perhaps serve to suggest to the reader the general tendency toward the abandonment of classical ideals in spoken drama which was going on in the last half of the eighteenth century. It will at least be realized that many other than musical problems are involved in the evolution of modern opera. The mere scanning of the titles of dramatic and operatic works of the period will show something of the conflict of classic reserve and modern impulse.

Since Gluck's reform was mainly accomplished in Paris, we may first mention the most important of his French contemporaries to contribute to the establishment of modernism. Egidio Duni (1709–1775), a pupil of Durante at Naples, began his career in Italy as a competitor of Pergolesi. Later visits to Vienna, Paris, and London established his fame, and after some experience at Parma (where the court was French) he settled in Paris in 1757. There he produced some eighteen comic operas, weak in orchestration and dramatic expression, but so charmingly tuneful that he gave great vogue to the form and may be regarded as one of the founders of the *opéra comique*[1] in France. François André Danican-Philidor (1726–1795), first known as a master of the game of chess, learned music as a page in the chapel royal and began in 1750 to devote himself to opera. He was regarded as the most original writer of his generation, introducing such novelties as an *air descriptif* into *Le Maréchal* (1761) and an unaccompanied quartet into *Tom Jones* (note the implication of the title). He had less of dramatic instinct or of sentiment than of constructive power; but he achieved a vast popularity. Pierre Alexandre Monsigny (1729–1817), of noble descent, included the study of violin as an accomplishment in the scheme of his excellent general education; went as a young man to Paris as *maître d'hôtel* to the Duke of Orléans; was so fascinated by the performance of *La Serva Padrona* that he took up the study of operatic composition with Gianotti; and after five months wrote and produced a great success, *Les Aveux indiscrets*. He was diffident of his powers, however, and after *Le Déserteur* (1769), *La Belle Arsène* (1773), and *Félix*

[1] This, like the Singspiel of the Germans, is opera with spoken dialogue. It was called *Opéra Comique* merely to distinguish it from the Grand Opéra, in which the dialogue was set to *secco recitative*. The plots of opéra comique are often altogether serious in nature. Cherubini's *Medea* was probably the first opera ever to have a really tragic ending, yet was technically opéra comique because it had spoken dialogue. But those qualities of incisive declamation and of clear, well-turned melody which the French had found wanting in Cavalli's music in 1660 had remained the ideal of French taste in all the intervening time, and are now—in some degree due to Gluck's influence—more finely represented than ever.

(1777), wrote no more. Yet his keen instinct for dramatic sense marks his work as a distinct contribution to French opera; and his influence was considerable both on contemporary taste and on later writers.

Most significant of all at this period was André Ernest Modeste Grétry (1741–1813). He was born in Liége, Belgium, where the hearing of operas by Pergolesi, Jomelli, and others fired him with an ambition to compose. He had been regarded by his first teachers as having no talent, and indeed could never learn counterpoint properly. Hearing Monsigny's *Rose et Colas* in Rome in 1759, he realized that his vocation lay in opéra comique. A first success with *Le Huron* in Paris (1768) was soon followed by *Le Tableau parlant*, a real masterpiece; and in 1771, with *Zémire et Azor*, he began the rapid production of over fifty operas, of which the best is doubtless *Richard, Coeur de Lion*. Most of these are comedies, but some pieces were also successfully written for the *Académie*. Though he is weak in harmony and melody, his characterization is extraordinarily vivid and his declamation striking. Méhul said of him that he "made humor rather than music"; but this very power earned for him the nickname "The Molière of Music," and it is probably he rather than Duni who is to be regarded as the true founder of modern French comedy opera.

Among the Italians, the greatest contemporary of Gluck was Domenico Cimarosa (1749–1801), born and trained at Naples, whose first success with *Le Stravaganze del Conte* (1772) inaugurated a career which soon placed him in a position of rivalry with Paisiello. He left Florence, where he had been active from 1784 to 1787, to succeed Paisiello at the court of Catherine of Russia, and went in 1792 to Vienna as imperial choirmaster at an enormous salary—a position contrasting garishly with that of Kammermusicus to the Emperor to which, upon the death of Gluck, Mozart had been appointed. In Vienna, Cimarosa wrote the most famous of his works, *Il Matrimonio segreto* ("The Secret Marriage") which long outlived his serious operas. His sense of humor is likened to Mozart's. Although it is only in the lighter field that he deserves to be compared with the greater master, he yet had a discriminating command of the orchestra, and his ensembles contribute to that development of the finale which we have already noted as beginning with Galuppi.

German opera had had but a precarious existence in the face of the general enthusiasm for Italian and French products. Keiser's ambition to establish truly German opera at Hamburg had come to naught, as we have seen; and after him the institution dwindled in importance. Owing to the influence of Hasse, during his residence from 1731 to 1763, Dresden became the greatest operatic center in Germany. Karl Heinrich Graun (now chiefly remembered for his Passion cantata *Der Tod Jesu*, which, until the last war, was still annually performed in Berlin) was made chapelmaster to Frederick the Great in 1740, and thereafter contributed both as composer and director to the advancement of opera in the Prussian capital. Leipzig, too, came into prominence as the nursery of true German opera through the activity of Johann Adam Hiller (1728–1804). He studied first at Dresden where he heard the operas of Hasse and Graun, and went in 1751 to the University of Leipzig where he gradually abandoned the study of law for that of music. Active in the promotion of public concerts (from 1763, after the Seven Years' War) he became director of the *Concert-Institut*. In 1781 these concerts were given in the then new *Gewandhaus* (Cloth hall—a reminiscence of the days of the craft guilds) which later became the most famous concert hall in the world. (The present building was opened in 1884.) Hiller's operatic production mostly preceded his conductorship at the Gewandhaus. He wrote in the form of the Singspiel, for the largely untrained company of the Leipzig theatre. Yet his treatment of the necessarily simple forms of the Lied was such as to give dramatic character and a somewhat expanded form to a type of expression in itself essentially popular and German. Of his fourteen Singspiele, the *Dorfbarbier* ("Village Barber") and *Die Jagd* ("The Chase") are perhaps the best, the former having kept the stage for more than a hundred years. He was also a prolific writer of sacred and choral music, and left many instrumental compositions. Besides all this he found time to edit what was probably the first musical weekly, *Wöchentliche Nachrichten und Anmerkungen die Musik betreffend*, from 1766 to 1770; to produce significant treatises on singing and violin playing; and to publish many careful editions of classical works into which, however, according to the complacent aesthetic attitude of the time, he introduced many alterations and improvements. (Thus Mozart supplied additional accompaniments for Handel's *Messiah;* but these are less destructive of the original character.)

MOZART'S OPERAS

Little can be discerned, in all the foregoing, of any direct or purposed aim in opera. We can see that many of the tenets of classicism had been either abandoned or forgotten, and that the very progress of dramatic and musical thought had already outmoded that aspect of Gluck's work which adhered to classical ideals. But there was no new estimate, such as Gluck's, of the whole problem of opera; and only an empirical attempt to embody the new developments of drama and music in operatic form. Genius indeed, and not theory, was needed for the crystallization of the changing ideals; and that quality, in this period, is to be found chiefly in the work of Mozart. We have seen that his contribution to the perfection of the sonata was made rather out of supreme musical instinct than out of theory;

and the same instinct, in an even higher degree, contributed to the solution of the problem of opera.

We have already noted (page 352) his participation in the composition of an oratorio (*The Observation of the First Commandment*); his music for *Apollo and Hyacinthus;* his first real opera, *La Finta Semplice* (the story of a lady who "feigned simplicity" to gain her desire); his first Singspiel, *Bastien and Bastienne;* and his first opera for Milan, *Mithridates.* After *Mithridates,* which is fully in the Italian style, and is described by Jahn as "full of milk-and-water heroism, still further debased by gallantry in powder and gold lace," Mozart, now returned to Salzburg, wrote at Maria Theresa's command a "theatrical serenade" *Ascanio in Alba.* It was performed amid the festivities in honor of the marriage of the Archduke Ferdinand at Milan in 1771, and quite outshone Hasse's *Ruggiero* written for the same occasion. For the coronation of Archbishop Hieronymus, his new and detested patron at Salzburg, he wrote (apparently with some indifference) *The Dream of Scipio.* In the autumn of the same year (1772) he went again to Milan to produce *Lucio Silla,* which, like *Mithridates,* was a great success. It will be noted that the Italian style is almost wholly followed up to this time, *Bastien and Bastienne* being the only German opera and, aside from *La Finta Semplice,* the only comedy so far produced.

A considerable forward step is seen in the comedy *La Finta Giardiniera* ("The Make-believe Gardeneress") written for the Munich carnival season of 1775. True characterization both of persons and action here begins to take the place of his more generalized manner (essentially classical and Italian) of dealing with these values in earlier works. If the next work, *Il Re pastore* ("The Shepherd King"), had less of dramatic interest, it was due to the conventionality of Metastasio's libretto and to the fact that it was composed as a "festival opera" in honor of Archduke Maximilian of Salzburg. In 1779 or 1780 he wrote incidental music to a heroic drama *King Thamos,* and in 1780 a two-act comedy *Zaïde,* of which the spoken text is lost, for performance by the newly organized forces in Salzburg. In this work "melodrama" (the musical accompaniment of spoken words) is used in place of recitative. It was J. J. Rousseau who in his *Pygmalion* had initiated this novel union of words and music; but Mozart's enthusiasm for the type was aroused by the work of George Benda, whose *Ariadne in Naxos* and *Medea,* composed in this style, are even yet to be regarded as remarkable efforts. For a time indeed Mozart thought melodrama to offer the solution of the problem of operatic recitative; but *Zaïde* is his only work in which this style is used. (The grave-digging scene in Beethoven's *Fidelio* and the incantation scene in Weber's *Freischütz* are later examples of melodrama.)

All these earlier works pale before *Idomeneo* written, like *La Finta Giardiniera*, for Munich. The text was arranged from the *Idomenée* set by Campra in Paris in 1712. The fable is classic, and the treatment a highly original blend of French and Italian methods, showing a perhaps largely unconscious acceptance of Gluck's principles. The overture is in one movement, severe and earnest, leading directly into the opera; the arias are free in form, and the accompanied recitatives often of extraordinary fire, unequaled even in Mozart's later work. The characterization is distinctive, the ensembles significant in their relation to the action, and the orchestra—now as large as he ever used, except that it lacks the clarinets—is employed with rare skill, both in texture and color. In conveying the dramatic purport of the text the music often surpasses Gluck's. Yet there is no indication that it is directly modeled after the older master's work. Indeed, in October, 1781 (*Idomeneo* was produced in January), we find Mozart writing to his father: "In opera, willy-nilly, poetry must be the obedient daughter of music. Why do Italian operas please everywhere, even in Paris, as I have been a witness, despite the wretchedness of their librettos? Because in them music rules and compels us to forget everything else"—a statement which is directly opposed to Gluck's fundamental thesis.

Nevertheless, Mozart's dramatic music is as far as possible from being intended merely to please. If he was more complaisant than Gluck in providing opportunities for his singers to shine, he was yet as careful as his circumstances would permit to be directly and even literally expressive. For example, in his next opera *Die Entführung aus dem Serail*, he speaks thus of his intent in writing Belmont's song *O, how anxious, O, how fiery:* "You know how I have given expression to Belmont's aria— there is a suggestion of the beating heart,—the violins in octaves. . . . One can see the reeling and trembling, one can see the heaving breast which is illustrated by a crescendo; one hears the lisping and sighs expressed by the muted violins with flute in unison." We have heard, since Mozart's day, music which is far more literally descriptive; but it is evident from this that Mozart was far from intending the "pure" music which alone many later commentators have been inclined to see in his work.

Die Entführung, as we have already noted, was written for Vienna where the Emperor Joseph had substituted a "National Vaudeville," as he called the German opera, for the ballet and the Italian opera. This move was less significant as a sign of declining Italian influence than appears on the surface. Hiller's efforts toward making the Singspiel into a true German opera were too meager in dimensions, and lacked too much of the Italian brilliancy to which Vienna had long been accustomed, to be acceptable there. Salieri, although a pupil of Gluck, was too much an

Italian in taste to adapt himself to German styles; and the Emperor, himself a well-trained musician, had been brought up on Hasse and Piccinni. Hence, the obstacles thrown in the way of the performance of *Die Entführung*, and hence also something of the retrogression toward Italian diffuseness (by comparison with *Idomeneo*) to be noted in the music.

It is difficult to realize that the accomplishment thus far chronicled is that of a youth of twenty-five. True drama, dealing with realities of human experience, is seldom produced by infant prodigies. Long accustomed to the easy triumphs of the prodigy, Mozart was even now only entering upon a man's career. He had little experience upon which to estimate the odds against him. Vienna in his day was perhaps the most unfortunate spot he could have chosen in which to work out, independently of patronage, the career of a professional musician. Paris, however, had proved inaccessible, and no other center was as yet large enough to offer full occupation for his energies. Mozart was neither a sycophant nor a manager by nature; but in the Vienna of his day—as was amply proved by the careers of men like Salieri, Clementi, and many others—material success was only possible to one who combined these attributes. He had already justified his unbounded confidence in his own musical powers; but he had no idea that these alone could not give him success. It is doubtless to his new and bitter realizations of this fact that we owe not only the new intensity of his later music, but also that finer organization of the musical substance which the new intensity of expression demanded. That sense of form and organization which is so brilliantly exhibited in the later symphonies is his resource for the still more brilliant organization of the later operas.

Even the great success of *Die Entführung* was insufficient to maintain German opera in favor in Vienna. The Emperor himself preferred the easy fluencies of the Italian style, and in 1783 an Italian company was assembled for opera buffa. Mozart's comment, after describing the pitiful examples of German opera which had brought about the change, is: "It is as though, knowing that German opera is to die after Easter, they wanted to hasten its end by their own act: and they are Germans—confound them!—who do this. My own opinion is that Italian opera will not survive long, and I shall always hold to the German; I prefer it, although it is certainly more trouble. Every nation has its opera, why should we Germans not have ours?' But the Italian opera prospered nevertheless; and to this fact was due Mozart's composition of three operatic fragments, *L'Oca del Cairo* ("The Goose of Cairo"), *Lo Sposo deluso* ("The Deluded Spouse"), and *Il Regno delle Amazone* ("The Realm of the Amazons"), during the years 1783 and 1784. Salieri, Cimarosa, and Sarti held the stage while Mozart was thus shelved. German opera was again launched in

1785, but the works were again largely inferior (Dittersdorf's *Doktor und Apotheker* being the only one which survived) and Mozart was not asked to contribute. As a sop to his pride the Emperor was pleased to command a comedy for performance at the palace of Schönbrunn. This was *Der Schauspieldirector* ("The Theatrical Manager"). Actors and actresses, seeking engagement, perform trial pieces before the manager, quarreling as well as competing before the trial is ended. The music is remarkably humorous, but the occasional nature of the action is so obvious that the work cannot be performed as a regular opera. Salieri produced a little Italian work on the same occasion which, having a really witty libretto, was a greater success.

At this ebb tide of Mozart's fortune, a complication of intrigue placed the librettist Da Ponte in relation with him. They agreed to collaborate on the subject of Beaumarchais's comedy *The Marriage of Figaro* (a sequel to *The Barber of Seville*) which had been forbidden performance as a play because of its loose moral tone. Da Ponte, in favor with the Emperor, induced him to modify his judgment, and the opera, written in six weeks, was produced on May 1, 1786, in spite of the most disgraceful intriguing opposition. Its success with the public was overwhelming; but the cabal which had nearly prevented its first production succeeded in keeping it off the boards during the next two years. This, perhaps the most perfectly constructed of Mozart's operas, we may examine more closely.

In the midst of such a rapid development of intrigue and situation as the plot presents, merely sparkling music such as Paisiello had set to the *Barber* would doubtless have sufficed. But Mozart was not content with such music. Without the slightest loss of verve in the action, he yet managed to differentiate his characters psychologically: to give them, even though their utterance is mostly in the simplest of diatonic melody, some subtle quality which reflects not merely the general emotion involved at the moment, but a definite, personal character. Even in the complicated ensembles of the finales, character is not forgotten.[2] It is in these finales

---

[2] Adequate illustration is obviously impossible here. After grasping the plot, the student should compare, for instance, Cherubino's first aria, *Non so più cosa son, cosa faccio* ("I know not what I am, what I'm doing") with the more familiar *Voi che sapete, che cosa è amor* ("You who have known it, known what love is"), observing that the same exquisite diffidence and bewilderment breathes through both numbers. Figaro, the Count, and Bartolo, the principal male characters, are all basses; yet the music of no one of them is mistakable for that of another. In the finale of the second act, when the Count is convinced that he has accused his wife unjustly, observe how he changes his tone without losing his character; how Figaro, at his entrance, is still the same person; how subtly the Countess assumes an injured dignity instead of her earlier excitement and confusion in trying to prevent the Count from finding Cherubino in her room; and how Suzanna, with exquisite mockery, insists,

indeed that Mozart's new grasp of the whole operatic problem is most fully manifested. That of the second act of *Figaro* has eight movements, each sharply characteristic of the situation as it develops. These are not knit together by any thematic relationship, but each has its own rhythmic character, and is based upon one or more thematic figures which are worked out in much the same fashion as are the subjects of a symphony in the development section. Thus, while the music in the large is made continuously to connote the action, it has at the same time its own intrinsic interest, and works out its own ends in a way which is musically satisfying. No such extended development of the finale is to be found in any earlier work. The problem of a complete union of music and drama was not yet solved however, for in the earlier stages of the act the music, interrupted by spoken dialogue, gives still the old succession of separate, closed forms. But, as Dr. Tovey remarks, if the finales could be extended backward to meet the introduction they would give combined musical and dramatic form to the whole action. Without the achievement of extended symphonic structure, however, such expanded form would be impossible.

We can give but little space to the next and in some respects even greater work which followed *Figaro*. Although this masterpiece had been smothered in Vienna, it had been performed in Prague with great success. In consequence Mozart was invited by the management to compose an opera for Prague, and fulfilled his contract by the writing of *Don Giovanni*, which was performed there on October 29, 1787. The libretto was again by Da Ponte, derived from several versions of the popular medieval legend. Although the work is called an *opera buffa* there is little comedy in it, the cowardice of Leporello, Don Giovanni's servant, offering the only true instance. The dissolute Count is drawn with a large measure of psychological reality, which is so far reflected in the music that this principal character has no single great aria to sing; Donna Anna, Elvira, and Zerlina are clearly differentiated types; and the famous scene in which the statue of the murdered Commander comes to Don Giovanni's feast is as awful as anything in operatic literature.

The new opera was performed in Vienna in May, 1788, at first without success. Fifteen performances brought it into favor, however, but it was

---

Così si condanna chi può sospettar ("Thus he is condemned who so quickly suspects"). There is, of course, no elaborate machinery of leading motive; but observe in the third movement (*Allegro*) of this finale, the manner in which the legato phrase at the fifth bar (used over and over again, mostly in the orchestra) seems to suggest, in the midst of the confusion, the reality of the affection between the Count and the Countess. Here and in many other places will be found ample evidence of that relation of operatic music to symphonic development which is spoken of in the text.

not again produced in Vienna during Mozart's lifetime. The only official recognition offered him had been the post of chamber composer to the Emperor (conferred in 1787, after the death of Gluck, the previous incumbent). Several dances were written—the only work required of him in this position; but the chief works were the three great Symphonies of 1788 already discussed. In 1789 he went on a tour to Berlin, stopping on the way at Dresden and at Leipzig, where to his intense delight he heard Bach's motet *Singet dem Herrn ein neues Lied*. He at once demanded the parts of other motets (there being no score available) and studied them, spread out on the table before him. "Here," he said, "is music from which one can learn something!" At Potsdam, Frederick William II was so impressed with his abilities as to offer him the post of Kapellmeister at a salary of 3,000 thalers. Because of his consideration for the Emperor Joseph, Mozart felt obliged to decline. One cannot but wonder whether the happier conditions which its acceptance would have brought about might not have prolonged his life. The Emperor, in any case, showed no great appreciation of the sacrifice. *Figaro*, however, had been successfully revived, and probably owing to this the Emperor commissioned him to set another libretto by Da Ponte, *Cosi fan tutte*. The title really means "thus all ladies do"; but since no one can be sure, at the end, whether the two principal men (who, on a wager, have disguised themselves as Albanian noblemen and won each other's sweethearts) have returned to their first affection, the slang phrase, "Everybody's doing it," is not a wholly false translation. But Jahn's judgment that "the libretto, never rising above the ordinary opera buffa, has not seldom dragged the music down to its own level," can hardly be disputed.

In 1790, Leopold II succeeded the Emperor Joseph—an event of distressful import for Mozart. The new ruler had little taste for music, and dismissed many of his predecessor's appointees. Even the slight favor in which Mozart had stood with Joseph was sufficient to put him in disfavor with Leopold. An almost disastrous concert tour was the result, from which Mozart returned to Vienna poorer than ever. Fortune now threw him into association with a rascally actor manager, Emanuel Schickaneder, whose concoction of a libretto in German, *Die Zauberflöte* ("The Magic Flute"), Mozart was at length induced to set. During its composition two commissions were received, one for a *Requiem* (from an unknown patron, later proved to be Count Walsegg of Stuppach, who wished to perform the work as his own composition), and one for opera, Metastasio's *Clemenza di Tito*, to be performed at Prague at the coronation of Leopold II as King of Bohemia. Although this subject required a return to the style of opera seria, Mozart was obliged to compose it. Even here, however, he often made a virtue of necessity; and the first finale, although lacking the dramatic foundation which had made possible the greatness of those in *Figaro* and *Don Giovanni*, is striking and worthy of its author. With all this on his hands, *Die Zauberflöte* was nevertheless finished in time for performance on September 30, 1791. Although the story is fantastic to the point of absurdity, so that true characterization is impossible, Mozart made for this opera his most imperishable music. As with *Don Giovanni*, several performances were necessary before the appeal of the opera could be fully felt; but it soon became the most popular opera of the day, its hundredth performance being celebrated on November 23, 1792. But Mozart was not fated to enjoy the fruits of his success. On December 5, 1791, after an attack of inflammation of the brain, toward which he had been sickening for many months, he died. The beneficence of Baron Van Swieten, a patron of the composer, extended so far that he arranged, out of consideration for the widow's finances, a funeral "of the third class." As the services in St. Stephen's Church ended, a violent storm was raging. The mourners followed the body only to the gate of the churchyard of St. Mark's; placed in the common vault, it was soon confused with other nameless corpses; and to this day the last resting place of this most incredible of geniuses remains unknown.

The Magic Flute was not merely a triumph of German over Italian opera. Its subject, although not a German myth, is of that fantastic, fairy-tale character which was soon to become the favorite theme of popular German literature. Thus Mozart's dramatic work, beginning with a full acceptance of the classic style, in itself exhibits many features of the transition to romanticism. Classicism, defined in the sense of the classic drama of France, virtually disappeared in his latest works; but defined more largely, in terms of musical ideal, classicism is still probably the stylistic character most justly to be ascribed to them.

OPERA IN FRANCE—CHERUBINI, MÉHUL, AND LESUEUR

Three other writers, slightly younger than Mozart, contributed in various degrees to the general overthrow of the classical ideal. Greatest of these was doubtless Luigi Cherubini (1760–1842). Born in Florence, and trained by Sarti at Bologna in the most rigid of contrapuntal traditions, he nevertheless attacked the problem of opera, producing from 1780 to 1788 eleven operas all in the current Neapolitan manner. During this time he had worked with success in London, but settled in 1788 in Paris which thereafter became his home. With quick versatility he adopted the French style (*Démophon*, 1788), in which his great contrapuntal powers were offered larger opportunity than in the Italian. His strong sense of orchestral effect, too, combined with his other abilities to make of

Lodoiska (1791) a work of startling novelty and power to the Parisians. The greatest works of this second period are *Medea* (1797), which we have already noted as the first opera to have a really tragic ending; *Les deux Journées*, known in Germany and England as *Der Wasserträger* or *The Water Carrier*—the only one of all his works to have a satisfactory libretto, and in consequence the only one long to survive on the stage; *Anacréon* (1803), and *Faniska*, produced in 1806 in Vienna. Under monarchy and revolution he had continued his activity unabated; but the dislike which Napoleon felt for him depressed him severely and impelled the journey to Vienna. The disturbed conditions there accounted for the comparative failure of *Faniska*, as well as for the failure of Beethoven's *Fidelio* in the previous year. Cherubini had heard *Fidelio*, apparently without much enthusiasm. Beethoven, on the other hand, esteemed Cherubini above all other contemporary writers for the stage.

Returning to France, Cherubini gave his chief attention again to sacred music, although he occasionally produced an opera. His active association with the Conservatoire gave him opportunity for valuable educational work, crowned by an important treatise on counterpoint. In addition there are many large instrumental works, all magnificently constructed but largely marked by the peculiar reticence in expression which was characteristic of the man. By temperament, which is after all the most significant attribute of the musician, Cherubini was a classic. The passion for dramatic truth often caused him, as it did Gluck, to eschew musical beauty for its own sake; indeed, he seems in this respect the most rigid of Gluck's followers. Yet the range of his style, indicated by two such different works as *Medea* and *The Water Carrier*, is very great; and although the essential spirit of romanticism is lacking in his remarkably intellectual structures, his sense of dramatic reality and his highly picturesque orchestration make his work the most tangible link between classicism and romanticism.

Étienne Méhul (1763–1817), after a youth of struggle, went to Paris in 1778 to finish his education in piano and composition. Hearing Gluck's *Iphigenia in Tauris* in 1779 he approached the composer, receiving sound advice and, after having formed his determination to become a writer of opera, some actual instruction from that master. After a long period of the most painstaking study, he made an instant success with *Euphrosine et Coradin* (1790), and in the next seventeen years produced twenty-four operas. Of these by far the greatest is *Joseph*, which still lives on the French stage. Indeed, it was held by M. Tiersot to be superior in dignity and sonority to Handel's great oratorio *Israel in Egypt*. Lacking sprightliness and charm, Méhul was at his best in dealing with somber and passionate themes. His orchestration is often novel to the point of questionableness—as in *Uthal,* where the violins are absent from the orchestra throughout; but the doubtful passsages are more than compensated for by many new and striking uses of the instruments. Berlioz doubtless gained many suggestions from Méhul.

Jean François Lesueur (1760–1837), lacking the imagination of Méhul and the technical learning of Cherubini, exhibited in opera that love of picturesque and striking orchestration which he had earlier shown in church music. His *La Caverne* was even more successful than Méhul's opera on the same subject. *Ossian, or the Bards* (1804), whose title will show the author's sympathy for one phase of early romanticism, won for him the favor of Napoleon, for whose coronation as Emperor later in the same year Lesueur also wrote a Te Deum and a Mass. His theory appears to have been more romantic than his practice; but as the one teacher at the Conservatoire whom Berlioz could respect, he did more than he was perhaps aware of to inaugurate romanticism.

Examination of the dates of production of the important works of the writers whom we have just been observing will show that none are later than the first decade of the nineteenth century, although several of the composers lived much beyond that time. This may be taken to indicate that the progress of the transition which they had inaugurated had become more rapid than they could follow. Born in the days of expiring classicism, they had all imbibed in youth the classic spirit; bound by its unconscious fetters they were compelled to look on, in their later years, at the triumph of a romanticism which they had helped to create but which they could not embody in their own creations. What Mozart might have done, had he lived out a normal life, we can only surmise. The only one of the inheritors of the classic tradition who was great enough to maintain and even to lead the extraordinarily rapid movement of transition was Beethoven.

BEETHOVEN'S DRAMATIC MUSIC—*Fidelio*

Beethoven's dramatic music is by no means to be found only in his one opera, *Fidelio,* nor even in his many dramatic overtures. The young man who in 1798 wrote the *Sonate Pathétique* possessed the sense of tragedy in an uncommon degree; and there are countless passages in the later instrumental works which could have come only from the mind of a true dramatic musician. The oratorio *The Mount of Olives* is marred, as an oratorio, by its overdramatic presentment of the Christ. Almost at the same time Beethoven composed his first work for the stage—the ballet *Prometheus.* It is a representation of the spiritual elevation of man, symbolized in two statues which are brought by Prometheus to Parnassus, there to be endowed by Apollo and the muses with finer attributes. The music consists of an Overture and sixteen numbers. It was produced in March, 1801, and repeated twenty-eight times during that and the next year. A libretto for a true opera had been long fruitlessly sought. Beethoven would have none of the farcical or licentious stories (such as that of *Figaro*, which he deplored), but wished for something which would involve truer and deeper emotions.[3] This he found at length in *Léonore, ou L'Amour conjugal*, by a French librettist J. N. Bouilly, the author of the book of Cherubini's *Water Carrier*. It was produced in November, 1805, a week after Napoleon's army had entered Vienna. Naturally, the moment was wholly unpropitious. After three performances the opera was withdrawn. With its original three acts reduced to two, it was mounted again in 1806; but owing to an ill-judged dispute with Baron Braun, the director of the theatre, over the division of the receipts, Beethoven again withdrew the work. Still further revised, it was again revived in 1814. Some indication of the care expended on the work is to be seen in the fact that Beethoven wrote, in all, four overtures for it. That for the first performance was the one now known as *Leonora, No. 2*. This was considerably intensified for the Vienna performance of 1806, taking the form now known as *Leonora, No. 3*. The *Leonora, No. 1*, which differs greatly from the others, was written for a projected performance of the opera in Prague in 1807. Cherubini remarked of the *Leonora, No. 3* that nobody could tell what its fundamental key was; and a feeling that the earlier overtures were too heavy prompted the writing of the *Overture to Fidelio* in quite another vein.

The tale is that of the heroic rescue of Florestan from unjust imprisonment and slow starvation at the hands of the wicked governor of the fortress, Don Pizzaro. Leonora, Florestan's wife, dressed as a boy, excites the affections of Marcellina and the cupidity of her father Rocco, the jailer, and is thus allowed to enter the fortress. Don Pizzaro, learning that Don Fernando, the Minister of State, is about to visit the fortress, and fearful that his prisoner will be discovered, proposes to Rocco to kill Florestan. Rocco refuses, but agrees to help dig the grave if Don Pizzaro will himself kill Florestan. Leonora (or Fidelio, as she is known to Rocco) overhears the plotting, anathematizes the villain in a tremendous recitative *Abscheulicher, wo eilst du hin?*, and induces Rocco to allow her to accompany him to the dungeon as his helper. In the dungeon Florestan

---

[3] He had been attracted by a subject offered by Schickaneder (librettist of *The Magic Flute*) but gave this up for *Fidelio*. And Paër tells an amusing story of Beethoven's behavior while listening with him to his opera *Achilles*. Beethoven's enthusiasm was vented in incessant exclamations of "Oh, but it is beautiful!" "Oh, but it is interesting!" and, at last, "I must compose this opera myself!" But the incident is only another instance of Beethoven's keen interest in drama.

sings a pitiful song, half of woe, half of faith and hope. Rocco and Leonora enter, shuddering at the cold and darkness, and begin to dig the grave. Florestan, unseen, begins again to sing of his lost happiness; Leonora hears his voice and is in transports, but must conceal her excitement. Rocco allows her to give bread to the prisoner. Pizzaro enters, reveals himself to Florestan as his bitter enemy, and is about to stab him when Leonora throws herself between them. Pizzaro would kill them both; but Leonora has a pistol and holds him at bay. At that moment is heard from the distance the sound of the trumpet announcing the arrival of the Minister. A change of scene provides a more suitable place for the happy denouement.

It was not dramatic sense but stage experience which Beethoven lacked. His characters are less subtly mirrored in the music than are Mozart's; even the intention of character suggestion seems entirely abandoned in the quartet in the first act, which, although each of the four persons involved is expressing his own inmost feeling, is cast in the form of a four-voiced canon. Nor had Beethoven, in writing for the voice, that imaginative feeling which he displayed in writing for instruments. The interest in this play lies rather in situations and events than in any subtleties of character; in the exhibited moral of triumphant love rather than in the perplexities of psychological conflict. Hence, the great scenes are forcefully presented, even without too detailed a characterization. In its fine sincerity, the whole opera is in vivid contrast to the horde of flippant and superficial works which were current in that day. It lacks almost every quality which would relate it to the classical ideals of the eighteenth century, but hardly attains to true romantic character.

The Rise of Romantic Opera—Carl Maria von Weber

We have perhaps sufficiently pointed out the existence of romantic tendencies in the opera following Gluck to show that there was an irresistible trend toward the new manner. In France, Germany, and England characteristic expression of romantic feeling occurred, first in literature—because words are the most natural, though not the most subtle, means of utterance—and later in other arts. And everywhere there was the same general abandonment of the classic tradition, in the wake of newly aroused interest in novel aspects of contemporary life. In addition to details already given, one may picture the movement as illustrated in the progress of the novel from Richardson to Scott, or from Le Sage to Victor Hugo; and in the change of the poetic spirit from Ossian and Percy to Byron, Keats, and Shelley. But Germany, since it was perhaps the least classical in spirit of the European nations, possessed the most nearly virgin soil for the cultivation of the romantic flower. Possessing also the most highly perfected musical language which had as yet been developed, it was natural that the Germans should produce a romantic opera which, once it had achieved birth, should grow and flourish as in no other land.

We have noted Mozart's ultimate preference for German over Italian opera. Beethoven, who esteemed *The Magic Flute* above all of Mozart's other works "because it was purely German," showed the consistency of his belief not only in *Fidelio* but in his Overture to Collin's *Coriolanus* and in the Overtures and incidental music to Goethe's *Egmont* and to Kotzebue's *King Stephen* and *The Ruins of Athens*.

But the first pure romanticist in opera was Carl Maria von Weber (1786–1826). His father, Franz Anton, was the uncle of Mozart's wife Constance. Franz Anton was an excellent viola player, and hoped to find in this first child of his second marriage a prodigy to compare with Mozart. His talent, however, was slow in appearing, and the father's life— that of a director of a wandering dramatic troupe—was ill suited to the pursuance of the child's education, either in music or in general. He had brief periods of excellent training with Heuschkel at Hildburghausen (1796) and with Michael Haydn at Salzburg (1798). At Munich he had lessons in composition with Kalcher, producing among various compositions an opera (*The Power of Love and Wine*—an extraordinary subject, whatever its treatment, for a boy of twelve) which was later destroyed. A temporary interest in the process of lithography caused a removal to Freiburg; but association with a competent operatic company speedily reawakened his musical interest, and the result was the composition of another opera, *Das Waldmädchen*, which was produced in 1800 in Freiburg, in Chemnitz, and in 1805 in Vienna. After another period of wandering he went again to Vienna in 1803, associating with Josef Haydn (whom he admired) and somewhat with Beethoven (whom at this period he disliked, both as man and composer). Most significant, however, was his study with Abbé Vogler, a composer, organist, and theorist of great renown, "by whose advice," he says, "I gave up working at great subjects, and for nearly two years devoted myself to diligent study of the various works of the great masters, whose method . . . we dissected together, while I separately made studies after them, to clear up the different points in my own mind."

It was through Vogler that Weber obtained in 1804 the post of Kapellmeister at Breslau. Here he gained much experience in conducting and began the composition of his first mature opera *Rübezahl* ("The Turnip Counter"), an old fairy tale of the Riesengebirge. It was never performed, and only the Overture and three numbers remain. The supernatural situations foreshadow those in *Der Freischütz* and *Oberon*. He went next to

Stuttgart as private secretary to Duke Ludwig and to King Frederick of Würtemberg. Here he fell for a time into deplorable dissipation, but with characteristic energy redeemed himself, and not only took to philosophic reading but, with the assistance of friends, composed a new opera *Silvana* to a new version of the story of the earlier *Waldmädchen*. This, though put into rehearsal, was not performed. Weber was unjustly accused of a fraud with regard to a loan; was imprisoned, acquitted, but banished. He went to Mannheim, and then to Darmstadt, where Abbé Vogler was living and where he had some intercourse with Vogler's afterwards famous pupil Meyerbeer. A "Harmonic Society" was formed of which he and Meyerbeer were members, and which had somewhat the same aims as Schumann's imaginary *Davidsbund;* and large schemes for the betterment of musical criticism were projected—among them the founding of a musical journal, which however never came into being. Weber shows himself to have been the first composer of importance to cultivate literary and critical powers. It was at Darmstadt that he became acquainted with the story of *Der Freischütz,* upon which was later based his greatest operatic success.

At Mannheim, whither he had been invited to give a concert, he produced the remodeled Overture to *Peter Schmoll* (his second opera, 1801), and wrote a part of a one-act opera *Abu Hassan* which was completed in 1811. Failing to secure a promised appointment as Kapellmeister until 1813 he alternated concert tours with brief periods of residence in Munich, Leipzig, Prague, and other cities, occasionally producing an opera and appearing often as pianist. Early in 1813 he was offered the directorship of the Opera at Prague—an institution which had sadly deteriorated since Mozart's day. Here he disclosed the great gifts as conductor and manager which his early association with the theatre had already unconsciously cultivated. In a few months he learned the Bohemian language— a feat afterwards repeated with the English tongue when he composed the opera *Oberon.* A visit to Berlin in the summer of 1814 revealed to him the isolation of his life at Prague. *Silvana* was performed; he became interested in the subject of *Tannhäuser* for a new opera (a project never carried out); wrote ten songs from Körner's *Leyer und Schwert* (six of them for men's chorus) which at once became immensely popular throughout Germany; and returned to Prague with some prospects of becoming Kapellmeister at the Court Opera in Berlin. During the next year he wrote a stirring cantata *Kampf und Sieg* in celebration of the victory of Waterloo—another composition revealing to the German people his intense patriotism. It was repeated in Berlin on June 18, 1816 (Waterloo day) with vast acclaim, further enhancing his reputation and prefiguring the great triumph which was to occur five years later. In

December he learned that he had been appointed Kapellmeister of the German opera at Dresden, a position which he held until his death.

Dresden, a stronghold of Italian opera since the days of Hasse, had remained until now indifferent to German opera. The task of rooting the German style firmly in the affections of court and people was no easy one. To the indifference of the court was added the active opposition of Francesco Morlacchi, since 1811 director of the Italian stage. Weber's energy, his command of every detail of production and his unfailing geniality and tact enabled him in a short time to put German opera on an equality with Italian. His spirits were doubtless sustained by his happy marriage to a singer, Caroline Brandt. Most of his compositions during the first Dresden years were of an occasional nature—a Mass for the King's name day, and a Jubel-Cantata, to which is prefixed the familiar *Jubel* Overture which ends with a pompous version of *God Save the King*. Association with Friedrich Kind, a conspicuous literary figure in Leipzig, brought about the resumption of Weber's interest in the story of *Der Freischütz*. The libretto was made early in 1817; but the music, composed only at intervals, was not complete until 1820. In the meantime, on a commission from Count Brühl in Berlin, he had written the Overture and incidental music to Wolff's play *Preciosa*—"more than half an opera," as Weber said. Its performance on March 14, 1821, was successful in itself, but still more important as paving the way for *Der Freischütz* which was given on June 18, achieving a success which no German work had ever before attained. In Berlin, as in Dresden, there was the same opposition of Italian to German opera. Gasparo Spontini (of whom we shall speak presently) after many deserved successes, had been made director of the opera in 1820. His reputation was enormous; but it faded rapidly after the performance of *Der Freischütz*, and because of this signal triumph Weber's work is undoubtedly to be regarded as marking a turning point not only in the attitude of Germany toward its own opera but also in the acceptance of opera in the romantic style.

The story is based on an old German legend—that of a fiend who, in exchange for their souls, sells to huntsmen bullets which cannot miss their mark. Victims can postpone their day of reckoning by finding another victim. In the opera, Caspar, already doomed, induces Max (who has failed to win in the contest for the position of chief huntsman) to bargain for the magic bullets. In a weird scene in the Wolf's Glen we see seven bullets cast—six for Max in the contest; the seventh for Samiel, the fiend, to direct as he pleases. Agathe, Max's sweetheart, has had premonitions of trouble, dreaming that, in the shape of a dove, she was shot by Max. In the contest three bullets have hit their mark. The next, fired by the Prince's direction at a dove, fails to strike Agathe (who is protected by a wreath of sacred roses given her by a hermit) and strikes Caspar instead. Max tells the secret of the bullets and is forgiven.

In its opposition of simple virtue to supernatural evil, the story is altogether in the vein of current German romanticism, whose roots lay deep in the mythology and folklore of the German people. The honest love of Max and Agathe—the main interest, of course—carries on against the physical background of the German forest, and against a psychological background of mingled superstition and religion. And not only are these emotions of love, superstition, and religion fully expressed in the music, but there is also a full characterization of the principal personages. Even without a change in the lilting 6–8 measure of the duet which opens the second act, Aennchen's lightheartedness is vividly contrasted with Agathe's heaviness of spirit; Max's aria *Durch die Wälder, durch die Auen* ('Thro' the forests, thro' the meadows") has far more of the suggestion of his ingenuous nature than appears on the surface; even Caspar—hardly more than a stage villain—seems real; and the famous scene in the Wolf's Glen is incomparable in its vivid illustration of the grip of the supernatural on the peasant mind—and on our own. The music is remarkably plastic in adapting itself to the sense of the words; the old aria form, with its perfunctory return upon itself, is either abandoned or effectively disguised.

Most important of all for the future association of music and drama, is Weber's use of something very closely approaching to the definiteness of the *leading motive*. Whenever Samiel appears, either in response to Caspar's invocation or to work his evil spells upon Max, there is a shuddering phrase in the orchestra (in which Weber for the first time exexploited the hollow chalumeau register of the clarinet) which, since Samiel utters no word, is especially vivid as a musical embodiment of the fiend. While musical characterization was hitherto by no means unknown, and while something of this same purpose can be seen in the heavy chords which accompany the appearance of the statue of the Commander in *Don Giovanni*, this phrase and others in *Der Freischütz* seem to have more definite meaning in relation to the drama than any which had ever as yet been devised. In his freedom of formal structure then, and in his sharper and more literal association of musical phrases with persons or features of the drama, Weber took a further step toward the overthrow of musical self-sufficiency in opera. We shall see when we come to the study of Wagner that his work is but a vaster exemplification of Weber's ideas. Wagner's theory, expressed in far more elaborate and philosophical language, will be found essentially to agree with the simple statement of Weber's ideal of "an art work complete in itself, in which all the parts and details of the related and involved arts, mingling together, disappear, and, in a sense submerging themselves, create a new world."

It was not given to Weber to realize his ideal. His next opera *Euryanthe*, commissioned for Vienna, was made on the scale of grand opera (the music being continuous throughout). In many respects it is far superior to *Der Freischütz;* but its libretto is unskillful, and the story (from an Old French romance retold by Boccaccio, and again by Shakespeare in *Cymbeline* where Imogen is somewhat the counterpart of Euryanthe) is lacking in those immediate appeals to the superstitious imagination which are incessantly present in *Der Freischütz*, and also in the truer human interest of the earlier work. The comparative failure of *Euryanthe* is perhaps sufficiently explained by these facts; but it also must be recognized that it contains much of Weber's best music, and that in abandoning the Singspiel form, as well as being constructed upon a higher dramatic ideal, it was really ahead of its time.

Depressed by its lack of success, and alarmed for his health, he accepted a rather lucrative commission to compose an opera for Covent Garden in London. His physician warned him that the effort would mean his death; but he could not bear the prospect of destitution for his family. The subject was another Old French tale (Huon of Bordeaux), under the title *Oberon*. To compose its English text he was obliged to learn the language, which he did with surprising thoroughness in a few months. This opera was also in Singspiel form—indeed it was more a play with incidental music than an opera, some of the principal actors having no singing parts. Also, the libretto was sent him piecemeal, so that even while writing he had no full idea of the meaning of the text. Naturally the work was unsatisfactory; yet again and again it reveals the unerring dramatic instinct as well as the vivid musical imagination of its composer. The Overture (like the Overtures to *Der Freischütz* and *Euryanthe*) is everywhere known; and Rezia's great aria *Ocean, thou mighty Monster* had scarcely been approached for vividness in the work of any other man. But his physician's prophecy proved true. Weber died at London in June, 1826, unable to return to his family for whom he had undertaken the journey.

Weber's achievement looms so large in historical perspective as almost wholly to overshadow the work of his German contemporaries. Romantic opera, however, could hardly have become the full expression of national taste without the added contribution of many other men. Of those who greatly furthered the movement, the following are the most important. E. T. A. Hoffman (1776–1822) was one of the most versatile geniuses of whom we have record. Poet, novelist, painter, singer, conductor, manager, and critic—all with a considerable degree of distinction—and thoroughly romantic in attitude in all these activities, he was perhaps the most widely influential man in his own time in the propagation of the new ideas. His operas are all Singspiele, romantic as to plot; but since they date from 1801 to 1811 they are lacking in musical freedom of structure and the essential "strangeness" of suggestion. His many fantastic tales had more influence on his successors, Schumann especially being largely influenced by the *Lebensansichten des Kater Murr* ("Tomcat Murr's Views of Life, with Fragments of the Biography of Johannes Kreisler") which was in some sense the inspiration of the *Kreisleriana.*

Louis Spohr (1784–1859), after attaining much of that fame as a violinist and instrumental composer which we have already noted, and after two unsuccessful attempts at opera, produced his first dramatic masterpiece, *Faust,* in 1816 under Weber's direction. The book (by Bernard, differing widely from Goethe's version of the story) was weak; the music, on the other hand, vividly suggestive, so that the work had a long run of popularity. Temporary success only attended his next work, *Zémire et Azor;* but with *Jessonda* (1823) he reached the highest point of his creative career. This opera maintained its position for many years, earning the sincerest commendation of all sound musicians, including Richard Wagner. The story—that of the rescue of the widow of an East Indian Rajah from the fate of being burned with her husband—lacks the usual supernatural features of the current romantic plots, but is all the more convincing to later generations. Spohr's dislike of Beethoven, his intense admiration for Mozart, and his curious theoretical respect for musical form, all contributed to the restriction of his range of dramatic expression. It was no inconsiderable genius which could surmount these temperamental obstacles.

Schubert's *Alfonso and Estrella* and *Fierrabras,* if envy and malice had not prevented their performance, might have influenced the early history of German opera. As it was, work of far less significance held the stages of Germany: operas of Konradin Kreuzer, Lindpaintner, Loewe (the great ballad writer), Albert Lortzing, Franz Lachner, and many others—all satisfying contemporary taste but contributing nothing of note to its refinement. Only one figure remains of significance in the development of German opera before Wagner—Heinrich Marschner (1795–1861). Of his three greatest works, *The Vampire* (1828), *Templar and Jewess* (1829, founded on *Ivanhoe*), and *Hans Heiling* (1833), the last-mentioned (with a fable not unrelated to that of Goethe's *Faust*) is especially vivid, being still occasionally performed. Wagner's admiration for Marschner was great, and his debt to him, in his early years. considerable.

Operatic Progress in France—Boieldieu, Auber, Hérold

But while these works are the most direct precursors of Wagner's music dramas, romanticism was also affecting the style of operatic composition in France and Italy. French opera either contributes positively to Wagner's own works, or indirectly to the formation of his exhaustive theories of music drama. Since Paris still remained the operatic center of the world, its opera was naturally more fruitful in this suggestion than the Italian. Yet this Parisian opera was not exactly French. We have seen that the first great figure in the history of French opera was Lully, an Italian; that his style dominated that of the lesser Frenchmen (such as Campra and Destouches) who followed him, until Rameau, about 1735, began to write for the stage; that Rameau's really thoughtful work was nearly overthrown in popularity by the advent of the Italian troupe in 1752 which precipitated the *Guerre des Bouffons;* that the triumph of French taste was won by another foreigner, Gluck; and that another Italian, Cherubini, although less popular than native composers such as Grétry, Monsigny, and Méhul, was easily their superior in intellectuality and musicianship. We have noted also the gradual decline of the classical idea of tragedy, and the mingling of tragic and comic element in the opéra comique. Out of this confusion of taste, inevitable in a time of revolution, came a new classification of opera. The lighter opéra comique, whose plots were of the type of *The Barber* and *Figaro*, acquired the sentimental tone peculiar to the romanticism of the early nineteenth century, and became ultimately the *drame lyrique*. On the other hand, the taste for more serious subjects (formerly dealt with in the accepted tragic manner) now found satisfaction in the *historical* opera—a genre whose parallels in the fields of painting and the novel will not be unfamiliar. In the lighter style native Frenchmen held their own; in the heavier, the palm was again given to foreigners.

Of the many composers who contributed to the lighter French opera, three only demand special notice. François Adrien Boieldieu (1775–1834), after youthful successes in his native Rouen, went to Paris where he had instruction from Cherubini. *La Famille suisse* and *Le Calife de Bagdad* pleased the public, but not Cherubini, to whose censure were due three years of study before Boieldieu produced his next work. In 1803, after *Ma Tante Aurore*, he went to St. Petersburg as conductor of the opera, returning in 1811 to Paris. Several works of no particular note followed; but these were followed in 1825 by his masterpiece *La Dame blanche* ("The White Lady"), whose book is derived from Scott's novels *The Monastery* and *Guy Mannering*. The opera *Jean de Paris* (ranked by Schumann with *Figaro* and *The Barber*) shows almost equally great mastery of appealing melody, sound characterization, and subtle treatment of the orchestra.

Unlike Boieldieu, Daniel François Esprit Auber (1782–1871) produced no operas in his early years. The first was written for private performance in 1811, and it was not until 1820 that *La Bergère châtelaine* gave him an assured position among musical dramatists. Again, much credit for this mastery is due to the instruction received from Cherubini. Fortunate enough to have the collaboration of Eugène Scribe, whose renown as librettist rivals that of Metastasio in the eighteenth century, Auber produced about forty operas, chiefly opéras comiques, of which the most important are *Le Maçon*, (1825), *Fra Diavolo* (1830), *Le Cheval de Bronze* (1835), and *Les Diamants de la Couronne* (1841). But the work upon which his later reputation largely rests is a historical opera *La Muette de Portici* (better known as *Masaniello*), in which revolutionary sentiment is portrayed with a power hardly even suggested in his other operas. This was produced in 1828, and a performance of it in Brussels in 1830 had some direct force in instigating the riots which drove the Dutch out of the country.

Boieldieu and Auber may be regarded as the last of the great masters of the old opéra comique. Less significant in achievement, but equally gifted, was Louis Joseph Ferdinand Hérold (1791–1833). All the world has heard the overture to *Zampa* (produced 1831). In France, however, *Le Pré aux clercs* is regarded as his finest work. Other members of the large group who were actively promoting opéra comique were Henri Montan Berton (a violent opponent of Rossini); Nicolò Isouard (rather a follower of Grétry than a progressive); Rodolphe Kreutzer (to whom Beethoven's *Kreutzer* Sonata is dedicated); Charles Simon Catel (less important as a composer than as the author of a treatise on harmony which superseded that of Rameau); and three Italians, Giuseppe Blangini, Giuseppe Catrufo, and Michele Carafa.

THE HISTORICAL OPERA—SPONTINI

The serious opera, distinguished from the opéra comique less through the nature of its plot than through the fact that it had no spoken text, was a genre apparently more congenial to the French public than to native French composers. Opera with spoken text had indeed more popularity with the generality of music lovers in England, France, and Germany than the continuously musical Italian type; but in Paris, where older cultural traditions had greater force than elsewhere, a large and influential group still supported the severer style. No influence could have maintained currency for the old classic manner; but neither could any force extinguish the memory of its grandeur, or the desire for some contemporary style of opera which should at least recall that grandeur. Among the types of plot which were found suitable for this continuance of the older tradition many were of a distinctly historical character—the events depicted having, to contemporary minds, something of the same interest as had tales of ancient mythology to those for whom classical education had given ancient legend almost the force of historical reality. The most popular of the new works, at least, were of the historical order. These, doubtless because both in characterization and description they demanded the composers' fullest energies of expression, were most significant in their influence on later works. As we have said, the greatest writers of French historical opera were not Frenchmen.

The first to be mentioned among the older generation of historical or serious composers is Gasparo Spontini (1774–1851). After youthful successes in Italy he went to Paris in 1803, where he found that much alteration of his hitherto purely Neapolitan style would be needed. *Milton* (1804) proves that he was able very rapidly to effect this change; and that the larger manner stimulated him to a far more profound imaginative invention was seen in the next work *La Vestale*, one of his several masterpieces. Gluck and Mozart were now his models. His subject—a tale of the desecration of the sacred fire—was a mixture of legend, history, and romance; his treatment so vivid as to achieve, in spite of opposition from both singers and jealous cliques, an almost unprecedented success. It was performed in 1807. *Fernando Cortez* (1809, later remodeled) was more literally historical in theme, and not less appealing. These two works gave Spontini great repute in Paris. Their massiveness and martial splendor were particularly acceptable in that Napoleonic era. A shortlived conductorship of the Italian Opera (united with the Comédie Française) revealed many disagreeable traits in Spontini's character, but his position as an artist was maintained. One or two minor works only intervene between the production of *Cortez* and his last Parisian opera *Olympie*, probably his most imposing effort. This was based on Voltaire's tragedy, the operatic text being far inferior to those of *La Vestale* and *Cortez* (the work of Étienne di Jouy). It was almost unsuccessful; but the impression made by the earlier operas on King Frederick William III of Prussia was such that Spontini was invited in 1820 to assume the conductorship of the Berlin Opera. In spite of serious disagreements with Count Brühl, the general director, *Olympie* was performed on May 14, 1821, with vast success. Five weeks later, however, occurred the first performance of Weber's *Der Freischütz*, whose direct appeal to German sentiment proved far more significant than Spontini's more spectacular and astonishing effects. But one great work was written after this reverse in his fortunes—*Agnes von Hohenstaufen*, obviously a German historical subject. It is regarded by many as his greatest work; yet so unpopular had Spontini become, through his overbearing demeanor at the Opera, that it was unsuccessful. Eight years later (1837) a revised version was performed; it was vastly improved, but not more favorably received. In 1841 he was actually driven from his conductor's post, and left Berlin shortly after. Thereafter, although respectfully regarded everywhere, he passed from active influence in the musical world. He was the last of those to whom the classic ideal was a living inheritance.

ROSSINI, BELLINI, AND DONIZETTI

Without a spark of respect for classicism, but possessed of inordinate talent, a ready wit, and an immediate understanding of the public, Gioacchino Rossini, in contrast to Spontini, vividly represents the antithesis between the dying classic ideal and that of the modern world. Passionately fond of music, he hated all the drudgery of counterpoint and all the accepted machinery of composition. He learned to sing and to play the horn, the piano, and later the 'cello. His enthusiasm for the quartets of Haydn and Mozart was so great that he was nicknamed *Il Tedeschino* —the little German. His affability and talent made him many friends; and through one of these he was commissioned to write an opera for Venice. *The Matrimonial Market*, accordingly, was produced in 1810—an opera buffa which was very well received. Rossini took full advantage of this auspicious start. Opera after opera poured from his facile pen, some failing, more succeeding; and as early as 1812 he won a signal triumph at La Scala in Milan with *La Pietra del Paragone*, in which for the first time (but not the last) he made use of his famous crescendo in the finale. *Tancredi* (Venice, 1813) was received with mad enthusiasm; *Elisabetta, regina d'Inghilterra* (Bologna, 1815) was equally successful (here, for the first time, the recitatives are accompanied by the strings); and with *Il Barbiere di Siviglia* (to the same libretto as that which Paisiello had set) he won, after an inauspicious first performance, the greatest triumph of his career. Paisiello's *Barber* was destined to be quite forgotten. *Cenerentola* ("Cinderella"), produced in Rome in 1817, is the only other comic opera of Rossini which can rival it. In these and his other works he borrowed without scruple, either from his own earlier works or from other masters; but the fact is far less important than the use he made of his borrowed material.

Most of Rossini's work thus far was in comedy; but several attempts in the serious style had been made, and a significant contribution toward the modernization of this genre was *Otello*, produced at Naples in 1816. In the production of this work Isabella Colbran, his future wife, had a principal part. It was she indeed who had aroused Rossini's interest in serious opera. The public could not endure the tragic ending, and Rossini was complaisant enough to provide another for the performance in Rome. *Armida*, highly romantic, and *Mosè in Egitto* ("Moses in Egypt," an oratorio with theatrical setting) show the trend of his mind; and *Ermione* (Naples, 1819), with its almost complete lack of vocal ornament, suggests a revolt from his earlier willingness to please at all costs. The revolt was temporary, however, or at least not complete. He produced more works for Naples—*Ricciardo e Zoraide, La Donna del Lago,* and *Maometto secondo*—until the revolution of 1820 drove his patron, the King, from the city.

Barbaja, the director of the theatre, thereupon arranged a visit of his operatic company to Vienna; Rossini, whose fame was already high at the Austrian capital, accompanied them. A violent Rossini fever was the result, bad (as we have seen) in its effect on Beethoven and Schubert, but tending in some measure to intensify Rossini's more serious purposes. In Vienna he began *Semiramide*—except for *William Tell,* his most important serious opera. It was produced in Venice in 1823, without much success. Rossini, embittered, resolved to write no more operas for Italy. A commission from London was accepted which came to nothing because of the failure of the theatre, but the flattering reception he had received in Paris, on the way, resulted in a directorship of the Théâtre Italien, followed by a post of "First composer to the King" which kept him in Paris until 1829. His assimilation of the French style is seen in his last great work *William Tell,* produced at the *Académie* in 1829. Here he has given up all those easy means of making mere effect which largely mar his earlier works. The music, it is true, is not always suited to the situations—the Overture, for instance, having little to do with the theme of the play—but the ideas themselves are worked out to logical musical conclusions, and the sincerity of the effort is apparent in every bar.

Before leaving Paris he had made an arrangement with the French government to write only for the French stage, and to write an opera every two years. *William Tell* was the only work written under this agreement. Charles X was deposed in 1830; the new government repudiated the contract, and Rossini went to court to establish his rights. In 1835 he won his suit; but hearing Meyerbeer's *Huguenots* early in 1836, he came to the strange and irrevocable decision to write no more operas. He had himself produced Meyerbeer's *Crociato in Egitto* at the Théâtre Italien, learning thus to know something of his rival's powers. Though he composed much in other styles (the strangely unequal *Stabat Mater,* some other choral pieces, and much piano music) he contributed nothing more to the progress of musical thought. That contribution may be summed up as, first of all, a great stimulus to the art of singing (in the sense, chiefly, of virtuosity, but not without relation to expression); a thorough modernization (not largely prophetic, but fully contemporaneous) of theme and general expressive handling in Italian opera; a new and colorful vividness in orchestration; and the use of effective accompaniment for the *recitativo secco*. He wrote with great facility. The *Barber* was put on paper in thirteen days—"probably," said Donizetti, "because he is so lazy." Indeed, his indolence was almost equal to his genius; and to his laziness is due his early indifference to stricter training, his half-cynical acceptance of himself as only greater than his meaner contemporaries, his sudden resolve to compose no more opera, and his later serious indulgence in mere sensuality. He himself thought that the *Barber*, parts of *Otello*, and *Tell* would be the only works of his to survive—a singularly keen judgment; but it was no mean genius which created the *Barber*.

No other stage in Europe—neither La Scala in Milan, nor the Operas of Vienna, Berlin, or London—inspired such widespread European respect as the Paris Opéra; and no Italian composer could achieve European distinction until he had been heard in Paris. Parisian taste, as we have seen, repudiated most purely foreign importations and demanded concessions to its own manner, such as we have seen in the cases of *La Vestale* and *William Tell*. That trend toward the *drame lyrique*, however, shows another aspect of French operatic interest; and to this two Italians contributed an essentially Italian influence while they were at the same time induced to make certain changes in their own manner. The first of these composers was Vincenzo Bellini (1801–1835). Possessed of a natural gift of melody, Bellini acquired little else in the way of a composer's equipment; but this one gift sufficed. Trained at Naples, he produced there his first opera *Adelson e Salvina* in 1825. Another in the following year gave him a commission for La Scala. *Il Pirata*, which was produced there in 1827, created a furore, and was soon heard in Paris and London. *I Capuletti ed i Montecchi* (Venice, 1830), and *La Sonnambula* and *Norma* (both produced Milan, 1831) with their flood of simple, haunting tune, gave Bellini a vogue with the general public which had hardly been matched and which is highly indicative of the spread of operatic interest in the direction of the more sentimental type of romanticism.

In 1833, after an extended visit to London, Bellini went to Paris where by Rossini's advice he was commissioned to write an opera for the Théâtre Italien. After some study of Parisian desires, especially in the matter of orchestration and dramatic (or theatrical) effect, he produced *I Puritani* (1835)—obviously historical in plot but feeble in dramatic interest. Again, owing to its melodic charm, the work was hugely successful, the exquisite voices of Rubini (a remarkably high tenor) and Madame Grisi (a favorite of Rossini's) also contributing much to its popularity. *I Puritani* was Bellini's last opera. Contracting a severe illness during a visit to an English friend at Puteaux, he died, not yet thirty-five years of age. The world has long ceased to thrill to Bellini's tender tunes, finding them insipid and characterless, washed only in an odor of romance.

The second of these more purely Italian composers was Gaetano Donizetti (1797–1848). Trained at Naples like Bellini, and showing rather more comprehension of the problems of musicianship, he completed his studies at Bergamo and produced his first opera *Enrico di Borgogna* in 1818 at Venice. Only moderate success attended this and many other works produced at Rome, Naples, and other Italian cities, until the appearance of *Anna Bolena* (Milan, 1830) which was soon a European favorite. Another historical opera, *Lucrezia Borgia*, written in 1833 for Milan, was taken in 1840 to Paris; but its performance there was forbidden by Victor Hugo (author of the tragedy from which the libretto was taken) so that its title had to be changed to *La Rinegata* ("The Renegade") and the Italians at the court of Pope Alexander VI to Turks. *Lucia di Lammermoor*, probably the most popular of all Donizetti's operas, was written for Naples in 1835. The famous Sextet, and the almost infamous Mad Scene will suggest to the reader both the qualities of Donizetti's melody and his lack of taste and of true musical expression for a dramatic situation.

After 1840, although he still traveled much, Donizetti lived chiefly in Paris. *La Favorita* was his first work to have its initial performance there. Although its change in style is not remarkable, it failed (although highly successful in Paris) to please Italian listeners. *The Daughter of the Regiment*, in a lighter vein, was slower of acceptance, though its sprightliness was at last fully revealed in the singing of Jenny Lind, Patti, and others in London. *Linda di Chamouni* was well received in Vienna in 1842, as were certain religious compositions in the strict style which revealed to the German critics a power not suspected in the gifted Italian. In 1843 he returned to Paris, producing a serious opera *Dom Sebastien* which was a failure, and a lighter work *Don Pasquale*, whose brilliance and gaiety pleased Paris beyond measure. *Maria di Rohan*, his last important opera, written in the same year for Vienna, is said to show something of the earnestness and vigor which Verdi later displayed in greater degree. Neither Bellini nor Donizetti contributed much that was permanent to the serious opera; but their successes are a reflection of a strong current of operatic taste which Verdi was soon to reveal as more significantly appreciative than it appeared to be at the moment.

MEYERBEER

While this picture of operatic activity at the opening of the thirties shows much confusion and uncertainty of taste, it shows also a large and growing appetite for operatic pleasure. None of the artists so far mentioned had been able to produce an opera in which all the varied and conflicting interests of Germans, Italians, and Frenchmen could be focused into a single ideal impression. Such an achievement was perhaps impossible; but for a time that ideal seemed to have been attained by Giacomo Meyerbeer. He was born in 1791 (the year of Mozart's death) in Berlin, the eldest son of a rich and cultivated family. (His real name was Jacob Liebmann Beer; he added the prefix "Meyer" in recognition of a legacy from a relative of that name.) He showed both inordinate aptitude as a pianist and distinctive talent for composition—gifts which his parents took great pains to cultivate. Zelter, Bernard Anselm Weber, and finally Abbé Vogler at Darmstadt, were his teachers. His diligence was unbounded, so that he learned the technique of stricter writing and composed an oratorio and many exercises in fugue and cantata forms before turning to opera. His first operas *The Admiral* (1811) and *Jephtha's Vow* (1812), and a comic opera *The Two Caliphs* (1813)—all written in accord with Vogler's precepts—were Singspiele which made no especial mark. *The Two Caliphs* failed in Vienna in 1814. Thereafter by Salieri's advice he went to Venice, to learn how to write for the voice. Rossini's *Tancredi* revealed many new possibilities and reawakened his failing self-confidence. Abandoning the style of the Singspiel, he proceeded to adopt that of Italian opera and rapidly became Rossini's only rival. Six operas in the Italian style were produced between 1818 and 1822. The best of these, which he afterwards called his "wild oats," was *Margherita d'Anjou;* but neither these nor his earlier works survived on the stage. A transition from the Italian manner, now growing wearisome to him, is seen in *Il Crociato in Egitto* ("The Crusader in Egypt") which, although possessing many strong dramatic features to which the Italians were generally indifferent, was produced with unbounded success in Venice in 1824. Rossini himself produced the *Crociato* at Paris in 1826; and this performance, which Meyerbeer attended, determined much of his future.

Meyerbeer soon took up his residence in Paris, studied not only the French operatic style but French history and literature, and produced at last, in 1831, *Robert le Diable*—a mixture of legendary, heroic, and allegorical characteristics—which took Paris by storm. Musically, it shows hitherto unexhibited command both of declamation and melody, vivid instrumentation, and climactic structure. The most complete amalgamation of Italian and French styles which had as yet been achieved, it showed little of that German seriousness and penetrating sentiment which one might have expected from a composer born and trained in Germany. But Meyerbeer was always the clever assimilator of current styles rather than the possessor of a distinctive style of his own. He took infinite pains, however, to make every detail of his work effective, disputing with Scribe, his librettist, over the tiniest turns of phrase, and making and remaking his music with the same meticulousness. It was thus natural that even after such a success as that of *Robert le Diable*, Meyerbeer should produce no other work until 1836. In that year appeared *The Huguenots*—probably his finest work, and the one which, as we have seen, determined Rossini to write no more opera. The tale is permeated with the horrors and intolerances of the Massacre of St. Bartholomew; and these stark and primitive emotions are intensified for us in the spectacle of the love of Raoul, a Protestant nobleman, and Valentine, the daughter of one of the Catholic leaders. The music lacks the subtler qualities of individual characterization, but is extraordinary in its vivid illustration of the more striking and terrible aspects of the scene. The dark fervor of the Protestants is often voiced in the melody of Luther's great hymn *Ein' feste Burg*. This work probably represents the pinnacle of historical opera.

Only two great works were added to this not very large list of operas —*L'Africaine* (which was begun in 1838) and *Le Prophète* (the book also by Scribe) which he began and completed in 1843. A three-act German opera, *Ein Feldlager in Schlesien*, was written for Berlin, where Meyerbeer had been appointed Generalmusikdirector in 1842; but this does not compare with the two greater works. *The Prophet*, produced at Paris in 1849, is somewhat akin to *The Huguenots* in theme, being based on the life of John of Leyden. Its almost unrelieved somberness and its lack of an interesting youthful heroine made it less popular, though the treatment is equally grandiose. Some parts of the *Feldlager* were used in the composition of *L'Etoile du Nord*, produced at the Opéra Comique in 1854. Another comedy, *Le Pardon de Ploërmel*, more widely known under the title *Dinorah*, was given in 1859. Neither was wholly suited to his powers, which were most fully stimulated by historical themes. He seems to have realized this, working laboriously at *L'Africaine* until little remained of the original conception. This is also generally historical in plot, Vasco da Gama being the hero; but the treatment is less purely illustrative and spectacular than in the earlier works, and it is the most truly musical of all. His death occurred during the last preparations for the first performance in May, 1864; the work was produced only in 1865. By this time, Meyerbeer's creative leadership in opera—undeniable in the thirties—had been surpassed. A truer concept of dramatic psychology and of the musical expression of character had arisen, and was already largely exemplified, chiefly in the work of Richard Wagner but also in that of some lesser men. Meyerbeer's work in the light of these later developments was soon to appear hollow and artificial, no matter how firm and imposing its glittering surface might be. It is his very competency in illustration which makes him unable to express in music the truer realities of drama. Yet there is no doubt that *The Huguenots*, compared with *I Puritani*, for example, represents a long step toward the emancipation of opera from the superficialities which had for so long been imposed upon it by convention.

CHAPTER XXVII

The Wagnerian Music Drama

The Larger Problem of Form in Opera

IN their attempts to adjust the form and substance of opera to that profound change in dramatic taste which we have just been observing, it will have been seen that most of the composers were following the time-honored practice of the British in political crises—they were "muddling through." Among all the long list of writers from Gluck to Meyerbeer, there were few who directly pondered Gluck's thesis, or attempted to add anything to the theory of the relations of music and drama. Mozart voiced what was doubtless an instinctive rather than a reasoned conviction when he said that "in opera, willy-nilly, poetry must be the obedient daughter of the music." For he was equally emphatic in insisting that his music embodied the very spirit of the words. Weber conceived opera as an ideal union of all the arts involved; but to effect this union he also relied upon instinct rather than reason. The lesser artists, even though they showed a sincere desire to lead rather than merely to follow existing taste, did little more than adjust their style and expression to apparent public desire. The essential problem of opera remained unpondered.

This is not strange. The opera composer is primarily a musician, not a theorist; and, like his public, is largely the follower of convention in musical expression. We have seen enough of the gradual development of musical forms to realize how, once they have been largely perfected, they become crystallized and almost rigid. This rigidity is only a reflection of the mental inertia of the average listener, who follows with pleasure only that form of musical discourse which he can assimilate with ease. Popular forms, however, are not necessarily the most simple. Repeated contact can make even complex forms popular. The jazz of today is a much more complex type of music than the simple dances and songs of our grandfathers. The madrigal of the sixteenth century was the most

477

widely popular musical form ever invented until it was superseded by the opera. But that supersession was not wholly due to the mere simplicity of the operatic aria; it was due rather to the aptitude of the aria for a new range and character of musical expression. Neither, as we have noted, did the madrigal grow into the opera. There is no instance of a perfected musical form which, of its own momentum, has evolved into a new and more inclusively expressive form. The fugue did not grow into the sonata; it was superseded by the sonata, because again new conditions of life (in themselves unrelated to problems of musical structure) presented new types of emotion which music had to learn to express if it was to remain a living art. Perceiving these new emotions, the composer in any period first naturally attempts to adapt the existing, readily intelligible forms to the new problem of expression. But everybody knows what happened when the new wine was put into the old bottles. And the stage we have reached in the history of opera is that at which the old bottles were beginning to bulge.

More concretely, the forms of music in use by the dramatists of the early nineteenth century were modifications of the existing instrumental and vocal forms. The overture—when it was not a mere shapeless pasticcio of tunes from the opera—was a modification of sonata form. The vocal pieces, although they were no longer arias strictly of the old *da capo* order, were often but thinly disguised elaborations of the aria, and were at best a kind of *durchkomponirtes Lied* set to a text which constituted, after all, no more than a fragment of that continuous representation of developing action, the whole act of the drama. Accompanied recitative had largely superseded the *recitativo secco;* but that recitative, while it could palliate the intolerable drop from the plane of musical stimulation to that of bald speech which was the fault of the Singspiel and the opéra comique, could not disguise the fact that the real music (the aria) often stopped just at the moment when the action was most urgently going on, because the musical form of the aria had come to an end. To the uncritical majority this made little difference. They had become accustomed to expect music rather than drama at the opera. But it was not to such listeners that Gluck's ideas had been addressed. Many more critical minds had begun to perceive the necessity of a dramatic musical form more extended than any existing purely musical form. They began to envisage a form coextensive with the whole act, or even with the whole drama. This vision had been partially realized, as we have seen, in the extended finale. As yet, however, these finales consisted of an uninterrupted succession of several smaller forms, each nearly complete in itself —although there might be interrelation in the shape of repeated thematic material or repeated fragments of earlier sections.

Essentially, it was this great expansion of musical-dramatic form which Wagner was to attempt and in large measure to accomplish. The whole history of his attempt—of the slow expansion of his vision to a point where the elements of the problem were at last seen in something like due proportion—is complex and difficult to follow. Still more difficult is the ultimate criticism of his conclusions, and of his actual results as they appear in the light of his conclusions. But not only the present-day problem of opera, but most of the peculiar problems of modern music arise in one or another of the Wagnerian innovations. Hence, his efforts and theories may not lightly be passed over.

WAGNER'S TRAINING AS MUSIC DRAMATIST

Wagner was born in 1813 at Leipzig. His father died shortly after, and the widow married Ludwig Geyer, an actor, poet, and painter of Dresden, who was sincerely concerned for the boy's future but was unable, before his death in 1821, to discover any definite trend in the youth's talents. At the Kreuzschule in Dresden, Wagner showed much interest in Greek, German poetry, and tragedy in general, but little affection for music. He tells us that he began to write a tragedy, largely inspired by Greek models, which was so sanguinary that the last act had to be carried on chiefly by the ghosts of the personages who had already perished. Nevertheless he acquired a real knowledge and a deep appreciation of this ancient art. Removing again to Leipzig in 1827, he continued his education at the gymnasium and at the university, and was now for the first time deeply moved by music—especially by the Symphonies of Beethoven, which he studied minutely. Heinrich Dorn, then teaching at Leipzig, later Wagner's successor at Riga and at last his bitter opponent, says of him, "I doubt whether there was ever a young musician who knew Beethoven's works more thoroughly than Wagner in his eighteenth year. The master's overtures and larger instrumental compositions he had copied for himself in score. He went to sleep with the quartets, he sang the songs, and whistled the concertos (for his piano playing was never of the best)." Beethoven's *Egmont* Overture had suggested to him that music was the essential thing needed to give meaning to his great tragedy, upon which he was still engaged. To write this music, he felt it needful "to clear up a few principles of thorough bass"; an attempt to do this for himself proving futile, he had lessons, first from Gottlieb Müller and later from Theodor Weinlig, Cantor at the Thomas Schule (Bach's old position). Weinlig is extolled by Wagner for his sane, progressive, unpedantic manner of teaching—not by laying down precepts, but by carefully correcting and guiding the student's own efforts. Although Wag-

ner's attention was thus first directed chiefly toward instrumental composition (he wrote a Symphony, several Overtures, a Piano Sonata, and
other smaller compositions), it is certain that Weinlig's influence was
most beneficial in stimulating Wagner's imagination and in supporting his
self-confidence. The Symphony once figured on a program at the Gewandhaus, but displayed little that was significant for the future.

Wagner's entrance upon a professional career (in 1833) was facilitated
by his elder brother Albert, a tenor singer at Würzburg, who procured
him a position as chorus master in the theatre of that place. He filled this
position competently, beginning to acquire that knowledge of conducting and of theatrical production generally which he was later to exhibit
in such marked degree. In the previous summer he had already drafted
a libretto for an opera *Die Hochzeit* ("The Wedding") at Prague, and
some of the music was written; but his sister Rosalie's disapproval of the
subject caused him to abandon the work. He now began his first completed opera *Die Feen* ("The Fairies"). It was never performed during
the composer's lifetime, but was given at Munich in 1888, showing real
attraction for the public, as well as the merely historical interest which
naturally attached to its belated production. His next attempt, *Das Liebesverbot* ("The Forbidding of Love"), was a result of the hearing of
Bellini's *Montagues and Capulets* and of Auber's *Masaniello*. The superficiality of Wagner's music, in comparison with Beethoven's, was obvious
enough; but he was now, like Meyerbeer with his Italian operas, in the
midst of his sowing of musical wild oats; and, greatly desirous of success, he was somewhat indifferent to the means of procuring it. The plot
is based almost wholly on the more licentious elements of Shakespeare's
Measure for Measure.

In 1834 a more responsible post was undertaken—that of Musikdirector
at the Magdeburg theatre. In the spring of 1836 the theatre became bankrupt, closing with a chaotic performance of *Das Liebesverbot*. He next
found a berth at Königsberg, whither several of the Magdeburg troupe
had migrated—among them a young actress, Minna Planer, with whom
Wagner had fallen in love, and whom, after having been assured of the
position of conductor at the theatre, he married. Minna's devotion to
Wagner was undoubted. So also was her inability to understand the more
and more fantastic visions of operatic greatness which were beginning to
ferment in his mind. Their future life was a strange medley of disagreements and reconciliations, ending only with a long separation and Minna's death in 1866. The theatre at Magdeburg also went bankrupt, and
Wagner, on Dorn's recommendation, was chosen director of a new theatre at Riga, on the Russian side of the Baltic.

Rienzi AND *The Flying Dutchman*

With Wagner as conductor and Minna as leading actress for the purely theatrical productions, the position at Riga was a distinct step in advance. Wagner produced here some of his instrumental compositions; but his mind was set on greater success than Riga could offer, and he began the writing of a grand historical opera *Rienzi* (based on Bulwer-Lytton's novel), which was to compete with Meyerbeer, but which was altogether beyond the resources of the establishment at Riga to produce. The story is that of a popular hero, Rienzi, espousing the cause of the people of Rome against the aristocratic families of the Orsini and the Colonni. Wagner's enthusiasm for this subject is not without interest in connection with his later behavior during the May Revolution of 1849 at Dresden. Characteristically leaving behind him considerable financial obligations, he left Riga in the summer of 1839, bound for Paris where he hoped to secure a performance of his as yet uncompleted *Rienzi*. The journey in a sailing vessel was tempestuous, giving extraordinary vividness to the sailors' tale of *The Flying Dutchman*, a version of which he had already read in Heine, and which was to form the basis of his next operatic work. After a week in London, the Wagners went to Boulogne, where Meyerbeer, now the oracle of the Parisian operatic stage, was spending the summer. Meyerbeer professed great interest in Wagner's work and promised many favors with the managers in Paris. Whatever may have been Meyerbeer's intentions, his promises brought no results. No theatre in Paris was able to produce *Rienzi;* or if able, none was willing. For two years he and Minna lived on the edge of destitution, Wagner making arrangements of popular airs from current operas, and writing critical and other articles for various journals. This latter channel of expression for his constructive ideas was later to be much cultivated. He finished *Rienzi* in 1840; found it already somewhat repugnant to his rapidly expanding sense of what opera should be, and turned to *The Flying Dutchman* as a subject which could be treated more in accordance with his ideals. M. Pillet, the director of the Opéra, took such a fancy to the libretto of this work that he proposed to buy it—to be set by a French composer! (It was given at Paris in 1842 with music by Dietsch—after Wagner, vainly protesting, had been paid 500 francs for his book.) Wagner completed all the music except the Overture in six weeks, and, hopeless of any success in Paris, sent this to Berlin for approval as he had already sent *Rienzi* to Dresden. In addition he composed some songs and one great orchestral work, *Eine Faust Ouverture*—intended to be the first movement of a *Faust* Symphony which was never completed. In 1842, however, *Rienzi* was actually accepted and put into rehearsal at Dresden; and Wagner left Paris in high hopes.

The performance of *Rienzi* in October, 1842, was a veritable triumph for Wagner. The whole work was drenched in spectacularity, of the kind to which Meyerbeer had accustomed the public; and although there are many moments in which the later Wagner is dimly to be recognized, so little of this finer sensibility is on the surface that the public took the opera without question as a work in the most approved contemporary taste.

Der Fliegende Holländer, on the other hand, which had had only an acceptance of courtesy without thought of immediate performance at Berlin, but was immediately put into rehearsal at Dresden, produced at its performance in January, 1843, a far different effect. Wagner had already perceived the meaninglessness of mere spectacle and the necessity of more penetrating psychological character drawing. He was perceiving, that is, the real difference between opera of the old order and true music drama. But although *The Flying Dutchman* represents a bold step in the new direction, it is far from showing full comprehension of the greatness of the problem. The Overture is an astonishing symphonic poem of the sea; and amid the turmoil of the elements the leading motive of the ill-fated Dutchman sounds forth the weird personality of the hero in unmistakable identity. The play itself is less convincing. Wagner intended a sort of allegory of the redemption of erring man by constant woman: a theme which, indeed, permeated most of his later work. But we do not readily identify ourselves with the hero, and are consequently at a loss to explain the strength of Senta's devotion, which impels her to leap into the sea after the departing hero who has appeared rather pettish in his conviction that his suit has failed. The redemption, however, has been accomplished. The spirits of Senta and the Dutchman ascend out of the sea to heaven before our eyes.[1] We are dimly aware that their earthly union could scarcely have been happy; but the sense of tragic necessity is nevertheless lacking, and the redemption is more remote than we desire. Naturally, in its embodiment of this unusual theme, the music is widely different from that of *Rienzi.* The hero, repellent as he is, is at least characterized as a distinctive figure, and Senta, especially in the wonderful Ballad in the second act, is vividly drawn as the passionate and devoted woman whom Wagner intends. Daland, the mercenary father, is probably incapable of musical representation, even by a maturer Wagner; and Eric, the disappointed lover of Senta, hardly has a chance to attain individuality. The music, although continuous and with infrequent

---

[1] Mr. Newman amusingly calls our attention to the fact that Senta's death achieved redemption for nobody below the rank of captain.

drops into the baldness of mere recitative, still lacks that largeness of form which is to make of a whole act of *Tristan and Isolde* an almost indivisible musical unit. The successive closed forms or "numbers" of the older opera still appear, somewhat hidden under the apparent continuity of the music. But the principle of the leading motive—the use of characteristic musical phrases, identified with persons or forces of the drama in such a way that the orchestra, instead of merely accompanying the singing, is often able to comment illuminatingly upon the action—is far more fully employed than in *Rienzi* and shows sign of becoming the ruling principle of the musical structure. In freshness and vigor, too, the music as a whole is of unbounded promise. *The Flying Dutchman*, if it was hardly the ideal "art work of the future," was certainly not of the past.

Tannhäuser AND Lohengrin

Wagner's rejection of merely historical plot is perhaps the most significant fact of his development thus far. To see that a drama is something more than a pictorial history, and that it is fatal to submerge the deeper psychological forces of drama in a stream of dramatically unmotivated historical incident, was a considerable feat of penetration in an opera writer of the early forties. In choosing popular legend as the source of his plot Wagner was not merely following the trend of romanticism. He felt that he was appealing to profounder human instinct than that which is revealed in historical incident, however striking—that he was dealing with the primal impulses of individual human action. This conviction continued to grow in him; and his next drama *Tannhäuser* is accordingly a continuation of the purpose already pursued in the *Dutchman*.

In Paris he had come upon the story of *Tannhäuser* in a popular form. Parallel study of the romantic labors of the Minnesinger suggested a historical background for his plot, and the result was one of the most convincing of all Wagner's stories. Again the theme of redemption is the underlying idea. Tannhäuser, knight and Minnesinger, has wearied of the smug conventionalities of society and has fled to the court of Venus. Here he is discovered, already convinced of his error and yearning to escape to earth. Returning, he is warmly received by his old associates in spite of his behavior, and learns that Elizabeth, whom he had deserted, still loves him. But when taking part in a contest of song held by the Minnesinger, he unaccountably bursts out with a sudden paean in praise of Venus. Scandalized, the knights are about to kill him; but Elizabeth intervenes, and secures the lightening of his sentence to that of banishment. He is ordered to join a band of pilgrims on their way to Rome, there to seek absolution for his sin. When the pilgrims return, Tannhäuser is not among them. Elizabeth, whose saintly prayers have been offered incessantly in his behalf, watches the procession with saddened heart. Furtively, at night, Tannhäuser comes alone, meeting his old friend Wolfram to whom he tells the tale of his pilgrimage—how in spite of his most sincere repentance, the Pope has told him that his sin can no more be forgiven than his dry staff can put forth leaves and live again. Desperate, he is hastening to the Venusberg; Venus herself appears to beckon him, and Wolfram's effort to hold him back is failing, when behind the scene there is heard a choir imploring Heaven to receive the soul of Elizabeth who, in an anguish of love and pity for Tannhäuser, has just given up her life. Venus vanishes at the sound; Elizabeth's body is borne in, and Tannhäuser dies beside it. But as a sign of his redemption, his staff has blossomed. It will be seen that it is far easier to assimilate the allegorical episodes of the Venusberg into the human figure of the hero than is the case with the *Dutchman*.

Tannhäuser was performed at Dresden in October, 1845. Wagner had hoped, in spite of the only partial success of the *Dutchman*, to find the public fully in sympathy with this more perfect embodiment of his new ideas. Instead, the public was bewildered and the critics fell foul of the work with a zest that augured ill for Wagner's future. The Overture was thought long, awkward, atrocious; the opening scene in the Venusberg (which Wagner later enlarged for an ill-fated performance in Paris) was too new in tone to be understood, and fell flat, and Tannhäuser's narration to Wolfram—music which now seems incomparably the most expressive in the opera—was quite incomprehensible. In spite of the Pilgrim's Chorus, the March, and the Song to the Evening Star, no melody could be found in the opera. Wagner was profoundly disappointed, but realized that another kind of effort than that of opera-making lay before him—an effort to make the public understand the opera as more than a mere evening's entertainment. Circumstances soon arose which gave form to this effort. *Lohengrin*, a finer embodiment than he had as yet achieved of his new theories, was steadily progressing; but the final formulation of the theory itself came as a result of Wagner's participation in the May Revolution of 1849 and his consequent exile as a politically dangerous character.

Superficially, the fable of *Lohengrin* is perplexing. We see a knight who comes from afar in response to the prayer of Elsa, falsely accused of the murder of her brother Godfrey. The knight accepts the challenge of Frederick, her accuser, on condition that no one shall ask to know his name, his race, or anything about him. Elsa being vindicated in the trial by battle, marriage with the knight is the not unexpected sequel; but the condition of anonymity is still imposed by him. Elsa's curiosity and fear are roused by Ortrud, Frederick's sister, to such a pitch that after the wedding Elsa cannot refrain from demanding to know the name of her spouse. Her husband thereupon tells the assembled court that he is a knight of the Grail; that it is his mission to offer aid to injured virtue; that he is the son of Parsifal, and that his name is Lohengrin. But his vows require of him that he keep his identity a secret. Having revealed it, therefore, he must be gone. Leaving to Elsa his horn, sword, and ring, he is about to depart when Ortrud sneeringly suggests that if he had stayed he might have restored Godfrey. Kneeling, Lohengrin silently prays. The white dove of the Grail hovers over his boat; and the swan which had drawn it is restored to the human form of Godfrey, who had been thus bewitched by Ortrud. Drawn by the dove, Lohengrin's craft sails away, and Elsa sinks lifeless in Godfrey's arms. Beneath this improbable tale, Wagner felt that he had hidden a profound truth about the reality of human devotion. Lohengrin desired to be loved, not for his knightly prowess but for himself alone; Elsa, freely giving her whole self, could not endure that less than the whole self of her husband should be given in return. The tragedy lies in the lack of complete trust.

Wagner's music goes far toward making clear the confused argument of the drama. In subtlety of suggestion, whether of the characters themselves or of the mystic influence of the Grail, it is far beyond any of his earlier music save perhaps Tannhäuser's narration. Individual, closed forms almost disappear in the continuous stream of the music. Only occasionally is there the baldness of recitative. The action is relatively rapid. The scenes, especially those of the second act, are in themselves of great interest. If Wagner had written nothing after *Lohengrin*, we should have been compelled to admit a long advance in the progress of opera toward drama.

WAGNER'S FINAL THEORY: *Opera and Drama*

Thrown out of active contact with music by the Revolution, Wagner now found both time and incentive to study the whole problem of music drama as it appeared in the light of history and contemporary practice. The result was *Oper und Drama*, certainly the most penetrating discussion of operatic theory which had ever been written. This larger work amplified the thesis which had already been propounded in two shorter works, *Art and Revolution* and *The Art-work of the Future*. Wagner's conclusions were reached through a most elaborate argument which took into account both the contemporary opera and the history (as Wagner saw it) not only of opera but of musical ideas in themselves. And since his thesis underlies not only his own works but much of the music drama and even of the instrumental music of his followers, we must attempt a brief summary of his ideas.

His first postulate is that "The error of the Art-genre of opera lay in the fact that a means of expression (Music) had been made the end; the end or objective of expression (the Drama) had been made a means." The musical foundation of opera had been the aria; and this aria itself had been designed to display rather the singer's perfected art than any truth of feeling. Its text also, the work of cultured poets, was addressed not to the hearts of humanity but to the cultured sensibilities of a select social group; but even this value was lost in the overweening conceit of the singer, to whose pride of vocalization both textual and musical meaning had to be sacrificed. Even Gluck's reform "consisted only in the 'revolt of the composer against the caprices of the singer. . . . In the relation of poet to composer there was not the slightest alteration. . . . It was only Gluck's followers who took advantage of their opportunity to enlarge the closed forms of music." A long discussion of the works of Cherubini, Méhul, Spontini, Mozart, Rossini, and Meyerbeer follows, showing that although in their work these forms are truly expanded, and the recitative more closely amalgamated with the aria, the essential flaw in the art form remains—"that a mere means of expression has attempted, out of itself, to dictate the purpose of the drama." With a discussion of melody as arising either out of the mere desire to give formal and sensuous pleasure (this type being the sterile, formal melody of the operatic singer) or out of a desire to express something in the emotional experience of man that lies outside the realm of purely musical feeling (the type whose invention exalts Beethoven as the real discoverer of the possibility of true musical expression, but not of the true means of expression)—with this discussion the first division of his book *The Opera and the Nature of Music* ends. He turns next to the examination of the Drama.

The Stage-Play and the Nature of Dramatic Poetry is the title of the second division. "Modern Drama has a dual origin: one natural, belonging to our own historical development, the Romance; and one alien, engrafted upon our culture through reflection, the Greek Drama. The true germ of our poetry lies in the Romance; but in the struggle to make this source as tasteful as possible, our poets have repeatedly fallen into a more or less exact imitation of the Greek Drama. The highest efflorescence of that drama which derives from the Romance we have in Shakespeare's plays; at the farthest possible remove from this drama we meet its complete antithesis, the Tragédie of Racine." Describing at length the work of all the greatest dramatists from Shakespeare to Goethe and Schiller, Wagner comes to the conclusion that the spoken drama is in the same plight as the opera—subject to the whims and talents of actors; concerned with spectacle and effect rather than with truth and reality of feeling. With such drama, true music can have nothing to do. And the impotence of the current drama will be found, in the last analysis to be grounded in the substance itself of that drama. This substance, as was just said, is the Romance. He proceeds, then, to search for the true basis of drama.

"Man is the Poet in a two-fold sense: through observation and through communication. The *natural* poetic gift is the power of creating, out of outward sense-impressions, an inner imaginative vision of these impressions; the *artistic* gift is the power of communicating this vision to others." But artistic representation is intelligible only to those whose natural poetic imagination has already conceived the vision. "Greek tragedy is the artistic realization of the content and the spirit of the Grecian Myth"— the myth being an expression of the natural poetic gift (through observation) of the whole people. It reflects indeed the popular attitude toward religion, nature, and the whole of life; and its center, after all, is man. In the Christian myth, on the contrary, both man and nature are reduced in importance; earthly life is of no consequence, and the greatest glory of life is only to be won through death, the negation of life. Here no concept of life as a unification of physical, moral, and intellectual interests is possible. Nature observation becomes physics and chemistry; religion becomes theology and philosophy; community life becomes politics and diplomacy; art is only knowledge and aesthetics; and the myth itself becomes a historical chronicle. To represent man and his circumstances as they are externally, not as they appear to the true imagination —this is henceforward the task of both historian and artist. The Romance therefore presents to us not men but citizens; not the reality of life, but the mechanism of history. The poet's art has turned into politics; and we shall have no more true poetry until we have no more politics. The Romance, which proceeds inward from the outside—from a complex detailing of circumstances to the representation of an individuality which is all but submerged in those circumstances—is thus the opposite of the Drama, which proceeds outward from the inside: building, against the background of a simple, immediately intelligible environment, an ever richer development of individuality.

In the Drama, we must understand through feeling. Understanding says to us, "this *is* so," only when feeling has said, "this *must be* so." Feeling, however, is intelligible only through itself: it understands no other language. Dramatic action therefore can be made intelligible only when it is directly addressed to the feeling; and the dramatist must contrive his plot accordingly. Merely historical plot, since it is addressed to the intellect rather than to the feeling, is lacking in purely human appeal. But since the intellect itself perceives only the details of the action as facts or realities, the observer's fantasy must correlate these facts through an act of the imagination—through a vision of these factual realities; and the creation of this vision is itself a kind of miracle. This miracle, however, differs from that upon which religious dogma rests, in that it does not transcend the normal processes of nature. It is merely the full awakening of the understanding through feeling. Word speech—in which of course the spoken drama is cast—is chiefly addressed to the understanding. Feeling, but meagerly fed through word speech, is most readily and fully excited through tone speech. That full awakening of the understanding through feeling (*Gefühlsverständniss*) which is the Drama—the imaginative miracle which every observer must in some sense perform for himself —can thus be stimulated only through a combination of word speech and tone speech.

Word speech and tone speech had a common origin: the instinctive outcry, in which elemental thought and feeling were vented. The gradual interruption and punctuation of this outcry through consonants gave word speech. Tone speech, on the other hand, arose through the expansion and formal organization of the vowel element of speech into musical tone-sequences. The loss in feeling suggestion which language suffered, as it gained in definitional meaning, was to some extent made up through the invention of rhythm and alliteration (*Stabreim*). (End rhyme is a later refinement of poetic art, even less suggestive of the inherent feeling quality of the words.) For complete utterance—for the full expression of that union of thought and feeling which constitutes the individual's imaginative concept of reality—a reunion of these two modes of speech (which were originally one) is necessary. This union may be likened to that of man and woman (word speech being the masculine element while tone speech is the feminine) depending upon fertilization for true productivity. The fruit of this union is the Drama of the Future.

This union is discussed in the third section of the book *Poetic and Musical Art in the Drama of the Future*. The ever-widening separation between poetry and music is first more minutely studied. Both poetic versification and purely musical forms are each condemned as mere cultural satisfactions, appealing only partially to men's whole sensibilities, and incapable of giving true and full expression to that final imaginative concept of human reality in which the facts of experience are fused into an understanding of experience. The opera, as it had been developed up to Wagner's day, was in no sense a true union of these masculine and feminine elements of expression, but only a silly flirtation between them. It was Beethoven who first perceived the barrenness of music; who, in his great instrumental works of the earlier periods, strove with titanic effort to make of music that which by itself it could never be—a completely and

independently expressive art—and who, in his Ninth Symphony, by unit-
ing poetry and music, intimated to the world the true solution of the
problem of expression. Music and poetry are like two travelers who have
set out from the same point in opposite directions. They meet on the
opposite side of the planet. Each has seen half the earth. They exchange
experiences and go on, to complete the circuit of the globe. Meeting
again, they are now undivided. Each has seen all the earth: the poet has
become musician and the musician, poet; and each is now the completely
artistic Man. At that point where they first met, their medium of intercourse was that melody which we have in our own (Wagner's) day.
Parting again, each now takes the path just traversed by the other. The
poet embarks upon the ship in which the musician has traveled—the ship
which is to cross the boundless sea of Harmony. That ship is the Orchestra; or, to change the figure, Harmony may also be regarded as the
sea itself—an element which determines the nature of melody. But since
melody (word-tone-speech) is the core of Drama, harmony (or the agent
of harmony, the orchestra) is itself an essential foundation of Drama.
Our present opera melody is so purely instrumental, and so disrelated to
word sense, as to be more intelligible and more popular when played
by instruments than when sung. This is not true of dramatic melody,
whose color should be that of the voice, not that of instruments, and
which ought to be conditioned by the natural (not the artificial poetic)
accentuation and meaning of the words—a true word-tone melody.

But the orchestra has also its own field of expression. It deals with that
which is verbally inexpressible, and is thus related to gesture—another
vehicle of expression for that which is beyond words. With Dance—
which is the gesture of the whole sentient body—music was associated
from the first. In conventional opera however the close association of
music with the dance pantomime and its conventional figures has robbed
music of most of its suggestive force. This suggestion of bodily move-
ment-impulse needs to be reunited to word-tone melody, if full expressiveness is to be achieved. The Drama of the Future therefore must be created
by an artist who, beginning with a truly poetic concept, realizes it in music which is representative not only of the sense of the words but also of
the manifold suggestions of gesture—and this gesture is not merely that
of an individual, but the *polyphonic* gesture of the whole group of persons engaged in the action. The orchestra, with its manifold capacities for
comment on the action, thus becomes the modern counterpart of the
Chorus in the Greek Drama.

The artist's problem then is the creation, out of these many strands of
interest, of a single form of dramatic expression. "The living core of
dramatic expression is the verse-melody of the actor: to this is related, as

foreboding or anticipatory suggestion (*Ahnung*), the absolute melody of the orchestra; and out of this verse-melody is derived, as a recall (of already achieved action), the thought conveyed by the instrumental motive." No absolute melody, designed for purely musical satisfaction, can fulfill the purposes of Drama. The poetic thought, out of which the whole drama must spring, conditions the form not only of the melody but of the whole dramatic structure, which thus becomes an organic, living action.

The gist of this long argument (in the original, some 300 pages) is that only the drama can fully represent human thought, feeling, and action; and that in the production of such drama, the three arts of Dance, Music, and Poetry (alliteratively expressed in Wagner's phrase *Tanz- Ton- und Tichtkunst*) must combine. The essentially novel form which this combination demanded had been gradually striven for in the whole succession of Wagner's works up to the time of his flight from Dresden. In *Lohengrin*, for example, there is less music in the rounded, closed forms of the Italian opera than in his earlier works. The melody is more immediately expressive of the text, although it is less continuous as pure melody; the foreboding function of the orchestra is fulfilled in the orchestral prelude (not an overture), which fills us with the sense of the mystic influence of the Grail; and the function of recall is performed by the frequent occurrence of musical phrases, earlier associated with Lohengrin, Elsa, Ortrud, and other characters which, as the opera proceeds, take on an almost verbal definiteness of meaning. The form of the music, often expanded so that a whole scene, such as that between Ortrud and Frederick at the opening of the second act, is developed out of a few phrases, is still really musical, although its great dimensions make it difficult to comprehend for the hearer accustomed to shorter, more conclusive pieces. But far as this music is from the type of melody hitherto invariably to be found, it is still equally far from being a full exemplification of Wagner's ideal.

The Ring of the Nibelungs

There can be little doubt that Wagner's theorizing in *Oper und Drama*, aided him in the perfection of his method. The next work after *Lohengrin*, the colossal *Ring of the Nibelungs*, is fully in accord with his thesis. The subject is drawn from Germanic mythology; the action as a whole —characters, objects, forces, even the scenic background—is typified in representative musical phrases called *leading motives*, more or less easily associated with their respective objects, and the whole substance of the music is developed out of these phrases. At those moments when the action develops to lyrical fervor there is truly lyrical music (as in the love scene in the first act of *Die Walküre*); but for the most part the musical process is almost exactly that of an enormously extended symphonic development. The various leading motives are usually introduced in conjunction with some feature of the play which serves to establish the connection between music and action; and, as these themes become more numerous, opportunities are greatly multiplied for orchestral comment on the progress of events through recall of the themes. Only through such a plan of structure would it have been possible to create a work of such magnitude. For the *Ring* consists of four long music plays: a Prologue, *Das Rheingold*, uninterrupted for the more than two hours of its music, and three immense three-act dramas which gradually complete the action initiated in *Das Rheingold—Die Walküre, Siegfried*, and *Die Götterdämmerung*. The fable is too intricate to be condensed adequately here. Its source is in the Germanic myth, the *Nibelungenlied;* the versification is largely in the old alliterative form which is characteristic of those poems; and the music is almost wholly built up out of what, for so immense a scheme, must be regarded as a remarkably small number of leading motives. Of formal, rounded melody there is none save in those scenes where a purely lyric manner is indicated. The thread of the musical idea lies for the most part not in the voice parts but in the continuity of the harmony supplied by the orchestra; and with the aid of this complex instrument—now enlarged and treated with a richness hitherto unknown in operatic scores—Wagner largely achieved that ideal of "endless melody" which, as an expression of the verbally inexpressible in a continuous action, was his ideal in *Oper und Drama*. Magnificent and imposing as the *Ring* must be allowed to be, it has certain faults—largely due to the fact that the poems were written in inverse order, beginning with *Die Götterdämmerung* and ending with *Das Rheingold*—which prevent it from being the ideal embodiment of his theory. The plot is somewhat confused, and the narration often repetitive; the purport of the whole is highly allegorical and hence capable of various interpretations; and—partly because of the vastness of the whole project—Wagner's command of his own new method of composition was not yet supreme. But all the objections which can be urged are as nothing when compared with the positive achievement: unquestionably the greatest operatic design which had ever been conceived.

It was not destined to be completed for many years, however. He worked steadily on the *Ring* and on several lesser critical essays until the spring of 1857, when the music of the great tetralogy was finished as far as the larger part of Act II of *Siegfried*. But the problem of making a living and of introducing his work favorably to the musical world was greatly aggravated by his exile. A journey to London in February, 1855, whither he was invited to conduct a series of concerts for the Philharmonic Orchestra, gave him but little opportunity to propound his own ideas. The chief critics of the London press were prejudiced against him; and though his conducting, especially of the Beethoven Symphonies, proved a revelation to the public, he returned to Zürich little better off in either purse or reputation. The stories of Tristan and Isolde and of Parsifal—legends from the Arthurian Cycle—had attracted him even while he was at work on *Die Walküre*. It now seemed so impossible that the colossal *Ring* could ever be performed that he resolved (partly because of a curious invitation from the Emperor of Brazil to compose an opera for Rio de Janeiro) to set the *Ring* aside and take up the shorter, possibly more popular theme of *Tristan*. The poem was finished early in 1857, and the music of the first act was completed in the winter of the same year. Much assistance, material and spiritual, was offered by many sympathetic friends, the chief of whom at this period were a German banker Otto Wesendonck and his wife Mathilde. The sympathy between Wagner and Mathilde was so great that the proprieties were sorely endangered; and Wagner had to give up the charming house which the Wesendoncks had offered him and go to Venice for the further prosecution of his work. The second act of *Tristan* was finished there, and the third in Lyons in August, 1859. The Emperor of Brazil, however, had now made other arrangements; and Wagner was no nearer his goal than before.

Tristan, *Die Meistersinger*, and *Parsifal*

Tristan probably represents Wagner's ideas of music drama more perfectly than any other work. Of it he said: "I readily submit this work to the severest test based on my theoretical principles. Not that I constructed it after a system—for I entirely forgot all theory—but because I here moved with entire freedom, independent of theoretical misgivings, so that even whilst I was writing I became conscious how far I had gone beyond my system. . . . The entire extent of the music is as it were prescribed in the tissue of the verse—that is to say, the melody [the vocal melody] is already contained in the poem, of which again the symphonic music forms the sub-stratum."

The fable is simply told. Tristan, who had once been Cornwall's champion against Morold, an Irish knight come to collect tribute from Cornwall, had sent back Morold's head in place of the tax. Himself grievously wounded, he had sought aid from Isolde, princess of Ireland, who, like her mother, was skilled in simples. Isolde discovered that it was Tristan who had killed Morold (reputedly her fiancé); but so pitifully did the wounded Tristan gaze up at her from his pillow that her heart was melted, and she fell in love instead of killing him. Tristan was healed; and now as the opera opens he has again visited Ireland as an emissary of King Mark (Tristan's uncle), and is bringing Isolde to Cornwall as Mark's bride. Outraged, Isolde commands her maid Brangäne to prepare a death potion which Isolde intends that she and Tristan shall drink together. But Brangäne cannot bear to do this, and substitutes for the death drink a love potion which had been intended for Isolde and Mark. After darkly veiled discussion of the differences between them, Tristan and Isolde, unaware of the substitution, drink the love potion, and are thus thrown into each other's arms on the very eve of the landing in Cornwall where Mark awaits his bride.

In the second act, the court goes on a hunt at night; Tristan visits Isolde, and they discuss their fatal passion until, in the gray dawn, the hunt returns and the two are discovered together. Melot, who has concocted the plan of the hunt, accuses Tristan, who makes as if to fight him; but as Melot thrusts, Tristan throws up his guard and is wounded. In the third act, Tristan, carried to his own estates in the island of Careol by Kurwenal, his serving man, hovers between life and death. Kurwenal, as the last act opens, has sent for Isolde to come and heal him. Much of the music is taken up with an amazing representation of Tristan's delirious agony. At length Isolde's ship is seen. Tristan, at the news, rises from his couch and tears the bandages from his wound. He dies just as Isolde enters. Mark, to whom Brangäne had at length confessed her deception, comes in another ship. In the fight which ensues (for Kurwenal does not understand Mark's coming) Kurwenal is killed. Isolde, who had sunk inert on Tristan's body, is aroused from her trance, and in an ecstasy of love sings away her last breath.

The music is wholly woven out of the relatively few leading motives which typify the essential persons and forces of the drama. And it is so contrived that, without losing contact for a moment with the dramatic action, it assumes a musical form which is in itself almost as coherent and logical as that of a Beethoven symphony. The dimensions of each symphonic piece—coextensive with an act of the drama—are colossal; but the process, once the themes themselves have been clearly announced, is largely that of the development section of the symphony, and the hearer thus follows, in listening, an entirely familiar thread. But the most important feature of the music is its amazing accuracy of expression, first in the perfect aptness of the themes themselves, and secondly in the incredible intensity of their passionate development. Every resource of existing musical art, especially that of harmony, is drawn upon for the production of such new effects; so that *Tristan* may fairly be said not only to mark the culmination of the long history of music drama up to its time, but also to provide the foundation for many new departures in the future, in instrumental music as well as in opera. The range of modulation (employed without any undue straining of the hearer's attention) is proportionately as expanded as that achieved by Bach in the *Well-Tempered Clavichord*. The orchestra, almost as large as that demanded for the *Ring*, embodies these shifting harmonies in a tone substance whose color is as subtle and as varied as that of the modern painters. And at the same time, by a subtle and almost unconscious process of definition, the leading motives acquire an exactness of meaning in relation to the action which gives to the music, especially at supreme moments, a power of suggestion almost overwhelming.

Naturally, such novel values were not to be grasped by everyone at first contact. To the hearer whose mind is set in advance in the expectation of hearing simple, straightforward melody lightly accompanied, Wagner's music seemed but a tangle and a confusion of sounds. Exactly that change in the conventional attitude toward musical ideas which Wagner advocated in *Oper und Drama* was prerequisite to the comprehension of his work. But so painstaking was his effort not to distort, more than was absolutely necessary, the existing course of musical thought, that when his greatest works at last began to be heard it was not the public which objected to them, but only the critics, who could not change their attitude (consecrated by their own august approval) without making the impossible confession that they had been mistaken. Few contemporary musicians, however, showed themselves capable of grasping the new attitude. Schumann and Spohr in the earlier years had shown a considerable understanding, and Liszt had become the uncompromising champion of the new art. But it was largely through Liszt's pupils and followers—younger men, more accessible to new ideas—that the great movement was carried on.

Wagner's experience in Paris in 1861 shows to what lengths opposition to him could go. After many fruitless efforts to gain the approval of the operatic directors, Wagner at last was rewarded by a command from the Emperor that *Tannhäuser* should be mounted. (Rehearsals of Berlioz' *Les Troyens* were shelved because of it.) In order at least partially to comply with the Parisian convention that there should be a ballet in every opera, Wagner had greatly enlarged and intensified the opening scene of the first act. (This music, known as the "Paris Version" of *Tannhäuser*, is made with all the skill of the composer of *Tristan*. It greatly overtops the rest of the music in interest, in consequence, and is comparatively seldom used for stage performances.) But the convention was that the ballet should occur in the second act rather than the first. The Jockey Club, one of the most munificent supporters of the Opéra, headed the opposition to a man who insisted on placing his ballet in such a position that they could not dine comfortably before witnessing it. The performance, which had cost untold sums and had had 164 rehearsals, was interrupted with hisses and catcalls, and after a third attempt Wagner withdrew the opera. *Tristan* fared, for a time, even worse. After fifty-seven rehearsals in Vienna it was abandoned as too difficult to perform; and in other cities it did not even get into rehearsal. (It was finally produced at Munich, June 10, 1865.) But the sentence of banishment which had kept him out of every German state was at length lifted—at first in all states other than Saxony, and in 1862 in Saxony itself.

He found his earlier works popular almost everywhere. At Vienna in 1861 he heard *Lohengrin* for the first time. But the writer of those works was not the same man as the great musician of the future, hoping against hope to have his newer creations understood. Finally, despairing of ever being able to finish the *Ring*, he published the text as a literary work (1863) saying, "I can hardly expect to find leisure to complete the music, and I have given up all hope that I may live to see it performed." In the next year, however, the young King Ludwig II of Bavaria, newly come to the throne, invited Wagner to come to Munich and finish his work. He had already begun *Die Meistersinger von Nürnberg*, his only comedy opera, and hoped to finish the *Ring*. But again petty opposition of all sorts was raised against him, so that he removed to Triebschen near Lucerne, where *Die Meistersinger* was finished in 1867. It was produced in 1868. Its method, in spite of the great difference in subject, is essentially the method of *Tristan*. The charming tale is that of the triumph of a young singer over the antiquated rules of the guild of the master singers—a tale which can readily be seen as an allegory of Wagner's own life. The music, equally charming, seems to come from an even larger understanding of humanity than is manifest in *Tristan* itself. These two works, with the *Ring* which was finally completed in 1874, are doubtless Wagner's greatest masterpieces. He had gone to Bayreuth in 1872, where at last it had become possible to build a theatre suited to the performance of his works as he desired them;[2] and in 1876 the *Ring* was at last performed in its entirety. Even with such resources, the financial returns were far below the outgo, and he was again obliged to tour as a conductor, visiting London in 1877. Here he read privately the poem of his last opera *Parsifal*. The sketches for the music were finally completed in 1879, the orchestration being finished only in 1882. It was performed at Bayreuth in the summer of that year. In the following February Wagner died in Venice.

---

[2] In this theatre, conductor and orchestra are quite invisible to the spectators—a condition which quite removes one very important distraction from the mind of the spectator. It can hardly be denied that Wagner's theorem of music drama often places his opera in the orchestra pit instead of on the stage. The construction of the Bayreuth theatre goes far to remove this objection.

In *Parsifal* we find the old theme of redemption treated in still another manner. It is not now perfect devotion, or mutual trust, or the sloughing of the shackles of social convention from the spirit of the purely human figure, which is to achieve the great end. It is simplicity and goodness of mind and heart, which transcend intellect and perceive by instinct rather than reason the true nature of the human problem as Wagner now saw it. Parsifal, a "pure fool," finds in his simplicity the strength to resist the temptations of Kundry (herself obeying, in her attempt to seduce him, the magic power of Klingsor, a renegade knight of the Grail); and comes also to "know through sympathy" the agony of Amfortas, King of the Grail knights, who has also come under Klingsor's spell and has been wounded by the sacred spear. His unsullied purity enables him to abolish Klingsor and his magic castle; and his slowly learned sympathy enables him to heal the wound of Amfortas and to cleanse the stains of Kundry. Both die in peace as Parsifal himself assumes the position of chief of the knights. The music is somewhat more uneven than that of the preceding great works; yet in many passages—notably in the expression of Amfortas's agony in the first act, and in the rendering of the atmosphere of Good Friday in the last—it attains a penetration or an exaltation, as the case may be, which is held by many to transcend any of Wagner's earlier achievements in expression. It was Wagner's express desire that—probably owing to the unlikelihood of securing proper conditions for performance elsewhere—*Parsifal* should be produced only at Bayreuth. In 1903 however it was given in New York, and has since been played in most of the important theatres of the world.

The impression given by actual performance of Wagner's dramas is seldom as impressive as the student, reading score and text, and using his imagination to the uttermost, will expect. Modern stage craft, with all its efficiency, cannot always prevent the spectacle from lapsing into absurdities as laughable as those which amused La Fontaine. In consequence, a profounder appeal to the hearer's imagination is often made by the orchestral performance, even without words, of excerpts like the *Liebestod* than by production of the scenes as Wagner intended them. In spite of his laborious argument about the union of the arts, it appears that he failed to accomplish that perfect union. As poetry, surely, few of his passages could stand alone; and few if any add in the slightest to our awareness of the whole dramatic meaning. His action is often halting, repetitive, conditioned by theatrical or musical opportunity, and psychologically unsound. It is only as a tone poet that he almost invariably achieves his expressive purpose. His works are vastly more truthful in expression than any earlier operas; but that he had not only solved the problem of the music drama but, as he fondly believed, had created the definitive form of the art work of the future—such a contention must be thankfully denied. How ironical it would have been that the great apostle of artistic freedom should have established for all posterity the binding rules of artistic endeavor!

It should be noted, moreover, that Wagner was contemplating in his last years a return to the symphonic form. The thesis of *Opera and Drama*, logical as it appeared to his mind at the time of writing, was really untenable. He then believed in art, not as a mere ornament of privileged life but as a necessity—indeed the highest necessity—of that larger spiritual existence which ideally should be attainable by all humanity. His defense of his thesis was so impassioned as to deceive himself as well as his admirers. But old age gave a truer perspective of the problem. The glib assertion that music and poetry, originally one, had been separated by that mere accident of conventional life which had brought into existence the government and the society of his day (a society in which art occupied a far from ideal position), and that the present highly organized forms of music and poetry represented no more than superficial demands for aesthetic pleasure within that society—that assertion was no adequate basis for a sweeping rejection of those forms, and gave no real foundation for his belief in music drama as the one great art form of the future. He nowhere expressly retracts his earlier thesis; but the trend toward the symphony proves that he recognized its instability.

Of the many kinds of assistance, material and spiritual, which were offered to and accepted almost without thanks by this extraordinary man; of his incredible selfishness in the pursuit of his ideals, and of his still greater devotion to them; of his impatience with any adverse criticism, combined with a passionate eagerness to learn the solution of his problem —a problem which he believed to be a vital concern of all humanity—of all this there is no space to speak in detail. Of the sheer novelty of his musical thought—his innovations in musical structure and form, and the ideas as to the nature of musical expression out of which his innovations sprang—we have tried to give some suggestion. His contributions to musical art can hardly be summarized in a sentence; but it can carcely be controverted that his whole achievement sprang from his understanding of music as something more than a formal art—as something, indeed, possessed of a power of expression which related it intimately and essentially to the experiences of life. He valued the classical literature of music, not for its abstract beauty but for its expression, finding in the *Well-Tempered Clavichord* and in the symphonies and quartets of Mozart and Beethoven intimate and ineffable revelations of that fundament of feeling which in *Parsifal* he was at last to exalt as the highest of human capacities. Since he handled the whole problem of musical form with great freedom in pursuing this ideal of expression, and since of sheer necessity he contributed vastly to the expansion of musical form, it was natural that the work of his successors should show an even greater disregard for the classical traditions of form. Much of that later work has attracted the attention of the world chiefly by its formal anarchy; but it begins to appear that whatever of that work is to survive in the affection of the great world must possess also some measure of that true expressiveness which it was always his first aim to impart.

CHAPTER XXVIII

Anti-Wagnerian Tendencies
Johannes Brahms
Giuseppe Verdi

I N the spring of 1860 there appeared in the Berlin *Echo* the following manifesto:

> The undersigned have long followed with regret the pursuits of a certain party, whose organ is Brendel's "Zeitschrift für Musik."
> The above journal continually spreads the view that musicians of more serious endeavors are fundamentally in accord with the tendencies it represents, that they recognize in the compositions by the leaders of this group works of artistic value, and that altogether, and especially in North Germany, the contentions for and against the so-called music of the future are concluded and the dispute settled in its favor.
> To protest against such a misrepresentation of facts is regarded as their duty by the undersigned, and they declare that, so far at least as they are concerned, the principles stated by Brendel's journal are *not* recognized, and that they regard the productions of the leaders and pupils of the so-called 'New German' school, which in part re-enforce these principles in practice and in part again and again enforce new and unheard-of theories, as contrary to the innermost spirit of music, strongly to be deplored and condemned.
>
> Johannes Brahms
Joseph Joachim
Julius Otto Grimm
Bernhard Scholz

The statement appeared prematurely. Many more signatures had been solicited, and the manifesto, thus bolstered, was intended for publication in one of the musical journals, not in the daily press. Its effect was far more detrimental to its authors than to the men it attacked. But it serves as a vivid illustration of the sharp division of opinion which had arisen in the musical world respecting the legitimate aims and purposes of music— a division brought about by the works of Wagner and Liszt, and doubtless much intensified by Wagner's polemics against the sterility of contemporary music.

The language of the statement is largely that of Joachim; but the instigation came from Brahms. How had it come about that a young man, not yet thirty, could dare to take up the cudgels against artists twenty or more than twenty years his senior—men whose achievements had won for them great, if as yet somewhat debatable, reputations? The answer is by no means wholly to be found in the life of Johannes Brahms. But his attitude, at least at this time, was that of a great number of sincere lovers of music: an attitude of indignation toward those who openly disparaged the achievements of the great masters of the past, who insisted that much might be expressed in sound which the masters had not recognized as within the legitimate scope of music, and that the rules and principles of structure which had guided those masters must be revised. How Brahms came to adopt this attitude, then, is a question whose answer may reveal much of the current of musical thought of the mid-century.

Brahms as a Student

Brahms was born in 1833, the son of a jolly, sturdy, not particularly cultured double-bass player of Hamburg who had somewhat unaccountably married a quiet, industrious, and instinctively refined woman seventeen years older than himself. It was taken for granted that the boy would become a musician; but there was no parental dreaming about the child's genius. He was to follow honorably his father's calling; that was all. When the father, impressed by his interest in musical sounds, began to teach the boy his notes, he found that six-year-old "Hannes" already knew his scales, could tell the name of any note he heard from any instrument, and had already invented for himself a system of notation. Of all the instruments, the boy loved the piano best. So he was sent—by a kind fate —to one Otto Friedrich Willibald Cossel, a man with a passion and a genius for teaching, who guided with a sure hand the astonishingly rapid development of the boy's talent both for playing and for composition. Although he had appeared but three times in public by the time he was ten, his playing had attracted the attention of musical circles in Hamburg, and a proposal was made that the boy be taken on a concert tour which, it was planned, might even extend to America. Cossel, aghast at this early exploitation of one whom he knew to be a genius and who would be ruined by such a misdirection of his interests, finally hit upon the expedient of sending Johannes to the most eminent of Hamburg teachers and theorists, Eduard Marxsen, whose reluctant acceptance of the young pupil put a stop to the project of a tour. Marxsen, a thorough master of the classical principles of composition, would have nothing to do with such adventurers as Schumann and Chopin, and gave his pupil, as examples worthy to be followed, only the music of Bach and Beethoven. Brahms, altogether susceptible to the romantic fever of the day, continued his lessons with Cossel, doubtless preserving much sensibility which would otherwise have been smothered. But he was also a docile follower of Marxsen's precepts, and learned from him what many of his contemporaries never learned, the real purport and substance of the classical style. When Mendelssohn died in 1847, Marxsen was bold enough to say, "A master of the art has gone; a greater arises in Brahms."

The real fruit of all this labor lay in Brahms's acquirement of an extraordinary power of self-discipline—not only in music but in reading and in all those matters of behavior which were involved in the development of manliness. He even took the pains of a Demosthenes to coerce an unruly boyish voice into the deep and sonorous speech which he deemed worthy of a man. Playing for mere pittances in cafés and bars, giving poorly paid lessons, he yet managed to read extensively and to compose, without thought of publication, inordinate quantities of music. For instance, he set almost the whole *Buch der Lieder* of Heine; and this work, with all the rest, he one day complacently consigned to the furnace. An artistic conscience so sensitive is hardly recorded in the annals of music. At the same time, such restraint can hardly have been exercised without damage to the freedom of fancy and the sheer fluency of invention which are any composer's most precious possession. None but a great mind could have preserved its elasticity under such discipline. But Brahms survived.

First Venture into the World—Schumann's Prophecy

In 1853 Brahms joined Edouard Reményi, a noted Hungarian violinist, on a concert tour. At Celle occurred the famous feat of playing the piano part of the C minor Violin Sonata of Beethoven in C sharp minor—accomplished without a thought of its remarkableness by the young musician whom Marxsen had taught to transpose to any key the fugues of the *Well-Tempered Clavichord.* At Hanover, Reményi took Brahms to visit the already famous violinist Joseph Joachim. Here began a friendship which was perhaps the most fruitful in Brahms's whole life. Joachim, fully recognizing the gifts of the young man who was only two years younger than himself, gave him recommendation to many friends and sent him directly to Weimar to visit Liszt. He was received with every courtesy.

Suddenly feeling too shy to play his own music, which Liszt asked for, he was given an illustration of that artist's powers; for Liszt took the manuscripts of the E flat minor Scherzo and the C major Sonata, and played them at sight. Plunging then into his own newly finished Sonata in B minor, Liszt played for a time, but turning to catch some hint from his youthful visitor of his reaction to the music, the master found the boy peacefully asleep in his chair! So began a division between the two— the antipathy, surprisingly, being all on Brahms's side—which was never removed. Brahms also fell out with Reményi at Weimar, and returned to Göttingen to Joachim. His friend now warmly recommended him to Schumann at Düsseldorf. With much misgiving, for he had once sent to Schumann for criticism some compositions which the master had returned unopened, Brahms at length presented himself at Schumann's door. But he found here a far different atmosphere from that of Weimar—simple, homelike surroundings and entire concern with the substance and the spirit of music, which contrasted sharply with the electric air of Liszt's drawing room and the incessant, although unmentioned, preoccupation with the public. All the native kindliness and the still deeper concern for musical art which had so often manifested itself in Schumann's enthusiastic commendation of young artists—an interest and a hope which had never yet found a wholly satisfying object—was poured out unreservedly for his young visitor. Nor was this commendation confined to the immediate occasion. Sensing perhaps something of the fate that was so immediately in store for him, and deeply moved at the discovery of one who appeared able to bear the leader's torch, Schumann wrote for the *Neue Zeitschrift* an article which not only praised without stint the young man's works, but spoke of him as "a musician [who] would inevitably appear [and] to whom it was vouchsafed to give the highest and most ideal expression to the tendencies of the time, one who would not show us his mastery in a gradual development, but like Athene, would spring fully armed from the head of Zeus." This article was published in October, 1853.

Although Schumann's intention was wholly kind, the effect of the article was not wholly fortunate. An unknown young man was exalted above older and more experienced artists; his actual production was too meager to give support to the contention made in his behalf; and by implication the whole "futuristic" movement of Liszt and Wagner was condemned. Brahms himself was probably more terrified than pleased. What reason had he to believe that he could live up to such a prospectus? Genius must indeed be certain of itself; but most of Brahms's training had been directed toward teaching him that certainty of oneself is not genius. The only certainties he had encountered appeared in the method of classicism, as expounded to him with much show of authority by Marxsen. To accomplish what Schumann had predicted of him, the young man felt that he must have recourse to some greater authority than his own native talent; and he accordingly set about acquiring a fuller mastery than he had as yet attained of this tried and proved method. A strong romantic impulse is apparent in the early piano works and songs which he had submitted to Schumann. This impulse he now set himself not wholly to suppress, but to curb. Clarity of line, exactness of statement, correctness in every detail of structure—these must be exhibited in every work which came from his pen; for any masterpiece must at least be flawless in these respects. Youthful impulse—in itself lovable enough to mitigate many faults and exuberances of expression—can scarcely survive such rigorous correction. It was therefore a dangerous method which Schumann had unconsciously imposed upon his protégé.

It happened also that Fate demanded of Brahms another effort at repression. In February, 1854, Schumann's complete mental unbalance had shown itself in his leap into the Rhine. During the two years which followed before his death, Clara Schumann was supported in her misery by the constant devotion of Brahms. It would have been strange indeed if the high regard with which their intercourse had begun, intensified by the new attitude of protection and sympathy which her pitiful circumstances had aroused, had not changed at last into a more consuming passion. This did, in fact, occur; and the passion was mutual. (Clara, after all, was only fourteen years older than Brahms; and Brahms was in many ways a very old young man.) But after the death of Schumann, marriage was as impracticable as an affair before his death had been unthinkable. "He took leave of the beloved; she kept the friend." But something had been drained from that friend's soul, so that the only other impulse toward marriage which he ever felt—that for Agathe von Siebold, whom he met in the summer of 1857 at Göttingen—subsided and died unspoken.

Thus secretly maimed, the young man set out upon a career. He was invited to the little principality of Detmold as director of the musical events there. He conducted a small chorus, gave lessons to the Princess and many of her followers, and composed some pieces for mixed voices, some songs, and the two orchestral Serenades, his first essays in orchestral composition. Schumann had strongly urged him to attempt a symphony, giving the rather startling counsel that if the beginning were only bravely made, the end would come of itself. Prophecy more unlikely to be fulfilled than this, in the case of such a careful creator as Brahms, it would be hard to imagine. But he had made the attempt. The ultimate result was the great Piano Concerto in D minor, which he had first cast as a gigantic sonata for two pianos, next as a purely orchestral symphony, and finally as the Concerto. At Hanover, under Joachim's direction, his playing of the Concerto had made a deep if somewhat bewildered impression. It was desirable to repeat the work in a more significant center; and arrangements were made for its performance in Leipzig at the Gewandhaus. Whether because of his own insufficient playing (which seems unlikely) or because of the opposition of a clique of "futurists" (with which, certainly, Liszt had nothing to do) the performance was, in Brahms's words, "a brilliant and decided—failure." The first major appearance of Schumann's apostle was actually hissed. This was in January, 1859, less than a week after the performance in Hanover. His own comment nearly hides the bitterness he felt; but it can scarcely be doubted that that bitterness, mingled with the repressions of which we have spoken, contributed a strong impulse toward the taking of that unfortunate step, the issuance of the manifesto of 1860 quoted at the beginning of the chapter.

The works which Brahms had completed up to 1860 include three Piano Sonatas, the Scherzo in E flat minor, four Ballades, three sets of Variations (all for piano); five groups of solo songs, and several works for duet, quartet, or chorus of voices, with and without accompaniment; a Trio (B major), two Piano Quartets, and a Sextet for strings in B flat; two Serenades for orchestra, and the Piano Concerto in D minor. Taken in their order of composition, one would expect them to reveal—as is the case with the works of Beethoven's first period—both the rapid acquisition of technical mastery and the gradual clarification of artistic purpose. They do indeed reveal these qualities; yet the progress exhibited, while not exactly unsure, sometimes seems clouded and confused by the existence behind the created substance of some titanic creative effort, a purpose which is seldom triumphantly achieved. The spontaneity with which the creation was obviously begun has been to some degree suppressed, either by doubt of the rightness (according to Marxsen) of the results, or by some obscurer doubt of the justness or even of the value of what was being said. This characteristic is of course not predominant. It is often indeed indistinguishable, and in the great D minor Piano Concerto is triumphantly overcome. But it underlies much of the austerity of Brahms's usual language, and, representing an almost constant purpose, is an essential element in the highly individual style which was so painstakingly coming to formation.

THE CHORAL DECADE, 1860–1870—THE *German Requiem*

A new disappointment befell him in Hamburg. The conductorship of the Philharmonic Orchestra was given, unaccountably, not to Brahms but to Julius Stockhausen, a great singer, who had already shown the same interest in Brahms's songs as Vogl had shown in Schubert's. Hopeless of obtaining due recognition in Hamburg, he had gone by Joachim's advice to Vienna (where the news of the choice of Stockhausen reached him). And, after playing there his Piano Quartets and making a considerable impression as an interpreter of Bach and Schumann, he was invited to assume the conductorship of the Vienna Singakademie. Although it compensated somewhat for his disappointment in Hamburg, the offer was not wholly fortunate. This society held only the second position in importance in Vienna. Brahms arranged programs of Bach's cantatas and Passions which were ill calculated to attract the public or to arouse its enthusiasm; he was neither an experienced nor an inspiring conductor; and although re-elected, he resigned the conductorship in the summer of 1863. Only once more did he ever accept a regular appointment. This was in the winters of 1872 to 1875 when he conducted (with far greater success) the concerts of the greater Viennese chorus, the Singverein of the Society of the Friends of Music. But he was now widely accepted as a composer and was able to live upon his royalties. He made many visits to friendly German cities, lived in quiet friendly intercourse with a few musicians and music lovers in Vienna, and made music for himself and for them which attracted also the growing attention of the world. The only other external event which had any apparent effect on his creative mind was the death of his mother in 1865. The fruit of his sorrow was the *German Requiem,* a work which after a few years was to establish the justification of Schumann's prophecy.

The *Requiem* (whose text is a selection of biblical verses, chosen by Brahms himself and representing his very unorthodox but profoundly sincere religious philosophy) was begun shortly after Schumann's death, was completed after that of his mother, and became the most apt and fitting commemoration of those who had fallen in the Franco-Prussian War of 1870. An ill-advised performance of the first three movements, under Herbeck at Vienna in 1867, had been a disastrous failure. But the next year the whole work was given in the cathedral at Bremen, making an overwhelming impression; and thereafter Brahms's position was no longer debatable. It was amply supported by several other large choral works, mostly completed during the decade 1860–1870. These are *Rinaldo,* a cantata set to Goethe's text—the nearest approach to operatic music which Brahms ever made; the *Rhapsodie* for alto solo, male chorus, and orchestra (text from Goethe's *Harzreise*)—extraordinarily passionate in tone, and strongly influenced by *Tristan,* although there is no hint of direct borrowing; the *Song of Destiny (Schicksalslied)* to a poem by Hölderlin —a companion piece, in its implications of faith, to the *Requiem,* and in its musical substance to the *Rhapsodie;* and finally the *Triumphlied* (1870, after Sedan). Several important chamber works also belong to this period: the Piano Quintet in F minor—a piece of terrible earnestness which, like the Concerto in D minor, assumed two tentative forms (those of a string quintet and a duet for two pianos) before its final molding; the second String Sextet in G; and two String Quartets in C minor and A minor—Brahms's first published efforts in this form, in preparation for which, however, he had written and destroyed about twenty complete quartets. There are but two works for piano solo in this decade—the *Variations on a Theme of Handel*, Op. 24, and those on a theme of Paganini (still to be reckoned as one of the most difficult studies ever written). It is perhaps fanciful, but it seems quite true, to say that works like the *Harzreise* Rhapsodie and the *Schicksalslied* with its exalted orchestral peroration, the A minor Quartet for strings, and a few others are at last showing a gradual release from that iron-bound seriousness which pervades the D minor Concerto and which is seldom missing in the earlier works until it finds at once its culmination and its emancipation in the *Requiem*.

The heedless, simple gaiety of Viennese life was thoroughly congenial to the convention-hating Brahms. Seldom appearing before the public, and then never in the popularizing guise of the wizard, he lived with and for his friends and his music; but long contact with the Viennese spirit cannot but be infectious, and gradually that cloud of bitterness into which the renunciations of his youth had plunged him was lifted. One of the first unmistakable evidences of this, and of the joyous nature that dwelt beneath the stern exterior, is to be found in the perennially delightful *Liebeslieder* Waltzes, for piano duet and mixed quartet ad libitum. The buoyancy of these incomparable dances is surely caught from his good friend Johann Strauss. Their exquisite texture, and their many hints of a deeper poetry than Strauss knew, are his own. They took the Viennese public by storm, and had not that unfortunate effect of distracting attention from the greater works which, in spite of their charm, one must attribute to the famous Hungarian Dances. Occasionally, too, he added another to that growing list of wonderful songs which had begun with Op. 3, and which was to place Brahms among the greatest masters of that form.

The Symphonies—The Last Piano Pieces—Chamber Music

Having been dominated for a decade by interest in choral works, he now turned to the field of instrumental music—as yet only partially conquered; for in spite of many endeavors he had produced no symphony. The orchestra was to him a portentous instrument. Indeed, it almost seems as if he thought of it not as an instrument in itself, but as the unwieldy aggregation of instruments which appears to the eye of one who first enters a symphony hall. There are many reasons for this. He had been trained as a contrapuntist—as one who conceived the fabric of music in many endless strands of simultaneous melody. Each instrument, to him, must contribute vitally to the whole sum of idea; must have a real part to play; and would be degraded by being submerged in some mere business of color-making. Keenly sensitive to the individual tone qualities of the instruments, he was prevented, by his continual regard for line, from realizing in his own structures the extraordinary wealth of tone colors which are at the command of one who composes largely with color effects in mind.[1] Although he was already master of orchestral line, he was thus no virtuoso in dealing with the orchestra. Also, he had a vast respect for the symphony as the highest of instrumental forms, and had no intention of contributing to the orchestral literature such flimsy structures as were every day put forth by students and even so-called masters of composition. At heart he almost feared, though by no means on the same grounds as Wagner, that the history of the symphony had ended with Beethoven's Ninth. His first attempt at a symphony had ended in a piano concerto. His next had lain for years in his mind; dormant or only slowly germinating. It was to be brought to completion as the C minor Symphony only after trustworthy experience with the orchestra had been attained.

The two Serenades, the Concerto in D minor, and the orchestral accompaniments for the choral works were his only orchestral efforts thus far. The first major work in that field is still not a symphony but a set of variations on a theme by Haydn—a theme known as the *St. Anthony Chorale.* The variation form, so consummately handled by Beethoven, had proved uncongenial to most of his successors and was becoming almost obsolete. Brahms alone among the greater minds had clung to it, and with the Handel variations and fugue for piano had won the ungrudging admiration of Richard Wagner himself. The Haydn variations show all the restraint (even amounting to timidity) in orchestration of which we have spoken; but their structure is a delight to the musician, and the charm of the old-world theme still lives. The work offers little suggestion, however, of the power and force which were to be displayed in the C minor Symphony, which appeared at last in 1876.

In this symphony it is certainly not fanciful to see a reflection of that long struggle for mastery, both of himself and of his art, which we have

---

[1] Such composition is, of course, as legitimate as composition for the piano which takes into account the additions to the indicated sound substance which are provided by the pedal. These values were used with great originality by Brahms in his piano compositions; but the parallel values in orchestral writing were seldom attempted.

seen the composer undergoing. Never before (or since) has a symphonic movement been so concentrated. The introductory section, beginning with a vivid wrenching apart of many voices which all begin on the one tonic, C, depicts a tension as great as it is within the power of music to suggest. Thereafter, three other motives are briefly presented (the last, on the three rising notes, G, E flat, g, being singularly indicative of a gathering of triumphant force); and out of this material, by various devices, the whole first movement is developed. In this gnarled structure (as rigid in its logic as any Bach fugue) there is to be seen the very spirit of Brahms's philosophy up to this time—his utter rejection of all triviality; his conscientious devotion to the fundamentals of art as he understood them; and, at any rate in the last movement, a strong sense of the final achievement of his difficult goal. Toward the end of the slow movement, into whose somber texture the distortion of the opening phrase of the symphony is often woven as kind of a leading motive, a solo violin hints at release. The third movement is not a scherzo in the Beethovenian sense, but a sort of intermezzo: not without humor, but more in keeping with the whole suggestion of the work than a true scherzo could be. This replacement of the scherzo by a more related type of movement is a frequent characteristic of Brahms's sonata structures (chamber music as well as symphonies) and is almost as striking a contribution to the emotional relativity of the whole work as was Beethoven's substitution of the scherzo for the minuet. The last movement has a long introduction, whose function is to prepare for the triumphant entry of the great song —palpably suggestive of the main theme of the *Finale* of Beethoven's Ninth Symphony—in which is represented the emancipation of spirit to which we have already alluded. Naturally, the work was slow in winning popularity. But it offered, as it was doubtless intended to do, a vigorous refutation of Wagner's thesis that after the Ninth Symphony no more true symphonic progress was possible.

In the following year another symphony appeared. This is in complete contrast to the first, in character and in the ease and naturalness of its flow; but the structure, although apparently effortless, is as perfect as that of the first. It may be taken as a kind of pastoral symphony—without the literalness of Beethoven's in the representation of country scenes, but with a similar vividness in its suggestion of the well-being that comes from true contact with nature. The production of two contrasted works in the same form is frequent with Brahms. This is further illustrated in the *Academic Festival* Overture (largely on popular students' songs, such as *Was kommt dort von der Höh* and *Gaudeamus igitur*) written in recognition of the honorary degree of Doctor of Philosophy conferred on the composer by the University of Breslau, to which was opposed the

Tragic Overture, related not to any particular play but rather to the spirit of tragedy. The same opposition of character is to be seen in the Double Concerto for violin and 'cello, largely somber in tone, to which the noble Concerto for violin—in many respects the greatest of works in this form —offers a significant contrast. The Second Piano Concerto in B flat also dates from this decade. It offers, as perhaps no earlier work had done, an exposition of that quiet loftiness of mind which the composer at last attained. In 1883 appeared the Third Symphony—a refutation, if one were needed, of Hugo Wolf's criticism of Brahms, *Er kann nicht jubeln* ("He cannot exult"); and in 1884–1885 came the contrast to this—the wonderful E minor Symphony, under whose quiet exterior the hearer at length comes to find more suggestion of mature feeling than is perhaps to be found in any other work in this form.

The same complete and vivid conveyance of meaning, under a surface which studiously avoids all superficial appeal to the attention, is to be found in the last piano compositions. From 1862–1863, when he wrote the Paganini variations, until 1877, Brahms wrote no music for the piano. In that year appeared a group of Fantasias, Op. 76—small pieces of very diverse character, remotely analogous to the Bagatelles of Beethoven and also, in a way, akin to the *Intermezzi* which he had substituted for the scherzo in the sonata sequence; and in 1878 the two popular Rhapsodies, Op. 79. In 1892–1893 appeared a considerable number of such pieces, mostly entitled *Capriccio* or *Intermezzo*, but including one Ballade and the fiery Rhapsody in E flat which concludes the series. Small in dimensions as these pieces are, they represent an extraordinary variety of moods and at the same time constitute a distinct addition—in a very unobtrusive vein—to the expressive possibilities of the piano.

Chamber music—his chiefest passion, as it was also Beethoven's—now began gradually to be produced in greater profusion. Three Violin Sonatas (the last two, in A major and D minor, dated 1886 and 1887, contrasting as do many works already mentioned); a third Piano Quartet (in C minor, begun in 1859, and only finished in 1875 when the bitter experiences out of which it had been engendered had somewhat lost their sting); four Trios, one with clarinet instead of violin; one more String Quartet (in B flat); two Quintets, one for strings and one with clarinet; two Sonatas for clarinet and piano (written like the other clarinet pieces especially for his friend Richard Mühlfeld) and a second 'Cello Sonata— all this wealth of chamber music was produced from 1880 on, and shows even more clearly than the piano pieces the composer's increasing absorption with music itself and his increasing indifference to the public.

Brahms's work aroused no such furore, either of controversy or of acclaim, as did that of Wagner. The two men were antipathetic to each other, and especially in the earlier years their aims seemed to be widely divergent. Yet there existed between them a sincere mutual respect—a respect which was unfortunately not shared by the hot partisans of each. Brahms proved the baselessness of Wagner's theory that music independent of the drama was dead, and that the older forms could no longer be made to express significant ideas. Wagner, on the other hand, by frankly avowing the essential relation of music to human experience, endowed music, especially through the leading motive, with a new vitality of expressive purpose which certainly would have been lost if theorists of the type of Marxsen had been allowed to dictate the future of the art. Of course, neither had all the right on his side; and in the end their earlier divergence of purpose seems much diminished. Wagner (with some unacknowledged help from men like Berlioz and Liszt) established on a sure foundation the value of color as an element of musical suggestion. He also did what no other could have done to show the possibility of an enormously expanded form design in music. So overwhelming was the conviction which his work produced in the minds of his followers that it was not strange that his method should be regarded, by those followers, as the only possible method for the music of the future. Yet there is little relaxation needed in the older principles of musical structure to bring the extremest of Wagner's work into conformity with what, after all, is essential in those principles. But it was of inestimable benefit to the art that such work as that of Brahms should be produced, contemporaneously with Wagner's and even after it. Brahms showed—conclusively, one would think—that progress is not necessarily to be achieved by the discarding of older methods; but Wagner also showed that progress is not necessarily assured by adherence to those methods.

The essential lesson—that musical art has grown great enough so that purposes and processes as divergent as those of Brahms and Wagner (or even of their followers) can be contained within the legitimate boundaries of the art—has not been very well learned. Controversies over method, the direct descendants of the Wagner-Brahms controversies, are rampant in our own day. The apparently obvious inference—that none of the existing definitions of method is large enough to cover the existing situation —is obscured by the rancor with which the ultramoderns and their opponents attack each other. It is an apparently irrefutable deduction from history that the development of any institution is continuous; that new elements are absorbed into older organizations, altering the character of the old in proportion to their force, but never wholly obliterating the traces of what has gone before. Wagner could never have swept away —as he supposed himself about to do—the older art of formal music. But it was Brahms who most clearly showed the continuity of Wagner's art with older sources.

BRAHMS'S DISCIPLES AND PROPAGANDISTS—VON BÜLOW

But it must be admitted that the Brahmsian tendency has been followed by few composers of great distinction. He had during his own lifetime no co-worker who compared to him as Liszt compared to Wagner. Joachim, whose early compositions Brahms thought far more significant than his own, soon recognized his shortcomings and ceased to compose. Grimm and Scholtz, the other two signers of the manifesto, were of no real importance. There was none indeed who was capable of the titanic effort which Brahms had made to master the classical style, and at the same time to express really new ideas. Those who belong in the Brahmsian group, therefore, are sympathizers—partly through admiration of his work, and partly through opposition to the Wagnerian tendency—and are not true followers of his methods. Among these may be mentioned Franz Lachner (1803–1890), in his youth a friend of Beethoven and Schubert, and for thirty years court conductor at Munich; Wilhelm Taubert (1811–1891), prominent as a composer of operas and symphonies, but now only remembered for his *Kinderlieder;* Karl Grädener, prominent at Vienna and Hamburg, a prolific writer of chamber music; Woldemar Bargiel (1828–1897) a stepbrother of Clara Schumann, more closely associated than the preceding with Brahms but not more significant; Heinrich von Herzogenberg (1843–1900), industrious and skilled, but whose works Brahms himself condemned as "without one drop of blood" (his wife however, Elizabeth von Herzogenberg, was a talented pianist and one of Brahms's sanest admirers, whose honest criticism he always sought, and whose friendship he valued above that of all other women save Clara Schumann); and Robert Volkmann (1813–1883), a protégé of Schumann, who was prominent in the musical life of Pesth.

The greatest of propagandists for Brahms, however, was Hans von Bülow, one of the most eminent of pianists, conductors, and teachers. He was first a pupil of Friedrich Wieck, and later of Liszt; and was an enthusiastic supporter of Wagner. He married Liszt's daughter Cosima in 1857, finding in her not only a helpful exponent of her father's pianistic art but an illuminating interpreter of the ideals of Wagner. There came about a constantly closer association with Wagner himself. Bülow made a remarkable piano arrangement of *Tristan and Isolde,* and later conducted the first production of *Die Meistersinger.* With all these labors, and with many of the most intimate details of Wagner's creative work, Cosima was closely associated. She understood his purposes thoroughly, and her complete sympathy—very rare in those days—awakened in him that singular responsiveness and charm which even Wagner's enemies admitted was incredible. The inevitable result was the divorce of Cosima from Bülow, and her marriage to his best friend. The catastrophe culminated during Bülow's preparations for the performance of *Die Meistersinger*. The apparent callousness of Wagner and Cosima is hard to understand; but, lamentable as the event was, all three found at last a kind of justification in the undoubted fact that Cosima was essential to Wagner's work, and that without her the completion of the *Ring* would have been a task beyond Wagner's energies. Von Bülow, she says, "would never have lost me had not destiny brought me into contact with him for whom I was bound to recognize it as my mission to live and die." Less productive "missions," at least, have been recorded.

Partly, no doubt, out of a natural revulsion, but chiefly because of a true and sympathetic interest, Bülow, after recovering from the distress into which he was thrown, threw himself wholeheartedly into the propagation of Brahms's music. Many years before, he had played the first movement of the C major Piano Sonata in public. He had been intrusted with the direction of the court orchestra at Meiningen, and had there added to his already consummate abilities as a pianist an equal command of the art of conducting. His interpretations of Beethoven especially set a standard of finish and exactitude never before attained. The tenseness and tragedy of Brahms's First Symphony may well have had an especial appeal to the wounded mind of Bülow. He took it up unhesitatingly; dubbed it (unfortunately) "the tenth symphony"; and produced it on his extensive tours with the Meiningen Orchestra. His faith never wavered. Loudly proclaiming the gospel of the "three B's" (Bach, Beethoven, and Brahms) he fulfilled something of the same mission for Brahms which Liszt in earlier years had undertaken for Wagner—achieving what the reticent composer could never have accomplished for himself.

In some degree the rift between the two parties was thus widened. But the ultimate effect was rather to show the greatness of Brahms's work in itself, and to reveal the fact that, as artists, there was more of kinship than of difference between the two men. For Bülow's admiration for Wagner as a composer never diminished, even while his enthusiasm for Brahms grew to equal and even to exceed it. Wagner's sweeping rejection of independent musical forms as outworn and incapable of true expression could have been disproved in his day only through the work of a man comparable to himself in creative power, who could demonstrate the actual vitality of the older forms. No other figure of like stature with Wagner existed; and even Brahms, in many respects, was unequally matched with him. Brahms's reticence and diffidence are sharply contrasted with Wagner's volubility and unwavering confidence in his own mission. A vast deal of the conflict between the men and their supporters was concerned with the ill-judged arguments and recriminations over the theories and avowed principles which each leader supported. Relatively little was concerned with the actual values of the music which each produced. But when the music itself had finally received the unbiased attention it merited, it was seen that both Wagner and Brahms had added incomparable riches to the art. Wagner's dramas suffer not at all from such condemnation of his principles as was uttered by Brahms and Joachim in the manifesto of 1860. But the choral music, the symphonies, the songs, and the chamber music of Brahms—similarly condemned as sterile, by Wagner's theory—have suffered just as little from the contempt of the Wagner party. To many, indeed—but perhaps these are still not completely impartial judges—the music of Brahms with its flawless structure, its restricted exuberance (under which lives an evident intensity of feeling), its regard for beauty, and its refusal to make any meretricious appeal to the superficial senses, is, while not the greatest music, at least the most highly civilized music we possess.

Verdi

As the Wagnerian thesis with regard to the futility of all nondramatic music was combated in Germany, so his dramatic principles themselves were countered by the large body of supporters of that Italian tradition which Wagner had found so empty. No man of the meager caliber of Bellini or Donizetti could have produced work which, by any thinking public, would be regarded as effectively competitive with Wagner's. But somewhat as Brahms was able to show the vitality of the symphony and the time-honored forms of chamber music, so Giuseppe Verdi, without entering into any acrimonious debates over the theory of music drama, proved that there was real dramatic truth to be told in the traditional manner of the older Italian opera.

Verdi was born eight months after Wagner (October 10, 1813) at the little village of Roncole. The child of a poor innkeeper, his opportunities for musical education were slight. His love for music was manifested in the untiring pursuit of any grind organ which appeared in the village; in his eagerness to learn to play an old spinet which he somehow acquired as a boy and which he kept all his life; or in his forgetting his duty as assistant to the priest at Mass, because of the sound of the organ at the moment of the elevation of the Host. Lessons with the village organist produced such advancement that the boy was soon sent to a school in Busseto, where his hitherto much neglected education was well cared for and where he won the favorable attention of Ferdinand Provesi, director of the Philharmonic Society and organist of the Cathedral. This capable composer guided the boy's studies until he was sixteen, when a small scholarship was won which gave him the opportunity to go to Milan. At Milan he was refused admittance to the Conservatory on the ground that he showed no special aptitude for music. He went instead to a distinguished composer, Signor Lavigna, with whom he studied harmony, counterpoint, and the opera—especially Mozart's *Don Giovanni*. In 1833 he failed of election to the position which Provesi's death had left vacant. But his progress had been so impressive that Barezzi (president of the Philharmonic Society of Busseto, and a principal contributor to the fund which sent Verdi to Milan) had no hesitancy in permitting the young man to marry his daughter. The marriage took place in 1836.

After no more than the usual delays and disappointments, his first opera, *Oberto di San Bonifacio*, was given at La Scala in Milan. Its success was sufficient to justify a contract to produce three more operas. In the midst of his work on the first of these, both his children and his wife died within a little over two months. The first of the operas was a failure; he was ready to give up his career; but after a period of great despondency he wrote *Nabucco* (the usual Italian diminutive for *Nebuchadnezzar*), with which work his career really began, and followed it with *I Lombardi alla prima Crociata*, his earliest permanent success. The manner of these works is in no way distinguished from the current Italian style. Their success was due to his natural and captivating melody, and of course to the sound musicianship which the conscientious pupil of Provesi and Lavigna had acquired. But there is no hint of any such purpose of reform as was already fermenting in Wagner's brain.

The greatest work of this early period is doubtless *Ernani*, based upon Victor Hugo's romantic drama. The opera was almost more successful than the play itself, being produced at fifteen different theatres in nine months. Many operas—far too many—in the same general style followed this first masterpiece. The most important are *Attila*, which gave the cue for much patriotic demonstration against Austria in the line, "Keep thou the universe, but leave Italy to me!" and *Luisa Miller*, adapted from Schiller's *Kabale und Liebe*. Some progress toward a stronger style is to be noted in *Macbeth*, which is but a feeble treatment of the Shakespearian theme, yet shows new power in handling the orchestra. But it was not until 1851, when *Rigoletto* was first performed, that the composer's instinctive genius (as opposed to the more reasoned development of Wagner's powers) was fully manifest.

Verdi himself realized that a part of his success lay in the more varied and striking nature of the subjects of his new works. The drawing of the

characters of the Duke, of Rigoletto (his humpbacked assistant in seduction) and of Gilda, Rigoletto's daughter who falls a victim to the Duke's
insatiability, would have been impossible to the composer of the melo-
dramatic *Ernani*. Yet his method underwent no profound change such as
that of Wagner's in achieving this greater vividness. A subtler strain of
melody is invented to portray the heedlessness of the Duke; but there is
no hint of the pondered structural intricacies of *Lohengrin* (completed
three years before *Rigoletto*) or of *Das Rheingold*, which soon after this
time began to shape itself in Wagner's brain. The same skill and inven-
tiveness are shown in *Il Trovatore* and *La Traviata*, both produced in
1853 and both retaining popularity to this day. The *Sicilian Vespers*,
written for Paris, suffered because of its subject (a massacre of the French
by the Sicilians); *Simone Boccanegra* was a failure in its first form, but
was later worked over and has again recently made a deep impression,
almost throughout the operatic world. *Un Ballo in Maschera* ("The
Masked Ball"), after its political allusions had been thinly disguised, was
produced in 1859 with the greatest acclaim.

So great was Verdi's fame that he was now requested to compose operas for three widely distant cities. *La Forza del Destino* was produced at
St. Petersburg in 1862. *Don Carlos* was wildly acclaimed at Paris in 1867.
But the third of these "foreign" works was not only the greatest success,
but marked another stage in the development of the composer's manner.
This was *Aïda*, written for the opera in Cairo and produced there in
1871. Not merely in magnificence and in impressive spectacularity, but
in actual expressiveness, *Aïda* is far in advance of the earlier works. It is
not through any such device as that of the leading motive that this vivid
expression is achieved, but rather through a more subtle adjustment of
the suggestion of melody itself to the matter at issue. Of "new method,"
then, it is scarcely possible to speak; Verdi's later method is only the
earlier method perfected. But in the course of this drama the mere
abandonment to musical pleasure, irrespective of the sense of the action,
is more and more rare. There is no laborious development of musical
matter in the symphonic sense (requiring, often, more of the hearer's
attention than he can well spare from observation of the drama itself),
but rather a closer approach to the embodiment of the sense of the action
in a comparatively simple musical fabric, clearly designed and easily followed. Even more is this true of the two last operas—*Otello* (1887) and
Falstaff (produced in 1893 when the composer was eighty years old).
For the last two he had the invaluable service of Arrigo Boïto as librettist.
The reduction of Shakespeare's tragedy, and the comedy *The Merry
Wives of Windsor*, to operatic proportions was an apparently insurmount-

able task, unless (as in the case of Ambroise Thomas's *Hamlet*) the sense
of the original were to be ignored; yet both the Moor and the clown
retain their essential qualities, and especially in *Falstaff* it was possible
for Verdi to achieve a characterization which is altogether convincing
and is universally admitted to be an achievement of the first order.

It is perhaps falsely suggestive to include mention of Verdi in a discussion of anti-Wagnerian tendencies. Wagner was at first wholly unknown
to his Italian contemporary, and, when he became known, was greatly
admired. Verdi undertook no polemic opposition to Wagner's work
or even to his theories. Wagner was accepted as one who had found a
remarkable solution of the problem of opera. Verdi merely showed that
he could not regard Wagner's as the one and only solution, by solving
the problem himself in quite another and a somewhat more traditional
way. To have shown that the Italian tradition of opera was a living tradition, and that the many Italian operas of the earlier years of the century
were faulty in their sentimental or bombastic or overornamental treatment
of their themes rather than in their adherence to the Italian tradition
itself, was a great service. To have shown, similarly, that—whatever may
be the futility of really absolute music—the traditional forms of independent instrumental music were also fully alive, was the inestimable service to music rendered by Johannes Brahms. Neither Brahms nor Verdi
had followers of their own great stature. But the simultaneous existence
of three such great artists is an indication of the breadth and significance
to which musical literature had attained at the close of the nineteenth
century.

These three, however, by no means indicate the whole range of musical
thought in the period. Russia was emerging from musical dependence
(chiefly on Italy, as we have seen); and France itself, reluctantly following the ideals if not the methods of Berlioz, was approaching a musical
renaissance of remarkable interest. Italy, England, Scandinavia, Spain,
and America were likewise reawakened. Science began to contribute materially to the clarification (and pseudo science to the confusion) of
theoretical ideas; historical methods were for the first time applied to the
study of musical developments; musical organizations devoted to study,
performance, or propaganda multiplied rapidly, and the musical public
—consisting in Beethoven's time of a small circle of enthusiasts led by a
few aristocratic patrons—gradually became the enormous and unwieldy
body which we know today. With so many forces at work producing
such diverse results, competent judgment of their intensity and probable
effect is impossible. But some awareness is necessary of the many varied
styles and theories of musical thought which are current, and whose

interaction will determine, perhaps in the comparatively near future, whether the future is to show a continuity with tradition or a complete break with it.

Russia having formed during the nineteenth century the principal tributary to the main stream of musical effort, we shall turn now to a sketch of that interesting and latterly extremely vital development.

The Rise of Nationalism

RUSSIAN MUSIC FROM ITS BEGINNINGS TO THE TWENTIETH CENTURY

A SWIFT retrospect of the course of nineteenth-century music, as
far as we have traced it, will show that during most of that
period two widely divergent styles of composition had dominated musical Europe—styles which may be designated generally as Northern and Southern, or more specifically as German and Italian. This
divergence had existed indeed ever since the sixteenth-century conflict
of the Netherlanders and the Italians. It is true that French music came
in some degree, and especially in opera, to reflect the national taste; but
this music, although distinguishable enough from the Italian, was rather an
offshoot from the Italian manner than in a style recognizable as indigenously French. English music similarly, dominated in the eighteenth century by Handel and Haydn, and in the nineteenth by Beethoven and
Mendelssohn, failed to attain any distinctively national characteristics, and
remained an offshoot of the German stock, even more subordinate to its
parent than was the French.

The reasons for this condition are not far to seek. Musical backwardness
did not lie (as was often popularly supposed) in any racial inferiority, but
merely in the lack of a pervasive musical culture in these nations. Italy
possessed a long tradition of musical achievement; and Germany had a
singularly rich and cultivated heritage of folk music—music which in the
course of the Protestant revolution had been available for the expression
of the profoundest of popular sentiments. To the Italian and the German,
consequently, music was an indispensable element of cultured life. To
the Frenchman and the Englishman on the other hand, music, however
enjoyable, was an ornament and a luxury of life. Ornaments and luxuries
from abroad are mostly more prized than homemade products. Moreover,
the perfection of style which had been attained in the two main fields of
production was so great that none of the lesser nations—however great

their love of music, their technical accomplishment, or their ambition to produce independent work—could fail to recognize the superiority of the two dominant styles.

Gradually it became recognized that merely to equal the foreign masters in technical finish was not enough for the achievement of a really national art. Nationally distinctive music must rest, either upon the folk song (as in Germany), or upon some equally spontaneous and universal type of popular expression whose characteristics could be reflected in artistic music. Dissatisfaction with imported products was only an evidence of the desire for a fuller expression of national feeling. But this dissatisfaction was growing; and the ideal of a national music—whether or not it was to be founded upon a sound basis—began to be propagated in many countries during the last half of the nineteenth century.

The first of these conscious efforts was made in Russia. We have had but little occasion so far to speak of the course of music in Russia. This we must now observe from its beginnings if we are to understand the peculiarities, both of the Russian style in general, and of the peculiar art —half instinctive, half derivative—which conscious study of the nationalistic problem produced.

A nation whose territory is so vast that more than twenty widely different dialects are spoken within its borders; whose institutions and traditions differ largely in different regions, and still more largely from those of Western Europe; and whose religion (Greek Catholicism) is likewise far removed in dogma and ritual from the Catholicism of the Western Church—such a nation must either develop a very different type of musical thought from that which we have so far studied, or, if it adopts the Western idiom, must show many highly individual peculiarities in expression. Widespread illiteracy among the Russian population gave rise, of course, to a wealth of orally transmitted legend which is the source of much of the written literature. Folk songs and folk dances, similarly unstudied, represent the native impulsiveness in all its crudity. But of the development of indigenous Russian music, little has so far been exactly studied.

Perhaps the most complete picture is to be found in certain collections of Russian songs, phonographically recorded and later notated, made in the Russian prison camps in Austria during World War I. These collections, assembled and critically studied by Professor Dr. Robert Lach of the University of Vienna, show an extraordinary diversity of musical character and a wide range of technical accomplishment. The basic scales are sometimes pentatonic, sometimes heptatonic. The rhythms are sometimes those of the Gregorian chant (a single time unit corresponding to the single beat of the bar, but without arrangement into any symmetrical beat-groups such as we have in 2-4, 3-4 or other regular measures), sometimes in frequently varied patterns (successions of 3-4, 2-4, 5-4 or other measure groups), and sometimes in regular measure throughout. In the simpler songs there is the most incredible monotony of motive repetition. One, for example, the song of a young peasant who has seen a fair damsel on a balcony and dreams of winning her, has seventeen successive repetitions of the notes D, C, B, A (with no variant save that certain notes are more or less frequently repeated) and each phrase ends with the two quarter notes B, A. The singer of this song sang eight others, all showing the same basic pattern, sometimes extended to the compass of a fifth, but always in the same descending phrases ending with longer notes. More primitive musical ideas than these could scarcely be found among the most aboriginal tribes. (The reader will note the resemblance of this music to that which we found at the very outset of our study, based on the interval of the descending fourth.) Other singers, from various regions of the Russian Empire, sang more varied songs, some displaying an almost equal monotony of motive repetition; others a higher variety when the same rhythm pattern is provided with different melodic curves; others, songs in which several motives are combined and alternated to produce a melody altogether akin to our own song form.

Altogether remarkable is the harmonic treatment. Almost every essential step in the long history of harmonic development seems to be illustrated: the parallelism of fifths and fourths which gave the earliest organum; the procedure characteristic of the *Ars nova* and the earliest Netherlanders, with the frequent occurrence of *faulx bourdon;* the later, more independent polyphony; and the still more modern, essentially harmonic structure. Professor Lach suggests—with much plausibility—that at least certain of these processes may have been somehow transplanted to the Caucasus at the time when they were current in Western Europe, and may have been preserved there almost unaltered: musical fossils, as it were. No proof can be adduced; but it is hardly likely that under such very different conditions the musical evolution of Russia should show, without direct influence, such marked similarity to that of Western Europe.

For the Russians, as we have said, are Greek Catholics, so that the religious as well as the social traditions of Russia remained largely isolated from Western influences. Both in melodic character and in the various systems of notation, the earliest church music shows large individuality of effort, even the Byzantine influence being relatively slight and confined to externals of ornament. One peculiarity in the development of Russian church music is that instruments were never allowed in the churches.[1] When we remember the great influence of instruments on the later forms of Western religious song, and consider how far this amalgamation of voices and instruments affected the whole formal structure of secular as well as religious music, we see how widely the current of Russian musical thought differed from that of the West.

The first effective contact with Western musical art was made through the efforts of Peter the Great. This, however, was merely a contact. The Empress Anne (1730–1740) imported an Italian opera company; and Italian music, often set to Russian stories, formed the substance of the Russian operas for almost a century thereafter. We have noted the engagement at St. Petersburg of successful Italian opera composers such as Galuppi, Traetta, Paisiello, Sarti, and Cimarosa. The activity of native Russians was even less significant than was the work of native Germans, like Hasse, during the period of Italian domination. There was thus no strong development of the native Russian idiom, and no effective attempt at Russian adoption of the far more highly finished artistic methods of Western Europe, until the nineteenth century.

GLINKA AND DARGOMIJSKY

The true beginning of the Russian national movement is attributed to Michael Glinka. He was born in 1804, the son of a retired army officer who was sympathetic with the boy's musical tastes. Glinka heard much native music played by a band in the employ of his uncle. His general education was good, and he had instruction in piano (from John Field himself) and in violin; but none at first in musical theory. It was only after some years of office work that he decided to devote himself wholly to music. In 1830 he went to Milan, studying with Basili, director of the Conservatory, and becoming well acquainted with Bellini and Donizetti and their music. Although he was somewhat influenced by this music, his idea of becoming a true exponent of Russian art was growing. He went through a rapid survey of musical theory with Dehn in Berlin, and returned to St. Petersburg, associating with Pushkin, Gogol, and other leaders of contemporary literature. The result of this association was Glinka's first opera *A Life for the Czar*. The story is that of one Ivan Soussanin who, to prevent the assassination of the Czar, Michael Romanoff, joined the forces of the invading Poles and led them into a remote forest, where his plot was discovered and he was put to death. The opera was

[1] Doctor Archibald Davison of Harvard University, in his book *Protestant Church Music* (E. C. Schirmer, 1933) reaches the conclusion that Russian church music is one of the two or three highest and most idealized types of religious expression.

produced in 1836. Its patriotic theme and its music—largely drawn from popular airs—gave it extraordinary popularity. Glinka was appointed director of the Imperial Chapel Choir. Traveling to Little Russia and to Finland in search of new voices, he acquired much new musical material which was at length assembled in his second and much more thoroughly Russian opera *Russlan and Ludmilla*. Probably because this music lacked the traces of Italian influence which are present in the *Life for the Czar* (characteristics to which the Russian public was long accustomed), and also because of its confused libretto, *Russlan* was almost a failure. Yet the music is both more mature and more original than that of the earlier work. In vividness of color, in its manner of thematic development (which is more vivacious and less mechanical than the contemporary German fashion), and in the thematic substance itself the work is highly individual. The Overture shows all these qualities, and contains probably the first instance of the use of the whole-tone scale—a tone sequence which was later to be much employed by Debussy and other moderns.

After the production of *Russlan* Glinka traveled again, first to Paris where he established cordial relations with Berlioz, and later to Spain, whose national idiom he found most congenial. Two so-called Overtures, *Jota Aragonesa* and *A Night in Madrid*, show how thoroughly he felt the spell of Spanish rhythms; and the frequency with which later Russian composers take up Spanish themes is said by some to be due to Glinka's example. He produced no more operas. (Incidental music to *Prince Kolmsky* was written before his foreign visits. It is said to contain his best music.) He began another when, after a three-year residence in Warsaw, he returned to St. Petersburg; but gave it up in response to a new enthusiasm for church music. To study this field he went again to Dehn in Berlin; but at a concert of his own works arranged by Meyerbeer he caught a severe chill and died in February, 1857.

In the circle of his musical friends in St. Petersburg were three men destined to carry on his ideas and to establish on a sure foundation that national art for which Glinka had striven. These were Seroff, a critic; Dargomijsky, Glinka's successor as leader of the new movement in Russian opera; and Balakireff, in many ways the chief inspiration of the group later known as the "Nationalists." Seroff was a very learned, very polemic, very self-contradictory critical writer, who first despised and later lauded Wagner, and who took the same changing attitude toward the Russian national movement. His service was largely that of an awakener of public interest; but he also wrote—with almost no preliminary training—two remarkably successful operas: *Judith*, which is somewhat Wagnerian in manner, and *Rogneda*, which repudiates Wagnerism.

Dargomijsky (1813–1869), at first satisfied to compose amateurish songs, was inspired by Glinka to perfect his technique, and entered the field of opera with *Esmeralda* (based on Hugo's *Notre Dame de Paris*) which, largely in the manner of Meyerbeer, was a failure. His next attempt, however, *Russalka*, based on a Russian legend and using Pushkin's verse, was dramatically very effective, and musically in a vein which truly continued the movement which Glinka had originated. But its lack of Italian suavity made its first reception dubious. The composer left for a tour of Western Europe which was successful only in Belgium, and came back to find his *Russalka* enthusiastically approved by a new group of nationalists, the "Five," whose support encouraged him to enter upon his last opera *The Stone Guest*. In pursuit of his aim to make operatic music interpret the words, he had devised a new species of "melodic recitative," supported by a highly colorful orchestra, but not subordinated to the orchestra as is often the case with Wagnerian melody. *The Stone Guest* (which Dargomijsky left slightly incomplete, and which was finished by Cui and orchestrated by Rimsky-Korsakoff) was consequently condemned as being a "recitative in three acts." But his method—with many differences— foreshadows that of Debussy in *Pelléas et Mélisande;* and at least in its humor and satire the work is a distinct contribution to Russian musical literature. Humor and satire, as well as the emotions more usually expressed in music, also characterize Dargomijsky's songs, of which he left a large number.

THE "FIVE"

The famous "Five" who began in the sixties to exert a large influence on the course of Russian music, were a group of men none of whom were professional musicians and only one (Balakireff) a "learned" composer. A military officer (César Cui), a scientist in medicine and surgery (Alexander Borodin), a naval officer (Rimsky-Korsakoff), and an administrative officer (Modest Moussorgsky), largely under the guiding spirit of Mily Balakireff, completed the group. It will be noted that the most widely known of all Russian composers, Tchaikovsky, who was the contemporary of the "Five," was not included in the group. This was because the progressive party felt that Tchaikovsky (and also the famous pianist and composer Rubinstein) were so steeped in German musical methods as to be unable to represent the true Russian spirit.

Balakireff (1837–1910) came of a well-to-do family and was given every opportunity for study. After taking a degree at the University of Kazan he met Alexander Oulibicheff (a biographer of Mozart and a violent opponent of Beethoven) at whose country estate he found a fine musical library and a private orchestra. Making full use of the practical and theoretical opportunities thus offered, he was soon introduced by his host

to Glinka, and went to live in St. Petersburg. Here his nationalistic sentiment (doubtless aroused by Glinka) had full expression. It took the
form, however, of music not merely on Russian themes, but upon the
characteristic music of other lands. He wrote an overture on Spanish
themes which Glinka had given him; the extraordinary pianoforte fantasia
Islamey, one of the most original virtuoso pieces in the literature of the
instrument, filled with that oriental coloring which is so often to be found
in later Russian music; and, later, an overture on Czechish themes. He
published a large collection of popular Russian songs, made incidental
music for *King Lear,* and, as a very important contribution to Russian
musical life, founded the St. Petersburg Free School of Music, in connection with which performances of modern Russian works were given. His
most characteristic works are doubtless *Islamey* and the symphonic poem
Tamara, also on an oriental theme. He also wrote two Symphonies, in C
and D minor, a Piano Concerto, several overtures, and many piano pieces.

César Cui (1835–1918), at length Lieutenant General and Professor of
Military Engineering, was the son of a Napoleonic officer who, wounded
at Smolensk, was unable to return with the French army on its disastrous
retreat. The father was something of a musician, so that the boy's studies
were encouraged. His ambition was much fired by a meeting with Balakireff in 1856, and by his marriage to a pupil of Dargomijsky. Two symphonic scherzos were followed by a comic opera *The Mandarin's Son,*
very much in the style of Auber. He wrote several other operas, the most
important being *William Ratcliff* and *Angelo;* but his style was too light
for this or for extended orchestral composition of a high order. Indeed,
his style is far more French than Russian. It was his fiery defense of the
nationalist movement rather than his compositions which made him of
such importance to the new cause. He was not a sound critic; but his
opposition to the Italianism under which the Russian spirit was smothered
did much to bring native works to the popular attention. Also, by ac-
quainting the Countess Mercy-Argenteau, an eager musical enthusiast who
lived in Belgium, with the works of the "Five," he served to introduce
modern Russian music to the Belgians and to Western Europe.

Alexander Borodin (1833–1887) is musically a far more significant figure. His musical talents were recognized and encouraged by his mother,
but when the medical career was chosen for him he embraced it without
opposition. As a student at St. Petersburg, however, he had many musical
associations and at first showed a decided inclination for German music.
After taking his degree he went on an extended scientific tour of Western
Europe, returning in 1862 as lecturer at the St. Petersburg Academy of
Medicine. He now became acquainted, through Balakireff, with the nationalistic movement, began to study with his new friend, and soon began

a Symphony which was at last performed in 1869. It was warmly received, in spite of the opposition of the reactionaries who still longed for Italian sweetness. After composing several remarkable songs his attention was drawn to opera, and the subject of *The Epic of the Army of Igor* (a twelfth-century Russian hero somewhat akin to King Arthur) was deeply studied. The project was temporarily shelved, chiefly because of an invitation to compose the last act of a ballet *Mlada* in which Cui, Moussorgsky, and Rimsky-Korsakoff were to collaborate. Although the work never came to performance, Borodin's part was completed and the dramatic stimulus given by his colleagues' praise was sufficient to reinterest him in *Igor*. His many official duties, together with his frail health, made it impossible to work rapidly. Indeed, *Prince Igor* was left unfinished at Borodin's death. But enough was done so that Rimsky-Korsakoff and his pupil Glazounoff could prepare it for performance. The Polovtsian Dances from this opera are familiar to every concertgoer. For so influential a man, his work is remarkably slight: two Symphonies, two String Quartets, about twelve songs and some piano pieces, together with the ballet finale (which was also completed by Rimsky-Korsakoff) and the opera. He was at variance with some of his colleagues—notably with Dargomijsky—in the matter of operatic recitative; but in essentials he was thoroughly Russian in sentiment, and shows a singular keenness of color perception and of suggestive character, both in chamber and operatic works and in the orchestral *Sketch of the Steppes of Central Asia*. His work was warmly welcomed in Belgium by the Countess Mercy-Argenteau, and was much praised by Liszt who performed his Second Symphony at Weimar.

Modest Moussorgsky (1835–1881)—shortest lived, most passionately devoted, most original, and most unfortunate of the "Five"—is latterly coming to be regarded as the most influential of that group on the later course of Russian music. Passing his earliest years far from the city and in contact with the peasantry, he acquired what was ultimately to prove a dominant interest in the raw substance of Russian life. Although the boy was intended for the army, his father provided also for his musical education. His early facility as a pianist was well cultivated, and his large gifts of improvisation sometimes took the form of staves and notes on paper. His preparations for the military profession were thorough, and although he continued his musical studies little was done to instill in his mind either any exact knowledge of the principles of musical form as they were understood by the professors, or any profound respect for the forms themselves. He took music as he found it, enjoyed German symphony and Italian opera, and began to ponder the problems of music and the idea of nationalism only when, in the winter of 1857, he met Dargomijsky. He began to study the works of Glinka and of his new friend. At the same time, in more or less systematic study with Balakireff, he made a really analytical study of classical masterpieces, gaining a new insight into musical principles. By comparison with this new and profound interest, his military studies began to pall upon him. It was not long before he gave up his commission; but his mastery of composition was quite unequal to the making of any profit-yielding reputation, so that from this time on he had always to struggle with financial adversity.

A deep sympathy with the lower social orders was soon awakened. Literature of the realistic school sharpened his awareness of the sometimes sordid, sometimes unconsciously poetic, impulses which motivated the lives he saw; and—doubtless largely through the examples already set by Dargomijsky—he began to see music as something justified, not by its formal perfection but by its fidelity to life. The *Peasant's Cradle Song* (really a complaint of the peasants against their hard conditions of life), and *Savishna* (a terrible rendition of the amorous suit of a half-witted youth to the village beauty) were among his first attempts to make music speak the language of life. An opera on Flaubert's *Salammbô* was begun but never completed; a choral work, *The Destruction of Sennacherib* and a symphonic poem *Night on the Bare Mountain* (a weird revel of witches and goblins who are dispersed by the sound of the church bell) show growing mastery of the realistic expression toward which he was striving. *Marriage,* an intended setting after the manner of Dargomijsky of the exact text of a play by Gogol, reached only the end of its first act; but the adoption of an ordinary theme of everyday life for musical setting was in itself a novelty, and the treatment is said to be extraordinarily vivid, even though the prose text with its rapid and humorous dialogue demanded incessant changes of rhythm and most unusual melodic lines.

In 1868 Pushkin's *Boris Godounoff* was suggested to him as the basis of an opera. Its first version was completed in a year. Dargomijsky heard it and saw in it a fulfillment of his own ideals in writing *The Stone Guest.* The work in its first form lacked feminine interest, but after some revision it was completed and performed in 1874. Its complete unconventionality was the cause of much division of opinion; but the subsequent, though much belated, acceptance of the work has made the world aware that it represents a distinct contribution to the vexed problem of opera. The musical substance has little of that self-contained symphonic development which Wagner achieved—a development so complete in itself that it hardly gives the hearer liberty of attention for the drama itself. Yet, on a less imposing scale, the principle of the leading motive is consistently employed; and the declamation is on the whole far more realistic than Wagner's. Intellectually the music is far less of an achievement, forming a less complete and sensitive embodiment of the whole emotional purport of the drama; but considered as a single factor in a complex scheme of word, tone, and action, it is probably true that Moussorgsky's music forms a far more assimilable element than Wagner's.

Only one more opera was fated to come from Moussorgsky's pen— *Khovanstchina. Boris* is the tale of a regent of the Russian throne who had ascended to power through the murder of the half-witted heir of Ivan the Terrible. *Khovanstchina* is the tale of one of Boris's reforms and its effect on the people. Nikon, appointed to the Patriarchate of Moscow by Boris, revised the liturgical books of the Greek Church, provoking a schism which lasted until the twentieth century. One of the families which resisted the new movement was that of the Khovansky. Opposition to the policy of Westernization, pursued by Peter the Great, was led by this family. *Khovanstchina* means, then, the intrigues of this family. Moussorgsky himself contrived his text, the suggestion and the historical material being provided by Vladimir Stassow, art historian and writer of music. The music is somewhat less revolutionary than that of *Boris*, in that it is musically more consistently developed. But the same vividness of invention and characterization is manifest. The work has been less popular, however, than *Boris*.

Smaller pieces show the same remarkable power of musical drawing. Sketches of child life, especially interesting by comparison with Schumann's whose attitude is that of a sympathetic observer, while Moussorgsky's is that of the participator in all the games and punishments; a delightful piece of musical satire, the *Peep Show*, which ridicules the critics of the new movement; and *Pictures at an Exhibition*, a musical reproduction of ten paintings exhibited by the composer's friend Victor Hartmann —such works as these show, in a smaller compass, that same extraordinary power of suggesting reality without sacrificing musical interest which makes the operas unique. There is no doubt that Moussorgsky is the immediate inspiration of the modern Russian group.

Youngest of the group of nationalists was Nicholas Rimsky-Korsakoff (1844–1908). Destined for the navy by family tradition, he was nevertheless encouraged to develop his obviously superior musical talents. Living in the country, his first musical experiences were somewhat meager; but when he went to the Naval College in St. Petersburg he managed to study both piano and 'cello and to do some desultory work in composition. In 1861 he was brought into contact with the little coterie of nationalists, began serious and energetic study with Balakireff, and even continued this work on the cruise which was a necessary part of his naval cadetship. He composed his First Symphony—which is the first work in that form by a Russian composer—on that tour, and it was played under Balakireff at one of his Free School concerts. The first fruit of the newly stimulated nationalistic attitude was a symphonic poem *Sadko*, upon which theme the composer afterwards produced an opera. A fantasia on Serbian themes followed, which won the favorable notice of Tchaikovsky. Thereupon Rimsky-Korsakoff turned his attention to opera.

Just how far he was to follow the principles of Dargomijsky was his greatest problem, both now and later. He had not that instinctive feeling for eloquent and descriptive recitative which Moussorgsky was to show; but being in close association with that artist, his ideals were doubtless much the same. Hence, *Pskovitianka*, his first opera, follows largely the method of recitative. (The tale is that of the threatened deprivation of the liberties of the city of Pskov by Ivan the Terrible.) It is the choral writing and the harmonic color rather than the somewhat dry recitative which gives vitality to the work. His easy mastery of orchestration was also rapidly maturing, and it was at this time (1872) that he took up the orchestration of *The Stone Guest*. The symphonic suite *Antar*, often spoken of as his second symphony, followed. Suddenly he began to feel that his technique was deficient, and began the assiduous study of counterpoint—a curious move, quite opposed to the principles of the nationalists who were averse to all that smacked of the Western idiom.

Rimsky-Korsakoff took over the Free School concerts in 1874, and immersed himself in teaching counterpoint, preparing also a great treatise on instrumentation. Naturally he was able to compose but little. In 1878, however, appeared his second opera *A Night in May*, based on a tale of Gogol. The subject is fantastic, and the music far less in the style of recitative. In 1882 was produced the opera *Snegouroschka* ("The Snow Maiden")—an allegorical fairy tale of spring. In the following year he became assistant director of the Imperial Chapel, and a year later refused the headship of the Moscow Conservatory. He accepted, however, at the invitation of the wealthy publisher Belaieff, the conductorship of the "Russian Symphony Concerts," organized for the production of native works. All this was a further distraction from composition, and the theoretical study and teaching—requiring an exact formulation of technical principles—was a deterrent from that pursuit of the nationalistic ideals which he had at first supported.

The composer completed various works of Borodin, among these the orchestration of *Prince Igor*, adding, it has been said, certain emendations of his own which are not wholly in accord with Borodin's intentions. Two of Rimsky-Korsakoff's most widely known orchestral pieces, the *Capriccio espagnol* and *Scheherazade*, soon followed. The extraordinary brilliance of the orchestration, especially in the *Capriccio*, earned from Tchaikovsky the most unstinted praise, and made these works stand out as stimulating examples of what, with Berlioz and Wagner, had already begun to be a new departure in composition. The orchestra, that is, becomes the tool of the virtuoso, as the solo instruments had done; and the virtuoso conductor was soon to appear. Neither of these works is directly national in character; but Glinka had long ago set the example of dealing with Spanish themes, and the oriental atmosphere not only pervades much of Borodin's music but gives a distinctive flavor to many features of Russian literature and custom. Some of this influence no doubt is imbedded in the Byzantine ritual; some is preserved in the strange mixture of pagan with Christian mythology, revealed in many Russian customs observed at the celebration of feast days. The latter peculiarity is illustrated in Rimsky-Korsakoff's overture *A Russian Easter* which, in the composer's words, is intended to depict "this legendary and heathen side of the holiday, this transition from the gloomy and mysterious evening of Passion Saturday to the unbridled pagan-religious merrymaking on the morn of Easter Sunday." There is at least nothing antinational or merely imitative of Western ideas in these works.

From 1889 until his death, Rimsky-Korsakoff's efforts were almost all in the field of opera. Twelve operatic works were completed in these nineteen years. Most of these are on Russian themes. The exceptions are *Mozart and Salieri* (a dramatic duologue by Pushkin, in which Salieri is made to poison Mozart), and *Servilia*, a tale of Rome under Nero. Of the works on Russian subjects, the most important appear to be *Sadko* (upon which subject he had already written a symphonic sketch), *Tsar Saltan* (whose subject might have come from the *Arabian Nights*), *Kitej* (whose legend is that of a city made invisible to its besiegers through divine aid), and *The Golden Cockerel* (another fairy tale). It will be seen from these subjects that Rimsky-Korsakoff was of a different mind from Moussorgsky with regard to the expressive purpose of dramatic music. Fancy rather than reality inspired him. His method consequently varies with his theme, being sometimes lyrical, sometimes declamatory in the manner of Moussorgsky, and sometimes Wagnerian.

TCHAIKOVSKY

From the very diverse personalities of the "Five," it will be seen that the results of their work were far greater than were contemplated in the somewhat narrow program of nationalism with which they set out. They were more truly nationalistic than they knew; but it was perhaps unfortunate that in their conscious efforts they formulated a definition of their aims which excluded from their number a composer of such distinctive gifts as Tchaikovsky. He, together with Anton Rubinstein, was dismissed as a slavish follower of German methods. Cui remarked, "It would be a serious error to consider Rubinstein as a Russian composer; he is merely a Russian who composes." And this verdict, coinciding with our present almost complete indifference to the music which Rubinstein composed, seems justified. As a very great pianist Rubinstein will be remembered, and his influence, though not as great as that of Liszt on the pianistic art, is likely to prove permanent. But neither his twenty operas nor his six symphonies (save the Second or *Ocean* Symphony which has the distinction of having been forgotten all over the world) have shown any permanent vitality. Yet the influence of Anton Rubinstein and his brother Nicholas on Russian music was profoundly important, since they were the founders of the Imperial Russian Musical Society (founded 1861), and were directors of the Conservatories of St. Petersburg and Moscow.

Peter Ilyitch Tchaikovsky (1840–1893), accused by his compatriots of a lack of national feeling, has nevertheless largely provided the Western musical world with its fundamental concept of the Russian character. Whether that concept is sound or not is a question to be settled by posterity. Tchaikovsky did not accept the doctrines of the "Five"; but his music certainly reflects the Russian temperament at least as fully as that of Cui, who was verbally an ardent champion of nationalism but was musically allied to France. And the Westerner is at a loss to understand how the oriental leaning of Balakireff and Borodin, or the Spanish enthusiasm of Rimsky-Korsakoff,[2] is thoroughly representative of Russian character, while the *Marche Slave* or the *Pathetic* Symphony must be described as the work of an expatriate. Foreigners seldom offer definitions of nationality which satisfy the nationals themselves; but neither do the nationals see their own characteristics in the light in which they appear to foreigners. And the foreigner is inclined to think that the vastness and diversity of Russia should be large enough to include so sharply marked a personality as Tchaikovsky, who certainly belongs to no other people.

No prodigy, he developed his musical powers only indifferently in connection with his studies in jurisprudence, which were pursued with equal patience but without zeal. Gradually, however, he came to see that he was destined to be a musician. Only in 1861 did he begin the study

[2] There are, indeed, many actual points of contact between the Russian idiom and those of Spain and also of the Orient. The Byzantine influence, apparent in Russian art and architecture, was also exerted in Spain, so that a certain common bond may justly be felt to exist between the composers of the two countries. The various strains of oriental blood appearing in the strangely mixed Russian population will account for the frequent appearance in Russian music of such oriental suggestion as is to be found in the *Russian Easter*. But just as we feel that our own nationality is an entity hardly to be fully expressed in music through the use of Indian or Negro themes, so we feel that the Russian character (whatever that may be) is not significantly to be suggested by music from alien sources.

of theory. Two years later he abandoned the minor position which he had held and began to devote himself wholly to music. He completed his course at the Conservatory in 1865, and in the following year was offered the post of professor of harmony at the newly founded Conservatory of Moscow. It is significant that during his youth he had no intimate contact with Russian folk music, knew nothing of Bach or Beethoven, but was a frequent visitor to the Italian opera. Mozart, among the classic writers, was his idol. To these influences must be attributed his always prominent lyrical bent, and the somewhat diffuse structure which characterizes almost all his work.

In 1868 he came into contact with the leaders of the nationalist movement. His Second Symphony was based on Little Russian folk songs and dates from the ensuing period; it contrasts with the first (called *Winter Daydreams*) which is the product of the shy, self-centered individual which Tchaikovsky then was and which he always really remained. His sympathies were not unreservedly with the Five, even at first; and though his personal relations remained cordial, he grew always further from the ideals of this group. His work was very heavy; yet he managed, in addition to much teaching, to complete before 1875 four operas (one was destroyed), a String Quartet, the Third Symphony, and the famous Piano Concerto in B flat minor. Owing to the usually sympathetic energies of Nicholas Rubinstein, his works had had competent performance and were generally well received by the Russian public. Abroad he had had little success. Vienna, Berlin, and Paris rejected his works, but England and America had showed real interest. His later great reputation rested upon the favor of his work with those whom he was held to be incapable of representing truly—his own countrymen. But its appeal was due rather to its fervent lyricism than to any nationalistic enthusiasm, whether aroused by propaganda or, as in the case of Moussorgsky, by a profound conviction of the relation of art to the life of the people.

Love affairs seem to have played but little part in Tchaikovsky's life. He was smitten by the charms of Désirée Artôt, leading soprano at the St. Peterburg opera; but he was little disturbed when he learned that she had suddenly married another singer in Warsaw. In 1877 he married a woman "with whom," as he said, "I am not in the least in love"—and left her after nine weeks, almost mad with disillusionment. His greatest feminine friendship was for a woman whom he never saw—Madame Nadejda von Meck, the wealthy widow of an engineer, who, deeply convinced by his music, at length contrived to settle upon him a considerable pension which relieved him of the necessity of teaching and left him free to compose. His gradually increasing popularity led to several tours abroad—taking him at last as far as New York—where he found his music more and more enthusiastically received. But his shyness never was cured, and he was always homesick as soon as he had left Russia.

Although Tchaikovsky met many great musicians on his tours, he seems to have had no musically fruitful intimacies after that with Nicholas Rubinstein. He took no part in the raging Brahms-Wagner controversies, respecting Brahms but disliking his music, while he disliked Wagner and his views but was much moved by his music. So he lived, intellectually alone, feeding upon his own lyrical sensitivity and expressing almost always his own personality only. Self-centered and self-fertilized, his genius underwent little change. His technical powers grew, of course, with the years; but there is discoverable no such difference in imaginative attitude as underlies the various periods which distinguish Beethoven's style. His structure is often described as weak. MacDowell's remark, "Tchaikovsky's music often sounds better than it is," is a natural result of the comparison of Tchaikovsky's symphonies or concertos with those, for example, of Brahms. Rigorous logic, as well as a keen sense of proportion, is lacking in the Russian's work; but the critics do not note that, the basic idea being almost always lyrical, such themes must have their own process of development. The result is not in the highest sense a symphony; but the public has sufficiently indicated that, whatever it may be called, the music has immediate and enduring appeal.

As a dramatic composer Tchaikovsky exhibits the same qualities. *Eugen Onegin*, his most successful opera, is (as the composer described it) a series of *Lyrical Scenes* from Pushkin's most masterly poetic tale. With really dramatic subjects such as *Joan of Arc* or *The Oprichnik* or *Mazeppa* he failed, largely because of his persistence in the use of Italian forms, and because the texts offered too little opportunity for the display of his one great gift of lyricism. The last operas, *The Queen of Spades* (also based on Pushkin) and *Iolanthe*, are again in his own manner. The former is almost as popular in Russia as *Eugen Onegin*. In the allied form of the ballet his limitations are less disturbing. *The Sleeping Beauty*, and especially the *Nutcracker*, from which a suite was extracted that has proved one of the most widely popular pieces in dance literature, show the same quick sensitivity which is the first quality to appeal to us in his other works. There is but one Overture on a dramatic theme, *Hamlet;* but that is called *Overture Fantasia* and is not far removed from the symphonic fantasias *Romeo and Juliet*, *The Tempest*, and *Francesca da Rimini*, which are indistinguishable from symphonic poems.

Of the six Symphonies, only the last three are frequently to be heard. The last, the *Pathetic*, with its lugubrious *Finale*, is often called the "suicide" symphony from the fact that three days after its not too successful first performance the composer drank a glass of unboiled water, contracted cholera, and died within a week. (But Tchaikovsky was firm in his opinion that this was "the best thing he ever had composed, or ever should compose"; and this does not represent a suicidal state of mind.) The Fifth Symphony, with its Fate motto dominating all the movements, is really far weaker in moral resistance. Its slow movement, however, probably represents as fully as any other the high tide of Tchaikovsky's genius. The Fourth, too, especially in its *Scherzo* (in which the strings are played *pizzicato* throughout), shows much originality of invention. All the orchestral work shows a most perfect command of the problem of orchestral writing, though in none is there the conscious display of virtuosity which is to be seen in Rimsky-Korsakoff's *Spanish Caprice*.

There are three Concertos for piano, of which only the first (in B flat minor) has been widely heard. The one Concerto for violin is almost equally popular, and the *Rococo Variations* for 'cello and orchestra stand high in the literature of that instrument. His chamber works are few— three String Quartets, the Piano Trio dedicated "to the memory of a great artist" (Nicholas Rubinstein), and the String Sextet called *Souvenir de Florence*. Something over a hundred songs, and a few religious pieces; a large number of piano solos, including one very long Sonata; and four Suites for orchestra which contain numbers rivaling many of the symphonic movements, complete the list of Tchaikovsky's contribution to Russian literature. The vexed question of its true nationality may be left to be settled by interested disputants. The fact remains that Russia as a musical nation was introduced to the Western world largely through the work of this one man.

In the music of Russia up to the end of the nineteenth century, then, we have first of all a singularly diverse folk music capable of a vast variety of developed treatment. But until the eighteenth century little activity in learned fields is to be seen; and the cultured art is almost wholly derived and borrowed from foreign sources. There is no slow and tested growth of a practice of composition, based on the popular song and addressed to minds desirous of finding in music a finer expression of native custom, feeling, or understanding. The harmonic processes and the phrase designs of the earliest Russians, as well as of Glinka and his followers, are essentially Western, exhibiting no more individual differences than do the works of contemporary Germans and Italians. The one outstanding originality is that of Moussorgsky who, achieving a really convincing dramatic recitative, may perhaps be compared to Dargomijsky as Monteverdi may be compared to Peri or Caccini. The dance, of course, in a nation which retained its primitive peasantry for so long, would show unlimited suggestion to the artist seeking a new theme; and we shall find the Russian ballet attracting even greater interest than did the same activity in eight-eenth-century France.

We shall also find that as the musical consciousness of Russia grows, the borrowed forms of Germany will appear less adequate for the expression of distinctively Russian feeling. The rounded symmetry of the German forms is the product of centuries of effort, not merely toward the mastery of the materials of music, but toward a completely elaborated, fully thought-out philosophy. Naturally such forms cannot contain the spas-modic, rebellious, pessimistic, hilarious excitements to which the untutored Russian is subject. Russia has had no great philosopher, although its philosophic sentiments—profoundly different from those of Western Eu-rope—have been expressed with great force in the form of socialistic theory by Karl Marx, or by novelists like Tolstoy, Turgenieff, Dostoievsky, and Gogol, and by equally striking poets and dramatists. With no firmly established conventions of form, with no traditional background of mu-sical theory (Russia has had but one great theorist, Taneieff, whose work at the Moscow Conservatory was of the soundest, and whose treatise on imitative counterpoint in strict style has earned the fullest recognition of German theorists)—without anything comparable to the slow and half-unconscious development which the musical art of Western Europe had enjoyed, the modern Russians have had to contrive a new idiom, sound enough in all its details to compete with the far more naturally evolved musical speech of the West. The Russian music of today cannot be judged as to its fulfillment of this task. It is too untried. But the great diversity shown by its newest composers is ample evidence that Glinka and the Five began a most fruitful movement. It is also evident that Tchaikovsky, whether typically Russian or not, contributed incalculably to the accept-ance of Russian music in the West.

CHAPTER XXX

The Rise of Nationalism
Continued

LESSER TRIBUTARIES TO THE NINETEENTH-CENTURY STREAM

BOHEMIA—SMETANA AND DVOŘÁK

THE great aim of all nationalistic art seems to be to attain to international recognition. How much that is purely national must be sacrificed in such a process is a question too complex to be debated here. But it is obvious that the vast machinery of publication, the establishment of highly trained orchestras in every music center, the travels of virtuosi, and the growth of literary and critical interest in music must all contribute to the internationalization of the greatest works. In a restricted sense music becomes indeed the "universal language"; and wide acceptance abroad is perhaps the truest measure of excellence that can be applied to any artist's work. Without attaining to the dimensions of the greater national contributions, the music of many lands has nevertheless made its mark upon this general speech; and many honored names are to be recorded of those who have brought their local idioms into the musical language of the world. Such influences arise sporadically. It is therefore impossible to deal with them systematically or in any exact order of importance.

Having just spoken of the Russians, it may be best to continue with other Slavic contributions. Bohemia has produced two very famous composers, Smetana and Dvořák, and several striking contemporary figures. Friedrich Smetana (1824–1884) was an energetic leader against the domination of Italian opera. He was an organizer of concerts, director of the most finished chorus in Bohemia, critic and musical correspondent for leading journals, pianist, conductor, and a composer of much music that is widely loved. His greatest interest was in opera, of which he wrote eight examples. The most famous is *The Bartered Bride*, whose exhilarating Overture is known everywhere. This opera has been produced on many foreign stages. He was accused by some compatriots of Wagnerian leanings, but was in intent at least a champion of native art. Both in his operas and in other works, Bohemian rhythms and melodies abound. He wrote a series of symphonic poems, *My Fatherland*, celebrating the history and the landscape of his country. The best known of these is *The Moldau*, which pictures the rise of this river in two sparkling springs and follows its course until it reaches Prague. His string quartet *From My Life* depicts his own life history. In the last movement, a long-held high E is a very literal allusion to an affection of the ear (and perhaps of the mind, though he was of course unaware of this) which brought about complete deafness. He became insane at last, suffering thus the greatest afflictions of both Beethoven and Schumann.

Antonin Dvořák (1841–1904), of humble origin, displayed precocious talent for the violin, was at length allowed to study in Prague, became a member of Smetana's orchestra, and, while supporting himself by the greatest efforts, still managed to compose incessantly in the largest forms. Several early symphonies and an opera were destroyed; but at length he produced a patriotic cantata *The Heirs of the White Mountain* which, strongly nationalistic in tone, was a great success. An opera *The King and the Collier*, after having been wholly rewritten, was also successfully produced. It earned a small pension for its author who, sending his works to the Viennese society which granted the pension, found in one of the judges, Johannes Brahms, an interested and helpful friend. Soon he received from Simrock (Brahms's publisher) a commission for a series of *Slavic Dances* for piano duet. These became almost as popular as the *Hungarian Dances* of Brahms. It is chiefly to his vivid feeling for his country's dance rhythms that his larger compositions owe their success. Two of these dances in particular, the *Dumka* and the *Furiant*, occur as elegiac slow movement and wild scherzo in many of his chamber compositions.

Five Symphonies—of which the best known is *From the New World*— were written between 1875 and 1893. The *New World* was written in New York, where from 1892 to 1895 the composer had assumed the direction of a newly founded National Conservatory. Many of the themes are strongly suggestive of the Negro spirituals which have since become so popular. Dvořák denied, however, that he used these themes directly: "I tried to write only in the spirit of these national American melodies." Nine operas, the remarkable cantata *The Spectre's Bride*, the oratorio *St. Ludmilla* (written for an English choral festival and somewhat uncharacteristic of the composer), a setting of the *Stabat Mater*, and a host of songs—this large volume is Dvořák's contribution to vocal literature.

There are also many overtures (the *Carneval* being probably the best known) and several sets of *Slavonic Dances* for orchestra, many chamber works for various combinations (the so-called *Negro* Quartet, the Piano Quintet, and the Sonatina for piano and violin are the most familiar) and two Concertos, one (relatively unimportant) for piano, and one (highly interesting and original) for 'cello. The pieces for piano solo are small and unpretentious. Neither Smetana nor Dvořák assumed so belligerent a nationalistic attitude as the Five in Russia; yet their work appears to the foreigner equally suggestive of the national character. It is perhaps unfortunate that Dvořák's finest symphony has made him appear, to our eyes, chiefly as an exponent of America. For we have somewhat lost sight of the interesting Slavic figure which stands behind even that music, and is much more clearly revealed in less widely known works.

POLAND AND HUNGARY—PADEREWSKI

Poland has produced few figures since Chopin who come within our somewhat restricted view. Moritz Moszkowski and the brothers Philipp and Xavier Scharwenka are familiar to us through works which display a Western adaptation of the Chopin idiom and give a somewhat pale reflection of the Polish character. The widely popular Violin Concertos and other pieces of Henri Wieniawski are in the same category. A truer picture of Polish feeling—cast however in works which have made but little appeal to the world at large—is to be found in the music of Stanislaw Moniuszko (1819–1872), who wrote many songs and operas, culminating with *Das Gespensterschloss* ("The Castle of Ghosts"), produced at Warsaw in 1865. Sigismund Noszkowski (1846–1909) contributed somewhat ephemeral symphonies, symphonic poems, and other orchestral works. The progress of the art was greatly hindered by the lack of established orchestras or opera houses save in Warsaw. Krakow, Posen, and Lemberg assumed importance as musical centers only after the beginning of the twentieth century. The greatest figure in Polish music since Chopin is Ignace Jan Paderewski. His compositions have been somewhat hidden behind his extraordinary brilliance as a pianist. They are chiefly for piano. The ardently patriotic D minor Symphony *Poland*, if somewhat diffuse in structure, has many passages of real significance. His one opera *Manru* has had no impressive success.

The native music of Hungary suffered even more than that of Poland in its distortions at the hands of clever West-European writers. The fundamental scale of this music is pentatonic (G, B, C, D, F). Between these standing notes, sliding tones of indefinite pitch may appear. The rhythm, likewise, is originally that of speech, although a more exact time scheme (particularly, of course, in dance measures) is later added. Music of this sort was largely performed by the gypsies. Its elevation to the status of art music offered many difficulties, which were surmounted by virtuoso composers like Liszt through the abandonment of much that was really characteristic. (The application of our major-minor harmony to melodies in pentatonic scales must inevitably alter the character of those melodies, just as it alters the character of the modal melodies of the Church.) The attention of the world was attracted to Hungarian melody through the *Rhapsodies* of Liszt and the perhaps more exactly representative *Hungarian Dances* of Brahms. Indeed, the Hungarian idiom was even less fully exemplified by native composers of note during the nineteenth century than through these greater men. (Liszt, Hungarian by birth, was distinctly cosmopolitan in sympathy.) Ernst von Dohnányi (born 1877) is widely appreciated as a composer, but not as a representative of Hungarian style. The same may be said, with greater force, of Leo Weiner (born 1885). A departure from German principles of structure was necsary before the peculiar qualities of Hungarian music could receive artistic treatment. The efforts in this direction of the two founders of modernism in Hungary, Béla Bartók and Zoltán Kodály, will be mentioned in our discussion of the twentieth century.

FINLAND—JEAN SIBELIUS

Among the most noteworthy composers at the turn of the century must be reckoned Jean Sibelius, who was the first composer to attract the attention of the world to his native Finland as a country of musical significance. The history of this singular people, racially tinged by a Mongolian strain and maintaining their sturdy, almost sullen independence of character and institutions against the alternate pressure of Russia and of Sweden, is not widely studied. Neither has the musical history of the people been much investigated. It appears, however, that a very rich folk music exists; that certain instruments related to medieval examples current in Europe, but having their own peculiarities, became widely popular (the old *kantele*, five-stringed, and the *jouhikantele*, a three-stringed relative of the Welsh *crwth*, the *Bockhorn*, and certain pipes made of willow or birch bark); and that notation was studied and exemplified in neumatic characters as early as the eleventh and twelfth centuries. The influence of the Reformation was here somewhat less than in Southern Europe, the Gregorian element maintaining itself to a considerable degree in the Protestant hymns. Secular music was relatively little cultivated; but there was an important Ducal chapel at Åbo in the sixteenth century. The same city was the center of a vigorous concert life at the end of the eighteenth century. After the burning of Åbo the capital and the University were removed to Helsingfors, thereafter the seat of widely diversified artistic and intellectual interests. One important fruit of this activity was the collection, from the lips of the peasantry, of the Finnish national epic, the *Kalewala*, which was not only recognized throughout Europe as a poem of great interest, but was made the basis of many dramas and operas. Not until about 1882, however, did any composers appear who are of significance for us. Martin Wegelius and Robert Kajanus founded a distinctively nationalistic movement, much colored however by German influence, and by the art of Johann Svendsen, the noted Norwegian composer.

Sibelius (1865–1957) was a pupil of Wegelius, and studied also in Berlin and Vienna. Fully schooled in accepted methods of composition, he nevertheless lost none of his love for the popular melody of Finland and for the national ideals. His music accordingly reflects the folk melody, but does not directly adopt it as thematic material. The striking personality of the composer is apparent from the first. His earlier works comprise the *Kullervo* Symphony, the orchestral suite *Lemminkäinen* (including "The Swan of Tuonela") and other works directly derived from the *Kalewala;* several symphonic poems such as *En Saga*, the *Karelia* Suite, and the widely popular *Finlandia;* together with several choral works and the incidental music for a drama *King Christian II.* An unusual literalness of suggestion is subtly mingled with a consistently logical continuity of the music; and comprehensive structural power is amply manifested in the Second Symphony (1902), which marks the culmination of his efforts toward the expression of the mingled energy and tenderness which is characteristic of his people.

What is possibly an equally racial characteristic, but one which is more obviously seen as a personal disposition to mystic contemplation, now gradually comes to be the more dominant quality of his speech. The symphony, dealt with in a singularly direct and unimitative way, with none of the contemporary graces and orchestral decorations, is the most preferred form. (The number of Sibelius's Symphonies was long expected to reach eight, but despite rumors to this effect the projected work was never finished.) But there is also much dramatic music; that for *Pelléas and Mélisande, Svanehvit, Belshazzar's Feast,* and *Kuolema* ("Death")— from which comes the famous "Valse Triste." There are also orchestral poems: *Nightride and Sunrise* and *The Oceanides;* a Concerto for violin, a string quartet called *Voces intimae,* the choral work *The Captive Princess,* and many smaller pieces of all sorts. Sibelius belongs to no school, apparently finding in himself that individuality which more conscious modernists seek in collective propaganda.

He does not stand, however, as the only Finnish composer. Others, men of note but far less striking than their leader, are Armas Järnefelt (born 1869), known for his symphonic poem *Korsholm* and for a very popular *Praludium* and a *Berceuse;* Erkki Melartin, director of the conservatory at Helsingfors, who has written five Symphonies and many chamber works in all groupings; and Selim Palmgren (1878–1951), whose widely known *May Night* gives no hint of the varied powers he has shown in opera (*Daniel Hjort*), in the orchestral suite (of which his most important example is *From Finland*), and in the song. The most vivid personality among these younger men was Toivo Kuula (1884–1918, murdered during the war for independence). Pursuing his studies in France, his idiom was somewhat colored by the new movement there. *Osterbottnische Suiten* for orchestra, choral and chamber works, and immense compositions in the *a cappella* style are among his works. His solo songs, although they hardly bear comparison with those of Brahms or Wolf, are astonishingly true to their texts both in meter and sentiment, and deserve much more attention than they receive.

Scandinavia—Edvard Grieg

The Scandinavian contribution is somewhat more familiar. Danish, Norwegian, and Swedish components—based upon only slightly differing national conventions, and hence difficult to distinguish—make up the stream. There are many evidences of very early musical activity. Latin *sequences* dating from the twelfth century, madrigals and sacred compositions in the current polyphony of the sixteenth (by Danish pupils of Giovanni Gabrieli), importations of Italian opera in the eighteenth—all these show an active musical life. The great Danish organist Buxtehude, whose *Abendmusiken* Bach walked endless miles to hear, was the only outstanding personality among early Scandinavian musicians, however; and he was more a German than a Dane in musical speech. Not until the nineteenth century did the art music of Scandinavia come to exhibit truly national characteristics. In Norway, however, there is ample evidence of the existence of a very ancient musical practice; and a recent history of Norwegian music by Dr. O. M. Sandvik, Gerhard Sjelderup, and others undertakes to prove the startling thesis that polyphony originated in Norway—a thesis given some support in the account of Gerald of Cambrai regarding music heard in twelfth-century England and Wales, which was mentioned above.

Denmark, less isolated than the other Scandinavian communities, was naturally least able to preserve indigenous characteristics in its art music. The first efforts were made by a German, J. A. P. Schulz (1747–1800), whose *Lieder im Volkston* and Danish Singspiele are held to give a true reflection of the national spirit. Other Germans, C. E. F. Weyse (1774–1842) and Friedrich Kuhlau (1786–1832—known to us as the writer of sonatinas, but to the Danes as an opera composer of great popularity), contributed to the growth of a national consciousness. The first true Dane to make his country's idiom felt was Niels Wilhelm Gade (1817–1890), whose *Ossian* Overture won him a royal grant which gave him a period of study in Leipzig. Here he was warmly received by Mendelssohn, producing a Symphony and the cantata *Colomba,* and absorbing without question the principles first of Mendelssohn and later of Schumann. Returning in 1848 to Copenhagen, he shook off somewhat the foreign influence; but it is rather in his cantatas and songs than in his eight Symphonies and the rather voluminous chamber music that he shows his understanding of Danish folk song. His influence in the musical life of Copenhagen was very great. As director of the Royal Conservatory, many pupils gained inspiration from him, the chief of whom was Carl Nielsen. Highly individual in his point of view, he is reckoned by his countrymen as the greatest musical artist whom their land has thus far produced. Five Symphonies, large choral works, two operas, and much chamber music stand to his credit.

With the music of Norway the name of Edvard Hagerup Grieg (1843–1907) is universally associated. He was indeed the first—as Gade had been in Denmark—to attempt a high artistic structure on the foundations of the music of his own people. Like Gade also, he had his schooling chiefly at Leipzig, absorbed the Mendelssohn tradition (though he harbored a secret love for the works of Chopin and Schumann—then regarded by the dour professors at the Conservatory as too radical), and received his diploma in 1862. Somewhat unsettled in prospects, he visited Copenhagen, met Gade whose work he fervently admired, and was advised at once to produce a symphony. But here he also met Richard Nordraak, a fiery nationalist of like age with himself, whose zeal at once changed the young composer's whole purpose. "It was as if the scales fell from my eyes. . . . We abjured the Gade-Mendelssohn insipid and diluted Scandinavianism, and bound ourselves with enthusiasm to the new path which the Northern school is now following." Returning to Christiania after Nordraak's early death in 1866, he founded a musical society there, married a cousin, Nina Hagerup, whose remarkably characteristic singing was of the greatest stimulus to him, and began a period of rapid production which brought his name conspicuously before the world. The Piano Sonata, two Violin Sonatas, the Piano Concerto, the *Peer Gynt* Suite, and a large number of small *Lyric Pieces* which exhibit the kernel of Grieg's genius more clearly than his larger works—all those were produced between his twentieth and thirtieth years, and were hardly exceeded in interest by any of the later compositions. A third Violin Sonata (in C minor), the Ballade for piano (really a set of variations on a Norwegian song), a Sonata for violoncello, and a String Quartet represent a later stage of expression.

Now, in various degrees, is to be seen the effect of some strange influence on the composer's mind which induced him to elaborate and to adorn with rather irrelevant matter the very characteristic substance of his earlier inspirations. He transcribed his own songs—some of them gems of the first water in their lyrical directness and simplicity—making absurd pyrotechnical displays which have little interest in themselves and less relation to the idea out of which they originated. The most extraordinary efforts in this direction are probably the inexplicable additions of a second piano part to four of Mozart's Sonatas—the most ill-judged efforts, surely, ever made by a man of genius. He had little power of development, and was therefore unequal to the construction of works of the largest dimensions. A symphony by Grieg is as unthinkable as one by Chopin. Even the Sonatas show far more value in their lyrical themes than in the developments. But when he confined himself to a small compass, Grieg was able to reach great heights of intensity or charm. This is illustrated in the familiar *Peer Gynt* Suite. One is astonished to find, on analyzing the structure of these pieces, that they consist of hardly more than repetitions of the very few phrases which constitute the thematic material. "Åses Tod," for instance, has but two melodic phrases, the second of which is rhythmically identical with the first; and out of these, which build up to and recede from a climax of great intensity, a mood of grief is portrayed which is as convincing as musical expression can well be. The same process of structure will be found in the other three numbers of the Suite. This is not development—for development implies an addition to the meaning as well as to the intensity of a phrase, and often involves large changes in its form—but is indeed a kind of treatment which is perfectly suited to the lyrical themes which Grieg spontaneously invented.

His lyrical genius was no doubt stimulated, not only by Richard Nordraak and by the great Norwegian violinist Ole Bull (who was largely instrumental in the determination of a musical career for Grieg), but also by the similarly lyrical-minded composer Halfdan Kjerulf (1815–1868), who was trained in Leipzig (during the forties), and who profited much by the work of Schumann. Johann Svendsen (1840–1911), although not espousing the nationalistic cause, earned the respect of the musical world with two Symphonies, various other orchestral compositions (including three Norwegian Rhapsodies), and some excellent chamber music. Christian Sinding (1856–1941) has likewise pursued cosmopolitan rather than nationalistic ideals; though his work is mostly in smaller forms, he has written Concertos for piano and violin, some chamber music, and one opera *The Holy Mount*. Norway boasts also one of the few women composers of distinction—Agathe Backer-Gröndahl (1847–1897), whose songs and piano pieces have a distinct flavor of the Norwegian scene.

Sweden produced during the nineteenth century no figure comparable to Grieg. August Södermann (1832–1876), with songs and orchestral ballades based on national themes, was followed by Ivar Hallström who embodied national legends in operatic forms. The work lacked solidity, however, and importations of Wagner's operas and Liszt's symphonic poems somewhat overshadowed the native movement. Emil Sjögren (1853–1918), following the lead of Södermann, produced many songs and instrumental works in smaller forms; and Anders Hallén (1846–1925), with four operas, several symphonic poems, and songs, gave further weight to the movement. Relatively little mark was made outside Sweden until the Symphonies of Hugo Alfven (born 1872), the choral works of Wilhelm Stenhammar (1871–1927), and finally the songs and operas of Wilhelm Peterson-Berger began to attract attention to the Swedish idiom. The continental influence remained very strong in Stockholm, however; and the only Swedish composer to win great notoriety outside his own land has been Kurt Atterberg, whose five Symphonies, other orchestral works, and chamber music have been much performed, even in America.

The important contributions during the later nineteenth century of Italy (save for the work of Verdi, already discussed), Spain, and Portugal are so late in coming to the attention of the world that they may well be discussed in connection with the twentieth century. The case is the same with England, which only began to assert its musical significance to the outside world with such works as Elgar's *Enigma Variations*. France, therefore, remains the only nation to be considered in this necessarily confused picture of the rapidly swelling current of later nineteenth-century thought.

FRANCE—THE *Drame Lyrique*—GOUNOD, BIZET, SAINT-SAËNS

The symphony, brought by German composers to a height of organization equal to their earlier development of the fugue, was far less congenial to instrumental composers in other countries. In Russia the only significant symphonist was Tchaikovsky, who was regarded by his compatriots as scarcely a Russian. Smetana, Dvořák, and Sibelius—each in a highly individual way—adapted their ideas to the outline of the form; but there are few examples of the symphony by non-German composers which sustain comparison with the great works of the German masters. The bitter experiences of Berlioz at home are sufficient evidence of the fact that the symphony was a form hardly representative of French musical taste. The opera rather, as it had been since the days of Lully, was still the form in which the French found their most congenial musical expression. And the conditions which made Berlioz an anomaly in his own land, both as symphonist and dramatist, were obviously such as to render improbable any development of opera parallel to that of Wagner; for Wagner's music was essentially of symphonic character.

Nevertheless, neither romanticism nor that later phase of the Revolution which was manifested almost throughout monarchical Europe in 1848 was without its influence on French opera. We have seen how the classical ideal of the eighteenth century gave way before the forces of science and democracy, and how romantic and historical subjects, set to lyrical and spectacular music, took the place of the older conventional operas. Now the old grand opera and the opéra comique were merged; and the essential distinction in style became that between the lyric drama on the one hand, whether "pleasant" or "unpleasant" (to use Mr. Shaw's rather accurate distinction), and the farcical or comic opera in the lightest vein on the other. If France had had a musical background of its own, such as Germany had possessed, we may imagine that it would have been Berlioz who would have led the way in the new movement. As it was, leadership was assumed by a far less significant figure—Charles Gounod.

Gounod was born in 1818. In addition to a sound general education he was trained in music, first by his mother and later at the Conservatoire. In 1837 he won the second *Prix de Rome;* he studied there the old masters of the polyphonic school, and returned to Paris as organist and director at the Missions Étrangères. He had already composed several works of a religious nature, of which portions of one were performed at London in 1851. He had studied theology also, intending to enter the priesthood, but gave up the idea and devoted himself to the study of more modern music—especially Schumann and Berlioz. The stage being the chief avenue to success, he produced his first opera, *Sapho,* in 1851, followed in 1854 by *La Nonne sanglante,* neither being highly successful. *Le Médecin malgré lui,* a comedy after Molière, fared no better; but in 1859, at the Théâtre Lyrique, began the fabulous triumph of *Faust*—fabulous at first only outside France; for even this music was accused by the Parisians of lacking melody. Ten years later it was again mounted in Paris and had 321 consecutive performances. Of the many versions in varied forms which Goethe's drama has inspired (Spohr, Berlioz, Schumann, Wagner, Liszt, and many lesser figures have treated the subject) Gounod's is by far the most widely successful and the least imbued with the spirit of the original. Yet the style of this music was far richer in sentiment and in brilliancy than the current outpourings of Auber and Adam. It is true that Gounod's other operas all fall below *Faust* in interest. *Romeo and Juliet* (1867) is perhaps the best of these; *The Queen of Sheba, Mireille,* and *Cinq-Mars* contain numbers which are more or less frequently heard; but the later works *Polyeucte* (founded on Corneille) and *The Tribute of Zamora* only ring the changes on an already exhausted style. Yet a new era in French opera dawned with *Faust.* (Gounod died in 1893.)

Before continuing the tale of this new development in the higher style, we must pause to mention a few figures who contributed materially to the lighter manner. Jacques Offenbach (1819–1880), born at Cologne, came early to Paris, studied 'cello for a time at the Conservatoire, and entered the orchestra of the Opéra Comique where he learned by experience what he did not care to learn in his classes. Gradually, through small attempts, he gained the ear of the Parisian public, and produced at last over a hundred operettas, in which a captivating melodic vein is used lightly to veil a mordant sarcasm, wholly attractive to his Parisian audiences. *The Tales of Hoffmann* is the finest and the best known of these works; it was posthumously produced in 1881. He had a host of followers both in France and elsewhere. Alexandre Charles Lecoq (author of *La Fille de Madame Angot*); Edmond Audran (whose *Olivette* had a long run in New York in the nineties); François Chassaigne (composer of *Le Droit d'Ainesse,* known in England and America as *Falka*)—these are the principal French writers. But Offenbach's influence stimulated Franz von Suppé (called the "German Offenbach"), Johann Strauss (the "Waltz King"), and Karl Millöcker—all active at Vienna—to their often charming and spirited works; and it may be that the same influence also prompted the extraordinary successes of Gilbert and Sullivan in England. The comedy opera, at any rate, has been a conspicuous feature of the lighter musical life of the world since Offenbach's day.

The Ballet, which had been a necessary feature of the French grand opera in the earlier days, came also to have a separate existence. Léo Delibes (1836–1891), who wrote many operettas and even several operas (such as *Le Roi l'a dit,* and the exotic *Lakmé* from which comes the often heard "Bell Song"), is still more favorably known for the charming ballets *Sylvia* and *Coppelia,* whose graceful music, without a trace of vulgarity, was to prove a preparation for the great expansion in the Ballet, largely due to Russian but also partly to French influence, which took place early in the twentieth century.

From the reception which Wagner's *Tannhäuser* had received in Paris, it would be inferred that his style was not likely to find many imitators among the French. But not all French musicians obeyed the dictates of the Jockey Club; and Wagner's musical personality impressed itself—with varied force it is true, but indelibly—on the work of almost every French composer after Gounod. The first of these was Georges Bizet (1838-1875), the composer of *Carmen*. The child of a distinguished musical family, he won many prizes, including the *Prix de Rome*, at the Conservatoire; and the fruit of his Roman sojourn was a short but striking opera *Don Procopio*. A symphonic ode *Vasco da Gama*, written after his return to Paris, was unsuccessful; and his next opera *Les Pêcheurs de Perles* was little better received. Already the Wagnerian influence is apparent, and is to some extent responsible for the relative failure of the work. *The Fair Maid of Perth* which followed was equally tinged by the Wagnerian method but was better received, and Bizet was much heartened. *Djamileh*, a one-act opera, was too somber to appeal to the public; in it, however, Bizet escaped somewhat from the direct Wagnerian influence and prepared the way for *Carmen*. *L'Arlesienne*, incidental music to a drama of Daudet, convinced even Paris of his mastery as a composer, although the music has survived in popular favor only in the form of two orchestral suites. *Carmen*, commissioned by the Opéra Comique shortly after the performance of *Djamileh* in 1872, was three years in the making. It is one of the most remarkable operas in history—so universally popular that it is hard to understand that its first performance was a failure.[1] The astonishing vivacity of the music, its perfect fitness for the plot, its vivid color, its effective characterization—all these are the product of a dramatic imagination of a high order. Certain features, notably the "death motive," are unthinkable apart from Wagnerian influence, and only show how all-pervasive was the style of the German master. But Bizet was no imitator, but one who could assimilate an idea and submerge it in his own great individuality.

The most widely known of Bizet's successors is doubtless Jules Massenet (1842–1912)—far less keen in characterization but possessed of an endless resource of suave melody which has made his works, especially *Thaïs* and *The Juggler of Our Lady*, popular all over the world. Less directly influenced by Wagner, he borrows, like every other contemporary, at least something of the Wagnerian harmonic idiom. Similarly, Emanuel Chabrier (1841–1894), with his *Le Roi malgré lui* and still more with his orchestral rhapsody *España*, shows how Wagner has been adopted by the French in spite of themselves. Alfred Bruneau (1857–1934) is a frank and courageous follower of Wagner, disdaining the prettiness of his master's (Massenet's) melodies, and striving in quite a twentieth-century manner after stark reality. Thus disposed, he found a congenial collaborator in Émile Zola, whose *Le Rêve*, *L'Attaque du*

---

[1] The work was first produced with spoken dialogue—which, however, need have had nothing to do with its ill-success. Part of the music of *The Fair Maid of Perth* was used to turn *Carmen* into a "grand" opera.

Moulin, Messidor, Ouragan, L'Enfant Roi, Naïs Micoulin, and *La Faute de l'Abbé Mouret* were made into operatic texts, sometimes by other writers, sometimes by Bruneau, and sometimes by Zola himself. Prose rather than poetic texts he finds most suitable to his realistic purpose; and the Wagnerian symbolism of the myth is wholly discarded. Yet there is distinct adoption of the penetrating thematic invention of Wagner, and a most uncompromising use of dissonance—before the twentieth century dawned, a distressing shock to the French ear. It is probable that Bruneau would be more widely known if he had not sided with Zola in his championship of Dreyfus. Gustave Charpentier's *Louise* is vastly popular; it is, however, the only work of significance by this talented composer, whose range of vision is apparently confined to what can be seen of Paris from a window in Montmartre. (He lived from 1860 to 1956.)

That lack of symphonic background which we have already noted in France must have been remedied to some extent before the progress in opera, just described, could have been achieved. No Frenchman, it is true, has attained the symphonic distinction of a Beethoven or a Brahms; but important developments in instrumental music took place during the nineteenth century which prepared the way for the extraordinary development of instrumental art in the twentieth. The first instrumental writer of importance after Berlioz was Edouard Lalo (1823–1892), who began with an unsuccessful opera *Fiesque,* and then turned to instrumental composition. His *Symphonie espagnole* for violin and orchestra, his Concertos for violin and 'cello, and a Suite *Namouna,* arranged from a not very successful ballet, preceded a Symphony in G minor which was much liked by musicians. One operatic success was achieved, *Le Roi d'Ys;* but his talent, developed through assiduous study of Beethoven, Schubert, and Schumann, was chiefly in instrumental composition.

More significant by far was Camille Saint-Saëns (1835–1921), a prodigy almost comparable with Mozart, who played a concerto of that master's in public at the age of seven. Of extraordinary intellectual acumen, his interests outside music were as keen as his interest in art. He was a painter, a poet, a philosopher, and an astronomer, and contributed notably to the critical literature of his time. Musically he was stimulated (one should not speak of "inspiration" in relation to Saint-Saëns—he did not believe in it) by Berlioz and Liszt, and by Gluck and Mozart, rather than by Beethoven, the romantics, or Wagner. He believed wholly in "art for art's sake"; was capable only of intellectual passion; and chose to appeal to purely artistic sensibilities in his hearers rather than to their passions. Imperfection in form, in consequence, was to him inexcusable. Yet it is extraordinary to find this man who wrote "the soul is no more than a means to explain the production of thought," contriving such vivid imitations of passion as the famous aria "My heart at thy sweet voice," or such exquisite and truthful "imitations of nature" as *The Swan*. The symphony, the concerto, the sonata, the opera—all were to Saint-Saëns the means of producing "effects." And what effects he produced! Yet, probably because of his singularly intellectual attitude, Saint-Saëns has not, as have all the really great composers, any distinctive thematic invention. The themes, and of course even more the thematic developments, of Bach or Beethoven or Schubert or Wagner have the unmistakable imprint of their inventor's personality. It is impossible to conceive of such thematic character in relation to Saint-Saëns. Sometimes it seems an echo of Bach that we hear; sometimes it is Wagner or Mendelssohn or Gluck. Sometimes indeed it is someone whom we do not know; but it is not even then the personality of Saint-Saëns which we recognize, but at best the consummate craftsman—analytical master of all styles, actual possessor of none. Naturally, he founded no school of followers.

CÉSAR FRANCK

It is quite otherwise with César Franck (1822–1890). He was born in Belgium, at Liége. Showing remarkable talent for the piano, he was destined by his father for the career of a virtuoso. At fifteen he went to Paris where he won many prizes at the Conservatoire, both in playing and composition. His father forbade him to try for the *Prix de Rome*, foreseeing that the great pianist whom he hoped for would be submerged in the doubtful composer. Franck returned to Belgium for a time; but in 1844 went back to Paris, taking up the laborious life of a teacher, and presiding at the organ, at first at the Church of Notre Dame de Lorette, and then, from 1858 until his death, at Ste. Clothilde. But in addition to all this drudgery he found time both to study and to compose. He must also have had in his mind from early years a new ideal of musical composition; and this ideal—long obscure and indefinite, even to his own vision —he seems to have pursued with unceasing devotion, until at last, when he was more than fifty years old, he came actually to realize it.

It was not through the music of contemporary France that he came to this understanding. The fountain of his inspiration was Johann Sebastian Bach. The later Beethoven—a mystic like Franck himself; and Richard Wagner—a vast symbolist and visionary as well as a musical dramatist: these were his lesser gods. A man of profound and unquestioning religious conviction, he interpreted the sayings of these prophets in the light of his own faith. It was not in the mighty sweep of their rhythms that he found his inspiration, but rather in their swirling harmonies, arising in strange regions and resolving still more unexpectedly. Somehow, with harmony as his chief resource, his genius had to find itself. There was little in the musical current of the Paris of the forties which could feed this desire. Hence, his first works were neither attuned to the popular ear nor at all fully representative of his convictions. Yet the three Piano Trios (Op. 1, 1842) show not only a singular charm but some germs of the later style. His first choral work *Ruth* (1846) pleased Spontini and Meyerbeer, but not the professors or the public. At rather long intervals other choral works followed: *Rédemption*, called a symphonic poem; *Les Béatitudes*, an oratorio; *Rebecca*, a biblical idyll; and *Psyche*, also called a *poème symphonique*. Of these *The Beatitudes* is the most important. The text is so contrived as to present the sentences of Christ against a background describing the bitterness and strife of the world which the sayings are to heal. Satan himself is at last vanquished, and those triumph who have been persecuted for righteousness' sake. As may be supposed, Franck deals more convincingly with the celestial aspect than with the satanic; but the work has nevertheless true dramatic power. Franck wrote also two operas, *Hulda* and *Ghisèle*, which were posthumously produced.

Interspersed with these productions were a large number of instrumetal works. The organ compositions have taken a place in the affection of the organists almost beside the works of Bach. The piano music is meager in extent, comprising but two great pieces: the *Prelude, Chorale and Fugue* and the *Prelude, Aria and Finale*. The former of these is of extraordinary depth; indeed, it may be doubted whether any more significant addition to the literature of the piano has been made since Beethoven laid down his pen. The chamber music consists (aside from four early Trios) of a Quintet for piano and strings, a Sonata for piano and violin, and a String Quartet composed only shortly before Franck's death. These three are among the most perfect examples of Franck's perfected style. There are three purely instrumental symphonic poems: *Les Éolides*, *Le Chasseur Maudit*, and *Les Djinns* (the latter giving large place to a solo piano); a wonderful set of *Variations symphoniques* for piano and orchestra (Franck's nearest approach to the piano concerto form); and finally the Symphony in D minor, in which he carries to a hitherto untried degree the not unknown practice of introducing into the later movements themes from the earlier sections, a treatment which is known as *cyclic*.

Almost all the music by which Franck is known was written after he was fifty years old. *The Beatitudes* was written in 1870 and remained unpublished for ten years. The Quintet dates from 1880, the Violin Sonata from 1886, and the Quartet and the Symphony from 1889. Yet even at this late date Franck's new and striking idiom failed to appeal to his countrymen. Vincent d'Indy, his biographer, tells how after the first performance of the Symphony "the composer of Faust, escorted by a train of adulators, male and female, fulminated a kind of papal decree that this symphony was the affirmation of incompetence pushed to dogmatic lengths." Franck himself, unconcerned as ever with the attitude of the public, replied to his family's eager questions as to the applause the work had received: "Oh it sounded well, just as I thought it would." He could afford to wait, even though death lurked around the corner. For in a few years a new school of French music had arisen, of which he was to be regarded as the founder.

This school, however, was short-lived. The somewhat Teutonic character of Franck's thought, although accepted and propagated by such pupils as d'Indy, Chausson, Duparc, and Ropartz, proved less compatible with the French genius than his followers anticipated; and the impressionism of Debussy with its aftermath (to be described in the next chapter) became the really inseminative influence.

CHAPTER XXXI

The Transition to the
Twentieth Century

BRUCKNER, MAHLER, AND REGER

FROM the very strength and diversity of the nationalistic forces which we have just been observing, it might have been inferred with much assurance that a great collision was imminent. At the beginning of the nineteenth century distinctive national character was exhibited only in the music of Germany, France, and Italy; and the French and Italian activity was chiefly with opera. At the opening of the twentieth, as we have just seen, many nations (more than we have considered in detail) were producing a wide variety of forms, all designed to exhibit the national character in its fullest clarity. And much of this effort was aimed distinctly against that dominance of the sonata form which was so conspicuous a fact during most of the nineteenth century. So great had been the genius of Beethoven that his most favored form, the symphony, had come to be accepted as the instrumental form par excellence, not only in Germany but throughout the world. It had no rival, even in France and Italy (where, however, instrumental music was less highly regarded than operatic); and the "symphony" orchestra began to appear in every music center as the highest type of musical organization. In Germany, moreover, so strong was the habit of symphonic thought that Wagner adopted its most valuable feature—the process of development—as the essential method of operatic composition. It was scarcely strange that the world which derived much of its instrumental music from Germany should come to regard competition with the symphony as unthinkable.

Wagner's immense influence on the musical thought of the world is perceptible in almost any later composition. It was not strange then that composers of distinction should be found in the very symphonic form which he had thought moribund. The eldest of these was Anton Bruckner (1824–1896). His singular temperament, combining a devout religious attitude with a musical sensibility which made him a keen enthusiast for Wagner, is reflected in his very considerable body of religious music, and in the nine Symphonies (the last one incomplete) which were written at various intervals between 1866 and 1894. Melodies of inordinate length, a harmonic fabric largely modeled on that of Wagner, and a singularly copious use of the three-part form (also exemplified dynamically in the sequence of intensification, climax, and epilogue, with a very frequent *pianissimo* ending)—these are the outstanding characteristics of his style. The idiom of the Austrian folk song and the exalted tone of the hymn are also conspicuous elements. It was not until 1887, when Hans Richter gave the Seventh Symphony in London, that Bruckner attained to any wide notice. Since then his work has aroused particular rather than general interest; but his partisans are vehement in his support.

A more distinctive figure, who may prove to be one of the most important links between the nineteenth century and the twentieth, is Gustav Mahler (1860–1911), a part of whose last years was spent in New York as conductor of the Philharmonic Orchestra. Song constitutes the foundation of his thematic material; this is natural, since his earlier efforts were in the direction of the song, and many important additions to song literature were contributed at various intervals. Among these are the *Songs of Youth, Songs of a Wandering Apprentice* (text by the composer), a collection from *Des Knaben Wunderhorn*, the collection from the poet Rückert, and so on. Following his Eighth Symphony came *Das Lied von der Erde*, a song cycle for tenor and contralto on texts from the Chinese. With the exception of the fourteen *Songs of Youth*, indeed, the accompaniments are always orchestral; and the gradual progress to the great *Lied von der Erde* is thus evidence of the close relation in his mind between symphony and song. (He was withheld only by convention from listing this work as a symphony.)

Mahler completed nine Symphonies, and left an unfinished tenth. Both in form and in subject matter these works offer many striking novelties. The first derives much material from the *Songs of a Wandering Apprentice*. Its first movement departs from symphonic form through a greatly abbreviated recapitulation, and the scherzo has a humorous parody in canon. The second begins with a great funeral march; its scherzo represents St. Anthony's sermon to the fish; and the introduction of a song *Urlicht*, between scherzo and finale, gives for the first time in history a symphony in five movements.[1] The Fifth, Sixth, and Seventh are purely instrumental. The Eighth, on the other hand, is for double chorus, solo voices, and orchestra throughout; its first movement is based on the hymn *Veni creator spiritus,* and the last three (connected to form a single grand division of the piece) are on the last part of Goethe's *Faust.* Naturally such endeavors can succeed only through very considerable deviations from the classic form. We find therefore a foundation in simple vocal melody rather than in the sort of concentrated, epigrammatic "subject" of Beethoven; a harmonic substance largely derived from (but not imitating) Wagner, although the style is far less chromatic; a considerable use of very modern *linear* counterpoint, which often involves a close approach to what we shall presently describe more fully as *polyharmony;*[2] and a singular disposition to proceed at once to the development of a theme immediately after it has been announced. Old polyphonic forms such as canon and fugue are treated with new and interesting freedom. His orchestral fabric is woven chiefly of lines, with little use of blending tones—a condition strongly suggesting the later tendency toward the smaller chamber orchestra. He greatly disliked music which lacked richness of thematic material, conceiving the constant reiteration of the same motive an evidence of pedantry. Expressively, although he was by no means a realist, he was distinctly concerned with an actual subject; so that the various movements of his symphonies are often given titles, as we have seen. Far from being the literal sort of program composer, he is also far from orthodox in his attitude toward the symphony. Hence, he has thus far failed to win very wide esteem outside Germany; but it is probable that his contribution to later developments will be more fully recognized when the nature of those developments comes at last to be fully understood.

THE SONG—HUGO WOLF

The song, in its more usual form with piano accompaniment, was also greatly developed during the later nineteenth century. We have taken but little account of this form since our discussion of Schumann's contribution, save to speak of the very important works of Johannes Brahms. Robert Franz (1815–1892) enriched the literature by many examples, quietly and artistically in the mood of their texts, but without any great individuality or novelty of treatment. Liszt, Rubinstein, Wagner, Peter

---

[1] The thunderstorm in Beethoven's *Pastoral* Symphony is formally only an introduction to the song of thanksgiving which follows. Schumann's *Rhenish* Symphony, whose *Romanza* is only a preparation for the ensuing Cathedral Scene, is similar. Tchaikovsky's First Symphony *Winter Daydreams,* also an apparent exception to the above statement, is more a succession of mood pictures than a symphony.

[2] See p. 582 below.

Cornelius (1824–1874–a friend of Wagner, composer of a very successful opera *The Barber of Bagdad*, and of many choral works) and even Mendelssohn left many striking examples of the song. Karl Loewe (1796–1869), although he composed profusely in larger vocal forms, the opera and the oratorio, and also for instrumental ensemble, is best remembered for his vivid settings of ballads. *Edward, Archibald Douglas,* and even Goethe's *Erlkonig* are treated with a literalness that is at first sight repellent, but becomes, with study, appropriate and actually musical.

But none of these, nor Brahms himself, was so obsessed with the spirit of the song as was Hugo Wolf (1860–1903), whose gift was certainly of the highest order, and who has left (in approximately 240 solo songs, four works for chorus and orchestra, and one completed opera *Der Corregidor*) probably the most original and significant settings of words to music which have been done since Schubert.

Wolf's manner is essentially Wagnerian (he was a devoted admirer of that master, and a somewhat prejudiced opponent of Brahms); but this implies no weak imitation. Rather it may be said that Wolf is almost the only modern musician whose harmonic processes embody the essential principles of Wagner's method without unconsciously absorbing his peculiar sensuousness of color, or adopting his almost incessant use of secondary sevenths. As Wagner left much to be communicated to the hearer through the orchestra, so Wolf, while observing the most scrupulous declamation of his text by the voice, devises for every new song an extraordinarily characteristic accompaniment which embodies a large part of the total sense to be conveyed to the hearer. Thus the immediate meaning of the poem is expressed by the singer, while to that meaning is added a great intensification of its spirit through the accompaniment. It may well be doubted whether any other composer has so fully and naturally represented in music the sense of words. Wolf's command of instrumental technique was revealed in but a few compositions: in an early symphonic poem *Penthesilea,* in the *Italian Serenade* for string orchestra, and in one String Quartet, earlier than the symphonic poem but more vivid and original. Indeed, in the directness and clarity of his utterance, Wolf seems to have avoided some of the symbolic diffuseness which was doubtless inevitable in Wagner's dealing with the mythical themes of his operas. Wagner's ideal union of poetry and music, at least on the smaller scale of the song, seems to have been achieved.

It will have been noted that all these late developments of German music derive more or less directly from Wagner. Brahms, as we noted, had no distinctive followers. Yet in Max Reger (1873–1916) we find a strange figure who in many respects may justly be regarded as a modern Brahms. In his great admiration for Bach and in his consequent high development of modern polyphony; in his avoidance of directly expressed program and his preference for apparently abstract musical form; and in his strong preference for chamber music, Reger resembles Brahms. His harmonic scheme, as highly varied as Wagner's, derives from Bach (in the extraordinary fantasias for organ, or the deeply expressive slow movements of the Masses and cantatas); but it is adventurous in the extreme in its use of modulation. At the same time it shows a studied respect for the traditions of the musical language, and reveals the extent to which the established principles of musical structure can be legitimately expanded. He wrote but one sonata for orchestra, the *Sinfonietta*, Op. 90. But more than half of his 140 opus numbers are examples of chamber music; and in these the sonata form (in which are included many of the older polyphonic forms, such as fugue, passacaglia, canon, and chorale-vorspiel) is fully recognized, even though the intricacy and the large dimensions of the work sometimes confuse the hearer. Reger's work has suffered contemporary eclipse in popular favor, since it offers so little of the type of stimulation which, since his death, has been especially demanded. A certain preoccupation with the problem of music-making itself tends to lead him into a diffuseness particularly unwelcome at the moment. It can hardly be denied indeed that Reger too often wore the academic garb when composing, and produced amazing examples of musical rhetoric instead of compositions addressed to a world of living men and women. But it is again not impossible that a clarification of his method may offer a secure foundation for some of the important music of the future.

PROGRAM MUSIC AND OPERA—RICHARD STRAUSS

We have already noted two vigorous attacks, during the nineteenth century, on the exalted position of the symphony. Wagner theoretically denied the validity not only of the symphony but of all music which was independent of words, and proposed the music drama as the only solution of the problem of the music of the future. Liszt (preceded by Berlioz) in his symphonic poems founded a form, freer in organization than the symphony, which was likewise associated with verbal ideas though not directly with a text. Wagner however, in associating music with his text, employed on a gigantic scale the most vital process of symphonic composition—the process of development. He believed that in this association with words he was giving permanence to all that was valid in the symphony. Wagner's attack, too, could be more easily ignored by the "absolute" musicians than Liszt's; for Wagner's works were stage plays—operas; and he might safely be regarded as proposing no more than innovations in opera—an institution which had a long history and which could be left to take care of itself. But to these same absolute musicians Liszt, utilizing the same orchestra as the symphony itself, trespassed upon sacred ground: he was bringing a meretricious, tinsel-clad figure to set up in the temple beside the divine image.

There ensued a bitter battle—which has not yet been fought to a decision—between the advocates of "absolute" and of "program" music. We have seen one call to this battle sounded in Brahms's manifesto of 1860. Eduard Hanslick, a Viennese critic, published in 1854 a study entitled *Vom Musikalisch-Schönen* ("On the Beautiful in Music") which has been almost universally read by those who have any interest in what lies beneath the surface of music. Hanslick's thesis is practically that music can express (in the usual sense of the word) absolutely nothing. The power of music to suggest certain moods is not denied; but even this faint shadow of expressiveness is minimized. Against the "program" musicians this little book proved a powerful weapon.[3] It frankly placed the value of music in its form, its intellectual interest, its sheer aesthetic quality of tone; and it supported with such apparent conclusiveness the attitude of a great majority of professional musicians (whose interest in technique is high and rather exclusive) that counter-arguments were difficult to find. Yet the vogue of the symphonic poem did not wane; and in that stubborn fact was to be found, after all, one of the most convincing arguments against Hanslick's thesis.

During the last years of the nineteenth century there was great excitement over the work of a startling new composer who was treating the symphonic poem in a new way. This man was Richard Strauss (born 1864, at Munich); and his new development was nothing less than the application of the Wagnerian leading-motive system to the symphonic poem. Fired by the enthusiasm of Bülow under whom he was studying conducting at Meiningen, he had begun as an ardent admirer of Brahms. But he soon came in contact with Alexander Ritter, an opera composer of some note, who converted him to the principles of the futurists and set him experimenting with the new form. The transition was gradual. The early works (such as the String Quartet, the 'Cello Sonata, the Horn Concerto, the Symphony in F minor, and several songs) are sound but not very striking music in the orthodox manner. Something of the new spirit is to be seen in the Symphonic Fantasia *Aus Italien*, which introduces, among other literal impressions, the tune *Funiculi, funiculà* (by Luigi Denza, but which Strauss took to be an old folk tune).[4] The first of the

---

[3] A much more extended discussion—indeed, the first comprehensive discussion of musical aesthetic—is the work of the English psychologist Edmund Gurney, *The Power of Sound*. Gurney's conclusion in this matter is largely the same as Hanslick's.

[4] A suit for infringement of copyright ensued.

symphonic poems (the second to be published) is *Macbeth*, a not particularly adventurous or successful work. The next is *Don Juan*, in which the method of the leading motive is fully applied, and which still remains a frequently played number in the repertoire of every large orchestra.

With *Tod und Verklärung*, which depicts a dying man's memories of life, his struggle with death and his entrance into the hereafter, the method is more assured. Dissonance, more startling than any that had hitherto been heard, was employed with what afterward turned out to be sound logic. *Till Eulenspiegel* showed a most vivid sense of musical humor. *Also sprach Zarathustra*, an attempt to sum up the philosophy of the world in a half hour of music, startled the world by ending in two keys: B major and C major. *Don Quixote* presented, in the guise of a set of variations, an account of several of the adventures of that dolorous knight, in which the bleating of the sheep (composing, to the Don's mad apprehension, the hostile host of Alifanfaron) is represented with a literalness quite incredible, while the tilt with the windmills, the ride through the air, and other escapades are only slightly less vividly described. *Ein Heldenleben* ("A Hero's Life") presents a figure of truly heroic dimensions, whose life is, however, given over to the conquest of a group of not very doughty antagonists, almost certainly identifiable with the reactionary critics of Strauss's own music; and the *Symphonia Domestica*, representing a day in the composer's life, sets an orchestra of about a hundred pieces the task of describing among other things the squalling of the baby in its bath, and the comments of admiring relatives who think the baby is "Just like Mamma" or "Just like Papa." Strauss's humor, although sometimes unconscious, is perhaps his supremest faculty; but there are many admirable pages of serious music in these works. As has been suggested, he does not scruple to use most unorthodox progressions: not only consecutive fifths and octaves, but parallel sevenths (in *Heldenleben*) and above all a kind of counterpoint in which he takes no account of the dissonant relations between moving parts, but makes them march along to their appointed goal in complete defiance of orthodox rules of syntax. The horror of the theorists of the old school was extreme, but the delight of the public (which loves impudence) was great. For in spite of its "wrongness," this music was intelligible, and moreover, *sounded* with a wealth of orchestral color which had never as yet been heard. There was abundant passion, expressed in melody of great sweep and verve which these aberrant voices seemed to enhance rather than to disturb. Beside these glowing scores, few modern symphonies save those of Brahms (and not always even those) could hold their own with the heterogeneous musical public which had now come into existence. With this public the symphony had by no means fallen into disfavor; but it had lost its absolute supremacy even in Germany.

Strauss had also made rather imposing entry into the field of opera. His first two efforts, *Guntram* and *Feuersnot*, were considerably in the Wagnerian manner and evoked less comment than the symphonic poems. After the *Domestica*, however, came the opera *Salome*, in which the mature hand of the composer of the symphonic poem is applied in a new manner to that form (the music drama) from which the symphonic poem had largely been drawn.

The text of *Salome* is a one-act play by Oscar Wilde, originally written in French but issued also in English by the author. The play is singularly compact in action, and, although it is in prose, the language, rather precious, is almost poetic in rhythm. Extraordinarily little narrative is needed for the unfolding of the situation to the hearer. The music therefore has ample opportunity to intensify the swiftly moving emotional developments. Applying all the possible suggestiveness of music to the revolting plot of the play itself, Strauss produces a music drama which has probably no parallel in its excitement of disgust and sheer horror. (It was the purpose of tragedy, as Aristotle understood it, to excite pity and terror.) The only character who is convincingly presented to us is Salome herself —a hideous creation enough in the spoken play, but a creature of such utter depravity when illuminated by the music that we wonder how we have managed to stay in the theatre with her. Unfortunately, John the Baptist, who in the play makes a considerable appeal to us by unflinchingly rejecting Salome's seductions, is represented by most unconvincing music. Thus the utter immorality of the heroine, against which the needful contrast of the Saint's white sternness is lacking, glows with a phosphorescent light that almost makes us mistake putrefaction for health.

Although this opera in its moral aspect is scarcely endurable, it is nevertheless little short of amazing as a musical-dramatic creation. Its music, to be sure, is far less complex in suggestion than Wagner's; the themes, even at the best, are not forged in that white-hot crucible of the imagination from which were poured the figures of Brünnhilde, of Isolde, and of Kundry who is in some sense thinkable as a counterpart of Salome. But the union of music and action is almost complete; the movement of both is swift and undeviating in purpose; and there is no gainsaying the mastery over the problem of dramatic design which is here displayed. It is almost certainly Strauss's greatest opera, and is perhaps his greatest musical work. Yet, if George Sand was right in saying that there was more music in a tiny Prelude of Chopin than in all the trumpeting of Meyerbeer, it may be that Strauss will be longest remembered for his songs. Such finely lyrical pieces as *Traum durch die Dämmerung*, *Cäcilie*, and

Befreit, and such stark realism as that of the *Steinklopfers Lied* belong surely to high regions of art.

Of the later operas, the most important are *Elektra* (a new version, by Hugo von Hoffmannsthal, of the ancient fable) and *Der Rosenkavalier* (a comedy, by no means reticent, which Strauss believed to have some kinship with Mozart's works). More recent are *Ariadne auf Naxos, Die Frau ohne Schatten*, and *Eine Ägyptische Helene*. The later works show a distressing decline in power. The younger generation, even before this decline became manifest, rather followed him merely in his flouting of long-established conventions than accepted his actual creations as models.

Impressionism—Debussy

Strauss, however, was by no means the only iconoclast. In France, which since the days of Berlioz had produced but one symphony (that of César Franck) able to gain permanent favor both at home and abroad, a musical impulse even more original than that of Strauss was felt. Cast in no accepted form, but possessing many of the qualities which, since the days of Monet and Manet, had been called *impressionism* in painting, remarkable music was flowing from the pen of Claude Debussy (1862–1918). By 1894 he had perfected one of the most provocative of modern compositions, the *Prélude à l'Après-midi d'un faune*. This might be called a brief symphonic poem, since it has a definitely illustrative or *poetic* purpose. (It describes in music what the impressionistic poet Stéphane Mallarmé had tried to put into words: the Faun's recollection of a voluptuous experience of yesterday, which was either a reality or a dream, he can no longer tell which.) This Prelude represents the attainment of a freedom and individuality of expression toward which Debussy had been striving almost from the beginning of his study. He had been obliged hitherto to restrain his novel impulses, as may be seen in the cantata *Le Gladiateur* with which he won in 1833 the *premier second grand prix de Rome*. This work, although it displayed "more personality" than that of the first winner, Paul Vidal, was consciously modeled on lines laid down by the theories and conventions of the Conservatoire. More of such work, however, he could not and would not do. In 1884 Debussy won the first prize with the cantata *L'Enfant Prodigue*. His *envois* from Rome (works submitted to the Conservatoire to show his progress as an endowed student) were increasingly vague and original, and distressed the sober judges immeasurably. These works were *Zuleïma, Printemps*, and *La Damoiselle élue* (based on Rossetti's *The Blessed Damozel*). While there are many traces of the influence of Wagner (especially *Tristan*), of Franck, and even of Massenet, the author himself is distinctly in evidence as one who sees a path before him which he must follow. *L'Après-midi d'un faune* is the first certain expression of this new personality.

As we have hinted, the new manner of expression here displayed is generally called *impressionism,* and had earlier been applied to the work of certain painters. Debussy himself was much stimulated by the *Nocturnes* of Whistler; and also by certain literary types, of which the poem of Mallarmé above mentioned was a distinctive example. In all this work, whether of musicians, painters, poets, or sculptors, a related manner of execution is to be found. But any distinctive manner of expression must be in the last analysis a product of the artist's attitude toward the thing he wishes to express. We tried to show that romanticism and classicism were really based on rather opposed attitudes toward the subject, and that the technical process of the classicist or the romanticist is but the reflection of the artist's approach. Impressionism, then, must also be defined.

"Impressionist! The words, in a measure, explains itself. The man for whom, in the famous utterance of Gautier, the visible world exists. One receptive to stimuli from every source; roused to action by the force of immediate circumstance; staking all on the dramatic freshness of the new experience. The original as opposed to the conventional; personal freedom rather than traditional safety. Color instead of form, and instead of absolute space, atmosphere, luminosity and tone. Not objects themselves, but the *effects* of objects as seen through sheaths of tone." This quotation from Thomas Craven's *Men of Art* will suggest both the attitude and the manner characteristic of the impressionist. Impressionism, it will appear, is but an intensification of the attributes of the romantic idealist. For it is no longer the object itself, as the artist feels it, which the impressionist wishes to present to us. His own feeling of the object takes precedence over the object itself which he is presenting, and becomes the actual subject, or at least the main attribute of the subject, with which he deals. If we understand Gautier's phrase aright, the objective physical world attains existence only in the imagination of the beholder; and he whose vision is most actively stirred by the phenomenon of the external world is he for whom the world has fullest existence.

Such a definition is, of course, not fully true. Impressionism, in that light, would describe the raving of a madman as well as the fine perception of the artist. But with the necessary qualifications, which may probably be safely taken for granted, such a statement does give a description of the actual artistic purposes of the impressionist. For the realization of his vision the impressionist naturally makes large use of new and strange effects; he naturally omits much which would be essential to a literal statement of many features of his subject. For these features, if dwelt upon, would only obscure the vision which is his, which he wishes us to grasp, and which makes the world live for the moment in a new imaginative light.

With *L'Après-midi*, then, Debussy achieved the impressionism for which he had always been instinctively striving. The actual sources from which he drew his idiom (in so far as it was not actually invented) appear various. Wagner and Franck, Lalo, Chabrier, Fauré and Chausson, Moussorgsky and Borodin, and even the "Gamelan" orchestra of the Javanese [5]—all these contributed something to that extraordinarily flexible musical substance which he had to contrive as an embodiment of his vision. Several most unusual songs called *Ariettes Oubliées,* piano pieces of a rather distinctive stamp such as the popular *Arabesques* and the *Danse* in E major (originally called *Tarantelle Styrienne*), and a String Quartet preceded or accompanied the composition of *L'Après-midi.* In these works something of the genesis of Debussy's style can be studied.

Even before *L'Après-midi* Debussy had come upon Maeterlinck's *Pelléas et Mélisande,* and had been stirred by it to the idea of another kind of music drama than that which Wagner had left: one which should not "follow the usual plan of the lyrical drama, in which the music predominates insolently, whilst the poetry is relegated to the background and smothered by elaborate musical trappings. There is too much singing in musical dramas. All musical development that is not essential to the text is incorrect. Apart from the fact that any musical development which is at all protracted cannot possibly correspond to the mobile words." Ten years of the most painstaking effort were spent in setting this text according to the principles here suggested. They are not very different from the principles enunciated in Gluck's preface to *Alceste;* but Debussy's uncompromising adherence to them resulted in what must be regarded as the most unusual music drama ever created.

Description of such a work in words is futile. There are no arias, of course, no clearly developed musical ideas; there are, indeed, phrases typical of the principal characters or of striking situations which resemble the Wagnerian leading motives in purpose but not at all in design. The music forms a background for the drama, and seldom rises above that apparently mediocre position. Consequently it is not until we abandon our expectations of hearing ordinary singing and ordinary development of musical ideas that we are able to hear the drama at all as Debussy intended it. When we adopt the necessary attitude, however, and cease to look for what is not there, we find that a most remarkable addition has been made to the spoken drama. Every suggestion that lurks in the words of something too subtle to be spoken seems to be uttered by the music. The

---

[5] This remarkable group of instruments—all percussion, in vast variety, save for a sort of two-stringed viola—performed at the Exposition Universelle at Paris in 1889; Debussy was much interested in their unique performances.

drama, not only unimpeded by "too much singing" but impelled by forces that are often but dimly perceptible from the words alone, moves forward with a new reality. The music itself, at first apparently vague and shape-less, takes on (perhaps from its association with the play, perhaps because we adjust our ears to catch its unobtrusive suggestions) an intrinsically musical interest of the keenest sort. It does not appear, from the recent course of operatic history, that Debussy's method has been accepted by composers as a real solution of the vexed problem of music drama; but that may be only because no master capable of composing in this manner has appeared. The work is now widely acclaimed as a masterpiece. Whether the method is adaptable to more vigorous types of action may be debated; but it seems almost indubitable that Debussy found, in this one instance, a solution of that problem of balance between text and music in the drama which all his great dramatic predecessors had sought in vain.

The volume of Debussy's music is relatively small. A considerable num-ber of piano pieces, as original in their treatment of the instrument as Chopin's; several sets of songs; two pieces for clarinet and piano, a Trio for flute, viola, and harp, and a 'Cello Sonata; three Nocturnes (*Nuages*, *Fêtes*, and *Sirènes*, described by Jean d'Udine as a "delightful impressionist symphony"), the tripartite symphonic poem *La Mer*, the *Danse sacrée* and *Danse profane*, and the *Images* (*Gigues*, *Iberia*, and *Rondes de prin-temps*) for orchestra; and finally the choral work *Le Martyre de Saint-Sébastien* (in which the composer's rather original religious views found expression)—this, with the works before mentioned, is a fairly complete catalogue of his compositions. The volume is slight; but the significance is great. For in his management of the tonal substance, in his peculiarly flexible melodic line, and above all in his adaptation of music to a novel purpose of expression, the work of Debussy more than that of any other man initiated the present new era in composition.

The qualities of that new work are still greatly in dispute. No clear theory has as yet been formulated—though endless foggy ones have been promulgated—which can define or explain in every detail the new tenden-cies. It is not even certain that the old principles have been overthrown. That they have been relaxed, that relations of tone unthinkable to the musicians of the nineteenth century have become a commonplace to the ears of the twentieth, and that the possible range of musical expression has been greatly enlarged, no one can doubt. Nor is there question that Debussy, more than any other, must be credited with having given the major impulse in the new direction.

So much, at least, may be accepted as historically established. Upon the music of the twentieth century, however, historical judgment is impossi-ble. Never perhaps in the history of art has there been a period of such confusion in practice or of such perplexing conflict in opinion. We shall make no attempt to present a settled view of the period. Some account of the actual theories which have been propounded will be given, together with mention of what at the moment seems to be the most important work. The only principle to which we shall hold, in this attempt, is that history has never shown an absolute discontinuity in the progress of musical thought, and that it is therefore unlikely that such a break has occurred or is occurring in our own day.

CHAPTER XXXII

The Twentieth Century
on the European Continent

A Larger Musical Public

EARLY in the twentieth century there began to appear new facilities for the distribution of musical tones which have proved comparable in effect to the invention of the printing of musical notes. The phonograph was perfected to the point where it could record, with ever-increasing fidelity, performances of innumerable masterpieces of the musical literature. Radio, broadcasting "live" concerts and operas, brought music into homes hitherto without musical contact; television has more recently enhanced the aliveness of these performances. It is needless to emphasize the value of these communications, whether for the serious student or for the casual music lover.

The musical public has thus been incalculably augmented. Musical taste, however, if measured in terms of this enlarged body of listeners and of the surfeit of musical fare set before them, has hardly been proportionately enriched. Casual contact with masterpieces does not yield understanding of their masterly conception or performance. It may, instead, breed a kind of familiarity too easily mistaken for understanding; overabundance of offered fare may tempt to gluttony; and the nourishment of the spirit, which is reputedly the ultimate value to be absorbed from music, may be supplanted by a deceptive nervous delight—ephemeral, capricious, even habit-forming.

In any period the apparent musical public has doubtless been larger than the real. That discrepancy is probably greater today than ever before. Since the eighteenth century, at any rate, and to a considerable degree even then, the apparent musical public (often more lavish than the real in its offering of material support) has had a notable share in determining the nature and the quality of the musical fare to be provided. Its demands are today more ineluctable than ever; and there is on this account alone a certain confusion in the minds of composers, who are in danger of finding that they have caught the ear of the apparent musical public instead of the real. According to their own dispositions, then, they may either write down to the listeners they have attracted or, failing to catch the more sensitive ears, end by writing music for themselves. Any public, confronted by music addressed only to composers' ears, is likely to be bewildered.

A New Musical Language

During this period of unprecedented expansion in musical propagation, an even more revolutionary change has come about in the musical language itself. Like all revolutions of consequence, this one has its roots in earlier departures from convention. But while this change may—and probably must—ultimately show a natural continuity with those departures, the new methods seem to imply an attack upon older tradition so fundamental as to seem seismic. The only comparable change within objective historic vision is the transition from modality to tonality. That, however, as we have seen, was an inevitable consequence of the acceptance of harmony as one of the elements of music and was so gradual as to have been all but imperceptible—at any rate to the ordinary listener.

To many of the most advanced composers during the first 30 years of this century, the new methods were justifiable as an attack upon tonality itself, which as a basis of musical understanding appeared outworn and no longer productive. To destroy tonality thus seemed the first step necessary toward the creation of a new music able to reflect the spirit of a new age.[1]

How daring that proposal was seems to have been but dimly recognized by its proponents. It was evident that the whole course of har-

---

[1] During the period we are contemplating, two world wars have been waged, in our view, "to make the world safe for democracy." The enemy, in both, has appeared as autocracy. Communism, which is in theory a kind of political atonality, has since supplanted autocracy as the chief danger to the democratic way of life. It was applauded by democracy when it first "emancipated" the Russian people from autocratic rule. But, as an eminent French critic, Emile Faguet, remarked in the foreword to his study of the sixteenth century of French literature, à propos of the Renaissance as an escape from Scholasticism, "Emancipations generally turn out to be no more than changes of servitude."

To what extent these conflicts in politics are related to contemporary conflicts in art is a question to be answered long in the future. That there is a relation seems indubitable. But that an escape from the servitude to the earlier formulations of new artistic principle may already be necessary—and is actually in process—seems strongly indicated by the trends of the moment.

monic development, with its continual widening of the acceptable range of discord, was straining the boundaries of tonality—at least as tonality was understood by practicing composers. The "Brahmins" (far more than Brahms himself) had felt that the "futurists" (a nickname Wagner resented) were endangering the very being of music. Shrieks of dismay had greeted the dissonances of Strauss and Debussy, and with the appearance of Schoenberg's *Drei Klavierstücke*, Op. 11 (1909), many musicians (the writer of this book among them) were amazed and confounded. The very basis of musical orientation seemed to have been destroyed.

Influences Affecting Twentieth-Century Music

Ever since the seventeenth century, the basis of musical orientation had been accepted as that relation of tones in a musical sentence to a keynote or tonic which had been named tonality. Any music lover, listening to a succession of pieces by Mozart, Beethoven, Schumann, and Wagner, could see that with these composers musical sentences had become increasingly periodic, while at the same time the gravitational attraction of the tonic remained as the underlying principle of cohesion. The innovations of Strauss and Debussy were soon perceived as no more than extensions of the gravitational pull of tonality, and therefore legitimate. Those of Strauss, indeed, turned out to be akin to the "arbitrary" discord of the earliest harmonic structures—whether mere freaks of musical behavior or more intentional defiances did not much matter, for the general tonal basis was usually clear. Those of Debussy, however, did sometimes result in a more or less extended suspension of the sense of tonality and are now widely regarded as forming the most direct approach to the new musical manner. We must therefore examine them somewhat more analytically than was done in the last chapter.

To create suspense (as every reader of detective stories knows) is to awaken interest. Every musical composer has sought the same effect. The musical means to that end is the delaying of the final cadence of the musical sentence by evading the gravitational pull of the tonic—usually by unexpected modulation out of the apparent orbit of the moment.[2] What Debussy discovered was another species of evasion, so elusive as to be capable of—although it does not always attain to—a complete obscuring of the sense of tonal gravitation.

[2] Read the *Prelude* to the C♯-minor Fugue of Bach (W. K., Bk. I, No. 4). You will find there but two sentences: the first ending with the cadence in G♯ minor in bar 14, the second comprising all the rest of the piece. Then read the *Prelude* to *Tristan and Isolde*. The musical device is precisely the same.

The means to this end was quite simple. It was gained through the use of what came to be called a *six-tone* or *whole-tone* scale—a succession of six whole steps (for example, C-D-E-F♯-G♯-B♭-C) which arrives at the octave of the starting note, as does our diatonic (seven-note) scale, but which robs the final note of all sense of finality. Tonality, that is, has been for the moment obliterated. And if this scale be compared with the diatonic scale, its lack of tonality will be seen to lie in the fact that it contains no *leading-tone* whose half-step (as from B to C in the C-scale) unmistakably points out the tonic to the ear.[3]

But Debussy's discovery was only another step in a harmonic direction which had been pursued ever since the perfecting of the system of equal temperament had made modulation possible from any one to any other of 24 keys.[4] The whole course of development in musical syntax since that time may justly be seen as an exploration of the possibilities of

[3] Whether the whole-tone series is properly a scale at all may be questioned. It is, indeed, an orderly succession of tones from one note to its octave—which is one definition of a scale. But is it also possibly a kind of arpeggio—the notes of a chord taken in succession? At any rate, the "chord" here involved may be plausibly derived from nineteenth-century principles of chord structure, thus:

The familiar dominant ninth chord (as C-E-G-B♭-D in the key of F) may have its resolution-tendency (a strong indication of its tonality) much intensified by raising its fifth, G, to G♯—this G♯ then leading very pointedly toward A, the third of the chord of F. Arpeggiated in the given order, these notes are unmistakably tonal in suggestion. But if we take them in a scale-order, we shall have C-D-E-G♯-B♭—five of the six notes of the whole-tone scale described in the text. With these five, the tonic is still not greatly obscured. The missing tone is, of course, F♯—explicable as an augmented 11th above the root, C. But as soon as this note is added to the series, and, like the D, brought down an octave so as to lie within the scale-octave C-c, it produces a curious ambiguity. If it remains F♯ and thus stands a whole step from G♯, the B♭ loses its identity and becomes A♯, and C begins to sound like B♯. If we go down the series, similarly, the G♯ after the B♭ becomes A♭, and F♯, in this context becomes G♭. Logically, also, E, D, and C will become F♭, E♭♭, and D♭♭; and our "scale," which began with a C, ends on a note which is an audible equivalent of C but is really a D. Thus the ordinarily unmistakable identity of two tones an octave apart is so far obscured that this final note is no final at all, and tonality, whose indispensable basis is an unmistakable tonic, has disappeared.

The chord from which we built the series will, however, still remain a chord if we disperse its notes (as C-G♯-E-F♯-B♭-D). Its resolution-tendency is uncertain, but it is acceptable to the ear. And if the six notes are played within the compass of the octave after having been thus dispersed, the sense of the whole-tone "scale" as an arpeggio will be easily perceptible.

The chord of the augmented fifth and that of the diminished seventh similarly divide the octave into three major and four minor thirds, respectively. They, in consequence, do not exhibit a distinguishable *root* and are readily resolvable into quite other tonalities than that within which they first appeared. The six-tone scale, viewed as a chord, is similarly ambivalent but even more obscure since it has six possible "roots" instead of three or four.

[4] Debussy's color sense is far more significant than his whole-tone scale in the total valuation of his art. But that scale is more significant than his color in the evolution of atonality.

modulation. (This does not mean, however, that composers were occupied with this possibility alone.) Bach supported equal temperament, not only because he could foresee but because he could most pertinently use the resources of such expanded harmony for expression theretofore quite inconceivable.[5] Nineteenth-century composers, mostly under the compulsion of romanticism, pursued the search into endless highways and byways of chromaticism, finding ever new subtleties of feeling and extending the boundaries of modulation to the most remote regions of tonal gravitation.

It seems unlikely that Debussy, during the act of composition, had any purpose of destroying or even denying the postulate of tonality. In only one piece (*Voiles,* in the first book of *Préludes*) did he attempt to maintain the tonal ambiguity of his six-tone scale throughout, and the product of that work is merely monotony in the too-extended use of a single device. It does not in any way suggest the exhaustion of tonality, and nowhere else does he use the device except for its obvious value of temporary tonal suspension. Nevertheless his achievement, seen in a later perspective, can be interpreted as an essential, although quite unconscious, step toward that later type of structure which was soon to be hailed as the emancipation of music from the tyranny of the tonic.

The sense of tonality had always been much fortified by harmony, both in the excursions away from the established tonal center and in the returns to it. Dissonant harmony is far more propulsive than consonant. Dissonance, therefore, had multiplied during the nineteenth century to a point where it was almost incessant, and contrasts between varied intensities of dissonance had become accepted (notably in the music of Wagner and his followers) as the more stimulating equivalents of earlier contrasts between consonance and dissonance. Yet these harmonies were contrived and used within the conventional framework of tonality.

But then, if emancipation from the tyranny of the tonic was to be achieved, a new view of dissonance had to be developed. If there was no tonic for it to point toward, its very propulsiveness had to disappear or be directed into some new channel. Debussy's whole-tone scale did indeed seem to stretch out toward the boundaries of musical space; but it always began its excursion from a perceptible tonic base and generally returned either to that same base or to another, equally stable. And as long as dissonance retained its meaning as a condition of instability *re-*

---

[5] Read, for example, in the *Confiteor* of the *B-minor Mass,* bars 123–146, the transition at the first appearance of the words *et expecto resurrectionem mortuorum.* The device is merely that of enharmonic modulation; but through this resource Bach makes music look over the brink of eternity as no later composer has been able to do. By comparison, Strauss's apocalyptic vision (in *Tod und Verklärung*) looks like a dream from the *Arabian Nights.*

lated to consonance-stability, there was no escape from tonality. (The element of rhythm, however it might be complicated to accord with new behaviors of harmony or melody, could not directly contribute to such an escape.)

But again, the familiar forms of music—fugue, sonata, rondo, and so on —had themselves been shaped through dependence on contrasts of key and would become amorphous if that dependence were lost. Thus a really new music, rejecting tonality and equating dissonance with consonance, would have in addition to devise new patterns of form, dependent on whatever substitute could be discovered for tonality and the conventional tonal tensions of dissonance.

The foregoing has been presented, of course, in the light of the present, as a rationalized view of what would have to be accomplished if the brave proposals of the 'teens and 'twenties were to be realized. Many of these were put forth with such insouciance, and with so evident a desire to do something new at any cost, that the real problems at issue were quite ignored. It will perhaps be interesting, as a prologue to our study of the actual achievements, to summarize briefly some of the proposals.

EARLY TWENTIETH-CENTURY PROPOSALS FOR CHANGE

Themes and thematic development were to be abandoned as obvious and mechanical. Any direct reference to extramusical experience was to be forbidden, and that which had its roots in knowable emotion was to be so presented that its origin could be clearly ascribed to the subconscious. "The composer does not make music; music makes itself in the composer" was the attitude set forth in an exposition of the new principles by no less a figure than Arnold Schering. And according to their choice of method, many little groups of like-minded composers appeared, raising respectively their banners as neoromanticists, antiromanticists, syncretists, expressionists, and the like.

Neoromanticists and antiromanticists are still with us, and still unreconciled. The expressionists were those in whom music made itself (the subconscious apparently being able to "express" more significant awarenesses than were forthcoming from consciousness). The syncretists seem to have formed a sect of expressionists, since they strove for the utterance, through a kind of synthesis of stimuli, of a kind of truth not demonstrable in language and hence beyond critical attack. Anarchy, it now appears, was rampant; reconstruction was hardly envisaged.

Other types of effort will be suggested in their place; but it is time to turn from supposed possibilities to accomplished fact. Divergent national tendencies, apparent at the end of the nineteenth century, had become so deeply rooted that they could not but persist into the twentieth. Our discussion, therefore, will deal with "modernism" as it has emerged in the principal European and American countries.

Modernism in Germany—Schoenberg, Berg, Webern

The most radical of twentieth-century composers, the most logical in the expression and the pursuit of his ideals, and the most ardently admired by his followers, was Arnold Schoenberg (1874–1953). He began as a follower of Wagner, composing a string sextet with a title and a fairly definite program (*Verklärte Nacht*, 1899), and an hour-long symphonic poem (*Pelleas und Melisande*, 1903) which, although it occasionally uses the six-tone scale, has no real similarity to Debussy's opera. A huge song-cycle (*Gurrelieder*), begun in 1900 but completed only in 1911, outdid Mahler's *Eighth Symphony* in the enormous forces required for its performance.[6]

Then followed two Chamber Symphonies (1906, but the second completed only in 1940) and two string quartets (1904–05 and 1907–08) which showed a decided break with the manner of the earlier works. The first Chamber Symphony is the most indicative of the change. It requires but 15 players (in larger halls the strings may be somewhat multiplied), but the texture is highly polyphonic, the individual parts extremely independent, and the harmonies (although the key is announced as E major) are often constructed out of superposed fourths—a texture visually similar to the conventional superposition of thirds, but aurally very different in effect. This structure is expounded fully in Schoenberg's *Harmonielehre* (1911)—a manual which treats with great thoroughness the "classical" theory of the eighteenth and nineteenth centuries, and then presents the new structure as a logical outcome of the old. Tonality as a principle is not attacked; but the first Chamber Symphony, in its acidity, and the theory, in its exploitation of hitherto unusable tone-relations, both suggest that the citadel of tonality is being stormed.

The difficulties which the new method presents for the voice are great. Two stage works, too introspective and too subtle in their implicit action to be called operas, exhibit this character—*Erwartung*, called a "mono-drama" (a woman awaiting her lover), and *Die glückliche Hand*, called

---

[6] As an accompaniment for the manifold chorus (5 solo voices, 3 four-part male choirs, and 1 eight-part mixed chorus) the orchestra comprises 4 piccolos, 4 flutes, 3 oboes, 2 English horns, 2 Eb clarinets, 3 Bb clarinets, 2 bass clarinets, 3 bassoons, 2 contrabassoons, 10 horns, 6 trumpets, 1 bass trumpet, 1 alto trombone, 4 tenor trombones, 1 bass trombone, 1 contrabass trombone, 1 contrabass tuba, 6 kettledrums, tenor drum, side drum, bass drum, cymbal, triangle, gong, glockenspiel, xylophone, rattle, some large iron chains, celesta, 4 harps, and a proportionate number of strings.

a drama with music. Fifteen songs from *Das Buch der hängenden Gärten*, by Stefan George, and a Second string quartet in F♯ minor (also arranged for string orchestra) precede the dramas and lead to what is doubtless the culminant work of the middle period—*Pierrot Lunaire*. Here Schoenberg uses the so-called *Sprechstimme* which, however, is not always a "speaking voice" but must frequently sing "hair-sharp" on pitch. The work is a cycle of 21 songs (actually identified as *melodramas*)[7] accompanied by piano, flute (or piccolo), clarinet (or bass clarinet) violin (or viola) and 'cello. The mood of the verses (by Albert Giraud) is precious and decadent, and out of these, to quote Cecil Gray, "Schoenberg has created a whole world of strange fascination and enchantment, of nameless horrors and terrible imaginings, of perverse and poisonous beauty and bitter-sweet fragrance, of a searing and withering mockery and malicious, elfish humor, which the poet most assuredly never contemplated. . . . Even the creations of Poe seem colorless, mechanical, and soulless when placed by the side of *Pierrot Lunaire*." [7a] The form-patterns as well as the texture are widely varied, but classical devices are extensively used. Number 8 is a passacaglia, the continuous bass-theme being figurated in later repetitions; No. 17 has a canon in the unison between voice and viola, while halfway between the entrances of each of these two parts the clarinet takes up the inversion of the same theme; and No. 18 has a canon between the piccolo and the clarinet whose theme appears also in augmentation in the piano, while the violin and 'cello proceed in canon on quite another figure. Moreover, when the wind and string parts reach the middle of the piece their continuation is the exact reversion of their parts thus far while the piano continues its augmentation to the end!

Except for a few songs, written in 1913–1915, there followed a long hiatus in composition. It turns out that Schoenberg was dissatisfied with the logical unity of his work thus far—even though his designs appeared (as in *Pierrot Lunaire*) to be as rigorously constructed as musical substance permits. (Tonality, incidentally, had long since become indistinguishable.) Somewhere, evidently, there was an intrinsic flaw; and the composer apparently spent many years not merely in discovering this flaw but in evolving a still "purer" manner of handling the substance of tone.

The technique that emerged was that of the *tone row*—a sequence of the twelve tones comprised within our octave,[8] taken in some chosen order (which might or might not briefly suggest a tonic) and pursued

[7] Cf. p. 450.
[7a] Cecil Gray, *A Survey of Contemporary Music* (1924), p. 176.
[8] And thus identical in substance with our chromatic scale, but utterly different in implication.

without returning to any tone until the whole gamut of twelve tones had been heard. This row might also be inverted; it might be played backwards; and this retrograde version of the row might also be inverted. Any desired transposition of the row might be made, and the notes might be used, not only in succession but simultaneously, as chords. The following will illustrate the twelve-tone row and its three derived forms which are the bases of Schoenberg's structures in his final period. It is from his *Variations for Orchestra,* Op. 31 (1928).

* Observe that the diminished fifth, the diminished third, and the major third of the Original are presented, in the Inversion, as their audible equivalents: the augmented fourth, the major second, and the diminished fourth. That is because these and other intervals are reckoned, not as having the tonal purpose which an implied tonic would suggest (the E after B♭, in the perspective of tonality, would naturally move to F), but as being simple musical distances, involving merely a fixed number of half-steps.

Rhythmic disposition of the notes of the row results either in motives (extensible into phrases) or in chords—the chords invariably using as accompaniment notes of the row which are not contained in the motivic phrase. Any note may be immediately repeated in a rhythmic design; but no note, once used, may be returned to until the whole series is exhausted. Rows of fewer than twelve tones are possible, but they will be treated in the same manner as twelve-tone rows. And any note may be presented in any desired octave.

This will suffice to suggest the general procedure in twelve-tone composition. The method was invented (or, as Schoenberg said, discovered, for he felt it to be pre-existent) in the search for "a new procedure in musical construction which seemed fitted to replace those formal and structural differences provided formerly by tonal harmonies." With a little practice, the eye—even of the uninitiated—can learn to distinguish the countless varied forms which the row may assume. The ear, on the other hand, has a much harder task. The row—or the *basic shape* as it is often called—is often exhibited as a kind of preface to the composition, needfully, for the shape is only the basis of motives constructed from it, and unless the row appears at the outset as melody, it would be troublesome for the eye and all but impossible for the ear to discover.

As a replacement of older formal types of design, the above-mentioned *manipulations* of the row are really not new. Inversion is a frequent device with all polyphonic composers; and reversion, although far less frequent, was even in the fourteenth century a familiar device. But both the melodic shapes and the *chords*—the horizontal and vertical aspects of the tonal fabric—frustrate seriously the ear accustomed to relate both melody and harmony to a tonic. The twelve-tonalists admit that the basic shape is often not consciously perceptible. They feel, however, that structures based on that shape possess an intuitively perceptible logic and offer a really new stimulation which can no longer be provided by composition in the tonal manner.

It must also be said that neither Schoenberg nor any of his significant disciples supposed that good music can be produced by mere pursuit of the method. The method is a means through which musical ideas of real interest can be communicated. "Through it," Schoenberg said, "I am . . . able to compose as unhesitatingly and imaginatively as one does in one's youth . . ." and this statement, from a musician of Schoenberg's stature, does not admit of denial. It is true that many composers of unquestionable strength reject the system as overintellectual and unsuited to the expression of those emotions which, until the twentieth century, it was the generally accepted purpose of music to express. But every revolution in music has sprung, in part, from a new vision of the expressive purpose of music; Beethoven, at the opening of the nineteenth century, spoke of spiritual matters hitherto unenvisioned and was roundly condemned for his departure from the comfortable conventions then existing; and it would be strange indeed if the turbid current of twentieth-century thought and feeling should be confined, for its utterance, to the conventional language of the nineteenth.[9]

[9] Thus far, no accepted criterion has appeared by which intimations of emotion of any character can be positively identified as resident in the musical substance. That the world has sought and found such intimations—and with large unanimity of judgment as to their character—is, however, indubitable. Indeed, if it were not so, music would have no history; for it is expression itself, not the mechanics of expression, which interests the world.

New processes of structure strike the uninitiated as inexpressive and therefore repellent. Analysts of these processes (for example, Rufer, *op. cit.*, and Allen Forte, *Contemporary Tone-Structures*, 1955) do not attempt to correct that impression. Yet gradual exposure to these processes is revealing, in all the really strong music of our day, a meaningful reflection of new and strange awarenesses (perhaps overconfidently attributed to the subconscious, since the subconscious must have operated long before the psychologists discovered it) that confuse and disorient our former placid interpretations of life.

The essential novelty of the new music will one day be found to lie in its utterance of new meaning, rather than in its novel processes of tonal organization. For to the world of music lovers—still essential to the continuing history of music—the notion of *pure* music, disassociated from everything external to music and

Schoenberg's work in his later manner comprised an unfinished opera to his own text, *Moses and Aaron* (the two completed acts performed in 1957); several choral works (including *A Survivor from Warsaw*, for narrator, chorus, and orchestra; *De Profundus*, to a Hebrew text, *a cappella*); concertos for violin (1936) and piano (1943); a *Theme and Variations*, originally for band; some chamber pieces, notably a *Fantasia* for violin and piano; and orchestral transcriptions of Bach and Handel. His last composition was the first of ten projected "Modern Psalms," with texts by himself. The music, even of this, remained unfinished. It is for four-part mixed chorus with orchestra; but the words are also recited, concurrently but not simultaneously with the choral voices, by a speaking voice. Adequate illustration of his music being obviously impossible in our space, we quote as a convincing personal expression of the man's sincerity the text of this "First Modern Psalm":

O Thou my God! All the peoples praise Thee and establish Thee in Thy majesty. But what can it matter to Thee whether I also do this or not? Who am I, that I should believe my prayer to be a necessity? When I say, "God," I know that in that word I speak of the One, the Eternal, the Almighty, the All-knowing and Unimaginable, of Whom I neither can nor should form an image; of Whom I neither should nor can make any demand; Who either will fulfil or will not heed my most fervent prayer. And yet I pray, as every living thing prayeth; in spite of all, I pray for grace and for the accomplishment of miracles! And still I pray, for I would not lose the blessed sense of unity, of being bound to Thee. And still I pray . . .

The adjective *atonal*, meaning *without a tonic*, was for some time applied, indiscriminately, both to the Schoenbergian structures and to others which exhibited a similar freedom in the use of dissonance but were based on methods far less reasoned. It is clear that merely to destroy such a fundamental basis of musical understanding as tonality had provided could not of itself provide a new basis of understanding. But the difference between the strict observance of the twelve-tone technique and an unregulated riot of dissonance was hard for the unaccustomed ear to detect, and the question whether the twelve-tone process is a valid substitute for tonality is still answered by the great majority of music lovers in the negative. For the presence in an art work of a perceptible relation to knowable experience is essential if the interest of the music lover is to be aroused and maintained.

---

therefore from life, is an absurdity. Valid criticism of music, therefore, must take into account not only structure but meaning. This need is clearly realized in some contemporary composers' writings about music—as for example, in Aaron Copland's *Music and Imagination* (1952) and in Hindemith's *The Composer's World*. (The author will shortly publish, through the University of Minnesota Press, a study of *The Elements of Expression in Music* which attempts to probe this question.)

That twelve-tone music may evoke such real interest is clearly seen in the work of Alban Berg (1885–1935), the most widely admired of Schoenberg's disciples. His first ambition was to become either a poet or a painter. But the Berg family was musical, and he began, at 15, to compose songs. In 1904 he began his studies with Schoenberg. Berg rapidly absorbed his teacher's ideas and attained a considerable mastery by 1910 when his lessons ceased. Berg's health was always precarious, however; and although he was assigned only to desk service in the First World War, his work was interrupted, and the volume of his composition was consequently not great.

Most of Berg's songs preceded his Op. 1, a piano sonata. A string quartet (1910) and three orchestral pieces (*Präludium, Reigen,* and *Marsch,* dedicated to Schoenberg) were his chief prewar works. But in May, 1914, he had decided to write an opera based on a fragmentary novel by Georg Büchner (1813–1837), entitled *Wozzeck.* The tale is superficially sordid—Wozzeck is a poor soldier, living with Marie and their child in poverty; Marie is seduced by a gorgeously-appareled drum major; Wozzeck discovers the fact and murders Marie, only to drown himself when he realizes what he has done. The misery is pointedly emphasized in the last scene, where children—Wozzeck's boy among them—play in complete unawareness of what has happened.

The *closed* process of dodecaphony[10] as Schoenberg perfected it seemed to Berg too abstract for exclusive use in setting a drama to music. Consequently it is employed only when it fits the dramatic situation; but free composition, although often unmistakably based on tonality, is so skilfully managed that the transition from one to the other is seldom disconcerting. The voice parts are melodically rather angular, but they invariably correspond to the natural declamation of the text, and often achieve poignancy comparable to the most eloquent utterances in classic opera. Brief motive-patterns, whether rhythmic or harmonic, are patently designed for characterization in a manner closely akin to the Wagnerian leading-motive—so extensively that Redlich[11] finds Berg's work "in this respect, almost a return to Wagnerian orthodoxy." But in formal structure the difference is fundamental, for Berg does not build out of his motives a quasi-symphonic form for the whole act, as Wagner does. Instead, he achieves musical coherence through the shaping of sections of each act in one or another of the "abstract" classical forms.

The first act of *Wozzeck* consists of a suite in eleven selections, a rhapsody on three chords, a military march, a lullaby, a passacaglia theme

[10] Gr. dōdeka = 12 + phonē = sound.
[11] H. F. Redlich, *Alban Berg, the Man and His Music* (New York, Abelard-Schuman, 1957).

with twenty-one variations, and a rondo-like *andante affetuoso.* The second act is a symphony in five movements, and the third consists of six inventions. The second of these (Act III, Sc. 2—the murder of Marie) culminates in an unendurable crescendo on the one note, B—surely the most elemental evocation of terror in operatic literature. (This scene is called an "invention on one note," the B having formed a persistent pedal-point throughout the scene.) Although these forms become perceptible on reading the score, it was not Berg's intention that they should be heard merely as abstract forms. They are a means of securing musical coherence; but their detail is so managed as to support and illuminate the action, and they seem to fulfill that purpose as adequately as does the Wagnerian symphony on leading-motives.

Wozzeck was composed from 1917 to 1921 and was first performed in Berlin in December, 1925, under Erich Kleiber. It has won world-wide success—of course within a relatively narrow circle which as yet constitutes the public for work so far removed from traditional opera. Still the work makes a compelling impression on music lovers who are quite unaware of its technical complexities and thus forms a justification, perhaps sounder than any argument based on analysis and logic, of the system of construction it represents.

Berg almost completed another opera, *Lulu,* drawn from two plays of Frank Wedekind, *Earth Spirit* and *Pandora's Box.* The story, although animated by the same sympathy for the unfortunate, is far more repellent than that of *Wozzeck.* The music is with few exceptions derived from a single tone row—a fact which, perhaps more than the misfortune which left the opera uncompleted, may account for its failure thus far to attain the popularity of *Wozzeck.*

Two purely instrumental pieces out of a very slight total volume of work have greatly aided in establishing Alban Berg as the most "humanistic" of Schoenberg's disciples. These are the *Lyric Suite* for string quartet and the *Concerto* for violin and orchestra—the latter Berg's last work. In the period immediately preceding his work on *Lulu,* Berg completed a *Chamber Concerto* for piano and violin, accompanied by ten wind and brass instruments, and a concert aria for soprano and orchestra, *Der Wein,* set to three out of five poems of Baudelaire collectively entitled *Le Vin.* These have won the affection of the initiated but not of the public. The *Lyric Suite* and the *Concerto* for violin and orchestra have genuinely attracted both. Each is dodecaphonic only in part, and the tone rows themselves are so made as to yield a number of simple triads. Hence the unaccustomed ear is not bewildered by persistent atonality. The *Concerto* was commissioned by the American violinist, Louis Krasner, and first performed by him in Barcelona in 1936. The tone row of this work is as follows:

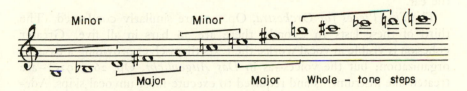

—four interlocked triads in the order minor-major, followed by a whole-tone progression which has but one step to go to complete a compass of three octaves. Tonality is hardly concealed in such a series.

Quite naturally, an opera of such dramatic force as *Wozzeck* offers such high interest apart from its music that it may well attract a far larger public than a purely instrumental work. But both the *Suite* and the *Concerto* have proved that the twelve-tone technique need not offend even the general ear.

If Alban Berg may be said to bring that technique closer to the musical expectation of the generality, Anton von Webern (1884–1945), the second of Schoenberg's immediate disciples, appears to gain distinction by a determined musical remoteness. His procedure was not at first founded on the tone row; but his earlier structures seem devoid of musical line (to say nothing of melody), and have consequently a form so disjunct as to be referable to nothing in the ordinary hearer's musical experience. But it appears that this music is not intended to be a formal design. It is an elusive fabric of tone, colored with the most meticulous care and giving to the ear somewhat the same stimulation as a pointillistic abstraction gives to the eye.

Webern was a fellow student with Berg under Schoenberg, and the two were close friends. He was a trained musicologist and a competent conductor (he directed the first performance of Berg's *Der Wein* at Vienna in 1932), and he seems to have enjoyed an equal measure with Berg of their teacher's regard. Rene Leibowitz[12] believes that a speculation in Schoenberg's *Theory of Harmony* (1909) as to the possibility of *Klangfarbenmelodien*—"tone-color melodies" constructed out of successions of tones of varying timbre as their primary principle—was an underlying idea in all Webern's work. This seems true, at any rate, of the six little pieces for string quartet, Op. 9 (1913), called *Bagatelles*. No. 3 of this group is eight bars long; it is based on two interval-progressions only —the fourth and the seventh—so dispersed that no rhythmic motives or

[12] In *Schoenberg and His School* (New York, Philosophical Library, 1949).

repetitive melodic suggestions appear; and color, although not highly variable in a string quartet, remains the principal impression conveyed to the ear.

The *Five Pieces for Orchestra*, Op. 10, are similarly condensed. The third of these lasts 19 seconds; there are 76 bars in all five. Greater cohesion is visible in vocal works, the texts themselves providing a basis of organization; but the voices—as in *Das Augenlicht*, Op. 26 (1935)—are treated like instruments and required to execute most unvocal skips. Adequate performance is thus extremely rare; but the piece was found highly impressive, even by opponents of its school of thought, when it was performed at a concert of the ISCM in 1938.

Webern finally adopted the tone row as a basis only after having apparently exhausted the possibilities of his earlier pointillistic structure. The most admired of his works in this manner are the *Symphony*, Op. 21 (1924) and the *String Quartet*, Op. 22. Canon (inverted) gives at least the visual aspect of thematic design; repeats (as in the sonata-exposition) similarly suggest symphonic form; but his music appears as the most esoteric structure in literature.

The twelve-tone technique is generally regarded as a peculiarly German method of composition, of which Schoenberg was the real inventor and Berg and Webern the chief exponents.[13] We have space for no more than mere mention of some of the younger writers in this style.[14] Although several of them have migrated either from or to Germany, and each may justly claim to have found expression for his individual imagination in the system, the German character seems to attach itself to the work of all. Two of the most important—Ernst Krenek and Egon Wellesz—will be discussed at some length when we come to study contemporary music in America and England. Each acknowledges his debt to Schoenberg, and each respects that master's warning against mere orthodoxy in the use of the system. A brief but fairly representative list of these younger men follows:

Boris Blacher (born 1903) speculates thus on the problem of "unrolling the series in time":[15] "One can imagine a co-ordinate system in which the metrical values are marked on the X-axis and the tonal values on the Y-axis; the result of these would emerge as living music." This speculation arose out of his effort to organize his ballet, *Lysistrata*. Such a

---

[13] A *Dodecachordal System* was invented independently of Schoenberg's thought by an Italian composer, Domenico Alaleona (1881–1928). But the German method is preferred by those Italians who pursue this manner of composition.

[14] The character of their works, as described by themselves, may be seen in Josef Rufer's *Composition with Twelve Notes* (London, 1954). Rufer is himself a Schoenberg pupil and an exponent of the system in many compositions.

[15] Cf. Stravinsky's position, p. 595.

theoretical image of structure is comprehensible even to an average man (like the writer of this book); that it would automatically yield "living music" is to that average mind unthinkable.

Luigi Dallapiccola (born 1904) has not adopted the serial technique exclusively, but has even there insisted on the imagination, rather than the system, as the composer's ultimate guide. Such works as *Sex Carmina Alcaei* and *Tre Poemi* have stimulated much interest in the technique in Italy, and he is regarded there as a leader in the movement.

Wolfgang Fortner (born 1907) pursued at first the technique of Reger, so brilliantly that he was named Professor of Composition at the Institute for Protestant Church Music in Heidelberg. He has used segments of the twelve-tone series as motives, essentially following the older scheme of phrase structure but still preserving the integrity of the series "as far as possible." He has written in his later manner three string quartets, sonatas for flute, violin, and 'cello (with piano), a 'cello concerto (1951), and a symphony (1947) which frankly admits its association with human misery and hope.

Hans Werner Henze (born 1926) is a pupil of Fortner. He is accounted one of the foremost composers of Germany. He has also his own manner of dealing with the series, akin to Fortner's. Traces of impressionism, polytonal passages, even echoes of jazz (in his ballet, *Jack Pudding*) may be found in his music. There is even the hint of a program in his Third Symphony (1952), which begins with a kind of vision of Apollo and ends with a magic incantation. An ingenious rhythmic design (a succession of measures containing 2, 3, 4, and 5 eighth-notes forms the basic rhythmic unit), as well as highly varied manipulation of the tone-series, is found in his second string quartet.

Similar individual views of the twelve-tone system will be found in the music of Hanns Jelinek (born 1901), an Austrian composer; Rolf Liebermann (born 1910), Swiss; Humphrey Searle (born 1915), English; as well as in the music of important European expatriates in America whose work will be mentioned later. Winfried Zillig made the following interesting comment on the system, suggesting that the forbidding mathematical aspect of it so often emphasized is falsely suggestive of its true nature:[16] "I am coming more and more towards the mysterious and compulsive connections with tonality, so that one could almost think that tonality might prove to be a special case of twelve-note music, just as the church modes were a special case of tonality." (Has music history indeed been viewing the evolution of the art in retrograde?)

The foregoing will suggest that the theorem itself of atonality must be

---

[16] Quoted in Rufer, *op. cit.*, p. 201.

abandoned as unsound. Schoenberg himself described the relation of the twelve notes in the "row" as "pan-tonality," and his followers—in various degrees as we have just seen—make many concessions to tonality in their manipulations of the series.[17] The theorem, indeed, has been rejected as a theorem by many composers whose "doctrines," in purpose evolutionary rather than revolutionary, have caused far less discussion than those of the twelve-tone school. Many of these composers, in line with the general trend of twentieth-century musical thought, have treated dissonance with a freedom which to unaccustomed ears is difficult to distinguish from the dissonance (as such) of the atonalists. They have also their followers, some of whom have mistaken unregulated dissonance and mechanically contrived design for purposeful composition. (These find their support in the apparent, rather than the real, musical public.) But all the musically animated workers are contributing to that greatly to be desired end—the reconciliation of divergent manners of musical speech to bring about a generally acceptable musical idiom in which that indefinable figure, the common man, may find (as throughout history he has hitherto found) immediately intelligible musical discussion of topics interesting to himself rather than merely to the musicians.

MODERNISM IN FRANCE

The End of Impressionism

From such glimpses as we have had of the musical consciousness of France, and of the awakening of that consciousness by Franck and Debussy, we shall expect the newer thought of French music to follow a very different course from that of German music. A Debussy produced in Germany is as unthinkable as a Schoenberg produced in France. But while the break with nineteenth-century tradition proved less violent than

---

[17] The objection to the tonal scale as "restricted" seems, indeed, to be based upon a somewhat unfair comparison with the twelve-tone series as "emancipated." For the twelve-tone scale, in obliterating the function of the tonic, must obliterate also the distinctions between such audibly equivalent (but tonally far different) intervals as the major second and the diminished third, or the augmented sixth and the minor seventh. These valuable distinctions are perceptible only in the orbit of tonal gravitation.

But the twelve-tone scale, when it escapes from that orbit, has indeed only twelve notes and no other intervals than those measured numerically in half-steps. The tonal scale, on the other hand, really has many more than twelve notes. For what in one context is C is, in others, B♯ or D♭♭; every other note may be similarly reoriented and renamed; and the "poverty-stricken" tonal scale thus shows 36 possible notes to the octave. We have already seen that Debussy's six-tone scale owes its ambiguity (so often hailed as the final step toward atonality) to a similar reorientation of its notes. (See Ftn. 3, p. 567.)

in Germany, the older aspect of tonality was here also attacked; and the uprooting of older conventions became—at least in practice if not in theory—nearly as complete. Some intervening steps may be traced.

Those conventions, especially as modified by César Franck, were fairly solidly established at the turn of the century. They were upheld by several of Franck's pupils and exerted, until after the First World War, an influence generally regarded as progressive. The most significant as a leader of musical opinion was doubtless Vincent d'Indy (1851–1931). His most enduring work now seems to have been the founding of the Schola Cantorum—originally a choir devoted to the study of Gregorian chant and the music of Palestrina and his time. In 1900 however the choir's scope was widened, and the objective became the musical education of youth. The Schola here came into conflict with the venerable Conservatoire as d'Indy sought to propagate the gospel of Franck and attempted to enlarge the horizon of French taste toward the comprehension of the symphony. Even before César Franck's notable example, d'Indy had composed a *Symphonie sur un Chant Montagnard* (1886). The work was for orchestra and piano (in no sense a concerto), but it emphasized the importance of symphonic form, and—far more than did Saint-Saëns's *Symphonie avec Orgue*—projected Beethovenian symphonic thought into the French musical stream. D'Indy was also an admirer of Wagner and incorporated something of his manner into his operas, *Fervaal* (1895) and *L'Étranger* (1901). Transformation of themes, however, rather than the Wagnerian leading-motive, was the basis of his structure. D'Indy was greatest as a teacher. His studies of medieval music and of earlier French masters were illuminating; his high view of the dignity of art and of its basis as essentially religious is apparent not only in his music but in his *Cours de Composition musicale;* and his catholicity of view may be judged from his sympathetic yet really Gallic study of Beethoven. D'Indy's most notable pupils were Albert Roussel and Arthur Honegger.

Ernest Chausson (1855–1899), more exuberant in temperament, yet hesitant and somewhat detached from the world, would doubtless have exerted a greater influence if his life had not been cut short in a bicycle accident. He left two symphonies of which the Second (Op. 20, in B flat) is still frequently heard; an opera, *Le Roi Arthus,* a quartet and a sextet for strings; and—the work by which he is best known—an admirable *Poème* for violin and orchestra. This was turned into a successful ballet, *Le Jardin aux Lilas* ("The Garden of Lilacs"). Guy Ropartz (1864–1955), longest-lived of Franck's pupils, spent his creative life in Brittany, but still kept somewhat abreast of current French thought. A *Choral Symphony* (1906) and an opera, *Le Pays* (1910), had a favorable radio revival in 1949; and a Fifth string quartet and a *Sinfonietta* (both dated 1948) reveal an astonishingly youthful mind in an aged body.

A significant transitional figure was Albert Roussel (1869–1937). He was a student at the Schola Cantorum for nine years and taught composition there until 1914, absorbing the Franckian tradition, but not becoming engulfed by it. Not only the impressionism of Debussy, but the leaner textures of later French composers are already foreshadowed in Roussel's *Divertissement* (1906) for piano and five wind instruments, and a choral work with orchestra, *Evocations* (1911). The latter work was a product, like the opera-ballet *Padmâvati*, of a sojourn in India. Service in the army (1914–1918) interrupted composition but determined his future course—alignment with the progressives. Yet his classical training forbade exaggeration, and three symphonies (in B minor, G minor, and A major) continue more than worthily the French symphonic trend of Franck and d'Indy.

Apart from, rather than opposed to, the Franckian trend was Gabriel Fauré (1845–1924), for long the director of the Conservatoire. He was a pupil of Saint-Saëns, but possessed a truer lyrical gift which was not submerged in the effort to gain technical mastery. The grand manner was too ostentatious for him, however, and his most characteristic works are his chamber pieces (two piano quartets, two string quartets), his piano music (for example, a *Theme and Variations* in C♯ minor), and his songs, so sympathetic as to give him the title of "The Schumann of France." In the earlier years of this century Fauré was vastly admired by his countrymen, but more recent movements show little trace of his influence. More truly identified with the twentieth century, but exerting influence rather as teacher than composer, was Charles Koechlin (1867–1950). He was a faithful co-worker with Fauré, and orchestrated —anonymously—many of the latter's works.

Until about 1920, the brilliance and clarity of the music of Maurice Ravel (1875–1935) seemed to indicate—along with the subtleties of Debussy—the probable trend of French music. This was only apparent, as we shall see; but each maintained the pointed suavity long admired by readers of French literature and opposed such qualities as the heaviness and obscurity of Germanic thought in a way which seemed to continue, quite naturally, the familiar opposition of the two cultures. That expectation has not been fulfilled. Both composers have "aged" far more rapidly than seemed possible; their manner, if imitated today, would appear grotesque; and yet—although Debussy's contribution to modern thought has been by far the greater—Ravel's popularity with what might be called the rear guard of modernism is high.

Ravel was, like Debussy, primarily a composer for the piano, and while

his orchestral works show consummate skill they are patently conceived out of that instrument. One of his first efforts—and, like the
Sonatine, one of his most perfect designs—was the *Pavane pour une
Infante défunte* ("Pavane for a Dead Infanta"—who, however, was
an imaginary person). In these pieces characteristics of his later style are
foreshadowed: a perception of the wide allusiveness of the dance as a
vehicle of expression, a disposition to look toward Spain for inspiration,
a Gallic restraint and clarity in melodic design, and, underlying all, a
temperament definitely passionate and romantic. *Jeux d'eaux* ("Play of
the Waters"), written in 1901, is less subtle but more vivid in color than
anything Debussy had produced. The *Valses nobles et sentimentales*
(originally for piano, but later orchestrated by the composer) venture
farther into the widening field of dissonance; there is even a considerable
excursion into bitonality; but all this sounds, today, like an echo of impressionism. This work, one may note, has as its motto a line from Reg-
nier—"the ever-delicious pleasure of a useless occupation"—which gently
suggests the decadence into which the major stream of French musical
thought had been lured and which was so soon to be vigorously com-
batted. There is a tinge of mordant humor in the *Alborada del Gracioso*
(from a set of five piano pieces collectively entitled *Miroirs*), and a strain
of neoclassicism in the suite, *Le Tombeau de Couperin* (1917). But these
still do not stray far beyond the confines of romanticism, and even in
the more pretentious suite, *Gaspard de la Nuit*, the wash of romantic
color hides from view both the sinister implications in *Ondine*, the starker
horror of *Le Gibet*, and the bitter irony of *Scarbo*.

Ravel's preoccupation with the dance, patent enough in the works just
mentioned, prompted not only the high idealization of that art in *La Valse*,
but its direct realization. His most extended work is the ballet *Daphnis et
Chloë*. The piano pieces *Miroirs*, *Gaspard*, and the *Valses nobles* all contributed to another ballet, *Adélaïde, ou le Langage des Fleurs;* and the
Boléro was written for the famous dancer, Ida Rubinstein. His handling of
the orchestra is both lucid and colorful in a thoroughly Gallic way; but it
is evident that his orchestral imagery required the prompting of some
extramusical purpose. He left but one orchestral work strictly designed
for the concert hall—the *Rhapsodie espagnole* (1907); and this, after the
Prélude à la Nuit, is a set of three dances—a *Malagueña*, a *Habañera*, and
a dance scene, *Feria* ("The Fair"). The tang of Spanish atmosphere is
evident—even more often than the titles of these works will suggest.
Ravel was born in the shadow of the Pyrenees. His family moved to
Paris when he was but three months old, but his mother was a Basque,
and a musician; and these facts may have some bearing on his work.

He left but two operas—*L'Heure espagnole* (1907), with its action persistently backgrounded by Spanish dance rhythms, and *L'Enfant et les Sortilèges* (1920–1925), a daintily told tale of a naughty boy whose misbehaviors are quite dreadfully punished by witchcraft. The texture here is *pointilliste*, with a skill unmatchable by any but a French composer. Ravel left also two concertos for piano (1931), one of which—written for Paul Wittgenstein who lost his right arm in the war—is for the left hand alone. It is musically the more important of the two. His last work, three songs to poems by Paul Morand forming a little cycle, *Don Quichotte à Dulcinée*, is in a genre not largely represented in his output. There is no unusual feature, technically, but the ironic attitude toward overdrawn romance is wonderfully expressed. His other songs, like Debussy's, are significant for their exquisiteness.

Ravel's chamber music is even slighter in volume. The early string quartet (1904) has now become a kind of classic example of advanced romanticism. But two later sonatas—that for violin and 'cello (1920–1922) and that for piano and violin (1923–1927)—are excursions into the new contemporary idiom, to whose definition they contribute little. (He said of the violin sonata that it was his purpose to emphasize the incompatibility of the two instruments—a purpose incompatible with Ravel's imaginative nature.) The *avant-garde*, far more than he realized, had outpaced him.

Of no particular influence on the future, but of a technical solidity and an expressive meaningfulness too striking to be ignored, was the music of Paul Dukas (1865–1935). One work—the inimitable *L'Apprenti Sorcier* ("The Sorcerer's Apprentice")—appeared in 1897 and is known the world over. The rest is ignored, except in France. Also in 1897 his Symphony in C—in three movements like that of Franck, but with no attempt (such as Franck had made) to combine slow movement and scherzo together—had been performed with no more than the respect due to a thoroughly competent example of a form not really congenial to French taste. In 1901 he produced a portentous piano sonata (the first significant example of that form by a French composer). This was followed by another huge piano piece, *Variations, Interlude, et Final sur une Thème de J. Ph. Rameau*—neoclassical, in contrast to the essentially romantic sonata. His notable opera, *Ariane et Barbe-bleu* (1907) was based on Maeterlinck's version of the story and was as exceptional in its general departure from conventional method as Debussy's *Pelléas*, for it cast each act in one of the "abstract" forms of instrumental music. (It is thus a precursor, in a general way, of Berg's *Wozzeck*.) In 1912 appeared a remarkable "dance poem," *La Peri*, again symphonic in manner, however unsymphonic the subject. Then came the war, and the rest of Dukas's career was that of a teacher.

One more figure—more significant than popular or even influential—in the transition of French music from Gallic isolation to a position of high importance is Florent Schmitt (1870–1958). In the soft atmosphere of impressionism, the firmness of his essentially diatonic harmony and his weighty orchestration assume a harshness which, in another light, would have impressed his countrymen more favorably. His setting of *Psalm XLVII* is permeated with a typically French sense of glory (not much discriminated whether the object is the nation or the Deity), and superficially suggestive of the magniloquence of Berlioz. *La Tragédie de Salomé*, in rhythmic complexity, seems a foretaste of the *Danse infernale* and the *Danse sacrale* from Stravinsky's *Fire-bird* and *Rite of Spring*. But Schmitt's teutonic structure was antipathetic to the rising generation, and he was revered rather than followed.

The Break with Impressionism—Satie and "Les Six"

In 1903 appeared *Three Pieces in the Form of a Pear* by Erik Satie (1866–1925). This composer had written, in 1887, three *Sarabandes* in which passages in consecutive ninth chords, in parallel motion, anticipated the lush impressionistic harmonies of which Debussy later made so much use. Four years later, in *Le Fils des Étoiles*, he wrote in the same parallel motion a succession of chords built up in fourths—again an anticipation of Schoenberg's first harmonic step away from Classic tradition. Although the *Pear* pieces were more provocative in their title than in their musical substance, they were nevertheless sufficiently rebellious, marking a strong distaste for the impressionism that by now was becoming so infectious that it was soon nicknamed "Debussyitis." And that distaste was the generating motive of the new movement, which was to prefer the lean to the lush.

Satie was regarded by many (who read his freakish titles rather than his music) as a charlatan; but he was serious enough to enter—in 1903—Roussel's counterpoint course at the Schola Cantorum and to pursue that study until he earned a certificate of proficiency. His eccentricity, however, did not abate, and such titles as *Véritables Préludes flasques (pour un Chien)* deflected interest from rhythms so novel that the music was written without bar-lines. His opposition to romantic and impressionist art was voiced, of course, in more significant tones than those offered by a few piano pieces. The most significant is a *Symphonic Drama in Three Parts, with Voices, on Dialogues of Plato*. Part I (from *The Banquet*) is Alcibiades's portrait of Socrates; Part II (from *Phaedrus*) is called "the Banks of Ilyssus"; and Part III (from *Phaedo*) describes the death of Socrates. The music is utterly simple and nondescriptive; the voices sing "as if reading"; and the greatest care is shown, in the vocal line, to follow the natural curves and inflections of speech. This is a far cry from the Wagnerian melody, so often patently contrived to fit the already constructed symphonic drama coming from the orchestra-pit. It may even be seen (with the *post hoc, propter hoc* logic of one who has a thesis to prove) as an anticipation of the Shoenbergian *Sprechstimme*. But it is more just to view these innovations as evidence of a sharp critical penetration into the weaknesses of the romantic and impressionistic manners, and as earnest attempts to correct excesses—even at the risk of excess in the opposite direction.

When France emerged as victorious from the First World War, her artists were no less jubilant than her politicians. In 1923 the music historian Paul Landormy felt justified in saying, "It may be affirmed that with regard to the value, abundance, and variety of its productions, France today takes first rank among the musical nations of the entire world." That affirmation has never been accepted by the entire world; but it would never have been made had not a peculiar type of propaganda been started which served to focus much of the efforts of French composers, and still more of the attention of the musical public, on the objective striven for by Erik Satie.

The catalytic event was an article in *Comoedia* by the critic Henri Collet, entitled "The Five Russians, the Six French, and Erik Satie." He suggested that a similar movement to that after Glinka in Russia should occur in France, its moving spirit being Satie who had in 1916 initiated a kind of *Davidsbund* of French composers who assisted each other in the public performance of their own works. "Les Six" were originally five, but might have been more (perhaps a musical *Pleiade?*); they neither sought collaboration nor set much store by Collet's notion of it; but the propaganda that ensued was intense and grew into something not unlike the war of the Gluckists and the Piccinnists.

The "Six" were Darius Milhaud and Arthur Honegger (both born in 1892), Louis Durey (born 1888), Georges Auric and Francis Poulenc (both born in 1899), and one woman, Germaine Taillefer (born 1892). Only the first two have exerted significant influence, but those two are of the first importance for the future.

Milhaud was a pupil of Gédalge, d'Indy, and Widor, gaining a sound orthodox training. But this was liberated during his sojourn in Brazil where as assistant to the Ambassador, the poet Paul Claudel, he found inspiration for his *Saudades do Brazil* (nostalgic pieces on Brazilian dances) and made incidental music for Claudel's *Agamemnon* and *Les Choéphores*. Returning, he found the temper of the Parisian public more attuned to novelties than to ancient classics. He met the demand with a ballet, *Le Bocuf sur le Toit* ("The Bull on the Roof), and with *Six petites Symphonies*, each in one movement, their title implying merely "sound-piece." These are of no great import, but their intent—that of releasing the French musical idiom from the Teutonic character imposed on it by Franck and his followers—proved decisive.

The new idiom is described as being either polytonal or polyharmonic. Polytonality appeared with the simultaneous performance of two or more melodies, each in a different key. Polyharmony presented simultaneously two or more chords, each orthodox in itself, but harmonically incompatible with each other. With polytonality, the hearer's attention is supposedly horizontal; in polyharmony, it is vertical. But it is clear that several polytonal melodies, heard together, must produce a semblance of harmony; and since the harmonies thus produced may show the essential disrelation of actual polyharmonies, the ear may be hard put to it to detect the difference. Yet both have a measure of historic justification. The device of the "pedal-point" with disrelated chords moving above it suggests a rudimentary polytonality, and polyharmony was at least suggested in the famous return of Beethoven's *Eroica* theme in the tonic against the dominant harmony of the fiddles.[18] But while these rather similar devices—sometimes including an analogous "polymodality"—were widely used, no excogitated system, such as that of the twelve-tone row, was promulgated.

Clarity—doubtless the most distinctive feature of French utterance on any topic or in any medium—cannot be attained by pursuing a formula. Weight however—similarly characteristic of German utterance—may be simulated by obscurity, which is easily attainable by the dogged pursuit of a formula. The formula of the twelve-tone scale generated a weighty

---

[18] Milhaud, arguing for polytonality in *La Revue Musicale* in 1923, contended that Bach, in one of his four *Sonatas* for piano which is in canon at the fifth, was producing polytonality—since one of the voices is in C while the other is in G. This argument seems specious; for the impression, to the average hearer and doubtless also to Bach, is not that of two keys, discriminated as such while simultaneously heard, but of a shift from one tonality to the other, or a state of suspension between the two, accordingly as the harmony is dominated by one voice or the other.

He illustrates the modern process by a brief example in which five melodic lines, individually in the keys of B♭, F, E, C, and D, are combined. A sixth part, also in B♭, is present; and if the two in that key were played so as to predominate, they might similarly dictate the hearer's idea of the tonality of the whole passage. But no hearer, however expert, could be expected to identify all five keys through the ear alone.

What the mind perceives in such a combination (compare the five combined themes in the Finale of Mozart's *Jupiter* symphony) is what the psychologist calls a *Gestalt*—a complex whole whose parts are heard, not as discrete entities, but as a whole. Similarly, the question with polytonal music is not the presence of discrete tonalities, but their combination into an acceptable whole. The real method, in such a combination, is not revealed in the mere exhibit of the constituent parts.

method of composition—more flexible than it at first appeared, but still rather a change of servitude than an emancipation from the trammels of tonality. Polytonality remained only a device, to be adopted or rejected at will, and imposing no obligation of dogged pursuit on the composer.

Milhaud uses this device frequently, along with all the others sanctioned by older conventions. The volume of his work is enormous, so that no more than a glimpse of its high lights is possible here. We have mentioned his music for *Agamemnon* and *Les Choéphores* (the first two dramas in the trilogy *Oresteia* of Aeschylus). The third, *Les Euménides,* was completed in 1922. These are dramas with music, rather than operas in the usual sense, since spoken words, whether accompanied by music or not, maintain the continuity of the drama. *Les Euménides* is widely regarded as Milhaud's greatest work. It marks the summit of his polytonal manner. Other operas (the term now used in its usual sense) are *Les Malheurs d'Orphée* ("The Woes of Orpheus," 1924); *Le pauvre Matelot* (The Poor Mariner," 1926), called a *complainte* in three acts; *Esther de Carpentras* (1937), called an *opera bouffe* but mingling much seriousness with its comedy; and *Médée* ("Medea," 1938), based on treatments of the story by Euripides, Seneca, and Corneille. There is also incidental music for Claudel's *Protée.* In the kindred genre of the ballet, there are *L'Homme et son Désir, Le Boeuf sur le Toit, La Création du Monde* (1923), *Salade, Le Train bleu,* and a version of Poe's *The Bells* (silver, gold, brass and iron), written at Mills College in 1945. In Paris, on a visit in 1948, Milhaud composed " *'adame Miroir,*" a strange fantasy enacted in a hall of mirrors by a sailor, his reflection, and "the violet domino," (Death). In the ballets—in contrast to the heavier operas—a small and characteristic orchestra is used, with much ingenious treatment of percussion.

Milhaud's list for orchestra is considerable: the six *Petites Symphonies* already mentioned; from 1939 to 1948, four symphonies in an approximation to classical form (the first commissioned by the Chicago Orchestra for its semicentennial, the last ending with a *Commémoration* of the revolution of 1848); several *suites* (some drawn from ballets); concertos for piano, violin, viola, and 'cello, and one for percussion; and countless scores for films.

For voices there are many cantatas, quartets, duets, and solo songs; for piano, two solo sonatas and a host of pieces either for solo or duet (*Scaramouche*—after Molière—is so well known as to be hackneyed); and our list may close with mention of 15 string quartets, the first dating from 1912, and the last two from 1948 and 1949. These two, although individually complete in themselves, may be played simultaneously as an octet!

Milhaud's long catalogue is imposing. It demonstrates an altogether exceptional musical aptitude. But it also suggests—and much of Milhaud's music proves—that aptitude can too readily become, in practice, a kind of heedless facility, comparable to the virtuosity of the performer who supposes that he can make music with his hands alone. *Les Euménides,* written when he was 30, seems the summit of his ascent. And his influence since coming to America, while wide, has not been deep.

Arthur Honegger (1892–1955), the only other member of "Les Six" to attain world-wide fame, seems in the perspective of the moment a more significant figure. He was born in Le Havre, but of Swiss parents who preserved their native independence of mind. He was 15 before his musical bent was fully revealed, but after that he pursued his classical studies—like Milhaud, in the classes of Gédage, Widor, and d'Indy—with more awareness of their solid value and less of youthful propensity to revolt than the other members of the famous group. In particular, Honegger admired and championed Wagner, in a day when the French (who had only belatedly made his acquaintance) were unanimous in repudiating him. He likewise looked on Bach as a guiding spirit—and not for his skill alone. His inclusion among the "Six" was of considerable material advantage; but he never manifested any allegiance to the supposed tenets of the group, which, indeed, were Collet's rather than their own.

Honegger's imagination was intuitively dramatic; his natural musical utterance, melodic; his constructive process, polyphonic. His harmonic horizon embraced all that was essential in the widening vocabulary of the twentieth century, but he pursued none of the fashionable—or the unfashionable—methods of structure. He apparently found—and taught, at Tanglewood in 1947—a kind of principle of musical necessity which had to be obeyed at all costs but for which no easy equivalent could be found in any of the current musical procedures. He occasionally employed polytonality, but not for the purpose of obliterating tonality; and the notion of really atonal music was to him as unthinkable as the rigid mechanics of dodecaphony. Such independence of mind, stimulated by imagination but controlled by undeviating adherence to principles rooted in established musical practice, was rare during the "roaring twenties."

His earliest compositions were songs, piano pieces, and chamber music, the latter comprising a string quartet (1917) and duet sonatas for various instruments with piano. His first resounding success was the orchestral "Symphonic Movement, No. 1"—a descriptive piece subtitled *Pacific 2–3–1* and superficially portraying a locomotive; but what it really described was the state of mind of the locomotive-lover. (Unfortunately the external object was more visible to the hearer than the internal; and the piece soon lost interest for the world.) "Movement No. 2," entitled *Rugby,* really failed; and "No. 3," which never got a subtitle, remains virtually unknown. But about the same time there appeared a dramatic cantata, *Le Roi David*—a most daring adventure in choral writing—which rapidly made its way into every musical quarter as a "modern" piece not only wholly listenable but, considering its vigorous dissonance, surprisingly easy to perform. The same abounding energy that animated *Pacific 2–3–1* is here devoted to a theme of true spiritual import.

Honegger's skill was mature enough by 1930 so that he was asked to write his First symphony for the fiftieth anniversary of the Boston Orchestra. Against the background of experiment current in that day, the bold assurance of this music is striking. But this is not the assurance of pedantry. It is the utterance of a man strongly—and in the *Adagio*, deeply—moved; moved, moreover, not by vague stirrings of the subconscious, but by an intense purpose which is too big to be named in any word but is nevertheless perceptible to any strong man who has known an abiding purpose. The density, especially in the first movement, is fatiguing; the hearer emerges shaken; but when he gets his breath he will say, "That is a symphony!"

There are four other Honegger symphonies, of which the *Symphonie liturgique* is probably the most significant. Its three movements are entitled *Dies irae* (but there is no appearance of the familiar liturgical tune), *De profundis clamavi*, and *Dona nobis pacem*. Charles Munch, to whom the work is dedicated, finds the music suggestive of revolt against a higher will, with a final, not unwilling submission. The Fourth is a "little symphony," written for the chamber orchestra of Basle and entitled *Deliciae Basiliensis*. Swiss melodies are engagingly used. The Fifth (1951) is called by the composer "*di tre re*"—not "of three kings," but "of three D's", that note being the pointed final of each movement.

Dramatic intensity, without the musical trappings of dramatic design, appears to be Honegger's objective in symphonic composition. When drama appears in its natural guise of words and action, he finds appropriate musical matter. But of the usual dramatic conventions and amenities he rejects as much as possible. The most important of his dramatic pieces (which do not for the most part assume the form of opera) may be listed, with comment much restricted, as follows: *Horace victorieux* was intended as a "mimed symphony," but the staging failed to materialize, and the work became a program symphony. The story, from Livy, is that of the Horatii and the Curiatii who fought to settle the strife between the Romans and the Albans. Eight sections describe not only the various phases of the fight but Horatius's murder of his sister, Camilla, who loved an Alban. *King David* was also first presented as drama, with wind instruments for accompaniment; in the cantata form, it was reorchestrated with strings. *Antigone* was composed as stage music for Cocteau's version of Sophocles's play, but, like *Judith*—at first also incidental music for Morax's drama—was built into a serious opera. *Judith* was performed by the Chicago Opera Company with Mary Garden in 1927. The theme—the murder of Holophernes—is fascinating but repellent, and the difficult score prevents frequent performance. *Amphion* (1931) is an opera-ballet; *Semiramis* (1934) is a ballet only; *Fedra* (d'Annunzio's version of the classic tale) is almost an opera; *L'Impératrice aux Rochers* (1926) is a "mystery" (the story of Emperor Aurelian's wife, Victoria, exiled to a rocky isle). But the most imposing of all is the music set to Claudel's version of the story of Joan of Arc, *Jeanne d'Arc au Bûcher* (1938). Throughout the long piece, Joan stands chained to the stake; the story appears in the guise of visions or memories which we understand to be coursing through her mind, but which are enacted for us. Joan does not sing, but choral and solo voices vivify the incidents related, and the music equals the masterly drama to which it is set.

Honegger's interesting instrumental piece called a *Monopartita*, a "Suite in one movement," dates, like the Fifth Symphony, from 1951. These works may perhaps indicate a tendency toward abstract musical thought—a considerable alteration, if this is true, from his former stand. But there is little doubt that he will be reckoned, not only as the most stalwart member of the "Six," but as one who, without a "system," showed the way to a reconciliation of systems in a commonly intelligible musical speech.

The other members of the "Six" are far less significant. The most conspicuous are Auric and Poulenc. Auric has written copiously for films, but he has made his music in such a fashion that it cannot interestingly exist by itself. Two ballets, *Les Matelots* ("The Sailors") and *La Pastorale* (which title hardly suggests the motion picture actors and the telegraphists who figure in it) perhaps gave direction to his later efforts. Poulenc has written much for piano, often most attractively; he had a considerable share in a collaborated ballet (by all the "Six" except Durey) called *Les Mariés de la Tour Eiffel* ("The Married Couples of the Eiffel Tower"); but his accomplishment—by no means without value—lies in the field of entertainment. Germaine Taillefer and Durey have receded into invisibility.

Outside the coterie of the "Six," the most conspicuous French composer of the earlier decades was Jacques Ibert (born 1890) who, besides many popular piano pieces, produced a symphonic poem, *The Ballad of Reading Gaol* (after Oscar Wilde), *Three Ballet Pieces* in piquant rhythms, and the popular orchestral suite, *Escales* ("Ports of Call")—impressions of three Mediterranean towns. Roland Manuel, a protégé of Satie, was an energetic propagator of the new music, but a less effective contributor of actual scores. Great things were prophesied also of Georges Migot; but the prophecy has not been fulfilled.

No attempt can be made here to picture the "present state" of French music. But the work of Olivier Messaien (born 1908) looms large in the foreground. He was a pupil of Dukas and Marcel Dupré. The major part of his work is deeply motivated by his Catholicism, and his musical idiom is accordingly derived (so far as it is derived) from whatever can contribute to that objective. Characteristic in this vein is a *Méditation symphonique, Les Offrandes oubliées* ("The Forgotten Sacrifice"), in three movements—"The Cross," "The Sin," "The Eucharist." Four similar *Méditations* deal with the implications of the Feast of the Ascension, and there are nine on the Birth of the Saviour. There is also a string quartet entitled *Pour le Fin du Temps* whose eight movements contemplate the saying of the angel of the Apocalypse, "There will be no more time." Various works for organ (he is organist at La Trinité) voice similar thoughts; *Visions de l'Amen* for two pianos and *Vingt Regards sur l'Enfant Jésus* for piano solo interestingly employ that instrument for an unusual expressive purpose. But secular ideas are not foreign to him, as may be seen in his *Fantaisie burlesque* for piano. Messaien is now Professor of Harmony at the Conservatoire, and has written a significant treatise on that subject—*Technique de mon langage musical.*

Jean Louis Martinet (born 1912) has shown remarkable command in a ballet, *Orphée*, which continues the romantic tradition of Ravel's *Daphnis et Chloë*. A set of Variations for string quartet seems to suggest a mind capable of symphonic effort. Henri Sauguet (born 1901) is as prolific as the English Benjamin Britten, writing in any demanded style or medium, and still escaping the banality ordinarily attendant on such diversified effort. In marked contrast is the work of Pierre Boulez (born 1926), a pupil of Messaien and Leibowitz, who has adopted fully the twelve-tone technique and is also a foremost worker in the field of electronic music. Two of his most important works are *Le Visage nuptial*, for two solo voices, women's chorus and orchestra, and a *Symphonie concertante* for piano and orchestra.

MODERNISM IN RUSSIA

Pursuing with some uncertainty the aims of the "Five," the hopes of the Russian nationalists were for a time centered on Alexander Glazounoff (1865–1936), a man of exceptional talent who enjoyed every assistance that could be offered, whether by his instructors and colleagues or by the wealthy publisher, Belaieff. Like Tchaikovsky, he did not wholly subscribe to the doctrines of the nationalists. Indeed, he became a devout follower of Brahms. Adopting German principles of structure (of the nineteenth, not of the twentieth century) he effectively disassociated himself from the progressive Russian movement.

A real departure from nineteenth-century ideals began with Alexander Scriabin (1872–1915). He displayed at first something of the delicate sensibility of Chopin, expressed in piano pieces of a not very extended imaginative range. Tours as a virtuoso pianist seem to have widened his horizon, with the result that in 1903 he resigned his professorship of piano at the Moscow Conservatory to pursue what appeared to be a very novel style of composition. He evolved a new type of chord structure, based not upon superposed thirds, but on a peculiar ladder of dissimilar fourths. These, however, were quite unrelated to Schoenberg's essays in such structure.[19] Through this novel harmonic structure Scriabin began to envision musical expression of subtleties of the soul which had hitherto escaped all realization. (The region of the subconscious, later invoked by so many explorers as the source of their "abstractions," would seem to be also the origin of Scriabin's later works; but they are so "romantic" in tone as to be repudiated by later delvers into that dubiously fertile region.)

Scriabin soon outgrew the influence of Wagner and Liszt, clearly apparent in the piano concerto of 1897 and in the First symphony, as he had the earlier influence of Chopin. His Second symphony has a definite, though highly metaphysical, program; but thereafter the huge orchestral pieces (*Poème divin, Poème d'extase,* and *Prometheus*) are increasingly absorbed in a kind of apocalyptic vision which leaves the ordinary world far behind. *Prometheus* demands an enormous orchestra with organ and is also to be accompanied by a *clavier à lumières*—a "light-keyboard"—which throws on a screen a prearranged scheme of color combinations and sequences designed to intensify the hearer's absorption in the message of the music. In his last work, the unfinished *Mysterium,* Scriabin intended an even more comprehensive synthesis of sense-stimulations

[19] The chord on which Scriabin's tone poem, *Prometheus,* is founded is derived from the harmonic series (see p. 188), and like the whole-tone scale of Debussy (which, however, is not so derivable) may be viewed either as a scale or a chord. This combination constitutes both the harmonic and the thematic basis of the piece. The chord itself, its scale form, and the tones of the harmonic series from which it is derived (Nos. 7, 8, 9, 10, 11, and 13) are shown below:

(through the addition of odors). How far he may have anticipated later musical tendencies remains a question for the analysts to answer fully. He seems to have few avowed followers.

Sergei Rachmaninoff (1873–1943), like Glazounoff, seemed at the turn of the century a possible continuator of the nationalism of the "Five." This remarkable man, one of the foremost pianists of the day, composed in many large forms as well as in the small pianistic shapes which first made him famous. His work showed the somber tints which the Western world was wont to associate with Russia; but this, to later eyes, was no more than the *Weltschmerz* of the romanticists and, so, anathema to all the more radical modernists. Yet his piano concertos (especially the Second) are in the repertoire of prominent pianists, as the Second symphony is in the repertoire of all major orchestras. His symphonic poem, *Die Toteninsel* ("Isle of the Dead"—after Arnold Boecklin's famous picture, which inspired Max Reger and many others) goes beyond his usually narrow range of expression and touches hitherto unvibrated chords of somberness. It dates from 1909, the year in which he first appeared in America as pianist; and the vast acclaim accorded to his playing may have diverted him from the difficult discovery of a more advanced idiom. The Third and Fourth Piano concertos, the Third symphony (1936), and the brilliant *Rhapsody on a Theme of Paganini* (the twenty-fourth *Caprice* for solo violin, which evoked Brahms's brilliant Variations) show in consequence a recognition of the advent of modern idioms rather than the adoption of any new attitude. His work in choral fields is well represented by his setting of Poe's *The Bells*, of which the English composer Joseph Holbrooke had earlier written a colorful choral version, and which Milhaud in 1945 was to turn into a ballet.

The decay of the older tradition is more noticeable in the work of Rachmaninoff's lesser contemporaries which reveals solid musical accomplishment rather than any real novelty of invention. Anton Arensky left many too-charming pieces for two pianos, some solo études, and a gently nostalgic Trio, but he was not at his best in his attempts at opera and symphony. Reinhold Glière is best remembered for his symphonic poem, *The Sirens*, and a ballet, *The Red Poppy*. Ippolitoff-Ivanoff's *Caucasian Sketches*, long popular, would now sound archaic. Alexander Gretchaninoff, although he essayed the composition of symphonies and operas, is still well and favorably known for his songs and his small-scale church pieces.

Out of this background, but stimulated by a vision of artistic purpose hardly derived from it, emerged one of the half-dozen or so commanding figures in twentieth-century music—Igor Stravinsky (born 1882). A superficial view of his work might readily suggest that it was the general product of inviting external circumstance, since so much was commissioned and designed for already established purposes. More penetrating interpreters and commentators, however, see in him the most fertile, varied, and prophetic mind of the time.

Although musical by inheritance and inclination (his father was a basso in the Opera at St. Petersburg), Stravinsky was destined by his parents for the law. Hence his first studies in piano and harmony were largely self-directed. In 1902, however, he met Rimsky-Korsakoff and presently became his pupil—in orchestration rather than in composition. An early Symphony in E flat, a *Scherzo fantastique*, and the vivid *Fireworks* show his progress with that master, whose death in 1908 left Stravinsky to shift for himself in a world as yet largely unknown. Having heard the *Scherzo* and the *Fireworks*, Diaghilev gave him a small commission (for *Les Sylphides*) and followed it with *The Fire-Bird* (1910) and *Petrouchka* (1911). These, brilliant in color and perfectly adjusted to the dance, made Stravinsky's name known everywhere as the most promising member of the *avant-garde*. This opinion was heightened (as was also the opposition) by the notorious first performance of *Le Sacre du Printemps* ("The Rite of Spring") in Paris in 1913. Higher than this in awakening excitement, no composer could go. But there was also intended a proportionate, if less visible, depth: an exploration into the primary regions of human impulse and, in the dance of death at the end, a vision of consequences ineluctable and terrifying.

Stravinsky's first opera, *Le Rossignol* ("The Nightingale," after Hans Christian Andersen) was completed after five years' interruption and performed in Paris in May, 1914. But the war supervened, involving not only the disruption of his plans but a gradual readjustment of his aesthetic beliefs and practices. His new convictions, catalyzed by a search for inspiration in Russian folk-poems, are thus expressed in his autobiography:[20]

I consider that music is, by its very nature, essentially powerless to *express* anything at all, whether a feeling, an attitude of mind, a psychological mood, a phenomenon of nature, etc. . . . Expression has never been an inherent property of music. That is by no means the purpose of its existence. . . . [Expression is] an aspect which, unconsciously or by force of habit, we have come to confuse with its essential being. . . . Music is given to us with the sole purpose of establishing an order in things, including, and particularly, the coördination between *man* and *time*. . . . Its indispensable and single requirement is construction. Construction once completed, this order has been attained, and there is nothing more to be said."

There is here an indubitable similarity to the underlying motive which drove Schoenberg toward the invention of the twelve-tone system.

[20] Igor Stravinsky, *Chronicles of My Life* (1936).

There is no similarity, however, but rather a complete divergence between the methods employed by the two men.[21] The transition is illustrated in Stravinsky's compositions of 1914–1918—years he spent in Switzerland—in which a drastic economy of forces (as compared with *Le Sacre*) is practiced, and in which the music appears to abstract itself from the external sense of either words or action. (The internal sense is on the contrary felt as heightened.) The *Histoire du Soldat* (1918) requires a narrator and only seven performers; it presents several stylized dances; *Les Noces* (1923), portraying Russian wedding customs, accompanies the dancing on the stage by four pianos, seventeen percussion instruments, and a chorus stationed with the orchestra. And the new aesthetic is uncomprisingly shown in the *Symphonies for Wind Instruments* (Boston, 1920) of which he said, "This music was not made to please or to excite passions. . . . It is an austere ceremony which revolves in brief litanies among the different families of homogeneous instruments." This work is dedicated to the memory of Debussy, in genuine homage, even though it is poles apart from impressionism.

A second opera, *Mavra*, a comedy in one act, was performed in 1922; thereafter he produced more stylized stage-pieces, such as *Oedipus Rex*, whose Sophoclean text Cocteau translated into Latin, but which Stravinsky treated "as purely phonetic material for the composer"; and *Perséphone* (1934), a dramatic poem on the Homeric hymn to Demeter by André Gide, for *recitante*, tenor, chorus and orchestra. (Here, the words have, for the hearer, far more than phonetic interest.) But the majority of his stage-works are for ballet—*Le Baiser de la Fée* (1928) on themes from Tchaikovsky; *Pulcinella* (1920), similarly after Pergolesi; *Jeu de cartes* ("A Card Game in Three Deals" 1937); the *Circus Polka* (1942) for Barnum and Bailey's elephants—which, the trainer ruefully admitted, they found to be "not their kind of music"; *Orpheus* (1948); and *Agon* (1957). But he returns to the genre of opera in 1951 with *Rake's Progress* (its text, after Hogarth, by W. H. Auden and C. Kallman).

The symphony as an independent form is chosen but seldom by Stravinsky. Besides the *Symphony in E flat*, Op. 1, and the *Symphonies for Wind Instruments* already mentioned, there are only the *Symphonie de Psaumes*, dedicated to the Boston orchestra on its semicentennial (1930) but "composed to the glory of God"; a *Symphony in C* (1940), and a *Symphony in Three Movements* (1946). But there are several concertos—for piano and orchestra and for piano and wind, a violin

---

[21] Schoenberg, in the 'thirties, spoke of himself as a constructor rather than a composer. Stravinsky had earlier recorded his complete distaste for the aesthetic underlying *Pierrot Lunaire*.

concerto, and a Capriccio for piano and orchestra—and of course many suites drawn from ballets.

Stravinsky's principal choral works are on religious themes: *Paternoster, Credo, Ave Maria;* a *Mass* for men's and boys' voices, with accompaniment for ten instruments; a *Canticum sacrum ad honorem Sancti Marci nominis* ("Sacred Song in Honor of the Name of St. Mark") for the Cathedral in Venice, and *Threni* ("Lamentations"—of Jeremiah) set to the text of the Vulgate. These latter works and the ballet, *Agon,* are written in a kind of serial technique said by some to derive rather from Webern than from Schoenberg. This approach is interesting, since while Schoenberg lived there was no meeting of minds between him and Stravinsky. (It was also rumored that Schoenberg, toward the end, meditated a return to tonality.)

The most conspicuous Russian composer after Stravinsky was Serge Prokofieff (1891–1953). He graduated at 18 from the St. Petersburg Conservatory with a well-grounded technique in composition. His first striking work was the *Scythian Suite* (1916), picturing in glaring colors a legendary and pagan Russia. He visited America in 1918, showing great pianistic skill in his Second concerto and in a number of vivid solo pieces (e.g. *Suggestion diabolique*). But he showed in the same year, in the *Classical Symphony*, an unexpected sympathy with older ideas. (He later commended the sonata form—with modifications, to be sure—as wholly sufficient for his purposes as a composer.) Prokofieff's widening interest in subject and an increasing deftness in the handling of his material were evident in his third piano concerto, his First violin concerto, and a Second symphony; an *Overture for Seventeen Instruments;* an "Incantation," *They Are Seven,* for tenor solo, chorus, and orchestra; and a ballet, *Pas d'Acier,* depicting Soviet heavy industry. He also wrote a *Divertimento* for orchestra in four movements; an opera on Dostoievsky's novel, *The Gambler,* which went deeper beneath the surface than the earlier ballet, *The Buffoon Who Outwitted Seven Other Buffoons;* and the engaging opera, *The Love for Three Oranges.* (This latter had been commissioned by the Chicago Opera and then delayed because of the death of Campanini, the conductor.)

Prokofieff's Fourth symphony, commissioned for the semicentennial of the Boston Orchestra in 1930, showed a further solidifying of thought which was still more evident in the Second violin concerto (1935). After long exile he returned to Russia in 1934, producing there his Fifth Symphony (1935) and his greatest dramatic work, an immense opera on Tolstoy's *War and Peace.* Increasingly, however, he was seemingly afflicted by the blight exerted by the curious restrictions of the Soviet aesthetic;

and although his Seventh symphony (performed in Moscow in 1952) was acclaimed by the Soviet press as having escaped "the fatal influence of formalism," an eminent American conductor characterized the work as showing "definite signs of the struggle between Prokofieff's genius and individuality and trying to work for his political bosses." Prokofieff's contribution to contemporary literature was valuable, perhaps especially as an initiation into the language of modernism. His influence on the future will apparently be less great.

Dimitri Shostakovich (born 1906) seemed for a time a rising star of the first magnitude. His First symphony, written at the age of 20, sounded as engaging as the early work of Robert Schumann. In the following year (1927) he voiced his assent to the Soviet creed in a *Symphonic Dedication to the October Revolution*. He then remained in high favor with the political powers until 1936 when his rather lurid opera, *Lady Macbeth of the Mzensk District* (already produced with high approval in 1934), was suddenly found to be infected with bourgeois ideas and to consist of "fidgeting, screaming, neurasthenic music." For similar reasons apparently, his Fourth symphony was withdrawn. The Fifth, however, won favor with the world at large. The Sixth has made no great stir. The Seventh, begun soon after the German invasion of Russia, was "conceived as a broad musical embodiment of majestic ideas of the patriotic war." When broadcast to the world by Toscanini in 1942, the Seventh seemed— during the war-fever of that day—to live up to the composer's prospectus. The Eighth was written in the same perspective and has also—like the Seventh—shown itself to be a book of illustrations. The Ninth, announced as intended to complete a trilogy, is in a quite different vein—gay, insouciant, and patently referable to the days between V-E and V-J during which it was written.

Shostakovich has composed a large body of piano music, fairly well represented by *Twenty-four Preludes* which seem to have been written almost at the rate of one a day, but which occasionally glow for their brief moment of life. There are at least two piano concertos—skillful and brilliant, but almost weightless. His chamber music is best represented by his piano quintet which won a huge prize from the Soviet government. It looks as if his career would show that the Soviets keep a poor school of composition, however impressive their work in performance.

Because of his birth in the Ukraine, and because he followed for a time a trend somewhat akin to that of Scriabin, this seems the logical place to speak of Karol Szymanowski (1882–1937), one of the most conspicuous of Polish composers of this century. Scriabin's influence, which supplanted that of Strauss, is notable in his Second symphony (1911), and in his first violin concerto (in one movement, 1922) which is probably the most opulently scored of any extant works in that form. A *Symphonie concertante* for piano and orchestra (1933) shows a more "modernistic" trend. After 1920 his home was in Warsaw where he became director of the Conservatory and developed a fruitful interest in Polish musical traditions, finding a remarkably novel manner of treating such national dances as the mazurka. Two operas (*Hagith* and *Król Roger*), three symphonies, an impressive *Stabat Mater*, many piano pieces and about 100 songs form a notable contribution to the literature of the earlier decades of the century. Other tendencies than his, however, have now supervened.

Alexander Tansman (born 1897) who spent six years in America— chiefly at Hollywood—has cultivated a more cosmopolitan style, having left his native Poland for Paris in 1919 and returned there from America in 1946. He has produced seven symphonies, two operas (*La Nuit Kurde*, and *Le Serment*—the latter, 1955), much chamber music, and many piano pieces, among them a *Sonatine transatlantique* in which the idiom of jazz is elevated to an unaccustomed height.

MODERNISM IN HUNGARY

Thus far in our study, important contributions to the stream of contemporary musical thought have appeared, in volume, somewhat proportionate to the size and the apparent cultural depth of the contributing nations. But the rule-of-thumb implied in this statement cannot be trusted too far. The old notion that music is the universal language implies not only that it can be widely understood, but that music of the highest significance may emanate from small tributaries to the musical stream. And this has proved true of Hungary in quite disproportionate measure, especially in the twentieth century.

An inverted notion of the real nature of Hungarian music seems to have ruled, even in Hungarian minds, until it was rectified by the investigations (ethnological as well as musical) of two great musical minds— Bartók and Kódaly—in the twentieth century. Briefly, that notion was an assumption that the true Hungarian music originated with the gypsies, and that it was debased by the Magyars. The reverse of this seems now to be proved true. The really native Hungarian idiom was completely obscured not only by the ornamental overlay provided by the gypsies but by the dominance of German musical thought in Hungary during the nineteenth century—the Rhapsodies of Liszt and the Hungarian Dances of Brahms (the accepted examples of Hungarian musical type) being drawn from the surface rather than from the depths, and being formalized by the prevailing German manner of organization.

The true ore had been so far covered by foreign convention that it could only be recovered by really scientific deep-mining. This was indeed accomplished—by such long effort that one can but wonder that the "miners" could thereafter erect any perfected structure on the revealed foundations. Yet there appeared out of this source a considerably novel musical idiom, fundamentally a "dialect" of the universal language, but with its harmonic element drawn from the implications of the newly discovered melody.[22]

Béla Bartók (1881–1945) surmounted exceptionally severe bouts with illness that plagued his naturally weak physique and acquired not only a commanding piano technique but a thoroughly grounded skill in composition. His first enthusiasm was for Brahms. This then shifted to Wagner, to Liszt, and to Richard Strauss whose *Also sprach Zarathustra* Bartók said made it possible "to see the way that lay before me." His first large work was a symphonic poem, *Kossuth*, celebrating that Hungarian hero in ten tableaux (1903). It was performed by the Budapest Philharmonic and also by Hans Richter in Manchester, England, in the following year. (It preceded his first discovery of Hungarian peasant music and remains unpublished.)

In 1904 Bartók first wrote down a Magyar song, as sung by a peasant girl. At once he seems to have grasped the implication that a whole native "literature without letters" must exist, and he began to seek out and record phonographically all the examples his travels to remote regions could discover. In 1906, in collaboration with Kódaly, he published *Twenty Hungarian Folksongs* which had originally been purely monodic. To be noticed by the musical world, they had had to be harmonized; and this had been accomplished by the collaborators with astonishing insight into both the peasant tunes and the types of harmony that could be applied to them without destroying their character.

In a way impossible to analyse, since genius had its share in the ultimate product and many other factors entered into it, this sort of harmonization —derived from these tunes rather than merely applied to them—became the foundation of a novel type of harmony applicable also to "learned" music. Most of the tunes were modal—centered upon notes other than the conventional tonic of Western music, and, like Gregorian chant, ruined by conventional harmony. For the harmony they needed, no model existed. Neither, of course, could they be merely surrounded with the vague blur of polytonality or reduced to the rigid system of dodecaphony. But out of the harmony first devised for this primitive music

[22] The organization of such a novel harmony is far too intricate a problem for discussion here. It is analyzed with high competence in *The Life and Music of Béla Bartók* by Halsey Stevens (1953).

grew a "vocabulary" of chords capable of use with contemporary melody—a vocabulary whose "roots" were primarily triadic, but which proved vastly more true to the large creative purposes of such a musician as Bartók than the decadent systems of the West.

Whether he bothered to analyze his own structural processes seems doubtful. He would never consent to teach composition. He feared that it would hinder his own creative efforts. Yet he was indefatigable in the search for truth—and when he found it was not in the least unwilling to communicate it. But to establish a system, even for his own use, seems to have been for him the erection of partial truth into a whole—an inadmissible practice for an artist in quest of the truth of life. Hence there is no Bartók school.

His compositions are less voluminous than those of many contemporary composers. They show, naturally, a gradual attainment of mastery, and Bartók's life may conveniently be divided into the three periods that are revealed in the work of so many great musicians. The first period of apprenticeship and escape from earlier influences (as of Brahms, Wagner, Liszt, and Strauss) ends with 1905. By that time he had made a wide reputation as pianist and was beginning to be known as a composer.

The second period extends to 1921. During this time Bartók devoted much effort to the collecting of folk songs and writing about them. (The full body of this work was unrealized until after his death. The publication of it in definitive form was begun only in 1951.) The major works of the period are stage-works: the one-act opera, *Prince Bluebeard's Castle* (1911), a singularly poetic version of the old horror story, remarkably illuminated by the music; a ballet or dance-pantomime, *The Prince Carved from Wood* (1914–1916), the tale of a Princess who loves, at first, not the Prince who woos her but a wooden figure he has carved, but who turns to him at the end; and a pantomime in one act, *The Miraculous Mandarin* (1918–1919), a tale enacted in a den of thieves where the Mandarin (the third captive of a girl kept by the thieves to allure victims) is fascinated, then robbed and smothered (but his eyes still seek the girl), then stabbed thrice (but he rises and pursues her), then hung from the chandelier (but he revives again and embraces her; this time she responds; his wounds begin to bleed, and he dies). There are also two string quartets (No. 1, Op. 7, 1908; No. 2, Op. 17, 1915–1917), several books of songs, both original and arranged, and similar collections of dances.

Bartók's third period may be said to begin with the two sonatas for violin and piano (1922–1923). These were in some measure designed as material for Bartók's extended tours which took him over most of Europe and briefly to America. The violinist was often Jelly d'Arányi, to whom both sonatas are dedicated. These pieces display the extreme of virtuosity, and perhaps also the extreme (for Bartók) of dissonance and all but atonal organization. But they are exceptional. The *Dance Suite* for orchestra (1923) was the first of his works to score a hit. It was written for the fiftieth anniversary of the union of Buda and Pest. The six dances are in no familiar dance-rhythms and have no titles, but they are dances nevertheless. They are linked together by a short strain used as a ritornello, and by this device the whole piece acquires unity. Echoes of Magyar, Rumanian, and even Arabic music can be detected by the initiated.

Music for String Instruments, Percussion, and Celesta (1936) is the most "abstract" in structure of all Bartók's orchestral works. Its thematic material is not twelve-tonal, but the whole first movement is woven as exclusively as is any twelve-tone piece from the four undulant motives of its chromatic theme. The others are more freely designed—the second a dance-like sonata form, the third a delicately colored *Adagio*, and the fourth a sort of rondo. The *Divertimento* for string orchestra (1939), like the preceding work, was written for the Basle Chamber Orchestra. As its title implies, it is an entertaining piece, without notable abstraction and indicating a kind of recession from the technical absorption previously ruling. It was the last orchestral work Bartók wrote in Europe.

The *Concerto for Orchestra* (1943) was commissioned by the Koussevitzky Foundation. It is the least obscure of all Bartók's orchestral pieces —not because he has "written down" to his American audience (he never wrote down, even for children), but because he seems now to have discovered the adjustments necessary in twentieth-century musical speech to make it intelligible to sensitive ears unable or unwilling to undergo initiation into the mysteries of abstract structure. The *Concerto* seems to suggest a path of escape from the jungle of abstraction which so many twentieth-century composers have mistaken for Parnassus.

There are of course many arrangements and excerpts for orchestra whether of songs or of stage-works; there are six string quartets—as indicative as are the orchestral works of the progress of Bartók's mind. There are three concertos for piano (the last, from 1945, slightly incomplete), and important concertos for violin and for viola; there are naturally a host of songs and a number of choral works—the latter culminating in the *Cantata profana* (1930). And last but not least—since the piano, even in the days of radio and phonograph, still offers the student his most immediate contact with a composer—are Bartók's contributions to piano literature. A kind of summary of this effort is to be seen in *Mikrokosmos*, a collection of 153 progressive pieces compiled between 1926 and 1937. This work, in the perspective of the twentieth century, is comparable in purpose to Bach's devoted effort—from the *Little Preludes* to the *Goldberg Variations*—to put the true substance of music into the actual hands and minds of music lovers.

Zoltán Kodály (born 1882), Bartók's colleague in folk song collection, is a far more important composer than his retiring nature, his somewhat restrained harmonic idiom, and his preoccupation not only with folk song but with sixteenth-century music have made him appear. His first great success was earned with the *Psalmus Hungaricus* (1923, for the semi-centennial of the union of Buda and Pest). It was soon performed all over the world. In 1926 came the hilarious opera, *Háry János,* from which a suite became similarly popular. His *Marosszék Dances* and *Dances of Galánta,* as well as his *Peacock Variations* on a Hungarian folk song, are his best known orchestral works. There are also important chamber works as well as piano pieces and songs. He has never been attracted by the various theorems of atonality; romantic and impressionistic flavors are unashamedly exhibited; but the music is patently that of an imaginative human mind.

Ernst von Dohnányi (born 1877), a spiritual disciple of Brahms and consequently less of an innovator than his successors, has nevertheless won a distinguished place both for his skilled pianism and his compositions, which are in all forms. An opera, *The Castle of the Voivod* (1922), *Ruralia Hungarica* (1924) for piano but scored for orchestra, and two symphonies (the Second, based on the philosophic theme of his choral *Cantus vitae* and first performed in 1957) are his principal works.

Modernism in Italy

With few exceptions, the composers of Italy have been composers of opera. Some, indeed, have made notable church music. A few, like Corelli and Vivaldi, have been real pioneers in instrumental fields. This preference for opera remained, somewhat mitigated, during the nineteenth century; and the twentieth has shown a much greater activity in instrumental music; but the old love for opera is not yet dead.

Modernistic trends were not, in consequence, particularly strong at the turn of the century. The fabulous success of Pietro Mascagni (1863–1945) with *Cavalleria Rusticana* (produced 1890) was to ring for many decades; Ruggiero Leoncavallo (1858–1919), with *I Pagliacci* (produced in 1892), was not less popular and was musically much more solid.

Giacomo Puccini (1858–1924), after several promising trials, leaped to the front with *La Bohème* (1896) and within a decade had produced two more prime favorites, *La Tosca* and *Madame Butterfly.* The virtues of these Puccini works are considerably veiled from the eyes of the more learned, who look for a more solid musicality than is there—and at the same time miss a peculiarly appealing mixture of melody and declamation, contrived with the continuity of the drama in mind, that is at least far more than merely clever. Puccini has the wisdom, of course, to select a swift and compelling story, so that his texts provide a good deal of the momentum we seem to perceive in the music; but for playability these operas are hard to beat. His next effort, *The Girl of the Golden West*, has been by comparison almost a failure; but *Turandot*, unfinished at his death and completed by Franco Alfano, has been recently revived and bids fair to equal the old favorites. Puccini is quoted as saying, "All the music I have written up to now seems a jest in comparison." Two operas by Ermanno Wolf-Ferrari, a composer German-Italian in music as well as in name, have hardly maintained their original rivalry with Puccini's. These are *The Jewels of the Madonna* and *The Secret of Suzanne*.

In Italy the symphony was not what might be called a popular form any more than in France. Yet the symphonies of Giovanni Sgambati (1843–1914) and Giuseppe Martucci (1856–1909) did turn the attention of the Italian people toward a native instrumental art. (The first permanent series of orchestral concerts in Italy was founded in Turin as early as 1872; and while the major emphasis was on operatic music—Wagner was more performed than Beethoven—other cities soon followed suit.) The most conspicuous of Italian composers in the new manner was, for a time, Ottorino Respighi (1879–1936) two of whose huge symphonic Poems, *The Fountains of Rome* and *The Pines of Rome*, were frequently played for two decades in the symphonic programs of Europe and America. The third of this series, *Roman Festivals*, soon turned out to be what the others actually had been—inflated examples of skilfully blended orchestral color, rather than musical structures of real coherence. Less imposing works—several based on Gregorian modes, such as the *Concerto Gregoriano* for violin—revealed Respighi as a sincere student, but by no means a provocative contributor to the newer musical thought of the day.

That provocation was to come from a slightly younger compatriot, Alfredo Casella (1883–1947). His first endeavors, fostered by his parents and encouraged by the venerated Martucci, were toward virtuosity as a pianist, although there was always a still deeper hankering to compose. On the death of his father, his mother took him to Paris where he entered the Conservatoire. While performing brilliantly the tasks there required, he caught from outside the new fever and made the acquaintance of Debussy, Ravel, Satie, and other notables. His first large work, the Rhapsody *Italia*, was, however, in a style opposed to the impressionism he had been steeped in; it is probable that he was influenced by the new ventures of Diaghilev, and particularly by Stravinsky's *Petrouchka*. Casella's confessed aim was to find a style intrinsically Italian and to bring it effectively to fruition in his native land. His failure to find recognition in Italy is singularly like the experience of Berlioz in France. His thorough equipment as pianist, conductor, and composer made him welcome elsewhere in Europe and in America; but while Casella gradually found not only kindred spirits among Italian composers but a small and sympathetic Italian public, the general attitude of his homeland was hostile. This was sharply evident at the performance of his "Heroic Elegy" (1917) written to commemorate the fallen in war. He and his fellow members of a "National Musical Society" were denounced as a "nest of futurists," and one journal actually suggested that he leave the country. Nevertheless, the Society gave twelve concerts, performing 102 Italian pieces during the three years of its existence; and Casella felt that with this activity "the renovation of the national consciousness really began."

Casella's chief contributions to this "renovation" were not, in his own estimation, works which directly borrowed from popular sources, but from "the sum of spiritual values which are commonly called tradition." [23] His three symphonies, of which the second is still unpublished, are neither "Italian" in this sense nor particularly tendentious; his chamber music, although he was an active performer in this genre, is rather small in volume and seems occasional in inspiration;[24] but his stage works have been favorably received everywhere. Of these, two ballets, *The Convent by the Water* (1912) and *The Jar* (1924), have yielded popular Suites. The first is satirical (a vein in which Casella excelled); the second is more mature in style, but still somewhat dependent on popular melody. He did not turn to the stage until 1928, when he began the three-act opera, *La Donna Serpente*, the tale of a fairy changed into a serpent because of her love for a mortal. (The fable, by Carlo Gozzi, had furnished the plot for Wagner's *Die Feen*.) It was produced in Rome in 1932, with indifferent success; but again the two aforementioned Suites went the rounds of the world's concert halls. A chamber opera on the fable of Orpheus was mounted at Venice, also in 1932, and was his only one to win general approval in Italy. The third, *Il Deserto Tentato*, a kind of martial "mystery . . . evoking the abstract voices of a virgin Nature, anxious to be fertilized by human civilizations," [25] seems less attractive

[23] Alfredo Casella, *Music in My Time* (University of Oklahoma Press, 1955) p. 229.

[24] His *Serenata* for clarinet, bassoon, trumpet, violin, and 'cello in 1929 won a prize offered by the Musical Fund Society of Philadelphia. Bartók shared the prize.

[25] *Op. cit.*, p. 214.

when viewed as an apology for the Italian conquest of Ethiopia. "Perhaps," the composer commented, "it is not really a theatrical work."

This very disjunct account of Casella's effort is a reflection of the effort itself, which was lofty in aim, wholly sincere, but impeded by opposition and by the uncertainty of one who hoped to orient intractable convention toward a new nationalism. His aim was not fulfilled, but the direction of Italian musical thought was changed. How much of that change is due to Casella is a question yet to be answered, when the still fluid idiom of "modern" music shall have crystallized.

Perhaps because Italian music has been long dominated by opera and has only recently followed the general European trend toward instrumental music, a similar uncertainty seems characteristic of the effort and the musical idiom of Gian Francesco Malipiero (born 1883). Failing his examination in violin at the Vienna Conservatory, he turned to the study of harmony, went home to Venice, took his diploma at Bologna, taught at Parma, and finally went back to Venice where he directs the *Liceo Musicale Marcello*, and has privately taught students in composition from all over the world. His first works, which he later rejected, were romantic. Studies of seventeenth- and eighteenth-century Venetian composers sharpened his scholarly interests and hastened his rejection of the romantic manner. Studies of still earlier music and of Gregorian chant seem to have shaped for a time an idiom in which curiously modal melody, a new freedom in the rhythming of syllables, and a strong aversion from orthodox processes of development based on themes are distinctive features. Extremely cursive melodic lines, with little emphasis on polyphony and a continuity thus not at first sight logical, are also noted by students of his work.

Malipiero did not tour the world as a virtuoso, as did Casella, but the volume of his work is much greater even though his external fame is less. He has written nine symphonies, inspired by various ideas—the Third, *delle campane* (bells); the Fifth for strings alone; the Eighth (1951) in one movement. There are many concertos (four for piano), seven string quartets, and many piano pieces and songs. There are also many choral works—a Requiem, a *sinfonia eroica* with Vergil's Aeneas for hero, a piece for chorus and orchestra on the Seven Deadly Sins, and an oratorio, *La Cana* ("The Last Supper"). But perhaps his most important works are his operas, for which he has mostly contrived his own libretti. Among these are a trilogy on the fable of Orpheus; *Torneo notturno* in seven "nocturnes"—The Serenade, The Storm, The Forest, The Tavern of Good Cheer, The Spent Hearth, The Castle of Boredom, and The Prison; two after Shakespeare—Julius Caesar and Antony and Cleopatra;

and *Mondi* (Worlds) *celesti ed infernali*, "in three acts, with seven women." There are also three comedies after Goldoni.

Malipiero is best known abroad, however, for his careful editing of the complete works of Monteverdi, and for a practical version of Cavalieri's *Rappresentazione di anima e di corpo* (see p. 247). Rigid scholarship raises eyebrows at some of his interpolations; but so eminent an authority as Leo Schrade based his monumental study of Monteverdi on Malipiero's edition.

Of considerable influence in Italy, but less conspicuous abroad, is Ildebrando Pizzetti (born 1880) who was for a time a co-worker with Casella toward the foundation of a new Italian music. Much chamber music and many songs, progressive but not distinctly in a new idiom, along with several operas—for example, *Fra Gherardo* and *Lo Straniero* ("The Stranger")—brought him to the attention of his compatriots. These works also attracted the interest of Mrs. Elizabeth Sprague Coolidge, the tireless supporter of new music, American and foreign, in Washington. In 1932, however, Pizzetti signed, along with Respighi, Pick-Mangiagalli and several others, a manifesto against the "cerebral" music of the day: "this art which cannot have and does not have any human content and desires to be merely a mechanical demonstration and a cerebral puzzle. . . . The romanticism of yesterday will again be the romanticism of to-morrow." (It is true that a gentler tone toward romanticism is taken today than formerly; but that tone reflects a broader definition of romantic art than was current in the 'thirties, rather than any disposition to turn the clock backward to a musical style wholly incompatible with the mentality of the present.)

Mario Castelnuovo-Tedesco (born 1895) is a man of a similar disposition, but of lesser powers, hindered from participation in the later development of Italian music because of his expulsion from Italy in 1939 owing to his Jewish ancestry. Operas, chamber music, concertos—one for violin, played by Heifetz, and one for guitar, written for Segovia—as well as settings of all the songs in Shakespeare's plays and overtures to at least seven of them—reveal an amiable and imaginative musical mind, but not one destined to affect the future of music.

In contrast to the above-mentioned men, perhaps the most fertile in suggestion for the future, and latterly one of the most significant participants in actual contribution toward a new musical art is the great pianist Ferrucio Busoni (1866–1924). During his lifetime he was barely recognized as a composer, his achievements as pianist far outshining his efforts in composition. Even today, he is rarely represented on programs; and his music—written before the developments in atonality and polytonality

which have largely determined the present course of the musical stream—
is in an idiom which, although new in comparison to the language of its
time, is strange to "modern" ears. Most of his life was spent as at least a
nominal resident of Germany; his understanding of German music was
complete and sympathetic; yet Busoni never forgot his Latin origin, and
his aesthetic outlook was by no means wholly Teutonic. His principal
works are: three completed operas—*Die Brautwahl* (1912), *Arlecchino*,
and *Turandot* (both 1917); a fourth, *Doktor Faustus* (by all odds the
greatest) was unfinished, but was completed by his pupil Philipp Jarnach
and performed in 1925; a formidable *Fantasia contrappuntistica* for piano;
and a number of songs to texts in several languages. But perhaps equal
support for new adventures in composition is offered by his *Entwurf
einer neuen Asthetik der Tonkunst* ("Sketch of a new musical aesthetic"),
and a collection of essays published under the title *Von der Einheit der
Musik* ("On the unity of music").

Goffredo Petrassi (born 1904) was one of Casella's co-workers toward
the "renovation" of the Italian musical consciousness. He has been largely
self-trained, but his technical competency is indisputable. He has written
five concertos for orchestra—modern counterparts of the symphony;
many choral works and songs; a piano concerto; and two operas—*Il
Cordovano* and *La Morte dell'Aria* (1949 and 1950). In his later works
Petrassi has leaned toward, but not systematically adopted, the twelve-
tone technique. Vittorio Rieti (born 1898), since 1939 resident in the
United States, was a pupil of Respighi. In a rather eclectic but very
effective style he has composed five symphonies, several operas and
ballets, and a number of grateful chamber works.

MODERNISM IN SPAIN

We have seldom had occasion to mention Spanish music since the days
of Morales, Soto, and Victoria, the illustrious members of the sixteenth-
century Papal Chapel. The savor of romance is indelibly printed on our
mental image of the land and its life; but while the rhythms of Spanish
dances have proved universally compelling, it has often been noted that
the most vivid portrayals of Spain have been provided by foreigners—
chiefly Russians like Rimsky-Korsakoff and Frenchmen like Debussy and
Ravel. Not until late in the nineteenth century did any Spanish composers of note emerge from the isolation suffered during the long interval.

The first of these to gain wide recognition was Isaac Albéniz (1860–
1909). His precocity, joined to an adventurous disposition, prevented the
acquisition of a wholly solid technique in composition; his pianistic gift,
however, was outstanding and in some measure helped him to solve in his

own way the problems of composition. His first works were operas, on conventional subjects; but acquaintance with Felipe Pedrell (1841–1922), a notable scholar, composer, and enthusiast for Spanish nationalism, fired his interest in native art and stimulated the composition of his most notable work, *Iberia*, a set of 12 piano pieces descriptive (or rather, interpretative) of life in various Spanish provinces or communities. Something of the impressionism of Debussy colors these works, but they are both national and highly original. Their pianistic color strongly suggests the orchestra, but actual transfer to that instrumental body robs them of the individuality which only a solo performer can give.

Enrique Granados (1867–1916), also a pupil of Pedrell, gained a more solid technique than did Albéniz, but had a far less vivid imagination. His fame rests similarly on a set of piano pieces, suggested by paintings of Goya and entitled *Goyescas*. An opera of the same title was based on these pieces. He left a few orchestral and chamber compositions, but his piano works—almost all on Spanish rhythms or songs—are his most compelling efforts.

Of loftier stature was Manuel de Falla (1876–1946), still another pupil of Pedrell. Having won distinction with his opera, *La Vida breve* (1905), he went to Paris where he formed sincere friendships with Debussy and Ravel and enlarged his style by adopting some of the characteristic procedures of impressionism. In 1914 he returned to Spain; but at the end of the Civil War he left to make his home in Argentina. His most famous works are two ballets, *El Amor brujo* ("Love, the Sorcerer") and *El Sombrero de tres picos* ("The Three-cornered Hat"), from which orchestral suites have been heard all over the world; the charming *Nights in the Gardens of Spain* for piano and orchestra (but not a concerto); and a concerto for harpsichord and orchestra, written for Wanda Landowska. De Falla also wrote penetratingly about various phases of contemporary music.

The gospel of Spanish music has been effectively spread by Adolfo Salazar (born 1890) who is a competent composer, but who has spent his chief energies in critical and historical writing. His four-volume study, *La Música en la sociedad europea*, is oriented to a broader view of musical history than is commonly taken by more severely trained musicologists; and his *Música moderna* (*Music in our Time*, 1946) offers a sane critical perspective over the whole modern scene. His *La Música de España* (1953) has not yet been translated.

❧ *CHAPTER XXXIII* ❧

The Music of England and the United States

W E TURN at last to the music of England and the United States—two nations which, from the eighteenth century on, have been viewed by Europeans as borrowers from, rather than as contributors to, the world's store of music.

ENGLISH MUSIC

England, as we have seen, had often figured as an actual leader in the musical thought of the world. The genius who contrived *Sumer is icumen in* was more than a hundred years ahead of his time; Dunstable taught the world much about the value of related discord; the Elizabethans were at least the equals of their formidable continental contemporaries in the most progressive form of the day, the madrigal; and Purcell must be reckoned similarly the peer of any seventeenth-century composer. But the elegance of French and Italian opera—like the finesse of French manners, language, and literature—bred a kind of self-consciousness in English taste that made native products look "homemade"; and Handel's German-Italian idiom, although occasionally tinged by the chlorophyll of the once-green musical thought of England, gained an ascendancy in that thought which was to endure for two centuries. Haydn, Beethoven, and Mendelssohn continued to enforce the subjugation of England to musical Germany. Nineteenth-century England produced a Byron, a Shelley, a Keats, a Tennyson, a Browning—but not their musical peers; and the vast social rectifications of the nineteenth-century industrial revolution, over against the sabbatarianism of the Victorian court, were movements beyond the power of English musicianship to interpret.

The Handelian oratorio had made choral singing the principal activity of amateur and professional performers alike. That this sort of effort put thousands in participating possession of music is a fact too often forgotten by those who deplore the narrowness of musical vision that resulted. Wonderfully trained choruses, largely composed of under-privileged operatives in drab factories, preserved the essential spark of musical life even though that spark was nourished by the soggiest and most conventional fuel. And English opera, when not a direct importa-tion from Italy, reflected only the most quotidian of imaginative interests. Its best examples were such works as *The Bohemian Girl* by the Irish composer, Michael Balfe, and *Maritana* by W. Vincent Wallace—feeble competitors even of *Norma* and *Lucia*. Sometimes, however, English genius glowed at the operatic level. Arthur Seymour Sullivan (1842–1900) contrived to speak a kind of simple musical truth irresistible in its appeal. Sullivan was described by Ernest Walker as "probably the most widely popular English composer who ever lived," and his popularity has not been extinguished by all the more raucous inventions of his successors. *The Mikado, Pinafore, The Pirates of Penzance*—these are titles which "ring a bell" in the musical memory of almost any man in the street. Even the wit of Sullivan's most famous librettist, W. S. Gilbert, is only a contribution to their popularity, for the subtle political satire which underlay almost all these productions is nowadays mostly lost. But no one today has ever heard *Ivanhoe*, Sullivan's vain attempt at a serious opera.

The last quarter of the nineteenth century, however, showed not only a vigorous renascence of effort but the beginning of a release from the bonds of foreign influence. England remembers gratefully such figures as Sir Alexander Mackenzie, Hubert Parry, Frederic Cowen, and Charles Villiers Stanford; the musicologists will perhaps trace some features of the newer music to them; but none of the composers of that generation is heeded today save Edward Elgar (1857–1934). His *Enigma Variations* (1899) struck a new and welcome note which continues to resound; his trilogy of sacred pieces, *The Dream of Gerontius, The Apostles*, and *The Kingdom* (although the first now seems far the strong-est of the three) altered, almost at a stroke, the stagnant tradition of choral writing begun by Handel and continued by Mendelssohn. His two symphonies, however, are too Brahmsian to stand by themselves, and his Violin Concerto (1910) remains his most significant instrumental work. Time has sadly faded his more popular *Cocaigne Overture* and the *Pomp and Circumstance* marches. Almost wholly self-taught, Elgar was really his only pupil and left little mark on his followers.

But the English genius, whether in literature or art, has always been too individualistic to submit to such general norms of expression as those of the French, whose national manner has been considerably formed and

safeguarded by the Académie, or of the Germans, who have more indirectly established what may be called a cult of intellectuality. And once
the yoke of servitude to continental tradition was thrown off, that genius
began again to reveal itself.

The English genius was revealed, but not well established, by Joseph
Holbrooke (born 1878) who in the first years of the century fought
valiantly for British music. But he was unequal to leadership in the
musical army. He had an undeniable gift of melody and a remarkable
flair for orchestration which were evident in his *Variations on Three
Blind Mice;* the overture (especially) to the choral *Queen Mab;* and
several works after Poe (*The Raven, Ulalume, The Bells*). A grand
dramatic trilogy, *The Cauldron of Anwyn* (*The Children of Don, Dylan,*
and *Bronwen*), set to a text from Welsh mythology by Lord Howard de
Walden, still commands the high respect of so independent a critic as
Norman Demuth; but it solved no problems of operatic structure. It is
too cumbrous for practical performance under present conditions, and
its fable (remotely akin to that of Wagner's *Ring*) is too obscure for
popularity. Holbrooke plowed much new ground, but planted ill-
selected seed.

More "intellectual," but narrower in imaginative range and of lesser influence—outside the circle of his admirers—was Cyril Scott (born 1879),
whose *Lotus Land* for piano was widely taken as the index of a commanding talent. His manner was impressionistic (priority in the use of
the whole-tone scale was claimed for him over Debussy); his vision (sometimes penetrating) was directed and perhaps hampered by a strong interest in occult philosophy; he would have no traffic with jazz (even his
Danse Nègre is untainted by it); and he was antipathetic to the new
musical syntax. His work has remained within the field of chamber
music, solo piano pieces, and songs (among them some highly sensitive
utterances); but on the present trend of English music his influence can
hardly be felt.

Yet Scott's work helped to form the background of the present; and
equally divergent and characteristic contributions to the English scene
came from such figures as Granville Bantock (1868–1946), a prolific
composer of choral works (for example, the tripartite *Omar Khayyám*),
symphonies (mostly programmatic), chamber music, and songs; Walford
Davies (1869–1941) who composed music for the morality, *Everyman*, and
Solemn Melody for organ and strings; and Donald Francis Tovey (1875–
1940) whose compositions (a symphony, an opera, *The Bride of Dionysus*, a 'cello concerto) were too learned for the public, but whose musical
learning, vast and varied—but suspect to the German musicological mind—
was communicated in some of the most readable discussions extant (e.g.,

the articles on music in the 11th edition of the Britannica, collected 1944).

Another facet of the many-sided English musical temperament was shown in the work of Frederick Delius (1862–1934). All his life he was an exile—he spent two years in Florida, where he had six months' instruction from an organist; two at the Leipzig Conservatory; and the rest in France. For his last 12 years he was paralyzed and ultimately blind. He was ignored by most of his countrymen until Sir Thomas Beecham, in 1929, organized a six-day Delius Festival in London. And yet Delius spoke of England in tones that somehow reflect the charm of that northern island which the Gulf Stream has warmed into the cradle of democracy. Having no "system," he had no disciples; seeing the importance (as did Grieg, who influenced him strongly) "of those things in music which are not music," he wrote for the most part about tangible realities; but, because he had an imagination that could penetrate beneath the surface of those realities, his music is never merely illustrative. His imagery is consequently obscure, both to the naïve and the sophisticated, and it is not strange that he should have enjoyed little recognition.

Delius's works are astonishingly numerous, considering the handicap under which he worked. Those which have been most heeded are the opera, *A Village Romeo and Juliet*, from which comes an orchestral intermezzo, "The Walk to the Paradise Garden"; *Appalachia*, a most poetic distillation from his not wholly poetic experiences as an orange-grower in Florida; *Brigg Fair*, a lusty English rhapsody; and *On Hearing the First Cuckoo in Spring*, for small orchestra and of small dimensions. There are many vocal works, of which *Sea Drift* (after Whitman) for baritone, chorus, and orchestra and the *Mass of Life* for soli, chorus and large orchestra are notable. There are also concertos for violin and for violin and 'cello, a considerable mass of chamber music, and many songs.

From the foregoing background at last a notable figure emerged—that of Ralph Vaughan Williams (1872–1958). His musical education was conventional, including a two-year sojourn in Berlin for study with Max Bruch. In 1909, after ten years of mature work, he went to Paris, where he had some not especially fruitful lessons with Ravel. But the most formative influence was his membership in the English Folk Song Society, which evoked not only the three *Norfolk Rhapsodies* but his ballad-opera, *Hugh the Drover* (featuring the operatic novelty of a prize-fighter), and made visible to his imagination the "things" his music was to deal with. That these were dateless things, yet all impregnated with his deep consciousness of England, is seen in his *Fantasia on a Theme by Thomas Tallis* (1910), and in his *London Symphony* (1910–1920) which, while picturing the modern town, remembers also Elizabethan times. Yet he went also to other sources for inspiration—to Walt Whitman for *Towards the Unknown Region* (1905–1918) for chorus and orchestra, and *A Sea Symphony* (his First, 1910); to Aristophanes for *The Wasps* (1909); and to liturgical texts for such works as an *a cappella* Mass, a *Te Deum*, a *Magnificat*, and a *Dona nobis pacem*.

What emerges is the most unstudied and the most convincing English style to be found since Henry Purcell. The most representative works produced by Williams's unflagging creative energy (a parallel to that of Verdi) are probably his symphonies, of which two have just been mentioned. The Third is a *Pastoral Symphony;* No. 4, in F minor, is perhaps his bitterest utterance ("I don't know whether I like it, but it is what I meant"); Nos. 5 and 6, in D major and E minor (1943 and 1948) are without announced "subject," but as meaningful as the others; No. 7, *Sinfonia antartica* (1951–1952) is partly derived from music for a film on Captain Scott's fatal adventure—music that chills you to the bone while it warms your heart to a realization of heroic purpose; and Nos. 8 and 9 are from 1956 and 1958.

Williams's operas are probably too indigenously English to succeed abroad, and too unromantic even for the English majority; but like those of Delius they display an independence of thought unimaginable in a composer enslaved by a system. A *dialogue en tableau*, *The Shepherds of the Delectable Mountains*, became in 1949 *The Pilgrim's Progress*, a "morality"; *Sir John in Love*, *The Poisoned Kiss*, and *Riders to the Sea* differ widely in theme and method, as do the ballets, *Old King Cole*, *Christmas Night*, and *Job* (a Masque for dancing). And besides these there is a great mass of church and chamber music, organ and piano pieces, and songs.

Vaughan Williams is often justly compared, for his independence and immediate realization of his own musical purposes, to Sibelius. He completed that emancipation begun by Parry and Stanford to free musical England from the fetters of Germanic tradition and kept pace with his younger contemporaries, Bax, Walton, and Britten, in their varied pursuit of an English musical idiom. Williams devised no system for himself and had none to transmit to others; but he did effectively illustrate a truth too often hidden from the followers of systems— that the language of music is rooted in the understanding, not merely of music as an art, but of experience which music transmutes into art.

The renascence of English music is a fact everywhere recognized. The new English idiom was hampered, as was music elsewhere, by the great wars; but it was never expelled, as were many continental types which necessarily had to root themselves in alien soils. On that account the new music of England has had a less forcible impact on American thought than the twentieth century music of many other countries. It may be that the deep racial kinship of England and America breeds, in both nations, a kind of superficial mutual dislike. But there are signs that a similar independence of thought is arising in our newer community, and that the advantages of a common musical directive may become more apparent as our common political ideals are clarified.

The measure of England's younger composers cannot be attempted here. Signs of their significance will appear in the brief account of their work which space permits. They will be presented in the approximate order of their birth.

Gustav Holst (1874–1934) seemed for a time to share with Vaughan Williams the leadership of the new English movement. His interest lay, however, outside as well as within the English scene, and his most effective work is thus the orchestral suite, *The Planets* (1914–1916), seen in the light of their astrological symbolism. Hindu legends are reflected in a chamber opera, *Sāvitri*, and in *Choral Hymns from the Rig-Veda;* interest in Greek drama, in choruses to *Alcestis;* but the major part of Holst's work is thoroughly English—for example, *St. Paul's Suite* for strings (celebrating a famous boys' school); a *Fugal Overture;* a symphonic poem, *Egdon Heath* (very dissonant); and his *First Choral Symphony* (after Keats, 1925), which remains his only effort in that form. Impressive also is his *Ode to Death*, after Whitman, for chorus and orchestra.

Less influential for the future, yet contributing to the vitalization of English musical thought, were John Ireland (born 1879) and Benjamin Dale (1885–1943). Bernard Van Dieren (1884–1936), although a Hollander by birth, settled in London and was regarded by Cecil Gray as one of the most fertile imaginations of his day. His radical tendencies, shocking to some, no longer appear extreme. Philip Heseltine (1894–1930)—writing under the pen name Peter Warlock—made many studies in old English music and composed many unforgettable songs which show the influence of Delius and Van Dieren.

Long regarded as the leader in British composition, but of late considerably reduced in stature, was Arnold Bax (1883–1953). He was extremely fertile in invention, producing seven symphonies from 1922 to 1939 (the last dedicated to the American People), a host of Overtures and other somewhat programmatic orchestral pieces, much chamber music, and many choral works and songs. His facile invention induced a loose texture, at variance with current tendencies and often obscuring the really vital elements in his imagination; but his Third symphony and the motets, *This Worlde's Joie* and *Mater Ora Filium*, stand very high in the affection of many.

Sir Arthur Bliss (born 1891), at first a pupil of Stanford, Vaughan

Williams, and Holst, returned from the war in 1918 to assume prominence as a decided liberal in composition, yet, as became his instruction, a respecter of tradition. He followed Bax as Master of the Queen's Musick, writing in that capacity several occasional pieces. Outstanding among his valuable additions to the national repertoire are his *Colour Symphony*, celebrating the heraldic meanings of four colors; such vocal works as *Madame Noy;* the choral symphony (with orator), *Morning Heroes*, and the opera, *The Olympians* (1949). Eric Blom thought his *Music for Strings* "the most striking English work since Elgar's *Introduction and Allegro*."

Alan Bush (born 1900) has made notable efforts to bring contemporary music to the masses. His strong communist leanings have alienated him to some extent from the more orthodox movements; yet his opera, *Wat Tyler*, while not performed in London, won a prize at the Festival of Britain (1951) and was performed (in German) over the Berlin radio. Two symphonies, a piano concerto with the unusual complement of a baritone solo and male chorus in the finale, and a violin concerto (B.B.C., 1948) show his trend toward a manner which he expounded in *The Crisis of Modern Music* (1946)—a plea for composition in which every note must be thematically significant.

At the moment, the most conspicuous figure in English music is Benjamin Britten (born 1913). Like Alan Bush, he studied composition with John Ireland, graduating from the Royal College of Music in 1934. In that year his *Fantasy Quartet* for oboe and strings was performed at the I.S.C.M. festival in Florence, and he reappeared at the festivals of 1936 and 1938. Exemption from war service as a conscientious objector did not prejudice his success with *Peter Grimes* (1945). Other operas—*The Rape of Lucrece, Billy Budd, Gloriana* (for the coronation of Elizabeth II), and *The Turn of the Screw*—seem to indicate that his rather facile manner is more suited to stage-works than to more abstract musical construction; yet his *Sinfonia da Requiem* strikes with assurance the solemn note. Britten's skill in handling the orchestra is well illustrated in *The Young Person's Guide to the Orchestra*—variations on a theme from Purcell, illustrating each instrument in a solo role, with a final fugue. A similar cleverness appears in *Let's Make an Opera* (this phrase seems to have superseded the original title, *The Little Sweep*), in which the audience is momentarily deluded into belief in its own power of composition.

Quite in contrast to Britten is still another pupil of John Ireland, Humphrey Searle (born 1915), whose earlier manner was decisively altered by study with Anton Webern in Vienna. He may justly be reckoned as a disciple of the twelve-tone school; yet his method is not without deviation from what is too commonly understood as the rigid intellectuality of that technique, and he also departs from it in some treatments of English melody. Searle has written two suites for strings; two piano concertos; a *Fuga giocosa* for orchestra; a symphony (1953); a setting of Edith Sitwell's *Gold Coast Customs* for speaking voices, men's chorus and orchestra; he has published a study of *The Music of Liszt* and an exposition of *Twentieth Century Counterpoint;* and he has provided the English translation of Joseph Rufer's *Composition with Twelve Notes.*

MUSIC IN THE UNITED STATES

"The American Scene," which the patriotic expatriate Henry James described some 50 years ago in not very complimentary terms, has vastly changed since his day. European scholars and artists—driven to our shores by the exigencies of war—have abandoned a former attitude of contempt, have become co-workers in our busy hive, and have enriched our activities incalculably. Particularly in the last decade—but perceptibly long before—the advent of such composers as Hindemith, Krenek, Schoenberg, Tansman, and Toch and such scholars as Apel, Bukofzer, Leichtentritt, Sachs, and Schrade opened many doors which unaided American effort had hitherto only set ajar. It is still too early for the effect of this influx to be seen in anything like historical perspective. Only now is it becoming possible to see even the beginning of the influence of European thought on America, and of American thought not only on the newcomers but on Europe itself. Cultural metabolism, as has often been noted in the course of our study, is again proving to be a very complex process.

No assessment is yet possible of that mutual American-European musical transfer. Signs of its operation are many, but they cannot be confidently interpreted. We can watch the clearing of the land and the tilling of the soil from which our music has sprung; we can recognize, among the many imported plants which for so long yielded almost all our musical nourishment, some surviving native species; but to classify the resultant hybrids, or to predict their future cross-fertilization, is still impossible. The history of music in America is a long and profitable tale; but the history of American music has only just begun.

The community "singing school," a quaint but priceless institution of early New England, was incorporated by Lowell Mason (1792–1872) into the curriculum of the public schools; and the fertilizing of our musical soil is in no small measure a result of the efforts of those who followed his lead. No burden of taxation is more generously borne by the American people than that devoted to education; and the share of that support which is devoted to music is, to say the least, remarkable. Orchestras, bands, choral groups, and individual talents are cherished and cultivated from the lowest to the highest grades; universities have admitted music into their curricula as of comparable significance with the humanities; and from this educational activity alone (although there are many others), music has become an indispensable item in the life of even the smallest communities.[1]

But the beginning of music in America was not in the public schools. It was in the churches; and even there the infant art would have been strangled in its cradle had the more rigid Puritans had their way. However, the Bay Psalm Book (the second book to be printed in America) appeared in Cambridge in 1640. Musical notation for 12 tunes was added in the edition of 1690, and by 1731 musical interest had so far widened that a public "concert of music on sundry instruments" was given in Boston. To the South a more liberal view ruled; and New York, Philadelphia, and Charleston (whose first public concert almost antedated that of Boston) gave encouragement to foreign musicians whose teaching seems to have been well remunerated.

Francis Hopkinson (1737–1791), a signer of the Declaration of Independence, claimed to be the first native American to become a musical composer. His modest efforts were outdone by William Billings (1746–1800), whose "fuguing tunes" have recently been treated in a more masterly but not more sincere fashion by Henry Cowell, William Schuman, and others. But the customs of our colonial citizens had not been of the type which finds expression in characteristic dances and tunes, so that even our first "national" air (*Yankee Doodle*) was apparently of British origin, as was later *The Star-spangled Banner*.[2]

Indeed, early America had but little of folk-music in the true sense—a music generated out of folk-experience and perpetuated without thought of "art." Its population was too heterogeneous, its cultural heritage too widely derived, and its activities and ambitions too practical for embodiment in the musical substance. Isolated regions—for example, the Tennessee mountains and the cattle ranches of the West—have indeed found

---

[1] The writer once served as adjudicator in a contest among the schools of a relatively small district of South Dakota. From one school came a string quartet, a piano trio, several soloists, and an orchestra of about 30 members. The enthusiasm of the performers was greater than their technical skill; but the impressive fact was that the village in which this (consolidated) school was situated had a population of 220!

[2] *Yankee Doodle* was used, both in the French and Indian War and at the opening of the Revolution, to ridicule the American soldiers' homespun appearance. But when the tables were turned, at the battle of Concord, the Americans took it over and kept it as their own. For the history of this and other patriotic tunes, see various monographs by O. G. Sonneck (1909), and also his *Early Concert Life in America* (1915).

tonal utterance for their contemplations; but their melodies (often un-consciously imported) awaken no nostalgia in unaccustomed hearers and have thus appealed infrequently to our art-minded composers. The music of the American Indian—our only indigenous music—is a foreign tongue to the nation at large. But the music of the Negro was developed in true folk-fashion in the social enclaves which slavery constituted.

This early folk music of the Negro found an immediate counterpart in the songs of Stephen Foster (1826–1864), songs which set the nation a-singing and inspired a host of similarly motivated "white" tunes such as *The Old Oaken Bucket*. Foster's harmonic vocabulary hardly extended beyond the primary triads; yet upon that foundation he wrote melodies like *Swanee River* and *Old Black Joe* which sing as spontaneously as any song of Schubert. Their A-B-A pattern, almost invariable, is borrowed from learned sources; their tang of melancholy is wholly dark-skinned; but by this simple conjunction of elements Foster became the first distinctively American composer. His popularity was greatly enhanced by the vogue of the Minstrel shows, given by troupes of "black-faced" singers with an interlocutor, whose type of comedy quickly became the greatest entertainment attraction in the country. Christy's Minstrels was but one of dozens of troupes that toured the nation, and Christy himself popularized many of Foster's songs. Dan Emmett, one of Bryant's Min-strels, wrote on a rainy Sunday in 1859 the tune of *Dixie*; and the Fisk Jubilee Singers, in the 'seventies, not only brought the Negro music back to their own race but took it abroad and sang it for Queen Victoria. It was through such efforts as these that America was made aware of music and induced to welcome the many foreign musicians (many from Ger-many, in the wave of emigration that followed the Revolutions of 1848–1849) who helped to found significant musical organizations.

Among these immigrants was Theodore Thomas (1835–1905) who, after touring as violinist with many famous singers, organized an orches-tra in New York which from 1869 toured the East and the Middle West. He also established the Cincinnati Biennial Festival and founded there the College of Music; he conducted the New York Philharmonic Society and the Brooklyn Philharmonic Orchestra; in 1885 he became director of the American Opera Company; and in 1891 he was appointed conductor of the Chicago Orchestra, holding that position until his death and bringing the institution to a perfection seldom if ever excelled.

These few items are but indices of the growth of musical interest in America, the background against which our American composers de-veloped. Since the contemporary scene must occupy most of our atten-tion, meager account must be rendered of the work of these men; but the honor due them is by no means to be measured by the space they fill in this account. For a time, we shall take them up in the order of their birth.

John Knowles Paine (1839–1906) studied in Germany and in 1861 brought back the type of musical learning that was to guide American effort for the rest of the century. He began teaching at Harvard in 1862 and became the first professor of music in an American university. Large choral works, two symphonies (No. 2, 1880)—probably the first significant American efforts in that form—and many chamber works and songs established his position as a true pioneer. Paine's influence was spread by such pupils as Arthur Foote, J. A. Carpenter, F. S. Converse, and D. G. Mason.

Arthur Foote (1853–1937), wholly trained in America, attempted no symphony but wrote an often performed Suite for strings in E; a symphonic prologue, *Francesca da Rimini;* many chamber pieces, some of which he performed with the Kneisel Quartet; and a number of the most sensitively felt songs to come from any American composer.

George W. Chadwick (1854–1931) might be called a sturdy romanticist. Besides long service as teacher and head of the New England Conservatory of Music, he left three symphonies (the First, 1886); a *Suite symphonique* which won the prize of the National Federation of Music Clubs in 1911; many overtures, and symphonic poems, and choral works; five string quartets; and about 100 songs, of which his *Ballad of Trees and the Master* (Lanier) was long cherished by singers.

Horatio Parker (1863–1919), spreading his influence from Yale, may be compared to Paine at Harvard. His chief works, however, were choral, the oratorio *Hora novissima* having won great acclaim both here and in England. His opera, *Mona* (1912), was the third American opera to be produced by the Metropolitan in New York, but neither this nor *Fairyland* (1913) won more than a *succès d'estime*. He might be called the last of the classicists.

Edward Alexander Macdowell (1861–1908) marks both the ending of the Germanic tradition and the beginning of a new American idiom whose completion, although not yet accomplished, appears to be approaching. His training was chiefly in Germany where his talent was so generously recognized that he settled in Wiesbaden as a teacher. But in 1888 he returned to America, working at first in Boston, then (1896) at Columbia University. He left this post, after a bitter disagreement with the administration, in 1904. His mind—whether from the distress of this incident or from an accident—rapidly failed, and after two blank years he died.

For two decades, Macdowell's compositions seemed to mark a new height in American musical thought. Thereafter a new idiom began to prevail which not only superseded his essentially romantic manner, but revealed weaknesses which had been concealed beneath the attractive surface his works always displayed. His influence has been perpetuated in the establishment of the Peterborough (N. H.) Colony—indefatigably promoted by his wife—more than by his actual writings. Yet, viewed in another perspective than that of the present, these writings are impressive, rather for their poesy than for their solidity as structures. For orchestra there are five symphonic poems (*Hamlet and Ophelia, Lancelot and Elaine, Lamia, The Saracens,* and *Lovely Alda*) and two suites (No. 2, the *Indian Suite*); two piano concertos; and a *Romance* (early) for 'cello and orchestra. Most of his choral pieces are for men's voices; there are many songs, several of which are to his own texts; but the major part of his work is for the piano, including four Sonatas (*Tragic, Heroic, Norse* and *Keltic*), many sets of small impressions (as *Les Orientales,* after Hugo; *Woodland Sketches; Sea Pieces*), and 12 Virtuoso Studies, all programmatically titled.

A considerable departure from the Germanic trend hitherto ruling American thought may be seen in the later works of Frederick Converse (1871–1940). *Flivver Ten Million* (1927) had perhaps a model in Honegger's *Pacific 2–3–1,* but this trend was not carried further. His opera, *The Pipe of Desire,* was notable as the first opera to be produced at the Metropolitan (1909). John Alden Carpenter (1876–1951) went farther with his "jazz pantomime," *Krazy Kat* (1921, on a current comic strip), and *Skyscrapers,* a ballet largely descriptive of the new age of mechanism (1926). His songs, especially those on texts by Tagore, are by comparison very gentle, but probably more accordant with his talent.

Converse and Carpenter, and still more their younger contemporaries, were speaking in a changed idiom. The basis of that idiom was still European, even though its variants had a distinctly American tang. But it sometimes reflects a rapidly burgeoning—and in learned eyes a rather weedy—native art which has turned out to be the most distinctively American music we have ever had. It came from what is ordinarily regarded as a lower social level, and in its essential nature it does not thrive above that level. Yet it has been grafted onto older stocks to which it thus imparts a new vigor; for this music is *alive.*

This distinctive American music goes by the unlovely yet somehow appropriate name *jazz.* But with its phenomenal growth in popularity, it has developed a great diversity in style, with the result that the learned in the jazz field now dispute vigorously the true meaning of the name. Recent authorities,[3] carefully tracing the history of this music and

[3] For example, Marshall Stearns, in *The Story of Jazz,* Oxford University Press, 1956; and Rudi Blesh, in *Shining Trumpets,* Knopf, 2nd ed., 1958.

analyzing its substance, seem to demonstrate convincingly that the original jazz-stock is a racially-rooted plant, brought from Africa with the institution of slavery, and dispersed, with the emancipation, to thrive as it might and acquire novel characteristics in the new soils upon which the seed was thrown.

Work-songs, with texts, rhythms, and melodies arising from and adapted to the communal tasks of the workers in Africa, were readily adjusted to the harder conditions of the slave-laborer in America. Naturally, an enrichment of the music beyond mere rhythmic accompaniment to strokes of pick and shovel made those strokes more endurable. This enrichment was of necessity *improvised*—upon slender bases of rhythmic and melodic pattern learned by ear and commonly accepted. Antiphony (the learnèd word for "response") was a natural feature in the design of the work-song. Variants from true pitch—flattenings of certain notes, surely indicative of physical and spiritual weariness—were common and survived in the "blues" of later jazz.

A species of Christianity, imposed upon but not wholly eradicating African tribal beliefs, was another solace for the woes of slave life. Here both song and dance were invoked for the utterance of the new thought. One outcome was the "spiritual" with its singularly metaphoric text (and equally metaphoric music); another was the dance. The border line between "sacred" and "secular," so carefully defined by puritanical whites, was unknown to the Negro, and the violent physical enactment of religious enthusiasm seen at prayer sessions had an indistinguishable counterpart in the dances which celebrated earthly joys. An apparently innate sensitivity to music and a similar aptitude for the bodily outlet of excitement will account in large measure for many somewhat primitive songs and dances which, at the turn of the century, remained almost uncontaminated by learned music.

A "white" counterpart of the dance-measures—possibly even derived from them—turned up at the same time. This was "rag-time." Viewed analytically, it was no more than a type of syncopation; viewed synthetically, as a communication addressed to a more privileged and more heedless (because less needy) audience, it served both to awaken and to satisfy cravings for excitement akin to those which had generated the spiritually far deeper outpourings of the Negroes. Being of related species, these types were capable of cross-fertilization. Some of the many types collectively called jazz were the result.

As the experts see it, although the pure strain survived, it was soon considerably overgrown by the hybrids. The eyes of the "consumers," indifferent to origins, accepted both indiscriminately. It is impossible in our space to suggest the taxonomy of these plants. Something of the pure strain can be described, along with a hint of the interminglings.

Both the name *jazz* (originally, *jass*) and the music itself originated in New Orleans somewhat before 1900. The rhythm resembled the syncopation of rag-time, but was really far more subtle, the improvised drumming being free of the tyranny of our bar-line. The melody similarly escaped at will the four-bar-phrase convention of learned music. The old tribal trick of flatting certain notes (chiefly the third and seventh) was even more conspicuous. The characteristic product was the "Blues"— strictly, a twelve-bar sequence of unvaried harmonies with new melody for each repetition. (A comparison with the Chaconne is at least suggested.) The words were melancholy; the tune even more so; but the purpose was rather to banish than to express grief. The reader will probably infer from this description a regularity which did not exist in jazz; for this music was invented and performed by people who could not read notes, and its spontaneity was the envy of those trained performers who could not improvise. Blues, spirituals, and dance-tunes (many of French origin, heard in the streets and in cabarets) were enlivened by this spontaneity, and bands began to form, divided into "rhythm-sections" (drums, plucked basses, guitar, banjo, and piano if available) and melodic sections (cornets or trumpets, trombones, clarinets, or even a violin).

In the 'twenties, Chicago became the jazz center of the country. White players (sometimes with orthodox training) formed groups which were similar but often much larger than the original bands. Paul Whiteman assembled a remarkable group and gave a formal concert in New York that put a new stamp of respectability on this sort of music. But while the concert bridged the gap between jazz and symphonic music, it also begat many new imitative varieties. A succession of new names appears, indicative of this resultant novelty. "Swing," Boogie-woogie," "Jump," "Bop" (often, but incorrectly, according to the initiated, called "Be-bop"), and more recently "Rock 'n' Roll" are names for the principal varieties, most of which, however, the experts insist are "jazz-which-is-not-jazz." But whether it is "is-jazz" or is "ain't-jazz," it has not only come up from its original slave cabin into the faubourgs but has long since been accepted across the Atlantic as the one feature of American music that is really original.

Originality, however, is a more difficult word to define than jazz; the fact of originality is even harder to identify; and originality of substance (apparently the criterion adopted by our European critics) may not be the only virtue requisite for originality—or at any rate for excellence— in new music. The ultimate business of music is the interpretation of life;

to discover and portray vital impulse is to be original; and this, in increasing abundance, is the evident purpose of our best American composers.

The Amercan scene has been much altered by the influx of both musicologists and composers from Europe. Our whole program of musical instruction, at first on the collegiate level but latterly in its earlier stages also, has been intensified by the generous contributions of such scholars as Willi Apel, Manfred Bukofzer, Alfred Einstein, Hugo Leichtentritt, Curt Sachs, and Leo Schrade; and our absorption of eminent European composers has been no less complete. We shall continue our study by examining their work and their influence. Two of the most important—Schoenberg and Milhaud—have already been considered. We shall take the others in the order of their birth.

Ernest Bloch (born 1880), although matured in Europe before coming to this country, has been a significant figure here and—perhaps more through his teaching than his actual composition—has contributed to the complex American stream. His treatment of Jewish themes— for example, in the Hebrew Rhapsody for "cello and orchestra, *Schelomo,* and the *Trois Poèmes Juifs* for orchestra—yields his most distinctive work. The "epic rhapsody," *America* (1927), although apparently written with complete sincerity as a tribute to his adopted land, failed to arouse the emotion he intended. His *Sacred Service* (a modern setting of a Hebrew ritual) shows again the cogency of his racial feeling. But his later works, especially his second *Concerto grosso,* speak convincingly in an idiom deeply earnest, although hardly American.

Ernst Toch (born 1887), after considerable successes in his native Austria, left his homeland when it fell under Nazi rule, went for a time to Paris, then in 1935 settled in the United States—for a while in New York and thereafter in California. His compositions are in all forms and include four operas, of which *The Princess on the Pea* has been the most favored in America; four symphonies—the Second, dedicated to Albert Schweitzer's ideals perhaps rather than to the man, the Third, winner of the Pulitzer Prize in 1955, and the Fourth, much thinner in texture but still richer in imagination; many smaller orchestral pieces, of which the "merry Overture," *Pinocchio,* has become a general favorite; concertos for 'cello and for piano; nine string quartets and many other chamber works; and a large number of piano pieces and songs. Toch's idiom, partially expounded in his book *The Shaping Forces in Music* (1948), is his own, carefully adjusted to his immediate expressive purpose but not excogitated, fully alive to present-day values in dissonance but fundamentally cognizant of tonality. His most daring experiment is perhaps his Suite, *Gesprochene Musik,* which explores the values of rhythm and dynamic contrast—two essential factors of the musical substance—stripped of their usual tonal garb. His influence, seen against the background of extravagant search for novelty, appears almost classic; measured in terms of the devotion of his pupils, it is hearteningly progressive—romantic in the new sense which is coming to be attached to that word.

The opposition to dodecaphony—vigorously expressed by those whose ears it offended, but more soberly by those who doubted its validity as a method of composition—found a leader in Paul Hindemith (born 1895) who, during what appear to be his most fertile creative years, was a resident and later a citizen of this country. Whether or not he would accept the role of champion, his influence on American music, both as performer, teacher, and composer, has been great.

As performer—mostly in his earlier years—Hindemith shone chiefly as violist; but there is hardly an important instrument which he has not handled with such competency as to prove that mastery, had he willed it, would have been within his grasp. As teacher, he has set forth—in *The Craft of Musical Composition* (1941, rev. 1945), and in *A Concentrated Course in Traditional Harmony* (1943, 1953)—a closely reasoned inquiry into the nature and behavior of the tonal substance.[4]

Hindemith's earlier work—that of the 'twenties—showed a disposition to rebel against tradition, rather than a clear constructive purpose. (The heady wine of atonality—by no means identical with dodecaphony—was generously imbibed by every progressive composer in that decade.) But from that period came also the admirable *Viola Concerto*, much performed by the composer both abroad and here, and the opera *Cardillac*, (revised in 1952). This is in a kind of Handelian manner, repudiating Wagnerian principles, but powerfully setting forth a significant theme. Other operas of this decade were *Hin und Zurück* ("Out and Back"), a one-act piece in which the action, having reached a sanguinary peak, is played backwards (the murdered wife comes to life and the husband puts the

---

[4] Since this does not constitute a "system," it is more difficult to summarize than are the principles of dodecaphony. The following thus gives no more than a hint of his theory:

Acoustical law is the basis of tonal organization. The diatonic scale is so based. Chords, however, are not of necessity tied to that scale, or built of superimposed thirds; neither do they differ essentially when inverted. The chromatic scale is derived from a single (fundamental?) tone and its harmonic series; and three degrees of relationship to the fundamental are determinable. The major triad, however, is the center of gravity, harmonically. Intervals have "quality," measurable in terms of "resultant tones"; and the strength of its intervals determines the strength of the chord. Melody (apart from its also essential component of rhythm) must respect these tonal priciples. Harmonic textures may be (as they always have been) either polyphonic or homophonic; and the general rhetoric of the musical discourse follows the pattern of logical thought in any field.

(For the distressing meagerness of this description a tolerable remedy may be found in Hindemith's *A Composer's World*, 1952, and especially in Chapter 5, "The Means of Production.")

revolver back in his pocket); and *Neues vom Tage* ("News of the Day") with rhythms sometimes provided by clicking typewriters and business letters sung by the chorus. (This was revised in 1954.)

A more profound work—perhaps the peak of Hindemith's operatic effort—was *Mathis der Mahler* (1938), on the life of the painter Mathias Grünewald. A triptych painted by Grünewald for the church altar at Isenheim suggested the book, which Hindemith himself made. (The painted figures in The Concert of Angels, The Temptation of St. Anthony, and The Entombment come to life and take part in the action.) A Suite from the opera, essentially a symphony, with its three movements titled after the pictures, is an enduring number in every orchestra's repertory. Not less impressive, however, is *Die Harmonie der Welt*, on the life of the astronomer Kepler and his belief in the medieval notion of the music of the spheres (see p. 56). From this, as from *Mathis*, a suite was drawn, also called a symphony, whose three movements deal with *Musica instrumentalis, Musica humana,* and *Musica mundana.* (The opera was first performed in Munich in 1957.) A *Symphonia serena* (1947) and a *Sinfonietta* (Louisville, 1950) complete the list of Hindemith's symphonic works. It should be noted that association between music and human event or experience is often acknowledged, and the belief that music has ineluctable relation to morals is not only implicit in the choice of such "subjects" but is frankly asserted, *passim,* in *The Composer's World* (the Harvard lectures, 1950–1951).

The whole volume of Hindemith's work is enormous. Perhaps the most representative of the vocal works are an oratorio (*Das Unaufhörliche* (1931) and *When Lilacs Last in the Dooryard Bloomed* (1946); but the *Cantique de l'Espérance* for mezzo-soprano, chorus and a double orchestra, and *The Demon of the Gibbet* (*a cappella*), along with the early *Melancholie* for contralto and string quartet, and *In Praise of Music* will suggest the diversity of his effort. There are many solo songs, of which the cycle, *Das Marienleben* (after Rilke, 1923, rev. 1948) is a notable example. More diversified still is the chamber music, comprising seven string quartets; seven sets of *Kammermusik* for different ensembles; sonatas for piano and each of the important orchestral instruments; and sonatas for violin, viola and 'cello unaccompanied. In addition to the Viola Concerto mentioned above there is another near-concerto, *Der Schwanendreher,* as well as full-scale concertos for piano, violin, and 'cello.

Little—perhaps none—of this music is distinctively American; Hindemith has returned, apparently for good, to Europe (Switzerland); yet his influence on American musical thought—doubtless to be accurately measured only in the future—has been great and may still grow.

Ernst Krenek (born 1900), of a different musical "faith" from Hindemith's, has also contributed notably to the stream of American musical thought. He won enormous renown with his early "jazz" opera, *Jonny spielt auf* (Leipzig, 1927; New York, 1928), but forsook its rather facile manner for the twelve-tone system (learned by association with Schoenberg, Berg, and Webern) in 1933. He was for some time solely devoted to this method but found many varied applications of it and at times reverted to the freer idiom. Krenek is a thorough student of the music of the sixteenth century, sometimes employing that technique in his own works, and making notable studies of the music of Ockhegem. His teaching (chiefly at Vassar and at Hamline University in St. Paul) has always been acclaimed as singularly lucid and tolerant, and he is a notable contributor to the literature of contemporary musical aesthetics. He prepared Monteverdi's *L'Incoronazione di Poppea* (1937) for performance in America by a touring European company and once completed an unfinished Schubert piano sonata to the satisfaction of severe critics. He has doubtless contributed much to the understanding and the adoption of the twelve-tone technique by American composers—not as a rigid, frigid construction-scheme but as a valid means of expression.

Krenek is a prolific composer. The variety and something of the character of his interests and his music are suggested by his eleven operas, of which *Charles V* is perhaps the most notable, while *Dark Waters* and *The Bell Tower*, with English texts, show his assimilation of the American scene; five symphonies (Nos. 4 and 5, 1947 and 1950); various other orchestral essays (for example, *I Wonder as I Wander*—very "modernistic" variations on a North Carolina folksong); four piano concertos (No. 4, 1950) and one for two pianos (1953); eight string quartets; six piano sonatas; choral compositions ranging from a *Proprium Missae* for women's voices to *The Santa Fe Time Table*, its sole text the names of the stations on that road from Albuquerque to Los Angeles.

The last of the European immigrants we have space to notice is Kurt Weill (1900–1950) who settled in America in 1935 (after expulsion from Germany, and sojourns in Paris and London) and with astonishing rapidity identified himself with American ways. His composing (in his own way) began at 10; his close connection with the theater during his student days was in accord with his own bent; but he went to Berlin in 1921 where he studied with Busoni and was chosen to conduct the first performance of his master's *Doktor Faustus* in 1925. His first opera, *Der Protagonist* in one act (1926), suggested the main direction of his future endeavors: at the left a showman strangles his sister for her guilty love; at the right, two characters simultaneously play a comedy. A satire on

American life by Berthold Brecht gave the book of *The Rise and Fall of the City of Mahagonny*, but his first great success came with *Die Drei-groschenoper* ("The Threepenny Opera"), a kind of rehash of *The Beggar's Opera* with a striking text also by Brecht. (Another text, by Marc Blitzstein, has sparked a recent revival of the work.) In America he collaborated with Maxwell Anderson (*Knickerbocker Holiday*, 1938) and (*Lost in the Stars*, 1949); with Moss Hart (*Lady in the Dark*); with Perelman and Nash (*One Touch of Venus*); with Ben Hecht (*A Flag Is Born*); and with Elmer Rice (*Street Scene*, 1947). A considerable number of purely instrumental works and songs show that his imagination ran in other lines as well as the theatrical; but his strongest impact on the public was with his operas. His adaptability was such that he may be said to have drawn more from American musical thought than he contributed to it; his influence is largely indirect; but the very popularity of his work, patently in a vein accordant with American effort, helped greatly to establish that effort in popular favor.

Returning now to our long neglected list of native American composers, we take up perhaps the most unique figure thus far to appear—Charles Ives (1874–1954). Village training in Danbury, Connecticut, did not sharply focus his talent but also did not blunt his unusual sensibilities. Formal study at Yale (1894-1898) raised more doubts than it settled as to the real sense of music, but did enhance his practical skills both as organist and composer. His doubts, taking some such mental shape as "Why do the books say you mustn't?" were resolved by "Let's try it, anyhow"; and the result was an earlier approach to polytonality and linear counterpoint than was dreamed of by the European "inventors" of those devices. Nor was this a mere experiment. The actuality of American life as he knew it was for him capable of musical expression—naturally, not in the manner of the books, but in the spontaneous fashion in which it was lived, with little regard for niceties of behavior and rhetoric and yet a strong dependence on fundamental decencies. Banality and lofty thought are not far apart in life," he seems to say, "Why should they not be neighbors in music?" At any rate, loftiness, measured against banality, seems to gain in stature; and the two are perhaps of the same blood.

Thus Ives's music, to the conventional ears of the turning century, was altogether incomprehensible and had to wait almost until his death for competent interpreters. That he poses fearsome technical problems cannot be disputed. In the *Holidays* symphony a brass band plays in complete indifference to the time or the tune of the celebration going on in the rest of the orchestra; and no conductor can helpfully "direct" such a directionless effort. Yet it somehow makes sense. The Fourth Violin

Sonata (*Children's Day at the Camp Meeting*), in the midst of music of considerable formal authenticity, muses nostalgically on *The Old Oaken Bucket* and *Work, for the Night Is Coming* and makes of them (or they make of it) an utterance of far higher import than either element could have done alone. His songs may suddenly demand the most extreme efforts of the voice, but the demand proves to be justified.

Ives had extraordinarily idealistic notions about the place of music in American life. Unable to sell his works, he made a fortune in the insurance business; then, even when his music at last was published, he refused to accept the royalties from it. Copies of his *114 Songs* were to be had for the asking. His is indeed a heartening life to contemplate.

He left five symphonies (identifiable by their titles rather than by their form); several *Sets* for orchestra, and for string quartet (one with piano); many piano pieces, of which the *Concord Sonata,* with its movements subtitled *Emerson, Hawthorne, The Alcotts, Thoreau,* is of outstanding significance; and several choral pieces such as the cantata, *The Celestial Country* (1899), and *General Booth's Entrance into Heaven,* accompanied by brass band. These titles will but lamely suggest the direction of Ives's interest. The music itself, although it could never have served as a model, is the most "national" music we possess.

Two other pioneers from the decade of the 'seventies must be noticed. Edward Burlingame Hill (born 1872), a Harvard graduate and until 1940 a professor of music there, was at first influenced by French Impressionism. His symphonic poems (especially the one after Amy Lowell's *Lilacs*) reflect that manner, and his book, *Modern French Music* (1924), showed how deep was his grasp. His taste was too intellectual for the multitude, but his works—three symphonies (No. 3, 1937) and a sinfonietta for strings, much chamber music, a few choral pieces, and an unexpected *Jazz Study* for two pianos (1924) show a catholic interest wholly beneficial to his many pupils. Carl Ruggles (born 1876), both composer and (latterly) painter, was almost from the first a radical harmonist. Uncompromising dissonance and a corresponding energy appear in most of his works—for example, *Men and Angels* for trumpets only (1922, rev., 1939); *Sun-Treader,* after Browning, for full orchestra (Paris, 1932); and *Organum,* orchestral (1949). These have been but seldom performed, but his repute among the younger composers is high.

More pathfinders were born in the 'eighties. Charles Tomlinson Griffes (1884–1920), one of the most sensitive imaginations America has produced, was early fascinated by French Impressionism as may be seen in his *Roman Sketches* for piano (1917). But from the same year came *The Kairn of Koridwen* (dance drama) and *Shojo,* a Japanese pantomime, both accompanied by small instrumental groups; and in 1919 came his most enduring orchestral work, *The Pleasure Dome of Kubla Khan*, whose colors time does not seem to fade. Exotic subjects stimulated him most strongly, whether in his piano pieces or his quite numerous songs; these subjects found no favor with the *avant-garde* of the 'twenties; but in the more just perspective of the present his stature does not diminish.

Louis Gruenberg (born 1884), a notable pupil of Busoni, returned from European study to assume a foremost place among those who looked to jazz as a source of Americanism. *Daniel Jazz* (1925) for tenor and eight instruments, *Jazzettes* for violin and piano (1926), and *Emperor Jones* (1933), an opera on O'Neill's play, are outstanding efforts in the adaptation of that narrow idiom to larger canvases. But there are also five symphonies, several symphonic poems, concertos for piano and for violin, and two string quartets.

Wallingford Riegger (born 1885), thoroughly grounded in performing ('cello), conducting, and composition both in New York and in Europe, returned to America to participate in the most advanced efforts of the 'twenties—even in the field of electronic music. His earlier works—for example, *Study in Sonority* for ten violins—found little favor; but after his Third symphony was chosen by the New York Music Critics Circle (1948), he began to emerge as one of our most solid musicians. He has experimented with the twelve-tone technique but has not adopted it extensively. Rhythm is his most striking asset, and nine of his works are for the dance; but there are three symphonies (the last, 1948) and many smaller orchestral pieces, two string quartets and other chamber music, and a number of works for organ, notable additions to the limited repertoire of that instrument.

Deems Taylor (born 1885) was conspicuous in the 'twenties for his suite, *Through the Looking Glass*, and his two operas, *The King's Henchmen* and *Peter Ibbetson*. Of late years he has receded from the foreground in which the success of those works placed him.

American composers born in the two decades 1891–1910 show a great variety of creative impulses and styles. Their education accorded with opportunity or inclination, unguided by any generally recognized norm such as that gradually established by the postwar years with the aid of the immigrants mentioned. Space demands brevity of discussion, and the exclusion of many reputable figures.

George Antheil (1900–1959), a pupil of Bloch, created a sensation with his *Ballet mécanique* (Paris, 1926, New York, 1927), a *Jazz Symphony*, and his first opera, *Transatlantic* (Frankfort, 1930). His second opera, *Helen Retires* (with John Erskine), showed much abatement of his adventurous style, and his work thereafter shows a considerably individual amalgamation of contemporary manners in harmony and rhythm, guided by a truer musical instinct than had been evidenced at first. Six symphonies, three string quartets, concertos for violin and for flute, bassoon and piano, several ballets—the last, *The Wish* (Louisville, 1955)—and four piano sonatas, are his chief works.

Aaron Copland (born 1900), not only by his compositions but by his lucid writings about music and his leadership in organizing musical efforts, has won the unofficial title of dean of American composers. His works cover every field, from piano music (for example, *Piano Variations*, 1930; *Piano Sonata*, 1941) to opera (*The Tender Land*, 1954). His most frequently performed pieces are probably his many ballets, the most familiar being *Billy the Kid* (1938), *Rodeo* (1942), and *Appalachian Spring* (1944, with Martha Graham). But many orchestral works rival these—as, for example, *A Dance Symphony* (from an unperformed ballet, *Grogh*), *El Sálon México*, his Third symphony (1946), and various suites drawn from the ballets. There are also interesting experiments—for example, *A Lincoln Portrait* (orchestral background for a verbal summary of the man poetized and quoted by Carl Sandburg), and *The Second Hurricane* (a high-school opera), as well as a tentative adventure into the twelve-tone technique in his Piano Quartet (1950). There is also music for many films, a small body of choral music, and a considerable number of chamber-pieces. Matter, with Copland, generally originates style, but this does not imply looseness or a merely illustrative manner.

Henry Cowell (born 1897), whose "tone clusters" played with clenched fist, flat hand, or whole forearm striking the keyboard won him early notoriety, has proved, indeed, one of America's most provocative composers. His sound and inquisitive musicianship was for some time hidden under this strange exterior, but it has emerged unscarred to reveal an earnest and wide-ranging mind. Cowell's total production is astounding—over 1,000 works in all genres, besides several books: for example, *New Musical Resources* (especially fertile in rhythmic suggestion) and a competent biography of Charles Ives. His Fourteenth symphony is from 1956; there are many quaintly titled orchestral works, including eight examples of the *Hymn and Fuguing Tune* (after Wm. Billings); there is much chamber music, almost always for unusual combinations, and of course many piano pieces, for he is a skilled pianist. Cowell's one opera, *O'Higgins of Chile*, and his choral works are not widely known. His later style, like that of Antheil, is more conventional, but is still too individual to attract disciples.

Howard Hanson (born 1896), appointed Dean of the Eastman School of Music in Rochester, New York, in 1924, has used his eminent position to focus public interest on American music in many important ways.

The School is one of the country's leading centers for musicology; the Orchestra, often under his direction, has given premier performances of countless American works; as teacher he has guided successfully a large number of pupils; and as composer he has enriched the repertoire with many soundly constructed and expressively significant contributions. Hanson's music is never that of the stylist, but it does not lack style, however varied its source; his technique is always sure, shunning the merely experimental. His most favored medium is the orchestra—his work includes many symphonic poems and five symphonies (the Fifth, 1955, entitled *Sinfonia Sacra*); but there are concertos for organ and for piano, a considerable number of choral works and chamber pieces, and the opera, *Merry Mount*, given at the Metropolitan in 1933. To no one is the advancement of music in America more indebted.

Roy Harris (born 1898) began his musical study only after service in World War I. Abandoning projected academic studies, he worked for a time with Arthur Farwell, then went to Nadia Boulanger in Paris where he "found his voice", and returned to America in 1929. He rapidly reached a high place in both popular and professional regard, in part because his style, although highly individual, never strove to catch what might be called the overtones of modernism. Its basis is fundamentally diatonic, often attaining color from modal borrowings and striking the unaccustomed ear as being simpler than it really is. Harris's invention is prolific, exploring every field but that of opera, and he was in the 'forties the most frequently performed of American composers. Seven symphonies, three ballets, many smaller orchestral pieces and chamber works, choruses with orchestra and *a cappella*, music for a film, and piano pieces and songs comprise his output. He has also filled a remarkable number of teaching positions.

Walter Piston (born 1894) is eminent both as composer and teacher. His style is eclectic, but discriminating; his imagination tends toward abstraction, but does not dwell in an ivory tower. His First symphony was performed in 1938—at an age when many composers have already attained Beethoven's magic number of nine; his Sixth is from 1955. Piston is predominantly an instrumental composer, with many lesser orchestral pieces and a remarkable variety of chamber works, including three string quartets. His only dramatic essay is a ballet, *The Incredible Flutist*. The incredible Leonard Bernstein is among his many notable pupils.

Roger Sessions (born 1896) holds among American composers a position analogous to that of Schoenberg, of whom Ernest Newman remarked that no composer had ever been so much talked about and so little performed. The analogy holds further, for Sessions's austerity of style is founded in an unswerving devotion to the search for that which seems to him musical truth. Thirty years ago, he defined his conception of that search:

"Younger men are dreaming of . . . a music which derives its power from forms beautiful and significant by virtue of inherent musical weight rather than intensity of utterance; a music whose impersonality and self-sufficiency preclude the exotic; which takes its impulse from the realities of a passionate logic; which, in the authentic freshness of its moods is the reverse of ironic and, in its very aloofness from the concrete preoccupations of life, strives rather to contribute form, design, a vision of order and harmony." [4a]

His language, like his music, is difficult. His words, indeed, acquire lucidity only as his music, at last becoming lucid, defines his words. And whether one has then read his meaning out of them, or one's own meaning into them, remains uncertain. But the certainty of a devoted spirit is ineluctable.

Being a perfectionist, Sessions has written relatively little, but an unwonted facility seems to have developed in the last few years. There are four symphonies—1927, 1947, 1957, 1958; two operas, *The Trial of Lucullus* (one act, 1947) and *Montezuma* (four acts, 1947); a piano concerto (1956); a string quintet (1957); and these exceed in volume almost all his previous work. His aesthetic attitude is summarized in his books, *The Musical Experience of Composer, Performer, Listener* (1950) and *Reflections on the Music Life in the United States* (1956); his basic theory, in *Harmonic Practice* (1951).

Randall Thompson (born 1899) speaks, often significantly, in what might be called the musical vernacular, recognizing (perhaps because he writes so often for voices) knowable experience as possessing the germs of musical evocation, and eschewing conscious attempts at exploration of the subconscious. His major effort is in choral music—for example, *The Peaceable Kingdom* (1936) and *Alleluia* (1940), both for *a capella* chorus, and *The Testament of Freedom* (1943) for men's voices and orchestra. But there are also three symphonies, a *Jazz Poem* for piano and orchestra, a string quartet entitled *The Wind in the Willows*, and several other chamber works. He has also an opera, *Solomon and Balkis* (1942) and has written incidental music for *The Grand Street Follies* and *The Straw Hat*.

Virgil Thomson (born 1896), long the most thoughtful of American music critics, has considerably revealed the basis of that competency in musical compositions of singularly diverse character. Long resident in Paris, he learned to suggest his thought succinctly rather than to exhaust it (and his hearers) by "saying everything." His opera, *Four Saints in Three Acts* (to "words" by Gertrude Stein), shows a penetrating sense

---

[4a] Quoted in Aaron Copland, *Our New Music* (1941), p. 107.

of humor; his *Symphony on a Hymn Tune* reveals his interest in the real roots of music; and his *Three Pictures for Orchestra*, considerably constructed on the veiled harmony of mutually exclusive triads, present their "objects," *Sea Piece with Birds, The Seine at Night*, and *Wheatfield at Noon*, in a remarkably similar perspective to that achieved by contemporary painting. Piano pieces, film music, songs, and *Hymns from the Old South* for mixed chorus *a cappella* prove his versatility, and several penetrating books demonstrate the depth of his thought.

The foregoing are probably the principal figures to have shaped our present musical trends. Their creative diversity precludes any stylistic unity based on conformity either to any structural system or to any regulated view of the American scene. Such a scene could be drawn only by composers of predetermined opinions, whether as to the scene itself or the manner of its delineation. Neither in England nor in America would a soviet aesthetic be tolerated.

Their younger contemporaries and followers show the same diversity, and the same repugnance to regulation. They show, also, what looks like a surer technical command. Such a skill has its dangers as well as its advantages, for skill is discernible by the apparent musical public as well as the real, and—as has often happened—its exploitation fosters acceptance of the appearance as the reality.[5] The list is long—so long that only an arbitrary selection is possible here. It is also growing, healthily; and Sydney Smith's contemptuous question, "Who ever reads an American book?" has long since lost its sting, even when transferred to American music. The composers selected will be mentioned in the order of their birth; a summary of their achievements will be attempted at the end; but no critical judgment of their value is intended.

Paul Creston (born 1906), of Italian parentage, is almost wholly self-taught in composition. His solid technique shows penetrating study of musical masterpieces of many eras; but his idiom has patently been colored by his own musical personality. He has written five symphonies, the Third (1950), entitled "Mysteries," dealing with the Nativity, the Crucifixion, and the Resurrection. The Fifth was first performed at Washing-

---

[5] No aesthetic touchstone has been discovered by which true artistic substance can be distinguished from dross. Yet that very discrimination is the basis of artistic wisdom. That such wisdom is gradually attainable is indicated by the persistent favor which both the learned and the unlearned accord to "great" composers—e.g., Beethoven. That Beethoven was an impeccable stylist is apparent to the learned; but this is not the ground upon which the multitude accord their favor; nor does learned opinion, however closely reasoned, establish popular favor. It only helps to fortify it—or, as in many instances recorded in this book, to impede by its narrowness the attainment of wisdom. Hence learning—inevitably conditioned by the pre-established apparatus of learning—is uncertainly pointed toward discovery of the touchstone, which hides somewhere in the vague wisdom of humanism.

ton in 1956. Two *Choric Dances*, a *Concertino* for marimba and orchestra, a concerto for saxophone, and a *Fantasia* for trombone and orchestra suggest the variety of his interest, a *Missa pro defunctis*, its depth. There are many chamber works and piano pieces.

John Verrall (born 1908) has had varied study both at home and with Kódaly in Budapest, and wide experience as a teacher. Two symphonies; three operas, *The Cowherd and the Sky Maiden*, *The Wedding Knell* (after Hawthorne), and *Three Blind Mice* (1955) performed at Seattle; a *Sinfonia festiva* for band; several choral works and chamber pieces in various forms; and a study of *Form and Meaning in the Arts* make up a notable contribution to our American literature.

Elliott Carter (born 1908), a pupil of Walter Piston and Nadia Boulanger, and holder of two Guggenheim fellowships, shows a marked personality as well as a varied susceptibility to musical suggestion. His rhythmic vigor is outstanding, and his ingenuity whether with instruments alone or in combination with voices is not only striking but meaningful. Several ballets (the latest, *The Minotaur*, 1947); a symphony (1944); *The Defense of Corinth* for speaking voice, men's chorus and piano 1942); and a remarkable piano sonata (1946) have been followed by many chamber pieces for unusual as well as conventional groups: for example, a string quartet and a piece for four kettledrums. Jazzy rhythms, rather than the distinctive rhythms of jazz, striking voice-leading, harmony with modal antecedents—all fused by a vivid imagination—yield music unmistakably American.

William Schuman (born 1910), at present director of the Juilliard School in New York, is one of the most conspicuous composers of the day. He won immediate recognition in 1939 with his *American Festival Overture* and has constantly enhanced his reputation with music in many forms, but of one integrity. Ballets in collaboration with Anthony Tudor and Martha Graham, six symphonies, a violin concerto, and a concerto for piano represent his more conventional manner. In contrast (but not less characteristic) are a *Circus Overture* and *The Mighty Casey* ("a baseball opera") and, perhaps most characteristic of his temperament, the *William Billings Overture* and the *New England Triptych*, both highly cognizant of the solidity of that early American figure. There are also many choral works, as well as four string quartets and piano pieces.

Samuel Barber (born 1910), like William Schuman, won immediate recognition with an overture—to *The School for Scandal* (1933). The somewhat conservative manner of this and other early works—for example, the *Adagio for Strings* (from a string quartet) and a piano suite, *Excursions*—was gradually and logically intensified by inner effort rather than external influence; and the result is a technical command of the highest proficiency coupled to an imagination which refuses to lose itself in structural speculation. A native lyrical gift was evident in *Dover Beach,* for voice and string quartet (1931), and was confirmed in *Knoxville: Summer of 1915,* for soprano and orchestra (1948). Instrumental skill was similarly developed in two *Essays* for orchestra; dramatic intuition was revealed in the ballet, *The Serpent Heart* (with Martha Graham) from which, by re-creation rather than extraction, came *Medea's Meditation and Dance of Vengeance,* in effect a symphonic poem culminating in the highest intensity. Upon this broad foundation was built the opera, *Vanessa,* produced at the Metropolitan in 1957 with much acclaim, but in Europe with but little success. (Curiously, the libretto, by Gian-Carlo Menotti, a most successful opera-composer, seems to bear the blame.) A modern type of oratorio, *The Prayers of Kierkegaard* (1954), is an impressive utterance of undogmatic religious feeling. A piano sonata of great technical intricacy but of a depth hardly sought by those who consider the piano merely a percussion instrument, concertos for violin and for 'cello, and a relatively small number of songs comprise Barber's contribution to our literature which raises the eyebrows of the esoteric but often deeply satisfies the generality.

A great number of composers, born in the 'teens of the century and later, impart increasing vigor to American music. Their effort is notably sustained by many local and national organizations, for example, the Koussevitzky Foundation, the board of the Louisville Orchestra, and the American Music Center which operates under a grant from the Ford Foundation. In the careful administration of these, it is worth noting that no such pre-established aesthetic criteria as those set up by the Soviet State are recognized. Neither is American*ism* defined nor doctrinally established, either by these composers or by competent critics; for toward its definition not only the composers but also the public—both real and apparent—will have their share. Yet, against the composite background of our culture the fact begins to emerge.

This is illustrated by the remarkable career of Gian Carlo Menotti (born 1911, in Italy) who had all his mature training in the United States. His Italian background is evident in all his work which is predominantly operatic. He invariably composes his own libretti—with a skill at least equal to his musical settings. His greatest successes are: *Amelia Goes to the Ball, The Medium, The Consul, Amahl and the Night Visitors,* and *The Saint of Bleeker Street.* His musical style has its roots in the *verismo* of the later Italians; his orchestra is always small, making frequent performance feasible.

To offer a long list of contemporary composers would be easy; to evaluate their work in any certain historic perspective, impossible. The man of the hour is Leonard Bernstein (born 1918), whose two symphonies, *Jeremiah* and *The Age of Anxiety*, promised more than his growing fame as conductor has allowed him to fulfill. Alan Hovhaness (born 1911), seeking elusive musical truth, destroyed more compositions than most men write in a lifetime and began again around 1940 to incorporate the varied lore of the East (he is Armenian by birth) along with the forthrightness of William Billings in compositions of high intricacy—for example, *Lousadzak* (Coming of Light), *Prelude and Quadruple Fugue*, and *Ad Lyram* (1957).

Morton Gould (born 1913), known to every disc-jockey for his brilliant orchestrations, has not unsuccessfully attempted the symphony (his Fourth is for band) and has produced an impressive ballet, *Fiesta*, at Cannes in 1957. Gardner Read (born 1913) exemplifies the knowledge compiled in his *Thesaurus of Orchestral Devices* in so many stylistic directions that his musical personality emerges with difficulty. Norman Dello Joio (born 1913) has sometimes successfully escaped the danger of his Italian temperament (and the lure of the apparent musical public's taste) in works of notable solidity (for example, a *Magnificat* and *Three Symphonic Dances*), in several ballets (for example, *Wilderness Stair*, with Martha Graham), and in several operas (two on Joan of Arc). Gerald Strang (born 1908), for some years Schoenberg's assistant, has held consistently to his master's principles of formalism (*Mirrorism* aptly names an essay in which the technique of reversion is exploited.)

Harold Shapero (born 1920), a pupil of Hindemith, Krenek, Boulanger, and Walter Piston, adopted for a time the twelve-tone technique and went on to contrive a manner of his own which maintains the austerity of abstraction but acknowledges the reality of emotional suggestion. Lukas Foss (born 1922) is of European birth and early training, but since 1937 a resident of this country. The lucidity of his piano-playing is also considerably manifest in his compositions which are often very intricate polyphonically; his dissonance shows a logical origin; and his larger designs are patently organic. A symphony, two biblical solo cantatas, *Song of Anguish* and *Song of Songs*, two piano concertos, and a string quartet show his predominant bent; but there is also an opera, on Mark Twain's famous yarn, *The Jumping Frog of Calaveras County*.

These names have been selected, in part for their eminence, but also for the variety in style and purpose represented in their work. There is still another field of musical interest only recently opened— that which emerged under the name *musique concrète* but is by its newer devotees called electronic music. *Concrète* has a fairly exact English analogue in *concrescence*—a growing together; and what is here so grown is an elaborately calculated substance of electronically-originated tone, recorded on tape and then combined in ways which often produce either sounds or tones beyond the capacity of any natural tone-source to utter. How far the suggested analogy with atomic fission and recombination holds is as yet undetermined. So, perhaps, is the ultimate musical value of the effort. But it has engaged the serious attention of highly competent composers, searching for new tonal values; and it has often happened that at demonstrations of the technique, those who came to scoff remained to pray.

In Europe, the movement is headed by Karl Heinz Stockhausen (born 1928) of Cologne; in France, by Pierre Boulez (born 1925)—both men being recognized composers of advanced technique. In America the leaders are Otto Luening (born 1900), a versatile composer, conductor and teacher, and Vladimir Ussachevsky (born 1911), since 1947 on the staff of the music department at Columbia University. Mr. Ussachevsky is likewise a thorough musician and a composer of indubitable skill.

The foregoing presentation is, to one deeply interested observer, a sketch of the American scene. An adequate picture should include not merely the United States but Canada, and Latin America, all of which have contributed, in no small measure, to the general awareness of music as a representation of some of the deepest interests of humanity. There is neither space for such a picture nor the skill to draw it. Our complex social philosophies—in the last analysis, the soil that nourishes all the arts—have been on both continents and for more than a decade confused and disoriented, in the midst of material plenty. A resultant cynicism—more often spoken than felt, for the heart, worn on the sleeve, retreats into folds of silence when daws begin to peck—taints much of the artistic purpose of Europe. Cynicism often hides its inner bitterness under a cloak of sardonic humor, jeering at the outworn mantle of romanticism. The cynic (literally, the dog) now has his day; but beneath the surface there is much similarity between him and the romantic, and signs of rapprochement between the two are a distinctive and encouraging mark of American music.

Bibliography

The following is intended to offer a practical selection from the vast literature about music to which the reader of this book may care to turn. Since practicality is aimed at, a great majority of the works listed are in English, and a similar majority of those date from the twentieth century. For those who wish to pursue more detailed or intensive study, ample bibliographical references will be found in Gustav Reese's *Music in the Middle Ages* and *Music in the Renaissance*, W. Apel's *Harvard Dictionary of Music*, and the fifth edition of T. Baker's *Biographical Dictionary of Musicians* (Slonimsky, ed.). The new edition of Grove's *Dictionary of Music and Musicans* (1954) offers dependable summaries of recent studies in almost every field. Briefer comment will be found in Oscar Thompson's *International Encyclopedia of Music*.

Those who have access to the great collections of music usually described as *Denkmäler* will find in the *Harvard Dictionary* (under "Editions, Historical") a summary of the contents of these collections which will serve as a workable index. The basic treatises in musical theory will be found in the same work under "Scriptores" and "Theory, Musical."

Periodical references are listed at the end of each of the bibliography subdivisions and are keyed as follows:

JHS	*Journal of Hellenic Studies*
M&L	*Music and Letters*
MQ	*Musical Quarterly*
Mu. Times	*Musical Times*
PMA	*Proceedings of the Royal Musical Association (London)*

I. GENERAL HISTORIES OF MUSIC

Adler, G., *Handbuch der Musikgeschichte*, 2 vols., 2d ed. (1929).
Ambros, A. W., *Geschichte der Musik* (1860–1909).
Bucken, E., *Handbuch der Musikwissenschaft* (1931).
New Oxford History of Music, Vol. I, *Ancient and Oriental Music* (1957), Vol. II *Early Medieval Music up to 1300* (1954).
Oxford History of Music, 1st ed. (1901–1908); 2nd ed., 7 vols. (1929–1932). All references to Vol. II of the *Oxford History of Music* in *The History of Musical Thought* are to the more comprehensive 1st ed.
Riemann, H., in Einstein, ed., *Handbuch der Musikgeschichte* (1919–1932).

ONE-VOLUME MANUALS

Einstein, A., *A Short History of Music* (1938).
Finney, T. M., *A History of Music*, 2d. ed. (1947).
Gray, Cecil, *The History of Music* (1928).
Láng, P. H., *Music in Western Civilization* (1941).
Leichtentritt, H., *Music, History, and Ideas* (1938).
Nef, K., *An Outline of the History of Music* (1935).
Prunières, H., *A New History of Music* (1943).

II. ANTHOLOGIES OF MUSIC

Ambros, A. W., in O. Kade, ed., *Geschichte der Musik*, Vol. V (1882).
Davison, A. T., and Apel, W., *Harvard Anthology of Music*, 2 vols. (1946–1950).
Einstein, A., *Beispielsammlung zur ältern Musikgeschichte* (1917–1930).
Gleason, Harold, *Music Before 1400* (1945).
Parrish, C., and Ohls, J. F., *Masterpieces of Music before 1750* (1951).
Riemann, H., *Musikgeschichte in Beispielen* (1929).
Schering, A., *Geschichte der Musik in Beispielen* (1931).

III. GREEK MUSIC

Macran, H. S., *The Harmonics of Aristoxenos* (1902).
Monro, D. B., *The Modes of Ancient Greek Music* (1894).
Reinach, Th., *La Musique grecque* (1926).
Schlesinger, K., *The Greek Aulos*, Intro. by Mountford (1939).
Winnington-Ingram, R. P., *Mode in Ancient Greek Music* (1936).

Antcliffe, H., "Music in the Life of the Ancient Greeks," *MQ* (Apr., 1930).
Barry, Phillips, "Greek Music," *MQ* (Jan., 1919).
Clements, E., "The Interpretation of Greek Music," *JHS*, XLII, 133.

IV. CHRISTIAN MONODY

Apel, W., *Gregorian Chant* (1957).
Dickinson, E., *Music in the History of the Western Church* (1927).
Fortescue, A., *The Ceremonies of the Roman Rite Described* (1934).
Idelsohn, A. Z., *Jewish Music* (1929).
Julian, John, *A Dictionary of Hymnology*, 5th ed. (1925).
Reese, Gustav, *Music in the Middle Ages* (1940).
Robertson, A., *The Interpretation of Plain Chant* (1937).
Schrembs, J., *The Gregorian Chant Manual* (1935).
Suñol, G., *Textbook of Gregorian Chant* (1930).
Tillyard, H. J. W., *Byzantine Music and Hymnography* (1923).
Wagner, P., *Einführung in die Gregorianischen Melodien*, 3 vols. (1912–1921).
———, *Introduction to the Gregorian Melodies*, trans. of Vol. I of above (1907).

Ward, Justine, *Gregorian Chant According to the Principles of Dom André Mocquereau of Solesmes* (1923).
Young, Carl, *Drama of the Mediaeval Church*, 2 vols. (1933).

Bonvin, L., "The 'Measure' in Gregorian Music," *MQ* (Jan., 1929).
Briggs, H. B., "The Structure of Plainsong," *PMA* (Feb., 1898).
Phillips, C. H., "The Aesthetics of Plainsong," *M&L* (Apr., 1934).
Swan, A. J., "Music of the Eastern Churches," *MQ* (Oct., 1936).
———, "The Znamenny Chant of the Russian Church," *MQ* (Apr., 1940).
Tillyard, H. J. W., "Mediaeval Byzantine Music," *MQ* (Apr. 1937).
Wellesz, E., "Some Exotic Elements of Plainsong," *M&L* (July, 1923).

V. CHRISTIAN POLYPHONY TO 1600

Andrews, H., *My Lady Neville's Book* (1926).
Baxter, J. H., *An Old St. Andrew's Music Book*, facs. of Wolfenbüttel, 677 (1932).
Beck, J. B., *Le Chansonnier Cangé*, 2 vols., facs. and transcr. (1927).
———, *The Play of Robin and Marion* (1928).
Bridge, Sir F., *Twelve Good Musicians from John Bull to Henry Purcell* (1920).
Bukofzer, M., *Geschichte des Englischen Diskants und des Faubourdons* (1936).
Davey, H., *History of English Music*, 2d ed. (1921).
Einstein, A., *The Madrigal* (1921).
Ellinwood, L., *Musica Hermanni Contracti* (1936).
———, *The Works of Francesco Landini* (1939).
Farmer, H. G., *Historical Facts for the Arabian Musical Influence* (1930).
———, *Music in Mediaeval Scotland* (1930).
Fellowes, E. H., *The English Madrigal Composers*, 2d ed. (1948)
———, *William Byrd*, 2d ed. (1948).
Glyn, M. H., *About English Virginal Music and Its Composers*, 2d ed. (1934).
———, *Complete Keyboard Works of Orlando Gibbons* (1925).
———, *Pieces for Keyboard Instruments by Thomas Weelkes* (1924).
Gombosi, O., *Jacob Obrecht* (1925).
Gray, C., and Heseltine, P., *Carlo Gesualdo, Musician and Murderer* (1926).
Hewitt, H., and Pope, I., *Harmoniche Musices Odhecaton* (1942).
Hughes, Dom A., *Worcester Mediaeval Harmony* (1928).
Jeppesen, K., *The Style of Palestrina and the Dissonance* (1927).
Lowinsky, E. E., *Secret Chromatic Art in the Netherlands Motet* (1946).
Morley, Thomas, *A Plaine and Easie Introduction to Practicall Musicke* (1597); Fellowes, ed. (1937); Harman, ed. (1952).
Schrade, L., *The Organ and Organ Music in the Mass of the Fifteenth Century* (1942).
Stainer, Sir J., *Dufay and His Contemporaries* (1898).
———, *Early Bodleian Music*, 2 vols., facs. and transcr. (1901).
Trend, J. B., *The Music of Spanish History to 1600* (1926).
———, *Orlando de Lassus*, 3d ed. (1930).
Warlock, P. (pseud. for P. Heseltine), *The English Ayre* (1926).

Andrews, H., "Elizabethan Keyboard Music," *MQ* (Jan., 1930).
Anglès, H., "Hispanic Culture from the Sixth to the Fourteenth Centuries," *MQ* (Oct., 1940).
Bukofzer, M., "John Dunstable and the Music of His Time," *PMA*, LXV, 19
———, "Popular Polyphony in the Middle Ages," *MQ* (Oct., 1940).
———, "Sumer Is Icumen In: A Revision" (Berkeley, University of California, 1944).
———, for complete list of works see Boyden, D., *MQ* (July, 1956).
Ellinwood, L., "The Conductus," *MQ* (Apr., 1941).
———, "Francesco Landini and His Music," *MQ* (Apr., 1936).
Ficker, R., "Polyphonic Music of the Gothic Period," *MQ* (Oct., 1929).
Gastoué, A., "Three Centuries of French Mediaeval Music," *MQ* (Apr., 1917).
Gombosi, O., "Dance and Dance Music in the Late Middle Ages," *MQ* (July, 1941).
———, "Machaut's Messe Notre-Dame," *MQ* (Apr., 1950).
Hannas, R., "Cerone, Philosopher and Teacher," *MQ* (Oct., 1935).
Láng, P. H., "The So-called Netherlands School," *MQ* (Jan., 1939).
Leichtentritt, H., "The Renaissance Attitude Toward Music," *MQ* (Oct., 1915).
Levitan, J. S., "Okeghem's Clefless Compositions," *MQ* (Oct., 1939).
Schofield, R., "Provenance and Date of Sumer Is Icumen In," *Music Review* (May, 1948).
Smythe, Barbara, "Troubadour Songs," *M&L* (July, 1921).
Yasser, J., "Mediaeval Quartal Harmony," *MQ* (Apr., 1937; July, 1937; Jan., 1938).

VI. ACOUSTICS

Bartholomew, W. T., *Acoustics of Music* (1942).
Buck, P. C., *Acoustics for Musicians* (1918).
Helmholz, H. L. F. von, *On Sensations of Tone*, new ed. (1948).
Jeans, J., *Science and Music* (1937).
Miller, D. C., *The Science of Musical Sounds*, repr. (1934).
Ortmann, O., *The Physical Basis of Piano Touch and Tone* (1925).
Redfield, J., *Music, an Art and a Science* (1928).
Stevens, S. S., and Davis, A. H., *Hearing* (1938).

VII. AESTHETICS, PHILOSOPHY, AND PSYCHOLOGY

Allen, W. D., *The Philosophies of Music History* (1938).
———, *Our Marching Civilization* (1943).
Carritt, E. F., *Philosophies of Beauty* (1931).
———, *What Is Beauty?* (1932).
Collingwood, R. G., *The Principles of Art* (1938).
Croce, Benedetto, *Aesthetics as a Science of Expression and General Linguistic*, trans. by Ainslie (1922).
Gehring, A., *The Basis of Musical Pleasure* (1910).
Gurney, Edmund, *The Power of Sound* (1880).
Hanslick, E., *The Beautiful in Music*, Eng. trans. by Cohen (1891).

Hospers, J., *Meaning and Truth in the Arts* (1946).
Langer, Suzanne, *Philosophy in a New Key* (1942).
——, *Feeling and Form* (1953).
——, *Problems of Art* (1957).
Meyer, L., *Emotion and Meaning in Music* (1956).
Mursell, J. L., *The Psychology of Music* (1937).
Paget, Violet (Vernon Lee, pseud.), *Music and Its Lovers* (1932).
Pratt, C. C., *The Meaning of Music* (1931).
Puffer, E. (Mrs. Ethel Dench), *The Psychology of Beauty* (1905).
Santayana, G., *The Sense of Beauty* (1896).
Schoen, Max, *Psychology of Music* (1940).

VIII. OPERA

Brockway, W., and Weinstock, H., *The Opera* (1941).
Dent, E. J., *Foundations of English Opera* (1928).
——, *History of the Opera* (1942).
——, *Mozart's Operas*, rev. ed. (1947).
Grout, D., *A Short History of Opera*, 2 vols. (1947).
Krehbiel, H. E., *A Book of Operas* (1909).
——, *A Second Book of Operas* (1917).
Newman, E., *Stories of the Great Operas*, 3 vols. (1929–1931).
——, *More Stories of Famous Operas* (1943).
——, *17 Famous Operas* (1955).
Streatfeild, R. A., *The Opera*, rev. by E. J. Dent (1932).

Prod'homme, J. G., "250 Years of the Opera" [in France], *MQ* (Oct., 1919).
Prunières, H., "Lully and the Académie de Musique et de Danse," *MQ* (Oct., 1919).
——, "Opera in Venice in the 17th Century," *MQ* (Jan., 1931).
   (Other references to periodical literature on individual composers will be found in Section X, Biography.)

IX. TWENTIETH-CENTURY MUSIC

Abraham, G. E. H., *This Modern Music* (1952).
Copland, A., *Our New Music* (1941).
——, *Music and Imagination*, Harvard Lectures (1952).
Demuth, N., *Musical Trends in the 20th Century* (1952).
Dent, E. J., *Terpander; or The Music of the Future* (1927).
Dyson, G. *The New Music* (1924).
——, *The Progress of Music* (1932).
Ewen, D., *The Book of Modern Composers*, rev. ed. (1950).
——, *The Complete Book of 20th Century Music* (1952).
Forte, Allen, *Contemporary Tone Structures* (1955).
Goss, M., *Modern Music Makers* (1952).
Hindemith, P., *A Composer's World*, Harvard Lectures (1952).
Howard, J. T., *Our American Music*, rev. ed. (1954).
——, *Modern Music* (1956).

Krenek, E., *Music Here and Now* (1939).
Lambert, C., *Music Ho! A Study of Music in Decline* (1934).
Pannain, G., *Modern Composers* (1933).
Salazar, A., *Music in Our Time* (1946).
Slonimsky, N., *Music Since 1900*, 3d ed. (1949).
Thompson, O., *Great Modern Composers* (1941).
Toch, E., *The Shaping Forces in Music* (1948).
Weissmann, A., *The Problems of Modern Music* (1925).
Yasser, J., *A Theory of Evolving Tonality* (1932).

X. BIOGRAPHY

ALBENIZ, Isaac (1860–1909)
Jean-Aubry, G., "Isaac Albeniz," *Mu. Times* (Mar. 1918).

ANTHEIL, George (1900–1959).
Antheil, G., *The Bad Boy of Music* (1945).

BACH Family
Geiringer, Karl, *The Bach Family* (1954).
Terry, C. S., *Origin of the Family of Bach Musicians* (1929).

BACH, Johann Sebastian (1685–1750)
Boughton, R., *Bach, the Master* (1930).
Buhrmann, T. Scott, *Bach's Life Chronologically* (1935).
David, H., and Mendel, A., *The Bach Reader* (1945).
———, *J. S. Bach's The Musical Offering* (1945).
Forkel, J. N., *J. S. Bach, His Life and Work*, trans. by Terry (1920); also
contained in H. David and A. Mendel, *The Bach Reader* (1945).
Hindemith, P., *J. S. Bach* (1952).
Parry, C. H. H., *Johann Sebastian Bach*, new ed. (1934).
Pirro, André, *Johann Sebastian Bach, the Organist and His Works for
Organ*, trans. by Goodrich (1902).
Rothschild, F., *The Lost Tradition in Music: Rhythm and Tempo in
Bach's Time* (1952).
Schweitzer, A., *Johann Sebastian Bach*, trans. by Newman (1923).
Spitta, P., *The Life of Bach*, 3 vols., trans. by Bell and Maitland (1899,
reprinted 1951).
Terry, C. S., *Bach, a Biography*, new ed. (1933).
———, *Bach, the Chorals* (1921).
———, *Bach, the Magnificat, Lutheran Masses and Motets* (1929).
———, *Bach, the Mass in B minor* (1924).
———, *Bach, the Passions* (1926).
———, *Cantata Texts of Johann Sebastian Bach, Sacred and Secular, with
a Reconstruction of the Leipzig Liturgy* (1926).
———, *The Music of Bach* (1933).
Whittaker, W. G., *Fugitive Notes on Certain Cantatas and the Motets*
(1925).

BARTÓK Béla (1881–1945)
Haraszti, E., *Béla Bartók* (1938).

Seiber, M., *The String Quartets of Béla Bartók* (1945).
Stevens, H., *The Life and Music of Béla Bartók* (1953).

Bartók, B., "Hungarian Peasant Music," *MQ* (July, 1933).

BAX, Arnold (1883–1953)
Bax, A., *Farewell My Youth* (1943).

Evans, E., "Arnold Bax," *MQ* (Apr., 1923).

BEETHOVEN, Ludwig van (1770–1827)
Bekker, P., *Beethoven,* trans. by Bozman (1926).
Berlioz, H., *A Critical Study of Beethoven's Symphonies* (1913).
Burk, John W., *Life and Works of Beethoven* (1943).
d'Indy, V., *Beethoven, a Critical Biography* (1913).
Grace, H., *Beethoven,* Master of Music Series (1904).
Grove, Sir G., *Beethoven and His Nine Symphonies* (1896).
Harriot, E., *Life and Times of Beethoven* (1935).
Hull, A. E., *Beethoven's Letters, Selected and Edited* (1926).
Lenz, W. von, *Beethoven and His Three Styles,* Calvocoressi, ed.
   (1909).
Marliave, J. de, *Beethoven's Quartets* (1928).
Mies, P., *Beethoven's Sketches, an Analysis of His Style* (1929).
Newman E., *The Unconscious Beethoven* (1927).
Rolland, R., *Beethoven,* trans. by Hull (1927).
———, *Beethoven the Creator,* trans. by Newman (1929).
———, *Goethe and Beethoven,* trans. by Pfister and Kemp (1931).
Schauffler, R. H., *Beethoven, the Man Who Freed Music* (1929).
Schindler, A., *Life of Beethoven,* trans. by Moscheles, 2 vols. (1841).
Schrade, L., *Beethoven in France* (1942).
Sonneck, O. G., *Beethoven; Impressions of Contemporaries* (1926).
———, *The Riddle of the Immortal Beloved* (1927).
Sullivan, J. W. N., *Beethoven's Spiritual Development* (1927).
Thayer, A. W., *Life of Beethoven,* Krehbiel, ed., 3 vols. (1921).
Tovey, D. F., *Beethoven* (1945).
Turner, W. J., *Beethoven, the Search for Reality,* new ed. (1933).

BELLINI, Vincenzo (1801–1835)
Lloyd, W. A., *Vincenzo Bellini* (1908).

Gray, C., "Vincenzo Bellini," *M&L* (Jan., 1926).
Einstein, A., "Vincenzo Bellini," *M&L* (Oct., 1935).

BERG, Alban (1885–1935)
Leibowitz, R., *Schoenberg and His School* (1949).
Redlich, H. F., *Alban Berg, the Man and His Music* (1957).

Hollaender, H., "Alban Berg," *MQ* (Oct., 1936).

BERLIOZ, Hector (1803–1869)
Barzun, J., *Berlioz and the Romantic Century,* 2 vols. (1950).
Berlioz, H., *Mémoires,* E. Newman, ed. and annot. (1932).

————, *Les Soirées de l'orchestre*, new trans. by Barzun (1956).
Elliot, J. H., *Berlioz* (1938).
Turner, W. J., *Berlioz, the Man and His Work* (1934).
Wotton, Tom, *Hector Berlioz* (1935).

Tiersot, J., "The Berlioz of the Fantastic Symphony," *MQ* (Oct., 1933).

BIZET, Georges (1838–1875)
Cooper, M., *Bizet* (1938).
Dean, W., *Bizet* (1948).
Parker, D. C., *Georges Bizet: His Life and Works* (1926).

Klein, J. W., "Nietzsche and Bizet," *MQ* (Oct., 1925).
Tiersot, J., "Bizet and Spanish Music," *MQ* (Oct., 1925).

BLOCH, Ernest (1880—)
Bloch, E., "Man and Music," *MQ* (Oct., 1933).
Gatti, G. M., "Ernest Bloch," *MQ* (Jan., 1921).
Newlin, D., "The Later Works of Ernest Bloch," *MQ* (Oct., 1947).
Sessions, R., "Ernest Bloch," *Modern Music* (Nov., 1927).
Stackpole, R., "Ernest Bloch," *Modern Music* (Nov., 1927).

BORODIN, Alexander (1833–1887)
Abraham, G., *Borodin, the Composer and His Music* (1927).
Brook, D., *Six Great Russian Composers* (1946).
Calvocoressi, M. D., and Abraham, G., *Studies in Russian Music* (1935).

Abraham, G., "Prince Igor, an Experiment in Lyric Opera," *MQ* (Jan., 1931).

BRAHMS, Johannes (1833–1897)
Antcliffe, H., *Brahms* (1905).
Colles, H. C., *Brahms* (1908).
Erb, J. L., *Brahms* (1905).
Fuller-Maitland, J. A., *Johannes Brahms* (1911).
Geiringer, K., *Johannes Brahms* (1936).
Hill, R., *Brahms* (1933).
Kalbeck, M., *Johannes Brahms* (*Leben*), 8 vols. (1904–1914).
May, Florence, *The Life of Johannes Brahms*, new ed. (1922).
Murdock, W., *Brahms*, with study of piano works (1933).
Pulver, J., *Johannes Brahms* (1933).
Schauffler, R. H., *The Unknown Brahms* (1933).
Specht, R., *Johannes Brahms* (1930).

BRITTEN, Benjamin (1913—)
Mitchell, D., and Keller, Hans, eds., *Britten, a Commentary* (1953).
White, E. W., *Benjamin Britten* (1948–1954).

BRUCKNER, Anton (1824–1896)
Newlin, D., *Bruckner, Mahler, Schönberg* (1947).
Redlich, H. F., *Bruckner and Mahler* (1955).
Wolff, W., *Anton Bruckner, Rustic Genius* (1942).

BUSONI, Ferruccio (1866–1924)
Dent, E. J., *Ferruccio Busoni, A Biography* (1933).

Gatti, G., "The Stage Works of Ferruccio Busoni," *MQ* (July, 1934).
Leichtentritt, H., "Ferruccio Busoni as a Composer," *MQ* (Jan., 1917).
Rosenfeld, P., "Busoni in His Letters," *MQ* (Apr., 1939).

BUXTEHUDE, Dietrich (c. 1637–1707)
Buszin, W., "Buxtehude," *MQ* (Oct., 1937).

BYRD, William (1543–1623)
Fellowes, E. H., *William Byrd, a Short Account of His Life and Work,* 3d ed. (1936).
Glyn, Margaret, *About Elizabethan Virginal Music,* rev. ed. (1935).
Howes, F., *William Byrd* (1928).

Westrup, J. A., "William Byrd," *M&L* (July, 1943).

CASELLA, Alfredo (1883–1947)
Casella, A., *Music in My Time* (1955).

Gatti, G., "In Memory of Alfredo Casella," *MQ* (July, 1947).

CHAUSSON, Ernest (1855–1899)
Barricelli, J. P., and Weinstein, Leo, *Ernest Chausson* (1955).

CHERUBINI, Luigi (1760–1842)
Bellasis, E., *Cherubini,* new ed. (1912).
Crowest, F. J., *Life of Cherubini* (1890).

CHOPIN, Frédéric (1810–1849)
Abraham, G., *Chopin's Musical Style* (1939).
Cortot, A., *In Search of Chopin* (1951).
Hadden, J. C., *Chopin,* rev. ed. (1934).
Huneker, J. G., *Chopin, the Man and His Music,* rev. ed. (1925).
———, *The Greater Chopin* (1908).
Karazowski, M., *F. Chopin, Life, Letters and Works,* 3d ed. (1938).
Niecks, F., *Chopin as Man and Musician,* 2 vols. (1907).
Weinstock, H., *Chopin, the Man and His Music* (1949).

COPLAND, Aaron (1900—)
Berger, A., *Aaron Copland* (1953).
Smith, Julia, *Aaron Copland* (1955).

Berger, A., "The Music of A. Copland," *MQ* (Oct., 1945).

CORELLI, Arcangelo (1653–1713)
Pincherle, M., *Corelli* (1955).

COUPERIN, François, "Le Grand" (1668–1733)
Tiersot, J., "Two Centuries of a French Musical Family—the Couperins," *MQ* (July, 1926).

COWELL, Henry Dixon (1897—)
Ewen, D., *American Composers Today* (1949).
Slonimsky, N., *Henry Cowell*, in *American Composers on American Music* (1933).

DEBUSSY, Claude (1862–1918)
Cortot, A., *The Piano Music of Claude Debussy* (1922).
Gilman, L., *Debussy's Pelléas et Mélisande* (1907).
Lockspeiser, Edward, *Debussy*, rev. ed. (1951).
Myers, R. H., *Debussy* (1948).
Seroff, V., *Debussy, Musician of France* (1956).

Gatti, G., "The Piano Works of Claude Debussy," *MQ* (July, 1921).
Jean-Aubry, G., "Some Recollections of Debussy," *Mu. Times* (May, 1918).
Newman, E., "The Development of Debussy," *Mu. Times* (May, 1918; Aug. 1918).
Prod'homme, J. G., "Claude-Achille Debussy," *MQ* (Oct., 1918).

DELIUS, Frederick (1862–1934)
Hutchings, A., *Delius, a Critical Biography* (1948).

DUFAY, Guillaume (*c.* 1400–1474)
Van den Borren, C., "Guillaume Dufay, Light of the 15th Century," *MQ* (July, 1935).

DVOŘÁK, Antonin (1841–1904)
Hoffmeister, K., *Antonin Dvořák*, trans. by Newmarch (1928).
Šourek, O., *Dvořák's Life and Works*, abridged and trans. by Paul Stephan (1954).

ELGAR, Sir Edward (1857–1934)
Buckley, R. J., *Sir Edward Elgar*, new ed. (1925).
McVeagh, Diana, *Edward Elgar, His Life and Music* (1955).
Maine, B. S., *Elgar, His Life and Works*, 2 vols. (1933).
Young, P., *Elgar, O. M.* (1955).

FALLA, Manuel de (1876–1946)
Pahissa, Jaime, *Life and Works of Manuel de Falla*, Eng. trans. (1954).
Trend, J. B., *Manuel de Falla and Spanish Music*, new ed. (1934).

Istel, E., "Manuel de Falla," *MQ* (Oct., 1926).

FAURÉ, Gabriel-Urbain (1845–1924)
Koechlin, C., *Gabriel Fauré*, Eng. trans. (1945).

Copland, A., "Gabriel Fauré, a Neglected Master," *MQ* (Oct., 1924).

FOSTER, Stephen Collins (1826–1864)
Howard J. T., *Stephen Foster, America's Troubadour*, new ed. (1953).
Morneweck, Evelyn F., *Chronicles of Stephen Foster's Family*, 2 vols. (1944).

Gombosi, O., "Stephen Foster and 'Gregory Walker'," *MQ* (Apr., 1944).

FRANCK, César Auguste (1822–1890)
   Demuth, N. *César Franck* (1949).
   d'Indy, V., *César Franck*, trans. by Newmarch (1910).
   Vallas, L., *La véritable histoire de C. Franck*, Eng. trans. (1951).

GERSHWIN, George (1898–1937)
   Ewen, D., *A Journey to Greatness, George Gershwin* (1956).

GIBBONS, Orlando (1583–1625)
   Fellowes, E., *Orlando Gibbons—His Life and Work* (1925).
   ———, *Orlando Gibbons and His Family* (1951).

GLINKA, Michael (1804–1857)
   Abraham, G., and Calvocoressi, M. D., *Masters of Russian Music* (1936).
   Brook, D., *Six Great Russian Composers* (1946).
   Montagu-Nathan, M. G., *Glinka* (1916).

GLUCK, Christoph Willibald, Ritter von (1714–1787)
   Cooper, M., *Gluck* (1935).
   Einstein, A., *Gluck* (1936).

   Istel, E., "Gluck's Dramaturgy," *MQ* (Apr., 1931).

GOUNOD, Charles François (1818–1893)
   Gounod, C., *Autobiographical Reminiscences* (1896).
   Tolhurst, H., *Gounod* (1905).

   Tiersot, J., "Gounod, a Centennial Tribute," *MQ* (July, 1918).

GRANADOS, Enrique (1867–1916)
   Mason, E. L., "Enrique Granados," *M&L* (July, 1933).

GRÉTRY, André Ernest Modeste (1741–1813)
   Rolland, R., "Grétry," in *Musicians of Former Days* (1915).

GRIEG, Edvard Hagerup (1843–1907)
   Abraham, G., ed., *Grieg, a Symposium* (1948).
   Horton, J., *Grieg* (1950).
   Johansen, D. M., *Edvard Grieg* (1938).

GRIFFES, Charles Tomlinson (1884–1920)
   Maisel, E. M., *Charles Tomlinson Griffes* (1943).

   Bauer, Marion, "Charles T. Griffes as I Remember Him," *MQ* (July, 1943).
   Upton, W. T., "The Songs of Charles T. Griffes," *MQ* (July, 1923).

HANDEL, George Frederic (1685–1759)
   Abraham, G., *Handel, a Symposium* (1954).
   Bairstow, E., *The Messiah* (1928).
   Chrysander, F., *Georg Friedrich Handel*, 3 vols. (1858–1867, reprinted 1919).
   Dent, E. J., *Handel* (1934).
   Deutsch, O. E., *Handel—A Documentary Biography* (1954).
   Flower, N., *George Frederic Handel*, new ed. (1947).

Larsen, J. P., *The Messiah* (1957).
Myers, R. H., *Handel's Messiah* (1948).
Rolland, R., *Handel* (1923).
Streatfeild, R. A., *Handel* (1909).
Taylor, S., *The Indebtedness of Handel to . . . Other Composers* (1906).
Weinstock, H., *Handel* (1946).

Coopersmith, J. M., "Handelian Lacunae," MQ (Apr., 1935).
Leichtentritt, H., "Handel's Harmonic Art," *MQ* (Apr., 1935).

HANSON, Howard (1896—)
Cowell, H., *American Composers on American Music* (1933).

Alter, M., "Howard Hanson," *Modern Music* (Jan.–Feb., 1941).
Tuthill, B. C., "Howard Hanson" in *MQ* (Apr., 1936).

HARRIS, Roy (1898—)
Copland, A., *Our New Music* (1941).
Cowell, H., *American Composers on American Music* (1933).

Slonimsky, S., "Roy Harris," *MQ* (Jan., 1947).

HAYDN, Franz Joseph (1732–1809)
Brenet, M., *Haydn*, Eng. trans. (1926).
Fox, G. G. A., *Haydn* (1929).
Geiringer, K., *Haydn, a Creative Life in Music* (1946).
Hadden, J. C., *Haydn*, new ed. (1934).
Sondheimer, R., *Haydn, a Historical and Psychological Study Based on His Quartets* (1951).

Strunk, O., "Notes on a Haydn Autograph," *MQ* (Apr., 1934).
See also Haydn number, *MQ* (Apr., 1932).

HINDEMITH, Paul (1895—)
Evans, E., "Hindemith," in W. W. Cobbett, *Survey of Chamber Music* (1929).
Rosenfeld, P., "Neo-Classicism and Hindemith," in *Discoveries of a Music Critic* (1936).

Cazden, N., "Hindemith and Nature," *Music Review* (Nov., 1954).
Reich, W., "Paul Hindemith," *MQ* (Oct., 1931).
Stuckenschmidt, H. H., "Hindemith Today," *Modern Music* (1937).

HOLST, Gustav (1874–1934)
Holst, Imogen, *Gustav Holst* (1938).
———, *The Music of G. Holst* (1951).

HONEGGER, Arthur (1892–1955)
Hill, E. B., in *Modern French Composers* (1924).
Matter, J., *Honegger*, in French (1956).

d'INDY, Vincent (1851–1931)
Demuth, N., *Vincent d'Indy* (1951).
Hervey, A., *French Music in the 19th Century* (1903).

See also *MQ* (Apr., 1915; July, 1932; Apr., 1939).

IRELAND, John (1879—)
Cobbett, W. W., *Survey of Chamber Music* (1929).
Holbrooke, J., *Contemporary British Composers* (1925).

Townshend, N., "The Achievement of John Ireland," *M&L* (Apr., 1943).

IVES, Charles (1874-1954)
Cowell, H., *American Composers on American Music* (1933).
———, H., and Cowell, Sidney, *Charles Ives and His Music* (1955).
Goss, M., *Modern Music Makers* (1952).

Slonimsky, N., "Charles Ives, America's Musical Prophet," *Musical America* (Feb. 15, 1954).

KEISER, Reinhard (1674-1739)
Loewenberg, A., *Annals of Opera*, new ed. (1955).

KODÁLY, Zoltán (1882—)
Waldbauer, I., in W. W. Cobbett, *Survey of Chamber Music* (1930).

Calvocoressi, M. D., "Zoltán Kodály," *Monthly Musical Record* (Apr., 1922).

KRENEK, Ernst (1900—)
Evans, E., in W. W. Cobbett, *Survey of Chamber Music* (1930).
Krenek, E., *Self-Analysis* (1953).
Rosenwald, H., in D. Ewen, *The Book of Modern Composers* (1950).

Erickson, R., "Krenek's Later Music," *Music Review* (Feb., 1948).
Weissmann, A., "Ernst Krenek," *Modern Music* (Dec., 1928).

LANDINI, Francesco (1325-1397)
Ellinwood, L., "Francesco Landini and His Music," *MQ* (Apr., 1936).

LASSUS, Roland de (1532-1594)
Einstein, A., *The Italian Madrigal*, 3 vols. (1949).
Reese, G., *Music in the Renaissance* (1954).

LAWES, Henry (1596-1662)
Evans, Willa McC., *Henry Lawes, Musician and Friend of Poets* (1941).

LISZT, Franz (1811-1886)
Corder, F., *Ferencz Liszt*, new ed. (1933).
Hervey, A., *Franz Liszt and His Music* (1911).
Huneker, J. G., *Franz Liszt* (1911).
Newman, E., *The Man Liszt* (1934).
Raabe, P., *Franz Liszt*, 2 vols., Ger. (1931).
Searle, H., *The Music of Liszt* (1954).
Sitwell, S., *Liszt*, rev. ed. (1955).

Tiersot, J., "Liszt in France," *MQ* (July, 1936).
Weingartner, F. von, "Franz Liszt as Man and Artist," *MQ* (July, 1936).

LULLY, Jean-Baptiste (1632–1687)
    Rolland, R., in *Musicians of Former Days* (1915).

    Prunières, H., "Lully and the Académie de Musique. . . .," *MQ* (Oct., 1925).

MacDOWELL, Edward (1861–1908)
    Cooke, J. F., *Edward MacDowell, a Short Biography* (1928).
    Gilman, L., *Edward MacDowell, a Study* (1909).
    MacDowell, Marian, *Random Notes on Edward MacDowell and His Music* (1950).

MAHLER, Gustav (1860–1911)
    Engel, G., *Gustav Mahler, Song-Symphonist* (1932).
    Mitchell, D., *Gustav Mahler, The Early Years*, Vol. I of projected biog. (1958).
    Newlin, Dika, *Bruckner, Mahler, Schoenberg* (1947).
    Redlich, H. F., *Bruckner and Mahler*, Master Mus. Series (1955).
    Schoenberg, A., in *Style and Idea* (1950).
    Stephan, P., and Gruenfeld, P., *Gustav Mahler* (1913).
    Walter, B., *Gustav Mahler*, Eng. trans. (1957).

    Wellesz, E., "The Symphonies of Gustav Mahler," *Music Review* (Jan.-Apr., 1904).

MALIPIERO, Gian Francesco (1882—)
    Prunières, H., "Gian Francesco Malipiero," *MQ* (July, 1920).

MÉHUL, Étienne-Nicolas (1763–1817)
    Ringer, A. L., "Étienne Nicolas Méhul," *MQ* (Oct., 1951).

MENDELSSOHN-BARTHOLDY, Jacob Ludwig Felix (1809–1847)
    Erskine, J., *Song Without Words, the Story of Felix Mendelssohn* (1941).
    Petitpierre, J., *The Romance of the Mendelssohns* (1947).
    Radcliffe, P., *Mendelssohn* (1954).
    Young, P. M., *Introduction to the Music of Mendelssohn* (1949).

MEYERBEER, Giacomo—original name, Jakob Liebmann Beer (1791–1864)
    Cooke, J. F., *Meyerbeer* (1929).
    Hervey, A. M., *Giacomo Meyerbeer* (1913).

    Istel, E., "Meyerbeer's Way to Mastery," *MQ* (Jan., 1926).

MILHAUD, Darius (1892—)
    Krenek, E., in D. Ewen, *The Book of Modern Composers* (1942).
    Milhaud, D., *Notes Without Music* (1953).

    Bauer, M., "Darius Milhaud," *MQ* (Apr., 1942).
    Mason, C., "The Chamber Music of Milhaud," *MQ* (July, 1957).

MONTEVERDI, Claudio (1567–1643)
    Bukofzer, M., *Music in the Baroque Era* (1948).
    Prunières, H., *Monteverdi, His Life and Work* (1926).
    Redlich, H. F., *Monteverdi, Life and Works* (1952).

Schrade, L., *Monteverdi, Creator of Modern Music* (1950).

See also *MQ* (July, 1952; Jan., 1955).

MOUSSORGSKY, Modest Petrovich (1839–1881)
Abraham, G., and Calvocoressi, M. D., *Masters of Russian Music* (1936).
Calvocoressi, M. D., *Moussorgsky*, compl. Abraham (1956).

See also *MQ* (Oct., 1932; Jan. 1934; July, 1939).

MOZART, Wolfgang Amadeus (1756–1791)
Blom, E., *Mozart*, 2d ed. (1947).
Davenport, M., *Mozart* (1932, reprinted 1956).
Einstein, A., *Mozart: His Character, His Work* (1945).
Jahn, O., *W. A. Mozart*, 3d Germ. ed., rev. by H. Abert (1919–1921); further rev. by A. A. Abert (1956).
———, *The Life of Mozart*, trans. by Townsend (1891).
Köchel, Ludwig Ritter von, *Chronologisch-thematisches Verzeichniss sämmtlicher Tonwerke W. A. Mozarts*, 2d ed. (1905); rev. and enlarged by A. Einstein (1937, 1947).
Wyzewa, T. de, and Saint-Foix, G. de, *W. A. Mozart, Sa vie musicale et son oeuvre de l'enfance à la pleine maturité*, 5 vols. (1912–1946).

OBRECHT, Jacob (1452–1505)
Murray, B., "New Light on Jacob Obrecht's Development," *MQ* (Oct., 1957).

OCKEGHEM, Johannes (1430–1495)
Krenek, E., *J. Ockeghem* (1953).

PAGANINI, Niccolò (1782–1840)
Courcy, G. I. C., de, *Paganini: the Genoese* (1957).
Day, L., *Paganini of Genoa* (1929).

PALESTRINA, Giovanni Pierluigi da (c. 1525–1594)
Coates, H., *Palestrina* (1938).
Jeppesen, K., *The Style of Palestrina and the Dissonance*, 2d ed. (1946).
Pyne, Zoë, *G. P. Palestrina, His Life and Times* (1922).

PISTON, Walter (1894—)
Goss, M., *Modern Music Makers* (1952).

Carter, E., "Walter Piston," *MQ* (July, 1946).
Citkowitz, I., "Walter Piston—Classicist," *Modern Music* (Jan., 1936).

PIZZETTI, Ildebrando (1880—)
Gatti, G., *Ildebrando Pizzetti*, Eng. trans. (1951).

PROKOFIEFF, Sergei (1891–1953)
Abraham, G., *Eight Soviet Composers* (1943).
Montagu-Nathan, M., *Contemporary Russian Composers* (1917).
Nestyev, I., *Sergei Prokofieff*, Am. ed. (1946).

PUCCINI, Giacomo (1858–1924)
Specht, R., *Puccini*, Eng. trans. (1933).

Gatti, G., "*The Works of G. Puccini*," *MQ* (Jan., 1928).

PURCELL, Henry (*c.* 1659–1695)
Arundell, D. D., *Henry Purcell* (1927).
Holland, A. K., *H. Purcell, the English Musical Tradition* (1932).
Westrup, J. A., *Purcell* (1937).

RAMEAU, Jean-Philippe (1683–1764)
Shirlaw, M., *The Theory of Harmony* (1917).

Masson, P. M., "Rameau and Wagner," *MQ* (Oct., 1939).
Tiersot, J., "Rameau," *MQ* (Jan., 1928).

RAVEL, Maurice Joseph (1875–1937)
Demuth, N., *Ravel* (1947).
Goss, M., *Bolero: The Life of Maurice Ravel* (1940).
Shera, F. H., *Debussy and Ravel* (1925).

RIEGGER, Wallingford (1885—)
Cowell, H., ed., *American Composers on American Music* (1933).

Goldman, R. F., "The Music of Wallingford Riegger," *MQ* (Jan., 1950).

ROSSINI, Gioacchino (1792–1868)
Bonavia, F., *Rossini* (1941).
Toye, F., *Rossini: A Study in Tragi-Comedy* (1934).

Dent, E. J., "Rossini," in *Heritage of Music*, Vol. III (Oxford University Press, 1951).

ROUSSEL, Albert (1869–1937)
Demuth, N., *Albert Roussel: A Study* (1947).

Landormy, P., "Albert Roussel," *MQ* (Oct., 1938).
Petit, R., "Albert Roussel," *Modern Music* (Nov.-Dec., 1937).

SAINT-SAËNS, Camille (1835–1921)
Hervey, A., *Saint-Saëns* (1921).
Lyle, W., *Camille Saint-Saëns, His Life and Work* (1923).

SATIE, Erik (1866–1925)
Myers, R. H., *Erik Satie* (1948).

SCARLATTI, Alessandro (1660–1725)
Dent, E. J., *Alessandro Scarlatti, His Life and Works* (1905).

SCARLATTI, Domenico (1685–1757)
Kirkpatrick, R., *Domenico Scarlatti* (1953).

SCHOENBERG, Arnold (1874–1951)
Armitage, M., ed., *Arnold Schoenberg, a Symposium* (1937).
Leibowitz, R., *Schoenberg and His School*, Eng. trans. (1949).
Newlin, Dika, *Bruckner, Mahler, Schoenberg* (1947).
Wellesz, E., *The Origin of Schoenberg's 12-tone System* (1958).

Hill, R. S., "Schoenberg's Tone-Rows," *MQ* (Jan., 1936).

Jalowetz, H., "On the Spontaneity of Schoenberg's Music," *MQ* (Oct., 1944).

SCHUBERT, Franz Peter (1797–1828)
    Brown, M. J. E., *Schubert: A Critical Biography* (1958).
    Deutsch, O. E., *The Shubert Reader* (1947).
    ————, *Schubert: Memoirs by His Friends* (1958).
    Einstein, A., *Schubert: A Musical Portrait* (1951).
    Flower, N., *Franz Schubert, the Man and His Circle,* new ed. (1949).

    Schaeffer, E., "Schubert's *Winterreise,*" *MQ* (Jan., 1938).
    See also *MQ,* Schubert No., XIV (Oct., 1928).

SCHUMAN, William Howard (1910—)
    Schreiber, F. R., and Persichetti, V., *William Schuman* (1954).

    Broder, N., "The Music of William Schuman," *MQ* (Jan., 1945).

SCHUMANN, Robert Alexander (1810–1856)
    Brion, M., *Schumann and the Romantic Age* (1956).
    Fuller-Maitland, J. A., *Schumann,* new ed. (1913).
    Niecks, F. W., *Robert Schumann* (1925).
    Schauffler, R. H., *Florestan: Life and Works of Robert Schumann* (1945).
    Young, P. M., *Tragic Muse: Life and Works of Robert Schumann* (1957).

    Abraham, G., "Schumann's Jugendsinfonie in G minor," *MQ* (Jan., 1951).

SCRIABIN, Alexander Nikolaievitch (1872–1915)
    Hull, A. E., *Scriabin, a Great Russian Tone-Poet* (1916).
    Slonimsky, N., "Alexander Scriabin," in O. Thompson, *Great Modern Composers* (1941).
    Swan, A. J., *Scriabin* (1923).

SESSIONS, Roger (1896—)
    Copland, A., "Sessions and Piston," in *Our New Music* (1941).

    Brunswick, M., "Roger Sessions," *Modern Music* (May, 1933).
    Schubert, M. A., "Roger Sessions," *MQ* (Apr., 1946).

SHOSTAKOVITCH, Dmitri (1906—)
    Martinov, I., *Shostakovitch,* Eng. trans. (1947).
    Seroff, V., *Dmitri Shostakovitch* (1943).

    Slonimsky, N., "Dmitri Shostakovitch," *MQ* (Oct., 1942).

SIBELIUS, Jean (1865–1957)
    Abraham, G., ed., *The Music of Sibelius* (1947).
    Arnold, E., *Finlandia, The Story of Sibelius* (1941).
    Hannikainen, I., *Sibelius and . . . Finnish Music* (1948).
    Ringbom, E., *Sibelius,* Eng. trans. (1954).

    Askeli, H., "A Sketch of Sibelius the Man," *MQ* (Jan., 1940).
    Meyer, A. H., "Sibelius: Symphonist," *MQ* (Jan., 1936).

STRAUSS, Richard (1864–1949)
Armstrong, T., *Strauss's Tone-poems* (1931).
Blom, E., *The Rose Cavalier* (1930).
Gilman, L., *Aspects of Modern Opera* (1908).
Huneker, J., *Overtones* (1904).
Newman, E., "Richard Strauss and the Music of the Future," in *Musical Studies* (1905).
Niecks, F., *Program Music in the Last Four Centuries* (1907).
Rolland, R., in *Musicians of Today*, Eng. trans. (1914).

STRAVINSKY, Igor Feodorovitch (1882—)
Myers, R. L., *An Introduction to the Music of Stravinsky* (1950).
Stravinsky, I., *Chronicles of My Life* (1936).
———, *The Poetics of Music*, Harvard Lectures (1948).
Stravinsky, Theo., *The Message of Igor Stravinsky* (1953).
Strobel, H., *Stravinsky: Classic Humanist* (1955).
Tansman, A., *Igor Stravinsky*, Eng. trans. (1949).
White, E. W., *Stravinsky, a Critical Survey* (1948).

Blitzstein, M., "The Phenomenon of Stravinsky," *MQ* (July, 1935).

SULLIVAN, Sir Arthur Seymour (1842–1900)
Sullivan, H., and Flower, N., *Sir Arthur Sullivan, Life, Letters and Diaries* (1927).

TCHAIKOVSKY, Peter Iljitch (1840–1893)
Abraham, G., *The Music of Tchaikovsky* (1946).
Brook, D., in *Six Great Russian Composers* (1946).
Newmarch, R., *The Life and Letters of Tchaikovsky* (1908).

THOMSON, Virgil (1898—)
Copland, A., "Thomson and Blitzstein," in *Our New Music* (1941).

Barlow, S. L. M., "Virgil Thomson," in *Modern Music*, Vol. 18 (1941).
Glanville-Hicks, Peggy, "Virgil Thomson," *MQ* (Apr., 1949).

TOCH, Ernst (1887—)
Pisk, Paul, "Ernst Toch," *MQ* (Oct., 1938).

VERDI, Giuseppe (1813–1901)
Bonavia, F., *Verdi*, 2d ed. (1947).
Gatti, G., *Verdi*, Eng. trans. (1955).
Humphreys, D., *Verdi, Force of Destiny* (1948).
Sheehan, V., *Orpheus at Eighty* (1958).
Toye, F., *Giuseppe Verdi* (1931).

VIVALDI, Antonio (?1669–1741)
Pincherle, M., *Vivaldi*, Eng. trans. (1957).

WAGNER, Wilhelm Richard (1813–1883)
Bekker, P., *Richard Wagner, His Life in His Work* (1931).
Ellis, W. A., *Life of Richard Wagner*, 6 vols. (1900–1908).
Kapp, J., *The Women in Wagner's Life* (1931).
Newman, E., *Wagner as Man and Artist* (1924).

———, *The Life of Richard Wagner*, 4 vols. (1933–1946).

Wagner, R., *Autobiography*, trans. of *Mein Leben* (1911).

———, *Prose Works*, trans. by A. Ellis (1895–1912).

WALTON, Sir William Turner (1902—)
Howes, F. S., *The Music of William Walton*, 2 vols. (1942).

Avery, K., "William Walton," *M&L*, (Jan., 1947).

Evans, E. E., "William Walton," *Mu. Times* (1944).

Foss H. J., "William Walton," *MQ* (Oct., 1940).

WEBER, Carl Maria von (1786–1826)
Stebbins, L. P., and Stebbins, R. P., *Enchanted Wanderer: The Life of C. M. von Weber* (1940).

Weber, Max M. von, *C. M. von Weber, ein Lebensbild*, adapt. by J. P. Simpson, as *Weber, the Life of an Artist* (1865).

Coeuroy, A., "Weber as Writer," *MQ* (Jan., 1925).

Einstein, A., "C. M. Weber," *M&L* (Jan., 1937).

WEBERN, Anton von (1883–1945)
Leibowitz, R., *Schoenberg and His School* (1949).

Searle, H., "Webern's Last Works," *Monthly Musical Record* (Dec., 1946).

Wiesengrund-Adorno, "Berg and Webern—Schönberg's Heirs," *Modern Music* (Jan., 1931).

WILLIAMS, Ralph Vaughan (1872–1958)
Foss, H., *Ralph Vaughan Williams: A Study* (1950).

Howes, F., *The Dramatic Works of Ralph Vaughan Williams* (1937).

———, *The Later Works of Ralph Vaughan Williams* (1937).

Young, P. M., *Vaughan Williams* (1953).

Dickinson, A. E. F., "Toward the Unknown Region," *Music Review* (Nov., 1948).

Kimmel, W., Vaughan Williams's Melodic Style," *MQ* (Oct., 1941).

Appendix

I. CUSTODI NOS

The following, like *Ut tuo propitiatus*, is from the early twelfth century, and is one of the earliest known compositions for three voices:

CUSTODI NOS

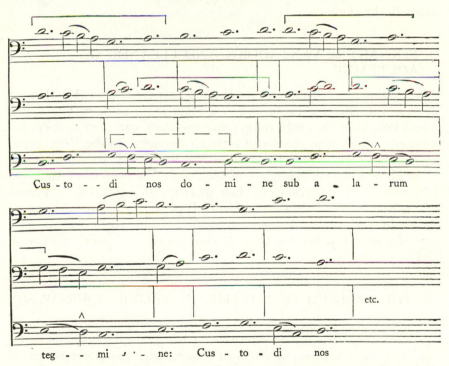

Keep us, Lord, in the shelter of Thy wing; keep us [all to the end of this world as the apple of Thine eye.]

The problem of rhythm is here simplified, rather than solved, by giving to each syllable of the text one full (triple) beat. But the trochaic meter of the verse thereby becomes indistinguishable from the iambic or any other poetic foot, since there is neither any distinction between long and short syllables nor between heavy and light. Note that there is no attempt to extend the seven triple beats which represent the seven syllables of the verse so as to make the "eight bar" period which modern feeling rather insistently demands.

The problem of dissonance, much complicated by the presence of three voices, was evidently something of a puzzle to the composer. He follows, approximately, the principle soon to be laid down by the theorists, that concord must appear on the strong beat of the rhythm, with discord relegated to the weak beats. But the discords on *do-mi-ne* and elsewhere show that this rule is not yet absolute.

Most interesting of all is the feature of imitation. This device, which will become of the highest import for musical structure, is here apparently used for the first time. The more conspicuous phrases are marked in the music by brackets.

II. BERNART DE VENTADORN AND ELEANOR OF AQUITAINE

According to a biographical sketch by a later troubadour, Uc (Hugh) de Saint Cire, Bernart was the son of a baker at the castle of Ventadorn. The Viscount of the castle, recognizing his talent, gave him most cordial support until an affair developed between the poet and the Viscountess. Bernart, banished, went to the court of Normandy and became the favorite of Eleanor, the granddaughter of Guilhem IX of Poitou and Aquitaine (the first of the troubadours). Her marriage to Louis VII of France having been annulled, she married Henry II of England, to which country she is said to have taken Bernart with her, but in any case took her interest in poetry and song, and may thus have influenced considerably the course of English music.

III. THE PROBLEM OF RHYTHM IN TROUBADOUR MUSIC

The presence of some rhythmic beat in verse is unquestioned. But verse in old Provençal was neither quantitative (though the distinction between long and short syllables was one of approximate time) nor accentual (though the dynamic speech accent seems to have been more pronounced than in modern French), but was based on the number of syllables in the line. This measurement (called *compas* in Provençal) is insisted on as an important characteristic of all *vers* in the *Leys d'amors* ("Laws of Love Poetry"), a fourteenth-century treatise in the Provençal tongue.

The first of the troubadours, Guilhem IX, wrote between 1087 and 1127. John Cotton's treatise and the *Ad organum faciendum* date from about 1100, and indicate only the remotest beginning of the problem of combined melody which, in the thirteenth century, will give rise to a completed theory of modal rhythm. Thus, theoretical recognition of the system of rhythm which is supposed to govern the troubadour music appears only after the decline of troubadour poetry into insignificance.

That does not prove, of course, that Provençal music had not such a rhythm. But some direct relation between the troubadours and the learned musicians would surely be indicated if the learned musicians were actually drawing their ideas from these poets. No such indication appears. The first learned theorist who deigns to notice popular music at all is Johannes de Grocheo who, writing about 1300, remarks that by comparison with the learned music of the polyphonists, popular melody was *non ita praecise mensurata* (not so precisely measured). And the *Leys d'amors*, complaining that in its author's day no one knew, any longer, how to compose the tune of a *dansa*, says rather contemptuously that "since they cannot do this, they have turned the tune of the *Dansa* into the tune of a *Redondel* with their minims and their semibreves of their motets." He also says that the *canso*, like *vers* in general, "ought to have a slow, quiet, new [that is, original] melody, with beautiful and melodious elevations and descents, and with beautiful transitions and pleasing pauses." This hardly implies that a primarily musical rhythmic drive was the characteristic of troubadour melody.

Index

663